Routledge Revivals

Shamans, Lamas and Evangelicals

First published in 1985, *Shamans, Lamas and Evangelicals* tells the little known yet fascinating story of a missionary venture to Eastern Siberia in the year 1818. Two missionaries, one English, one Swedish, with the tiresome voyage across the Baltic behind them, set out with their wives to face the daunting prospect of a 3000-mile journey by sledge across the rough snow roads of Siberia in the depths of winter.

The mission was unusual in its conception. Established by the London Missionary Society and the backing of the Tsar, Alexander I, its aim was to bring the Christian gospel to the Buryats, and, once that was accomplished, to cross into China, evangelize the Mongols there, and then set about the conversion of the Chinese. The mission failed, but it was nonetheless an extraordinary episode. It is the story of men who first had to learn Russian in order to teach themselves Mongolian, who brought up their families, founded schools, treated the sick, and translated the entire Bible into Mongolian, printing the Old Testament on their own local press. This is an interesting historical reference work for scholars and researchers of Russian history and Mongolian history.

Shamans, Lamas and Evangelicals
The English Missionaries in Siberia

C. R. Bawden

First published in 1985
by Routledge & Kegan Paul.

This edition first published in 2024 by Routledge
4 Park Square, Milton Park, Abingdon, Oxon, OX14 4RN

and by Routledge
605 Third Avenue, New York, NY 10017

Routledge is an imprint of the Taylor & Francis Group, an informa business

© C. R. Bawden, 1985

All rights reserved. No part of this book may be reprinted or reproduced or utilised in any form or by any electronic, mechanical, or other means, now known or hereafter invented, including photocopying and recording, or in any information storage or retrieval system, without permission in writing from the publishers.

Publisher's Note
The publisher has gone to great lengths to ensure the quality of this reprint but points out that some imperfections in the original copies may be apparent.

Disclaimer
The publisher has made every effort to trace copyright holders and welcomes correspondence from those they have been unable to contact.

A Library of Congress record exists under ISBN: 0710200641

ISBN: 978-1-032-64143-0 (hbk)
ISBN: 978-1-032-64150-8 (ebk)
ISBN: 978-1-032-64146-1 (pbk)

Book DOI 10.4324/9781032641508

Shamans, Lamas and Evangelicals
The English Missionaries in Siberia

C. R. Bawden

Routledge & Kegan Paul
London, Boston, Melbourne and Henley

First published in 1985
by Routledge & Kegan Paul plc

14 Leicester Square, London WC2H 7PH, England

9 Park Street, Boston, Mass. 02108, USA

464 St Kilda Road, Melbourne,
Victoria 3004, Australia and

Broadway House, Newtown Road,
Henley-on-Thames, Oxon RG9 1EN, England

Set in Linotron Plantin
by Input Typesetting Ltd, London
and printed in Great Britain
by The Thetford Press Ltd
Thetford, Norfolk

© *C. R. Bawden 1985*

No part of this book may be reproduced in any form without permission from the
publisher, except for the quotation of brief passages
in criticism

Library of Congress Cataloging in Publication Data

Bawden, Charles R.
Shamans, lamas, and evangelicals.
Bibliography: p.
Includes index.
1. Missions to Buriats.   2. London Missionary
Society—History—19th century.   3. Novoselenginsk
(R.S.F.S.R.)—Church history.   I. Title.
BV3035.N68B39   1985   266'.023'420575   84–11609

British Library CIP data available

ISBN 0-7102-0064-1

To my wife

Contents

	Preface	x
	Acknowledgments	xvi
	Dates and Measurements	xviii
1	Early Plans	1
2	I. J. Schmidt and the Kalmucks	30
3	The Beginnings of the Mission	47
4	The Missionaries: Stallybrass and Rahmn	62
5	The Missionaries: Swan and Yuille	83
6	St Petersburg and the Buryat Zaisangs	99
7	The Journey to Irkutsk	123
8	From Irkutsk to Selenginsk	131
9	The Buryats of Transbaikalia	147
10	The Missionaries Separate	169
11	Family Life in Siberia	193
12	Missionary and Lama	217
13	Preaching to the People	237
14	The Mission Schools	250
15	Translating the Bible	279
16	Printing the Old Testament	298
17	The External Relations of the Mission	322
18	The End of the Mission	343
	Maps	356
Appendix	The Printing of the Bible in Mongolian	358
	Bibliography	359
	Index	367

Illustrations

PLATES

between pages 46 and 47

1. Contemporary surveyor's plan of the Selenginsk mission site
2. (*a*) John Paterson (*Evangelical Magazine*)
   (*b*) Ebenezer Henderson (*Evangelical Magazine*)
3. (*a*) William Swan (*Evangelical Magazine*)
   (*b*) Cornelius Rahmn
4. (*a*) Edward Stallybrass (*Evangelical Magazine*)
   (*b*) Sarah Stallybrass (Edward Stallybrass, Memoir of Mrs. Stallybrass, London, 1836)
5. (*a*) View of the Selenginsk mission in the 1820s (A. Martos: *Pis'ma o vostochniy Sibiri*, Moscow, 1827)
   (*b*) Selenginsk in about 1880 (James Gilmour, Among the Mongols)
6. (*a*) The Selenginsk mission site in about 1900 (G. S. Rybakov, 'Angliyskie missionery v Zabaikal'skoy Oblasti', 1905)
   (*b*) The mission site today
7. (*a*) One of the mission houses at Selenginsk in about 1900 (Rybakov)
   (*b*) The monument erected by Robert Yuille in memory of his wife, Martha
8. (*a*) The dedication to Edward Stallybrass on the Mongolian manuscript given to him by the two zaisangs
   (*b*) Badma's letter to William Alers Hankey with William Swan's translation.
9. View of the lamasery on the Chikoi (P. S. Pallas, *Sammlungen historischer Nachrichten*, II, 1801)
10. View of the lamasery at the northern end of Goose Lake (Pallas, II)
11. Interior of the main temple of the lamasery on the Chikoi (Pallas, II)
12. Interior of a Mongolian tent (Pallas, I, 1776)
13. Two consecutive recto sides of the censored manuscript of Edward Stallybrass's Old Testament translation

Illustrations

14 Title page of the report on the work of the Selenginsk Academy
15 An examination paper worked by Dakba, a student at the Academy
16 Page 1 of the first edition of Genesis, with Schmidt's imprimatur dated 1833
17 Page 1 of the second edition of Genesis, with Schmidt's imprimatur dated 1840
18 Title pages of the Mongolian New Testament of 1846
19 The preface to Robert Yuille's Mongolian primer with his letter to the Rev. S. C. Malan (Bodleian Library, Misc. Asiat. d. 392)
20 Dedication, recopied by William Swan, in one of the dictionaries presented by Robert Yuille to the Royal Asiatic Society
21 (*a*) Page 1 of Edward Stallybrass's manuscript Mongolian hymn book
   (*b*) A page from Charlotte Ellah's copy of Schmidt's Mongolian dictionary
22 Sketch of a Buryat student reading the Scriptures, by Robert Yuille
23 Last page of the deed of grant of land at Selenginsk to the missionaries by the Emperor Alexander I
24 Copy of a letter, with translation, in William Swan's hand, from D. N. Bludov, conveying the imperial permission to continue the mission

MAPS

1 Sketch map showing the principal places through which the missionaries passed on their first journey from St Petersburg to Irkutsk   356
2 Sketch map showing the area of the missionaries' activities   357

Preface

Selenginsk, a drab, run-down little Siberian garrison town, situated not far from the frontier with Outer Mongolia, on the far side of Lake Baikal, must be one of the most unpromising stations ever to have been occupied by agents of the London Missionary Society. Yet in 1814 that Society, advised by two clergymen with considerable experience of Russian life and politics, the Rev. Robert Pinkerton and the Rev. John Paterson, that Irkutsk or its neighbourhood promised to be one of the most important missionary stations in the world, decided to establish a mission to the Buryat Mongols of eastern Siberia. The four men who went out to man it were generally known as the 'English Missionaries in Siberia', though one of them, Cornelius Rahmn, was a Swede, two, William Swan and Robert Yuille, were Scots, and only one, Edward Stallybrass, was an Englishman. The mission was intended not only to convert the Buryats, and perhaps other Siberian tribes, but to serve as a point of entry into the Chinese empire. It was hoped that from Siberia, Outer Mongolia could be occupied, then Peking, and then the whole of China proper. It was a grandiose concept, destined to fail, because it was based on a false appreciation of the political, religious and social circumstances of the time.

Though the mission never fulfilled the sanguine hopes placed in it, it was the subject, in its time, of much confident publicity, and, later, of antiquarian reminiscence. Even when the Directors of the Society became disillusioned at its lack of growth and success, none of this disappointment was allowed to detract from the 'intelligence of a delightful and encouraging character' which continued to be received from Siberia, and to be reprinted in the Society's Reports and in other publications. In the end, the mission was terminated and the missionaries withdrawn, with few tangible results apart from the translation of the Bible into Mongolian, and soon it was more or less forgotten. In the 1864 edition of the Rev. William Brown's comprehensive *History of the Christian Missions*, it was dismissed, along with a number of other short-lived ventures, with the words: 'As they furnish

Preface

few details of special interest different from other missions, we do not think it necessary to give any particular account of them.' C. H. Robinson's book of similar title, published in 1915, while not ignoring the mission, completely distorted its character, denying that the missionaries had done anything at all except translate the Bible. Two decades of preaching, teaching and itineration were summed up in the words: 'No actual attempt to evangelize the Mongols was, however, made till the coming of James Gilmour in 1870.'

In spite of their remoteness and seclusion, the missionaries were visited from time to time by travellers in Siberia, and, after their departure, the mission house at Selenginsk became one of the local sights. Opinions about them varied. Captain Peter Gordon, who passed through Selenginsk in 1819, and stayed with the Stallybrasses, was so captivated by their way of life that he wished, for the moment at least, that he could stay and help them. A few years later, Captain John Dundas Cochrane passed the same way in the course of his notorious pedestrian journey through Russia and Siberia, and decided that the missionaries were simply wasting their own time and other people's money.

Little mistakes about the missionaries' names, the names of the places where they lived, and their activities, mar the accounts of most travellers, even of those who actually made their acquaintance. Alexei Martos spent a few hours at the mission house in December 1823 and recalled Sarah Stallybrass, by name and patronymic, as Sara Filippovna, though in fact her father's name was Thomas. The Norwegian Professor Christoph Hansteen, who, together with Lieutenant Due and the German scientist Adolph Erman, was investigating the magnetic system of Siberia in 1828, met Yuille, and recorded his name as July. Martos called him Yulii. Erman thought that Yuille's companions were brothers, and that their name was Stanybrass. C. H. Cottrell was in St Petersburg in 1841, at the same time as Stallybrass and Swan were passing through on their way home, and presumably met them. Yet he wrote of them as if they had spent the entire period of their service at Selenginsk, and as if the printing press had always remained there, neither of which was true. S. S. Hill was in Siberia in 1847, only six or seven years after the suppression of the mission. He criticized the missionaries for not having done anything to teach the Buryats useful subjects such as reading, writing and arithmetic, something which they had realized at an early date to be essential, and which they had been doing for some seventeen years by the time of their expulsion.

After its closure, the memory of the old mission would often be revived in print but, with one or two exceptions, later writers were just as inaccurate as its contemporaries had been. James Gilmour, a later missionary to the Mongols, devoted a whole chapter of his book *Among the Mongols* to it in 1883. But even what he wrote is not free from misconceptions, while other, less authoritative accounts are, almost without exception, marred by petty errors. Wrong dates are given, and place names muddled. Most accounts

Preface

say that the Old Testament was printed at Selenginsk, while Henry Lansdell relegates the printing to Verkhneudinsk. All are mistaken. Again, we are told that the mission was established as the result of an appeal to the Missionary Society by the Bible Society, and that the printing press was sent to Siberia from London by the Bible Society. The Bible Society itself had nothing to do with the founding of the mission, while the press was bought in St Petersburg by agents of the Missionary Society, and forwarded from there.

Even John Paterson, the father of the mission, muddled its chronology, relying, no doubt, on imperfect memories of his own early days. Recalling the impact made on the Buryats by I. J. Schmidt's translation of the Gospel according to St Matthew into Kalmuck, he says that it was this which first inspired him to advise the Missionary Society to send a mission to them. But it cannot have happened like that. The mission was decided upon in 1814, while Schmidt's translation was not published until the following year. In the present century, Franz Larson, who at one time was helping revise the Stallybrass and Swan translation of the Bible for the Bible Society, thought that Robert Yuille had died on service in Siberia, whereas he actually died in Glasgow in 1861. Alfred Kingston's *History of Royston*, Stallybrass's home town, tells us that his eldest boy was given the 'family name' of William Carey. Actually William Carey was Stallybrass's second son, and was named after the celebrated Baptist missionary at Serampore, as his father tells us himself.

The only two reliable printed sources for the history of the mission are a chapter by Richard Lovett in his *History of the London Missionary Society*, published in 1899, and an article in Russian by V. I. Vagin, based on Russian government archival sources, published in 1871.

One reason for the occurrence of so many elementary mistakes is the fact that almost everything which was written about the mission was based on previously published material, not on original documents. Most of what was published came from biased, partisan sources, from the Missionary Society itself, or from persons associated with the mission, like Paterson, or John Crombie Brown, the Society's agent in St Petersburg, or Mrs Swan herself, and was intended to inspire, not merely to satisfy curiosity. Uncomfortable facts, especially those concerning Robert Yuille, were suppressed, and Yuille's side of the story was never told. The inner history of this extraordinary mission, and something of the external circumstances surrounding its foundation, its active life, and its suppression, can now be more reliably reconstructed from the surviving papers connected with it. These complement, contrast with, and often flatly contradict, what has previously appeared in print. Contrary to the opinion expressed by William Brown, the study of the history of this mission furnishes much more than a few 'details of special interest'. A mission whose history embraces such names as those of the Emperor Alexander I, Prince Alexander Golitsyn, the Orientalist I.

Preface

J. Schmidt, and George Borrow, as well as those of its own members, cannot be dismissed as commonplace, while the period during which it flourished was an exceptional one. Alexander's conversion to Bible study and mysticism coloured a whole decade of Russian political and religious history, and the Missionary Society, advised by the perspicacious Paterson, was quick to exploit the possibilities offered by this unique development. Unlike other Protestant ventures, the mission to Siberia even survived the Orthodox reaction which set in towards the end of Alexander's reign, and achieved its greatest success, the printing of the Old Testament in Mongolian, with the specific approval of his successor, Nicholas I.

The present study is based mainly on three archives. The most important source has been the archives of the Council for World Mission, incorporating those of the London Missionary Society. The three boxes of Incoming Letters from Russia contain the missionaries' official correspondence with their superiors in London, together with some personal letters, and various other papers relating to the mission itself, its pre-history, and residual matters which followed its closure in 1840. The file is unfortunately incomplete. Internal references show that a few letters, including some which might have been of considerable importance, are missing. The files of Outgoing Letters from the Directors to the missionaries have suffered much more severely from the ravages of time, but fortunately they are, comparatively speaking, unimportant. To some extent they are merely admonitory in tone, meant to encourage and console their recipients, and where they are factual they often comprise transcripts of resolutions which can be read more conveniently in Board and Committee minutes. The relevant papers in the files of Candidates' Papers, while modest in extent, are invaluable sources for the early lives of the missionaries, and useful information is to be found in the files of Home Letters and elsewhere. Board Minutes, incorporating reports from the Northern and Eastern Committees, and the Minutes of the Committee of Examination, record the decisions taken by the Society in respect of the mission. Something has survived in manuscript of the missionaries' Journals.

The second important collection of archival material is that of the British and Foreign Bible Society, which contains not only the correspondence between that Society and Stallybrass and Swan, but also some early correspondence connected with the evangelization of the Kalmucks, and the manuscript original of Paterson's Memoirs. The latter incorporates a few early letters sent by Swan to the second Mrs Paterson before her premature death.

The Ohio Wesleyan University, Delaware, possesses a small but uniquely valuable collection of Stallybrass family letters.

These archives have lain, not entirely unread, but largely unexploited, for nearly a century and a half. To have been in a position to read through the entire correspondence in its original form has been a moving and unforgettable experience. One cannot handle with indifference such things as a bill or a letter of advice in the handwriting of I. J. Schmidt; the manuscript translations of the Old Testament censored by Schmidt, and signed on every page by him; a letter from Peter Gordon of Calcutta, dated from Okhotsk in November 1818, describing his unsuccessful attempt to land in Japan in search of a mission field; the local surveyor's coloured plan of the Selenginsk mission station, and a deed of gift of the land, drawn up in Russian and English, and signed by Prince Golitsyn; the examination papers worked by the Buryat pupils at the Selenginsk Academy; and above all, the almost uninterrupted series of letters from the missionaries themselves. These few cardboard boxes contain all that is memorable of twenty extraordinary years in the lives of three remarkable men – their hopes and fears, their achievements and disappointments, and, in the case of one of them, the personal tragedy.

The papers themselves, then, belong to the 'mortal things which touch men's hearts'. But at the same time, they prompt hard questions. What motivated these men to devote their lives, risking the lives of their families as well, to mission work in distant Siberia? How did they justify their uninvited interference in the lives of strangers? They were not eccentrics, but members of recognized churches, exponents of the growing body of Christian opinion which, in the face of opposition even from within the churches themselves, saw the conversion of the whole world as a divinely ordained and realizable task. The objective in Siberia was not to teach, or to heal, though the missionaries had to do both. It was to preach the gospel, obtain conversions, and so save souls from imminent perdition. What in human terms might look like arrogant meddling appeared to the missionaries as humble obedience to the divine command to go into all the world and preach. The task was urgent. As Paterson wrote, defending the Moravians of Sarepta against the imputation of impetuosity in having renewed the Kalmuck mission in 1815 before funds were available: 'We certainly never hinted that they should wait until something positive was fixed upon. They had already delayed the matter too long and many thousands had left this world without hearing of a Saviour in consequence of this delay.' And Swan too: 'O, it is dreadful to think of the multitudes that have already gone to perdition because no man cared for their souls. Their blood can be traced to the doors of Christian churches – to the closets and the studies of Christian ministers – to the shops and families of Christians in secular life!'

Convictions of such intensity expressed themselves in a condescending pity for the perishing heathen', and a relentless contempt for the 'systems', Buddhism and shamanism, whose 'lies and nonsense' kept them in spiritual subjection. The missionaries spoke from a position of assured superiority. They *knew*, without a doubt, that they were right and the others were wrong. It was a 'dark world' which lay around them, where they had to 'wage war'. The lamas were the 'emissaries of Dalai Lamaism', responsible for the 'works of Satan', and what they practised was 'craft'. The unfortunate

Preface

people were 'wholly given to idolatry and superstition of the grossest kind', and were the mere dupes of the lamas.

This was a Christian mission in the purest sense, uncontaminated with secular objectives. Living under a foreign authority, the missionaries escaped any reproach of furthering imperialistic ambitions. They did not trade, or help others to trade. They did not even charge for the education they gave, but on the contrary, subsidized their poorer pupils. Challenged rather than disheartened by their numerical inferiority, compared with the lamas, they set about what amounted to a radical social, moral and religious revolution amongst the Buryats. As Swan wrote:

> Think for a moment what a work is entrusted to missionaries. They aim at nothing less than changing the moral face of the world. When they establish themselves in a heathen country, they set themselves to subvert the established belief of the people on the most important of all subjects – they give the lie to the gods the people worship, and to their sages who taught them to do so – they lay the axe to their most deeply rooted prejudices, oppose their favourite dogmas and ancient customs – they say and do that which is equivalent to pouring contempt on their most venerated institutions, and drawing down infamy on their priesthood, and ruin on their craft – and all to introduce a new, a foreign religion.

Radicalism of this sort left no room for compromise. The missionaries were self-conscious agents of God, and would persist in their purpose as long as God willed it. Failure was not, in their estimation a possibility, though tangible success might be postponed indefinitely. Nevertheless, worldly odds proved to be against them, and in the end they had to give up the struggle, leaving little evidence of their stay in Siberia.

Acknowledgments

The present study has been made possible only through the interest and generosity of those institutions which are in possession of the documents on which it is based, and which allowed me every facility in making use of their archives. In particular I wish to record my thanks to the Council for World Mission, and the Library of the School of Oriental and African Studies, University of London, which now holds the archives and the library of the London Missionary Society; the Bible Society; the Bodleian Library; the Ohio Wesleyan University, Delaware; the Royal Asiatic Society; and the Taylor Institution Library, Oxford. The book would have suffered from many more imperfections that it does but for the help of the many individuals who so kindly answered my enquiries, drew my attention to obscure sources, supplied me with material which would not otherwise have been accessible, or assisted in other ways. In particular, I would like to thank most warmly the following ladies and gentlemen: Professor Pentti Aalto, Mr Ivon Asquith (Oxford University Press), the late Professor Robert Auty, FBA, Professor Sir Harold Bailey, FBA, Dr S. Batalden, Mr B. C. Bloomfield (formerly Librarian, School of Oriental and African Studies), Miss Kathleen Cann (Archivist, the Bible Society), Miss Gillian Davies (formerly Librarian, Royal Asiatic Society), Mr R. F. Dell (Principal Archivist, Strathclyde Regional Archives), Mr G. A. Dyer (Archivist, the University Library, Sheffield), the Rev. Joel Eriksson, the Rev. Emyr Evans (formerly Minister, the United Reformed Church, Iver), Mr A. L. Fleck (Curator, Hitchin Museum), Mr Paul Fox (Photographer, School of Oriental and African Studies), Mr David Gilson (Assistant Librarian, Taylor Institution Library, Oxford), Mr A. S. Gur'yanov (Director, Nauchnaya Biblioteka, Kazan), Professor A. T. Hatto, Mrs Shelagh Head (Local Studies Librarian, Hertfordshire County Council Library Service), Professor Dr Walther Heissig, Mr Allan Hofgren (Press Secretary, Evangeliska Fosterlands-Stiftelsen, Stockholm), Mr D. L. L. Howells (Assistant Librarian, Taylor Institution Library, Oxford), Dr Caroline Humphrey, Miss Helen Hundley, Mr Alan Jesson (Librarian, the Bible

Acknowledgments

Society), Miss Elizabeth Johnson (Cartographer, School of Oriental and African Studies), the Rev. G. A. Jones (Minister, the United Reformed Church, Royston), Dr Philip Jones (Brasenose College, Oxford), Professor John Krueger, Mr R. O. MacKenna (formerly University Librarian and Keeper of the Hunterian Books and MSS, University of Glasgow Library), Dr W. H. Makey (City Archivist, City of Edinburgh District Council, Department of Administration), Mr John Massey Stewart, Mrs M. J. P. Matz, the Rev. Dr A. Morton Price (Principal, Scottish Congregational College), Mr Howard Nelson (British Library), Miss Andrea Nixon, Dr Richard Pankhurst (Librarian, Royal Asiatic Society), Mr J. G. Parker (Research Assistant, Royal Commission on Historical Manuscripts), Dr David Postles (Archivist, Sheffield City Libraries), Dr A Pyatigorsky, Professor Igor de Rachewiltz, Mr Alpo Ratia, Professor John Reed (Ohio Wesleyan University), Dr Staffan Roseń, the Rev. Mats Selen (the Swedish Church, London), Mrs R. E. Seton (Archivist, School of Oriental and African Studies), Miss A. C. Shrubsole, CBE (Principal, Homerton College, Cambridge), Mr T. H. Simms (Honorary Archivist, Homerton College), Professor Denis Sinor, Mrs Agnes Stallybrass, Mrs Catherine Stallybrass, the late Oliver Stallybrass, Mr William Stallybrass, Professor Bengt Sundkler, the Rev. Bernard Thorogood (formerly General Secretary, Council for World Mission), Professor Edward Ullendorff, FBA, and Mrs Ullendorff, the Rev. J. Van Hecken, Mr Peter Walne (County Archivist, Hertfordshire County Council Record Office), Miss Jean R. Yuild (Reference Librarian, Edinburgh University Library), and one correspondent who prefers not to be named.

Photographs are reproduced as follows: Plates 1, 8(*b*), 14, 15, 22, 23 and 24, from the archives of the Council for World Mission (incorporating the archives of the London Missionary Society), by kind permission of the Council for World Mission and the Library of the School of Oriental and African Studies, University of London; Plate 3(*b*) by kind permission of the Swedish Church, London; Plates 6(*a*), 7(*a*), 16, 17, 18 and 21(*a*) by kind permission of the British Library; Plates 8(*a*) and 21(*b*) by kind permission of the Taylor Institution Library, Oxford; Plate 13 by kind permission of the Bible Society; Plate 19 by courtesy of the Curators of the Bodleian Library, Oxford; Plate 20 by kind permission of the Royal Asiatic Society.

The painting on the jacket is reproduced from MS C I, 12, by kind permission of the Fürstlich Fürstenbergische Hofbibliothek, Donaueschingen.

Dates and Measurements

In 1752 the Gregorian calendar, or New Style (N.S.), was adopted in Great Britain, but in Russia the Julian calendar, or Old Style (O.S.), continued in use throughout the period of the duration of the mission to the Buryats. There was thus a regular difference of twelve days in the way a date could be recorded, with the New Style date being *apparently* twelve days later than the Old Style. The missionaries, and the other correspondents of the London Missionary Society in Russia, were not consistent, either individually or with each other, in the way they dated their letters. Sometimes they put both dates, with the Old Style usually, but by no means always, preceding the New Style. They occasionally made mistakes in calculating the effect of the difference of twelve days. Sometimes they used a single date, usually, but again by no means always, adding the letters O.S. or N.S. to indicate which calendar they were using. As a result, it is impossible to date every letter accurately in relation to one or other calendar, and dates are given in the form in which they occur in the letter quoted.

A pood was equivalent to 36 lb, a desyatin to 2.7 acres, and a verst to 3,500 feet or a little over one kilometre. The money used by the missionaries was the paper rouble, whose exchange value varied over the years, as explained in Chapter 11.

1
Early Plans

A hundred years ago, one of the best-known British missionaries was undoubtedly the Reverend James Gilmour of the London Missionary Society (LMS), who went out to China in 1870 and spent twenty years among the Chinese and Mongols of Inner Mongolia. Two Anglican societies, the Society for Promoting Christian Knowledge and the Society for the Propagation of the Gospel in Foreign Parts, had been in existence throughout the eighteenth century, but it was only at the end of the century that a vigorous missionary movement began to emerge, inspired by the Evangelical Revival. The first of the new societies to be established were Nonconformist or Evangelical in character. The Baptist Missionary Society of 1792, and the non-denominational London Missionary Society itself, founded in 1795, were followed only in 1799 by the Anglican Church Missionary Society. The new societies proved to be nurseries of unexpected talents. Grammarians and lexicographers like William Carey or Robert Morrison, pathfinders and explorers like John Williams and David Livingstone, all discovered in service abroad in the mission field the opportunity to realize potentialities which might never have found appropriate employment had they stayed at home. Gilmour was one such man.

Gilmour's fame, though, resulted, not from his success as a missionary, which was unremarkable, but from the wide popular appeal of his book *Among the Mongols*, which appeared in 1883, went through several editions in the following years, and was last reprinted in 1970. It has survived the years, and is still one of the best books ever written about Mongolia. A collection of essays, put together after Gilmour's death by his biographer Richard Lovett, and entitled *More about the Mongols*, did not enjoy anything like the same success, but Lovett's biography, *James Gilmour of Mongolia*, was perhaps the most popular of all books connected with the famous missionary. It ran into several editions, partly, no doubt, because it was pushed as a Sunday School prize. For children there was another posthumous book, this time about Gilmour's family life: *James Gilmour and his Boys*. The LMS had its own special edition of this book, which was intended for

Early Plans

presentation to Sunday School children who collected money for the Society's missionary ship, *John Williams*. It had a pre-printed form on the fly-leaf, with spaces for recording the name of the diligent child, and the sum of money collected. There were other books about Gilmour too, including one by his missionary friend, Mrs Bryson, who was with him at his death. For a time, in the last years of the nineteenth century, James Gilmour *was* Mongolia, as far as the British reading public was concerned, and he brought the land and the people to life for that public more vividly than anyone else has ever done.

But, in spite of the publicity surrounding his name, and his identification in the title of his biography, with the scene of his labours – a fashionable pattern for missionary biographies for many years – James Gilmour was not, and never claimed to be, the pioneer in the Mongolian mission field. It was just that he knew the country through and through, and was able to describe, in vigorous, fluent and attractive prose, what he had seen and experienced there. Besides, his life had many of the inspirational qualities which appealed to the pious imagination of Victorian mission enthusiasts. Here was a boy from a small Scottish village, Cathkin, near Glasgow, converted while a student, and inspired to minister to the heathen in remote northern Asia. He toiled at first alone, then with a devoted wife whose health was ruined by the rigours of the mission field, and who died young. There was a baby, little Alick, who sickened and died two years later. There were two older boys, who had to be sent home to go to school, leaving their widowed father to toil on alone. And, finally, there was the gallant Gilmour himself, grizzled and worn by twenty years in the roughest of mission fields, dying, in harness, before he was fifty years old. The family was a united one, on earth and in heaven. Gilmour once wrote to his sons: 'Tell Grandpa if he comes to Heaven first to take our love to Mama and tell her that we are all coming by and by.' Heaven was near at hand: it was an extension of Scotland, and the assured destination. The angels, Gilmour wrote to little Jimmie and Willie, would stop and talk to Mama and little Alick, and would ask her: 'Has he any brothers, and sisters?' and Mama would reply: 'Two brothers at school in Hamilton, Scotland.' It was an edifying story; it was well told by Lovett and by Gilmour himself, and it put Mongolia on the map for English readers for the first time.

Gilmour's work among the Mongols was inspired by, and to some extent built upon, that of an earlier mission, also sent out by the LMS. The English missionaries in Siberia, as they came to be known, had operated among the Buryat Mongols of Siberia, just inside the frontier with China, from 1818 to 1840. At that time the Mongols of China were inaccessible to mission work, just as, in Gilmour's time, the Mongols of Siberia were to be inaccessible. But the people were of the same stock, and though their spoken dialects were different, those of them who were literate used the same form of the written language, and the same script. Gilmour owed these earlier missiona-

Early Plans

ries certain debts. Perhaps the heaviest was the fact that they had translated the whole of the Bible into Mongolian. They had printed the Old Testament in Siberia with their own hands, and the New Testament was printed for them in England. The later missionary was spared years of preparatory work.

A whole chapter of Gilmour's book *Among the Mongols* is devoted to this early mission. It begins as follows:

'A mission among the Buriats, a Mongolian tribe living under the
authority of Russia, was commenced by the Rev. E. Stallybrass and
the Rev. W. Swan, who left England in the year 1817–1818. The mission was established first at the town of Selenginsk, and afterwards also on the Ona; but in 1841 the Emperor Nicholas broke up the mission, and the missionaries retired from the field.'

Such is the brief official record which the London Missionary Society is wont to produce, when occasion arises to refer to its first endeavours for the conversion of the Mongols. The history of this most interesting mission has never been written, – probably never will be written. No attempt at a history is made here; but as this old mission is often asked about, perhaps the few particulars that have in various ways come to the knowledge of the present writer may have interest for some of his readers.

Gilmour attributes the brief chronology of the mission which he gives to the LMS itself, but it is doubtful whether this paragraph is a literal quotation from any of the Society's papers or publications, and it probably represents Gilmour's own version of what he thought was the official view. On the face of it, there is no need to question the accuracy of this uncomplicated summary of the fate of the earlier mission to the Mongols, but, even on the basis of comparison with contemporary published material, let alone unpublished documents, it can be seen to be inaccurate. If, in fact, the life of the mission had been as harmonious as Gilmour's chapter implies, his errors and omissions would be of little consequence.

But there had been a darker side to the story, which had been successfully concealed from the public. For nearly the whole period of its existence, the small mission group had been riven by professional differences and personal incompatibilities, which had almost destroyed it. After some years, the missionaries had found it impossible even to go on living together, and they had taken up separate stations. They had naturally had to justify this step to the Directors of the Society, and they had done so on the grounds that the sparse population and the nomadic way of life of the people argued in favour of a number of outstations, rather than a larger group of missionaries concentrated in one place. This was a plausible argument, and was actually a realistic assessment of the local situation. But it was not the effective reason for the dispersal of the missionaries, and in that sense the Directors were

Early Plans

misled. They did not remain in ignorance of the true state of affairs for long, however, and over the course of the following years they were compelled to take patient steps to remedy the defects in the composition of the mission. In the end, one of the trio of missionaries was actually expelled from the service of the Society. Locally, the mission's reputation suffered from its obvious internal disunity, but at home nothing discreditable to it was ever allowed to appear in print.

Gilmour's chapter does not prepare us for this sort of revelation. On the contrary, it presents a picture of ability, devotedness and perseverance, even of heroism, on the part of the early missionaries, all words used by Gilmour himself. So his chapter misleads, for it creates a quite false impression of a band of like-minded evangelists, working harmoniously together as a team, with a single, obvious aim in view. Is it conceivable that Gilmour deliberately distorted the picture, altering the facts? It seems unlikely, for everything we know about him suggests that he was a man of absolute integrity. But the question must be investigated.

Let us look first at the mistakes which Gilmour made. Firstly, the mission was not commenced by Messrs Stallybrass and Swan, but by Stallybrass and the Rev. Cornelius Rahmn, a former Swedish army chaplain. Admittedly, Rahmn stayed no longer than a year in Siberia, before his wife's chronic ill-health forced him to leave the field. But he worked subsequently as the Society's missionary at Sarepta on the Volga for a few years. Then he ran a mission for the Swedish community in St Petersburg until the Russian authorities forbade him to do so any longer. Moving to England, he was employed for some years at the headquarters of the LMS, before taking over the pastorship of the Swedish Church in London, and also acting as chaplain to the Swedish and Norwegian Legation. He spent the last years of his life in Sweden, in charge of the parish of Kalv. Rahmn may not have achieved a great deal in Siberia, but he had been Stallybrass's companion in St Petersburg for a few months; he and his wife had shared with the Stallybrasses the discomforts of the long and exhausting journey by sledge over the winter snow-roads from the capital to Irkutsk; the two missionaries had jointly had the honour of being received by the Emperor Alexander I in Moscow and of firing his enthusiasm for the mission. Stallybrass valued Rahmn highly as a companion and fellow-missionary, and felt lost for a while when he had to leave Siberia. Rahmn was an exemplary Christian and servant of the LMS, and there was no reason to ignore his part in the founding of the Siberian mission. It can have happened only by oversight, and the omission argues for Gilmour's honesty as an author: there was nothing to hide.

Secondly, the mission was first established, not at Selenginsk, but at Irkutsk. Again, there was nothing discreditable about this false start. When the mission was founded, almost nothing was known in London about the Buryats, and some of what was believed was wrong. For example, the Society

Early Plans

was quite confused about the nature of the religion practised by the Buryats. It was thought that their shamanist religion was 'intimately connected with that of Dalai Lama, and somewhat akin to Brahminism'. The truth, as the Society's missionaries soon discovered, was quite different. Lamaism, the 'religion of the Dalai Lama', was a missionary religion itself amongst the shamanist Buryats. The two heathen faiths were rivals, not aspects of the same thing.

Irkutsk was one of the chief cities of Siberia, with its own Governor. The Society's advisers knew of it by repute, and it was a natural long-distance choice for the site of the mission. But almost at once these advisers learned, no doubt from the two Buryat *zaisangs*, or petty chieftains, who were sent to St Petersburg in late 1817 to help translate the New Testament into Mongolian, that, although Buryat could be heard in Irkutsk, the city was not the best choice for a Mongolian mission, and that it would be better to penetrate more deeply into true Buryat territory. Within a year the mission had been moved, first to Selenginsk, a little run-down garrison town on the far side of Lake Baikal, which few people in England can ever have heard of up till then, and soon afterwards to a site on the opposite side of the river from the town. This isolated position had the advantage that the missionaries were not living on top of the small Russian community of Selenginsk, and so ran less risk of becoming involved in the affairs of the Greek church.

Thirdly, the outstation on the river Ona was not the only one, though it had been Swan's, and Mrs Swan, from whom Gilmour must have got much of his information about the old mission, may have remembered it more clearly on that account. But why did Gilmour fail to mention, by name, the separate mission station on the river Khodon, to which Stallybrass migrated, and where the Old Testament was printed? Unlike Ona, which lay untenanted for some years, it was consistently occupied; there had been a lively school there; and it was more significant, as the site of the printing-press, than Swan's station on the Ona. Gilmour provides the clue to this mistake himself. He tells how he went once to what was called Onagen Dome, mixed Mongolian and Russian for 'the house on the Ona', and found there two tombs, one with a Latin inscription, and one with a Russian one. The former grave was that of Sarah, Edward Stallybrass's first wife, the latter that of Charlotte, his second wife. Both women had died, and been buried, at Khodon. So Gilmour had simply made a mistake. Either he thought that Ona and Khodon, which in fact were only about twenty-five miles apart, formed one station, or else he gave the wrong name to the place he visited. In either case, the explanation is perfectly innocent.

Finally, and an insignificant detail, it was in 1840, not 1841, that the mission was suppressed, though in the event Stallybrass and Swan and their families left the mission field early in the latter year.

But later on, in Gilmour's own account, there are more intriguing inconsistencies, and statements which do not stand up quite so well to examina-

5

tion. Almost at the beginning of the chapter he mentions the mission cemetery at Selenginsk: 'On the banks of the Selenga, and within easy reach of the town of Selenginsk, is a substantial stone-built inclosure containing four graves – those of Mrs. Yuille, two of her children, and one of the Rev. E. Stallybrass.' Who was this Mrs Yuille? Gilmour has so far failed to tell us. In fact, she was the wife of the third member of the trio of missionaries who manned the mission to the Buryats, the Rev. Robert Yuille, who, with his wife Martha, had been sent out in 1819, and had accompanied Swan from St Petersburg to Selenginsk in the winter of 1819–20. Gilmour then goes on to write: 'There is also inside the protecting wall a stone pyramid of decent height, with a Latin inscription, so obliterated as to make it impossible to discover whether it marks the resting place of Mr. Yuille, or merely commemorates the erection of the monument by him.'

Strangely enough, such a pyramid still stands near Selenginsk, the last relic of the mission station. This must be the monument of which Gilmour speaks, yet its Latin inscription is almost entirely legible, and can be seen to be dedicated to the memory of Martha Cowie, faithful wife of Robert Yuille, 'nata in Scotia in urbe Glasguae'. How could Gilmour, who was there in March 1871, have failed to read, because it was 'obliterated', what can be read today? Why did he apparently know, or affect to know, so little about Robert Yuille, who spent over a quarter of a century among the Buryats, not all of it, admittedly, in the service of the Society? Of him, Gilmour writes, almost dismissively:

> Besides Stallybrass and Swan, there was a Mr. Yuille connected with the mission. . . . Mr. Yuille, who had charge of the press, remained in Siberia after his colleagues had returned to England. The convert Shagdur, in a letter written to Mr. and Mrs. Swan, a year after their departure, speaks of having met Mr. Yuille at Udinsk, and says he had no intention of leaving soon. He was pledged not to teach religion; but to work for the education and elevation of the people; but after a short time he too was withdrawn, and so ended the labours of the missionaries in Siberia.

These remarks are inconsistent with Gilmour's doubts, expressed a page or two earlier, as to whether the monument at Selenginsk marked Mr Yuille's grave or not. If he had been withdrawn from the mission field, it could not possibly have done so. And if he had not been withdrawn, but had died in Siberia, who would have had the ability, or taken the trouble, to erect a substantial monument with an inscription in Latin?

There is a hidden background to these uncertainties. The sad truth was that Mr Yuille had proved, almost from the beginning, to be an uncomfortable companion to his fellow missionaries. His appointment had been a mistake, and ultimately everyone concerned knew that it had been. John Paterson, who, more than anyone, had conceived the idea of the mission to

Early Plans

the Buryats, and brought it into being, claimed in his manuscript memoirs that he had always had his doubts about Yuille. Under the year 1819 he wrote: 'How it was it is perhaps difficult to say, but Mr Yuille never gained my esteem, nor could I ever look on him as a well qualified Missionary for Siberia. Experience has shown that I was not wrong, but there he was by appointment of the Society.' This was a retrospective judgment. Paterson's memoirs were not a diary, but were composed towards the end of his life. Nor had anyone spoken quite like this against Yuille when his appointment had been considered and made. He had been recommended two or three times by the Rev. Dr David Bogue, in whose Seminary at Gosport he had studied for the mission service, and though there are hints in some of the Board Minutes and those of the Committee of Examination that Yuille was a difficult character, these are significant only with hindsight. But Paterson was right. Yuille was tragically unfit for his post, and in time the Directors were brought to accept this fact and, in the end, to dismiss him. His companions in Siberia were never in any doubt about the matter, even wondering, in later years, whether he was not perhaps mentally deranged. John Abercrombie, the Circassian printer from Karass, who had worked for the Basel mission at Shusha, and joined the Siberian mission in 1834 to operate the press, was reduced to despair within a few weeks by Yuille's bullying. Yuille bullied the Buryats as well, literally beating Christianity into them, and they nicknamed him *khatuu bagshi*, 'the tough teacher'. Publicly, though nothing was, or could be, said, which might throw doubt on the integrity of the mission, Yuille's name was simply allowed to slip quietly out of the pages of the Society's annual reports, and after the mid-1830s he was, publicly at least, ignored, though his affairs were to harass his colleagues and the Directors for years to come.

Practically everything that Gilmour has to say about Yuille is wrong, or, to put it more charitably, is sufficiently divorced from the truth to give quite a false impression of the part he played in the mission. It is true that Yuille was in charge of the printing-press, but it was only for a short while. His overbearing, even violent, behaviour made it impossible for Abercrombie to go on working under him, and his obstinate insistence on his right to make arbitrary alterations to Stallybrass's translation of Genesis, without consulting his colleague, and ignoring the fact that he was tampering with a text which had been passed by the censor, and his refusal to promise not to do the same with other books of the Bible, forced Stallybrass and Swan to withhold further copy from him until the Directors had been consulted about the case. The Directors' response was to instruct Yuille to give up the press, which was then transferred from Selenginsk to Stallybrass's station on the river Khodon. The printer moved there too, and all the remaining books of the Old Testament were printed, not at Selenginsk, but at Khodon. The colophons to the various fascicles which came out over the years between 1835 and 1840 all faithfully record the name of the place where the printing was carried on, but only in Mongolian, which was, and still is, a language hardly known in western Europe. The fact that the press had been moved to a new location was never denied, but it was never given much publicity either, apart from the announcement in the Society's 42nd Report, issued in 1836, to the effect that 'for the more correct printing of the Mongolian Scriptures, the press has been moved to Khodon, where Mr Abercrombie, the Printer, is now proceeding with the Old Testament'.

As a result, practically all reputable reference books and library catalogues give Selenginsk as the place where the Mongolian Old Testament was printed. The error occurs as early as in George Bullen's *Catalogue of the Library of the British and Foreign Bible Society*, printed in 1857, and continues in Darlow and Moule's great catalogue of the printed versions of the Bible, and in the printed Catalogue of the Library of the British Museum. Darlow and Moule even provide an ingenious, but false, etymology to explain the puzzling fact that the colophons name Khodon and not the traditionally accepted Selenginsk as the printing place.

Nor was it true that Yuille was 'withdrawn', or that this supposed withdrawal took place a short time after the departure of his colleagues, or that, with his departure, the work of the mission came to an end. The work of the mission was brought to a decisive end when Stallybrass and Swan left Siberia at the beginning of 1841. Yuille had taken no recognized part in it for the preceding few years. For a long time he had been engaged in an obstinate battle with the Directors over his refusal to come home for discussions, principally about his alleged mismanagement of the press, and after a long correspondence between London, St Petersburg and Siberia, he was finally expelled from the Society's service with effect from September 1838. He hung on in Siberia for another eight years, somehow supporting himself and his son Samuel Bogue Yuille, perhaps by teaching, perhaps by doing some doctoring, or perhaps by printing, for he had set up a rival press after he had lost control of the mission press. At all events the local Buryats are said to have remembered him kindly after his departure. But he no longer had any connection with the Society, and, indeed, he had done his best to frustrate the printing of the Old Testament, by refusing to release to his colleagues a quantity of paper belonging to the British and Foreign Bible Society (BFBS) which he held at Selenginsk, and which they desperately needed at Khodon when time was running out for them. In the end, the Russian authorities, too, lost patience with Yuille, and ordered him out of the country. He drifted back to Scotland, only to plague the Society afterwards for arrears of salary, for he never recognized the validity of his dismissal. Yuille drops out of sight in the Society's papers after his return home, and his apparent rejection of the Society's final offer of a financial compromise. He surfaces again for a moment in 1859 in the minutes of the Council of the Royal Asiatic Society, to which he tried, unsuccessfully, to sell forty-five Manchu, Mongolian and Tibetan books for the sum of £50.

Early Plans

Yuille died in Glasgow in 1861, but his death is not recorded in the Society's printed Register of Missionaries.

Evidently, then, Gilmour knew something, but not very much, about Yuille's part in the mission. What were the sources of his information? Gilmour was literally right in his belief that a history of the early mission had never been written, but, though he would not have had access to the Society's papers, a great deal had in fact appeared about it in print during its lifetime and afterwards. From 1816 to 1844 there was, almost without a break, a series of reports on the foundation of the mission and its activities in the *Evangelical Magazine*. Between 1821 and 1833 the Society's own *Quarterly Chronicle of Transactions* carried extracts, some of them quite lengthy, from the journals of Stallybrass and Swan, and also from those written by Rahmn at Sarepta. The mission was regularly referred to in the Society's Reports from 1818 to 1841. There were articles of less significance in the *Missionary Magazine* from 1836 to 1839, and in the more popular *Missionary Sketches*.

Gilmour could have read any of these publications, and probably did read some of them, for he certainly prepared himself before accepting the Society's invitation to go to Mongolia. Replying to this invitation on 29 September 1869 he wrote:

> Last night I received your letter communicating the request of the Committee that I should go to Peking with the view of reopening the Mongolian Mission. I have read the papers you kindly sent me on this subject, and also various articles on Mongolia, its inhabitants etc. and from these I have received the impression that there are many and great difficulties connected with the undertaking, so much so, that had the choice been left with myself, I would have preferred some post in the mission field surrounded with fewer difficulties and involving less responsibility.

Gilmour does not identify these discouraging articles.

Gilmour gives no hint that he had read what was an almost contemporary account of the mission in book form, *First-Fruits of a Mission to Siberia*, by the Rev. J. C. Brown. Brown had been closely concerned with the affairs of the mission in its later years, and at one time had even thought of going out to Siberia himself. He was Pastor of the British and American Congregational Church in St Petersburg, and acted as agent of the LMS there from 1833 to 1840. He was away on leave of absence from his church for about a year in 1836 and 1837, but otherwise all the mission correspondence, in both directions, had passed through his hands, and had been read by him, during almost the whole of the period when Yuille's case was under scrutiny. But his book had been published far away, in Capetown, in 1847, and in any case it was not a history in the true sense. It was, rather, a eulogy of the selfless missionaries, and an elegy for their mission, which had been suppressed by the Russian government only a few years earlier, just as it seemed to be on the verge of achieving success in terms of conversions. It says very little at all about Yuille, and the only hint of his differences with the Society, and one which the reader might easily fail to notice, was the remark: 'Mr Yuille was desired to leave his station and visit England.' Brown's book was, and always has been, extremely rare. It is not, for example, listed in the printed Catalogue of the Library of the British Museum. Swan had, however, owned more than one copy, and in March 1865 he sent a spare one as a gift to his friend, William Lockhart. It is this copy which is preserved today in the Library of the Council for World Mission, though it is impossible to tell when it came into the possession of the London Missionary Society. It seems hardly likely that Swan, who died early in 1866, would have left his widow without a copy of this unique book about their joint mission, written by a friend and colleague, and if Gilmour ever saw it, he probably saw it in Mrs Swan's library. But even so, he would not have found anything in it which would have led him to a different estimation of the nature of the early mission.

For the sake of completeness, we should mention that Mrs Swan herself published, though anonymously, a pamphlet entitled *Reminiscences of the Mission in Siberia*, but Gilmour can hardly have made use of it, as it appeared, in Edinburgh, only in 1882 or 1883. The best factual account of the early mission is contained in a chapter on both the Mongol missions in Richard Lovett's *History of the London Missionary Society*, which was published in 1895, some years after Gilmour's own death.

None of the printed sources which might have been available to Gilmour goes to the heart of the matter, but, at the same time, he could have avoided some of the mistakes he made if he had made fuller use of them. He would have known that it was Stallybrass and Rahmn who opened the mission, and he would have appreciated that Yuille was not simply 'connected' with the mission, but had been a full member of it for nearly twenty years, and a properly ordained minister. But he would have found nothing, correct or incorrect, about Yuille's later activities, for, even before his dismissal, the Society was ignoring him in its publications, and justly so, for after 1833 he failed to send in any reports on his work, and proved as uncooperative as possible.

We can only surmise that what Gilmour said about Yuille was based on confused recollections of what Mrs Swan may have told him. He was certainly well acquainted with her, for he had met her several times in 1869, and it was she who urged the Society to select him to reopen their mission to the Mongols. Moreover, there were one or two facts which Gilmour knew about Yuille which were drawn from the Swan family correspondence, and not from any publication of the Society, to whom they would have been of no interest. In March 1842, a little more than a year after the Swans had left Siberia, their favourite convert, Shagdur, wrote them a long letter, which

Early Plans

Brown reprinted in his book. One of the things Shagdur told them was that he had seen Yuille and his son Samuel in Verkhneudinsk, and, he added, 'it seems he does not intend to go away very soon'. This is the letter to which Gilmour refers in his book. Whether he read it in Brown's *First-Fruits*, or whether Mrs Swan showed him the original, it says nothing about a second thing he knew, that Yuille had allegedly been 'pledged not to teach religion', and this knowledge can have come only from Mrs Swan. Probably, then, Gilmour adapted some vague information, which he had gathered from Mrs Swan, and whose accuracy he had no reason to doubt, so as to form a coherent account of the mission. Mrs Swan may have shaded the truth. Indeed, she must have done so, once the name of Robert Yuille had been mentioned. There is a perfectly understandable reason for this.

For Hannah Swan, as for her husband and for Edward Stallybrass, the mission was not a matter for dispassionate historical examination. It was the work of God in their hands, a task of supreme importance, to which they had devoted themselves absolutely, and anything which they said or wrote about it could have had only one object, the furtherance of the mission cause. What they felt about their duties as missionaries had been uncompromisingly expressed by Swan in his original application to the LMS, in answer to the question: 'State your views of the obligations which the calling of a Missionary includes.' Swan replied that 'being embarked in a great and noble cause' a missionary should 'make every other pursuit bend to it – that he consider his talents, his time, his property, his influence to be disposed of only in the promotion of it, without considering himself at liberty to engage in pursuits of a scientific, commercial or general nature, any further than these may be necessarily connected with his own immediate and sacred work, as a Missionary of Christ'. Stallybrass and Swan realized these high principles in the conduct of their lives. They could have become scholars in a field of learning where they were the pioneers. They had compiled their own grammars and dictionaries of the Mongolian language, working through Russian and Manchu, languages which they had also had to learn on the spot. They had been the first Englishmen to study the lamaist scriptures of the Mongols, and to read their secular literature, and though others before them, like John Bell of Antermony, had witnessed shamanist séances, their descriptions of what they had seen amongst the Buryats were the best and fullest to have been published in English. They could have made a name for themselves in the world of learning as brilliant as that of their early teacher, and censor of their translations, Isaac Jacob Schmidt. Yet they deliberately refrained from seeking what they looked upon as worldly success and worldly fame. Valuable as it might have proved, they never published any of their linguistic work, for they considered it as merely ancillary to their great task of translating the Bible into Mongolian, and academic preoccupations would have been a distraction from the work of God. Yuille, on the other hand, did have scholarly pretensions, and this was a contributory reason why his colleagues distrusted him: he was not single-minded. Against the background of self-effacement on this scale, we cannot be surprised if Mrs Swan, in her conversations with Gilmour, felt herself to be serving a higher cause than that of mere historical factuality, and did not tell him all she knew. Her aim would have been to inspire, not just to inform, and this must be the innocent explanation for the inexact picture of the early mission which Gilmour painted, and which the popularity of his book perpetuated.

If this assessment of what happened, and why, is correct, then Gilmour's failure to read the Latin inscription on the monument at Selenginsk can be dismissed as a mere bagatelle. He may simply have used the wrong word, and written 'obliterated' where 'obscured' or 'overgrown' would have been more apt. But whatever the explanation, there is no general pattern of falsification into which this trifling error fits, and not the slightest reason to distrust Gilmour's honest intentions in telling the story as he did.

Gilmour succeeded in bringing to life the heroism of his predecessors in the mission to the Mongols. His book inspired his public to admiration of their work, and undoubtedly popularized his own mission. But his chapter is a tantalizing one. There is so much unsaid which one would wish to know, so many obvious questions unasked and unanswered. He does not tell us how or why Stallybrass and Swan came to be stationed in the depths of Siberia in the first place. They are just there, suspended in history, with no background to their adventure. How did it all come about? A land-locked part of the Russian empire, separated from England by a two or three months' journey by sledge over the winter snow-roads to the capital, St Petersburg, followed by a voyage of uncertain duration through the Baltic, or a cold trek across the frozen roads of northern Europe, seems an unlikely choice for a pioneer mission field. It does, though, appear less eccentric when it is remembered what obstacles were put in the way of missionary enterprise in the growing British maritime empire in the early nineteenth century. Until 1813 the monopolistic East India Company had been entirely opposed to the development of missions, and had refused to carry missionaries in its ships, or allow them to settle in places under its control. As a result of this policy, William Carey and his colleagues, for example, had been obliged to settle in Danish Serampore rather than elsewhere in India. Missionaries were unwelcome in the West Indies, too, where they were suspected of disturbing the large population of negro slaves. One of them, the Rev. John Smith of the LMS, was arrested in 1823 in George Town, Demerara, and so badly treated in gaol that he died early in the following year. His wife was even prevented, by order of the Governor, from following his body to the grave.

Though Siberia during the reign of Alexander I may have been physically remote, it was not such a dangerous place. But, while the Buryats, as shamanists and lamaist Buddhists, were pagans, and so a legitimate target for evangelization, Russia itself was a Christian country, whose established

Early Plans

church followed doctrines and practices which were very different from those of the independent churches to which the missionaries belonged. The latter were bound to be resented as interlopers, to be regarded as competitors, and to arouse the suspicion that their activities would tend to discredit the Orthodox church. Why did the Society think the experiment worth trying? Siberia was *terra incognita* to most Englishmen at the time. Even John Paterson, the mission's patron, had very hazy ideas about the Buryats and their language. How, then, did the Buryats come to be selected as the target people? Why was Irkutsk chosen as the site of the mission? How was permission obtained to set up the mission, and how was it maintained?

A general answer to this series of puzzling questions is to be found in a consideration of the peculiar religious situation which obtained in the ruling circles of Russia in the first quarter of the nineteenth century, and also of the strange personality of the Emperor Alexander I himself. Sovereign over a country committed to the Orthodox faith, Alexander had developed pronounced mystical and evangelical leanings. Even before his famous association with Julie von Krüdener, which began in 1815, he had come under the influence of the converted Prince A. N. Golitsyn. Golitsyn introduced him to the Bible in 1812, at a most critical time in his reign, when Napoleon had begun his invasion of Russia, and for some years Alexander lived in an exalted atmosphere of biblical and mystical enthusiasm. Princess Sofiya Meshcherskaya, with whom he read the Bible, was the sister of Princess Golitsyn.

As the defeated French retreated from Moscow, the Russian Bible Society was founded in St Petersburg, in December 1812, with imperial sanction. It met for the first time in January 1813, with Golitsyn as President, I. J. Schmidt as Treasurer, and Paterson, and Pastor Pitt of the Anglican church in the capital among its members. In the course of the next few years, Bible Societies were to spring up throughout the Russian empire, even, by 1820, in far distant Okhotsk on the Pacific coast of Siberia. Enthusiasm for the Bible cause prevailed for over a decade, fading only in the face of Orthodox reaction towards the end of Alexander's reign in 1825, and at the beginning of that of Nicholas I. During that atypical decade, Protestant missions were allowed to function in various parts of the empire. There were the Moravians who had been at Sarepta since the time of Catherine the Great, the Scots at Karass and also at Astrakhan and Orenburg, the LMS at Selenginsk and Sarepta, and the Basel mission at Shusha, south of the Caucasus. All profited from imperial patronage, but suffered inevitably from the fragility of that patronage.

The mission to the Buryats was not, then, an eccentricity, for whose existence special reasons have to be sought, for it belonged in a pattern of expanding Bible Christianity in Russia which was conditioned by the historical processes of the day. But the questions posed about its nature are still of great individual interest, and answers to them can be found in the missionaries' correspondence with their own Society and with the BFBS, in a few private letters which have survived, in committee minutes, and in contemporary literature.

What can be recovered reveals a fascinating web of chance, personal friendships and family relationships, which combined with the favourable situation at the time to result in the foundation of the mission, and its survival long after the death of Alexander I. Many names met with in connection with the foundation of the Russian Bible Society will figure in the story of the mission as well. Alexander himself, Golitsyn, Schmidt and Paterson were all involved. We can catch glimpses, too, of the daily life of the missionaries, and of the strange social and religious milieu in which they worked, and follow them in their various activities, as they translated the Old Testament and printed it, preached and taught, visited lamaseries to negotiate or dispute with the lamas, and travelled throughout Buryatia. One facet of the story, however, remains obscure. The missionaries' relations with the local authorities, whose deterioration must have been what led eventually to the suppression of the mission in 1840, are touched upon only at a few points in the correspondence, and then sometimes allusively rather than explicitly. The missionaries feared that their letters would be intercepted and read, and were very circumspect in what they reported about their relations with the civil authorities and the Orthodox church. Once or twice they used shorthand for security's sake, but mostly they just kept off certain themes. Again, there must have been correspondence with the local authorities, and if there was, and if any papers survive, they will probably be found only in Siberian archives, which are, at the present time, impenetrable. Thus in one important respect our view of the mission must be an unbalanced one.

The mission achieved only very limited success. The reasons for this are to be sought not so much in the damaging dispute which threatened at times to paralyse it, as in the circumstances of its conception. The force of tradition amongst the Buryats, and the vitality and organizational strength of the Buddhist church, were greater than had been imagined at the outset. Another obstacle to success was the missionaries' inability, in the face of Russian legislation, to baptize their converts. But even more important was the fact that the original evaluation of the scope and prospects of the mission had been greatly inflated, and for this fatal exaggeration John Paterson must, most probably, be held responsible.

The mission to the Buryats was not a haphazard strike into remote pagan territory for its own, limited, sake. The Buryats were, of course, the primary target, but their conversion was intended to lead on to bigger things. One of the original reasons for establishing the Siberian mission was the central position of Irkutsk, not only for evangelizing the various tribes of Siberian heathen, but also for penetrating China at a time when there was no access through the coastal ports. From the Buryats, it might be possible to reach

Early Plans

the Mongols of China. And from there it was not far to imagining the conversion of the Chinese court and then the people, through the medium of the Manchu language, which was correctly believed to be somewhat similar to Mongolian, but incorrectly considered to be the linguistic key to China. It was a grand design, based on false premises.

For one thing, Manchu was not spoken by 'a great proportion of the inhabitants of China', though Swan advised the Directors in 1821 that it was. It was becoming more and more of an irrelevance as the dying language of a thin imperial and aristocratic upper crust. Evangelization of the Chinese people could be accomplished only through the medium of the Chinese language. For another thing, China was to remain as inaccessible through its Siberian frontier as it was from the coast until the 1840s, after the First Opium War, and once China had been opened from the coast, the land route through Siberia and Kyakhta would have been superfluous, even if the mission had lasted that long. Swan was able to warn the Directors as early as 1820 that there was no hope of getting into China by way of Kyakhta, the only crossing point, but by then they had committed men and resources to a mission whose intended purpose could, at best, be only partially fulfilled. The Society did not withdraw its Siberian mission, though it regretted having founded it, and denied it the means to expand.

There were perfectly practicable, if tiresomely long, routes to the border with China. The difficulty lay in crossing it. Stallybrass and Swan's experience showed that a Siberian mission could be maintained from London, given proper support in St Petersburg, and Selenginsk could also be reached, though with greater difficulty, from the other end of the continent. The eccentric Calcutta merchant-captain Peter Gordon, a great enthusiast for mission work, had, in 1818, brought copies of Robert Morrison's Chinese New Testament by sea to the Russian port of Okhotsk, and from there had forwarded them to Selenginsk. Gordon took a broad view of mission matters, and the object of his voyage had been to try to effect a landing in Japan, or, failing that, to find a maritime station in the north Pacific from which Korea, Japan and eastern Siberia could be evangelized. He favoured a site somewhere on Sakhalien, which would be controlled from Irkutsk.

There seems to have been no reaction to this grandiose design, but the missionaries at Selenginsk got their Chinese Testaments, and gave a few of them to members of the Russian Ecclesiastical Mission, which passed through Kyakhta on its way to Peking in 1820 to relieve the previous mission. So Morrison's Testament reached Peking, but this had been a unique opportunity which could recur at best only once every ten years, and it was of no real significance. Wandering Mongols occasionally carried a tract or a gospel across the frontier, but that, too, was a chance event, and quite unimportant. The furthest the missionaries were ever able to penetrate into the Chinese empire was a few hundred yards to Kyakhta, on what were no more than rare one-day sight-seeing trips. The obstacle to entering China

Early Plans

was a political one, the Chinese insistence on the exclusion of foreigners, and this policy applied at Kyakhta just as much as it did at Canton, and was respected by the Russians. John Paterson misread the situation when, in 1815, he characterized the forthcoming mission as 'far more promising than any yet occupied by the Missionary Society, India excepted, and the most promising of all as far as China was concerned'. It was destined never to have more than a purely local function.

When the London Missionary Society was founded, in 1795, it declared its sole aim to be 'to spread the knowledge of Christ among the Heathen and other unenlightened Nations'. In so doing, it was acting in conscious obedience to Christ's injunction, expressed in Mark 16:15: 'Go ye into all the world, and preach the gospel to every creature.' There was thus, from the doctrinal point of view, nothing surprising or exotic in the selection of the Buryats as a mission field, and the reasons for the choice are to be sought in the Society's estimate of the practical circumstances of the time. In the course of the years, the Society came to concentrate on a small number of extensive fields of activity, on China, India, the South Seas, and Africa including Madagascar. But to begin with, it followed a different policy, sending missions out on uncoordinated tasks, as and when these seemed to warrant the commitment of its scarce resources in men and money. This policy resulted in what the Society's historian, C. S. Horne, termed 'desultory, and one might almost say, abortive, efforts'. Russia belonged to this category. From the very beginning, the Society had had its eyes on the pagan peoples of the Russian empire as a viable field, though experience soon showed that this enthusiasm for Russia had been misplaced, and that as a mission field it was expendable.

The early records of the Society are disappointingly terse. Board Minutes record suggestions which were made, but not necessarily the reasons why they were made. And, if the mission field proposed was not occupied, there may be no indication of why the suggestion was not followed up. Thus we know only that, on 25 September 1795, it was resolved to attempt a mission to what was uncertainly termed 'Tartary by Astracan'. Eight months later, on 3 May 1796, the Rev. Dr John Love, who had acted as the Society's provisional Secretary at its preliminary meetings, and had been elected its first Foreign Secretary in September 1795, presented a memoir concerning the northern coast of the Caspian Sea, first to the Directors, and then to a General Meeting. The Directors were authorized to act on the proposal if they thought fit, but there is no hint that any further action was taken. Nor can we be sure quite what they meant by 'Tartary', for this was an elastic concept which, at different times, could refer to anywhere and everywhere from the southern Russian steppes to the border regions of northern China. It is quite possible, though, that even at this time, it was the Kalmucks, a Mongolian people who lived a nomadic life to the west of the lower reaches of the river Volga, and so, in general terms, north of the Caspian Sea, whom

Early Plans

the Directors had in mind. They were familiar at least with the name of the Kalmucks through their connection with the United Brethren, or Moravians, and in particular through their interest in the Moravian settlement at Sarepta, near Tsaritsyn, on the western side of the lower Volga.

Not only had a mission field to be decided upon, but so had the method by which it was to be occupied. Two quite distinct modes of operation were feasible. In the end, the London Missionary Society would send out ministers, single or married men who had been ordained and had followed a course of missionary training at home. Such men would be supported from the home base by salaries, leaving them free to devote all their time to strictly missionary tasks, to learning the local languages, translating the Scriptures if that had not yet been done, evangelization, teaching, and pastoral, and ultimately also medical, care. But in its earliest years, the Society, like other patrons of missions, was attracted also by the method of founding mission colonies overseas. These colonies would be manned by farmers and craftsmen, men with the skills necessary to turn the new Christian settlement into a secure and, if possible, self-supporting base for the ministers who also formed part of its complement. William Swan discussed both methods in his theoretical and practical handbook *Letters on Missions*, and found the colony type of station to suffer from inherent handicaps. His chief objection was that there would almost certainly be a conflict in the choice of site. An area which offered the best prospects for its own economic development would not necessarily be an ideal mission settlement as well. Nevertheless, he could not help being fascinated by the idea, and he even cherished the vision of individual churches, with their ministers and congregations, emigrating as communities to some heathen land, where their Christian example would 'leaven the mass' of the pagan population. 'Were fifty or a hundred British churches thus "to give themselves to the Lord," and establish themselves in well-chosen spots in pagan countries, what might not be expected, with the blessing of God, from such a measure?'

This was an uncharacteristically utopian flight of fancy on the part of the usually sober, even sceptical, Swan, and nothing of the sort ever actually occurred, but the Society did, in its first years, experiment with the colony type of mission, when it sent its first missionaries to the South Sea Islands in the ship *Duff*. Success here was at first very uncertain, and some of the missionary-workmen proved unstable members of the community. But still, when, in 1803, the Society began to consider seriously the question of sending a mission to Russia, it was the colony type of mission which it visualized, and the enquiries which it instituted were directed mainly towards trying to ascertain what civil and economic privileges its craftsmen and missionaries might expect to enjoy in such a colony, and what were the agricultural, industrial and commercial possibilities of the region concerned.

It is not surprising that the Society thought along these lines, for under the Empress Catherine II it had become Russian policy to encourage the establishment of foreign colonies in underdeveloped parts of the Empire, and many colonies, mostly of Germans, had been founded in south Russia, principally in the neighbourhood of Saratov, on both sides of the Volga. Of these, the best-known, though it was atypical in its nature, was the Moravian settlement at Sarepta, further down river. Sarepta had a dual role. The Russian initiative, to which the Moravians had responded from their headquarters at Herrnhut, was an economic one; Sarepta was intended to be a centre of development. The Moravians, while recognizing this, and organizing the new colony on what were intended to be commercially viable lines, accepted the invitation primarily for religious reasons. Sarepta was not, though, founded as the headquarters of a mission, but with the intention that it should form 'a regular church or congregation which should shine as a light in a dark place, holding forth the true light of the gospel to Christians, heathens and Mahomedans in those eastern regions'. If and when it became rich enough to support actual missions, it would try to evangelize the surrounding lamaist Kalmucks, but such was not its primary purpose. Still, Sarepta was the model presented to the LMS by the Russians, when the Society began to pursue its enquiries about a Russian mission.

The United Brethren had tried earlier in the eighteenth century to establish themselves somewhere in Russia, but without success, and it was not until 1764 that they were formally invited, by Catherine the Great, to set up a colony. The site chosen, and first occupied in the following year, was on the western bank of the little river Sarpa, which flowed northwards into the Volga, some way below the town of Tsaritsyn, later known as Stalingrad, and now renamed Volgograd. In the present century, Sarepta was renamed Krasnoarmeiisk, and it is now a part of Volgograd itself. The colony's name was chosen and confirmed by the Lot, the usual Moravian method of ascertaining whether an initiative was in accordance with the Divine Will, at Herrnhut in 1766. There is an evident allusion in its name to that of the river on which the settlement stood, but it had a more significant, scriptural basis in the passage in the First Book of Kings 17: 'Arise, get thee to Zarephath, which belongeth to Zidon, and dwell there; behold, I have commanded a widow woman there to sustain thee.'

Sarepta's situation was not unfavourable. The climate was pleasant, much more healthy, for example, than that of Astrakhan. The land was fairly fertile, though less so than had at first been thought. Its excessive salinity meant that Sarepta would have to rely on manufacture and trade rather than agriculture, while the brethren could not compete with the Kalmucks in cattle-raising, being unable to range as widely over the pastures. But there was water, enough of it to run an artificial supply into the colony, and to operate a flour-mill and a saw-mill. A mineral spring, which was named Catharinenbrunnen after the Empress, but was usually known as the Gesundbrunnen, or Health-well, was discovered a few miles from the colony, and by 1796 it was attracting as many as 300 patients a year who came to Sarepta to take the waters. The colony lay in the midst of a large number of Kalmucks – nearly 100,000 families, it was estimated at the time – who would ultimately present a worthy target for missionary enterprise, and who in the meantime might provide a market for Sarepta's products. Finally, Sarepta lay at a road junction. One road led southeastwards towards Astrakhan, while the main highway led northwards towards Tsaritsyn and metropolitan Russia, and southwards towards the Caucasus and Persia. Sarepta's inn, her blacksmith and her bootmakers were assured of regular custom.

The colony had its fair share of disasters and difficulties to contend with. No sooner had it been founded than, in 1771, a large part of the Kalmuck population deserted the Russian empire, and began their epic trek back to China. The German population narrowly escaped deportation. The Kalmuck prince Bambar, who was pasturing at the time on the opposite bank of the Volga, and who had enjoyed medical treatment from the colony's doctor, planned to abduct him, and the rest of the skilled population, to serve in his horde when they reached the end of their journey somewhere in Inner Asia. Bambar was frustrated when the Kalmucks on the west bank of the Volga failed to join in the flight. Sarepta was saved, but it lost a large proportion of its Kalmuck customers for goods such as tobacco and vodka.

In September 1774 the colony was thoroughly plundered by the rebel Pugachev. Before they fled from their homes, the Moravians buried equipment and valuables in pits in the ground, but the rebels discovered most of the hiding-places, and what they could not carry off they smashed up. Fire was a recurring menace to Sarepta and its outstations. The Sarepta mills were destroyed in 1803, though the settlement itself was spared. Three years earlier, the Brethren's house at Saratov was burned down, while in 1812 there was a double disaster, accidental fire at their property at Astrakhan, and the complete destruction of the outstation in Moscow as a result of the French occupation of the city. Finally, two-thirds of Sarepta was burned down in 1823.

There were economic difficulties to contend with, too. The Kalmucks formed only a sparse, shifting population, especially after the diaspora of 1771, and for some of Sarepta's products, especially bricks, there was little demand outside the colony. The water supply proved to be insufficient to run the mills economically. At St Petersburg, the Moravians suffered from the incompetence of one of their agents. J. H. Hasse, their commissioner, or trade-agent, in the capital, managed to reduce the agency there to bankruptcy by 1801, and it took years of prudent work on the part of his successor, the Dane Asmus Simonsen, to restore the community's credit. All these disasters and crises meant that, over the years, the Moravians could afford very little in the way of missionary work among the Kalmucks, and in 1822 they gave up the struggle altogether, finally discouraged by the realization that Russian legislation would prevent them from baptizing the few converts they were beginning to make, and whom they would inevitably lose to the Orthodox church.

With all its problems, the Moravian settlement grew into a clean and neat little replica of a provincial German town, with a pious and industrious population. It was visited in 1773 by the German savant P. S. Pallas, who called it a 'superb colony'. Twenty years later he found Sarepta greatly improved. In the centre of the town was a market place with a fountain, shaded by trees. The main streets, which were laid out in a grid pattern, were lined with poplars, and each family owned its own cattle, and there were little private gardens along the Sarpa. A thriving commercial community was growing up. The first enterprise had been a communal store, which began business in 1766. Candle-making, distilling of vodka, and brewing followed. The inn was built in 1770, and a pharmacy was opened in 1776. There was a brick factory, and the two mills on the Sarpa which have already been mentioned. All the usual crafts were represented: there were bakers and butchers, tanners and locksmiths, tailors and stocking-makers, and so on. Dr Wier, the colony's physician, built up a private practice alongside his communal duties. A little way away from the settlement, along the path to the spa, lay a village called Schönbrunn.

It was no wonder that Sarepta became a familiar and welcome oasis to travellers in that part of Russia. Ebenezer Henderson and John Paterson, both great promoters of Bible work in northern Europe and Russia, approached Sarepta one hot day in the late summer of 1821, while on their journey from St Petersburg through south Russia and the Caucasus on Bible Society business. Afterwards, Henderson wrote:

> The afternoon was excessively hot, and we still felt greatly fatigued, notwithstanding the refreshment we had procured at Tsaritzin; but there was something indescribably soothing in the prospect of Sarepta, which beautifully opened on our view as we approached it, and inspired us with the delightful hope of enjoying a season both of physical and spiritual resuscitation. Passing the country-seat and village of Otrada, the church and houses of which are sweetly surrounded by poplars and vineyards . . . the road led us near a neat little farm, belonging to the Moravians; and about five o'clock we had the pleasure of stepping into the *Gemein Logie*, an excellent inn, fitted up quite in the German style.

Of the town itself, Henderson wrote:

> Fine tall poplars line the streets, and ornament the square; and the vineyards and gardens give it an appearance most enchanting to the eye that has been accustomed to wander in vain in quest of a single bush for hundreds of versts in the surrounding steppe.

It was Sarepta's character as an oasis of good order and homely comfort in the midst of wild and inhospitable steppe country which caught the fancy of other travellers as well. Two years after Henderson called there, Sarepta was devastated by fire, and many of the inhabitants left it for good. Some time between 1838 and 1843, the colony was visited by Xavier Hommaire de Hell, a French civil engineer and geologist then in Russian service, and he, or rather his wife, who was anonymously responsible for the descriptive parts of their joint book, was as charmed by Sarepta as Henderson had been. She felt saddened by the sight of the blackened ruins of two factories, which the Moravians had been unable to rebuild, and which boded ill for the future, but she found the town itself delightful:

> Picture to yourself a pretty little German town, with its high gabled houses, its fruit trees, fountains, and promenades, its scrupulous neatness, and its comfortable and happy people, and you will have an idea of Sarepta: industry, the fine arts, morality, sociability, commerce, are all combined in that favoured spot. . . . Everything breathes of peace and contentment in this little town, on which rests the blessing of God. It is the only place I know in Russia in which the eye is never saddened by the sight of miserable penury . . . . Every house is a workshop, every individual a workman. During the day every one is busy; but in the evening the thriving and cheerful population throng the walks and the square, and give a most pleasing air of animation to the town.

But, even as early as this, Sarepta's best days as a unique institution were over. The inevitable dichotomy between spiritual and commercial interests, which Swan had anticipated would weaken any religious colony, was already leading to a change in the character of Sarepta. For one thing, it was impossible to prevent what was essentially a commercial concern from attracting undesirable elements. One such adventurer, whose name is known, and whose activities threatened to give Sarepta a bad name, especially with the Kalmucks, in its earliest days, had been Johannes Jaehrig, who later served P. S. Pallas as assistant and interpreter. Not much is known of the early life of Jaehrig, who died in a lama temple at Kyakhta in 1795, perhaps because his Moravian contemporaries preferred not to perpetuate his memory. He had compiled some notes on the Kalmuck language while at Sarepta, which proved of some use to the colony's missionaries, and Pallas himself had a high opinion of his linguistic abilities. Benjamin Bergmann, the other pioneer of Mongolian studies in the German language, was less enthusiastic. Precisely what Jaehrig had done to make himself unwelcome in Sarepta we do not know. But according to Alexander Glitsch, who was a member of the family which owned Sarepta's most celebrated commercial enterprise, its mustard factory, and who compiled its centennial history, which was published in 1865, he had taken part in the mission to the Kalmucks merely as a pretext to cover his 'frivolous, depraved intercourse with that people', much to the dismay of the Brethren.

There were other, similar, individual disappointments. In 1818, Brother

Hübner had to be withdrawn from the mission field because he had become too fond of the bottle, with all its consequences. But much more significant than these isolated personal shortcomings was Sarepta's gradual but inexorable departure from its early ideals. Its character as a commercial settlement meant that the population became more and more mixed. As early as 1816 the Moravian element in the population was outnumbered by non-Moravians, the majority of the strangers being Germans from the colonies to the north, and Russians. The younger generations felt less and less sympathy, as time went on, with Herrnhut, and the connection became a formal, administrative one, kept up only at a high level. Sarepta continued as a Moravian community almost to the end of the nineteenth century, but its changing internal composition, and the conflict between its loyalties to the Russian state and those to Herrnhut, which tried to maintain a control, especially in financial matters, which was no longer acceptable, finally provoked a crisis in the situation. In 1892 the authorities at Herrnhut terminated Sarepta's membership of the Moravian unity. Two years later, the Protestants of Sarepta joined the Lutheran church, and the sole Moravian colonial experiment in Russia came to an end.

Today, the name of Sarepta has fallen into oblivion, and it is hard to appreciate what an important position this little German settlement, planted in the remote Kalmuck steppes, held in British Nonconformist missionary circles at the beginning of the nineteenth century. Admiration for the Moravians was not uncritical, and some hard things were said, for example, by John Paterson about what he felt was the free and easy way in which Moravian translators treated the Word of God. Richard Knill, the first regular agent of the LMS in St Petersburg, was equally, though less explicitly, suspicious of some aspects of Moravian behaviour. At that time, 1823, the Society still maintained Rahmn as its missionary to the Kalmucks, living at Sarepta, but not associated in his work with the Moravians. On the surface, everything was harmonious, but beneath it there were some misgivings, keenly felt, though ambiguously expressed. Writing home in June 1823, Knill felt obliged to say:

> As for Mr Rahmn's situation at Sarepta, I do not know that it was ever *cordially approved* by the United Brethren. There is something to me very dark about that station. The woman in the Apocalypse had the world under her feet, but it seems to be quite the contrary at Sarepta. However, it becomes me to say nothing as I have not seen it, – and we are also indebted to the U.F. for their Chapel at St. Petersburg.

But these were only personal misgivings, and differences with the Moravians were no obstacle to mutual cooperation. At the institutional level, both the LMS and the BFBS maintained close relations with the Moravians at Sarepta and elsewhere in Russia for two decades. Both societies patronized the colony. The BFBS voted money in 1808 to finance the casting of a fount of

Early Plans

Kalmuck type, with which the Moravians hoped to print their projected translations of the Scriptures. Directors of the LMS were prominent among those who organized the collection of money for the rehabilitation of the Moravians in Russia after the disasters of 1812, and the Society subsidized the renewed mission to the Kalmucks, which was sent out from Sarepta in 1815. On the other hand, the Moravians gave much practical help to the members of both societies in Russia. The house of Asmus Simonsen, their commercial agent in St Petersburg, assisted in many ways, not least by accepting the bills of the missionaries in Siberia, and sending them regular supplies of bank notes. Paterson, Knill and others were always sure of a welcome at Sarepta House in the capital, and when the independent congregation which Paterson had begun to gather together in 1815 in the house of a Mr Brown, one of the English residents, outgrew its accommodation, the Moravians allowed the little English church the use of their chapel there. And, finally, it was Sarepta's existence, and knowledge of its constitution, which provided the Society with a sound basis of fact from which to assess the offer made by the Russian authorities when negotiations were opened in 1803.

It is impossible to tell what motivated the Society to initiate these discussions with the Russians. Early volumes of the Moravian journal, *Periodical Accounts relating to the Missions of the Church of the United Brethren*, which contain news about the progress of Sarepta and its mission work, are in the Society's library today, and most probably belonged to it at that time too, but something more specific than this must have happened to explain the Society's move. There may have been two coincidental spurs to action. One is perhaps to be discovered in a letter, copied to the Society, dated 16 July 1802, which was sent by the Rev. C. F. Gregor, Minister to the Congregation at Sarepta, to the Rev. C. I. Latrobe, in Fetter Lane, the Moravian headquarters in London. This letter describes a visit paid by two Scottish missionaries, Henry Brunton and Alexander Patterson. The two men were on their way, with a 'young African companion', to Astrakhan and beyond, intending to establish a Christian settlement somewhere in the Caucasus or Persia. The Moravians were rather sceptical about the venture. The two travellers had not bothered to inform themselves about Moravian customs and missionary methods and experience before turning up in Sarepta. Indeed, they seemed never to have met a Moravian before. They had not prepared themselves by finding out anything about any of the people amongst whom they would eventually settle. They were thought to have no definite ideas about missionary work, though this was an unjust criticism at least as far as Brunton was concerned, for he had had several years' experience as a missionary in West Africa. Finally, the two men knew no foreign language – at least, none that would be useful to them where they were going.

Nevertheless, these were the beginnings of the Scottish colony at Karass in the Caucasus, a colony which obtained a grant of land from the Russian authorities, and privileges similar to those of Sarepta, and it may have been partly the news of this visit to the Moravian colony which persuaded members of the Society that it might be worth pursuing enquiries themselves. Siberia had not yet entered their thinking: their interests were still limited to a missionary settlement in European Russia, somewhere along the Volga.

The second impulse to action may have been personal initiative on the part of the Rev. Alexander Waugh, a founding director of the Society, and an influential member. He was also chairman of the Committee of Examination, the Committee which, among its other duties, recruited new missionaries and arranged their training programmes, for twenty-eight years before his death in 1827. A group of papers preserved in the Society's archives together with the letter from Gregor suggest what may have happened, though the story cannot be followed up in full either there or in any committee minutes.

Some time in 1803, Waugh claimed to have observed that the new Emperor of Russia, Alexander I, influenced by one of his advisers, N. N. Novosil'tsev, was apparently well disposed towards that policy of developing Russia through the medium of foreign colonies to which Sarepta owed its existence. Novosil'tsev was a member of Alexander's so-called Unofficial Committee of advisers, and was to visit London in 1804 on a diplomatic mission. William Pitt thought him to be a man for whose inexperience and youthful enthusiasm allowances should be made, but nevertheless then, and for some years to come, he had the ear of the Tsar, and Waugh had access to him, at least indirectly. It is just possible, too, that Novosil'tsev may, quite independently, have had a personal interest in the Kalmuck Mongols of the Volga. The pioneering book by Benjamin Bergmann, *Nomadische Streifereien unter den Kalmüken*, published in Riga in 1804–5, which gave a comprehensive view of the geography of the Kalmuck steppes, an account of Sarepta itself, and a survey of the history, customs, religion, epic poetry, and literature of the Kalmucks, rivalled only by Pallas's encyclopaedic work on the Mongols in general, was dedicated to Novosil'tsev in his capacity as President of the Imperial Academy of Sciences at St Petersburg.

Waugh began his enquiries with the Russian authorities through an acquaintance of his, a Mr Davidson, who was at the time in charge of the imperial farms at St Petersburg. Davidson got Waugh to supply him with a list of questions which, in the surviving copy, is drawn up in French, and headed:

La Société des Missionaires de Londres se proposant d'introduire la
religion chrétienne parmis les Tatares et les autres paiens qui habitent
les rives du Volga, désire préalablement avoir des réponses aux
questions suivantes proposées par Mr Waugh dans une lettre à Mr
Davidson.

Early Plans

This form of words suggests that, although it was Waugh who conducted the negotiations, and who had probably initiated the project, the scheme had been officially adopted by the Society, and that the enquiries were made on its behalf and with its backing. It is clear, too, that mission work was to be the main object of the proposed settlement, and that the Society wanted a site in the Volga region.

Davidson passed the questions on to Novosil'tsev, and when the Russian diplomat came to England in September 1804, Waugh received from him some papers which he passed on to his fellow Directors, together with a memorial of his own, dated 20 December 1804. This memorial has become separated from the other documents in the case in the Society's archives, so that one cannot be absolutely sure which were the papers which Novosil'tsev handed over, but they probably included, in spite of the seven months' delay, a letter in English, signed by him, and dated St Petersburg, 25 February 1804, which refers to 'the enclosed papers' which he is directed to forward, and which reveals that the Emperor himself had approved the Society's proposal; the list of questions together with the answers to them; and a scheme of the privileges, described as consistent with those granted to Sarepta, which the colony would enjoy. The scheme of privileges is drawn up in French, and there is also a rough English translation, with a few notes on passages which apply specifically to the Moravians and would not be relevant to the Society's missionaries, and a more polished version of the same translation. There is no definite evidence as to how these last two documents originated, but the stilted and incorrect English of the rough translation, and the confident manner in which the notes grant exceptions to the privileges as they would relate to the mission colony, suggest that this version, at least, was also an official document, emanating from St Petersburg.

The general tone of these papers was reassuring. Like those of Sarepta, the privileges were generous, though perhaps not exceptionally so. The Scottish colony at Karass, for instance, was to enjoy a comparable status. The colonists would be confirmed in the perpetual possession of the lands granted to them by the Emperor, and, unlike the Moravians, who enjoyed corporate possession only, as was their custom, they could dispose of this property individually, but only to other members of the same colony. They would have complete freedom to practise their religion, to build towns, villages and other dwellings, and churches with steeples – so specified, no doubt, in order to distinguish them clearly from churches of the Orthodox faith, with their characteristic domes – and schools. In general, they would be subject to the laws of the Empire, but they would be allowed to have their own administration, free from outside interference except when the interests of the Empire were in question. They would enjoy full civil rights in their colony and throughout the Empire. Their own authorities would have the power to issue internal passports, and could apply for passports for colonists to leave the country, which would be issued to them by the appropriate offices. The colonists would be allowed to engage in internal and external trade without having to belong to the Guild of Merchants, and carry on crafts and industries of all sorts, with a restriction placed only on the distillation of brandy, which was already farmed out. Interlopers would be forbidden to set up inns or salt-stores, or other public or private buildings on their lands, without their consent. They would be exempt, but not debarred, from military and civil service, and not subject to the billeting of troops. They would be able to sell their property and leave Russia, if they wished, on the payment of three years' interest on capital acquired in Russia, and the effects of dead colonists could be shipped home in the same way. They would be allowed to have an agent from among their own number residing at the capital, and, finally, they would be exempt from taxation for at least the first twenty years of the colony's existence.

These privileges constituted, almost exclusively, a definition of the future colony's political and commercial status, and, whether or not it was noticed at the time, one essential condition was left unmentioned. Nothing was said about liberty to proselytize and to baptize any converts who might be made. As things turned out, failure to establish this point meant that the Moravians' missionary efforts were entirely frustrated when, in 1822, they applied for, and were refused, permission to baptize their few Kalmuck converts. No doubt the same fate would have overtaken the Society's colony.

The Russian replies to Waugh's questions also suggested that the authorities would interpret very liberally the privileges they were ready to grant. The Society was assured that the Russian government would not only not object to the settlement of some thirty to sixty families, but would actively assist the project. Protection of all kinds was promised to the colonists, though they were advised to keep quiet about their missionary purpose, perhaps so as not to alarm the native population, but more probably in order not to arouse the jealousy of the Orthodox clergy. Swan was to encounter the same cautious reaction when passing through Tobolsk in 1820. He found the Governor receptive to the idea of sending a missionary there, to work amongst the local Muslims, but reported that 'he hesitated however upon our pressing the matter home. . . . He is afraid of exciting jealousies and suspicions among the clergy and on that account declined for the present to give his recommendation or to promise his influence to further such an undertaking. He himself not being of the Russian but of the reformed church, may from motives of delicacy be less inclined to interfere in ecclesiastical matters, or where the interests of the Church may be supposed to be concerned.'

Forthcoming though they were, the Russians did not comply with the Society's request for a mission site somewhere in the Volga region. They agreed to a colony 'in the vicinity of the dwellings of the Tatars' but interpreted this provision to indicate a site further to the east, beyond the

Early Plans

Urals, in western Siberia. They did not, at least in the papers available today, specify the exact location of the colony, but directed the Society's attention towards the Government of Tomsk. Local advantages, they assured Waugh, included a mild climate and fertile soil. The colonists would be able to develop profitable industries, such as tanning, textiles, soap-making and fat-rendering, based partly on the raw materials produced by the herds kept by the local population, and they could engage in brewing and distilling as well. The presence of 20,000 troops along the Irtysh line would provide them with a market for their produce, and towns and markets would be within reach along the Russian and Siberian waterways. There were also plenty of heathens for them to exercise their benevolence upon – 'la Société pourra d'autant plus facilement parvenir à son but que dans ces contrées il se trouve quantité de paiens' – and these Tatars were peaceful folk, from whom no danger was to be anticipated. The Russian reply contrasted the local Tatars with the 'so-called Tatars of the Volga, who include those of the Caucasus, and these are all Mohammedans and strongly attached to their religion'. This may seem rather a disingenuous excuse, for the west Siberian Tatars were Muslim too, though their religion was diluted by a strong dash of older shamanistic beliefs and practices which still survived amongst them. However, there seems to have been no attempt to deceive the Society. Swan, on his first journey to Siberia, found that the Tatars of Kazan, at least the less sophisticated rural ones, were 'less firmly attached to the religion of the false Prophet than the Mahomedans who live nearer the headquarters of his delusion', and there were other factors, too, which marked them out 'to the friends of the Bible as objects of peculiar attention'. Perhaps the same applied to other Tatar peoples still further east.

Why, though, should the Russians wish to divert the Society's colony away from the Volga region, and why should they offer such an unconvincing excuse as the resistance of the Tatars of the Caucasus to Christianity? It was not as if the Society was deliberately seeking a site in the Caucasus. It would no doubt have been content with one among the thousands of Kalmucks who, as lamaist Buddhists, were thought to be more open to evangelization. The Kalmucks had hardly been touched so far by the few missionaries whom Sarepta could spare. But the Russians may have decided that the Sarepta privileges implied a prior right to work amongst the the Kalmucks, and that to allow competition might provoke complaints. On the other hand, the Russian preference for Siberia may have been based on economic considerations. They may simply have felt that the Volga region had already been colonized to a sufficient extent by the Germans who had come in during the reign of Catherine the Great, and that the benevolence of the Society might be better exercised in a less developed area.

Even though the project was never realized, one wonders just where the favoured site might have been, but there is no convincing answer to this question. In his memorial covering the Russian reply, Waugh wrote, confusingly, that 'the place which they seem to prefer before the neighbourhood of the Volga is a station on the Tura near the Ienesei in the Govt of Tomsk'. If by this he meant the well-known river Tura, it is surprising to find it associated with the Yenisei, from which it is separated by several hundreds of miles. But neither the Russian reply, nor Novosil'tsev's covering letter, mentioned the Tura in this connection. The very vague way in which the papers allude to the proposed site leaves it open to doubt whether a site on the Tura, or one much further east, near the city of Tomsk, was intended. But the fact that the figure of 150 roubles is given as an estimate of the maximum cost of conveying a family of four persons, with five poods of luggage, from St Petersburg to *Tomsk*, suggests that the mission would have been situated somewhere near that city, and not where Waugh thought it was to be.

Waugh passed on to the other Directors the text of the Russian reply together with comments on it. He also added something apparently of his own, suggesting that the site chosen was worthy of consideration for yet another reason, apart from those of the mild climate and the fertile soil which had been urged. This was 'its vicinity to China, to the northern frontiers of which it is immediately contiguous; the opportunity of introducing the Gospel to China thro' the great intercourse which is carried on between that immense country and St. Petersburg, on the neighbourhood of the road of which intercourse is situated the place of the proposed settlement'. It is here, in this memorial, that, for the first time, we become aware of that will-o'-the-wisp promise of being able to enter China from the north, which lured the Society on for two decades, but never proved anything more than a mirage. Certainly, cities like Tomsk lay along the main route from European Russia to China, but entry into China was practicable only at the frontier post of Kyakhta, south of Lake Baikal, and strict supervision of foreigners was enforced there. China maintained a chain of police posts along the frontier on either side of Kyakhta, just inside Mongolia proper, for the express purpose of preventing unauthorized movement across the frontier. Frontier relations between the two empires had been regularized by the Treaty of Kyakhta in 1727, and it is hardly likely that Novosil'tsev would have encouraged Waugh to think of Siberia as constituting the back door into China, knowing, as he must have done, that it would be contrary to Russian interests to permit, or even to connive at, what would be construed as interference in the internal affairs of the Chinese empire. Wherever the idea now formalized had originated, it could only lead the Society to a dead end.

Even while recommending the advantages which the proposed mission site would enjoy, Waugh was not happy with the plan itself, and doubted the wisdom of the Society's committing itself to so risky a venture. He wrote:

Early Plans

It is probable that the idea of sending a colony will be deemed unsuitable to the object of the Missionary Society. But a limited number of Missionaries may be sent out with the settlers, and with them alone a connexion with the Society established and maintained. . . . There are many things, however, to be taken under consideration before any definitive measure be adopted. Mr Davidson will very readily introduce a committee of the Directors to his Excellency Novossilzov, who will supply them with every information, and grant by authority of the Emperor all the legal securities which may be deemed requisite. A door seems to your memorialist, in the gracious providence of God, to stand open, into these extensive dark and idolatrous regions; and with intire confidence in the zeal and candour of his honoured associates, he leaves it, under God, to the spiritual discernment of the Directors, to dispose of the opportunity presented to them as to their own minds it shall seem best.

There the matter rested. There seems to be no further mention of it in the Society's papers, and it may not have reached the stage of formal discussion in committee. Waugh was evidently reluctant to give his personal approval, and the Directors may have decided that what they had been offered, while superficially generous, would almost certainly commit them to the support of a hazardous and expensive commercial venture, far from home, which held no promise of missionary success. The privileges had been copied mechanically from those granted to Sarepta, a settlement whose priorities were quite different from those of the Society, and this lack of imagination on the part of the Russian authorities at the outset may have led the Directors to anticipate inflexibility and obstruction once they had given a hostage to fortune. By the end of 1804, then, interest in Russia as a mission field had faded away, and nothing might have been undertaken in that direction had it not been for the meeting, unconnected with Missionary Society business, of three remarkable men, the Scottish Congregationalist John Paterson, the former missionary at Karass Robert Pinkerton, and the Dutch Moravian Isaac Jacob Schmidt.

2
I. J. Schmidt and the Kalmucks

The name of Dr I. J. Schmidt will be remembered by readers of Herbert Jenkins's classic *Life of George Borrow* as that of the unhelpful member of the Russian Board of Censors who promised to advise Borrow how to set about obtaining permission to print the New Testament in Manchu translation in St Petersburg in 1834, on behalf of the British and Foreign Bible Society, but never bothered to do anything more about the matter. Schmidt was one of those whom Borrow had in mind, the actual translator Stepan Lipovtsov being the other, when he wrote to the Rev. Joseph Jowett, his correspondent at the Bible Society: 'You cannot conceive the cold, heartless apathy . . . which I have found in people to whom I looked not unreasonably for encouragement and advice.' Borrow's biographers have tried their best to excuse Schmidt's dilatory behaviour. Jenkins wrote that he was 'apparently very busily occupied with his own affairs, which included the compilation of a Mongolian Grammar and Dictionary'. Miss Eileen Bigland offered a more circumstantial but largely imagined explanation of Schmidt's incivility. For her, it was the compilation of the Grammar alone which engrossed Schmidt's attention, and he 'needed a violent prod in the ribs before he so much as lifted his head' from the task.

In fact, Schmidt's Grammar had been published nearly three years earlier, in 1831, and can have had nothing to do with his supposed snub to Borrow, though certainly his Dictionary was not to appear in print until 1835. If the truth be known, his neglect of Borrow stemmed from his natural egoism, rather than from preoccupation with any particular task, and Borrow appreciated this. Schmidt, he told Jowett, was 'so involved in a multiplicity of business' that he had been unable to find the time to offer him advice or information.

Borrow was not the only one to complain of Schmidt's insensitivity to the needs of others. In an undated letter from St Petersburg to his friend John Paterson, written probably at the beginning of 1833, and so a year or so before Borrow experienced his rebuff, William Swan offered a candid esti-

I. J. Schmidt and the Kalmucks

mate of Schmidt's character in terms rather freer than he might have employed in his official correspondence:

> The immediate cause of our protracting our stay here, you I presume are already acquainted with. I am now working hard at the Mandjur SS [Sacred Scriptures] and hope to finish it in time to travel by the summer roads – My application for liberty to print the Mongolian SS has been at last successful – Schmidt is to be the censor, and this arrangement makes it very desirable that *his* work should be commenced while I am here – I have written to Siberia for MSS and hope soon to have Stallybrass's Pentateuch to begin with. *This* is a *collateral* reason for my remaining a few months here of no small weight – Schmidts views of translation and ours are not exactly the same, and our criticisms of his N. Test, in part, as he supposes, occasioned its suppression – so if his love to the cause do not triumph over his love to retaliate, he may easily find occasion to retard or even yet prevent the printing of our version.

These were hard words – unjustifiably hard as it turned out. Schmidt proved to be a much more accommodating censor than the missionaries had anticipated. Certainly he was slow to act, but he realized this, and in the press of his own work he allowed Edward Stallybrass to take over much of the task of censoring the translation himself, when he was in St Petersburg in 1836. But even so, we find William complaining about Schmidt again in that year, in almost the same words as Borrow had used: 'Dr Schmidt, the authorized censor of our version, although disposed to advance the printing of it, is yet so much occupied with his other engagements as to leave him but little time to attend to it; in consequence of which the press has been obliged to stand still waiting for copy.'

Schmidt's disregard of others probably lay in his very character. He was self-centred, and, so it seems, rather selfish. More seriously, he could even claim other men's work as his own. But the little scene drawn by Jenkins and Miss Bigland of the preoccupied scholar poring over his remote researches to the neglect of more pressing affairs, while inappropriate in this context, is not inapt. It serves to recall what sort of a man he was.

Schmidt was one of the great Orientalists of the nineteenth century. Apart from the two books just mentioned, he was the author of a long series of articles and books concerning the languages and cultures of the peoples of Inner Asia, principally the Mongols and the Tibetans, whose excellence earned him a doctorate from the University of Rostock, and membership, in St Petersburg, of the Imperial Academy of Sciences. His name is familiar to every student of the Mongolian language today as that of one of the founders of their discipline. Much of his work has been overtaken by time. His pioneering Mongolian–German–Russian dictionary, for example, was made obsolete within fourteen years of its publication, by the much more

I. J. Schmidt and the Kalmucks

comprehensive Mongolian–Russian–French dictionary of the Polish scholar J. E. Kowalewski, which was printed at the University of Kazan in successive volumes during the 1840s and is still the standard reference work. But much of what Schmidt did still retains its usefulness a century and a half later. It was he who opened the eyes of western European readers to the unsuspected riches of Mongolian literature. He was the first to appreciate the value of the Mongolian tradition of historical chronicles, and his text-edition, with a translation into German, of a seventeenth-century chronicle, published in 1829, was considered worth reprinting in 1960. In spite of its many shortcomings, it is still a classic in its field. It was Schmidt, again, who made the great central Asian epic of Geser Khan accessible to European readers, while his translation of the classic collection of Buddhist tales, the *Ocean of Stories*, is still enjoyable today.

But with all his learning and talent, Schmidt had his faults. He was cantankerous and intolerant. Never prepared to admit that he might be wrong, he was always ready to enter into bitter, even abusive public controversy with other scholars with whom he disagreed. Twice in his lifetime he clashed openly with the celebrated Russian Sinologist the monk Iakinf Bichurin. The first of these two quarrels involved Rintsin Wangchikov, the brightest pupil at the school run by the missionaries at Selenginsk, and concerned the so-called 'Stone of Genghis Khan'.

This was an inscribed stone monument, dating probably from the middle of the thirteenth century, and so one of the oldest, if not the oldest, examples of writing in the Mongolian language. It had been discovered in the basin of the Argun river in eastern Siberia early in the nineteenth century and brought to St Petersburg, where it was displayed at the exhibition of 'Products of Home Industry' held in 1839. The subject of the inscription was the commemoration of an extraordinary feat of Mongolian archery. At an assembly held by Genghis Khan, a certain Yisüngge had shot an arrow to a distance of 335 *alda*, or double arm-spans. The actual interpretation of the inscription, though, proved a matter of controversy. Two translations were in existence. One was Schmidt's, and the other had been made by Rintsin, who had passed it to Bichurin. On the initiative of the president of the organizing committee of the exhibition, both translations were put on display together with the stone. Schmidt took immediate umbrage at what he chose to interpret as a correction of his work, and published an intemperate open letter addressed to Bichurin, in which he accused the learned monk of entering into competition with him, and defended himself furiously against criticisms which had never been made. For some time, Bichurin hesitated to reply, until friends urged him to do so, lest silence be taken as assent. His mild retort ended that particular controversy.

After his death, Schmidt was censured by his fellow Moravian, the missionary and Tibetan scholar H. A. Jäschke, for the way he had commented upon two Tibetan dictionaries which had preceded his own

I. J. Schmidt and the Kalmucks

work. One, which had been compiled by an anonymous Roman Catholic missionary, and had been printed at Serampore in 1826, was indeed imperfect, as might be expected of a dictionary of a hitherto almost unknown language, which had been drawn up almost without assistance of any sort. 'Nevertheless,' wrote Jäschke, 'any one who knows by experience what time and toil such a work must have cost, though its design remained unfulfilled and its object unaccomplished, will not easily be able to repress his indignation at the tone, in which this book in the preface to his Grammar is recklessly and absolutely condemned by Professor Schmidt.' And he goes on: 'High praise, however, is awarded by the Professor to a second work, the Tibetan–English Dictionary by Csoma de Körös, which appeared in 1834. This work deserves all eulogy; but the Professor's manner, which imitates that of a master commending a pupil, is, though on other grounds, as unwarranted and as offensive in this as in the former case.'

Schmidt, obviously, was not an easy man to get on with. It must be recognized, too, that his reputation resulted, to some extent, from the fact that the main body of his work appeared in German, and so was not, like that of some of his compatriots, concealed in the obscurity of Russian, a language which was more or less ignored in western Europe at the time.

There were other, and for our purposes more significant, aspects of the character and interests of Schmidt. He was a pious Moravian, and a practical businessman and banker. He served as Treasurer of the Russian Bible Society during the whole period of its existence, from 1813 to 1826, and he translated much of the New Testament into both Kalmuck and classical Mongolian, supervised and corrected what his assistants had translated, and saw both editions through the press. Marriage connected him with Robert Pinkerton, and Bible work brought him into contact with John Paterson, and the mission to the Buryats was an offshoot of their common interests.

Isaac Jacob Schmidt was born on 14 October 1779 in Amsterdam. His father, Jan Schmidt, had originally been an Arminian, but he joined the United Brethren in 1763 at the age of twenty. Jan's wife, Anna Van Dam, whom he married in 1778, was also a convert, who had become a Moravian in 1769, coincidentally at the same age as her husband. Jan worked first as a book-keeper in the service of a fellow Moravian, but later he set up in business on his own account, and amassed something of a fortune. The year 1795 brought double disaster. His wife Anna died, after having given birth to six sons and a daughter, and the French invasion and occupation of the Netherlands brought about the collapse of his business and reduced the family to penury. In 1800 Jan escaped from his depressing circumstances, taking up a commercial post on the island of Java, where he remarried. The young Isaac Jacob, who had been educated at the Moravian school at Neuwied on the Rhine, had, in the meantime, begun to prepare himself for a life in trade, studying business and languages. But an opening he had been looking forward to failed to materialize, and instead, in 1798, he accepted

I. J. Schmidt and the Kalmucks

an invitation to join the Moravian settlement at Sarepta as a commercial assistant. He took Russian nationality in St Petersburg, and spent the rest of his life in Russia, dying there in 1847.

At first, Schmidt had only frustrating routine work with which to occupy himself at Sarepta. But when he was given the task of making the rounds of local Kalmuck chieftains in order to collect payments due from them to Sarepta, he discovered, in his contacts with this Mongolian nation, both the intellectual stimulus and the raw material which nourished his life's great work, and, fortunately, he had enough spare time to enable him to exploit his opportunity. Schmidt spent three summers and a winter, between 1804 and 1806, amongst the Kalmucks, studying their language, history, customs and religious beliefs. He built up a considerable collection of manuscripts, no small achievement considering how reluctant the Kalmucks were to let strangers see their books. Unhappily, this library was completely destroyed in the great fire of Moscow in 1812. He also began to compile the records and notes on which his later scholarly work was based.

In 1807, Schmidt was promoted and transferred to Saratov, and in early 1812 he made a good marriage to Maria Helene Wigand. His wife's father was Johann Wigand, the son of a preacher, who had been born in Germany in 1744. After studying theology in Halle, Wigand became a tutor in the family of a Russian general, and moved with him to St Petersburg and Moscow. In 1767 he entered the service of another family, at Kharkov, and here, influenced by J. F. Pauly, a Moravian teacher at the monastery school, he became attracted to, and joined, the United Brethren. In 1782 he was appointed Professor of History at the University of Moscow, and at the same time he served as chaplain to the Moravian community in Sarepta House there. Between 1793 and 1800 he was Agent at St Petersburg, where his duties were both administrative and clerical. In the latter year he moved to Sarepta, where he served as second superintendent until his death in 1808 at the age of sixty-four. Wigand was an influential and highly respected member of the colony, and, apart from that, he chanced to have numbered at one time among his pupils Nikolai Ivanovich Treskin, Civil Governor of Irkutsk from 1806 to 1819.

From Saratov, Schmidt moved in early 1812 to Moscow. After only a few months there, he was appointed commercial agent in St Petersburg, to succeed Asmus Simonsen in the management of Sarepta's trade interests there. Schmidt left Moscow hurriedly for his new post only a few days ahead of the invading French army in September. He travelled in the company of a new-found friend, John Paterson, who had been in the old capital for a mere three days, on Bible Society business. The threads were beginning to draw together.

The Kalmucks, amongst whom Schmidt had lived and studied, are a Mongolian nation, an Asiatic people living in Europe. At that time, they

I. J. Schmidt and the Kalmucks

were the best-known of all the Mongolian peoples, more familiar by far than the Buryats of Siberia or the eastern Mongols within the frontiers of China.

There have been various attempts to explain the origin and meaning of the name of the Kalmucks, none of them conclusive. In practice, the term is used to distinguish those Oirat, or West Mongolian, tribes which, for about 150 years after the end of the sixteenth century, migrated westwards, in larger or smaller groups, from their original homeland in Jungaria, the steppe-country between the Altai and the T'ien-shan ranges. They finally settled, if that is the proper word to use in connection with a nomadic people, perpetually on the move, in south Russia, astride the lower Volga and in the Don basin. Not all the West Mongols took part in these migrations. Some moved, instead, south-eastwards into the Kokonor region of north-west China, where they played a part in Tibetan religious politics in the seventeenth century. Others remained on the home pastures. The latter, the so-called Jungars, built up a short-lived state which, in the first half of the eighteenth century, presented a serious challenge to the Chinese empire, under its foreign, Manchu, dynasty, for the control of Inner Asia. Given wiser leadership, the Jungars might have achieved at least a position of equilibrium, but selfish indulgence in family feuding and petty power politics weakened their cohesion, and left them open to conquest by the disciplined Manchus, who were led at that time by two of the greatest rulers China has ever known, the K'ang-hsi and the Ch'ien-lung emperors. After several decades of intermittent warfare, the Manchus determined to settle the issue once and for all. They achieved total victory, and consolidated it by a policy of reduction which, by 1759, eliminated the Jungars for ever as a political and military force in Inner Asia. A little over a decade later, in 1771, a large part of the Kalmuck nation deserted the Russian empire, and migrated back towards Jungaria, where the Ch'ien-lung emperor took them under his protection. Only those Kalmucks who lived on the eastern side of the Volga, though, joined the flight. Those on the other side were reluctant to move, and it was these Kalmucks who formed the sparse and scattered mission field around the infant Moravian settlement at Sarepta.

The Kalmucks were, and remained after their westward migration, a typically Mongolian people, sharing many characteristics with both the eastern Mongols of Inner and Outer Mongolia, and the Buryats of Siberia. They were horse-riding nomads, living principally from their flocks and herds. They ate meat and milk products, and they fermented and distilled the milk of their mares to make their traditional alcoholic drinks. The standard Kalmuck dwelling was the tent, or *kibitka* as it was known in Russia. Just like the *ger* of the eastern Mongols, this consisted of a framework of trellis walls, topped by an umbrella of rafters which supported a wheel-like roof ring. The whole was covered with sheets of felt. The Kalmucks were almost entirely mobile. Even their lamaseries were housed in tents, and could be carried around when the hordes moved their location. After

I. J. Schmidt and the Kalmucks

the dispersal of 1771, though, the Kalmucks came more and more under direct Russian authority, and, as time went on, Russian and western European influences began to make themselves apparent. By the early nineteenth century, one Kalmuck prince, at least, Major Tümen of the Khoshut, had his own permanent palace, built on an island in the Volga, some miles north of Astrakhan. Hommaire de Hell and his wife visited it, probably in the early 1840s, on the occasion of some festivities there. They just missed the steamer which carried a crowd of notables up from Astrakhan, and had to follow by ordinary boat. What they found was an elaborate palace, built in the Chinese style, with a detached pagoda or pavilion half hidden amongst the trees, where the old prince lived in religious seclusion. Inside, the French visitors could not imagine that they were being entertained by Kalmucks, so sophisticated and European was everything around them.

The form of the Mongolian language spoken by the Kalmucks was rather different from the dialects of the eastern Mongols, but recognizably of the same stock. For writing, they used the same alphabet, the one introduced by order of Genghis Khan in the early thirteenth century, though in a phonetically more exact form, which had been worked out in the mid-seventeenth century by one of their own learned lamas, the famous missionary and translator of the Tibetan scriptures who was known as the Zaya Pandita. Their written language was very similar to the literary Mongolian used by the eastern Mongols and the Buryats, differing from it mainly in matters of spelling.

The Kalmucks had been converted to the lamaist form of Buddhism, brought to them from Tibet, before they migrated to Russia, and they brought with them religious beliefs, sacred books, and cult practices, which they possessed in common with their contemporaries in Mongolia itself. The Buryats, on the other hand, were to be affected by Buddhism only rather later, during and after the eighteenth century. There were shamans as well as lamas amongst the Kalmucks, spirit masters who functioned as intermediaries with the unseen world in the crises of everyday life, and many people still retained and worshipped shamanist idols, or *ongon*, images made of cloth or felt.

The shamans, practitioners of the 'Bookless Faith', or the 'Black Faith' as it was also called (to distinguish it from the 'Yellow Faith', reformed or Gelugpa lamaism, with its extensive body of scriptures), were adepts at such practical arts as rain-making or magic healing. They could work themselves into a trance-like state of possession, during which they exercised the supernatural powers they were reputed to possess. They could cure the sick, or even save the dying, by searching for the straying soul whose absence from the body was thought to be the cause of the disaster, and bringing it back; or, if the sufferer died, the shaman was the expert who knew the way to the world beyond and all the dangers which had to be avoided along the road, and who could guide the departing soul to its destination. Many of

I. J. Schmidt and the Kalmucks

the popular religious cults and rituals practised by Mongols further east were familiar to the Kalmucks too. These rituals predated the introduction of Buddhism, but some of them had been taken over and adapted by the lamas and incorporated into Mongolian Buddhist beliefs and practices. Thus the Kalmucks were familiar with the custom of erecting *obos*, that is, cairns constructed according to ritual precept, which served as shrines for the local deities to dwell in and receive worship. Of old, the ritual of obo-worship had been accompanied by bloody sacrifices of animals, whose reeking carcases would be draped over the cairn, but with the introduction of Buddhism a milder ethos prevailed, and the slaughter of living creatures was discouraged. The obo itself came to be looked upon as a symbol of Mount Sumeru, the central peak of the Buddhist cosmos. Fire-worship, a service also involving the sacrifice of a sheep, and the dripping of its fat or of butter on to the blazing fire, and intended to avert bad luck and ensure prosperity, was a domestic ritual carried out by lamas or shamans or by the head of the family. The Kalmucks also knew all the same tricks of casting horoscopes, of magical diagnosis of demoniac possession and illness resulting from it, of fortune-telling and all the divinatory and geomantic skills associated with the disposal of the bodies of the dead and the exorcism of malignant souls, as were current elsewhere in Mongolia, and the handbooks which they used were versions of those used by the eastern Mongols.

When Edward Stallybrass and Cornelius Rahmn reached the Buryats in 1818, they discovered that they were not the only missionaries there. They were in competition with an energetic Buddhist clergy. They were outnumbered and outmanoeuvred by those whom they slightingly termed the 'emissaries of Dalai Lama', who were busily and far more effectively engaged in winning over the people from their more primitive shamanistic beliefs. Amongst the Kalmucks the situation was both more advanced and more stable. There, the Buddhists had already won the battle, and the surviving shamans no longer presented an organized challenge to them. But, generally speaking, the problems facing the Protestant missionaries to these widely separated Mongolian peoples were very much the same, and it may be useful to look briefly at the strengths of lamaism and at how the Moravians fared with the Kalmucks, before examining missionary success and failure amongst the Buryats.

No missionary to a Mongolian people could be indifferent to the challenge of shamanism, but it was far less formidable than that presented by the lamaist church. Shamanism was a religion without scriptures, without ecclesiastical organization and priestly hierarchy, with no philosophical appeal to the intellect, with little recorded history apart from some legends and, especially among the Buryats, shaman family-trees, and with no international connections. What the shamans practised was essentially a this-worldly craft. They claimed to help people in the crises of everyday life through their intimacy with the all-important and all-pervading spirits, and their ability to manipulate them. They claimed, amongst other things, to be able to treat disease, but their methods were limited to influencing and expelling the demons of disease. They were not, as many lamas were, skilled in diagnosis, or knowledgeable about pathology, herbs, and mineral drugs. They had a cosmogony, and indeed a most complex one, but nothing that could be called a theology. They were not concerned with spiritual problems such as those of sin and salvation. By the late eighteenth century, shamanism had sunk to the status of a fragmented folk-religion, of no political significance. Things had not always been so. In the days of Genghis Khan there had been powerful, aristocratic shamans, like the notorious Teb Tenggeri, who organized a plot to subvert the rule of the great emperor, and lost his life when it failed. Some of Genghis's immediate successors in the thirteenth century maintained court shamans, whom they consulted before taking any important decision. These court shamans would foretell the future by scorching the shoulder-blade of a sheep, and interpreting the resulting cracks, just as their humble descendants did on the Mongolian steppes only a generation or so ago. But those days had long since passed, and by the eighteenth century it was the tightly organized, politically conscious Buddhist church which formed the dominant ideological influence everywhere in the Mongolian world, except in some parts of Buryatia.

Kalmuck, Buryat and east Mongolian lamas, and, by extension, the whole population, all felt themselves to be an integral part of the greater lamaist ecclesia, and looked to Tibet, and above all to the Dalai Lama, for inspiration, leadership and legitimation. The same scriptures and the same philosophical treatises formed the basis of the education of every ambitious lama, whether Tibetan or Mongolian. The Mongolian language was widely used in lamaseries, but Tibetan was the official language of religion, and exerted a unifying influence comparable to that of Latin in western European Christianity. In fact, in some ways the Buddhist church resembled that other great world religion, the Roman Catholic church, in its clerical structure, the nature of some of its beliefs, and the character of some of its services. And just as the Catholic church, while vulnerable here and there to reform or heresy, remains an indestructible rock, so its Oriental counterpart, the Buddhist church, enjoyed an inner vitality which would not be sapped by the nibblings of a few Protestant missionaries of alien culture.

The lamaist church among the Mongols possessed inner strengths which were connected with the way it had come into being. Lamaism had been cultivated amongst the Mongols as a court religion as far back as the thirteenth century. Then, after the collapse of the Mongolian Yüan dynasty in China, in 1368, it led a tenuous existence until, three hundred years later, it experienced a sudden, explosive revival, and expanded to embrace not only the ruling classes, but also the common people in almost every corner of the Mongolian world.

In the second half of the sixteenth century, various princes in different

I. J. Schmidt and the Kalmucks

parts of Mongolia had outgrown the shadowy authority of the nominal emperors, the successors of Genghis Khan. They rejected the miserable feuding which had brought the Dark Ages to the steppe lands. Power was moving into the hands of able and energetic local rulers like Altan Khan of the Tümet in Inner Mongolia, or Abudai Khan of the Khalkha in Outer Mongolia, who were building up new centres of culture in their individual khanates. For an ideology commensurate with the political status they intended to enjoy, they turned to the only acceptable model, to Tibet, where the Gelugpa, or Yellow, sect of reformed Buddhism was steadily asserting its predominance over other sects. Some of these Mongols were politically and militarily powerful enough to influence the course of events in Tibet to suit their own purposes, and so it came about that, in 1576, Altan Khan was able to take the decisive step which ensured that Mongols everywhere were to become adherents of the lamaist church, and remain so for the next three and a half centuries.

Legend tells how Altan Khan had first become personally acquainted with Buddhism three years earlier when he captured two lamas during the course of a campaign against the Shira Uighur people of west China. One of these lamas preached the doctrines of the faith to his captor, and converted him. In 1576, Altan Khan's nephew, a prince known as Khutuktu Setsen Khungtaiji, is said to have persuaded his uncle that it would be meritorious and advantageous to invite to Mongolia the leading high lama of Tibet. The latter, though such a development was as yet unplanned, would become the titular Third Dalai Lama.

The arguments deployed by the Khungtaiji show that, to his mind, Altan Khan, having achieved a situation of military and political stability in relation to his most significant rivals, China to the east and the Oirats to the west, had accomplished his political destiny, and should turn his thoughts to higher things. What he suggested was the following:

> You have taken your revenge on the Chinese who once conquered our city [i.e. Peking] and have established relations with them. You have avenged yourself on the Oirats, who seized Karakorum, and have overcome them and brought them into subjection. But now your years have increased, and you are approaching old age. The wise say that what is necessary for this and the future destiny is the Faith. Now it appears that in the western land of snows [i.e. Tibet] there dwells, in corporeal form, the Mighty Seer and Merciful One, the Bodhisattva Avalokiteshvara. Would it not be wonderful if we were to invite him, and re-establish the relations between Church and State as they once existed between the Emperor Khubilai and the Lama Pagspa?

Superfically, this quotation from the chronicle which Schmidt translated looks like an appeal from the younger to the older man to turn his thoughts to spiritual matters and his own salvation in the face of approaching death.

I. J. Schmidt and the Kalmucks

But in fact it was a profound political statement. It proves, for one thing, that Altan Khan enjoyed the power, prestige and self-confidence to invite the highest lama in Tibet to undertake the arduous journey to his khanate without anticipating a refusal. But far more significant than this evidence of the sudden resurgence of the eastern Mongols as a force to be reckoned with in Inner Asia is the framework which the Khungtaiji proposed for the new arrangements to be made for Mongolian society. He was advocating the deliberate revival of a political system which had been elaborated during the reign of China's most magnificent emperor, Khubilai Khan – Marco Polo's master – and which was to inform Mongolian politics down to the present century. This system was known to the Mongols as the 'Two Principles', and it consisted in an alliance between the Buddhist church and the secular power to form a dual authority in the state.

The 'Two Principles' were never practically effective under Khubilai himself, for he was the emperor of China rather than of Mongolia, but from the late sixteenth century onwards they set the standard to which any acceptable government had at least to aspire. To act according to the 'Two Principles' was, however, no guarantee of political success, for karma, the weight of the deeds of a previous existence, might preponderate. That was true of Ligdan Khan, the last emperor of the Mongols, who died in 1634. It is recorded of him that 'he exercised the Two Principles of government to a high degree, but through the force of karma, acts of insubordination multiplied among the khans and commoners of the Six Ten-Thousands, and, unable to keep them in peace, he dominated the six great peoples by brutality, occupying the throne for thirty-one years'. Nevertheless, acceptance of the 'Two Principles' was a *sine qua non* of political respectability right up to the year 1911, when Outer Mongolia became a monarchy, and its one and only king, the Eighth Jebtsundamba Khutuktu or Living Buddha of Urga, wielded both powers himself.

What the Khungtaiji was doing was seeking the sanction of Mongolia's imperial past for the innovations he was determined to introduce. There was written authority for the 'Two Principles' in a handbook of statecraft which dated back to Khubilai's time, known as 'The Tenfold Virtuous White Chronicle of the Faith'. The Khungtaiji himself had re-edited this book from two manuscripts which had somehow managed to survive the chaotic years since the collapse of the Empire. The settlement made in 1578 between Altan Khan and the high lama was in agreement with the ideas contained in this treatise. Altan Khan, the recently converted Mongolian prince, conferred upon the high lama the new title of Dalai Lama, and this was also applied retrospectively to his two predecessors. The new Dalai Lama, conscious of the political capital to be gained from association with the great Khubilai, proclaimed that he was himself a reincarnation of Pagspa Lama, the former emperor's Tibetan adviser, and that Altan Khan was a reincarnation of Khubilai himself. The Khungtaiji and one or two other intermediaries were declared to be reincarnations of early Buddhist interpreters. Many fundamental changes in the structure of society were made at this time. Old customs, such as that of slaughtering camels and horses and burying them with a dead person to serve him as an escort, were abolished, and new ones were introduced. A clerical hierarchy was instituted, comprising four ranks of monks, each of which was declared equal in status and privileges to one of the ranks of the existing secular nobility. In a speech to Altan Khan, the Dalai Lama stressed that this was not the first time they had met, but that they had known each other in many previous existences. Their identity as Khubilai Khan and Pagspa Lama was only the latest such association, but it was at that time that the Khan had conferred upon the Lama the title of State Preceptor, a golden seal, and a diploma, and had placed him at the head of the clerical administration.

From the point of view of Altan Khan, the immediate effect of this agreement with the new Dalai Lama was to proclaim his legitimacy as the rightful heir to the imperial power wielded by Khubilai, thus challenging the reigning, but ineffectual, emperor, Tümen Jasagtu Khan. But this was a matter of the moment only, and there were long-term results of far greater significance. Roused by the example of Altan Khan, other Mongolian princes were quick to establish relations with the vital intellectual and spiritual force represented by the Lamaist church, to encourage the spread of lamaism in their territories, and to persecute and try to eradicate shamanism. Even the emperor himself turned Buddhist, and invited the Dalai Lama to visit him too. The invitation was accepted, but the Dalai Lama died on the way, and the aristocracy of Tümet seized the opportunity to have a member of the family of Altan Khan, and hence also of Genghis Khan, founder of the Mongolian nation, declared to be the fourth incarnation of the Dalai Lama. Thus within thirteen years of the conversion of the first Mongolian prince to Buddhism, a Mongolian aristocrat had come to hold the highest position in the Tibetan Buddhist hierarchy.

At this time, too, Abudai Khan of the Khalkha introduced Lamaism into his khanate, and caused the huge lamasery of Erdene Juu to be built. He placed it, with the advice of the Dalai Lama, next to the site of the old imperial capital Karakorum. This was of practical advantage, in that the stones of the ruined city could be reused for building the lamasery, but there was a deeper significance in the choice of situation. Located where it was, Erdene Juu was a reminder of Mongolia's great past.

Wherever Buddhism prevailed among the Mongols, so did the idea of the 'Two Principles', linking and enmeshing the secular and the clerical authority. The two were interdependent in the organizational sense, but it could happen, also, that they were linked by family relationships. Thus, in Khalkha, the church was headed by the Jebstundamba Khutuktu, the title accorded to the high lama whose rank and prestige were similar, and second only to, those of the Dalai and Panchen Lamas of Tibet. The first, and

I. J. Schmidt and the Kalmucks

undoubtedly the greatest, Khutuktu was the son of the Tushetu Khan Gombodorji, ruler of one of the three khanates of Khalkha. When he died in 1723 at the age of eighty-seven, he was succeeded by the child of a son-in-law of the K'ang-hsi emperor. There could hardly be a clearer demonstration of the prestige of the Buddhist church, and though neither Kalmucks nor Buryats were directly subject to the authority of the Khutuktu, there was immense satisfaction to be felt in membership of a church ruled by a high lama of his calibre, and lamas from both nations would go on pilgrimage to visit the Khutuktu and worship him, or to study at his lamasery city of Urga.

There were other reasons why Mongols, Kalmucks and Buryats were to prove impervious to Protestant Christianity, whoever it was who attempted to convert them, but what protected them above all was their sense of belonging to a community of the faithful which stretched geographically far beyond the frontiers of Mongolia, and infinitely far backward and forward in time; which was the great source of colour and ceremonial in their lives; and which was an inseparable element in their national self-consciousness.

With their scanty resources, it would have been impossible for the Moravians to evangelize even those Kalmucks who were within easy reach of Sarepta, but, apart from that, their very philosophy of missions hindered their efforts. It was not Moravian policy to select missionaries on the strength of their scholarship. What they felt was needed in the mission field was not erudition, but a sound knowledge of the Scriptures, and a personal appreciation of the truths contained in them. Studious habits were thought to be an inferior qualification to those of the craftsman for the rigours of missionary life. In following this principle, the Moravians considered that they were observing biblical example. As they themselves put it,

> as to the persons employed, the Brethren found no objection to send Missionaries that had not received a learned education, provided they, in their degree, answered the description given by the Apostles sent forth by our blessed Saviour himself, to go into all the world, and preach the Gospel to every creature; who, though of mean extraction, and no human learning, were nevertheless endowed with the Spirit of God, and had learnt his will concerning man's salvation, by a diligent search in the Holy Scriptures, and a blessed experience of the divine effects of the gospel in their own hearts.

This preference for tough colonists rather than learned ministers was the expression of a different philosophy of missions from that of the London Missionary Society, and William Swan, in his *Letters on Missions*, found occasion to show how the Moravians limited their own effectiveness by valuing manual skills and personal devotion above learning:

> If we advert to the pretensions of the missionaries in question to general

I. J. Schmidt and the Kalmucks

learning, here, I believe, they will be found defective; and to their deficiency in this point, perhaps, is to be attributed their having done so little in the way of translating the Scriptures and other books, and introducing generally the knowledge of letters among their congregations gathered from among the heathen. Besides, as if conscious of their inability in this respect, the fields of exertion they have chosen are the very spots where the want of literary acquirements would be least felt. Their Greenlanders, etc., have no books or learning of their own, like the Hindoos, Chinese, and other pagan nations, high in the scale of general improvement, skilful in the arts of civilised life, and among whom learning raises its possessor to a proud elevation above the unlettered multitude; not but what learning might be turned to good account in Labrador or South Africa, but the want of it may there be more readily dispensed with than in Benares or Serampore.

Learning could not be dispensed with amongst the Kalmucks. They might not stand on the same intellectual level as William's paragons of worldly scholarship, the Hindus and the Chinese, but at the same time they were culturally far ahead of the illiterate Eskimos, and if the Moravians imagined they could treat them as primitive, uneducated folk, they were much mistaken. They found them to be believers in a precisely and intricately constructed faith, expressed in well-ordered and dignified ceremonial. Even the Kalmuck music, strange as it was to European ears, impressed them with its sophistication. Nor were the Kalmucks strangers to scholarship. They counted among their great men of learning the Zaya Pandita Namkhaijamtso, who had not only been invited to preach and teach amongst the Khalkha, as well as his own people, but who, in the last twelve years of his life had personally translated, or supervised the translation of, more than 170 Tibetan books. Namkhaijamtso, who lived from 1599 to 1662, had been an exceptionally gifted scholar, but there were other Kalmuck lamas who were expert in the Buddhist scriptures, some of them having studied in Lhasa at the feet of the Dalai Lama himself, thus acquiring an almost superhuman reputation for wisdom and holiness. The Moravians, on the other hand, were outsiders. Few of them had a thorough knowledge of Kalmuck. They did not understand the Buddhist theology they were trying to undermine, and, until 1815, they did not possess even a single book of the Bible in printed form, which they could distribute as a challenge to the voluminous lamaist scriptures and prayers. They suffered from every possible disadvantage.

It was in 1768 and 1769 that the first attempts were made to preach to the Kalmucks. Three unmarried Brethren, Conrad Neitz, Christian Hamel and J. F. Maltsch, began to study the language, and the first two lived for a time among the Kalmucks. A *zaisang*, or subordinate official, named Tochmut, had settled, for reasons of health, just opposite Sarepta, on the right bank of the river Sarpa, and a number of Kalmucks, most of them invalids, had gathered near him. Neitz and Hamel built a hut of tree-bark near this settlement and moved in, prepared to live as Kalmucks. They found life hard. The monotonous diet of animal food disagreed with them, and they were plagued by lice, which flourished in the dirty conditions, but which it was a sin to kill. The Kalmucks were a rowdy lot at the best of times, and worse when they were drunk. At Sarepta they would race on horseback through the streets, yelling and whooping and scuffling with each other. Once a drunken Kalmuck princess even invaded the Sisters' House, and tried to force the modest female Moravians to sing for her. In their home surroundings, free from any restraint which the unfamiliarity of the German settlement might have imposed on them, they were even more intractable. It is not surprising that the Brethren could do little with them.

In 1771, nearly all the Moravians' Kalmuck acquaintances disappeared from the scene in the course of the great migration to China. A few years later, encouraged by Moravian headquarters at Herrnhut, the Sarepta community attempted to establish a regular mission, and four of the Brethren, including Neitz, who turned out to be their best Kalmuck scholar before the arrival of Schmidt, were deputed to make a thorough study of the language. It was now that the bane of neglect of learning became apparent. The Moravians still had no grammar of the language, and for vocabularies they possessed only some very inaccurate lists of words drawn up by the now dead Maltsch and the deplorable Jaehrig. In the end they persuaded an old lama to help them, and they took the opportunity of their lessons to try to convert him. But it was no good. 'He had no ears to hear, being an old, self-righteous, self-holy and very superstitious man.'

It was thought that one way to reach the hearts of the Kalmucks would be by offering them medical advice and treatment, and one or two of the Moravians, especially Neitz, undertook to act as intermediaries between the people and Brother Wier, the Sarepta doctor. An experience related by Hamel illustrates the indifference to what the Moravians were trying to do:

> On the occasion of a journey which I was making in the horde connected with the business of the store, I was called to a moribund cleric, who had already been treated by the Kalmuck doctors without any benefit. Now there were 9 of the most important Gelung i.e. priests with him, considering what else should be done. Eight declared that medicine was of no further use, and that only *khürüm*, that is, prayers said by the clergy, paid for at great expense, would help. Then the 9th, by name of Ishi gelung, who had some years previously been with the Dalai Lama in Tibet, and enjoyed great respect, said: 'Any number of *khürüm* are held for the sick, and it is no use at all. It would be much more beneficial if, like our fathers, we prayed to God without acquisitiveness. But where is our old doctrine? Why do you immediately think of

I. J. Schmidt and the Kalmucks

holding *khürüm*? For no other reason than to obtain money and cattle. It's just the same even with the Dalai Lama today. No! If there is any help for our sick people, it is to be found with the Germans, and that is why I sent for my friend Christian. What do you think?' Hesitantly they agreed. I then examined the patient as well as I could, sent an urgent message to Dr Wier, who sent the necessary medicine, which was blessed with good results. Ishi gelung often came to me, and liked me, but he would have nothing to do with the gospel of Jesus and his mercies, even though he could not refuse his approval of individual passages. He was no hypocrite. He did not praise his heathen religion, but said himself: 'We are all cheats.' Nevertheless, he continued to live, like other Kalmucks, in many sins.

Gradually, the missionaries came to be more trusted by some of the Kalmuck lamas, and were even able to borrow books from them, and from these they began to get a better idea of the complexities of the Buddhist religion. Like others, they were not only struck by the superficial similarities between Buddhism and Catholicism, things like the use of the rosary in prayer, but they even came to the conclusion that parts of the Buddhist scriptures seemed to have been taken from Christian doctrines and 'only to have been distorted to suit the perverse notions of the nation'. Yet, for all their efforts, they made only one convert, a poor blind girl whom they saved from being exposed on the steppes to die, and she, no doubt, had little choice in the matter. By about 1800 they had decided to give up their adult mission, and to concentrate on teaching children instead. But the school run by Brother Wendling failed in its turn, and the good folk of Sarepta found fulfilment in what was called diaspora work, serving the spiritual needs of the German colonists in the neighbourhood of Saratov, rather than in dissipating their energies among the unresponsive heathen.

A final mission was undertaken between 1815 and 1822, subsidized by the London Missionary Society. This time, some success was achieved. The reported conversion of Schmidt's two Buryat assistants, one of whom actually entered the Orthodox church three days before his death, encouraged some Kalmucks to profess their belief in Christ, but the Russian authorities would not allow them to be baptized into any church other than the Orthodox church. In the face of this insuperable obstacle, the Moravians abandoned their mission altogether in 1822.

In the end, the Moravian missionaries were defeated by intervention on the part of the Russian government, just as the English missionaries were to be defeated eighteen years later, but in any case they were fighting a hopeless battle. In half a century of sporadic campaigning they had succeeded in attracting only a few unfortunates or renegades. In general, the Kalmucks resented their presence and ridiculed them, so that the Brethren came to wonder if they were not 'throwing that which is holy before dogs, and pearls

I. J. Schmidt and the Kalmucks

before swine'. The Kalmucks never took their efforts seriously, to the distress of the Moravians. They were intrigued, as the Buryats were to be, by features of Christianity which reminded them of their own faith, and they were amused by Bible stories which they liked to hear told. But they remained absolutely convinced of the superiority of their own religion, and were impervious to the unfamiliar concepts which the missionaries put before them. The latter were on occasion politely invited to 'go home'. In one of their diaries we read:

> Sunday the 24th one of our best friends among the Gellongs spoke several hours with us about religious things – only, like others, he does not like to hear of Christ. The 27th we were frequently ask'd if we do not soon purpose returning to our friends elsewhere? And when we speak of the only way of salvation, they reply: 'Did you but spend your money at home, and keep your Religion to yourselves.'

By the end of the eighteenth century, then, the Moravians had done very little preparatory work, and had achieved practically nothing in the way of missionary success. But the foundation of the British and Foreign Bible Society in 1804 offered them new hope, and in 1806 they applied to the Society for help in the preparation and printing of an as yet untranslated version of the Scriptures. The Bible Society's enquiries disclosed a pitiful state of affairs. All the Moravians possessed seems to have been a translation by Neitz of part of their harmony of the Gospels, and perhaps a few other passages from the Bible. They had no means of printing anything, and though they were able to answer that many Kalmucks, especially, could read, they were not at all sanguine that they would pay any attention to the Bible.

The prospects looked bleak, but nevertheless the Bible Society approved a grant of £60 to Sarepta in 1808 for the purchase of a fount of Kalmuck type. In return, the Moravians took up the Society's suggestion of making a new start by translating the Gospel according to St Matthew in full, and they entrusted I. J. Schmidt with the task. Schmidt finished the translation before he left Moscow in the autumn of 1812, and, as soon as a fount of type was ready, he had the Gospel printed and published in St Petersburg, in an elegant quarto edition with a magniloquent Latin title page.

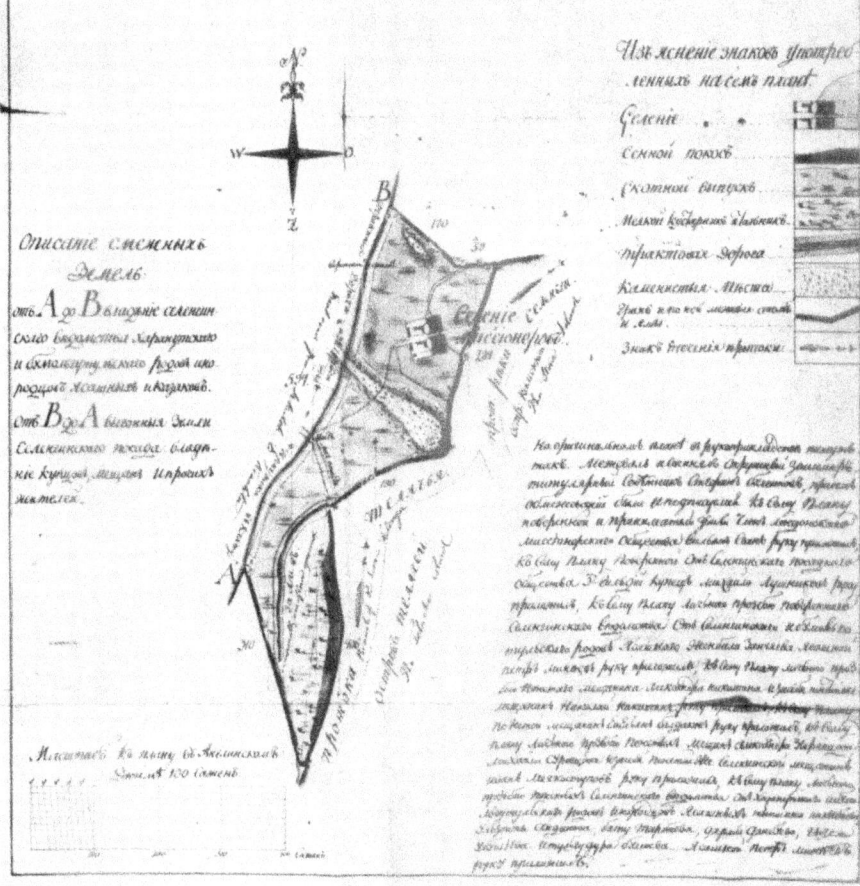

1 Contemporary surveyor's plan of the Selenginsk mission site

2 (a) John Paterson

2 (b) Ebenezer Henderson

3 (a) William Swan

3 (b) Cornelius Rahmn

4 (*a*) Edward Stallybrass

4 (*b*) Sarah Stallybrass

5 (a) View of the Selenginsk mission in the 1820s

5 (b) Selenginsk in about 1880

6 (a) The Selenginsk mission site in about 1900

6 (b) The mission site today

7 (*a*) One of the mission houses at Selenginsk in about 1900

(*b*) The monument erected by Robert Yuille in memory of his wife, Martha

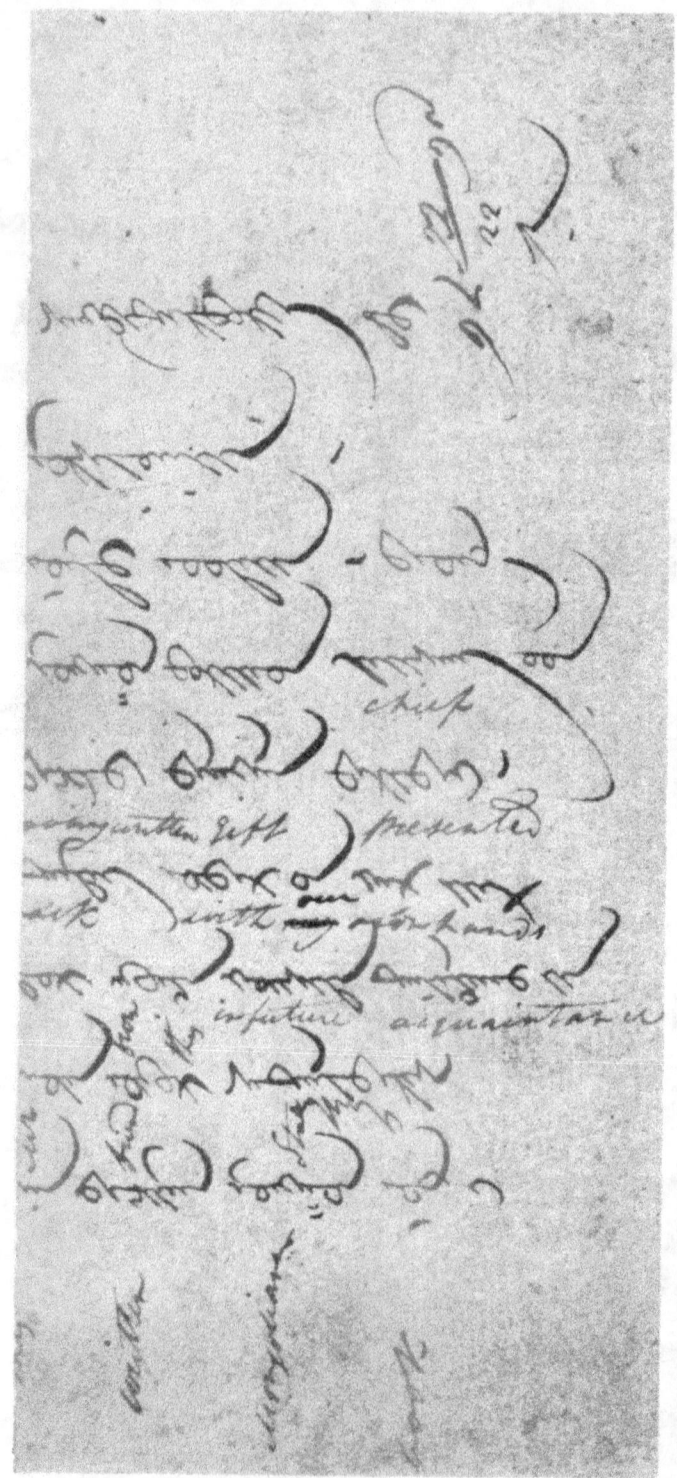

8 (a) The dedication to Edward Stallybrass on the Mongolian manuscript given to him by the two zaisangs

Translation

It is my great chance to whom the expression of your highly-valued great wishes, commenced to me by my brother. My dear... we are wills together as brothers of affection by our mutual desire to do all that ever god... The bark of his which formerly completely turned on his own pedal. The other enemy God made us wish to come hither, and hither are come; and we are now begging... the fact of our in new Jesus Christ and in thy attitude in entrance law, and praying to him always as our only Saviour. Farewell myself with humbly and respect that

Mongolian Buriat Lousang Badma
Marchemache

9 View of the lamasery on the Chikoi

10 View of the lamasery at the northern end of Goose Lake, showing, in the foreground, lamas with musical instruments, and women, bidding farewell to a visitor

11 Interior of the main temple of the lamasery on the Chikoi

12 Interior of a Mongolian tent, showing, centre, the apparatus for distilling kumis, and, left, the dual image of the shaman idol Immegildschen

13 Two consecutive recto sides of the censored manuscript of Edward Stallybrass's Old Testament translation. Part of chapter 30 of Proverbs is followed by the beginning of chapter 31. At the top of each page are the Mongolian numerals for 31. I. J. Schmidt's title and name are spread over the two pages, reading Aka/demik, Kollezhskiy Sovetnik i Kavaler Yakov Shmit

A Report of the First Three Years Proceedings, of the Selenginsk Academy, Instituted in December 1823; for the Instruction of the Youth of the Heathen Tribes of Siberia.

To the Directors of the London Missionary Society, and other Friends of the Selenginsk Mission, through the medium of John Venning Esq. St. Petersburgh.

December 1826.

14 Title page of the report on the work of the Selenginsk Academy

15 An examination paper worked by Dakba, a student at the Academy

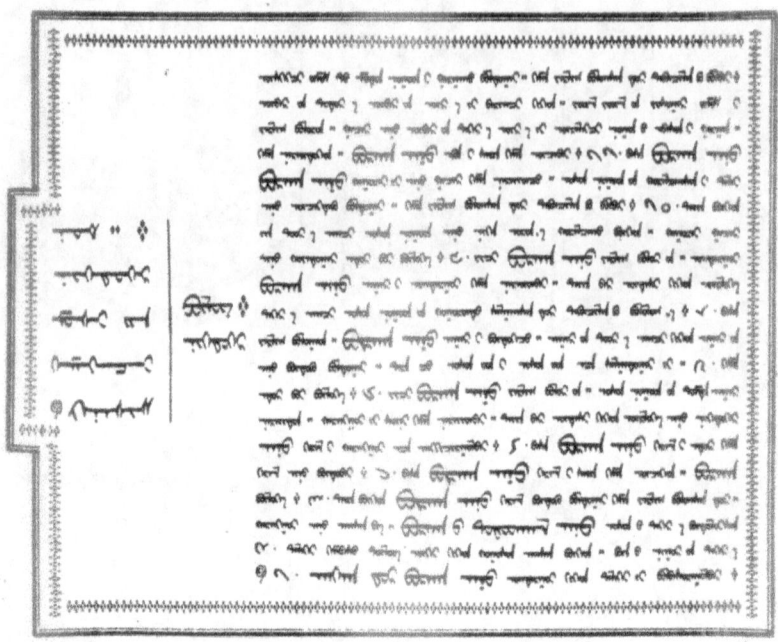

16 Page 1 of the first edition of Genesis, with Schmidt's imprimatur dated 1833

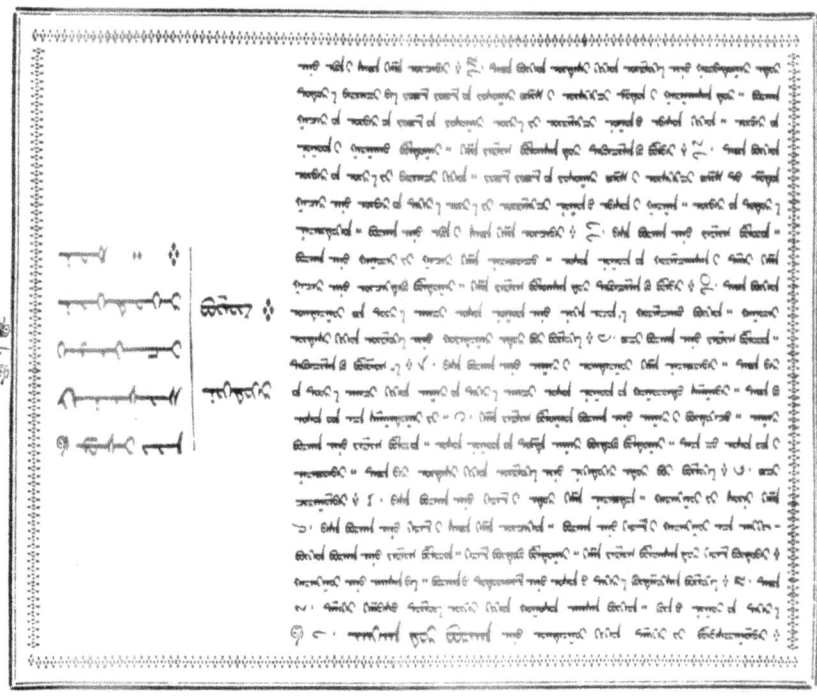

17 Page 1 of the second edition of Genesis, with Schmidt's imprimatur dated 1840. The name of God, printed in large characters in the earlier edition, has been reduced to uniformity with the text

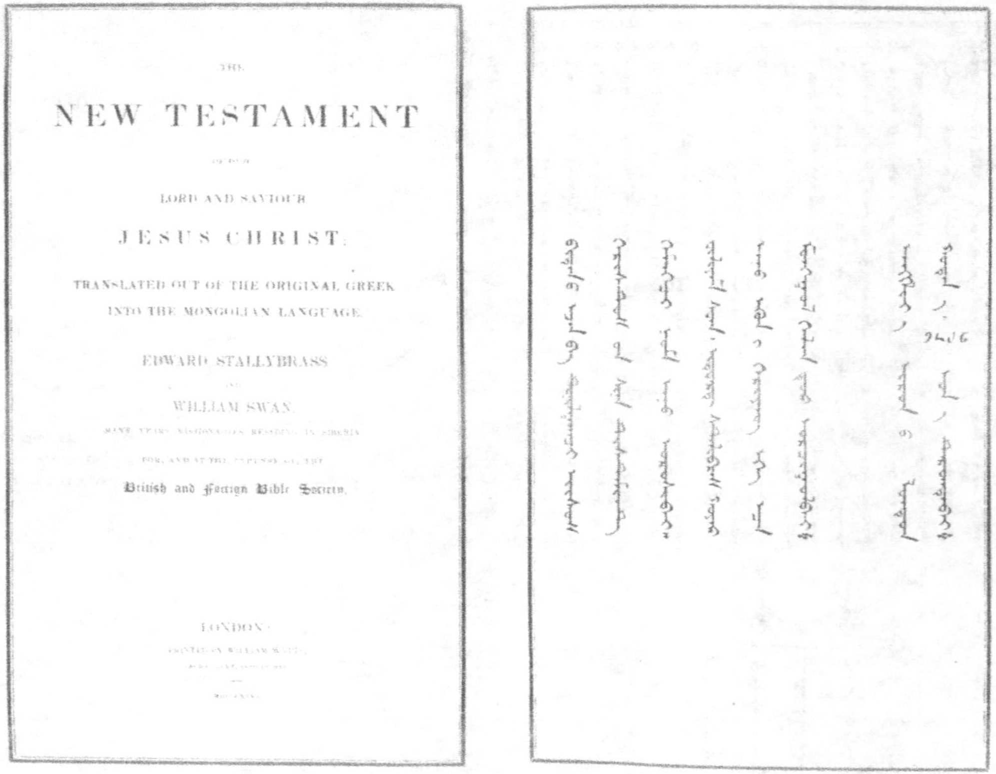

THE

NEW TESTAMENT

OF OUR

LORD AND SAVIOUR

JESUS CHRIST:

TRANSLATED OUT OF THE ORIGINAL GREEK
INTO THE MONGOLIAN LANGUAGE

BY

EDWARD STALLYBRASS

AND

WILLIAM SWAN

MANY YEARS MISSIONARIES RESIDENT IN SIBERIA

FOR AND AT THE EXPENSE OF THE

British and Foreign Bible Society.

LONDON:
W. M. WATTS, CROWN COURT,
TEMPLE BAR.
1846.

18 Title pages of the Mongolian New Testament of 1846

19 The preface to Robert Yuille's Mongolian primer with his letter to the Rev. S. C. Malan

A Tibet=Mongolian Lexicon
commonly called
Dok-bar-la-ba.
with a preface and grammar —
Copied and revised
from a printed copy under the
inspection of
Robert Yuille Missionary
in the service of the London
Missionary Society
and presented by them
To the
Royal Asiatic Society
of Great Britain and Ireland

Selenginsk – Dec^r – 1829 —

Presented to the
ROYAL ASIATIC SOCIETY
by the Revd R. Yuille
7 July 1832

20 Dedication, recopied by William Swan, in one of the dictionaries presented by Robert Yuille to the Royal Asiatic Society

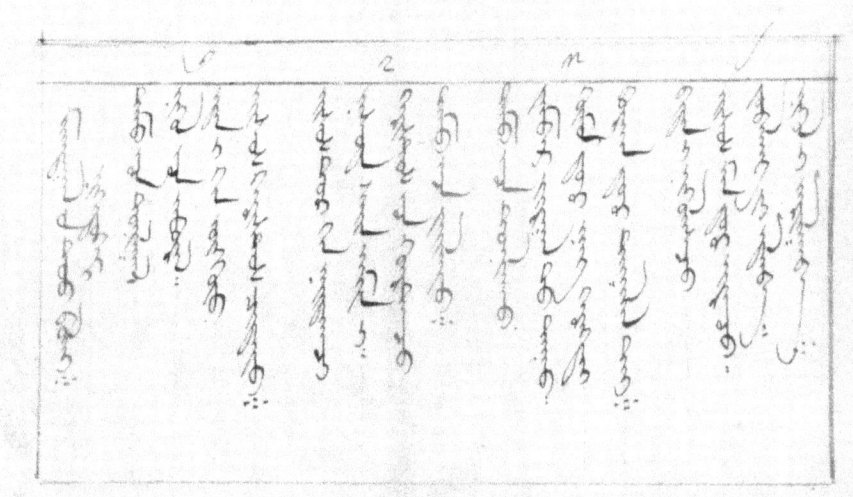

21 (a) Page 1 of Edward Stallybrass's manuscript Mongolian hymn book. The first verse reads, in translation: 'Rescue from hell, deliverance from sin. Who can grant this? Jesus Christ can.'

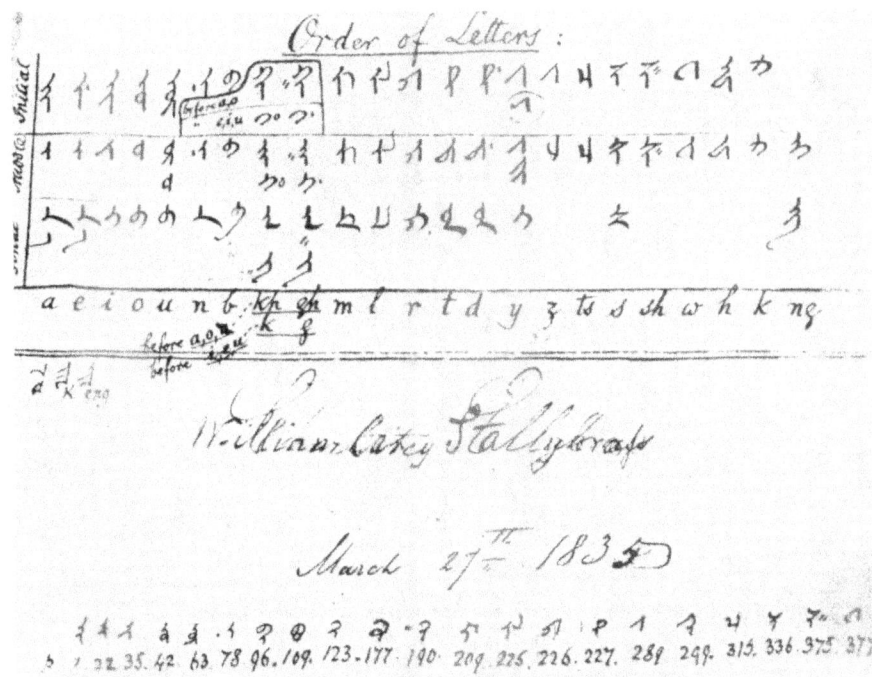

21 (b) A page from Charlotte Ellah's copy of Schmidt's Mongolian dictionary, showing her name overwritten with that of her stepson William

22 Sketch of a Buryat student reading the Scriptures, by Robert Yuille

Вашимъ въ Селенгинске, making
инство, уведомить them part of this
какъ о сей изъяви favour of my Sove-
Государя Импе- reign Imperial Master.
ратора.

Да даруетъ Господь May our Lord and
Спаситель нашъ Saviour give His
Божіе Свое на все, что blessing to all what
делается на земли is done on earth for
во славу Имени Его the glory of His holy
всесвятаго и для Name and for the
спасенія рода чело- salvation of mankind.
веческаго! Да позна May soon all the
ютъ вскоре все на- nations know Him
роды Его, яко Иску- as the Redeemer of
пителя душъ ихъ, и their souls, and His
Царствіе Его да при- kingdom come to rea-
детъ исполнить ожи- lize the expectations
данія всехъ люби- of all who love Him!
ящихъ Его!

Съ истиннымъ почте- I remain with true
ніемъ пребываю esteem,
Вашимъ, Revᵈ Sir,
Милостивый Государь мой, Your
покорнейшимъ слугою obedient servant
Князь Александръ Голицынъ Prince Alexander Golitsyn

№ 124.

въ С. Петербургѣ   St Petersburg
19 Апреля 1822.   April 19. 1822.

23 Last page of the deed of grant of land at Selenginsk to the missionaries by the
Emperor Alexander I, showing the signature of Prince Golitsyn

Копія –

Милостивый Государь!

[Russian text of letter, handwritten]

№ 1137
30 мая 1831го

Его Пастору Свану

(Translation)

Dear Sir
 His Imperial Majesty upon my most humble report has, in condescension to your petition, willed that the Mission of the London Missionary Society in Selenginsk, continue its labours for the conversion of the Buriats to the Christian faith, and, besides this, His Majesty is pleased to permit the arrival of new missionaries from England for this purpose, with this (understanding) however, that they exceed not the bounds of operation and right granted them by the Emperor Alexander 1st of blessed Memory.
 Communicating to you this His Majesty's will I have the honour to will present respect
Dear Sir
Your most humble servant
(Signed) D. Bludoff

№ 1137
31st May 1831
(rec. 11th June O.S.)
Mr Pastor Swan

24 Copy of a letter, with translation, in William Swan's hand, from D. N. Bludov, conveying the imperial permission to continue the mission

3

The Beginnings of the Mission

It was before his transfer to St Petersburg as successor to Asmus Simonsen that Schmidt became acquainted with the two men to whom the Siberian mission owed its creation, Robert Pinkerton and John Paterson.

The Reverend Robert Pinkerton was one of a group of four missionaries who were sent out from Edinburgh in 1805 to reinforce the Scottish colony which Henry Brunton and Alexander Patterson had founded at Karass three years earlier, but whose complement had been much depleted by sickness and death. Life at Karass proved too great a strain on Pinkerton's health to allow him to make his home there, and in 1808 he left the colony. For a while, before devoting himself entirely to Bible Society work, he was a tutor in the family of Princess Meshcherskaya. Sofiya Meshcherskaya was a sister of Princess Golitsyn, and one of that group of earnest zealots whose enthusiasms found expression in the formation of the Russian Bible Society, in tract distribution, and in prison visiting. It was she who first encouraged Pinkerton, in 1811, to attempt to organize a Bible Society in Moscow, while for his part, Pinkerton enlisted her patronage, and her active assistance, in the tract cause. She composed many tracts herself, translated others from English, and made generous financial contributions to the work.

By 1811, Pinkerton was living in Moscow, and around that time he became related by marriage to Johann Wigand, one of whose daughters he married, and so to I. J. Schmidt through the latter's wife, Helene Wigand. The idea of a mission to the Buryats was already in Pinkerton's mind, some time before John Paterson ever set foot in Russia. Early in 1812 he had asked Schmidt for his comments on a number of questions about the Kalmucks on behalf of the Bible Society, and in a P.S., dated 8 April, attached to a copy of Schmidt's reply, he gave his reasons for considering the 'Kallmuck and other Mongolian tribes such as the Buryats and proper tribe of Mongols, about Irkutzk and on the borders of China, as more likely to receive the gospel than the various tribes of Mohammedan Tartars'. They were not intolerant of other faiths, as the Muslims were, and also they were 'gross idolaters' and polytheists who would, he thought, comparatively easily accept the superiority of the concept of a single divine being, once it was laid before them. His opinion was no doubt formed on rational grounds, but it took no account of the hold which Buddhism as a religion and as a social cement had upon the Kalmucks and other Mongols.

Pinkerton's letter shows that he was quite aware of the ethnic identity of Kalmucks, Buryats and Mongols, and the most direct source of this information would have been his brother-in-law Schmidt. Schmidt, as an expert on the Mongols, would certainly have been aware of this elementary truth, but in addition, as is apparent from his correspondence, he had a highly placed local informant and well-wisher in Irkutsk itself, in the person of Nikolai Ivanovich Treskin. Treskin was Civil Governor of Irkutsk under the notorious Governor General of Siberia, Ivan Borisovich Pestel, and he acted as Governor General during Pestel's habitual absence. Treskin had been a pupil of Johann Wigand, and still remembered his late master kindly. He was known to be a keen student of the Bible, and an active supporter of the Russian Bible Society, of which he was a correspondent. In a letter dated 29 May 1814, addressed to the Rev. C.F. A. Steinkopff of the British and Foreign Bible Society, Schmidt recalls that he had 'made the attempt to request him by a letter to give me some information concerning the state of religion of the People of Sibiria, particularly of the Mongol tribes to whom also the Burates belong'.

Probably, then, it was this combination of family and personal relationships, perhaps with a promise inherent in them of official good-will and support at the highest level in Siberia, which was responsible for turning Pinkerton's attention specifically to the Buryats as a potential mission field. In the early years it was in fact he, and not Paterson, who was the Bible Society's, and hence the Missionary Society's, expert on Russia and Siberia. Irkutsk was *his* choice, reached after 'having with much labour examined into the present state of the nations of Siberia', and the Directors were advised in 1814 to turn to a work of his which he had left in London in manuscript if they required more information about the peoples of Siberia, and especially about the tribes around Irkutsk. Thus, while Pinkerton did not take an active initiative in organizing the Siberian mission, he evidently had a prior interest in the idea of it, and one or two of the early letters from St Petersburg to the LMS on the subject are signed jointly by him and Paterson. In later life, Paterson was to claim that the plan had been his from the first, and that everything that had to be done to launch the mission had been done by him. This was a considerable exaggeration, as was his other, similar claim that 'all the burden of the Siberian Mission as well as the other missions in Russia' had fallen on himself.

Paterson, whatever his undoubted qualities as an organizer and a diplomat seems to have been of a competitive, monopolizing disposition. Pinkerton was not an easy man either, and almost from the beginning of their mutual acquaintance, which began in 1812, the two men grew jealous of each other,

The Beginnings of the Mission

each of them becoming suspicious of encroachment by the other on what he considered his own territory. Both were in fact great pioneers of Bible Society work in Russia, and from both of them we have books describing what they did. But in Pinkerton's *Russia: or Miscellaneous Observations on the past and present State of that Country and its Inhabitants*, published in 1833, Paterson is entirely ignored, as he is in the earlier *Extracts of Letters from the Rev. Robert Pinkerton on his Late Tour in Russia, Poland and Germany, to Promote the Object of the British and Foreign Bible Society*, 1817. In Paterson's posthumous work, *The Book for Every Land*, based on his memoirs, Pinkerton is mentioned only when it is absolutely unavoidable, and then in a grudging, almost denigratory way. The true situation comes to light in the still unpublished manuscript memoirs themselves.

Whether by accident or design, it was while Pinkerton was still living in Moscow, to which he had returned in late 1812 after the French evacuation of the city, that the Russian Bible Society was founded in St Petersburg, largely as a result of Paterson's energetic lobbying. When Pinkerton did arrive in the capital, Paterson kept him at arm's length, suspecting, in his own words, that Pinkerton 'would not scruple to supplant me if he could'. He looked on Pinkerton as a mere agent of his own designs, writing of his colleague's arrival in St Petersburg: 'This was unsolicited on my part, but, at the same time, not unwelcome; for although the object had been gained, his knowledge of the Russ could not but be of advantage to me in what yet remained to be done.' Not unnaturally, Pinkerton resented having been outmanoeuvred by the newcomer, and his resentment was exacerbated when Paterson's friend, Ebenezer Henderson, joined him in Russia in 1816, and then relieved him while he returned to England on a visit. Paterson blamed Pinkerton's furious reaction to Henderson's arrival for a collapse of his own already delicate state of health, while Henderson became disgusted at what his friend condemned as Pinkerton's 'arrogance'.

John Paterson was born in 1776 at Duntocher in the parish of Old Kilpatrick, near Glasgow. His parents were not well-off, but they saw to it that he got a decent secular education, which included some Latin, and instruction in religion. Having worked out an apprenticeship at what his friend and biographer William Alexander described simply as a handicraft, he entered the University of Glasgow in 1798. In Glasgow he came under the influence of the Evangelical movement, and was particularly attracted by the work of the LMS. While still an apprentice, he had been interested in religion, and had spent much of his spare time in study. He was especially fond of systematic or controversial theology, though in later life he regretted having spent so much of his time on this, instead of 'exploring the Word of God and enriching himself with its treasures'.

Paterson wanted to preach the gospel himself. He gradually moved from the Presbyterian church towards independency, and in 1800 he joined a class of young men who were being recruited by Robert Haldane for training as preachers. One of his teachers was the celebrated Greville Ewing, who, with Ralph Wardlaw, was one of the most active and inspirational supporters of the LMS in Scotland. For a while, Paterson had his own Congregational church at Cambuslang, but in 1804 he answered a call from the Congregational churches of Edinburgh to go out to India as an agent of theirs in a mission they had decided to found there. The companion selected for him had to withdraw on health grounds, and Paterson was asked to choose another from Haldane's classes. He selected Ebenezer Henderson, whom he had not known before, so founding a deep friendship, and a professional partnership whose work in the Bible Society cause extended over the whole of northern Europe, from Iceland as far east as Tiflis.

Paterson and Henderson set sail for Denmark in 1805. The East India Company's policy at that time of refusing to carry missionaries in its ships meant that the two men would have to take passage in a Danish vessel to Serampore on their way to their final destination at Surat. This roundabout route would have had the advantage of bringing them into contact with the Baptist missionary William Carey and his colleagues, but as it turned out they never reached India, and never even embarked on the voyage there. The Edinburgh churches were not a missionary society, and could not provide a broad and properly funded home base from which to support an overseas mission. Paterson and Henderson found Denmark a fruitful field of labour during their stay there in the second half of 1805, and wrote home asking their sponsors to supply other men to campaign in Scandinavia after they themselves had left for India. In reply, the Edinburgh churches wrote to say that they could not afford the cost of both ventures, and advised the two men to make themselves useful where they were, and not go to the East. Soon after that, some sort of internal discord arose in the Edinburgh churches which weakened them still further, and gradually Paterson and Henderson found themselves thrown on their own resources. Paterson had by now settled in Copenhagen, where he supported himself to begin with by teaching English, while Henderson, after a spell at Elsinore, where there was a British community, crossed to Sweden, and settled at Gothenburg. It was in Copenhagen, in 1806, that Paterson first discovered the spiritual and social virtues of the Moravians, for whom he developed a lasting admiration. 'Among them,' he wrote, 'we always found our best friends, and with them we always enjoyed religious friendship.' At one time, he and his first wife, Katarina Hollinder, who was Swedish, were even members of the Moravian society in Stockholm.

In 1807, Copenhagen suffered severely from its bombardment by English land and sea forces, and Paterson, who afterwards wrote a vivid eye-witness account of the attack, as seen from the Danish side, realized that there was little hope of continuing to work effectively in Denmark, and decided to follow his friend Henderson to Sweden. In Gothenburg, Henderson already had a circle of friends, and had begun to preach regularly in the so-called

The Beginnings of the Mission

English chapel. During the early 1700s, a prosperous community of English merchants had grown up in Gothenburg, and by mid-century it was numerous enough to need, and to be able to support, a church of its own. For ten years following 1749, money was collected for the purpose, but what in fact was built in 1759 was a town house incorporating a large chapel. The house did not stay in the possession of the congregation for long. In 1763 it was sold to a group of three of the members of the congregation, and a few years later it passed into the sole ownership of one of them, John Hall. Services were held in the chapel by English ministers until 1785, and after that date, until 1822, itinerant preachers made use of its facilities. It was here that Henderson preached, first in English and later also in Swedish, and here that, in 1811, he established his own tiny congregation.

Amongst Henderson's friends in Gothenburg, probably even as early as 1807, was a Scottish family by the name of Blackwood. Andrew Blackwood was an engineer who had come to Gothenburg in 1786 to help install a water supply, some twenty-two years before his more famous countryman, Thomas Telford, took the road to Sweden. His first contract was completed by late 1787, and Andrew then turned his hand to restoring an old mill, which he later rented. Unlike Telford, he settled down in Sweden and made his home there with his wife, who died in 1795, and two children, Betty born in 1779, and a son, Robert. Another friend of Henderson's was a pious young schoolmaster, Cornelius Rahmn, son of an army officer, and a former student of law at the University of Lund. Cornelius took holy orders in 1810, and was appointed supernumerary preacher to the Royal Artillery in Gothenburg. In 1815 he married Betty Blackwood. Probably through Henderson, Paterson got to know both the Blackwoods and Cornelius, and found the latter a man after his own heart. Cornelius had always cherished a longing to become a missionary since reading, as a boy, about the Moravian mission to Greenland, and when, in 1817, Paterson was looking for a companion to go out with Edward Stallybrass to open the mission at Irkutsk, it was on him that the choice was to fall.

From Gothenburg, Paterson travelled on to Stockholm, where he based himself for some years. His work on behalf of the British and Foreign Bible Society there led him on to plan the printing and distribution of the Bible in Finnish. Since the time of the Russian invasion of 1808, Finland had been detached from Sweden and under Russian occupation, and in 1812, a year which he later recognized as having been a turning-point in his life, Paterson decided, with the agreement of the Bible Society, to visit St Petersburg, in order to speed up arrangements for printing the Finnish Scriptures there.

Paterson knew the value of the right connections, and how to make them. He went to Russia with the backing of Count Steinheil, Governor of Finland, and of Baron Nikolai, the Russian ambassador to Sweden, and soon became acquainted with the most influential men in the Russian capital. He met

The Beginnings of the Mission

Prince Golitsyn, the Minister of Foreign Religions and the confidant of the Emperor Alexander; Privy Councillor Hablitz, who introduced him to the Anglophile Count Kochubei, a former member of Alexander's Unofficial Committee of advisers and one-time Minister of the Interior; and Vasilii Mikhailovich Popov, Director of the Chancery of the Ministry of the Interior. He reached St Petersburg in August 1812, soon settled his queries about the Finnish Scriptures with Golitsyn, and then opened up with him the wider question of the circulation of the Scriptures among the peoples of Russia itself, an enterprise which could, and did, entail the formation of a Russian Bible Society. Paterson was anxious to visit Moscow, in order, as he put it, to get a better knowledge of the country. The advancing French army under Napoleon was already at Smolensk, and Golitsyn tried to dissuade him from undertaking what he feared would be a futile journey. However, Paterson insisted, obtained the necessary papers and an introduction to Sarepta House in Moscow, and, on the same day that Napoleon began his advance from Smolensk, he and Katarina set out from St Petersburg towards the same destination.

Paterson must have had some more specific reason for undertaking this risky journey, and his motive was probably a desire to meet Pinkerton and pick his brains. Paterson was a stranger in Russia, speaking no Russian, and in need of someone more experienced than himself to show him the ropes. Pinkerton was the obvious choice. What Paterson does not reveal in his book is that Pinkerton had already been in correspondence with him earlier in 1812, and had put before him the outlines of his own scheme for setting up a Bible Society in Moscow. The main aims of this Society would have been to distribute the Scriptures and improving tracts in European Russia, and in Asia too if funds proved adequate, and to establish schools where they were needed. As with the mission to the Buryats, Pinkerton had a prior interest in the idea of establishing a Bible Society in Russia. This project, too, was to be taken out of his hands by Paterson, who, at that time, with his influential contacts in St Petersburg and the backing of the BFBS, was in a better position to take action.

In his book Paterson, characteristically, plays down the significance of this journey to Moscow, as well as that of the advice he got from Pinkerton. Of the latter, he wrote: 'He knew the Russian character well, and had formed some interesting connections among some of the leading people, for which his position in a Russian family as tutor gave him facilities; but although I got some valuable information from him as to the situation of the country, I got little as to my particular object, so that, as respected it, I certainly returned to Petersburg no wiser than when I left it.' Of the journey itself, he wrote: 'Altogether it was a most unpleasant journey, and one that was as unprofitable as it was unpleasant. I had accomplished nothing, and obtained no information as to the object I had in view.'

But what could he have hoped to achieve? All the men who mattered –

The Beginnings of the Mission

the Emperor himself, Golitsyn, Kochubei, Popov, and others who were to be the leading spirits in the Russian Bible Society – were in St Petersburg. With the French almost at the gates of the city, it is in any case a wonder that anyone had time to spare to talk about a non-existent Bible Society. Paterson could spend no more than two or three days in Moscow. He arrived on the evening of Wednesday 2 September, and was off again on the following Saturday. In that short time he paid a courtesy call on the Governor General, and also went to see Princess Meshcherskaya and her sister Princess Golitsyn, but neither of these calls can have been pretext enough for the hazardous dash across the line of march of the approaching French army. It may be only conjecture, but one is inclined to sense, behind Paterson's rueful admission that it had all been a waste of time – and a tragic waste of time, too, in a personal sense, for Katarina never recovered from the strain of the double journey, and died soon after – the suppressed recollection of a none too cordial reception from Robert Pinkerton.

But although Paterson did not admit it in his book, the journey to Moscow was to prove productive in one particular direction: it marked the beginning of his interest in a Siberian mission. Pinkerton could safely be ignored in his memoirs, but his correspondence with the LMS proves how much he relied on Pinkerton's advice and support in the initial stages of planning and organizing that mission. Another valuable acquaintance made in Moscow was that of I. J. Schmidt. Schmidt was just about to leave for St Petersburg, to take up his new appointment there, and the two men decided to travel back together. No doubt they would have come together in any case, for Paterson was to make his home in Sarepta House in St Petersburg until March 1813, but perhaps the shared experience of the journey and its dramatic circumstances forged a special bond of sympathy between them. They would have found little difficulty in understanding each other. Paterson probably knew German, for we know that he had engaged a servant who spoke both German and Russian to help him out on the journey as regards the latter language. Schmidt, too, probably already enjoyed the command of English which it is known that he possessed later in life. And it is hardly likely that their conversations did not extend to the Kalmucks and the Buryats.

During the coming months, much of the time which Paterson could spare from his main objective of promoting the Russian Bible Society, was to be devoted to elaborating plans for evangelizing the two Mongolian peoples. For one thing, he was closely concerned with the negotiations between Sarepta and the LMS which resulted in the Society's allowing the Moravians the sum of £300 to cover the outfit of their missionaries and the expenses of their first year's campaign. In another scheme, he worked together with Schmidt. That Kalmuck type, which the BFBS had agreed to pay for some years before, had never been manufactured. Now that Schmidt's Kalmuck St Matthew was in being, with a Russian Bible Society prepared to promote

The Beginnings of the Mission

it, there was a pressing need for a Kalmuck fount. Between them, the two men designed one and got it manufactured. Typically, Paterson claimed the credit for this himself, writing:

> Mr Schmidt had put into my hands specimens of the Calmuck, and after studying the nature of the writing, I succeeded in reducing it to such order that it could be cut in type, and printed in the usual way – an attempt which had not hitherto been made. I was also directed to a type-cutter, a self-taught German, a very clever, ingenious person, and by him, under the direction of Mr Schmidt, I had a fount cut, and the printing commenced in the course of the year.

There is nothing inherently improbable in this. While in Sweden, Paterson had studied the whole craft of printing and book-making, and knew what was required. However, Moravian records attribute the successful creation of the Kalmuck type to Schmidt alone. Both men were rather acquisitive of fame. It really does not matter today which of them designed the type, and saw it through all the processes of manufacture, but it is a pity that, preoccupied by petty personal vanity, they forgot to record the name of the German craftsman who actually did the work.

The formation of the Russian Bible Society in January 1813 evoked an ostensibly enthusiastic response from all over the Empire. Branch societies and auxiliaries were established in the larger localities, and correspondents were appointed elsewhere, while contributions in money poured in from all sides. No doubt many of the new Bible Society's supporters were genuine partisans of the cause, but, equally, it was a band-wagon which no career-conscious official could afford not to jump on. Even the non-Christian inhabitants of remote Siberia were credited with having greeted this, to them irrelevant, event with outbursts of joy which were realized in spontaneous donations of money. Several Buryat princes and lamas, amongst them Galsang Mardaev, the chief *taisha*, or prince, of the still largely shamanistic Khori Buryats, and a high Buryat lama, sent in generous amounts. These, and subsequent subscriptions and expressions of support for the Bible cause, created a quite erroneous impression in Europe, and especially in missionary circles in England, about the degree of receptiveness of the heathen peoples of Siberia to the gospel. They were seen as marking a significant development, and as being, perhaps, a token of greater things to come. I. J. Schmidt reported the event to the BFBS in 1814, and at just about the same time, Paterson and Pinkerton were using it as ammunition in their attempt to persuade the LMS that a mission to the Buryats would represent a worthwhile investment of scarce money and scarcer men.

Not everyone was taken in by the improbable enthusiasm with which the activities of Alexander's and Golitsyn's pet project were received all over the Empire. In 1819, Captain Peter Gordon, having spent some months in Okhotsk disposing of the cargo of his schooner, the *Brothers*, and with no

The Beginnings of the Mission

prospect of a passage by sea back to Calcutta, decided to make his way overland through Siberia to the Persian Gulf. Gordon was an odd character, merchant and ship-owner by profession, evangelist by predilection. Blustering and flamboyant, he reminds one in some ways of George Borrow, though he did not possess Lavengro's gift of words. He was an archetypal John Bull. Nothing scared him, especially not foreigners or authority. He was always on the side of right, and when, as happened at least three times in his life, he found himself arrested and imprisoned, he fought back defiantly. Gordon first comes to notice in 1816 with his book describing how he was captured off Beachy Head in 1809 by a French privateer, and how he escaped and walked to Rotterdam, masquerading as an American. Then, in 1820, he managed to get himself arrested near Astrakhan. The matter had something to do with his having sent a letter, in Kalmuck, so he says, to the Moravians at Sarepta, whom he was planning to visit. Whose letter it was he does not say, but the local authorities grew suspicious, arrested him, and moved him on. Gordon had bad luck with his indiscreet letters. His third and worst brush with authority came in 1827, when he was arrested on the orders of the assistant to the collector and civil magistrate at Madura in south India, and kept in custody for a considerable time without having charges preferred against him. On this occasion his detention resulted from his having injudiciously denounced the misdeeds of the authorities at Madura to the Governor in Council at Madras. Some years later, probably in 1836, Gordon was petitioning the House of Commons for his case to be reviewed, and in 1841, when we more or less lose sight of him, he had managed to get a petition to the same effect before the House of Lords.

Peter Gordon was an original. He was sardonic, cynical, choleric, and no respecter of persons, unless he happened to like them. Part of his eccentric purpose in trekking across Siberia in mid-winter was to try to open a trade route through Okhotsk and Kyakhta into China, but he also planned to call on Edward Stallybrass at Selenginsk. This at least he succeeded in doing. He spent several days at Selenginsk, visiting Kyakhta, where he became convinced that his commercial hopes could not be realized. When the time came, on Boxing Day 1819, to leave and cross Lake Baikal, Gordon could hardly tear himself away from the mission station. He wrote in his diary: 'Parted from these esteemed missionaries, with whom I could have been well contented to spend the remainder of my life, being persuaded that the propagation of Christianity is the highest benevolence and the noblest task of man.' Gordon was a man of instant enthusiasms and changing moods. Only a few weeks previously, Siberia had presented charms of a very different sort to him. While he was at Verkhneudinsk, he writes, 'two or three fine, unaffected young girls convinced me, that a winter at Verkni might be passed very agreeably'.

Transient as his emotions could be, though, Peter Gordon was consistent in his detestation of the Russian Orthodox church and all it stood for. His

The Beginnings of the Mission

Fragment of the Journal of a Tour through Persia in 1820 contains an amusing comparative glossary of English and Russian terms, covering everything from the Emperor, 'whom they consider to be God', down to Cossacks, or 'Locusts', Merchants of the second or third Guilds, or 'Pedlars', and so on. God, in Russia, he rated as 'a child's doll'. Religion was 'gross idolatry'; prayer was 'barefaced hypocrisy'. He ridiculed the Russian Bible Society as 'One of Alexander's hobbies. It yields next to the taking of Paris his choicest harvest of flattery.' Its auxiliaries were dismissed as 'dumb shews'.

Schmidt and Paterson, though, interpreted the donations from Siberia, improbable though they were, considering the religious alignments of the different parties concerned, as evidence of a new spirit among the Buryats, and this impression was clearly conveyed in their letters. In 1814, Paterson wrote to George Burder, the Secretary of the LMS:

> Among the many tribes in this neighbourhood the Buryats demand particular attention. They are a Mongolian tribe. It was a Buryat prince who sent in 800 rb. to the Bible Society and had subscribed 150 annually; and it was one of their high priests who sent in 400 rb. as an offering for himself and his brethren for the purpose, to quote his own expression, *of promoting the distribution of the Scriptures among all people.*

And he went on with an even more daring extrapolation:

> We have no doubt that viewing things in the light here represented you will see that there is at present a most important opening into those hitherto much neglected regions. Appearances among these people are calling to you *Come over and help us* and we are persuaded they will not call in vain.

This was a fundamental misinterpretation of what had happened, and Paterson's error was all the more significant because it was taken up and cherished as axiomatic, at least to begin with, by the missionaries themselves. So, three years later, Sarah Stallybrass could write to her sister Ann: 'The Mongolian and Manjur Tartars form a large part of the population, among whom the word of eternal life has not yet had circulation, and as you are already apprised they are hungering for this bread.'

Consideration of local conditions in Siberia at the time suggests that there was probably quite a different explanation for the Buryats' unlikely generosity. Pestel, from St Petersburg, and Treskin, on the spot, ran Siberia from 1806 to 1819 as if it were their own fief. Their policies were not unenlightened. Development of agriculture, the removal of trade monopolies, building roads and improving communications, fostering trade with China, and so on, were all worthwhile objectives. It was the way in which they were pursued that made them objectionable. Whether or not they altogether deserved it, Pestel and Treskin acquired the reputation of being cruel and ruthless dictators, and, amongst their subordinates, bribery and corruption were rife. Now Treskin was known to be a Bible enthusiast. Gordon himself found the ex-Governor, as he was when he called on him, to have an excellent knowledge of the Scriptures, and during the evening he spent with Treskin, who was still living in Irkutsk even after his replacement by Speranskii, a copy of the Bible was always at hand for reference. But Treskin had no illusions about the possibility of converting the Buryats. He told Gordon: 'No, no, the Boriats will never be converted, they are not such fools: they know that they are a great deal better than Christians, for they don't lie, steal or get drunk half as much. Why don't you send your Missionaries to India, why don't you turn Missionary as it is such a good thing – no, no, you are not such a fool, you find something better to do in the East Indies.'

This was not the image of the Governor of Irkutsk which Paterson, who did not know him, was promoting in London. Anticipating the arrival of the missionaries in Siberia, he had written: 'The Governor of Irkutsk is a zealous correspondent of the Bible Society – is a religious man – and as he has much in his power, being active Governor of the whole of Siberia in the absence of the Governor General, we may depend on their receiving every facility they want.' So they might, perhaps, if Treskin had remained in office, but it would probably not have done their reputations much good with the local people.

Treskin's personal piety may have been quite genuine, or it may have been prompted by a tactful desire to keep in with the trend at court, where Alexander was at this time, 1814, much under the influence of Golitsyn, the President of the Bible Society, and immersed in his Bible enthusiasms. In Siberia, it can have made little difference. The roubles donated by the Buryat taishas and lamas would have been extracted willy-nilly from the common people, and would have been intended, partly at least, simply to curry favour with the Governor, whose sympathies were well known. To imagine uneducated Buryat herdsmen, Buddhists or shamanists, voluntarily handing money to their superiors to be passed on to what would have appeared to them as a completely irrelevant organization, is sheer fantasy. Later on, they would gladly accept copies of the Scriptures from the missionaries because they had good uses for the paper and leather they were made of. It is difficult to imagine that they would have been moved by more pious considerations at an earlier date. As Peter Gordon remarked of another, similar incident: 'The truth is, that if the Boriats had known for what purpose the money was taken from them, they would much rather have paid for exemption from Bibles.'

In the summer of 1814, both Paterson and Pinkerton were in England, where they had discussions with the Bible Society and the Missionary Society on a number of topics, including that of a mission to Siberia. The Directors of the LMS asked them to prepare a memorandum on the subject, and on 7 November 1814 they wrote from St Petersburg, restating concisely the

The Beginnings of the Mission

substance of the conversations which had taken place in London. The letter is in Paterson's hand, but bears the signatures of both men. Having first declared themselves ready to take on the extra commitment of promoting the work of the LMS as far as was compatible with their primary responsibilities towards the BFBS, they put forward a definite proposal for a mission to Irkutsk, to be manned, preferably, by two unmarried missionaries, at a cost, probably, of not more than £200 a year. The main purpose of such a mission would be to spread the Gospel amongst the heathen peoples of eastern Siberia, and to translate the Bible into both Mongolian and Manchu. Pinkerton's enquiries had convinced him that Irkutsk would be the best site for this mission. It was centrally situated in Siberia, surrounded by a number of non-Christian tribes, and it was also, as he and Paterson supposed, though irrelevantly, the main centre of communication between Russia and China. The Buryats, from whom such generous donations had been received by the Russian Bible Society, were the obvious starting-point for such a mission.

There were, the two men felt, several other factors which pointed to the Buryats, and also, inexplicably, the Yakuts, as 'ripe for the reception of the gospel', but their arguments are remarkable for the eagerness with which they were asserted rather than for their aptness to the situation. They were thoroughly confused about the identity of the Buryat language. Paterson had allowed a very misleading account to be published in the 11th Report of the BFBS for 1814, an account which he corrected in his memoirs, but which, at the time, formed the basis of the Bible Society's, and hence also of the Missionary Society's, information:

> We have made an important discovery, viz. that the language of the Calmuck Testament is likely to be understood by some of the other Mongolian tribes in Siberia, and on the confines of China. The language appears to be the same in all respects; only the Mongols in Siberia, and on the confines of China, use the Mandjur character, which they call the purified Mongolian or Calmuc.

The truth was that written Kalmuck, or Oirat as it is also termed, and the literary Mongol used by the Buryats for writing, were not mutually intelligible, as was soon discovered when the Kalmuck St Matthew was tried out on some Buryat officials. Nor was the Manchu script ever used for any Mongolian language. Like the Kalmuck script, it was a refinement of the Mongolian alphabet. It dated back to the beginning of the seventeenth century, and was used exclusively for the non-Mongolian Manchu language, for which it had been deliberately developed.

Paterson was still under this delusion when he and Pinkerton reported to the Missionary Society.

> The language of the Buryats is nearly the same with the Kalmuc, into which a part of the new Testament is already translated, and will soon

The Beginnings of the Mission

be printed, only they use the Manjur character, which differs somewhat from the Kalmuc. As soon as it is fully ascertained that the language is the same and perfectly understood by them, we shall have so much of the New Testament as is translated, printed in their characters and sent to them.

In fact, the process of preparing the Testament for Buryat readers was to prove more complicated.

It was known that lamaist religious books were printed mainly in Peking, and that the Buryats imported them from China. One such book had got into the hands of Treskin, who had sent it on to I. J. Schmidt. From this premise the two men drew the wholly correct conclusion that 'these books are not only understood and read by the Buryats, but also by all the numerous tribes of the Mongols proper, the greater part of whom live under the protection of the Chinese Government'. Unfortunately, they went on to draw the false conclusion that mastery of 'this one language opens up a most extensive and important field for missionary labours. These are advantages which you know how to estimate.' They ignored, to the detriment of the funds of the LMS, the all-important political fact of the closed frontier between Russia and China, which would preclude any coming and going. It was sheer wishful thinking, too, to suppose that the Society could exploit the supposed connections between Buryatia and Tibet. 'Their religion', the two men wrote, 'is the Lamite religion, and their learned priests usually study in Thibet itself, which gives them a near connection with this country, so that through them we may be able to gain a more intimate acquaintance with Thibet, and even to obtain access to those hitherto almost inaccessible regions.'

A second important objective was to spread the gospel among the Manchus and in China generally, and in this respect, too, Paterson and Pinkerton let their enthusiasms run away with them, and consequently misled the Directors. For one thing, they thought that the fact that the Buryats could import books from China into Siberia meant that the converse was also true. 'The circumstances of their being able to obtain books from Pekin shows the possibility of sending your Chinese Testament from this quarter into the very heart of China, and even to Pekin itself.' For another, they shared the frequently held but illusory belief that Manchu, the language of the ruling dynasty, would prove to be the key to the Chinese mission field. They put forward a number of factually correct, but irrelevant, arguments, to support their much exaggerated estimate of the importance of the Manchu language, though they missed, as it happened, the only pertinent one. The best Mongolian dictionaries were bilingual Manchu–Mongolian vocabularies classified according to subject matter, which could be obtained from Peking in printed versions. The missionaries were to find such books indispensable in building up their own dictionaries. For other purposes, the Manchu language was to prove more or less useless, and in fact, even as early as 1817, the Directors had demoted the study of Manchu to a subordinate position, when they drew up their official instructions for Edward Stallybrass.

The Bible Society, though, was to spend a great deal of money twenty years later in the attempt to complete and issue a Manchu version of the Scriptures. Fortunately, the £2,600 which it cost them to support William Swan and George Borrow while they were copying out the Manchu Old Testament, and to cover the cost of printing the New Testament in St Petersburg, had a splendid, though unintentional, outcome. It was money well spent, though by accident. If the BFBS had not gone ahead with the copying and printing of the Manchu Scriptures, it would not have needed Borrow's services in St Petersburg, and if Borrow had not had the chance of proving himself in Russia, who knows if he would ever have been asked to go to Spain? Two fascinating series of letters would never have been written, and we should have been deprived of *The Bible in Spain*.

Paterson and Pinkerton rather made light of the difficulty of finding men whose characters would match the challenge of Siberia, and of the nature of that challenge. They made it all look so easy. 'We think', they wrote,

> that this mission should be undertaken by two unmarried missionaries, of decided piety, ardent zeal; of a steady and persevering disposition; who have some acquaintance with the world, have a liberal education and a turn for learning languages; being also apt to teach. They must likewise be willing to become all things to all men, in the apostle's sense of the expression, in order to save their souls. It may perhaps be necessary for them to comply, in some measure, with the asiatic manner of living and dressing, in order to conciliate the affections of the people they intend to benefit. The most of them are one half wanderers, feeding their flocks in the extensive Steppes in Summer, and living in Huts in winter. Your missionaries in preaching the gospel unto them may perhaps need to wander with them: now with a family this would be next to impossible; but single men will find little difficulty in accustoming themselves to this manner of life, particularly as the climate is excellent, very healthy and the country in many places very pleasant. Mr Schmidt was 4 years wandering with the Calmucks, and was never more comfortable in his life. If the Lord give success to the word of grace among them, there will then be a necessity for forming a settlement among them, the management of which should be committed to married men, and we do not think that it will be difficult to prevail on the converts to settle along with the missionaries, especially as they are already half settlers.

There is something of Dr Pangloss in these sanguine prognostications, intended as they were to convince the Directors that Irkutsk was the 'most eligible' place to set up a Siberian mission, and that the mission would prove

The Beginnings of the Mission

one of the most important stations in the world. Nevertheless, the two men added a warning: 'A year's residence at Irkutsk, and an acquaintance with the people, their language, and manners, will throw much light on every thing connected with this subject.'

Paterson and Pinkerton were on firmer ground in their appreciation of the immediate political situation in Russia. Their contention that the Emperor Alexander I would prove well disposed towards a mission to the Buryats, and would give it his warm support, was borne out by subsequent events. Alexander patronized the missionaries most generously. Whether the help which it was anticipated they would receive from Treskin would have been forthcoming was never put to the test, as he was dismissed in 1819, but they found an effective friend and protector in Mikhail Speranskii, Pestel's successor as Governor General.

The letter of 7 November was decisive, and on 26 December 1814 the Directors of the LMS formally resolved to open their mission to Siberia, and delegated to the Committee of Examination the task of finding suitable men to undertake it.

4

The Missionaries: Stallybrass and Rahmn

It was not easy to find candidates suitable for the Siberian mission: indeed, the LMS was short of young men willing to go out to any mission field. Five months after the Directors had taken their decision to open the mission, the Committee of Examination had been able to do no more than report that the Rev. Dr David Bogue, Tutor at the Missionary Seminary at Gosport, had included in a list of the names of men who would soon leave the Seminary, that of a Mr Mead, whom he recommended for Irkutsk. We are not told on what grounds this recommendation was made, and evidently it was not approved, for Mr Mead was ultimately sent to India. At the weekly Board Meeting held on 21 August 1815 it was decided that the question of an appointment to Irkutsk should be taken up at the next meeting, on the 28th. To judge by the absence of a minute to that effect, this was not done. A little later, Robert Yuille, who would eventually be sent to Selenginsk, offered himself as a missionary, and his offer was accepted on 15 April 1816, but in general terms only. He was not earmarked for Siberia, and, indeed, if he had not objected to it on the grounds of the tropical climate, he would have been appointed to Malacca.

The first missionary to be appointed to the Siberian mission was Edward Stallybrass. Edward was born on 8 June 1794, one of nine children, at Royston, where his father, William, was a deacon of the Congregational church. Only a few years before his birth, the church had been split over some points of doctrine. The deacons, presumably with William Stallybrass amongst them, and most of the congregation, seceded from what became known as the Old Meeting, and established their own community. This met in the New Meeting, a building erected in Kneesworth Street, which was opened for worship in 1792 or 1793. The first pastor was Thomas Towne, who also kept a school in Royston. Towne held office until 1830.

Edward must have had a thoroughly religious upbringing, but it was not till he was about seventeen that he underwent the experience of positive conversion.

The Missionaries: Stallybrass and Rahmn

> I hope I have some good reason [he wrote in his application to the LMS] to believe that about the seventeenth year of my life, the blessed Spirit of God applied to my mind, in a saving way, the great truths of the Gospel; at which time I was led to see my own lost and fallen state as a sinner in the sight of God; the impossibility of being justified in the sight of God, except by the righteousness of the Lord Jesus Christ; the importance of immediate application to, and implicit reliance on him as the only Saviour from the wrath to come.

Some two years after this revelation, Edward applied to enter Homerton College, with the intention of training for the ministry. His application was supported by the Rev. James Pearse of Clavering, who, for some reason, was said to be Edward's own pastor, in spite of the fact that he appears to have belonged to Mr Towne's congregation. It was read on 11 January 1814 at a meeting of the King's Head Society, which was responsible for the College, and Edward was accepted as a student, subject to a three months' period of probation, which he successfully completed. Little more is known of his career at Homerton, where he gave entire satisfaction, except that he was awarded a prize of £3 on 14 November 1815 in respect of his work during the two years he had spent there. For some time before that, Edward had been considering changing the direction of his future career and becoming a missionary, conscious of the overwhelming need for missionaries to go out and rescue the heathen, and of the lack of volunteers for the field. Eight days after the award of his prize he sent in his formal application to the LMS.

Edward's application is not a *curriculum vitae*, but a profession of faith. It tells us practically nothing about his early life, not even where he went to school, but a great deal about his religious convictions and his appreciation of the nature of the work of a missionary. The LMS had not yet drawn up the printed form on which later applicants, William Swan, for example, were asked to supply answers to specific questions, so that his application, in the form of a letter to the Rev. George Burder, the Secretary of the Society, is a free essay in self-assessment. Edward had a correct Evangelical theology, which he summarized as follows:

> The Bible I regard as a revelation of the mind and will of Jehovah to man; in which, I believe, are made known the glory and perfections of God – the state of holiness and happiness in which man was originally created, and the state of guilt and degradation into which he has sunk – the eternal purposes of God concerning him, and the development of these purposes – the incarnation of the divine Redeemer, his sufferings, his death and atonement which he thereby made, and his resurrection – the necessity of the influences of the Holy Spirit, whose office it is to enlighten, sanctify, and prepare for Heaven the benighted mind of man – the separation which will take place at the last day when all

they who have been the subjects of the Holy Spirit's influence will be received for ever into the presence and favour of God, but they, who continue finally impenitent, will be justly banished into everlasting ruin and despair.

He then outlined his reasons for wishing to become a missionary:

That which has induced me to alter my intentions, with respect to the scene, and the subject of my labours, is, a consideration of the importance of Missionary exertions, and the comparatively small number of persons, who appear disposed to engage in them. The subject has engaged my attention for the last year, more particularly during the last six or seven months; about which time I made known my . . .* concerning it to my Tutors, who wished me to give the matter due consideration, and to seek by earnest prayer to know the will of God concerning me.

Finally, Edward detailed the steps he had taken to ensure that he really did have a call, and his conception of the purpose of a missionary life:

I have endeavoured to divest my mind of everything which might tend improperly to influence me; I trust I have sought to become acquainted with the difficulties, which they, who engage in this most important work, must encounter; I have also tried to consider, and apply to my own circumstances, the encouragements and consolations which the word of God affords, to induce me unreservedly to devote myself to the promotion of His glory; and to me it appears, that the importance of the cause, and the encouragements to undertake it though arduous, by far preponderate; that with these sentiments it is my bounden duty to undertake it. The plan which is adopted for enlightening the heathen, by the translation of the Scriptures, and the preaching the gospel, appears to me to be the most likely (with the divine blessing, without which all efforts will prove fruitless) to promote that most desirable end; to the promotion of which, I have come to a determination, (if the Missy Society shall think it proper to patronize me), that, in the strength of divine grace, I will consecrate all the powers both of my body and mind.

Edward's application shows that he was a professional. The right sentiments were couched in appropriate terms. Here was a modest man, made confident, though with qualifications, through self-examination and prayer. He was warmly supported by the theological tutor at Homerton, Dr Pye Smith, and by the classical tutor, the Rev. William Walford. The latter, who knew him better, endorsed the application as follows: 'The writer of the above letter, Mr Stallybrass, is such a person as we shall regret to part with because he is in all respects suitable to the purposes of our institution: we shall however

---

* The paper is torn and missing here.

give him up to the Missionary Society with great satisfaction as a young man every way qualified by his piety, his talents and his prudence to forward the interesting objects which that society is pursuing.' Edward's letter was considered by the Board of the LMS on 27 November 1815, and referred to the Committee of Examination, which called him for interview twice in December, and then recommended that he should be accepted. As far as we know, he was not designated for Siberia at this time.

The King's Head Society, which managed Homerton College, had been founded in 1730 in London, where it met at the King's Head Tavern in Poultry, by a group of Congregational laymen, who were disturbed by certain doctrinal developments in their churches. At the same time as they accepted Edward's candidature, the Board of the LMS felt obliged to compensate this society for expenses which had already been incurred in training the young man whose services would not now be available to the churches at home. They also expressed the hope, in which they were not disappointed, that Edward would be allowed to finish his training at Homerton under Dr Pye Smith. In recognition of all this, they paid the King's Head Society £20 on account in September 1816. A further payment of £100 was made in January 1817, by which time Edward was no longer formally a student of Homerton.

Homerton College, nowadays situated in Cambridge, was at that time still in East London, and Edward had joined the Congregational church at Stepney, whose pastor was the Rev. George Ford. There he came to know a Mr Thomas Robinson, a tallow-chandler and one of the church deacons, and his daughter Sarah. In August 1816, Edward and Sarah became engaged – not, however, without a crisis of conscience for Sarah, who had to reconcile the claims of a call to the mission field with those of her father, who was getting on in years. Edward's destination had still not been decided, and the two young people were still single when, in October, the LMS abruptly decided to appoint him to Irkutsk, and asked him to be ready to sail for St Petersburg in three weeks' time. This unexpected decision had been prompted by the demands of Paterson and Henderson, who wanted the future missionary to be able to spend the winter in Russia learning the language, before setting out for Siberia. Up till then, Sarah had been expecting to leave England in the spring of 1817, and both the nature of her destination, and the prospect of having to let Edward go on in advance, unmarried, were disconcerting. 'I received the intelligence with some composure,' she wrote in her diary, 'though a continued renunciation of my own will I do not always feel.' However, she quickly reconciled herself to the blow.

As it turned out, Sarah was to be spared disappointment. Edward was ordained at the end of October, and on 11 November he called at the headquarters of the LMS to take leave of the Directors, only to be told that they had changed their minds, and that he was not to sail the next day, as had been planned. They were worried about the severe weather which had set in on the Continent, and thought it wiser to keep him back till the following year. In St Petersburg, Paterson was rather put out. Realizing that the Baltic might freeze over early and prevent ships coming up to Cronstadt, he had alerted correspondents in various Baltic ports to look out for Edward, should he have to land short of his destination. He was disappointed, too, that Edward would not be able to spend the winter familiarizing himself with Russia and its language, nor help him out in preaching to the English congregation in the capital. Still, there was nothing to be done, and he contented himself with advising the Directors that Edward should learn as much French as possible while still at home, as it would be useful in St Petersburg and on the way across Siberia. For some reason, the Directors resolved to send Edward back to Dr Pye Smith, advising him to study Russian and German.

The opportune last-minute change of plan did not leave Edward and Sarah free to marry at their own convenience. Some years earlier there had been a lengthy debate within the LMS on the subject of the advisability of early marriage for new missionaries, and in 1807 the Board had taken a policy decision that young men going out on their first appointment should, preferably, be unmarried, and that they should spend a year at their station before taking a wife. This would give them time to decide whether they had chosen the right station, and whether it was a suitable place to bring a European woman.

Edward wanted to marry before leaving England, and he attended a meeting of the Committee of Examination on 17 February 1817 to put his case for a suspension of normal practice. According to the minutes of the meeting, he argued that Miss Robinson's 'dispositions and qualifications' were such as to fit her to teach children, while the Committee took a broader, more practical view. Edward was urged to reflect on the possible consequences of marrying before he left home. The Committee suggested to him 'the great expediency both as it relates to the object of the mission and his own and her personal comfort that he should not marry prior to his leaving this country. He was desired to give the subject a serious and candid consideration and to attend this Committee on the 24 Inst.'

What this advice boiled down to was the anticipation that, during the course of the long journey to Irkutsk, the new Mrs Stallybrass, like any other new bride at the time, would probably become pregnant, with all that that would entail. To start the three months' winter trek by sledge over the Siberian snow-roads while expecting a baby, or with one to look after, was a horrifying prospect. The Directors may have recalled how poor Katarina Paterson, who had faithfully accompanied her husband from St Petersburg to Moscow and back – a much shorter journey – had lost her baby, and then died herself, as a direct result. In the end, though, they gave way. As it happened both Betty Rahmn, who had a baby daughter with her, and

The Missionaries: Stallybrass and Rahmn

Sarah, were pregnant when they left St Petersburg. It was an exhausting journey. The days were spent jolting over roads which were sometimes so rough that the sledges capsized. In the main towns they could often find comfortable lodgings, thanks to the imperial recommendation they enjoyed, but elsewhere they had to pass the nights in fusty Siberian post-houses, or in their own sledges. Sometimes they travelled right through the night. Both women reached Irkutsk sickly and jaded. Betty lost her new baby a few weeks after its birth. Cornelius and Edward were distracted from their proper duties by the worry of looking after their wives, and, though Sarah clung on, the Rahmns had to admit defeat and leave Siberia.

Before reaching a decision about the marriage, the Committee of Examination appointed a sub-committee of three of its members to interview Sarah. They reported in her favour, finding her 'a suitable person to be the Wife of Mr Stallybrass appointed as a Missionary to Irkutsk'. It was no wonder that they did, for Sarah Robinson comes over in her letters and her diary, extracts from which were published by Edward in a Memoir after her death, as an earnest young person of irreproachable, if cloying, piety. She belonged to a special world, to the inner circle of declared members of the independent churches of the time. Her self-portrait conforms to a familiar pattern – a self-confessedly iniquitous childhood, during which she rebelled against the strict upbringing of loving parents, ends in the recognition of her own sinful unworthiness. She is converted, becomes a grateful member of her church, and devotes herself thereafter to good works. Earnestness came to her early in life. While she was still at school she was advising and admonishing her sister Ann, and never stopped trying to keep her up to the spiritual mark: 'Are you mortifying the deeds of the body?' she asked her. 'Are you CRUCIFYING the flesh, with the affections and lusts? Are you putting sin to this ignominious death?' Her sisterly advice took on the proportions of a course of instruction: 'I had promised myself, in the commencement of this letter, to say something on the nature of this ordinance, but as the subject is too long for the limits of a sheet, I shall resume it in my next, begging you, in the mean time, to add *watchfulness* unto prayer.'

Sarah's experience was that of many of her Evangelical contemporaries, and the exalted language in which she records it echoes the rapturous outpourings of one after another of the obituaries of other estimable females, worthy persons, valuable ministers, dear youths, interesting subjects of memoirs, as they were variously termed, in the pages of the *Evangelical Magazine*, the principal independent and missionary journal of the day. She might well have been submerged in that throng of worthy mediocrities, but there was something which set her apart – the clarity with which she heard the call to missionary service, and the determination with which she followed that call. Sarah had a vision, and she followed it faithfully to the bitter end, her death in Siberia at the early age of forty-four, after a mission-life of almost uninterrupted ill health. She was a zealot.

The Missionaries: Stallybrass and Rahmn

Let us look a little more closely at Miss Sarah Robinson, now aged twenty-eight, not just for her own sake, but as a typical example of a young lady member of an elite group, whose thought-patterns she followed and whose in-language flowed so fluently from her pen. She was five years older than Edward, having been born on 7 April 1789. Birthdays, and the passage of time, oppressed her with thoughts of days wasted and opportunities missed, partly because, for all her energetic self-analysis, Sarah was under-employed. Until she went to Siberia, she had no regular outlet for her restless charitable impulses. In 1812 she wrote to Ann:

> The 7th of April summons pleasing and painful recollections to your sister. Yes, three and twenty years of a life spent almost in vain, cannot fail to produce the latter to a mind not callous to every feeling of gratitude to its Maker. How many times, during that period, has not the sun veiled his splendour on whole days of vanity and negligence; not to mention the abuse of a large portion in sinful diversions while in an unconverted state! Ah! what reason is there to admire the mercy of God in not taking me away in my sins.

Sarah's prose serves her badly. Its structured formality and lack of individuality make it read like a homily intended for publication, or as if she were preaching to some unseen but rapt congregation. Her outcries are a caricature of emotion. She comes over as a churchy marionette, not a real person. But now and again, through a chink in the façade, we glimpse the truth of her agonized nature. Sarah was anxious. The tension, as she summoned Ann to self-examination, was no pose. In her heart she nursed a desperate fear that she might yet lose her beloved sister throughout eternity. In one of Edward's private letters from Siberia there is a hint that Ann and her husband, Joseph Monds, were not as far advanced in piety as their missionary relatives. 'When, my dear Brother and Sister,' he wrote in 1821, 'shall we number you amongst those who have made an open profession of the name of our Lord . . .?' Read in conjunction with a letter from Sarah to Ann, written three years earlier from Irkutsk, this explains Sarah's deep concern for her sister's, and her own, everlasting happiness. Sarah wrote: 'Oh, how much more important has the salvation of each member of my family appeared to me, since I have been separated from them – if to be far removed from them on Earth causes grief, and pain, what would *eternal* separation do – My hearts desire and fervent prayer for each of them is that they might be saved!' So Ann was not yet saved, and Sarah was apprehensive.

Again, her debate with herself in her diary as to whether she was justified in leaving her elderly father, to go out as a missionary, reads like contrived casuistry. There is no heart in it, as she reaches the conclusion that 'he is in the hands of a merciful and gracious God, who has ever provided, and will still provide, for his wants'. And on the day she embarked for Russia, never to see her father again, she sent him a dutiful and rounded expression of her affection and gratitude. An unpublished letter written to Ann at the same time redeems all the cold charity of the formal farewell, and one hopes that Ann showed it to old Thomas. Sarah was deeply attached to her father, unhappy and anxious at leaving him to follow the call she could not deny, but quite incapable of telling him so, so she told her sister instead, pouring it all out in a single breath, incoherent but sincere:

> My dearest Ann,
> Receive these few lines to assure you all how much consolation and support I have and do experience yes I am happy and that comfort springs from God – tell dear dear Father I owe this consolation principally to him oh what shall [I] render to God for such a Parent – tell him how much I owe to that last smile it dwells on my imagination on my heart – tell him I am his encreasingly indebted and affectionate Child and I am yr devoted Sister
> in haste S Stallybrass
> adieu adieu.

Sarah had less exalted worries, too. Newly arrived in Irkutsk, she was still missing her father. Life was so novel and strange, and his advice would have been so useful. She and Edward, she writes, have to do so much for themselves. If they want veal, they have to fatten their own calf and kill it. If they want beer, they must brew it themselves. That reminds her. Could Father send them a good recipe for beer? They have not had a decent bottle since leaving St Petersburg, where it was almost as good as English beer. Edward's first attempt at home-brew has failed – probably the malt was not quite right. Edward, who never seems to have let up from his heavy role of missionary, must be held partly to blame if we misjudge Sarah. He must have discarded everything which he thought might detract from his wife's saintly image when selecting material for his Memoir of her, and as a result he has left us only a cardboard cut-out, not the full woman. The few surviving unpublished letters fortunately redress the balance a little.

Sarah was obsessed by her sins, though the extravagantly exalted language in which she recalls her fallen state arouses the suspicion that they were more imaginary than real, the obligatory prelude to a restoration to grace. She wallowed in her self-proclaimed unworthiness. She was 'the vilest of sinners'. She was amazed to find that salvation was available to *her*, of all people. She paints her childhood, doubtless a blameless one, as if it had been spent entirely in dissipation. Standards must have been almost unattainably high, or rhetoric impossibly inflated, for even Edward wrote of her as a girl that 'she appears, however, for some time after she had left school, to have desired to follow the course of this evil world'. And Sarah herself remembered her mother especially for 'putting restraints upon my carnal and vain propensities, and for engaging my youthful affections on the side of religion'. In spite of her religious upbringing and her conversion, Sarah found sin hard to avoid. It was much easier to pretend to be good. 'To cover my conduct and actions in the presence of my fellow-creatures, is no laborious part; but to suppress secret faults, as pride, self-complacency, lust, and envy, requires all the energy of the renewed man; and then, unless aided by the influences of the Holy Spirit, cannot be effected.'

The turning-point in her life was reached in 1808 when, at the age of nineteen, she experienced the same sort of conversion as did many of her contemporaries, including her future husband, and her future fellow-missionary, William Swan. She composed a fulsome statement of self-criticism on the subject of her fallen state, which she addressed to the whole church at Stepney, which she was seeking to join. In it, she wrote how she had come to realize the importance of self-examination, and 'looking into my heart, I found it to be deceitful above all things, and desperately wicked'. From the time of her conversion, she seems to have devoted herself to charitable works, 'constantly going about doing good, and searching out objects of distress, which, as far as her means allowed her, were relieved'.

Once saved, Sarah was on parade for the rest of her life, 'fervent in spirit and diligent in business', as Edward recalled after her death. When she was not running the house, supervising the servants, teaching the little Buryat girls, or giving out tracts 'to every class and description of persons who could read', she was urging her children along the paths of righteousness. 'Often she would take the children into her closet to converse and pray with them: the children esteemed it a privilege to be admitted into her room for these purposes.' So it went on, in spite of recurrent illness and discomfort, almost to the last moments of her life. But not quite, for these last moments, heartbreaking as they were in themselves, proved something of a disappointment to Edward. Poor Sarah's mind was confused by sickness and pain, and he could not hear her final declaration of faith:

> It would have afforded me pleasure to record her *dying* testimony to the power of that gospel which she loved. But this is not granted me. For some time before her death, her mind was beclouded, her delirium very high, and her speech incoherent. Notwithstanding, in the midst of her incoherency I was often cheered in perceiving the bent of her mind, the element in which she delighted to move, and the subjects upon which she delighted to dwell.

To her contemporaries and fellow Congregationalists, Sarah was no doubt what John Paterson called her, 'a charming young woman'. But, looking back at her over nearly two hundred years of changing values and patterns of behaviour, and seeing her in the neutral print of her letters, divorced from her background, and deprived of the comforting camouflage of her own milieu, into which she must have merged imperceptibly, we can perhaps forgive ourselves if we are tempted to see her as a bit of a prig. Even if her self-searching and the consequent torrents of self-revilement were only a

The Missionaries: Stallybrass and Rahmn

convention of her time and circle, she still, in a way, had a good opinion of herself. Who was she, cocooned in a God-fearing family, to proclaim herself the vilest of all sinners? What did she *really* know about lust? Hypersensitive about her own spiritual failings, and desperately concerned at the damnation awaiting the careless heathen, she could yet be aloof and insensitive to immediate suffering. One day, she passed a gang of exiles on their way to Siberia, men and women, some riding in carts, others on foot. Sarah's reaction was that of one exempt from liability to the same fate: 'While their deplorable situation excited our sympathy, the hardened and wicked look of both young and old seemed a confirmation of the justice of their punishment.'

It may be unfair to judge Sarah on the basis of one piece of anecdotal evidence, but Edward's own assessment of her capacity for pity is telling. He wrote of her: 'She possessed great compassion for the *temporal*, and much greater for the *spiritual* miseries of men. Many of the poor by whom we are surrounded will, I doubt not, deeply and sincerely lament her loss. She was able in some measure to relieve their temporal necessities. But often would the tears of pity flow for those worse miseries which she deeply felt but was unable to relieve. She earnestly desired to see greater facilities opened up for staying the spiritual plague.' Sarah had clear priorities in the exercise of her sympathy.

In unguarded moments, Sarah could drop hints of a sort of pride in the superiority of the missionary's life, and of satisfaction at the thought that she was sharing it, though she took care to depreciate the latter. 'It is but little, I know, that I can do in the great cause in which I have engaged; but our united efforts may contribute to advance the happiness of the poor, perishing heathen', she wrote with becoming modesty. But to her father she could also say: 'Will you regret that you have one child sent to these remote parts, to assist in conveying the glad tidings of salvation to a people who sit in "gross darkness?" Will you not wish that you had more to devote to this cause?'

Sarah was a child of her milieu. She accepted its beliefs, conformed to its standards, felt its emotions and spoke its language. She was a model church-member, and it cannot have taken her long to charm the sub-committee into agreeing that she would make an ideal missionary wife. Ideal, that is, in terms of her duty towards her church, her calling and her husband. She would never let any of them down. But it was quite another matter, and something she probably did not appreciate at the time, whether her exalted but rigid and narrow Evangelical spirit would find any echo in the hearts of Buryat herdsmen, unprepared for the strange phenomenon of a foreign, female missionary.

There could have been some truth, too, in Sarah's critical self-analysis. Pride and complacency were, she confessed, her besetting sins, and she may have been right. Her determination is not in doubt: a lesser spirit than hers would have been crushed under the weight of frustrating and lonely toil in Siberia, worn down by repeated pregnancies and chronic ill health. But this admirable quality may have had its counterpart. If we can believe some of the things which Robert Yuille said about the way she and Edward treated him and his wife, Martha, then Sarah must have been rather domineering, and status-conscious too. Unfortunately, Robert's letters, which are the only evidence of a less admirable side to Sarah's character, are not altogether reliable. It is quite possible that he had been mistaken in thinking he had a genuine call to the mission field. Certainly his colleagues, especially William Swan, had their doubts about his fitness from the very beginning. He was prickly and easily offended, aggressive and defensive at the same time, perhaps because he was conscious of an inner fallibility. This sense of insecurity is revealed in the way he rapidly developed a grudge against Edward and Sarah, a grudge which he cherished, so it seems, for the whole twenty-two years of the mission's existence, and longer.

One of the incidents which helped give rise to this grudge is described in a long letter which he wrote in 1829, soon after Martha's death, to the Rev. William Orme, then Secretary of the LMS. It began as a eulogy of the Christian virtues of his late wife, but soon declined into a peevish and childishly circumstantial account of how Sarah had, allegedly, manoeuvred Martha out of the management of a little school for girls which the missionaries had organized at the Selenginsk station. Sarah's imperious attitude rankled with him even after her death in 1833. In 1834 he unburdened himself in a local personal letter to William, in which he raked up several incidents from the long distant past:

> Have you forgotten the Plan which was laid down against us Even before we arrived at Selenginsk in 1820 viz Mrs S Wrote to a Friend that there were people coming to take charge of the household affairs of the Mission, and then They would have more time for correspondence etc. But that Friend of hers advised us not to come under such bondage, gave reasons for it – And you know that this very Plan was laid before me on the fourth day after our arrival at this place; and you cannot have forgotten how very much displeased Some persons were, because I could not agree to this Plan!

So far from being unable to forget the things Robert complained of, William denied that any of them had occurred at all, and it is conceivable that they were only the products of his morbid, introspective imagination. But he himself certainly believed in them strongly enough to complain to the Russian authorities, in 1839, that his colleagues had been influencing the Directors against him for the last nineteen years simply because he and Martha had rejected a suggestion that they should take over the domestic side of the mission's affairs as their sole responsibility. So it is possible that, in the beginning, these late fantasies had been triggered by some such snub

The Missionaries: Stallybrass and Rahmn

on Sarah's part, and that her protestations about her pride were something more than mere conventional rhetoric. No doubt she and Edward, and William too, all of them cultivated in their way, had a lot to put up with from the less polished Yuilles, and perhaps she did not bear with them too gladly.

This was not the only quarrel to disturb the mission. There had been friction with the Rahmns too, those 'pious and worthy persons' as Sarah called them, friction important enough to have been reported to Paterson, and to require long-range intervention on his part. Edward liked and respected Cornelius, and could have worked harmoniously with him, but Betty tried his patience. She suffered from her nerves, and seems to have made sure that everyone else suffered with her. She was always dying, whether at Irkutsk or Sarepta. In March 1819, Edward wrote home from Irkutsk that the doctor had advised 'her returning to St. P. as the only means by which her recovery can be hoped for'. A year later, Peter Gordon called on the Rahmns at Sarepta, and was impressed by Cornelius's 'disappointment at being kept out of his intended sphere, by the dying state of his wife'. There he was, 'panting to declare the glad tidings to the poor perishing Calmucs who surround him', but just about to move yet again, this time to Astrakhan, 'on account of the debilitated and nervous state of his wife'. Betty did not die in Russia. She hung on till the age of sixty-nine, by all accounts a good Christian woman and loving wife, and died at home, in Sweden in 1847, having outlived Martha Yuille, Sarah Stallybrass, and her successor Charlotte. Her brief association with the Irkutsk mission was clouded by her emotional instability. She demanded constant attention, and her recurring hysterical upsets not only distracted Cornelius from his calling, but ended in his venting his frayed temper on his companions.

Paterson's memoirs tell part of the story. Under the year 1818 he writes:

Received letters from Messrs Stallybrass and Rahmn from Irkutsk. Mrs Rahmn's health had completely failed. One of those nervous afflictions which rendered her unhappy and all about her miserable. Her poor husband of course suffered most. His sufferings made him discontented and apt to find fault with everything however trifling. The Stallybrasses being English their tastes and way of living were somewhat different. Mr Rahmn had written to me complaining of some things. This led me to write to them both giving them my advice and requesting them to come to some explanation with each other as I was convinced all their complaints arose from a misunderstanding which by opening their minds to each other would be removed and restore peace and comfort. The letters in question shewed I was right, for both confessed wherein they had been wrong and assured me that a perfect understanding was restored and that they were determined to proceed with their work in harmony and with zeal.

But harmony was not restored, and the ill-humour which went on simmering in Irkutsk was simply the continuation of mutual irritation which had first erupted in St Petersburg. Edward was far too loyal to complain about the Rahmns in his official correspondence, but, after they had finally left Irkutsk in 1819, he unburdened himself privately to Paterson. Betty had been ill for some days before their departure but, restless and fretful as she was, she was looking forward to the journey as a sort of rest cure.

> Her hopes with respect to the effects of the journey, and her desire to commence it, seems to have exceeded every other person's. This we thought a favourable sign, because as her complaint is in a great degree nervous, it may be productive of better. It may perhaps have seemed strange to you, and many other of our friends, that we should have continued to live as separate families under these circumstances.
> Without saying anything about Mrs S's inability to attend to the concerns of our own family during the greater part of the winter, we have had reason to retain the ideas which we were led to adopt at St. P. – it was then our proposal that we would live separately; and some circumstances which occurred during their abode with us for the last eight days have fully confirmed us in our former ideas, that it would be most conducive to our peace and unity to act as we have done. This, my dear friend, I write to *you* and to *you* only, because you have a peculiar sort of relation to both of us.

So a mere week of Betty Rahmn's company at close quarters was distracting enough to be the subject of correspondence with Paterson, thousands of miles away, and one can sympathize with Sarah's frustrations during those eight long days. How reassuring it is to see her slip off her pedestal of perfection every now and again, and behave like a normal, fallible human being! William may have had little incidents like this in his mind when he wrote, perceptively, in his *Letters on Missions*, that missionaries were not saints, but subject to human failings just like everybody else, and were not to be thought of as 'raised above all the common feelings of humanity and the infirmities of other men'.

When Edward attended the Committee of Examination for the second time, the 'probable inconveniences of marrying prior to his leaving the country were pointed out to him', but, obligingly, the Committee left it to him to make the final decision, and, as might be expected, he felt that he was 'under an obligation to marry immediately'. The marriage took place soon afterwards, on 5 March 1817, and on 16 May the young couple embarked on the ship *Oscar* for Cronstadt. On the way, the ship called at Elsinore, where they were entertained by an English merchant, a Mr T. Ellah. For Sarah there was an unperceivable irony in the meeting, for Edward was to marry Charlotte Ellah some twenty years later, after her own death in Siberia.

The Missionaries: Stallybrass and Rahmn

The voyage was no holiday. Edward was sea-sick for the first three or four days, but as soon as he recovered, he and a fellow-passenger, the philanthropist and prison-reformer Walter Venning, arranged with the captain to have the use of a room for services, and for preaching on the Sabbath day, and Edward 'had the satisfaction of turning the room which was about to become a scene of gambling into a sanctuary for God'. Sarah made a set at Sam, the captain's cabin boy. She found that he appeared 'to possess a heart susceptible of impression; but, alas, I fear not very abiding'. This led her to reflect upon the seafaring life in general:

> What a thoughtless, inconsiderate existence does a mariner's life appear! The oldest sailor on board, being asked what was the object of his chief ambition, replied, 'To be a great man – an admiral, or commander, or some such thing.' O my God! who has made me to differ? No ambition of my own would have taught me that a crown of righteousness is the chief glory; and that to be an heir of eternal life is the only thing worthy the solicitude of an immortal being.

Still, the ship's crew, thoughtless and inconsiderate though their lives may have been, were competent seamen, and they brought them safely to Cronstadt. After a last, stormy night at sea, they landed on 10 June, the twenty-four days from home representing the fastest passage made so far by any ship that season. At Cronstadt they were delayed for a day, waiting for passports, and they reached St Petersburg on the 11th. Paterson was in England and Sweden that summer, and they were welcomed first by Ebenezer Henderson, who was lodging at the Bible House, and then by Robert Pinkerton, who, though still taking an interest in the mission, lived a few miles out of town, and was less accessible.

Before he had been in St Petersburg for three full days, Edward had found time to call on a Russian general, whom he refers to incorrectly as General Soublikoff, and deliver a letter and a parcel on behalf of William Alers Hankey, the Society's Treasurer. The general was not at home at the time, but Edward was kindly received by his wife, the same lady whose name was later metamorphosed by the printer of his Memoir of Sarah into Madame Satlonkoff. Nikolai Alexandrovich Sablukov had retired from the Russian army in 1801 with the rank of Major-General, and had then used the opportunity of the brief period of peace in Europe to travel abroad. While in London in 1803 he had married Miss Juliana Angerstein, daughter of John Julius Angerstein, who was himself of Russian extraction. John Julius was a prominent member of Lloyds, and also a connoisseur and collector of fine art: thirty-eight of the paintings in his collection were acquired by the nation after his death, and formed the nucleus of the National Gallery. Presumably he and Alers Hankey were business acquaintances, while Miss Alers Hankey and Juliana were personal friends. Sarah and Juliana seem to have become fond of each other during the missionaries' brief stay in St Petersburg. Sarah refers to her as 'my most constant' Madame de Sablukov, and when the missionary party set out for Moscow and Irkutsk, it was Juliana who offered to complete an unfinished letter of Sarah's to Ann Monds, to tell her about her sister's last months in the capital. Her letter, in an angular, almost indecipherable hand, still survives.

The Stallybrasses do not seem to have made many friends in Russia, to judge by their letters. In one unpublished letter to her brother Thomas, written from Irkutsk in July 1819, Sarah, either overlooking Juliana Sablukov, or regarding her as English, complained that, after the departure of the Rahmns, she was left without a single woman friend, and there was no prospect of making new ones in Siberia. The only real friend she had made, she said, was Princess Meshcherskaya. There was an English woman married to a Russian, who had lived in Irkutsk for fifteen years, and whose young son Sarah had promised to coach in English, but she was as neurotic as Betty Rahmn, and presumably did not count. Things would be no better in Selenginsk, where cultured society was at a premium. There was the commandant, a Russian major whose Polish wife was a kleptomaniac. There was a young lady called Maria Ivanova, the daughter of a general, living with her grandmother. An artillery lieutenant called Vassilich was married to Maria's sister. He had served in Germany, and so, according the acidic Peter Gordon, to whom we owe this intimate sketch of the upper ten in Selenginsk, was comparatively civilized. There was a sub-postmaster who ranked as a postilion, and a rich shopkeeper called Voroshilov, who was ruled by his garrulous wife, and apart from that only one or two others who could be called even semi-genteel. The priest and the surgeon were beyond the pale, since they were nearly always drunk. Curiously enough, Edward and William never mention by name men of learning whom they must have known – Novoselov, Igumnov, Bobrovnikov, Kowalewski, Popov, nor, perhaps out of caution, do they ever refer, even remotely, to any of the Decembrists who were banished to Transbaikalia.

While the missionaries kept themselves very much to themselves in Siberia, the unusual religious climate at court, and its reflection in public life, allowed them to move in circles in the capital far above those to which the London tallow-chandler's daughter and her husband could have aspired had they stayed in England. If they did not make friends, they gathered acquaintances, of whom the Sablukovs were the first, who were extremely useful to them. Through Pinkerton and Henderson they got to know Prince Golitsyn, who was intimate with the Emperor himself, and later on they won the good will of men of the utmost importance, men like Mikhail Speranskii and Baron Paul Schilling von Canstadt. In other words, they and their mission were taken notice of by the highest in the land, a lucky chance where so much depended on pull and favour.

Edward took to Henderson at once, finding him a 'striking instance of genuine and devoted piety'. Ebenezer Henderson came from much the same sort of background as his older colleague and friend, John Paterson. He was a Scot, born in a little hamlet, or rather a mere pair of cottages, called The Linn, near Dunfermline, in 1748. His father was for many years a farm-overseer near Dunfermline, and was an elder of one of the local churches. Ebenezer's upbringing was extremely strict, and on one occasion home discipline nearly crippled him for life. Running away from his mother to escape a beating for something he had been up to, he fell into a tub of boiling whey and was badly scalded. After only three and a half years' schooling, partly at what was known as a road-side school, a substitute for the missing parish school, and partly at the Grammar School in Dunfermline, he was apprenticed to an older brother to learn clock and watch making. After some eighteen months, the two brothers quarrelled over an accident to a clock wheel, and Ebenezer returned home. His parents put him to learn the trade of bootmaking, but apparently he showed little skill in this either. Towards the end of the century he came under the influence of pious men such as James Haldane, Rowland Hill and Greville Ewing, who preached in Dunfermline, and in 1803 he joined Robert Haldane's seminary in Edinburgh as a candidate for the ministry. It was from here that Paterson picked him out as his companion in the abortive mission to India.

Henderson seems to have been of a more contemplative, studious nature than the dynamic, pushing Paterson, but the complementary qualities of the two men led to a partnership which was responsible for conceiving and carrying out a series of pioneering programmes of Bible work – the foundation of Bible Societies and the printing and distribution of the Scriptures – across the whole of northern Europe. They undertook long and exhausting journeys over some of the most difficult terrain in the old world. They made two noteworthy journeys together, one through northern Sweden and Lapland into Finland in 1808, just failing to get as far as Åbo, from which they were driven back by the invading Russian army, and the other from St Petersburg through Novgorod and the western provinces of Russia as far as the Crimea, Tiflis and Astrakhan, in 1821–2. The first of these journeys was described by Paterson, while the second provided Henderson with the material for his own travel book: *Biblical Researches and Travels in Russia*. Both men travelled on their own, too, Paterson in continental Europe, mainly in Scandinavia and Russia, and Henderson, most memorably, to Iceland in 1814–15.

In the late autumn of 1816, Henderson joined Paterson in St Petersburg to assist him in his work in connection with the British and the Russian Bible Societies. He stayed there on his own during the spring and summer of 1817, while Paterson was visiting Sweden and England, looking after the English congregation which was still meeting privately in Mr Brown's house. In his spare time, he was studying the Manchu and Mongol languages. During that winter, Henderson was becoming more and more conscious of having received a call to the mission field, and his convictions were reinforced when he received from Robert Steven, a Director of the LMS, an invitation to go out to Siberia as one of the Society's missionaries. By the time that Edward reached St Petersburg in June 1817, though, Henderson's hopes had been dashed. Edward would have welcomed him as a companion, but he took the negative decision with true Christian submission, writing as follows to Alers Hankey: 'He appears very much disappointed at not being able to accompany us to Irkutsk, as it had been the subject of his contemplation long before Mr Steven wrote to him on the subject. We could not forbear to regret, were it not for the recollection that the great head of the Church ever likes to manage her success, and that he will never suffer the cause of Zion to be impeded in its progress for want of suitable instruments.' Henderson, too, took the refusal of the Bible Society to give up its claim on his services in good part, accepting this as an indication of the 'leadings of Providence'.

The two men might have been rather less philosophically resigned had they known at the time that the reluctance of the BFBS to allow Henderson to transfer to the LMS had been inspired by the deliberate intervention of Paterson. On 31 January 1817, Henderson wrote to Steven, authorizing him to pass on the offer of his services to the Directors of the LMS, though reaffirming his loyalty to the BFBS. In going to Irkutsk, he said, his principal, even his exclusive object, would be to forward the aims of the latter society 'in a degree and to an extent which I could not possibly have done in any other situation'. He also wrote to inform Paterson, who received the letter while he was in Stockholm on his way to London, of his decision. This advance warning alerted Paterson to the possibility that he was in danger of losing his indispensable companion, and apparently also gave him time to think of a suitable substitute. He wrote back to Henderson, aiming to persuade him that he was better suited to Bible work in Russia than to missionary work in Siberia, and either then, or after his arrival in England, advised the BFBS not to let Henderson go. At some time, too, he proceeded to sound Cornelius Rahmn.

Paterson gives a circumstantial account of what happened, but, like so much of his reminiscences, it does not stand up to analysis. In his manuscript memoirs, Paterson recalls that he reached Gothenburg on 2 March, and then goes on to say:

> In Gottenburg I received another letter from Dr Henderson giving me an account of how things were going on in Petersburg, and informing me that he had made up his mind to offer his services to the London Missionary Society for the Siberian Mission. This I could not agree to and having mentioned the subject to my friend Mr Rahmn, I found that he was not averse to offer his services to accompany Mr Stallybrass. This gave me hope that I might prevent Henderson going to Siberia, at least for the present. Rahmn was every way suited for such a mission and

The Missionaries: Stallybrass and Rahmn

as for Mrs Rahmn I knew that she had for years been eager for the work.

He goes on:

> Another object which lay near my heart was Henderson's plan of joining the Siberian Mission. I brought the matter before the office bearers of the Bible Society who highly disapproved of his abandoning their service. They brought the matter before the committee when a resolution was passed refusing to give him up to the Missionary Society. I also brought the matter before the latter and arranged with them that they should enter into correspondence with Mr Rahmn and if possible engage him to accompany Mr Stallybrass. The only objection was his wife and child as I conceived that unmarried men would be preferable for commencing a new mission. But it came out that Mr Stallybrass was on the eve of being married to a charming young woman. To this I objected, on which Dr Pye Smith rose and strongly pled for his being allowed to take out a wife and did it in a manner which completely silenced one who was also on the eve of also being united to a helpmate and there the matter rested. I knew that I would get no thanks from dear Henderson for my interference but I only did what I considered to be my duty.

This makes a pretty story, with Paterson in the leading role, winning one trick by keeping Henderson as his companion, but letting the other one, the question of Edward's marriage, go for personal, sentimental reasons. Perhaps when compiling his memoirs he really thought it had been the prospect of his approaching second marriage to Jean, daughter of Admiral Greig, a Scot in the Russian service, which persuaded him to drop his objections to Edward's marriage. Or, also in retrospect, he may have imagined himself to have acted more subtly, to have realized that if he persisted with his objection to married missionaries in Edward's case, he would cut the ground from under his own feet in Cornelius's. And in that event, Henderson's candidature might be revived. But there are good reasons for concluding that events cannot have followed the neat sequence suggested by Paterson's narrative, and contemporary papers suggest a rather different pattern.

If his memoirs are to be trusted in the matter of dating, Paterson reached Gothenburg on his way home only on 2 March 1817. The question of Edward's marriage had been settled at a Board meeting of the LMS held on 24 February, and the marriage was celebrated on 5 March. So Paterson must have been mistaken in recalling his participation in a debate with Dr Pye Smith, as he had not even reached England by the time the marriage took place.

Secondly, a Board meeting of the LMS held on 17 March 1817 resolved to request the Secretary to ask the members of a deputation which was about to visit the Seminary at Gosport to look out for any student there who might seem a suitable companion for Edward. The official 'Hints' for the use of the members of the deputation, which were drawn up at the same time and dated the same day, contain, however, a note to the effect that 'this is not absolutely necessary now as Mr Henderson, now at St Petersburgh has offered to go to Irkutsk – This is a great acquisition.' So, by mid-March at any rate, Henderson was still in the running, and, as far as we can tell, Cornelius's name had not yet been mentioned. The significance of all this becomes more pronounced when we realize that Paterson had attended the meeting of 17 March, by invitation, and had evidently done nothing then to block Henderson's candidature or to promote that of Cornelius.

Some time before the end of May, the BFBS, either formally in committee, as Paterson says, or informally as Sarah writes in a private letter to Ann, had considered Henderson's application and had decided that it could not do without his services. Thereupon Steven suppressed Henderson's formal offer, which was in his possession, and the matter was at an end.

The first official mention of Cornelius's name comes in the minutes of a meeting of the Northern Committee of the LMS held on 11 August, when it was decided to recommend him to the Directors as a suitable companion for Edward. The Board accepted the recommendation at its own meeting held later the same day. This resolution must have been taken in response to a letter written from Stockholm by Paterson on 21 July on his way back to Russia. Proof of the connection is afforded by the fact that in that letter Paterson advised the Society to establish a credit of £150 in Cornelius's favour with the Gothenburg firm of Scott & Gordon, and that the resolution of 11 August recommended that very step. Thus several weeks had elapsed between the Society's abandoning its claim to Henderson and agreeing to appoint Cornelius. The language of Paterson's letter, too, suggests that this was the first time he had brought Cornelius's name to the attention of the Society, and it is safe to conclude that it was on his way back to St Petersburg, acting in his knowledge that the BFBS had refused to release Henderson, not on his way over, anticipating such an action, that he had first tried to recruit Cornelius for the LMS. Paterson thus appears in a much more sympathetic and less Machiavellian light than he does in his own memoirs.

In his letter he wrote as follows:

> I feel peculiarly indebted to you for your prompt compliance with the projected mission to Irkutsk, a station likely to be of such importance to the diffusion of the Gospel. It grieved me much to be under the necessity of quitting England before a suitable companion could be decided on, to accompany Mr Stallybrass to the place of his destination, which circumstance, unless obviated, might have retarded, perhaps

The Missionaries: Stallybrass and Rahmn

even might have rendered the mission abortive. Happy am I in having it now in my power to recommend to the Society a person in every respect qualified to accompany Mr Stallybrass. His name is Cornelius Rahmn, a clergyman of the Swedish Church now officiating as a curate in one of the churches in Gothenburg, a man of decided piety, universally respected, zealous in every good work. He has gone thro' the usual course of studies at the university of Lund and possesses more than ordinary talents. He informed me of his desire of engaging in missionary labours upon which I proposed to him the station of Irkutsk. He desired time to reflect on the subject and to seek direction from on high, promising to write to me to Stockholm and inform me of his decision. Before I inform you of his answer, I must premise that he is a married man, consequently must be accompanied by his wife and a child of about 20 months, should you accept his services. His wife is a Scotch woman, decidedly pious and also possessing a missionary spirit. He is about 27 years of age.

Paterson's letter provoked a flurry of correspondence between Sweden and London. In it he had quoted a letter from Cornelius to himself which included an expression of the former's intention to become a missionary, and this seems to have been a sufficient basis for the Directors to act upon. There was a real need for haste. At this time it was still intended that Edward should set out for Siberia as soon as the snow-roads were open for traffic, about the beginning of December, and as Cornelius needed a couple of months to wind up his affairs in Gothenburg, no time could be lost in appointing him.

On 29 July Cornelius wrote to George Burder, introducing himself, and asking for a quick decision. A letter could take as little as nine or ten days between Gothenburg and London, but, whether or not this letter was available at the Board's meeting on 11 August, Cornelius was appointed, and Burder wrote to tell him so on the same day. Cornelius acknowledged his appointment on 26 August, by which time he had also drawn the grant of £150 which he needed for his travelling expenses.

We have already briefly made the acquaintance of Cornelius Rahmn. He was the oldest of the four missionaries to Siberia, having been born in Gothenburg in 1785, the son of Gustaf Samuel Rahmn, a lieutenant in the Royal Swedish Artillery. In 1799, at the early age of fourteen, he entered the University of Lund, where, at his father's insistence, he studied law. He had, however, little taste for the legal profession. After leaving Lund he came under the influence of the Rev. J. U. Blomdahl, pastor in the parish of Starrkärr, not far from Gothenburg, and in 1803 he sought, and obtained, permission to act as a lay-reader in that parish. In 1805 we find Cornelius active as a teacher at Marieberg, near Gothenburg, and in 1807 he found employment as a private tutor at a place called Torpa. This was the time of the Russian campaign against Finland and Sweden, and Cornelius was undecided whether to pursue a career in the church, to which he was already inclined, or to take up his father's profession as an army officer. Partly as a result of advice from Blomdahl, he chose the former alternative. In 1810, at the minimum age of twenty-five, he was ordained, and was appointed chaplain with the Göta artillery, and served in that capacity until he joined the LMS.

Cornelius had had a good, broad education. He had studied Latin, Greek and Hebrew, and, as well as Swedish, he knew French, German and English, though he was rather rusty in the first two. Edward was rather critical of his command of English, too, finding him no more than capable of making himself understood. This may have been true of his oral English, but his letters and journals show that he could express himself easily, if not always correctly, in writing, and much more fluently than Edward could manage in French. He was also a faithful member of the Swedish church, though his contacts with independents of various persuasions – his English missionary colleagues and a circle of Moravian friends – had some effect on his religious views. It was through reading about the Moravian mission to Greenland that he first became interested in mission work, at a time when there were no Swedish missionaries in the field, and he always remained sympathetic towards the Moravians.

Cornelius had other responsibilities in Gothenburg, besides his chaplaincy. Since 1812 he had been the rector of the Prins Oskar School, a school founded by local officers for the children of soldiers. He was probably referring to this when he wrote to Paterson that he anticipated some difficulty in 'the resignation of my present pastoral charge and my connection with the Orphant School'. He had also founded, and still ran, a little Juvenile Bible Society, in association with the school. However, within two months of receiving Paterson's proposal he had managed to resign his various appointments, sell up his belongings, and set out for St Petersburg, by way of Stockholm, the Åland islands and Åbo, with his wife and little daughter, Hanna. They reached the Russian capital in mid-October.

5

The Missionaries: Swan and Yuille

While Edward and Cornelius and their families are settling down in St Petersburg during the summer and autumn of 1817, let us anticipate events and make the acquaintance of the other two missionaries who were to follow them out and join the mission after it had moved to Selenginsk, William Swan and Robert Yuille. Both men were Scots, and both firmly believed that they had been called to the mission field, but there the similarity between them ended. William was an educated man, experienced in business, clear-headed and articulate. He possessed an instinct for diplomacy and a tact and polish which enabled him to negotiate at the top level in Russia, and extract from Government almost everything which he and the Society wanted. He was a loyal servant of the Society, even when, as could happen, he disagreed with its policies; and because the Directors respected him and trusted his judgment, they took his representations seriously and made concessions which Robert Yuille could never have gained. Robert was a rough diamond, an ex-factory hand of some sort. He had enough push and enough random education to raise himself out of the common ruck of industrial Glasgow, to attend classes at the University there, and to become an ordained minister and a missionary. But that was the limit. Thereafter he was out of his depth, professionally and intellectually. He was semi-literate, awkward, self-opinionated and stubborn, and his life was an inexorable progress towards tragedy. As we shall see, the signs of coming disaster are apparent in the earliest committee minutes concerning him, and in his first letters to the Society. One cannot help feeling deep pity for Robert. He was the author of his own destruction, and he was too obtuse to appreciate what he was doing. Perhaps in the end, though, he precipitated and welcomed the collision with the Directors as the only way out of an intolerable predicament.

William Swan was a native of Fife, born at the Milltown of Balgonie, near Leven, on 21 June 1791. He attended the local parish school, where he made exceptional progress, especially in Latin, a subject in which the teacher gave him individual tuition. We know next to nothing about his parents, who both died before he became a missionary, except that they were extremely pious people, always willing to put up any itinerant evangelist who happened to be in the neighbourhood. William enjoyed a sheltered childhood, and then at the age of just thirteen his parents sent him off to Edinburgh University, intending him to train for the ministry. He was not happy at Edinburgh, nor was he at all enamoured of the career which had been chosen for him, and after one session his parents took him away, and started him off in business. Whether it was to an accountant that he was first apprenticed, as his obituary notice says, or to a lawyer, as he himself says in his application to the LMS, hardly matters today. Whichever it was, in six and a half years at Kirkcaldy, where he also worked on and off as a cashier and accountant for the Bank of Scotland, or later in Edinburgh, where he spent more than three years as an accountant, he gained a sound experience of business practice.

It was while he was at Kirkcaldy that William underwent the experience of conversion, an experience which, in his case, seems to have led to the rejection of secular pleasures as sinful:

> His decision of character was strikingly manifested at this time, and it was this that sustained him in a long and consistent course of well-doing, during a singularly blameless and devoted life. From his boyhood, he had had a great fondness for boats, and everything connected with shipping. During his residence at Kirkcaldy, he had, by the kindness of a friend, the use of a small yacht. This to him was a source of great enjoyment, and much, if not all his spare time, was spent in it. A young companion happened to have a similar yacht of his own – the two were consequently much together sailing in the bay. After Mr Swan's experience of the power of the truth, this favourite amusement was given up, and the leisure hitherto devoted to it was now spent in earnest searching of the Scriptures. . . . Often did he wonder how his companion, who had at the same time as himself become a communicant, could continue as formerly to give his *time* to that which, if not considered sinful in itself, became so, by the waste of that precious talent.

This extract from his obituary makes William sound dour and grim, and this impression is reinforced by his choice of pen-name, 'Zelotes', for his first published article, a piece on the obligations of a missionary. But he must have had an urbane and attractive side to his personality as well, for he earned the regard of that most self-opinionated critic of his fellow-men, George Borrow. In 1833 the two men met in St Petersburg, and worked together for some time making a manuscript copy of a Manchu translation of the Old Testament. Certainly, Borrow had a genius for identifying himself with whatever he happened to be doing at any particular time, and in St Petersburg as an agent of the British and Foreign Bible Society he played the archetypal evangelist and champion of Protestantism, just as he did to even greater effect in Spain a little later. But this would not have impelled him to declare that William was 'one of the most amiable and interesting characters' he had ever met, unless there was some truth in it. Borrow was no time-server, and he must have felt a genuine affection for the man he described as 'our beloved, sincere and most truly Christian friend'. What an incongruous pair they must have made, though, the flamboyant Romany Rye, with memories of Mumpers' Dingle and Isopel Berners still fresh in his mind, and the earnest evangelist, author of a maudlin memoir of his dear departed friend, Mrs Jean Paterson, as they sat together, poring over – a Jesuit translation of the Old Testament!

Not only did William give up yachting as a sinful waste of time, but he also sacrificed a promising career in finance, after having helped draw up the first actuarial tables for the Scottish Widows' Fund. In 1816 he moved to Glasgow, and entered the Theological Academy there, which since 1811 had been turning out young aspirants for the independent ministry, under the guidance of the Rev. Greville Ewing and the Rev. Ralph Wardlaw. It was not long after making this break that he decided to become a missionary, for somehow or other the LMS had got to know of his interest by the beginning of 1817, and were already keen to appoint him to Siberia. At the Society's request, Wardlaw interviewed him at this time, but William asked for his eventual appointment to be deferred. Just like Edward, he did not apply to go to Siberia: the decision was taken for him by the Missionary Society. He had been hoping to be sent to China, but confessed himself 'fully reconciled to the sphere mentioned in your letter, on recollecting its vicinity to the Borders of that vast Empire, and the probability of an opening presenting itself in that quarter'. Disappointment in his ultimate destination was not, though, the reason for William's request for deferment. He was looking forward to making translations into whatever would be the appropriate language, and felt he needed more time to deepen his knowledge of the original languages of the Scriptures.

A year went by before William submitted his formal application. After that, events moved rapidly. He was accepted on 16 March 1818, ordained, at Greenwich, on 3 June, and by 22 July he was already in St Petersburg. By now, the Society had begun to regularize its recruitment procedures and had adopted, in early 1817, a series of standard questions which candidates were required to answer. William was the only one of the four missionaries to Siberia to apply to the Society late enough to be faced with the printed 'List of Queries'. Edward and Robert had sent in individually composed letters before being interviewed, while Cornelius had been accepted solely on the strength of Paterson's recommendation and of brief written accounts of himself. He never came to England or met any of the Directors until after he had ceased to be a missionary.

The printed questionnaire contained nineteen questions. Some of these required factual answers to simple enquiries: did the applicant belong to a particular church, and if so, how long had he been a member; what was his attitude to infant baptism; how old was he; did his parents agree to his proposal, and were they in any way dependent on him for their support; what was his medical history, and did he think he could put up with the rigours of the mission field; and so on. Other questions were more searching, evidently designed to detect candidates whose sense of vocation, though superficially genuine, was in fact fragile or even suspect. The candidate also had to give a full account of his religious views and convictions, as far as the 'doctrines of the gospels' were concerned: in William's case the answer took the form of a separate letter nearly two thousand words in length.

William's 'confession of faith' was an orthodox re-statement of independent theology, and as such it must have reassured the Directors. But, the substance apart, they must have realized, from the evidence of this paper, that in William they were gaining a man of sharp intellect, sound judgment, and precision in drafting and self-expression. William's essay on his beliefs is remarkable for its orderly construction, its clarity of exposition, and its sensitive, accurate use of language. Starting from the basis of his acceptance of certain self-evident propositions – that natural religion implies the existence of God and of man's necessary duties towards him; that the Scriptures are inspired by God; and that they are the 'sure source of all the divine knowledge He has been pleased to put upon record for our use' – William develops his views upon man's fundamental depravity, and the availability of certain salvation through the power of God. Each step in his argument leads logically to the next, with the salient points underlined for emphasis. From the general exposition he moves on to his own individual case, examining the growing influence of the Holy Spirit upon his sinful nature, his conversion, and the growing realization that his purpose in life must be the 'salvation of sinners'. Here was a man not only fully convinced, but endowed with the ability to expound his conviction, point by point, in a logically irresistible manner. No wonder the Society jumped at him, and wished there were more recruits of his calibre. One can only wonder how the same men, Ewing and Wardlaw in Glasgow, and the Directors in London, were taken in by Robert's muddle-headed posturing.

Candidates also had to defend their sense of a call to the mission field. They were asked: 'As you must be aware that a wish to engage in Missionary work is in many instances founded on false premises; have you deliberately and solemnly examined your own motives and ends; and do they approve themselves to your conscience, as in the sight of God?' At the time, William could give only a provisional, though perceptive, answer. He had, he said, examined his conscience and believed that his wish to be a missionary was founded on the principle of love for God and for man:

> I desire to promote the glory of God in the conversion of sinners. I have subjected myself and still endeavour to subject myself to scrutiny in

The Missionaries: Swan and Yuille

> regard to my motives and ends. I am aware of the necessity and advantages of this, and it is my prayer that they may be made increasingly pure, and kept pure. I say *kept pure* because I feel my corruption is ready to admit *defiling mixtures* which did not enter into my original contemplations.

Even in this early, inexperienced assessment of his motives, there is inherent the apprehension that the would-be missionary might, even involuntarily, have mistaken the nature of what he confidently assumed to be a vocation, or that his motives might, in the course of time, become blunted or perverted. In other words, he might have applied for improper reasons, or, in the lonely mission field, safe from the supervision and criticism of his peers, he might find himself unable to live up to the original vision. William always kept this danger in mind, as in his answer he promised he would do, and a more mature analysis of true and false motivation in a missionary is to be found in his *Letters on Missions*. That work shows that much of what William found to condemn in men who became missionaries with inadequate motivation was drawn from experience in the field of the case of Robert Yuille. Though his analysis is general and anonymous, there is no mistaking where he had found his raw material. Large parts of the book form a character-study of his unfortunate colleague.

One of the most interesting answers given by William is the one he wrote in response to the requirement to state his views of the obligations inherent in a missionary career, and from which we have already quoted in Chapter 1. William classified the missionary's obligations under four heads: entire devotion to his work; unremitting diligence in it; noble faithfulness and courage in the discharge of it; and a simple dependence upon the blessing of God for the success of it. All other occupations and interests, scientific, academic, exploratory or commercial, had to give way to the demands of the mission field. One feels that William would have disapproved of the two-pronged ambitions of men like John Williams, the ship-builder of the South Seas, or David Livingstone. Just as he had given up sailing in favour of Bible study, so he, and Edward too, were to give up everything else, particularly the chance of becoming academic scholars in a virgin field, something they could easily have achieved. From the point of view of his calling, of course, he was right to see his duty as indivisible, and to observe throughout his time in Siberia the ideals he had so percipiently formulated in his application. But his reticence, and that of Edward, proved a loss to learning. The language, literature and culture of the Mongols, a field in which they were, in England at least, unchallengeable masters, was not to be systematically cultivated at any British university until after the Second World War, when, with the support of public money, a tenuous tradition was founded. The knowledge which Edward and William acquired so painfully died with them. The first useful Mongolian–English dictionaries, two of them compiled, ironically, by missionaries, and the third drawing heavily on Kowalewski's nineteenth-century dictionary, appeared only during the ten years from 1950 to 1960, and none of them was printed in England. The first comprehensive grammar of the Mongolian language in English also appeared during the same decade, and it was the work of a scholar of German-Russian origin, published in West Germany. All this might have been anticipated by a century or more, if Edward and William had interpreted their priorities a little more liberally.

But would it? There is no certainty that, even had they tried to publish their grammars and dictionaries at the time, these would have aroused any interest in contemporary academic circles. The Tibetan–Mongolian dictionaries which Robert sent home in manuscript copies in 1829 aroused no particular curiosity at the time, and have lain undisturbed in the library of the Royal Asiatic Society ever since, and his school text-books seem to have got lost. The sketches of life in Buryat lamaseries and of shamanist séances which were excerpted from the missionaries' journals and published in the Missionary Society's *Quarterly Chronicle of Transactions* have likewise been overlooked. There was, at the time, little or no perceptible demand in Britain or western Europe altogether for Mongolian linguistic scholarship for its own sake. This was recognized by both enemies and friends of the mission cause. Captain John Dundas Cochrane, RN, who once called on the missionaries in the course of his famous 'pedestrian journey' across Russia and Siberia, thought the whole Siberian mission to be misconceived: 'For my own part,' he wrote, 'so small are my hopes of their success, that I do not expect any one Buryat will be really and truly converted: for the sake of profit several may so pretend, but as long as they have their own priests and religious instruction, so long the Missionary Society will do no more good than simply translating their works, and acquiring the knowledge of a language useless to England.'

Cochrane might have been surprised to find his negative views of the value of the Mongolian language almost echoed by I. J. Schmidt, in his own introduction to his Grammar of Mongolian, which was published in St Petersburg in German in 1831. As Schmidt wrote: 'Whether or not any need will be met by the appearance of this Grammar I do not venture to assert, for the reason that no public demand for the satisfaction of such a need has ever been made known, to myself at any rate.' However, this opening sentence was a gambit in the true sense, a disarming concession, which was to be followed by an energetic defence of Mongolian as a language important not only on account of its practical utility, in particular for Russia, in trade and politics, but also because of its linguistic interest. Neither the utilitarian nor the academic argument would have swayed Edward or William. They each had manuscript copies of their grammar and dictionary, and that was enough for missionary purposes. Even if there had been any temptation to

The Missionaries: Swan and Yuille

publish, that would have been removed, as William himself admitted, by the appearance of Schmidt's Grammar in 1831 and his Dictionary in 1835.

Robert Yuille's letter of application, which is the source of all we know about his early life, was written from Glasgow on 26 July 1815. His parents were Scots, but at the beginning of the 1780s they had migrated to Ireland, probably to Dundalk, in connection with the thread-making trade. Robert was born in Ireland in 1786, and spent the first seven years of his life there. His family then moved back to Glasgow, still in the same line of business. Five years later he lost his father and elder sister, and bereavement was followed by misfortune. His mother was swindled out of what little capital she had by a relative, who persuaded her to let him run her business, and took the opportunity to line his own pockets. Mrs Yuille had just enough money left to pay off her debts, and she then got out of the thread business altogether, and somehow managed to establish her four sons as weavers, a trade which apparently needed hardly any capital to set up in. Not long after that she died, or, as Robert puts it in his ponderously awkward epistolary style; 'she paid the debt of nature and I hope followed her beloved Husband to the House of many mansions, which is prepared for the Righteous', while he carried on, first as a weaver, and then as an employee in some sort of factory.

Superficially informative, Robert's letter fails, as did many of his later communications, to tell his readers exactly what he was doing at any particular time, though it does suggest that his childhood horizons were very restricted. So was his religious milieu. His parents were, so to speak, dissenting Dissenters. They were Antiburghers, members of a splinter group of the Secession Church, which had, itself, broken away from the Established Church of Scotland in 1735. As a boy, Robert had not taken much interest in religion. He had been prevented from 'committing many of the sins of youth', as he put it, out of blind fear of God, and not through any more generous conviction. After his mother's death, he seems to have become more concerned with religion and its application to his own life. Impressed by a couple of sermons he heard, he thought of joining the Antiburghers, his parents' church. But then, as it happened, he fell under the influence of Ralph Wardlaw, and became a member of his independent congregation instead. Let us hear the story of Robert's conversion in his own words:

> Two sermons which I heard about this time were likewise of some
> benefit, the first was taken from Numbers 15–30,31, and the second
> from Revelations 3–16, after which I resolved to remain no longer a
> Presumptuous or a [luke]-warm sinner; but to make an open avowal
> of my attachment to Christ by joining myself in fellowship with that
> Church in which I had continued to hear the word preached after the
> death of my Parents – But being led by the spirit, for I confess the flesh
> at first was weak, under the Ministry of Mr Wardlaw, who by Faith

and Works has shewed me the way of God with more clearness, whose
Church I joined in Janry 1814, after having observed their Walk and
Conversation for more than a year, and with whom I could delight to
dwell – About four years ago I began to think of the Missionary Service
and to be employed in it I thought would yield me the greatest pleasure,
but concieving [sic] that I have not a capacity for it, and that God
would not have his name Magnified by my instrumentality would make
me say, thy will O God be done, thou knowest whom thou hast Chosen.
But when I heard any of the Servants of God praying to the Lord of the
harvest to send forth Labourers into his harvest, my desire for the
work would be renewed, and I would often solicit my Maker to make
his Grace sufficient for me, and to pour out his spirit upon me, and
to allow my feeble arm to assist in the Erection of the Lords Temple. I
continued in this state of mind for more than two years, when I placed
myself under a private Latin Teacher in order that my abilities in that
way might be tried, and finding my capacity, as I thought, not to be
inferior to the other two young men who were in the Class with me, I
determined, with the advice of some Friends, to Crave the assistance
and Protection of some Missionary Society. And having made my Case
known to my worthy Pastor he directed my attention to your Honoured
and Highly favoured Society, as being the only place from which much
good could be expected to result.

Luckily for Robert, his pastor, Wardlaw, was an active and influential promoter of the work of the LMS in Scotland. He had, in addition, gone through something like the same sectarian doubts and changes as the younger man, and seems to have felt a certain sympathy for him. Wardlaw was, in fact, a great-grandson of Ebenezer Erskine, who had founded the Secession Church, but in 1800 he left the 'Burghers', and joined Greville Ewing's independent congregation. In 1803 he took on the ministry of a church of his own. It was through him that Robert's aspirations were given a definite direction. It may have been their confidence in Wardlaw's judgment which persuaded the Directors to overlook the warning signs which are evident in this earliest of Robert's letters to them. But though they may have discounted its grammatical infelicities and the forced use of inappropriate scriptural tags, one wonders how those senior divines and experienced men of affairs could so easily have passed over the mixture of conceit and false humility in the character of a man who could speak of the guidance of the Holy Spirit and then, in the same breath, cite his own pleasure as the reason for choosing the career of missionary. Did they feel no qualms about the depth of Robert's integrity?

In his application, Robert was very reticent about his formal education. In fact, he said nothing at all about it, except for the Latin lessons. Did he perhaps think that the Directors would not be interested in where he had

The Missionaries: Swan and Yuille

gone to school, and for how long, or was there nothing to report? Had he applied a couple of years later, question 4 on the printed form would have elicited information about his education. All that we know of Robert suggests that, while he was no genius, he was something of an untaught and unteachable polymath, a wayward, undisciplined autodidact. He could turn his hand and mind to almost anything, from building and operating his own printing press to learning Tibetan, but his intellectual attainments are a matter for doubt. He certainly made great claims for himself. Above all, he reckoned to have translated Isaiah and the whole of the New Testament into Mongolian, though he never produced a copy of the former for inspection, and his colleagues were convinced that the latter had been the work of his pupils. Was it all pretence? Edward and William had no doubts about it. As far as they were concerned, Robert was ignorant and incompetent. If they were right, had he bluffed his way into the LMS, and been crippled ever afterwards by the lack of intellectual training and a formal grounding in school subjects? If so, how did he manage to conduct his school at Selenginsk so successfully? One of his pupils, Rintsin, is still remembered today, amongst his own people, as one of Buryatia's first modern intellectuals. Robert remains something of an enigma.

Curiously enough, Robert says nothing in his letter to the LMS about his time as a student at the University of Glasgow. The most likely explanation of this omission is that he had not actually entered the University at the date of his application. He matriculated in 1815, the year he wrote to the Society. Admittedly, he is entered in the University's records as being in the Greek class in that year, and the Greek class formed the second year of the University's four-year course, so that it is possible that he could have been a student in 1814 as well. There is, though, no certainty that he was, and the inordinate pride which he took in later years in his membership of the University suggests that he would have mentioned it if he had had a chance to do so.

In 1830, Robert had a contretemps with a certain Colonel Maslov, a gendarmerie-officer who had been sent on a tour of inspection of the administration in Siberia by the Emperor, and who seems to have treated Robert with less courtesy than he felt he was entitled to. The snub roused him to ineffectual fury, and he relieved his feelings in a characteristically irrelevant outburst to the Secretary of the LMS:

> Therefore I mention for the information of Colonel Masloff, (if necessary) That I was brought up in the ancient and large City of Glasgow in Scotland; that I am the son of a respectable and once well known citizen of that City; that my Private and Public Teachers were among the best that Glasgow had in my time; that I paid the regular, but high Fees, out of my own money, which are required in Glasgow for Education; that I was a Student in the University of Glasgow, when the *Present*

Emperor of Russia visited our ancient City; and I was one of that *crowd* of Students whom He saw within the walls of that University; that I also enjoyed, for nearly 3 years that course of Education which was given to Missionary Students, in the well known and well approved Academy of the London Missionary Society; That I was Ordained to Preach the Gospel of Christ by an Honourable Presbytery of Holy Ministers in London; that by my own particular Desire I was sent as a Missionary to Siberia; and that by the Grace of God, I have for the last Ten Years, at Selenginsk, endeavoured to do good to all men! so that, whatever the Colonel has heard of me, or may think of me, This, which I have now stated is the *truth*.

From the very beginning of his association with the LMS, Robert proved wayward and tiresome to deal with. He always had to be different. His name crops up repeatedly in the minutes of Board and committee meetings between 1815 and 1818, and almost every time it is in connection with some special treatment which he was soliciting for himself. After he had been accepted and had been enrolled as a student at the Missionary Seminary at Gosport, serious doubts arose about his fitness to be a missionary. It might have been embarrassing for the Directors to drop a man personally recommended by Wardlaw and Ewing, and pushed by Dr Bogue, the Tutor at the Seminary and one of their own number, but how the Society must have wished, in later years, that they had grasped the nettle before it was too late.

Robert's application was considered by the Committee of Examination on 4 August 1815, and Wardlaw was asked to provide a report on him, and on a Mr Fleming, another Scottish candidate. Poor Fleming, incidentally, proved another bad choice. While at Gosport, he was accused by some of his fellow students of Unitarianism, but after an investigation, in which Robert played a part which is today impenetrable, he was acquitted of that heresy. He was appointed to Malacca, but spent only a year in the field before being suspended in 1821 on account of insanity. He returned to England in 1822, and from then on disappears from the Society's records.

It was not until November that Wardlaw replied, promising to set up an interviewing board, and when the board met in March of the following year Robert failed to attend, explaining his absence by the fact that no invitation had reached him. How this could have happened, when the convenor of the board was his own minister, whom he must have been seeing regularly, is not explained. But, in the event, he and Fleming were both accepted, and entered the Gosport Seminary in June.

The first report on Robert's work, made by Dr Bogue in October, was favourable. He had 'good abilities' and was likely to prove a valuable missionary. But then the warning signs began to show. Only three months later, Robert was wanting a concession. He wrote to the Board asking if he

The Missionaries: Swan and Yuille

could go back to Glasgow and study there under Wardlaw and Ewing. Either the Board was not yet alert to his egotism, or they dealt with him gently on principle. He was requested to stay on at Gosport for another year, after which his application might be reconsidered. In fact, only six months later he put in the same request again, and on that occasion a policy decision was taken that all students should stay at Gosport until they had finished their studies.

A year later, in May 1818, Robert was appointed to Malacca, whereupon he wrote to the Board objecting to the appointment on account of the hot climate. By now he had spent two years training in the Missionary Seminary, and he must have known perfectly well that the main activities of the Society were concentrated in hot, or even tropical areas. There were only a few posts to be filled in cool or cold climates, such as the Ionian Islands, and, by rejecting Malacca, Robert was, by implication, laying claim to one of these plums. The Directors would have been justified in treating his request as selfish impertinence, but they took it at its face value, and Alers Hankey, the Society's Treasurer, undertook to sound Bogue out as to whether Robert might be better suited to Siberia. There was nothing vindictive in proposing this extreme contrast to tropical Malacca. Russia, together with Siberia, was looked on at that time as something of a health resort for missionaries who, like Richard Knill of Madras, could not stand the tropics any longer, and in fact Robert was getting preferential treatment.

Bogue's reply was evidently reassuring, and on 13 July the Committee of Examination resolved to recommend Robert for Siberia. It is a pity that Bogue's letter is no longer extant, so that the grounds on which he formed his opinion cannot be examined, because they appear not to have convinced the Board, to which the Committee reported. The Board sent the matter back for reconsideration. Meanwhile, Robert was inept, or cheeky, enough, to submit a third request to be allowed to finish his studies in Glasgow. This, too, was rejected.

The Committee of Examination consulted Bogue again, asking him to be more explicit in his assessment of Robert's suitability for Irkutsk, and, once again, Bogue made a positive recommendation which, like the earlier one, is lost. Bogue may have been a kind-hearted old teacher, who could not bear to report adversely against any of his students, or he may have had a particular liking for Robert. Certainly, Robert was always conscious of a special bond between his old tutor and himself, and years later he named one of his sons – his only surviving child, as it turned out – Samuel Bogue, after the older man. The Board, however, was now no longer inclined to be complaisant. When the Committee requested them to reconsider their recommendation of Robert, they responded by calling him to interview, 'in order that they might converse with him prior to his positive appointment to the Irkoutsk Station'. Having done so, on 23 November 1818 they threw the whole question of his appointment to Siberia back to the Committee for further consideration.

Robert must have known that his fate was in the balance, but he went on pushing his luck. In defiance of the Society's policy, he let it be known that he had become engaged to a Miss Martha Cowie, and was intent on marrying her before leaving for Russia. The Board probably did not know about this on 23 November, or, instead of referring the case back, they might have taken the action which they took a week later, on the 30th. Learning from the Secretary of Robert's engagement, they cancelled his appointment to Siberia, and decided to apply yet once more to Bogue, this time for two men, one each for Irkutsk and Malacca, posts both left vacant by Robert.

Robert's engagement constituted a direct challenge to the Society's policy, and by cancelling his appointment to Siberia, though not his acceptance as a missionary, the Directors met it squarely, at least for the time being. At the same time, they were receiving warning signals from Russia. In October 1818, both William Swan and Paterson wrote from St Petersburg, cogently arguing the case for sending out a single man as a companion for William. William, circumspect as ever, gave good reasons for his opinion, while hinting indirectly that all was not well at Irkutsk:

> You are aware of the nature of the Siberian Mission – It is not one where the work can be prosecuted by merely going to the place and sitting down in a settled habitation. The Missionaries must move about from place to place, and in a word it requires men unincumbered with families. If frequent exposure to difficulties and danger are to be calculated upon in our first attempts to establish this mission, it is obvious that *single* men should be sent; and therefore I hope that any future Missionary or Missionaries, who shall gird on their armour for this service, will not think of forming a matrimonial connection. It is to be hoped that the female missionaries who are already at Irkutsk will be rendered abundantly useful to the cause as well as comforts to their husbands and that their going will be overruled for good.

If William was not sanguine, Paterson, a more senior man, and able to talk to the Directors on an equal footing, was still more outspoken:

> I beg you will pay particular attention in the choice of a companion for Mr Swan that he be single and under no engagement whatever to any female friend. He must take both head and *heart* with him to Irkutsk. Our married friends cannot go and wander about in tents and unless they do this they cannot get at the language so completely as to be able to translate well.

William wrote again at the end of November 1818, by which time he had learned that it was Robert who was to be his companion. He had made Robert's acquaintance briefly earlier in the year, and, reading between the

The Missionaries: Swan and Yuille

lines of his letter, we can see that he had not been favourably impressed. He accepted the news with apprehension rather than pleasure:

> My acquaintance with Mr Y was neither so particular nor so long continued as to give me a thorough knowledge of his temper or habits or qualifications in general; although I must say, I saw no reason to judge unfavourably of him in any respect. I am not sure how he may stand affected with regard to the point upon which I fully expressed my sentiments in my letter to you above referred to – so far as this mission is concerned – If anyone holds a life of laborious usefulness dearer than his own personal comfort, he will not come out married, and if he does not, he need not set his face towards Siberia . . . . Females must be exposed to various dangers and sufferings, while at the same time they unavoidably cramp the exertions and in a measure tie the hands of their husbands.

So, from both sides, the Directors had unmistakable warnings of trouble to come. Yet Robert got away with it. The Board dropped its opposition to his marriage, and reinstated him, though not at once. One wonders why. Admittedly, the Directors were to take other questionable decisions about the mission later on. They paid for a printing press to be sent to Siberia, and then let it stand idle for ten years for want of a printer. They approved of the missionaries' opening schools, but denied them the funds needed to run them effectively. But their error over Robert's appointment was a fundamental and irreversible one, which all but crippled the mission. They knew him, and they must have realized that he would be even less amenable to reason and discipline in Siberia than he had been when under their direct eye at Gosport. Nevertheless, they went ahead and appointed him. The papers give no clue as to why, and we can only surmise that Robert was sent out simply because there was no one else available.

What happened was that Bogue was twice asked to recommend an alternative name, but by 15 February 1819 he had sent no reply. Time was beginning to run out. William's companion would need a few months in St Petersburg to acquire some Russian and to acclimatize himself. For reasons of convenience and economy, winter travel across Siberia was much to be preferred to summer travel, and if the missionaries failed to catch the snow-roads of 1819–20, a whole year might go by before Edward's one-man mission could be reinforced. The next we know of the story is that, on 8 April 1819, Robert wrote to the Society again, almost as if nothing had happened. He told the Board that Miss Cowie's friends wished him to marry her before leaving home, and the Board gave way. Robert was informed that 'although the Directors would prefer the mode of procedure at first proposed they will nevertheless not object to the modification suggested by his friends at Glasgow; it being understood that no additional expense be incurred to the Society on account of the young woman prior to her departure from England'.

The formalities dragged on. Miss Cowie had to undergo inspection, just as Miss Robinson had done, but fortunately Wardlaw and a colleague at Glasgow, the Rev. Dr Burns, were able to report favourably on her piety and her suitability as a missionary's wife, and the Board accepted their assessment. A new turn of events in Siberia provided a convenient pretext for formalizing the capitulation which had now taken place in London. In May 1819 it was learned that Betty Rahmn's deteriorating health would not permit her to stay in Irkutsk, and that she and Cornelius were going to return to St Petersburg as soon as possible. This meant that Sarah would be left without a woman companion, and accordingly the presence of the new Mrs Yuille would prove opportune.

William tried his best to demolish this argument. In March 1819 Edward wrote from Irkutsk to Alers Hankey to put his case:

> I have written to Dr Paterson, expressing my hope that Mr Swan might soon join us – If another Missionary is not engaged for Irkutsk, and the Society should think of sending another, perhaps the same objections to a *married* person would not exist as before. You will easily conceive that to Mrs S the idea of having another female friend would be exceedingly agreeable. I desire to bless God, however, that she is not *anxiously* concerned about that, and more desirous that the good of the mission should be promoted, than her own personal comfort secured.

Following normal practice, this letter was read in St Petersburg, and William added his own dissentient comments:

> I write this note at the suggestion of Dr P to hint to you the propriety of not communicating to Mr Yuille what Mr Stallybrass says respecting the proposal of a married missionary joining them, lest it should lead him to bring his companion with him or at any rate raise her expectation of joining him sooner than circumstances will actually warrant. The foregoing letter furnishes you with an additional proof of the disadvantage of having females engaged in *this* Mission *at present*. We must feel for Mrs Stallybrass – but sympathy for her cannot justify a measure in all other respects so much to the probable detriment of the cause.

But it was all in vain. Robert gained his point, and there he was, as Paterson ruefully recalled many years later, appointed to Siberia by the Directors, with all that was to follow.

Trouble blew up almost at once. Travellers to St Petersburg at that time needed a passport issued by the Russian Embassy in London. The Directors knew this, because Paterson had told them so in April 1817 when Edward was preparing to go out. But Robert had to be different, and he and

The Missionaries: Swan and Yuille

Martha set off for Russia without the proper documents, putting everyone concerned, and others besides, to a great deal of inconvenience. Of course, he blamed the Directors for not advising him properly. The story bears retelling, in Robert's own words. The ship reached Cronstadt on 27 April 1819, and

> there we began to meet with some difficulties for the want of a passport; the Capt was in danger of being detained on our account; for the Custom-house officers are not obliged to give what they call a clearance to the ship, unless the passengers can produce their necessary passports. This difficulty was soon surmounted by the interference of two of the Passengers, who were acquainted with several of the gentlemen in office. Being thus set at liberty from our watery habitation, we went with Capt Mack in quest of lodgings which we found at the house of Mr D. Stewart *inn-keeper*. Here the Capt and one of the above passengers sat in council with Mrs Yuille and myself, in order to project the best plan for obtaining our admission into the Russian Capital. It was thought advisable, after mature deliberation, that we should apply to John Booker Esq. the British Counsel [sic] at Cronstadt, whom they said would be happy to render us all the assistance that lay in his power; they spoke thus, from a knowledge of his general character. Accordingly we proceeded to Mr Booker's office, in which, and to whom I had been introduced on a former part of the day, as a stranger, but now as a stranger in distress. He entered into my situation with much sympathy and fervour, which no one else but Mr Booker could have done; for I consider him to be the most polite and obliging Gentleman I have met with either in Scotland Ireland or England. For his kindness to me I have already returned him my sincere thanks, and would wish to do it again through the medium of your Missionary Chronicle. He not only forwarded the letters, which I had prepared for Dr Paterson by his own Post, but also drew up a petition to Lord Cathcart on my behalf. This petition was written one copy in Russ for the Minister of Foreign Affairs, and one other in English for his Lordship, and these were accompanied with two letters, one of explanation to L. Cathcart and the other to Dr Paterson informing him what had been done, and desiring him to second the endeavours of the petition. These, with the assistance of my Dear Brother Swan, and Mr W. Venning, the Missionaries' friend, who I believe is known to you, in the absence of Dr Paterson, obtained, with some difficulty, our admission into the Metropolis; after we had been detained one whole week in Cronstadt. For altho' Mr Booker had written to Lord Cathcart, stating my object, as a Missionary having come to promote the Interests of the Bible Society etc., yet his Lordship having had no instructions concerning me, neither Public nor Private from Britain, he was, on that account, unable to satisfy the various demands

which were made about me. Here the matter would have rested, had not Mr Papoff, and His Excellency Prince Galitzin pledged their word of Honour and become responsible for my entering the country; this they were enabled to do, from the information they had respecting me from Friend Venning. I was introduced to Mr Papoff afterwards for the purpose of thanking him for his kind and timely interference on my behalf. He expressed his sorrow, because I had been so long detained at Cronstadt, but observed at the same time, that the Laws of Nations should be observed. I explained to him how it was, that I had come without a passport when he observed again that there was no harm done, only to myself. I think Mr Papoff may be ranked among the plain *meek men* of the earth, if I may judge from the short conversation I had with him. I shall only further add on this particular, that I hope the Directors will not allow another of their Missionaries to proceed to Russia without his necessary introduction, for it puts our friends to a great deal of trouble.

This was not a good omen for the future, and what made it worse was that the letter was dated 22 October. Robert had not bothered to report to the Directors for nearly three months after sailing from Leith on 8 August. At least he had the grace to confess himself in the wrong for not having written before:

> I would have written you on our arrival here, had it not been that Mr Swan mentioned it in a letter which he sent then to the Directors, and in another since: Nevertheless I know that I have transgressed in not writing myself long before this time. I beg your forgiveness and I promise to be more punctual in future.

There is a hint of a rebuke, probably from Paterson, in this apology. Robert had not made a good start.

6

St Petersburg and the Buryat Zaisangs

Edward and Sarah spent almost exactly six months in St Petersburg, learning Russian and familiarizing themselves with Russian ways. Edward also made himself useful by preaching to the English-speaking community there, first of all in Mr Brown's house, and then, with the permission of the Emperor, in the Moravian chapel, which was kindly lent for the purpose by the pastor, a Mr Mortimer, who was himself English. The congregation amounted to no more than eighty or a hundred out of some two thousand British residents, and even so it included a few Russian nationals, amongst them V. M. Popov, the Secretary of the Russian Bible Society, and the Sablukovs.

This new series of public services was in fact opened, not by Edward himself, but by a Mr Glen, a Scottish missionary, and a member of the Church of Scotland, who spent a few weeks in St Petersburg on his way to join the Scottish mission in Astrakhan. The British community was not renowned for its Christian devotion: indeed, quite the opposite was true, and some of its members, particularly the Scots, were considered the most irreligious element in the capital. Paterson was scandalized by the state of affairs. The gospel had not been 'preached to them in its purity' for several years, and the consequences of this neglect were 'visible and awful'. Thus, Sunday was, for the most part, not observed, and even if people did attend church in the morning, they were quite prepared to go to the theatre, or to card-parties, or to 'masquerades', in the evening. An additional scandal was that the British Hunt met on Sundays. Paterson could not bring himself to go into more detail, and left his correspondent, George Burder, to imagine for himself all that might follow from this ungodly behaviour.

Nevertheless, pagan as it was, the British community cherished its regional and sectarian prejudices and differences. Many were Scots, and would have nothing to do with the Church of England, while the church people suspected that Dissenters, like Edward, might be tainted with Methodism, of which they were reported to be rather scared. All in all, it was better for Glen, the Scottish churchman, to take the first step in holding public services. Edward took over from him on his departure, and William, in his turn, looked after the spiritual needs of the British independents while waiting to travel on to Siberia. It was not till 1820 that the LMS yielded to Paterson's urgings, and agreed to maintain a resident agent in St Petersburg, who could act, at the same time, as the regular pastor there, freeing Paterson to attend to his Bible Society work. Their first such agent was the Rev. Richard Knill.

Sectarian intolerance, a common characteristic of the devout, was of course no monopoly of the St Petersburg British, and, to be fair to the expatriates, it must be said that the missionaries whom they were welcoming into their midst were every bit as parochial and bigoted in their convictions as they themselves were. They disliked and distrusted the Orthodox and Roman churches as a matter of course, but they espied other, and even more dangerous, enemies of Christendom at work in Europe itself, not to mention among the heathen. As Sarah wrote to her sister Ann in July 1817, with all the experience of a couple of weeks abroad:

> It would be well if more of our dissenting Clergy were to turn their attention to foreign Stations. The harvest truly is great and the labourers scattered but here and there. I do earnestly wish that some judicious English Preachers who labour among a handful of People could believe it their duty to travel on the Continent of Europe, where Socinian and Arian sentiments are making rapid strides and doing more mischief than Catholics or Grecian Supporters.

Immediately after his arrival, Edward handed Popov a letter of introduction from the Directors addressed to Prince Golitsyn. The Prince was absent at the time, but before the end of June he was able to receive Edward, and to assure him of the good will of the Emperor, and of the latter's willingness to assist the mission in every way. From then on, Edward's main concern was to learn Russian. He intended also to start studying Mongolian with the help of I. J. Schmidt. Even if he did so, which is doubtful, he cannot have made much progress, as nothing had been arranged as late as the end of October, only two months before his departure for Siberia. He was also trying to improve his French and German. Ann's husband, Joseph Monds, must have been at home in both languages, for from time to time Edward, by his own admission an unwilling letter-writer even in his mother tongue, would make the effort to fulfil an evident promise to write to Joseph in one or the other. There are a few lines in German, in copperplate Gothic script, written from Irkutsk in April 1818, and a whole page in French from St Petersburg, written in October 1817. The opening words of the latter are enough to show that Edward's command of French was rather shaky. He begins: 'Mon chér Frere. Nous avons été tres beaucoup delectés par la reception de votre lettre . . .' Fortunately the Rahmns chose this very moment to turn up in St Petersburg, and Edward had an excellent excuse to drop back into English to comment on this exciting event.

In his official correspondence, Edward gave vent to his joy in meeting his new companion and his wife, and in fact he always got on well with Cornelius. But Sarah, in her family letters, hints that they were not over-enamoured of their new acquaintances. She found the Rahmns 'not so prepossessing at first as are some Persons', though, as the days went by, she began to like the Swedish couple better. This was just as well, for, as far as could be foreseen, the four of them were to be life-long companions in Siberia, where other congenial company would be scarce. Cornelius she described as a man of 'remarkably grave and amiable manners, about the middle stature, light hair, fair complexion, but a plain foreign face; very wide mouth and thick lips'. Betty, by contrast, was tall and thin and dark, but plain looking, and of a delicate constitution. What aroused general consternation, though, was the fact that almost as soon as she arrived she announced that she was pregnant. Edward passed on the indelicate news to Joseph in French: 'Her constitution is not very strong, but as she has been pretty much fatigued in her journey, we hope when she is settled she will be better. In addition to this, *elle est enceinte*, which contributes to her weakness, and which I rather think must make a difference in our journey.'

In fact, Betty's announcement necessitated a complete rearrangement of travelling plans which had only just been worked out in what were thought to be the best interests of the missionary party as a whole, and Paterson was actually in the middle of writing to Alers Hankey to tell him of these plans when she broke the news. Seeing that Edward and Sarah were far from strong – something which no one had mentioned before – and that Betty, though facing a lifetime in Siberia, did not seem up to enduring a great deal of hardship or a severe climate, Paterson had decided to let them all spend their first winter in St Petersburg, to see how they coped with the weather, and then send them on by easy stages. They could leave by the sledge-roads in February, and go as far as Tobolsk, where they could stop till late April if they found the going too rough, and finish the journey in early summer. Now everything was upset, and there was nothing for it but to brave the cold, and let them leave as early as possible in winter, in order to reach Irkutsk before Betty's confinement, which was expected in early May.

Giving birth along the road would have been a disaster for the neurasthenic Betty, though it would not have scared a real Siberian. Fifty years later, Victor Meignan, a rich young Frenchman travelling in winter from Paris to Peking for the fun of it, joined forces over part of the Siberian sledge-roads with a group of ladies. One was a Mrs Grant, a native of Kyakhta, and the wife of a Scottish merchant of that town. Her husband had founded, and still managed, the 'pony-express' which linked Kyakhta with Peking, and it was he who had given James Gilmour a temporary home during his rather miserable visit to north Mongolia in 1870 and 1871. Mrs Grant was accompanied by a Miss Campbell, and the third member of the party was Madame Nemptchinof, wife of a rich Kyakhta tea-merchant. Mme Nemptchinof was already pregnant when she decided on an excursion from Kyakhta to

Moscow, to visit her daughter, who was at boarding school there. She had had her baby en route, and was now going home with the new-born infant. The journey across Siberia was not quite as troublesome in 1873 as it had been half a century earlier, for the stretch between Moscow and Nizhni Novgorod could be done by train, but even so, as Meignan admitted, this was not the sort of adventure a French lady would have contemplated with any degree of assurance. Nor could Betty Rahmn.

But in fact the pregnancy was a blessing in disguise. Exhausting as the winter crossing of Siberia could be, it was less so than taking the summer roads. The sledge-roads might not be level – indeed in places they were, for example, churned up into snow-waves, which tossed the sledges about like boats in a choppy sea. But the summer roads, rutted and boggy, repaired perhaps with logs tossed into them higgledy-piggledy, could be even more trying. And then there were the mosquitoes. Moreover, in winter, the frozen rivers provided fairly smooth short cuts, while in summer travellers had to transfer into and out of boats to get along and across them.

Sarah was put out by Betty's news. 'One circumstance I cannot fail to deplore,' she told Ann, 'that my female friend is delicate in her constitution, and her situation at the present time renders her particularly so: had she known her circumstances, before Mr R offered his services to the Directors, I think she would scarcely have undertaken the journey to St Petersburgh, much less the remote one to Irkutsk.' But before the little party could set out, in December, Sarah herself was pregnant as well, and so ill that Paterson even thought of keeping the two women back for a year, and letting their husbands go on without them. The missionaries would have none of this, and persuaded Paterson that they must all travel together. Reluctantly, he agreed that they should, knowing that if things went wrong, and either of the women fell ill and died on the way, as was anticipated by some people in the capital, all the odium for the disaster would rest on his shoulders.

The Rahmns were, in fact, getting deeper and deeper into a false situation, something for which Paterson was personally responsible. His biographer, William Alexander, paints a very sympathetic picture of his character, in which he figures as a great bear of a man, slow, thoughtful, and decisive, but at the same time perhaps a trifle naive:

> His mental operations were not quick; he was wont to survey a subject calmly, continuously, comprehensively, before he came to a conclusion upon it; but once having seen his way to a decision, he went to it firmly, and adhered to it with indomitable perseverance. The most prominent characteristic of his mind was strong, robust sense, combined with great practical sagacity. . . . There was nothing mean, nothing selfish, nothing hypocritical, nothing tortuous about him; all was genuine, simple, straightforward and honourable. With all his native shrewdness, and after all the experience he had had of the world, he

retained, in a singular degree, that charity which 'thinketh no evil,' which 'believeth all things,' which 'hopeth all things.'

But Paterson's frank, open nature had its reverse side. Where his enthusiasm and affections were engaged, he was capable of self-deception, and his persuasive advocacy of a cause could degenerate into special pleading. We have seen how he over-sold Irkutsk as the centre of a mission which might lead to the evangelization of China. In the same way, he was blind to the evident demerits of Cornelius Rahmn as a missionary. Paterson liked him and respected him, and saw in him, as an individual, the makings of an effective evangelist. If only he could have taken a more detached view of his friend's family circumstances, he would have admitted to himself that all Cornelius's qualities and qualifications would, in practice, be nullified by the one factor he deliberately played down. Betty's neurotic, demanding nature would distract her husband from his professional calling whenever she felt she was taking second place to his work. Paterson was opposed to sending out married missionaries in the case of Edward and Robert, but he could find a pretext for making an exception where his friend was concerned: Mrs Stallybrass was, after all, going out with her husband, and she would surely welcome the companionship of a 'pious female friend'.

Again, Paterson had known both Cornelius and Betty for a long time, and must have been aware of her instability. In 1823 he could acknowledge her fatal influence over her husband in a letter to Alers Hankey, but, by that time, Cornelius was on the point of abandoning his second mission station, Sarepta. 'She is a good woman,' he wrote, 'and her heart is set on Missionary work; but she enjoys very bad health in general and is nervous in a high degree. Were I in her situation I think I would throw myself on the Lord and remain where I was rather than cause my husband to leave his post to save a life which has all along been such a draw back upon his mission, and in so far I would rather be disposed to blame her.' Cornelius, though, could do no wrong. 'Him I dare not blame. He almost idolizes his wife so that she has him completely under her control, and he is ready to sacrifice every thing, even his own life for her benefit. We must place ourselves in his situation and then judge him, and I am sure none of us who know the value of a pious and beloved wife will judge him harshly.' It did not occur to Paterson to question whether a man who idolized his wife to the extent of allowing her complete control over him was suited to the mission field, or, if it did, he suppressed the disconcerting thought. He could have found sound scriptural authority for thinking otherwise.

It was not till late November that Edward received his formal Instructions from the Society, dated 1 September, concerning the conduct of his mission. The Directors had been in no hurry to prepare them, knowing that Edward would be in St Petersburg for some time before continuing his journey, but they also explained to him that they had had no time to do so before he left

England. This seems rather a disingenuous excuse for delay, seeing that the document is based squarely, in some places literally, on a draft which Paterson had drawn up for the Directors and sent to them as early as 8 April 1817, from Axminster, where he had gone for the purpose of marrying Jean Greig.

Paterson's draft is rather fuller than the letter which Edward received. For one thing, it contains ephemeral advice, such as instructions as to how the missionaries, armed of course with a passport from Prince Lieven, the Russian ambassador, were to get from Cronstadt, where they would disembark, to St Petersburg. No doubt this guidance had reached them long since, in another form. 'They will stop', Paterson wrote, 'at the English Inn at Cronstadt, write immediately on landing to Mr Henderson, sending the letter by post addressed to the care of Messrs Asmus Simonsen and Co, and requesting he would come down and take them up to St. Petersburg. He will likely be down the next day. If he should not come down or send them they can go up in the steamboat and stop the night at one of the English Inns, where they will learn where the house of the Bible Society is.'

But the Instructions also omitted one matter of vital and permanent importance, Paterson's advice to keep out of Russian politics and religious affairs, and presumably this warning was conveyed to Edward separately, either in the letter which accompanied his Instructions, or by word of mouth from Paterson, Pinkerton or Henderson, whom he was told to consult. Paterson's advice was categorical. Edward should be strictly warned 'not to intermeddle with politics, or even to make his remarks, especially in their letters to their friends. No remarks must be made on the religion of the Russians. Things may be described, providing the description is faithful; but no commenting on them.' The missionaries heeded this warning throughout the life of the mission, no doubt to their own benefit, though as a result their letters sometimes lack topicality. But it was impossible, in the face of the determination of their enemies in Siberia to trap them, to avoid giving the appearance of disapproving of some of the practices of the Orthodox church, and in the end it was accusations of misdemeanours of this sort which served as a pretext for the suppression of the mission.

Edward's Instructions are interesting enough to quote verbatim:

The Directors of the Missionary Society had not an opportunity, before your departure from London, to prepare a letter of instruction respecting your mission to Irkutsk; nor did they then think it absolutely necessary, as it was intended that you should spend some months at St. Petersburgh, there to attain so much of the Russian language as would enable you to converse with persons of that country while in Russia, and when pursuing your further journey, so as to render an Interpreter unnecessary. By the time that this reaches you, we doubt not that you will have made considerable progress in the language, and by the time which may be proper to commence your long journey, you will, in that respect, be sufficiently prepared for it.

It affords us great satisfaction to inform you that we trust God has been pleased, thro' the instrumentality of our dear brother Mr Paterson, to direct us to a suitable missionary to accompany you, viz. the Rev. _____ of Gothenburgh. Being well recommended to us, he has been unanimously chosen as a missionary to Irkutsk. It would have grieved us much had you been obliged to enter on the arduous work before you alone; but we flatter ourselves that Mr _____ will prove a true fellow labourer, like minded with yourself, and disposed to enter on the work with his whole heart. It gives us also great pleasure to think that Mrs _____ will prove an agreeable companion for Mrs Stallybrass, when resident in a region so remote from all your former connexions. We are fully sensible of the sacrifices you both make; we believe that you sat down and counted the cost, and are confident that he whom you love and serve will strengthen you, will be your shield and reward, and that no good thing will be withheld from you.

Our dear friends Mr Paterson, Mr Henderson and Mr Pinkerton are so much better acquainted with the nature of the mission you have undertaken, that we must refer you for more particular directions to them; and such is the confidence we feel in the soundness of their judgment and in the integrity of their hearts, that we desire you, without reserve, to submit to their instructions in all things.

Thro' them you will obtain such letters of introduction to the Governor of Irkutsk, as we trust will secure a favourable reception. You will then devote all the energies of your soul to the acquisition of the Mongolian tongue, or language of the Burjats; and, as soon as capable of it, commence the translation of the Sacred Scriptures – the New Testament in the first place, into it. The importance, the unspeakable importance, of such an undertaking cannot but deeply engage your mind. That very much depends on an accurate and faithful translation, conveying as far as it is possible the mind of the Holy Spirit, thro' that medium, to the natives of the country, will so impress your heart, that you will not only use the utmost diligence, but the greatest caution also, and be induced constantly to implore the aid of Him, by whom they were originally inspired. And should you be spared to accomplish this business, you will have reason, throughout all eternity, to bless God that you did not live in vain.

To accomplish this task it will probably be necessary to form, for yourself, a grammar and dictionary of the language; and to effect this, you must of course engage the assistance of competent persons for your own instruction, and to give you their help in the work of translation. We are sensible how great and difficult the business before you is, but the utility of it is a consideration of greater magnitude than the difficulty; and when you reflect on the promised power and grace of our Divine Lord and Master, you will say, 'I can be all things thro' Christ which strengtheneth me.'

Before you are qualified to publish any translation (which must be done with all deliberation) you may be able, we hope, to preach the gospel in the language. Let this be a principal object of your pursuits, and rejoice in the hope of being able to speak to the people in their own tongue, the wonderful things of God, the glorious gospel of salvation, thro' faith in the blood of Christ.

It is the wish of the Directors that in every possible and practicable way, you would promote the interests of the Russian Bible Society – an institution that presents to the world the most sublime and glorious prospects. It will be your honour and your happiness to contribute to the utility of that noble establishment.

Your conduct, Dr Bror, in relation to persons professing the faith of the Greek Church must be very cautious. Should you be able to form a Church on those principles which we judge to be agreeable to the Scriptures, you must be careful whom you admit, that the Society may be as free as possible from all anti-Christian sentiments and practices. And as to your mode of living, it will probably be necessary to submit to many privations; but you will gradually be reconciled to the customs of the country. It may be needful to endure the irksome task of perusing their religious fables, and even of copying some of them with your own hand; but the end to be attained will reconcile you to the means, however unpleasant.

When you have surmounted the difficulties of acquiring the Mongolian language, we hope you may be enabled to proceed to the Manjur; but this is an after-consideration, and we shall be able to correspond with you on the subject.

We recommend to you, keeping up a correspondence with the Secretary of the Russian Bible Society and also with the Moravian missionaries, and with those from Scotland. We need not say, we hope you will write to us also as frequently as you can, and send us an abstract of your Journal, which we request you constantly to keep. It is a measure of considerable importance. On our part you will not be forgotten. We shall feel a deep interest in your welfare; in the health of yourself and Mrs
and of your Colleague and his wife, and we hope ever to remember you when we address the throne of grace. You have many precious promises for your support, and we feel persuaded that He whom you and we serve, in the gospel of Christ, will never leave nor forsake you.

Thus, the missionaries' priorities were, first, to learn the Mongolian language thoroughly, and, secondly, to apply this knowledge to tasks of an exclusively spiritual nature, to the translation of the Bible and to the preaching of the gospel. They were not going out as medical missionaries or as schoolteachers, though, as things turned out, they had to operate in both capacities. Nor, deep within Russian territory, were they ever to incur the reproach of acting as the vanguard of commercial or imperial expansion, except among a few suspicious Russian merchants. Theirs was a gospel mission in the strictest sense. But it is implicit in the terms in which their Instructions warned them that they might have to learn something about Buddhism, that they were expected to conduct their mission from a position of conscious superiority. In order to appreciate what they would be up against, they might have to brace themselves to read some of what the Directors disparagingly called the Buryats' 'religious fables', and even to copy some of them out with their own hands, distasteful as such a task might be. So, from the beginning, higher authority endorsed, or even prescribed, the attitude adopted by the missionaries, namely that deep study of the Buddhist scriptures was not relevant to the success of their mission. This stance necessarily defined the missionaries' overall policy. Their strategy would be quite different, for example, from that favoured by the Jesuits in China. There it had soon been seen to be expedient for the missionaries to identify themselves in dress, way of life, and learning, with the scholar class, in the hope of acquiring the prestige which might help them to convert the nation from the top downward. The missionaries to Siberia took a different line. They were to work by preference among the common people, where a knowledge of the intricacies of Buddhist theology would be irrelevant. Their appeal was to be to the individual conscience. They would not engage in scholastic debate at a high level, but would propound the gospel in what they saw as its absolute truth, to the ordinary people, not relating it to, or comparing it with, Buddhist doctrine and practice except in the most elementary way. Of course, conditions in early nineteenth-century Buryatia differed enormously from those of seventeenth-century China. There was no Mandarin class to emulate, no great tradition of secular learning to master. But such considerations are irrelevant, for the disdain with which the learning of the lamas, the spiritual leaders of the people, and the devotion of the people themselves to Buddhism, were treated, were the result of a preconceived assumption of superiority, not of an assessment of local conditions.

Some time before his Instructions arrived, Edward was asked by Popov to submit a formal request for assistance to the Emperor. In consultation with Paterson and Pinkerton, he drafted a letter in English, addressed to Prince Golitsyn, which Popov translated into Russian and forwarded. The letter began with a restatement of the general intentions of the missionaries to bring the gospel to the heathen peoples of Siberia. They felt, they said, that a desire to possess the Bible in their own language was already apparent among the Buryats – a misreading of events which will be considered below – and that this was an indication of God's will that the mission should be prosecuted. They went on to detail the methods they proposed to use – the by now familiar combination of language-learning, translation and preaching – and to promise to keep out of politics and not to interfere with the affairs of the Orthodox church. They then put forward their detailed requests. As strangers in the country they asked for privileged travelling facilities, and for letters of introduction to the Governor General of Siberia, the Governor of Irkutsk, and all the Governors through whose jurisdictions they would pass. They suggested that an introduction to the Archbishop of Irkutsk might come in useful, too. Otherwise they asked only that they might enjoy the Emperor's special protection in carrying out their mission once they had reached Siberia, though they anticipated that they might be glad of a grant of land on which to build a permanent mission station if their initial efforts proved encouraging enough. No mention was made in the letter of permission to baptize any converts they might make, and it may be that their advisers recognized that to agitate this point might jeopardize the mission before it ever got under way.

No official answer to this letter had been received by the end of November, when Edward sent a copy to London, but he had been informed privately that the Emperor had agreed to everything that had been asked of him, and had also invited the missionaries to have an audience of him when they reached Moscow. With this supreme encouragement, the little party set out by sledge from St Petersburg on 21 December 1817 O.S., reaching Moscow just a week later.

Edward and Cornelius were received by the Emperor on 5 January 1818, and both of them wrote accounts of the event. Cornelius's letter to his mother, written in Swedish, was published only in 1893, in his daughter's Memoir of him. Edward sent at least two accounts to the Directors, one in a letter dated the same day, and another in his Journal, which the Society published in a slightly edited form. Both men were deeply impressed by the fervent sincerity of the Emperor, who, 'with eyes sparkling with joy, and with animation which nothing but a feeling sense of the subject could excite, spoke of the promises made in the word of God, respecting the circulation of divine truth; and of the pleasure which he felt, and which every believer in them must feel, at this singular period, in seeing so many of them fulfilled'. Edward had been gauche enough in his report to patronize the Emperor to the extent of allowing that as far as he, Edward, could see, Alexander was truly sincere, and the editors of the Society's *Quarterly Chronicle of Transactions* prudently omitted the following short passage: 'And many private accounts which we have heard, and of the truth of which we have been assured, concur to prove to us, that his language was not the effect of the moment, but (as far as we can judge) was the index of the prevailing desire of his heart, and the general tenor of his conduct.'

Altogether, the interview with the Emperor was a most gratifying occasion for the two missionaries, for Alexander expressed not merely approval, but positive enthusiasm for their mission, and promised to do all he could to help them. He told them that he had issued orders to all concerned to grant them every facility they needed, and he also promised to pray to God on their behalf. He had been struck by the same coincidence which had persuaded Edward that the time was favourable for the success of the mission.

> His Majesty took particular notice of a circumstance which has occurred, which is that two Boriats have arrived from Irkutsk at Petersburg; their intention is to learn Russe, and to get acquainted with the Bible. They have already transcribed the gospel of Matthew from the Kalmuck into the Mongolian dialect, and if more of the Kalmuck should be translated, they will transcribe it also; and as soon as types can be made, the gospel of Matthew will be printed; this is a favourable circumstance for us. His Imp. Majesty observed that what was singular in it was that the Boriats were thinking of sending to Europe at the same time that you were thinking of sending to them.

The two Buryats were the *zaisangs*, or tribal chiefs, Nomtu and Badma, whose activities in St Petersburg were to become the subject of a great deal of enthusiastic but ill-conceived propaganda at the time. The exaggerated optimism engendered by the conversion to Christianity of these two Buryats may have done no great damage to the public image of the LMS, but it did deceive the missionaries themselves for a while, and allowed them to form a quite incorrect idea of the extent to which the Buryats as a whole were ready to receive the gospel.

In Paterson's memoirs we find a compressed and rather inaccurate narrative of the reason why the two Buryats came to St Petersburg, and what the effect of their stay was. He makes it appear as if the venture was motivated by the enthusiasm of the Buryat people at large, and as if the knowledge of it in England was what inspired the formation of the mission to Siberia. Under the year 1813 he recalls how subscriptions to the newly founded Russian Bible Society had come in from as far away as Kyakhta, and then goes on:

> As the Buryates are a tribe of the Mongolians and speak the same language with slight deviations as the Calmuc, as soon as the gospel of Matthew was printed we sent them some copies. At first they had some difficulty in making it out; but some of their most learned men at last mastered it. They were so much pleased with it that they wished to have it translated into their dialect, and appointed two of their most learned men to repair to Petersburg for that purpose. This gave the first idea of sending a mission to them, and I immediately wrote the London Missionary Society on the subject and my correspondence with them

issued in Messrs Stallybrass and Rahmn being sent to lay the foundation of the Mission to that people.

The same account appears in his published book, and there, too, it is situated so as to precede mention of his visit to England in 1814, and to appear to relate to 1813.

Things cannot possibly have happened in that sequence. It may be that Paterson, summarizing the important events of his life many years after their occurrence, confused the donations of money which preceded the journey of the two Buryats to St Petersburg with an earlier collection of contributions from the Buryats which was assigned to the general funds of the RBS. Schmidt's Gospel of St Matthew in Kalmuck was not printed until 1815, and it was only in October of that year that Paterson was in a position to send a copy to England. The Buryats cannot have got hold of it much, if at all, earlier. In other words, the translation had not reached the Buryats until a year or so after Paterson and Pinkerton had had those discussions in London, in the summer of 1814, which led to the establishment of the mission on 26 December 1814. The two learned Buryats did not reach St Petersburg until another three years had passed, that is, in early December 1817, just a week or two before Edward and Cornelius left the capital on their way to Irkutsk. It is thus quite impossible for their arrival to have had anything to do with the decision to establish the Siberian mission. Yet even J. C. Brown, who was for many years the Society's agent in St Petersburg and conducted the affairs of the mission there, also thought the two events were connected, writing in his book about the mission: 'The interest excited by the visit of Badma and his companion to Europe, led in 1819 to the establishment of a mission at Selinginsk, in the government of Irkutsk, between Lake Baikal and Kiachta, on the frontier of China, by the agents of the London Missionary Society.' The true story of the two Buryats, as far as it is ascertainable, is rather different from anything which was published at the time.

Nowadays, the impact of the two Buryats on the progress of Bible translation and evangelism among their own people is more or less forgotten, and they are remembered, if at all, only because of the boost which their arrival in St Petersburg gave to the academic work of I. J. Schmidt. They brought with them from Siberia a copy, acquired in Peking by Vasilii Novoselov, a student with the Eighth Russian Ecclesiastical Mission there, of a book known in Mongolian as *Erdeni-yin Tobchi*, that is, 'The Precious Summary', and presented it to Schmidt. This book was a history of the Mongols from their legendary origins up to the seventeenth century. It had been compiled in 1664 by Sagang Setsen, a nobleman from the Ordos region of west China, the territory inside the great northern bend of the Yellow River, which is still inhabited by Mongols today. Sagang Setsen was the great-grandson of Khutuktu Setsen Khungtaiji, the adviser and coadjutor of Altan Khan, and his book contains an authoritative, if biased, account of the conversion of the eastern Mongols to Buddhism, a historic development in which his own ancestor had played such an important role. In the next century, this chronicle attracted the attention of the Manchu emperor Ch'ien-lung, who caused translations of it to be made into both Manchu and Chinese. All three versions were cut on wood-blocks and printed, a rare occurrence as far as a secular book was concerned, for block-printing was, at that time, almost exclusively reserved for Buddhist religious texts.

Over the next few years, Schmidt exploited his good fortune in obtaining what was then a unique example of Mongolian historiography, and in 1829 he published the text in the original Mongolian, with a facing translation in German, and an extensive apparatus of explanatory notes. His *Geschichte der Ost-Mongolen und Ihres Fürstenhauses* was not only the first monument of Mongolian historiographical literature to be presented in full to European readers, but was also an encyclopaedic store of information about the history and culture of the Mongols, whose appearance in print helped to found modern Mongolian studies. At the time, though, it was not in recognition of the help they had inadvertently given to Western Orientalism that Nomtu and Badma became famous, but on account of their importance as symbols of what was confidently believed to be the impending conversion of the Buryat people to Christianity. For a few years they were centrally involved in the Bible cause, and their activities impinged also upon those of the missionaries to Siberia. However, with Nomtu's dismissal in disgrace in 1820, and Badma's premature death in 1822, this short association came to an untimely end, and it will be convenient to anticipate events by a year or two, and tell the greater part of their story here.

Nomtu Uutayin and Badma Morciunayin were *zaisangs*, or chieftains, of the Khoatsaiskii and the Kharganatskii tribes, respectively, of the Transbaikalian Khori Buryats. For a year or two after they reached St Petersburg, their names were broadcast throughout Protestant Christendom through the medium of the reports of the various churches and societies which had an interest in them. The tone of these reports is confident and uncritical, almost lyrical at times, representing the two men as model, indeed almost miraculous, converts to Christianity. But a reading of unpublished contemporary letters and journals not only puts a different complexion on the extravagant claims which were being made publicly, but suggests that the two Buryats were simply being made use of by the Russian Bible Society and its supporters in the interests of a religious and political movement which was no concern of theirs.

The first and fullest account of the train of events set in motion by the despatch of the Kalmuck Gospel according to St Matthew to the Buryats is to be found in volume VI of the *Periodical Accounts of the Moravian Brethren*, under the suggestive heading: 'Account of the manner in which the study of the Gospel was, by the power of God, made the means of awakening two

Saisangs (Mongolian nobles or princes), of the Chorinian Buräts; extracted from a Report by Brother Isaac Jacob Schmidt, of the Church of the United Brethren, and Treasurer to the Bible Society at Petersburg, to the Elders' Conference of the Unity.' The 'Account', which is dated 7 March 1818, that is, less than three months after the arrival of the zaisangs at St Petersburg, is accompanied by a letter from Schmidt on the same subject, and in the next volume of the same series there appears the text of a letter sent by the two Buryats to their prince, the *taisha* Dembil, chief of the whole Khori people. This letter is a pious effusion, in which Nomtu and Badma announced their conversion to Christianity, which they had already reported to the Russian Bible Society through their mentor, Schmidt, and advised their *taisha* to do the same. In fact, Dembil was already flirting with the idea of seeking baptism into the Orthodox church, though not for reasons of personal conviction. Dembil, as we shall see, was something of an opportunist and a rogue, who saw in conversion the most likely means of gaining influential allies in the capital in the long-running battle he was engaged in with his fellow-nobles and the mass of his subjects.

Schmidt tells us that copies of the printed Kalmuck Gospel had been sent, either by himself, as seems likely, or by others, to Treskin, the Civil Governor of Irkutsk. Treskin had arranged for the book to be passed on to scholarly members of two Buryat peoples, the Selenginsk Buryats who lived to the south-east of Lake Baikal, and the Khori Buryats who lived further towards the East, to see what they could make of them. At first, even these Buryats, who were reputed to be much better educated than those who lived in and around Irkutsk, had found it difficult to read the Kalmuck Gospel at all, mainly because of the unfamiliar appearance of the script. Fortunately, a well-known lamaist text, written in Kalmuck, and once the property of a Torgut zaisang who had taken part in the exodus from Russia, came to light, and by means of comparison with this, two zaisangs of the Khori Buryats, that is, Nomtu and Badma, succeeded in deciphering the Kalmuck script and reading the gospel. The new book excited some curiosity, and, stimulated no doubt by knowledge of where the gospel had come from, and through whose hands it had reached them, the supreme lama, or *Khamba*, of the Buryats, who resided at Goose Lake near Selenginsk, and the chief *taisha* of the Khori Buryats, 'each among his own people, and of their own accord, made a collection', which amounted to over 11,000 roubles, or the equivalent of £550. Schmidt says that the *taisha* concerned was Galsang Mardaev, but as he died in 1814 or at the latest in 1815, it seems more likely that it was the intriguer Dembil who helped raise the money.

The collection was put at the disposal of the Russian Bible Society, on condition that the Gospel of St Matthew, and, if possible, other books of the New Testament, should be translated into Mongolian, and printed in the traditional script familiar to the Buryats. The RBS referred the matter to a sub-committee, of which Schmidt was a member, and it was he who proposed that one or two learned Buryats should be sent for to undertake the work. The suggestion was unanimously approved, and Prince Golitsyn requested Treskin to put the matter in train. The choice, naturally enough, fell on the two zaisangs who had already examined the gospel, and willy-nilly they were plucked out of their Transbaikalian homes and sent off westwards. They reached St Petersburg early in December 1817, after passing through Moscow, where they were received in audience by the Emperor a few weeks before his reception of Edward and Cornelius.

As soon as they had settled down, the two zaisangs set to work, under Schmidt's supervision, to translate St Matthew from his Kalmuck into Mongolian. We may leave this aspect of their activities until we come to review the story of the translation of the Bible into Mongolian in the early nineteenth century as a whole, and concentrate here on the human complications which resulted from the bizarre chain of events initiated by the despatch of the gospel to Siberia. It seems that, even before the two zaisangs had left home, the experience of reading and studying the gospel had begun to have an unsettling effect upon them. Badma's father realized what was going on, and reprimanded him, warning him that he was already spoiled as far as Buddhism was concerned, and that if he was not careful he would be seduced into Christianity altogether in Russia. Both he and Nomtu had to put up with 'many severe and bitter remarks' from their families and their superiors. So perhaps, even before they reached St Petersburg, they were predisposed towards what actually happened, their defection from Buddhism and their conversion to Christianity.

The two zaisangs found themselves in a lonely, isolated and artificial situation in the capital. Nomtu was worse affected by their new life than Badma. Neither could speak Russian on arrival, and Nomtu never managed to learn the language at all. To begin with, they had no company except for that of the Kalmuck-speaking Schmidt and their interpreter, and they spent their time engrossed in the study of the gospel, trying to make sense of its unfamiliar concepts and reformulate them in their own language. Schmidt was their sole adviser. They took their linguistic and exegetical problems to him, and soon these became entangled with their own problems of belief and conscience. There was no relief from the intense atmosphere in which they lived and worked, no circle of Buryat, Buddhist friends with whom they could relax and recover their sense of proportion. The summons to the capital had deprived them of the stabilizing influences of Buryat society, and within a few weeks of their arrival they found themselves a prey to agonizing doubts about their religious convictions and spiritual identity. Buddhist practices were beginning to appear sinful to them, they were becoming confused by what used to be familiar Buddhist doctrines, and they were finding the gospel correspondingly easier to understand and accept. They took their worries to Schmidt, told him of their desire to become Christians, and asked his advice. Schmidt did not try to dissuade them, but he did warn them that, at the best of times, it was hard to live a Christian life, and that they could anticipate scorn and downright hostility on the part of their fellow-Buryats when they returned home. They replied that they were willing to take the risk, though they hoped they would not be called upon to do so in the near future, while their faith was weak. In his 'Account', Schmidt denies having brought any psychological pressure to bear upon the two zaisangs, writing: 'The work of the Spirit of God in the hearts of these men having originated altogether with Himself, I left the whole entirely to Him, without intermeddling in the least.' This may well have been the case. Loneliness and deprivation of all that was familiar to them could have been enough by themselves to demoralize the two men.

The precipitate conversion of the two zaisangs came as a propaganda gift to the promoters of missionary work, especially in England, and the opportunity was eagerly seized. Versions of Schmidt's 'Account' and of the zaisangs' letter to their taisha were published in the *Evangelical Magazine* for 1818 and in the BFBS Report for the year 1819. The two Buryats were paraded at the anniversary meeting of the RBS in the Tauride Palace in September 1819, where, as Paterson and Henderson informed the BFBS, and all the readers of its Reports, 'they evidently rejoiced in hearing that the sacred Book in which they have found the pearl of great price, was preparing for people of all nations and languages'. No one in authority seems to have had any scruples about exploiting the situation, either with regard to the sensitivities of the two zaisangs themselves, whose worries and doubts were flaunted for all to read about, or the reading public itself, which was being fed with what was, in Nomtu's case at least, a travesty of the truth. Nor do they seem to have appreciated the possibilities of farce, or tragedy, inherent in it.

Nomtu and Badma were mere symbols, and when Nomtu proved to be an unreliable symbol, he was silently dropped, while the reasons for discarding him were kept secret. In his memoirs, under the year 1817, Paterson cursorily dismissed the unhappy man who had been unequal to his curious destiny with the words: 'Nomtu returned home but did not turn out well.' But as long as there was publicity value in the two zaisangs, he had spoken in very different terms. Writing to Alers Hankey in May 1818, he said:

> Our two Burjats are quite decided in their determination to become christians and I hope they are such in heart already. I shall send you some documents soon which will charm you. They will soon return to their homes and there they wish to be baptized by the Missionaries in the presence of the elders of their people. They will immediately commence preaching the gospel to their own countrymen.

Paterson's 'documents' probably included versions of Schmidt's 'Account' and of the zaisangs' letter, and Alers Hankey could legitimately take pleasure in them as divinely sanctioned, if unexpectedly prompt, tokens of coming success among the Buryats. But Paterson's glosses on them were inept, and even irresponsible. Perhaps, in a moment of euphoric wishful thinking, the zaisangs *had* dreamed aloud of public baptism at the hands of Edward and Cornelius, to be followed by a campaign of evangelism among the Khori Buryat. But Paterson should have recognized this effusion for what it was – sheer fantasy on the part of lonely men who were, at best, over-anxious to please their employers, at worst, no longer fully in touch with reality, and he should have appreciated the risks involved in passing it on, as if it were objective fact, to the Treasurer of the LMS. He must have known that Russian legislation forbade the baptism of heathen converts into any other Christian church except the established one, so that there was no practical possibility of the zaisangs' dream-wish being fulfilled. Fortunately, no recognizable damage seems to have been done by this particular piece of distortion of the truth, though we cannot tell whether Paterson's exaggerated optimism had any effect upon the Society's assessment of its priorities.

Of the two men, Badma seems to have come up to expectations, though he never returned to Siberia, and so never took an active part in missionary work amongst the Buryats. He worked as a lexicographer in the service of Schmidt, and it was probably he who did the spade-work for what became Schmidt's dictionary. He translated several, if not all, of the books of the New Testament into Mongolian, and he was baptized, on his death-bed, into the Orthodox church. Of his religious convictions we possess curious evidence in his own hand. There are two pieces of writing deriving from one or other of the zaisangs which are preserved in libraries in England. One of these is a short Buddhist religious text now bound up in one of the books from Edward's library which belong to the Taylor Institution Library in Oxford. This manuscript has a dedication in Mongolian from Nomtu and Badma to Edward, written in what seems to be the handwriting of Nomtu, the elder of the two men. At that time Edward evidently knew little, if any, Mongolian, for he annotated the Mongolian text, word by word, in pencil, with its English equivalents. In translation the dedication reads as follows:

> This Mongolian manuscript was written by our own hands and presented to our true friend Stallybrass as a sign of mutual recognition in later days. The Mongolian zaisangs Nomtu Uutayin and Badma Morsiunayin. St. Petersburg, 22 December 1817.

The dedication has a sentimental interest, but it is of value apart from that, as it forms first-hand evidence that the two groups of Bible enthusiasts did actually meet in the Russian capital.

Badma's religious sentiments are expressed in a letter he wrote to Alers Hankey in September, which William Swan forwarded, with a translation, at the end of a letter of his own. The translation was published at the time. Though only approximately faithful to the original, it is worth recalling as an indication of what was thought to be Badma's state of mind:

It is my great desire to return the expression of your highly-valued good wishes, communicated to me by my brother Mr Swan. We are united together in brotherly affection by our mutual desire to do all the will of God. The bark of lies which formerly completely covered us has been peeled off. The all-seeing God made us wish to come hither, and hither we came; and we are now lying at the feet of our Saviour Jesus Christ, and in this attitude we embrace him, and pray to him always as our only Intercessor. I subscribe myself with humility and respect – the Mongolian Buriat Saisang Badma Murchinachi.

The letter is difficult to translate accurately, as it is an early attempt by a Mongol to express concepts of Christianity for which there was at the time no standard terminology, but the following version probably comes a little closer to the true sense of what Badma wrote:

On an occasion which caused my desires to be fully satisfied, I heard from my elder brother Swan here the precious words of my elder brother Mr Hankey, and so was gratified and satisfied to the bottom of my heart at having been joined with the number of you, my brothers, who desire the will of the Almighty. Renouncing the root of deception and stultifying oppression, we came hither seeking to become servants of God the Ruler of All. Wishing always that in your pure prayers you would from henceforth as before, remember us, who worship at the feet of the Lord Jesus Christ, and keep us near, I am Badma Morchiunayin, the Mongolian Buryat zaisang.

The missionaries in Siberia would have been glad of Badma's assistance on the spot, both as a translator and as an intermediary with his own people, as long as he refrained from joining the Orthodox church. The reputation of the baptized Buryats was so low that, if he had returned as one of them, his representational value would have been negligible, and he would have been an embarrassment to the mission. But the problem solved itself. On 7 November 1822, Robert Pinkerton called on Badma, no doubt by arrangement, to find him ill in bed, attended by an Orthodox priest equipped with a portable altar, who was administering the rites of baptism and Holy Communion in the presence of Prince Golitsyn, who was acting as godfather, and of Schmidt. Poor Badma was very low. He shed tears as he renounced his own name, which meant 'Lotus', on account of its heathen connotations, and took a Russian name rendered by Pinkerton as John Alexandroff. Three days after the ceremony he died.

Nomtu also became a convert, but rather a disreputable one. Life in St Petersburg did not agree with him. He was anxious about his family, and his inability to learn Russian isolated him from almost everybody else. This latter disability was hardly his fault, but it meant that he could not take a full part in the translation programme. There were other complications, too,

St Petersburg and the Buryat Zaisangs

and in 1819 it was decided that he should return to Siberia, travelling with William Swan and the Yuilles. The journey was not a happy one. William, always circumspect in what he wrote to his superiors, was silent about Nomtu's shortcomings, even as late as 18/30 March 1820, when, with the journey to Selenginsk behind him, he told George Burder: 'The Saisang Nomtu accompanied us no farther than Irkutsk – the road from that city to his own home not being the same with ours to this place any farther than Udinsk.' This is not a very plausible explanation, though it may have satisfied a correspondent in England who was not familiar with Siberian topography. Unless they took the unusual land route around the south of Lake Baikal, all travellers from Irkutsk to Transbaikalia, whether they were going to Selenginsk and Kyakhta, or further east to the Khori pastures, had to go the same way as far as Verkhneudinsk, and the journey up the Angara, across Lake Baikal, and then up the Selenga to that town represented the major part of the way to Selenginsk. Unless there was some reason to the contrary, it would have been well worth while travelling that road in company.

It looks as if the two missionaries had found a welcome pretext for ridding themselves of the society of Nomtu, and one hint of this is to be found in a letter from Edward to Alers Hankey. On 21 February/4 March 1820, only a day or two after his new colleagues had arrived, Edward wrote:

> You will perhaps have heard that there is not the ground for entertaining such hopes of one of the Dzaisangs as was once thought; the account of our Friends, respecting him is very discouraging: I have always been fearful that our friends were too sanguine, and more particularly so since I have known more of their character, circumstances, etc. May the Great Head of the Church be pleased to overrule this apparent evil for good!
> He was baptized at Irkutsk into the Russian faith.

It was probably the delay associated with Nomtu's baptism into the Orthodox church which provided the convenient excuse for dropping him at Irkutsk, rather than putting up with his company as far as Verkhneudinsk.

This is all rather opaque, but something must have gone very wrong for Edward to venture to rebuke colleagues at the capital in a letter to the Treasurer of the Society. Whom was he blaming? The word 'Friends' clearly refers to William and Robert, but who were the 'friends' who had misjudged Nomtu's character so disastrously? If Edward was thinking only of the extravagant propaganda which had been put about regarding the two zaisangs, he might possibly have been holding Paterson responsible, for he was the most vocal of the patrons of the Buryats, and he also had the ear of the Directors. But would he have criticized his own friend and mentor so crudely? It seems rather unlikely.

In any case, this was not the whole story. Nomtu had proved a general disappointment, but he had also behaved extremely badly on the journey to

Irkutsk, and it was really this which had disturbed Edward. As Robert wrote to David Langton, the Society's Assistant Secretary and Accountant:

> Here [i.e. at Irkutsk] we took farewell with our Travelling companion the *Sisang Nomtoo*. He was a Pest to us the whole length of the journey. The Directors have said too much about the Christianity of this man. Indeed, he has yet to learn Christ. This some of our Friends in Petersburg knew before; they ought therefore to have informed you, before so much was said of him, and us also before we travelled with him.

This tactless rebuke cannot have endeared Robert to the Directors, but he was right all the same, and it was well deserved. Nomtu was no credit to the Bible cause even while he was at St Petersburg, and everyone knew it, but no doubt it would have been embarrassing to admit it publicly, or inform London of what had gone wrong. The one curious feature of this contretemps is the fact that Robert had, apparently, not noticed what was amiss. Certainly, he had spent only three months in the capital, from the end of August to the end of November, and needed time to find his feet. But he must have seen that all was not well in the tight little circle to which he belonged. What he should have complained of was not the lack of warning, but the irresponsibility of whoever inflicted such an impossible travelling companion on the little missionary party.

Whose fault had it been? One might put the blame on Paterson, who was in charge of the mission's affairs, but for one thing. His own wife, Jean, was aghast at the folly of sending Nomtu back to Siberia in the same party as the missionaries. As she wrote soon afterwards to William: 'Had not the conviction that your Saviour would be near you operated most powerfully on my mind in overcoming every apprehension, it would, to this moment, have continued to revolt at your departure in such circumstances.' She would hardly have condemned a step taken by her own husband so roundly, and we can only assume that it was other members of the Bible Society in the capital who were responsible for taking the foolish decision.

Nomtu was known to be unstable, quarrelsome, inclined to drink too much, and at times dangerously violent. He seems to have been unable to get on with his companions at St Petersburg, particularly with Badma, and it was his unbalanced and disruptive personality, as well as his incompetence, which decided his superiors to send him back. He started to give trouble again soon after leaving St Petersburg, and William's private correspondence shows that this was not unexpected. Writing from Moscow to Paterson on 2/14 and 3/15 December 1819, William said: 'I am sorry to say also that Nomtu has begun to show symptoms of his former bad state of mind – Pray for him and for us – we shall do all we can to keep him right and are determined to suffer much before we take any measures but those of kindness with him.' In his first letter to Jean Paterson, a series cut short by her

St Petersburg and the Buryat Zaisangs

untimely death early in 1820, also written on 3 December, William enlarged a little on what was the matter with Nomtu.

> I think there is not much to be feared from Nomtu who seems to have suffered a kind of temporary derangement and to have lost the management of himself owing to the misunderstanding between him and his companions, but which is now I hope not so bad as it has been. I have seen enough of him however since we set off to convince me that he still cherishes a rancorous disposition towards them, although it is at present smoothed over – Today he entered upon a justification of himself, and a violent accusation of Badma, as having acted improperly towards him – although quite sober the subject threw him into a violent passion – Let us not forget to bear both of them particularly on our spirits before God – the first thing which struck me on hearing of what was wrong about him was that we had been deficient in prayer for them – and this occasioned in part the distress which I suffered on his (Nomtu's) account. He seems to understand the language of kindness, and I hope he will not be the worse for being in our company during this journey.

Even this, though, was not the whole story, and William was probably anxious not to alarm Jean Paterson by going into more detail. The fact was that Nomtu had homicidal tendencies. The full misery of that long sledge journey, cooped up with the disgruntled Buryat, is hinted at only in William's obituary notice, where the anonymous author states:

> One of the most trying passages in Mr Swan's career was the long journey from St. Petersburg, of upwards of 5,000 miles, to his station beyond the Baikal. It was not the great distance, nor the winter roads, that made it formidable, but the circumstance that it had been arranged that he should travel with a native Mongolian then returning to Siberia, who proved to be anything but a pleasant companion, from his personal habits and recklessness. To be shut up day and night in such a carriage as they had, with a man addicted to intemperance, and occasionally so violent as to threaten his companion's life, was a severe trial, and an exercise of self-denial, which, in after life, he frequently said, should not have been required of him.

Did the obituarist realize that this drunken ruffian was not just a chance Mongol who had unwisely been offered a supervised passage back to Irkutsk, but one of those same two Buryat zaisangs whose conversion had raised such high hopes in the pages of the *Evangelical Magazine* almost half a century earlier?

Nomtu surfaces now and again in later years in the mission's records, though never to his credit. On top of his other faults, he was a petty, and none too successful, trickster. In 1820 he was trying to wheedle copies of the Mongolian Gospels out of the missionaries, in order to pass them on to a 'certain Great General', who was supposed to be planning to distribute them. No one knew who the General was, and as by coincidence the missionaries happened to have run out of gospels, Nomtu did not get what he wanted. A year and a half later, though, he had come into possession of some gospels, and was discovered to be giving them away to local Buryats, and then going round a little later dunning the recipients for ten roubles a copy, explaining that he had to refund this sum to the missionaries. The trick failed, as the Buryats preferred to give him his books back, rather than part with what was then quite a large sum of money. Just how large it was can be seen from the fact that in 1832 Robert could engage casual labour at half a rouble a day to have a log house dismantled, and only had to pay one rouble a day to have eight sledgeloads of wood dragged across the frozen Selenga, a distance of well over a mile.

In 1822 Edward went one day to call on the chief taisha Dembil, who was at the time a candidate for baptism into the Orthodox church, and found him, as he wrote in his Journal, 'indulging in intoxication with Nomtu'. Nothing positive is recorded about Nomtu after this date in the papers of the mission, though there are one or two allusions to him. In 1823, Edward wrote home that Nomtu was 'to all appearance still in heathen darkness, and though he has a name that he lives is, to all appearances dead'. He was still active as an evangelist of sorts in 1827, for in that year, William wrote in his Journal, in an entry which was printed and published, that Nomtu was still zealously 'promoting his own views of the truth'. He gently and wistfully reproved the waste of his talents, saying that Nomtu's 'knowledge of Mongolian books, and ability to expose their errors, might be of use to the cause of Christ, if he were under proper direction'.

This was as far as the Missionary Society was prepared to go in admitting, publicly, that it had been taken in by Nomtu. Later on, in the same extract from his Journal, William had a little more to say about the zaisang. In April 1827 he called on the Khori taisha, who showed him a letter which Nomtu had sent him in 1822. 'The object of it was to explain the doctrine of the New Testament, in opposition to that of the Shigemoni system. The letter contains some apposite references to passages of Scripture, and points out the contrariety of the views exhibited there of the true God, to the dogmas of the Lama-books upon that head; that the God of the Scriptures and the gods they worshipped could not possibly be one and the same being.' The effect of this ostensibly good news would have been spoiled by William's next sentence, which the editors of the *Quarterly Chronicle* cannily omitted: 'This was all very good and had the writer not thrown a stumbling block in the way of his brethren by the kind of profession he has himself made, such statements coming from him would have had more weight.' This is only one example of the way in which the staff of the mission house sometimes edited letters and reports from missionaries, not only prior to publication, but, apparently, even before they were read in Committee, so as to give them a tendency different from that intended by the writer.

Reticent though the missionaries are about Nomtu, their occasional references to him suggest that he continued to impinge upon their lives, and in fact he was a kind of professional rival, a missionary agent of the Orthodox church, though this is never made clear in their correspondence. In one letter home, William reveals that Nomtu's baptismal name was Michael, but it is only from sources unconnected with the mission that we discover that Nomtu enjoyed the highest sponsorship available in Siberia, and had actually been allowed to take the name of the Governor General, Mikhail Speranskii, as his own. Information about him is sparse, but he seems either to have taken holy orders, or to have been allowed to dress as a priest in order to enhance his prestige, and to have worked as an assistant to Alexander Bobrovnikov, the Mongolist, in some sort of pastoral capacity. But advancing age, and his old disability, total ignorance of Russian, finally rendered him as useless in Siberia as he had been in St Petersburg, and in 1834 he was relieved of his clerical duties.

It is hard not to feel some sympathy with Nomtu, who was transported to St Petersburg to further the ambitions of others, and who was completely out of his depth there. Peter Gordon reckoned to have seen through the whole farce while he was in Siberia:

> Some time ago Treskin, when Governor, in his great zeal for the cause of the Bible society, sent twelve thousand rubles which he had collected and two Saisangs, chief officers of a Boriat tribe, to Petersburg, 'in order to facilitate a version, in compliance with the desire of a few Boriats, who had heard some chapters read.' The truth is, that if the Boriats had known for what purpose the money was taken from them, they would much rather have paid for exemption from Bibles. The Saisangs were torn from their families and bewailed as men who would be forced to apostatize. This circumstance was blazoned throughout England, and acquired for Treskin a high character for piety and zeal. Even the Emperor appeared to be deceived by it, and said to Messrs Stallybrass and Rahm [sic], that it was a remarkable coincidence, that God should incline their hearts to the Boriats, just at the time he stirred them up to seek instructors.

Gordon spent only a few days at Selenginsk at the end of 1819, visiting Edward and Sarah, and one wonders how he reached this conclusion. He claimed to know what the Khori Buryats thought about the event, but he spoke no Mongol and probably did not know Russian either, while Selenginsk, where he was staying, was a long way from the Khori pastures. William and Robert had not reached Selenginsk by then. Indeed, Gordon missed them, to his great regret, by a quarter of an hour, at a post-station near Tomsk on 12 January, and so they cannot have been his source of information either. Can Edward have been disillusioned so early? It seems unlikely. His letter to Alers Hankey, quoted above, suggests that he had heard things about the two zaisangs which had caused him to modify his opinion of them, but by the time he wrote that letter his hitherto unknown colleagues had joined him, and no doubt he was drawing solely on their rueful accounts of the journey. The only likely explanation is that Gordon picked up the story from Treskin himself, during the course of a convivial evening he spent with him in Irkutsk at the beginning of January 1820, when the two men discussed the religious situation in eastern Siberia. As we know, Treskin had no illusions about the attitude of the Buryats to Christianity, and he also held the Siberian Christian community in low esteem. 'How many Christians did you meet on your road between Ochotsk and this place?' he asked Gordon. 'Come, speak, real good Christians – be honest. Ah! not one!' It may have given the old cynic, who had recently been relieved of his appointment with Speranskii's arrival as Governor General, ironic pleasure to let his transient visitor in on the secret of the part he had played in the tragicomedy of the two zaisangs.

7

The Journey to Irkutsk

When the missionary party set out from Moscow on the long road to Irkutsk on Monday 19 January 1818 N.S., they were, in one sense, pioneers of Siberian travel. It was not that Siberia was by any means *terra incognita*. On the contrary, it had been very thoroughly explored, not least by two ambitious scientific expeditions which had been mounted by imperial order during the eighteenth century. J. G. Gmelin's expedition of 1733 to 1743, and P. S. Pallas's of 1767 to 1774, had resulted in the assembly and publication of a vast amount of information covering every aspect of the country, from its geological structure to the languages and religions of its inhabitants. The scholars from the Academy of Sciences had ranged over the whole of Asiatic Russia, but there were other travellers, on other business, who had kept more closely to the main artery of Siberia, the road from Moscow to Irkutsk and beyond, which the missionaries were to follow.

The only description, though, of such a journey, which might have been available to Edward and Cornelius, and which William certainly knew of, was that of John Bell of Antermony, published in 1763. Bell was a Scottish doctor in the service of Peter the Great, who had accompanied the Russian embassy to the court of Peking led by L. V. Izmailov, which had set out in 1719, and returned in 1722. But even if the missionaries had studied Bell's book before setting out, it would have been of only minor use to them in planning their own journey, encyclopaedic though it was. Like most Siberian travellers of the eighteenth century who put pen to paper, Bell had made his crossing of the sub-continent in exceptional circumstances, and the conditions which he had encountered as an embassy physician were rather different from those which Edward and Cornelius would face as private individuals a century later.

In fact, for a foreigner to cross Siberia on his own account in the eighteenth century was an extremely rare occurrence. John Ledyard, an American who had sailed with Captain Cook on his last voyage, nearly managed it in 1787–88. He got as far as Yakutsk before being arrested, hurried back to Europe, and pushed across the Polish frontier. But the missionaries would

The Journey to Irkutsk

not have known about him. Some of his papers disappeared in Siberia, and what survived had to wait nearly two hundred years for full publication, though a life of Ledyard appeared in 1829. Another European traveller whose experience might have served as a model was Jakob Fries, a doctor of Swiss origin, who took part in a recruiting drive through Siberia in 1774–76. Fries enjoyed no particular privileges, using the same sort of post-station, with the same facilities for changing horses, as were to be available to the missionaries, though for part of the way he took a more southerly route. But his travelogue, contained in a long letter to his parents, remained, like Ledyard's diary, unpublished until long after it had any topical value.

Half a century after their own day, the missionaries would have been better served, for by then the jaunt across Siberia had become commonplace. Officers going home on leave, rich young globetrotters, journalists, philanthropists, engineers and missionaries, often chose the land road across northern Asia. Some, like the prison visitors Henry Lansdell and George Kennan in 1879 and 1885 respectively, had business in Siberia, while others, like Lionel Gowing and Charles Uren in 1886, took that route because it promised to be an intriguing alternative to the familiar and boring passage home from China by sea. There was a vogue for Siberian travel reminiscences in the latter half of the nineteenth century, but Edward and Cornelius went out almost cold, with nothing at all in print to prepare them for what lay ahead.

What little guidance they had came from their friends, particularly Paterson and Pinkerton. Neither had actually travelled in Siberia, but the journey to Irkutsk was distinguished from travel in European Russia only by its greater length and tedium, and the advice of the older men would have been quite valid. The missionary party set out well prepared, and with the best credentials. They travelled in their own *kibitkas*, sledges protected by a hood and also by a thick curtain which could be fitted across the open front in really cold weather. At a pinch, one could make use of vehicles supplied at the post-stations, travelling 'by transfer', *na perekladnykh* as it was termed. Travelling by transfer was cheaper than buying or hiring a vehicle, but it had nothing else to recommend it, and most people tried to buy or borrow their own sledge in winter, or *tarantass* in summer. All that could be got at the post-stations was a rudimentary, poorly-sprung carriage, or, worse still, a completely unsprung cart, or *telega*, and every traveller who for one reason or another had to travel that way cursed his ill luck. One such unfortunate was George Kennan. Kennan was no weakling. As a telegraph engineer employed by the Western Union Telegraph Company in 1865 to survey a route for a line which was to join America and Russia through Alaska and Siberia, he endured the most horrifying winter experiences in northern Kamchatka and beyond, one of the coldest parts of the globe. But even he found travelling by *telega* almost too much for him:

The Journey to Irkutsk

On a bad, rough road an East Siberian *telega* will simply jolt a man's soul out in less than twenty-four hours. Before we had travelled sixty miles in the Trans-Baikal I was so exhausted that I could hardly sit upright; my head and spine ached so violently, and had become so sensitive to shock, that every jolt was as painful as a blow from a club; I had tried to save my head by supporting my body on my bent arms until my arms no longer had any strength; and when we reached the post station of Ilinskaya, I felt worse than at any time since crossing the Urals.

But that was not all. Travelling by transfer meant changing vehicles as well as horses at every post-station, unloading and reloading each piece of luggage every few hours, or some hundreds of times in the course of a long journey. Thomas Knox, an American newspaper reporter, kept count: between Irkutsk and Nizhni Novgorod alone, where he took the train, he passed 219 post-stations, changing horses each time.

Now packing a vehicle was an art. Boxes and cases with sharp edges had to be discarded, and all one's gear packed in flat leather bags. Bedded in hay, these formed the foundation for what was to be the traveller's bed for the duration of the journey. On top of this layer came a fur sleeping-bag, or a mattress and rugs and blankets. Soft pillows were needed to line the whole of the back part of the vehicle, and in the front part, under the driver's seat, space had to be found for all the odds and ends needed for a journey of several weeks – food, tea-pot, cutlery, and so on. Precious items had to be securely packed. When William and Robert, who, unlike James Gilmour in a later generation, were not teetotallers, arrived in Moscow after a rough ride from St Petersburg, they were dismayed to find that the jolting had smashed almost their entire stock of wines and spirits. It was bad enough to have to turn out every few hours to show the order for horses, and pay for the latter. To repeat the packing process as well, over two hundred times, at all hours of the day and night, in the depths of a Siberian winter, was not something to be looked forward to. And, finally if the accommodation at a night stop looked uninviting, as it often did, because the station was overcrowded, overheated, or infested with bugs, the traveller could always spend a more agreeable night under his furs in his own vehicle. The post cart had to be given up, so that this alternative was not available.

The Emperor had been as good as his word, and the party had been supplied with letters of introduction to all the governors and post-masters along their route, requiring them to help the travellers in every way, while the Governor General, Pestel, had sent special instructions to similar effect. Prudent travellers in Siberia were, in fact, accustomed to provide themselves with letters of recommendation, if they could, in order to smooth the way, and in particular to ensure a regular supply of horses. Thus Professor Hansteen and Lieutenant Due, who set out in 1828 to investigate the magnetic system of Siberia, armed themselves with letters of recommendation from Speranskii to all the post-officials in Siberia, and these worked like magic, saving them time and protecting them from swindling post-masters, even though Speranskii had ceased to be Governor General.

The missionaries took 3,000 roubles in cash, a letter of credit cashable at Tobolsk, and another order, issued by the Russian-American Company, which they could use at any of the Company's offices in Siberia. Finally, they had, through the generosity of government, been issued with what Paterson called a 'free passport' for horses, which he reckoned would save them two kopecks per verst for each horse, or more than 1,000 roubles over the whole journey. The value of the paper rouble, which was what the missionaries used throughout the time of their mission, tended to fluctuate, but in 1818 it stood at about a shilling, and a saving of £50 was very welcome.

Travellers using the Russian and Siberian post-stations had to obtain a *podorozhnaya*, or order for horses, Paterson's 'passport'. These orders were of three kinds. The most rapid conveyance was ensured by the possession of a 'courier' *podorozhnaya*. A team of horses was always kept in reserve at each station in case it was needed for a traveller, usually one on government service, who held such an order, and no delay was permitted in changing the horses. To travel 'courier' was not an unmixed blessing, if only because the unfortunate holder, and anyone with him, hardly dared stop for a meal or a proper rest, and most Siberian travellers had tales to tell of some unhappy fellow-creature who had crossed the sub-continent with almost incredible speed, and as much consideration as would be given to an express parcel.

What the missionaries received was presumably an order of the second type, the so-called 'crown' *podorozhnaya*. This had the advantage of giving the holder a prior claim to horses over the holder of the third type of order, the 'private' *podorozhnaya*, who would be denied his horses even at the very last moment if the holder of a crown order required them. Courier and crown orders were issued without charge, but a tax calculated on the number of horses specified in the order and the length of journey was levied on holders of a private order. It was this tax which Paterson was so pleased to have avoided, but the missionaries, like all other travellers still had to pay the tariff rate at each station for the number of horses specified in their order, at each change of team. They were travelling with two sledges and another for their luggage, and an order for ten horses. On some particularly demanding stages, ten horses were not thought to be enough, and the *smotritel'*, or post-master, would insist on supplying more, sometimes as many as twenty-four altogether. The missionaries do not recall ever having had to pay for the extra horses, though later travellers, Gowing and Uren, for example, often had to argue the point.

Edward wrote one or two letters home while on the journey, including a

The Journey to Irkutsk

long family epistle sent from Kazan to his sister-in-law Ann, which was copied by her brother Thomas for the Directors of the LMS, and a diary of the journey which the Society printed in its *Quarterly Chronicle*. But what with the biting cold which made writing a penance, the snow which obscured every feature of the landscape almost to the very end of the journey, the incessant worry about the comfort of the two pregnant women, and Edward's habitual reluctance to put pen to paper, his account turned out to be rather uninspiring, almost as devoid of detail and colour as the white world through which the party travelled. What it lacks in liveliness of observation and description it makes up with solemn testimony to the regularity of their religious observations under trying circumstances. So, somewhere east of Kazan, they found it imposible to stop one Sunday because of the over-crowded post-house, and had 'to spend that sacred day in travelling'. This became almost a pattern:

> We were several days obliged to travel on the Sabbath. Sometimes, indeed, we found it possible to obtain a room in a private house; but this was not often, as we travelled principally through villages, containing houses of one room only. Yet we hope we endeavoured to consecrate our different carriages as sanctuaries to God; and although from their violent motion, we could read but very little, yet we could raise our supplications to the throne of the Most High, sing his praises, and converse upon those subjects which were calculated to promote our best interests.

Still, this was the first English diary of a crossing of Siberia to appear in print since Bell's, and it deserves a better fate than the oblivion to which its single appearance, in a missionary magazine, has condemned it. No later traveller, reviewing the literature, seems to have noticed Edward's diary, which is a pity, for, in spite of its brevity and its occasional ponderous moralizing, it did tell its readers, for the very first time, what it was like to cross northern Eurasia as a private person in mid-winter.

The missionaries spent a couple of weeks in Moscow getting ready for the long journey. Cornelius's sledge had been ruined beyond repair on the road from St Petersburg, and it was not easy to find another one. The party finally set out around four in the afternoon on 19 January N.S. They took the usual road. Two days later they passed through Vladimir, but it was dark, and they did not stop, and so saw little of the city. Another two days brought them to the ancient town of Murom, or Moreham as Edward anglicized it. Here Betty felt so weak and ill that they had to call a doctor and interrupt their journey for a few days. There was a chance to look round this little provincial town, and talk to the priest and other local inhabitants. In the market place Edward was surrounded by inquisitive Russians, who asked him where he was going, and expressed astonishment that the missionaries could be travelling to Siberia *of their own free will*. Murom had sixteen churches and three monasteries, one of which Edward visited. He was impressed, but not edified, by the sight of the tomb of Prince Constantine of Vladimir, who had been martyred by the people of Murom. Nearly three hundred years after the event, his body had been exhumed, and then 'saintified', as Edward recorded with distaste.

At Murom, too, the missionaries made the acquaintance of the Governor, a General Sukov, who was also the President of the recently founded Bible Society there. The general invited them to call on him, but was thoughtless enough to suggest they come on Sunday. They replied that they were not used to paying visits on the Sabbath, but would be glad to come the next day. Not at all put out, the general invited them for the Monday.

By 26 January, Betty was well enough to travel again, and they set out for Nizhni Novgorod, which they reached the next evening. Nizhni made little impression. It had some handsome houses, and a large market, like Murom, and that was all Edward said of it. From there, they set out along the Volga for Kazan.

Edward was already experiencing, and becoming exasperated with, the ignorance and bovine stolidity of the drivers, from whom he could learn nothing about the places he was passing through. He asked one of them how many people lived in Nizhni, but the only answer was 'I don't know.' 'These men', he wrote, 'think one business is sufficient for one man, and if they know how to drive a sledge that's enough.' The brutishness of the average yamchik, or driver, called for stern measures. In the same letter to Ann, Edward wrote: 'It is difficult to maintain my character with them, "to be no brawler, and no striker." Sometimes they through carelessness, give us such shakes that I am oblig'd not merely to bawl, but also to thrash them, which they receive with all due submission.' Thomas must have been a tactful amanuensis. He copied the letter to his sister for the Directors to read, but, no doubt guessing that a resort to violence on the part of their missionary might upset them, he modified the sentence so as to read: 'I am oblig'd to call out I will thrash them which they would receive with all due submission.' But beatings, real or threatened, had nothing like the same effect as withholding the customary tip, or *na vodku* as it was known, had on the dull-witted drivers, who looked forward to the mere penny they would get after covering a stage of perhaps as much as thirty miles.

Kazan was a disappointment. The city had been badly damaged by fire two years before, and good accommodation was simply not to be had. Even the post-master had lost his house, and could not take the travellers in. Finally, they found two miserable rooms in a crowded house, but it stank so that they were all ill, and they were glad to leave and travel on towards Perm.

Between Kazan and Perm the cold became more intense, and one night Edward and Cornelius, who were sleeping in their sledges, had to get up and go inside, and sit up the remainder of the night in the post-station. It was on this stretch, too, that their difficulties with Sunday travel began. In Perm they had to replace their luggage sledge, which had been jolted to pieces. They were entertained at the house of a brigadier, and also met an ex-naval officer who spoke English. The latter had once sailed to the South Sea Islands, and this prompted Edward to tell him about the 'pleasing accounts which had been received from Otaheite'. To his consternation, the Russian saw things in a different light. He did not think the news was pleasing at all, and considered that the natives had been upset by the arrival of Europeans and would have been much happier if they had been left alone.

It was after Perm, at Kungur, that for the first time they experienced difficulty in getting horses. But here, and once or twice elsewhere, it only needed a flourish of the imperial seal, and the threat of a direct complaint to the Minister of the Interior, to elicit more complaisant behaviour from the obstructive post-master.

Leaving Kungur, the party made the imperceptible transition from Europe to Asia, and event which moved Edward to suitably grave reflections: 'It was with peculiar feelings that we passed the boundaries of Europe, that enlightened and highly favoured part of the world; but the hope of being instrumental in imparting its light to some far distant tribes, who are sitting in gross darkness, tended to dispel the painful sensations which we began to experience.'

On 18 February they were in Ekaterinburg, where they visited the imperial gem-stone factory, and made a few private purchases. The next stop was Tobolsk, where they were the personal guests of the General Post Director of Siberia, and dined also with the Governor, and met the Archbishop, who was also President of the local Bible Society. Being lionized had its drawbacks, and they had to make a special request to be allowed to keep to their rooms on the Sunday. To this the Post Director 'cheerfully assented, and afterwards told us a person of distinction had called to make our acquaintance; but that he had informed him, we were engaged at our devotions, and must not be disturbed'.

Passing through Tara, the missionaries approached the Barabinsk steppe. They were relieved to find that it was no longer infested by bandits, though ever since leaving Tobolsk they had been worried about meeting wolves and other wild beasts in the wastes of Siberia. Still, as Edward confidently wrote: 'Our God whom we serve and who delivered Daniel from the mouths of lions, is able to deliver us also, and we trust that He who hath delivered will yet continue to deliver.' His trust was not misplaced. They were twelve days on the road from Tobolsk to Tomsk, lonely days during which they passed through only a couple of towns and hardly saw another traveller. The roads were good, but the houses poor. Some had bladders stretched over the windows instead of glass, while some had only wooden shutters and nothing else. On 14 March they reached Tomsk, having encountered not a single wolf.

The Journey to Irkutsk

The Governor had personally made arrangements for their accommodation, and had ordered the city gate-keeper to keep a look out for them. He supplied them with provisions, and invited them to dinner on Sunday, a pleasure they naturally had to forgo. The Governor treated the travellers handsomely. He not only gave them a Cossack escort, but he sent another Cossack on in advance to see that horses were ready for them at each station. At Krasnoyarsk a Russian merchant had heard of their approach, and had arranged to put them up in his house, but as they had planned to travel through the night they had to decline his hospitality. At Kansk, the last station in the Tomsk government, they were looked after very hospitably by the officer in charge, who personally accompanied them to the border with the Irkutsk government.

Edward had expected conditions to deteriorate progressively the deeper he went into Siberia, and he was pleasantly surprised by the appearance of the Irkutsk goverment: 'Almost as soon as we entered this government, we saw a favourable change in the appearance of things; the villages were all regularly built, the streets wide and clean, and in the post-houses better rooms for the accommodation of travellers, and many other things which confirmed the ideas which we had been led to entertain of the character and activity of the Governor.' Only the weather was against them. The spring sun was beginning to melt the show, and in order to be able to use their sledges to the very last, they had to hurry on, travelling even on Sunday. They finally lumbered into Irkutsk on 14/26 March 1818, after travelling day and night over roads roughened by daily thaws and nightly frosts, and, at the very end, over a dusty track quite free of snow.

The journey had taken twenty-one weeks from St Petersburg, and Edward reckoned the distance at 6,189 versts or 4,105 English miles. Nothing untoward had happened on the way. The sledges had twice been overturned, but all in all it had been a quiet journey, and 'considering the situation of our Ladies and little child, and the severe weather, it appears almost miraculous that we should all have been thus preserved and brought hither not only with *good*, but with *improved* health. "He has kept all our bones, and not one of them is broken." ' Paterson was much relieved to hear of the party's safe arrival. Dr Leighton of St Petersburg, whom Edward had consulted before setting out, would probably not have been at all surprised at the good news, for he had forecast that, though Sarah might expect to feel 'poorly', she would do just as well on the journey as if she had stayed at home.

8

From Irkutsk to Selenginsk

Irkutsk had grown up at the confluence of two rivers, the Angara, which is the only river to flow out of Lake Baikal, and its tributary the Irkut, which joins it from the south. A smaller stream, the Ushakova, flows into the Angara from the north, near the city. Irkutsk had been founded as an *ostrog*, or fortress, in 1661. It became a city in 1686, and the centre of the province of the same name in 1764. By the beginning of the nineteenth century it had grown into a pleasant little city of some 15,000 inhabitants, possessing a cathedral and a dozen churches, and was the seat of a Civil Governor. From 1822 onwards, after the reforms initiated by Speranskii, it was the headquarters of the Governor General of eastern Siberia.

Throughout the nineteenth century, Irkutsk was to make a favourable impression upon most foreign visitors, especially upon those who, like George Kennan, first approached it from the barbarous north-east of Siberia, and found themselves plunged suddenly into a centre of cultured, sophisticated and even luxurious living. Adolph Erman, a German scientist who travelled with Professor Hansteen, and who reached Irkutsk from the west in 1828, was delighted with the city. He found everything 'much more pleasing to the eye, and more tasteful and expensive in its decoration than in Tobolsk'. The main streets ran parallel to the river, and though they were not paved, they were kept in good order, as were the wooden walkways provided for pedestrians. Most of the 1,900 or so houses were of wood, many of them detached, and with kitchen gardens to the rear. Some of the public buildings, like the grammar school and the offices of the Russian-American Company, would, in Erman's opinion, have been considered spacious and ornamental in any city in Europe. The glory of the city was its central square, with the Governor's residence standing on one side. Erman felt quite at home here, for not only did everything look modern and European, but one morning he heard a military band rendering selections from Weber's opera *Der Freischütz*, which had had its first performance in Berlin only seven years before.

Outwardly, Irkutsk was gay and prosperous, even a little too worldly to be entirely pleasing to the serious missionary families. There were frequent balls there, and the missionaries were invited several times to attend, but they always declined on the ground that such amusements were incompatible with their calling. Sarah was confronted, as she might have been anywhere, with the servant problem. There were plenty of servants to be had, but she found the 'lower class of people' idle as well as numerous. She engaged three servants, a Buryat lad who did the outdoor work, fetching water, running errands, or milking the cow, a woman to help with the cooking and do some gardening, and a little girl for the simple housework and for sewing. 'By these three, strange to say,' she told Ann, 'we have less work done than by one good English Servant, though it is a consideration, that the wages of all three together is less than for one English person.' Sarah regretted that she had left her industrious German maid with the Browns at St Petersburg, but she consoled herself with the thought that, by example and precept, she might be able to improve the Irkutsk servant class somewhat.

It was going to be an uphill job, though. Morals were slack, and Sarah was outraged at her maid's indecent brassiness. 'What would you have thought,' she asked Ann, 'the second night after your Servant entered the House, if she brought home a Child, and on enquiring if she had a Husband, the answer with a loud laugh was, that she had none – These things and many other equally unpleasant we must be content to put up with, if we hire free People – All the decent Servants are purchased when young, and brought up in the families.' Things would be no better at Selenginsk. As Peter Gordon put it: 'The female servants are a most wretched set; they do not possess the least sense of honesty, sobriety, or chastity; they are extremely impertinent, dirty, indolent, ignorant and fond of finery. Mrs. S——, than whom it would be impossible to find a better mistress, could seldom induce any one to stay with her above a few weeks together; the animal she had when I left her, was one of the general's slaves, yet she would occasionally take the pet and walk off.' Eventually, Edward and Sarah did discover a reliable housekeeper, but fear of salacious gossip forced him to dismiss her after Sarah's death in 1833. He told Ann and Joseph about it:

> For more than a year before my dear Sarah's decease, on account of her impaired strength, we had a young woman from Selenginsk living with us in the capacity of house keeper. She was in many respects clever, had become well acquainted with our house, manner of living, was kind to the children, and managed very well for them and their clothes, etc. But she was a *young* woman; and although as a *married* man she might have lived in my house without suspicion; yet when I became a *widower* scarcely 99 in a 100 would have believed she was kept for any lawful purpose; and to avoid the *appearance* of evil, I was obliged to part with her – You, my beloved friends, will start from the mention of such a subject with disgust. But such is the state of society universally, among

which our lot is cast – not merely heathen but also professedly Christian!!! Nor can I complain. For, judging me by their own standard – and they know no other, they would, from what daily occurs, have great reason for their conclusion.

Irkutsk was the commercial centre of eastern Siberia, especially for the traffic to and from China which was funnelled through the twin frontier posts of Kyakhta and Maimaicheng which lay just to the south-east of Lake Baikal. It had a fine market hall, or *gostinyi dvor*, built of stone, with rows of shops well supplied with goods from Europe and China, and the outdoor markets made a lively scene, with Russian dealers and housewives chaffering in mixed Russian and Mongol with the Buryats who brought in provisions for sale. Outwardly bustling and prosperous, Irkutsk began, during the 1820s, to experience an upsurge in intellectual activity as well. In the field of Mongolian linguistic and ethnographic studies alone, a field which closely interested the missionaries, the city could boast of local scholars such as A. V. Igumnov, Vasilii Novoselov and Alexander Bobrovnikov. Towards the end of the decade, this talent was reinforced by the arrival of a couple of young scholars, A. V. Popov, and Józef Kowalewski, an exiled Pole, both of whom had been detached from the University of Kazan to improve their knowledge of Oriental languages, especially Mongolian.

The missionaries hardly ever mentioned their Russian and Buryat acquaintances, except for their pupils, in their reports and letters home. But chance hints and clues in their papers and elsewhere prove that they must have known most of these pioneer Orientalists, and worked more or less closely with some of them. Igumnov and his circle were the founders, in Irkutsk, of a tradition of Mongolian scholarship which flourished later at the University of Kazan. This tradition was maintained not only by Europeans such as Kowalewski, but also by some young Buryat scholars who, sometimes in the face of considerable official discouragement, took up the hitherto neglected study of their own people, and so contributed to the development of their national self-awareness. So, for example, Dorji Banzarov, a young Buryat Cossack who had the greatest difficulty in obtaining exemption from the obligatory twenty-five years' military service to which his status condemned him, is still remembered today as the author of the first systematic study of Mongolian shamanism, based upon original texts which he was the first to examine. A Buryat lama, Galsang Gomboev, edited and translated an early Mongolian chronicle, the *Altan Tobchi*, or 'Golden Summary'. The missionaries' association with the founders of this school of Orientalists was of great help to them in their early days as students of Mongolian, and they, in their turn, contributed to its development by the training they gave to at least one budding Buryat scholar, Rintsin Wangchikov. Rintsin, who had been trained as a future evangelist, deliberately turned his back on the mission and took up a career in government and then as a school teacher. The mission to Siberia must be said to have failed in its main aim of converting the Buryats to Christianity, but, paradoxically, it probably served to promote just that development which the missionaries would so gladly have stultified, that is, the promotion and recognition of the language and culture of Mongolia, including shamanism and lamaism, as fields of study worth pursuing for their own sake. It is ironical, though understandable, that the missionaries' success in their stated aim of arousing a sceptical spirit in the minds of their pupils, should ultimtely have backfired on them. They were not, however, the only Europeans to be baffled by the strength of the 'Mongolian' element in the nineteenth century Buryat renaissance. During the 1840s and 1850s, Archbishop Nil of Irkutsk, who, incidentally, was responsible for the suppression of the mission in 1840, was trying to promote Orthodox Christianity among the Buryats. One tactic of his was to procure the conversion of influential men in the hopes that others would follow their example. He set his sights on Banzarov, but the young scholar stubbornly rejected Christianity.

A. V. Igumnov, a native of Siberia, was one of the earliest Russian Mongolists, a linguist, ethnographer and collector of books, and the central figure among the Orientalists of Irkutsk. Today he is largely forgotten, unjustly overshadowed by men of a later generation like his own protégé Kowalewski. Igumnov was born in 1761 at Kundarinsk on the Chinese frontier, east of Kyakhta, and grew up bilingual in Russian and Mongolian. His first official appointment was as interpreter at the frontier-office at Kyakhta, which he joined in 1777. From then until 1809 he enjoyed a varied career as magistrate and government official at Nerchinsk, Verkhneudinsk and Irkutsk. In 1781 he accompanied the Seventh Russian Ecclesiastical Mission to Peking as interpreter, following the example of his father, who had been a member of the Sixth Mission ten years earlier. A second visit to Peking, this time as interpreter to Count Golovkin's embassy of 1805, was frustrated, as for reasons of protocol the embassy failed to get any further than Urga. Igumnov kept up a correspondence with Golovkin in which he spoke critically of the way Pestel and Treskin abused their power in Siberia, and when this correspondence came under Treskin's surveillance, he was forced to abandon his career at Irkutsk and retire to Verkhneudinsk. It was only after Speranskii had replaced Pestel and begun his review of the administration of Siberia that Igumnov could return to Irkutsk, and ultimately resume his official career. In the meantime, he opened a school in Verkhneudinsk, where his pupils included the children of some of the Buryat taishas, and which, in a way, foreshadowed the English mission schools. At the same time, he was going on with his linguistic studies, and enlarging the Mongolian–Russian dictionary which he had started to compile before the turn of the century.

It was in 1818, while Igumnov was still at Verkhneudinsk, that Edward and Cornelius began their study of Mongolian at Irkutsk. They were pract-

From Irkutsk to Selenginsk

ically destitute of books. They had no grammar and no dictionary, and very little to read. Their reading matter consisted of eleven chapters of Genesis which their teacher had translated himself; a book of dialogues, which, from Edward's description of it, was probably a Mongolian version of the well-known Manchu–Chinese primer of conversation known as *Tanggû meyen*, or 'The Hundred Chapters'; and a Mongolian version of what was undoubtedly the travel journal of Tulishen, a Manchu ambassador from the court of Peking, who had led a mission to Ayuka Khan of the Volga Torguts between 1712 and 1715. That was all, and it was not a promising beginning. Probably the most discouraging thing of all was the lack of a dictionary, but, some time before the beginning of 1819, this want was partially relieved.

At the end of January of that year, Edward wrote to Alers Hankey to say:

Since I last wrote to you I have received the loan of a large vocabulary or Dictionary of Mongolian and Russ words, which has occupied a great deal of my time in copying, but is now nearly finished. In its present state it is not of much use to us, being entirely without alphabetical order; I hope however to arrange it alphabetically, and translate the interpretation into English, after which it may be of great use to the mission, at least until we can get a better. The number of words which I have obtained from this Vocabulary is about 7000 and about 3000 we had before obtained making 10000 out of 17000, of which the Mongolian language is supposed to consist.

Edward did not say from whom he had borrowed the dictionary, nor who had compiled it, and these questions cannot be answered with certainty. It would be tempting to assume that it was Igumnov, who had been working at the compilation of a Mongolian dictionary for so many years, who put his material at Edward's disposal and advanced his early studies so opportunely, but there is no substantial evidence for this. We know only that it would have been in Igumnov's character to do so, for he seems to have been generous with his material and certainly let Kowalewski use it a few years later. But we do not know for sure that Edward even met Igumnov at this time.

Edward's last letter before his January one had been written about three months earlier, at the end of October 1818, just after he and Cornelius had returned from an exploratory foray across Lake Baikal. They had stopped for a short while at Verkhneudinsk, then gone on through Selenginsk as far as Kyakhta, where they were refused permission to cross into China, and had returned to Irkutsk by the land route round the southern tip of the lake. In Verkhneudinsk they had been entertained by Mattias Hedenström, a gentleman of Swedish extraction, born at Riga in 1780, who had been banished to Siberia, and was at that time serving as an *ispravnik*, or police inspector, in Transbaikalia. Hedenström was a cultured man of wide intellectual interests, and also, as it happened, the owner of the house in Irkutsk which Cornelius and Betty were occupying.

Neither in his October letter, nor in the long extract from his Journal in which he described the tour to Kyakhta and back, did Edward mention the name of Igumnov, though this is no proof that he did not meet him, so chary was he of naming Russians in his letters. But if he did meet Igumnov, and if Igumnov had lent him his dictionary, it would have happened before the date of his October letter, not after it, as he told Alers Hankey, and he would surely have informed the Treasurer at the first opportunity, while the exciting news was still fresh in his mind.

There is another circumstance, too, which seems to exclude Igumnov. Edward made a point of telling Alers Hankey that the dictionary he had borrowed was not arranged alphabetically, and that it was a tiresome chore, though a necessary one, to put it into a more useful form. That a Mongolian dictionary should not be arranged alphabetically is not surprising. The Mongolian and Manchu–Mongolian dictionaries in common use in the East, which were compiled in China and printed in Peking, followed a traditional pattern of arrangement in which the words were grouped together under a large number, nearly three hundred, of subject headings. But we know, because Kowalewski tells us so, that Igumnov had actually arranged his dictionary alphabetically.

Manuscript Mongolian – Russian dictionaries were not easy to come by, even in Siberia, and if it was not Igumnov's which Edward borrowed, it can only have been one belonging to his teacher. Nowhere does Edward name this teacher. He tells us no more than that he was difficult to follow. This was partly because he gave all his instruction in Russian, partly also because, although he was credited with a sound knowledge of Mongolian, he did not know the language systematically, and was incapable of explaining linguistic difficulties. As Edward put it, he knew a thing was so, but not why it was so. This teacher was, in fact, the very same Vasilii Novoselov who had once been a student-member of the Russian Ecclesiastical Mission in Peking, and had brought back from there the manuscript chronicle which the two zaisangs had presented to Schmidt. After leaving China, Novoselov settled down in Irkutsk as a translator, and he went on living there, probably up to the time of his death, which seems to have occurred some time before 1828. He, too, had compiled his own Mongolian dictionary, working from a trilingual Manchu–Chinese–Mongolian source. Unfortunately, neither his work, nor Igumnov's, nor Edward's, is accessible today, so that the little puzzle of where Edward found his material cannot be answered with absolute certainty.

A year or two later, the missionaries acquired more authoritative reference material from Peking. At the end of 1820 the Tenth Russian Ecclesiastical Mission passed through Kyakhta on its way to Peking, and William gave the Archimandrite Kamenskii, who was at its head, 350 roubles of his own money to buy books. The returning Ninth Mission brought him four dictionaries, two of them Manchu–Mongolian, one with additional Chinese entries, and the fourth being an abridgment of the third. In all, he got fourteen volumes for his money, but the missionaries had to make their own alphabetical indexes. Edward and William each made a copy for his own use, in itself a volume of between seven and eight hundred pages. Characteristically, although William does name Kamenskii in his letters home, there is no mention of his having met either the celebrated Sinologist Iakinf Bichurin, who was returning with the Ninth Mission, nor Dr Voichekovskii, who was going out with the Tenth, and whom he was to run up against in different circumstances years later in St Petersburg.

The missionaries' relations with Alexander Bobrovnikov, the father of the more celebrated Mongolist Aleksei Bobrovnikov, are obscure, though they certainly knew him by name, and almost certainly knew him personally. Once or twice in their letters they mention that there was a teacher of Mongolian at the Irkutsk Spiritual Seminary, and this can only refer to Bobrovnikov, who held such an appointment there. In 1829 they admitted to closer knowledge of him. In that year, William wrote home to say that the 'Mongolian teacher at the Irkutsk Spiritual Seminary' had been entrusted with the task of revising Schmidt's Mongolian New Testament, and that the missionaries had been invited to help him. They had, however, declined the invitation, 'knowing the character and acquirements of the man'. What lay behind this ambivalent utterance it is impossible to tell.

Of the younger generation of Mongolists, Józef Kowalewski was known to the missionaries, though only Robert mentions him in his letters. Kowalewski was born on 9 January 1801 N.S. He entered the University of Vilno in 1817, and while still a student joined a secret patriotic society which had been organized by the Polish poet Adam Mickiewicz. This society was broken up by the police in 1823, and in the following year Kowalewski and some of his fellow-members were banished. Fortunately for himself and the future of Oriental studies, the banishment was relatively lenient. Kowalewski, who up to then had been a schoolmaster, with an interest in Latin and Greek literature, was sent to Kazan to study Oriental languages at the University. In mid-1828, he and Popov were sent further east, initially to Irkutsk, and from there he was able to explore Transbaikalia. It was at this time that he made the acquaintance of Robert Yuille, with whom he stayed for a couple of weeks in the summer of 1829. Kowalewski travelled as far as Peking, in 1830 and 1831, as a member of the Eleventh Ecclesiastical Mission. He became one of the most celebrated Orientalists of the nineteenth century, and is best remembered today for his monumental, and still indispensable, three-volume Mongolian–Russian–French dictionary, which he published in Kazan between 1844 and 1849. In his sixties, he suffered a wholly undeserved and devastating blow. On 19 September 1863 a bomb was thrown from a window of the house where he was living in Warsaw at the Russian governor, Count Berg. As a reprisal the military authorities ordered the immediate burning of everything in the house. All Kowalewski's books and manuscripts were destroyed, as was a piano which had once belonged to Chopin. By the time Kowalewski visited Transbaikalia, the three missionaries were fluent in Mongolian, and had also separated. Edward and William were no longer living in Selenginsk, and, apart from his friendship with Robert, which resulted in his bringing back from Peking over twenty books in Manchu, Mongolian, Chinese and Tibetan for the mission, he seems to have made little impact upon it.

Soon after reaching Irkutsk, the missionaries decided that the Siberian capital was not, after all, the ideal site for the headquarters of a mission to the Buryats. For one thing, it was a Russian city, but apart from that, the Buryats on the western side of Lake Baikal were reputed to be illiterate, and to speak a dialect so corrupt and mixed with Russian that it would be impossible to acquire a decent knowledge of the language from them, and inadvisable to try to translate the Scriptures into that sort of Buryat. As the missionaries were intending to run a scriptural mission, distributing Bibles and tracts over the wide area they could not cover with preaching, illiteracy among the population would prove a major obstacle. They decided, therefore, to follow advice they had received from Paterson, which he had no doubt got from the two zaisangs, and go and explore on the far side of Lake Baikal, looking in particular at the claims of Selenginsk as a mission centre.

The missionaries were probably right in their decision to try their luck in Transbaikalia, rather than on the west of Lake Baikal, but, if so, it was not for the reasons they gave, and one wonders on whose advice it was – for they were in no position to make an independent judgment – that they formed such an incorrect opinion about the state of Buryat culture amongst the Ekhrit-Bulgat Buryats who lived west of the lake. The one point on which they had not been misled was that of illiteracy. These Buryats had no writing, so that, from the narrow missionary point of view, it would have been difficult to proselytize amongst them. But, although the Buryats who lived in Irkutsk itself may have spoken a Buryat corrupted by Russian, there was nothing decadent about the mass of the people, or their language. They were the true guardians of everything that was old and traditional in Buryat life, everything which contributed towards the preservation of their ethnic and cultural identity. Shamanism flourished amongst them, unenfeebled by contact with alien lamaism, and it was this shamanism which informed the old oral literature – heroic epics, legends, shaman chants, and so on – which the Ekhrit-Bulgat, *par excellence*, cherished and kept alive. Their speech was a pure, uncorrupted Buryat, and continued to be so throughout the century. As the famous Buryat scholar Žamcarano remarked ninety years later: 'Buryat antiquity survived nowhere in its pristine vigour as it did amongst these Ekhrit-Bulgat. Later, I became convinced that what is old, and in particular the epic, had maintained itself better wherever the population still

From Irkutsk to Selenginsk

held to shamanism, and where literacy had not as yet blossomed.' Curiously, the missionaries seem to have remained oblivious to the unifying power of the old oral literature, which flourished on both sides of the lake, but is never talked about in their letters. For them, Buddhism was the cultural enemy, and possibly they underestimated the conservative influence of the ancient epics and legends of the Buryats. Had they remained on the west side of Lake Baikal, they would no doubt have adjusted their strategy, but in any case, they would have found the Cisbaikalian Buryats an even harder cultural nut to crack than those among whom they eventually settled, who proved resistant enough.

The two men set out for Transbaikalia on 28 August 1818 O.S., leaving behind them Betty, whose sickly baby had finally died three weeks earlier, after a distressing few months of life, and Sarah, who had just given birth to her first child, a boy whom they had christened Thomas Edward. The journey was uneventful. They went by post-coach up the Angara, and had a smooth crossing of Lake Baikal by galliot, just escaping one of those sudden and treacherous storms for which the lake is notorious. Then they went on by coach along the Selenga, following a track rather than a road, with their wheels at one time being covered by the water of the river. At Verkhneudinsk they called on Hedenström, who gave them first-hand information about the Buryats, about Selenginsk, and about the Buddhist religion as practised by the Buryats. Hedenström gave them their first sight of a statuette of the Buddha, whose name they transcribed at this time as *Jagjamooni*. He was

> sitting cross-legged, with four arms; two of which were clasped in his lap, and the other two lifted up. Upon his head was a cap of curious shape. The interior of the image was filled with flour and water, said to be mixed and put in by Dalai Lama's own hands, by which act it was in a peculiar manner consecrated. Such an image as this is reported to be sold in Kiachta for two horses.

Edward's information was so new and strange that the editors of the *Quarterly Chronicle* added a footnote, explaining who the Dalai Lama was. Another curious sight was that of

> several bones of calves, which had been formerly offered in sacrifice to their gods, upon which were written prayers in the Mongolian and Thibetan languages. We were told, that these prayers were a kind of soul-mass, or *requiem* for the dead. Such prayers together with the performance of other ceremonies at the burial of a Taischi, or other rich Buriat, are usually purchased by a third part of the cattle formerly possessed by the deceased. The burial of a Taischi, lately deceased, cost about 200,000 rubles; (or £10,000 sterling) a handsome legacy for the Lamas!

From Irkutsk to Selenginsk

From Verkhneudinsk Edward and Cornelius took a boat part way up the Selenga, then went ashore for the rest of the way to Selenginsk, which they finally reached after a clumsily mismanaged crossing of the river, during which their ferry boat struck a sandbank and remained stranded all night. As was usual in eastern Siberia at that time, there was no hotel or guest house at Selenginsk, and they were allotted lodgings, no doubt by the local police in accordance with normal practice, in the house of a merchant. A couple of days later they paid a call on the Khamba Lama at the important lamasery of Goose Lake, armed with a letter of introduction from Hedenström. Here, for the first time, they came face to face with the religion and the priesthood which were to cause them so much heart-searching and distress over the years. Here they saw their first prayer wheel, an object at that time so novel that, like other contemporary travellers, they felt themselves obliged to give a full description of it:

> It was a sort of slightly constructed barrel, placed within a stand supported by four legs. This barrel, we were given to understand, contained prayers. On the outside of it was fastened a string, which being pulled by the Lama turned the barrel, and thus he offered the prayers which it contained!

They saw, too, the wooden blocks from which the lamas printed their books, and many 'ugly looking *burchans* (or gods)'. One of the latter was of Chinese manufacture and had cost 150 head of sheep, an example of the regrettable generosity of the misguided faithful which they would continue to have occasion to deplore.

Everything was new and strange, from the appearance of the tents to the sights and sounds of a lamaist service, and Edward described it all for the Directors. For the first time, no doubt, he was given '*koumiss* (a kind of brandy distilled from milk)' to drink, and then some tea, 'of the common leaf, boiled with butter, milk, and salt'. 'After the tea, fried mutton, and boiled mutton, of a very fine sort, were successively brought, but both without bread.' The Khamba explained that he had not known they were coming, and so had not laid in any bread. They were invited to spend the night in the Khamba's tent, but were put off by the look of the cold, dirty room and retired to their carriage. Next day they got their first sight of a Mongolian tent.

> We rose from our *kabitkies* at 5 o'clock, and went into the tent, where we found a woman busy in preparing tea. In the middle of the tent was a hole dug, which contained a fire, on which was placed a large iron kettle. In the roof of the tent was a hole for the purpose of ventilation. Notwithstanding this, the tent was filled with smoke, but the people, from being accustomed to it, appeared not to mind. The tents are formed with poles, and covered with *voilock*.

From Irkutsk to Selenginsk

A footnote explains the Russian word *voilock* as 'a sort of thick substance made from cow's hair, beaten, with water'. This was a sort of felt, the usual Mongolian tent-covering, and it would soon cease to be a novelty.

The lamas put on a special service for the delectation of the missionaries, something which they often did for European visitors, but Edward and Cornelius were not edified by the spectacle:

> The chief Lama told us, that the Lamas would now perform the service, upon which the latter went to collect their instruments, laughing as they went. These consisted of cymbals, kettles, and two long trumpets, which made a most dismal noise. The Lamas said their prayers with a muttering voice, and with their eyes shut. At intervals they were accompanied by the instruments, which were sounded without any regular tune. The chief Lama stood by, muttering his prayers with apparent devotion. The whole was a scene of the greatest nonsense and confusion. We inquired how often they performed this service, and were told once every month, except what is called the *white month*, when sacrifices are offered, and then it is performed every day. The Lama observed, that on the former occasions comparatively few attend, but that in the *white months* the place is crowded. How did we wish, and hope, and pray that the mountain of the Lord's house might be established upon the top of *this* mountain, and be exalted above this *hill*, that the numerous tribes of *this* people might flow unto it. May our God hasten it in his time.

The missionaries kept the conversation with the Khamba Lama at a low level, as they were not yet ready to disclose their real purpose in coming to Transbaikalia. Erman, who called on the Khamba a few years later, and had no ulterior motives to hide, enjoyed a more wide-ranging interview, learning a lot about Buryat Buddhism and its relation to that of southern Asia. He was a little too free, though, in his remarks on the celibacy the lamas were supposed to observe:

> The Khamba reproved with an air of reserve the opinion which I expressed as to the inexpediency of the vow of celibacy. I afterwards learned from the high priest's Russian neighbours, that he labours under the suspicion of a domestic love affair, and it is just possible that he may have fancied there was some personal allusion in my jesting criticism.

Perhaps no one liked to warn him that he could have made an even more embarrassing blunder. It was no secret to the missionaries, or to anyone else, that the lamas were suspected of sodomy as well as fornication, and the Khamba, innocent as he may have been personally, may have suspected an even slyer dig than Erman had intended.

Selenginsk, the main object of the missionaries' tour, lay on the right-

From Irkutsk to Selenginsk

hand bank of the Selenga, and was not a prepossessing sight. All Edward could find to say of the town was the following:

> During the forenoon we took a walk in the town, which contains but few inhabitants. The market is small, and little business transacted in it. The sand lying about in the streets was almost over our shoes. The hills have a very barren appearance.

Selenginsk was, in fact, moribund. The town was almost as old a foundation as Irkutsk, having been first built as a fortress in 1666. As long as it was Russia's last outpost on the road to Mongolia and China, it had a role to play. For a hundred years after its foundation, northern Mongolia was seething with unrest, as Jungars and Manchus battled for supremacy over Inner Asia. But that troubled period came to an end in 1759 with the defeat of the Jungars and the suppression of an attempt at an anti-Manchu uprising on the part of a few Khalkha nobles and others, and Selenginsk settled down as a sleepy garrison town. Its importance as a frontier post and market town had already been undermined by the Treaty of Kyakhta, which was drawn up in 1727. This treaty settled the line of the Russo-Chinese frontier some distance south of Selenginsk. Any commercial function which Selenginsk might have had was usurped by the new town of Kyakhta, which grew up right on the frontier, adjoining its Chinese counterpart of Maimaicheng, while as an administrative centre and market town Selenginsk was overtaken by Verkhneudinsk.

No one had a good word to say for Selenginsk. Its fundamental weakness lay in its cramped situation, hemmed in by sandy hills on a low-lying plain which was subject to floods and erosion. Bell, passing that way a century earlier, had been just as dismissive as Edward, remarking:

> Selenginsky is situated on the east bank of the noble river Selinga, in a deep, barren, sandy soil, that produces almost nothing. The choice of this situation was extremely injudicious, for, had the founders gone but half a mile further down, to the place where now the inhabitants have their gardens, they would have had a situation, in every respect, preferable to the present. This place consists of about two hundred houses, and two churches, which are all of them built of wood.

Bell was right about the noble river, which reminds one of the Rhine above Koblenz. A hundred years later, Selenginsk, though, still consisted of just about two hundred houses, a thousand civilian inhabitants, and another thousand garrison troops. By then, one of its churches, the Cathedral of the Holy Saviour, was built of stone, as was the market hall, which had twenty booths. But two recent serious fires had done a lot of damage, and erosion was steadily completing the ruin of Selenginsk. When Captain Cochrane visited the place, he was told that only twenty years earlier, the centre of the town had lain where the centre of the river then was. There was no

From Irkutsk to Selenginsk

hope left for Selenginsk, and in the middle of the nineteenth century its inhabitants finally gave up the unequal struggle. The old town was abandoned, and a new one, Novo-Selenginsk, was established in its place, on the western bank of the Selenga, where it is today.

Edward approved of Selenginsk as a site for the headquarters of the mission. Its main advantage lay in its geographical position. At Irkutsk, the missionaries had felt cut off from any possible mission field, as it was impossible to get out amongst the Buryats. Selenginsk, though, was surrounded by two, and possibly three, large conglomerations of Mongols. In its immediate vicinity were some ten or twelve thousand Selenginsk Buryats. North and east of these lay the pastures of the even more numerous Khori Buryats, while to the south, just over the frontier, dwelt the true Mongols, the Khalkhas of Outer Mongolia. For the moment, the latter were inaccessible, and Edward was discouraged to find how anxious the Russian authorities were not to offend their Chinese opposite numbers. They would not, for example, allow him to distribute on his own account the Chinese New Testaments and tracts which he had received from Malacca through Peter Gordon. Treskin had offered to take care of the distribution himself if Edward would entrust him with the books, but knowing that the Governor had already received Chinese Scriptures from St Petersburg, and had deliberately failed to circulate them, Edward was understandably reluctant to hand over his small supply. For another thing, the Russian authorities at Kyakhta had prevented him and Cornelius from making a day trip across the border to Maimaicheng, something which most European visitors to that part of the world did as a matter of course, long before China was opened generally to foreigners. The excuse was that England and China were rumoured to be at war, and the two missionaries might be taken for spies. Even so, Edward still hoped that once he was living on the far side of Lake Baikal, near the frontier, things might be easier. Another temporary argument in favour of Selenginsk, this time as against a site somewhere among the Khori Buryats, was a rumour, soon to be discredited, that the Moravians were planning to send a mission to the latter. The Moravians looked on the two Khori Buryat zaisangs as their own converts, although both became members of the Orthodox church, and Edward felt that because of this they were entitled to priority among the Khori, should they wish to exercise it.

Plans for the future of the mission were still fluid. Edward advised the Directors that it might be more economical to build a house at Selenginsk than to try to rent one. Cash was so short in eastern Siberia that interest ran at 25 per cent per annum, and owners of property would not let it out on less favourable terms. This meant that, as the missionaries had been promised a free grant of land by the Emperor, the capital outlay in building a house would, notionally, be recovered in four years. But, for the moment, Edward counselled caution. Selenginsk had not been tested in practice, and might turn out to be no more convenient than Irkutsk.

From Irkutsk to Selenginsk

Meanwhile, at St Petersburg, William Swan and Paterson were wondering how best to organize the work of the mission in the light of Betty Rahmn's seemingly feeble hold on life. It turned out, after all, that the Moravians were not going to stake a claim to the Khori Buryats as a mission field, so that there was no reason why their pastures should not be occupied by the English missionaries, and Paterson proposed a division of the mission into two groups. Edward and Cornelius could stay at Selenginsk with the ailing Betty, while William and his as yet unidentified partner, who, it was still intended, should be a bachelor, could proceed to the pastures of the Khori and nomadize with them.

But Betty's state of health proved too fragile to permit even this makeshift arrangement. On 8 May 1819 N.S., Paterson wrote home with the sad, and, so he said, unexpected, news that Betty's illness, which had been showing signs of improvement during the early summer, had taken a turn for the worse as the move to Selenginsk drew nearer, and that, on the advice of their doctor, both families had decided that there was nothing for it but to cut their losses, and let the Rahmns return to St Petersburg. Predictably, Paterson shielded his friend against anticipated reproaches, drawing an emotional picture of the intolerable predicament in which he had found himself, through no fault of his own:

> I hope you will not judge harshly in regard to his conduct in this affair. I immediately endeavoured to place myself in his situation. A wife whom I doated upon confined to bed for a whole year, racked with pain, everthing done human skill could do for her recovery; getting worse instead of better; no probability of her recovery as long as she remained in otherwise a most healthy but for persons disposed to rheumatism, insupportable climate; my own usefulness as a missionary quite cut off by these circumstances; my medical attendant declaring a change of climate absolutely necessary; and urged to this by a partner I fondly loved; I must acknowledge that in such circumstances I would have acted as our friend has done, and I question if there be an individual among you who would have acted otherwise.

For a while, both Cornelius and Betty toyed with the romantic notion that he would take her back to the capital and put her into care there, and then come back alone and rejoin the mission in Irkutsk. Fortunately, even Paterson disapproved of this nonsensical plan, though he admired the couple's 'spirit' in proposing it, and felt that it proved that their hearts were truly in their work.

There was, however, a silver lining to be perceived encircling this dark cloud, even a double one. For one thing, although it was going to cost the Society a lot of money to withdraw the Rahmns, Paterson could console the Directors with the thought that their loss would have been heavier still if Rahmn had been trained at their expense. And then, at the very last moment, he had a bright idea. Why not write to Cornelius at one of the cities he would have to pass though, and divert him to Sarepta, to set up a mission there? It was no sooner said than done. Paterson had a word with Schmidt who, he said, 'highly approved' of the plan, and without consulting the Directors, wrote off to intercept Cornelius at Tobolsk, while Schmidt wrote to Sarepta to prepare the Moravians for his arrival there. Paterson put foward a suspiciously large number of plausible arguments in retrospective justification of the rash action he had taken. The climate of Sarepta would suit Betty far better than that of St Petersburg. She would find a supportive Christian community there, together with the best possible medical assistance. There was a 'watering place within a gentle walk of the town fitted for rheumatic patients'. (This would doubtless have been a boon if Betty had been suffering from rheumatism rather than hysteria, and had shown signs of being able to walk the five miles to the Gesundbrunnen.) The cost of living at Sarepta was only a third of what it was at St Petersburg, while the journey there from Irkutsk was shorter by 1,500 versts, which represented a further source of economy. Finally, Cornelius could go on studying Mongolian in its Kalmuck form at Sarepta, so that if Betty recovered, or if, as seemed more likely, she should die, he could 'immediately join his own Mission qualified for entering on his work among the Buriats whom he loves'.

Paterson managed to present the fiasco at Irkutsk as a blessing in disguise, and he confidently interpreted his last-minute improvisation as an expression of divine intervention and guidance. He told the Directors that he expected to receive their complete approbation of this latest plan. 'Who knows but it may lead to the salvation of thousands. God leads the blind in a way they know not.' But Cornelius had no better luck at Sarepta than at Irkutsk, and Betty's nervous instability drove him away from that station too a few years later. However, Betty Rahmn's flight from Irkutsk did at least facilitate a solution of the vexed question of Robert's determination to marry Martha Cowie before he left home, in defiance of the Society's policy. The Directors had agreed that Cornelius might take his wife with him, persuaded that Betty's company would prove a comfort to Sarah Stallybrass. Now that Betty had left Irkutsk, Sarah was once again alone, and there was no reason why Martha should not assume the role of companion. Accordingly, the Directors felt able, at their meeting on 14 June 1819, to sanction her marriage.

With his appointment to Sarepta, Cornelius ceased to have any formal connection with the mission to Siberia. He remained in the Society's service for several years, first in Russia, and then, from October 1826 to June 1834, as an assistant in their Foreign Department in London. In 1828, still, apparently, under the spell originally cast by Paterson, the Society's Northern Committee recommended that he should be sent out once again to join the Siberian mission. Fortunately, wiser counsels prevailed, and from that time Cornelius dropped entirely out of the story of the English mission to the Buryats.

The prospect of losing Cornelius worried Edward, for he had found in the older man not only a congenial friend, but someone wiser and more experienced than himself, to whom he could look for practical and spiritual guidance and support. When, in mid-May 1819, the Swedish couple finally left, he stayed on at Irkutsk, occupying himself with further language-study, and with the dull but essential task of re-sorting his dictionary. There was still no possibility of engaging in real missionary work, even though he had received some sheets of the Mongolian translation of St Matthew which was being printed at St Petersburg, for the local Buryats were unable to read the new book. Edward was listless, and could not settle down in Irkutsk again. His friends had gone, Sarah was continually unwell, and his teacher had had to leave Irkutsk and cross over into Transbaikalia as interpreter in what Edward called the 'Taisha's affair'. Altogether, as he wrote to Paterson at the end of May, he felt 'quite unhinged', and was looking forward to making a new start at Selenginsk at the earliest opportunity.

9

The Buryats of Transbaikalia

The so-called 'Taisha's affair' involved Dembil Galsanov, the chief taisha of the Khori Buryats, who held office from 1815 until his death in 1822, and whom we have already met, in Chapter 6, as a drinking companion of Nomtu's. Dembil was the son and successor of the chief taisha Galsang Mardaev, during whose term of office the first stirrings of curiosity about the Russian Bible Society had made themselves apparent among the Buryats, and he was the superior of Nomtu and Badma. It was he to whom they had addressed the celebrated letter in which they announced their conversion to Christianity and advised him to become a Christian as well. Dembil's doings were thus of some consequence to the English missionaries.

His 'affair' is touched upon only rather one-sidedly in the mission correspondence, where its implications for the spread of Christianity are emphasized to the almost total exclusion of its political aspects. Edward was no doubt mindful of Paterson's warnings when he wrote as follows to Alers Hankey on 6/18 May 1819:

> I have lately received a letter from His Excellency Mr Papoff in which he asks several questions respecting the state of affairs here etc, but I have not thought it desirable to entangle myself with political concerns but would rather give myself entirely to those things which more immediately respect the gospel of Christ. There appears to be much interest excited in St P. by the rejection of the *Tysha*, to whom the two Buriatt Chiefs addressed their letter. I understand His Imperial Majesty has given command to enquire into the cause of this conduct of the Bratsky. If the truth is found out, I think it will appear that the Bratsky were not the only persons engaged in the rejection. He was the Tysha of the largest race of the Bratsky, the *Chorinsk*, who are computed to be about 30,000. He has appeared particularly favourable to the introduction of the gospel among his people. If it should appear that he has been injured, I trust he will be restored to some situation in which he may still be useful in the same way.

The Buryats of Transbaikalia

It was just as well for Edward to write in this oblique way, for, as he surmised, the Bratsky, or Buryats, were by no means the only ones concerned in the taisha's affair, which developed into a political crisis which occupied the attention of the highest authorities in both Siberia and Russia. The missionaries were always worried that their letters might be opened and read by inquisitive Russian censors, and in this instance, as on other occasions too, they also warned the Directors not to publish even their watered-down remarks. Rather than risk appearing to take sides, or to even analyse the affair, Edward and William preferred to confine themselves to rather banal reflections.

If the truth be told, Dembil was a bully, a crook and a drunkard. The sort of thing he had become notorious for was organizing an assault on a religious ceremony at the Aga lamasery in the eastern part of the Khori pastures along with his aristocratic cronies, disrupting the proceedings, and beating up the congregation. But what provoked the crisis of 1818 to 1819 was his misappropriation of thousands of roubles of public money. Furious at this peculation, his people, commoners and nobility alike, banded together in an attempt to get rid of him, and Pestel, facing the possibility of civil disorder in a sensitive area next to the Chinese border, sanctioned the demand for Dembil's removal from office. Dembil, however, had already put it about that he was contemplating conversion and seeking baptism into the Orthodox church. Golitsyn instructed Pestel to rescind the order for Dembil's deposition, and in June 1819 the taisha was restored to his privileges, and proceedings against him were dropped. His application for baptism was not, however, accepted.

The crisis on the Khori steppes was not resolved by this action, and remained as one of the many individual problems awaiting the attention of the new Governor General Speranskii, when he arrived in Siberia later in 1819 in succession to Pestel, charged with the general task of reviewing the administration of Siberia, and making recommendations for its reform. Speranskii was not, in principle, opposed to the spread of Christianity. He approved, for example, of the efforts of the English missionaries to educate and enlighten the Buryats, and patronized them during his period of office and later. But he quickly saw through Dembil's pretence. The taisha's rejection of the old religion was simply a bid to curry favour with the authorities, and make it easy for them to turn a blind eye to his misdeeds. Dembil was not the only pseudo-convert at the time. There were others like him who had an eye to the main chance, and on the other hand there were involuntary converts who were deliberately made drunk, and baptized while they were in a drunken haze. On the whole, the converted Buryats brought no credit to the church they were joining, since everyone knew that their motives were usually corrupt, or the circumstances suspect. Dembil's affair brought the process of conversion into even greater disrepute, and this was bound to rub off on the English missionaries, who were not always clearly

The Buryats of Transbaikalia

distinguished from the Russians in the eyes of the Buryats. Speranskii temporized. Dembil was allowed to remain in office, but a second application for baptism, made in 1822, was also rejected. His opportune death in the same year, while still in his twenties, put a temporary stop to religious controversy amongst the Khori.

It is hard to tell how much of an impact Dembil's affair had on the progress of the mission. But, as chief taisha, he had plenty of scope for the exercise of his immature and malevolent nature, and seems to have done his best to frustrate men whom he probably detested because they possessed the integrity which he lacked, and whom he may even have feared because of their contacts in the capital. A letter written by William in April 1822, shortly before the taisha's death, alludes to what Dembil was capable of:

> There is one point more concerning the Chorinsky Buriats upon which I have not yet touched – but it is a delicate one. I refer to the desire of some of them with their chief Taisha a dissipated young man at their head, to enter the Greek Church by baptism – This is the result of no conviction of the truth of Christianity, but merely of political motives and could amount, if accomplished to nothing more than the change of a few forms and ceremonies. We have therefore much cause to regret it; but situated as we are you can conceive *why* I am not more explicit in writing how deeply and seriously this point may affect the mission. Our design is to destroy the works of the devil in this part of the world, and while his malice sets open enemies against us, his cunning will employ those who ought to be friends to thwart our efforts and mar the work. . . . What we have said about this should *not* be published.

Dembil was succeeded by Jigjit Dambadugarov, son of an earlier chief taisha. Jigjit was well disposed towards the missionaries, and even began to study English with them, but his political situation, following upon Dembil's disreputable flirtation with the Orthodox church, compelled him to be cautious in his dealings with them. Thus, Dembil's affair had proved, for the missionaries, a dramatic and subtle introduction to the complexities of the political, social and religious situation in Transbaikalia. For us, too, its contrasting elements – a traditional, but degenerating, native aristocracy confronting an expanding, alien, authority, and an intrusive religion in conflict with a still vigorous native faith – offer a convenient opportunity to suspend our narrative, and survey the Buryat scene at the beginning of the nineteenth century, and some of the historical events which had helped shape it.

The historic home of the Buryats lies around the southern part of Lake Baikal. When the Buryats first began to come under Russian influence during the seventeenth century, they were found to be occupying an extensive area stretching from the river Kan in the west, in the neighbourhood of Krasnoyarsk, to the Argun in the east. Their northern limit was at about the 57th Parallel, and thus well below the line of the northerly tip of Lake Baikal, while on the south they were more or less bounded by what was to become, by the Treaty of Kyakhta in 1727, the Russo-Chinese frontier. None of these limits can be taken as exact. Buryats lived then, and still live today, across the frontier in Mongolia itself. Both the Buryats and the related Mongols were nomadic, and as well as following their pattern of seasonal migrations, they occasionally moved to new pastures altogether, usually under political stress. There were noteworthy shifts of population in the seventeenth and eighteenth centuries from Cis- to Transbaikalia, and, more importantly, from Mongolia into Buryatia.

The Buryats were not the only inhabitants of Transbaikalia. Around Nerchinsk, in the east, there was a sizeable population of Tungus, known as the 'Fifteen Fathers', people speaking a language related to the Manchu of the Chinese court. Their way of life resembled that of their Buryat neighbours, and those few of them who could read were literate in Mongolian, not in their own language, which had not been reduced to writing. Like the Buryats, they were shamanists, worshipping a multiplicity of good and evil spirits, and also, like the Buryats, they were to become the target of lamaist missionaries during the early years of the nineteenth century.

This seemingly stable and conservative form of society was to be gradually but fundamentally affected from the early seventeenth century onwards by the intrusion of a new and alien element, in the shape of Russian explorers, traders, settlers and exiles. The initial occupation of Transbaikalia took only a short time in the middle of the century. By 1654, the Russians had opened up the country as far east as the river Shilka, where they built the fortress of Nerchinsk, while the erection of other fortresses, such as that at Selenginsk, helped to consolidate their hold on the country. But, in contrast to the speed of the first wave of penetration, it was only slowly that Buryatia began to evolve in a new direction under pressure from the intruders. For example, until well into the nineteenth century the Buryats, generally speaking, though with some exceptions such as the growing force of Buryat Cossacks, retained their traditional tribal organization. Each tribe was headed by a member of the old hereditary nobility, who usually bore the title of taisha, or, like Nomtu and Badma, that of zaisang. The Khori, comprising eleven tribes, and the Selenginsk Buryats, consisting in the early nineteenth century of eighteen tribes, were each under the authority of a chief taisha. When Edward and Cornelius arrived in Siberia, the chief taisha's administration, such as it was, was centred in his office, or *kontora*, a word rendered by the missionaries as 'comptoir'. Speranskii recommended the transformation of these offices into what was to be termed a steppe-*duma*, or council. But whatever the nomenclature, the reality of power seems to have lain in the hands of the local Russian police.

Of the Buryat peoples of Transbaikalia, the most important were the Khori and Selenginsk Buryats. There were other tribes in the area, whom the missionaries occasionally encountered, but whom they never really tried to evangelize. Around the mouth of the Selenga, and much mixed with Russian settlers, lived the Kudarinsk Buryats; north of them lived the Barguzin; there were a few families who stuck obstinately to their old beliefs, living on the 'sacred' shamanist island of Ol'khon in Lake Baikal; and southwest of the lake dwelt the Zakamennyi Buryats, who were known also as the 'Seven Fathers'.

The Khori were one of the original Buryat tribes, tracing their existence back to an eponymous ancestor, Khoridai, one of the three legendary progenitors of the whole Buryat people. They had long since evolved into eleven sub-tribes. In early times, the Khori had nomadized on both sides of Lake Baikal, but by the beginning of the nineteenth century their pastures lay to the east of the lake. Dembil, and his successor, Jigjit, who held office till 1835, had their kontora near the Ona river, a tributary of the river Uda upsteam from Verkhneudinsk, not far from the present-day town of Khorinsk.

South of the pastures of the Khori lay those of the Selenginsk Buryats. These, as their territorial designation, contrasting with the ancestral name of the Khori, suggests, came into being as a recognizable entity much later, at roughly the same time as the Russian advance into Buryatia. They were a composite people, brought together mainly by the migration into Buryatia of tribes who originated across the frontier in Outer Mongolia, and who merged with the local Buryats, some of whom were themselves recent arrivals from west of Lake Baikal. The original inhabitants were generally referred to as the 'Six Tribes' while the immigrants from Mongolia were known as the 'Eight Fathers', though the total number of tribes soon grew beyond the fourteen that this would imply.

Immigration from Outer Mongolia was of far-reaching importance, not only for the ethnic formation of the Selenginsk Buryats, but for the social and religious development of the Buryats as a whole, since many of the newcomers were bearers of lamaism, and gave the first impetus which resulted in the conversion of the Transbaikalian Buryats in the eighteenth and nineteenth centuries. The process of immigration reached its peak of intensity around the turn of the seventeenth century. This century saw the emergence of two rival powers in east Asia. In China, the native Ming dynasty had long been in decline, and its collapse was accelerated by the rapid expansion of the Manchus, a Tungus people whose original home was to the north-east of metropolitan China. By conquest or alliance, the Manchus gained the support of several of those Inner Mongolian princes whose pastures bordered immediately upon China, and in 1636 they proclaimed their own dynasty, the Ch'ing. This was the beginning of the end for the independent khans of Outer Mongolia as well. The growth of a new dynamic force in China, enjoying the allegiance of most of the princes of Inner Mongolia, produced a power vacuum on the north side of the Gobi

Desert. The three reigning khans of Outer Mongolia managed to keep up a semblance of independence for a while, but they could not resist Manchu expansionism, and gradually fell into a tribute relationship with Peking.

Beyond Outer Mongolia, to the west and south-west, there was emerging another power which, for a century or so, was to challenge the Manchus for the control of Inner Asia. Galdan, a prince of the west Mongolian Oirats or Jungars, began, about 1670, to rebuild the Mongol empire, with its centre not in Mongolia proper, but in Jungaria. The enfeebled khans of Outer Mongolia offered an obvious field for intervention and expansion, and the last two decades of the seventeenth century were a period of political intrigue and war which came to a temporary halt only with the death of Galdan in 1696. Galdan's interference in the affairs of Outer Mongolia brought ruin to the Mongols there. Inter-tribal warfare, and invasion and occupation by both Oirats and Manchus, led to many groups of Mongols fleeing from their old homes into Russian territory, where they agreed to pay tribute and to become subjects of the Tsar in order to escape from unbearable conditions in Mongolia. It was this influx of refugees which formed, with the indigenous population, the basis of the new tribal group which was to be known as the Selenginsk Buryats.

With minor variations, Buryats of all tribes formed a homogeneous ethnic group, speaking mutually intelligible dialects, and all leading much the same sort of life. Most were nomadic pastoralists, herding horses, cattle and sheep, though there were exceptions. Some Buryats were farmers, while others, especially the Kudarintsy, were fishermen skilled at making their own equipment. Yet others had given up traditional pursuits, and had become Cossacks, guarding the Chinese border. Other changes occurred in the course of time. The Transbaikalian post-stations, for example, were manned by Buryat riders and drivers, while great numbers of Buryats became lamas. This meant, for some of them, spending their lives in the growing number of lamaseries, attending services, copying books, studying and practising astrology or medicine, and so on. Many, though, were lamas in name only, and continued to live and work at home, just as if they were laymen.

Some Buryats were, by the beginning of the nineteenth century, living in wooden huts, but the standard Buryat home was still the *ger*, or felt tent. It was in connection with the construction and furnishing of the tent that William, a century and a half before present-day anthropologists made the same observation, noticed how conservative the Buryats seemed to be by nature. All the tents were constructed in the same way, and from the same materials. The walls were made up of sections of wooden trellis-work, lashed together end to end so as to form a circle. To the peaks of the wall-laths were tied rafters, whose upper ends were slotted into the wooden wheel which formed the smoke hole of the tent. The wooden skeleton was then covered with pieces of felt. Access was through a low doorway, closed by a wooden door over which flaps of felt hung down outside.

The Buryats of Transbaikalia

The interior arrangement of the tents was uniform as well, and when, with social and religious change, new items were introduced into the tent, they found their appropriate place within the traditional layout, where they would for a while compete with what they were due to displace. In this century, the altar with its Buddha statues at the back of the tent has given place to a table with family and other photographs. In the early nineteenth century, the intrusion of lamaism into what had been a shamanist society initiated a similar process. In some tents, shamanist idols could be found hanging up alongside the lamaist altars. These were the tents of people who were only just then making up their minds to abjure the old faith and adopt the new, and who were still afraid of the power of the old idols, or *ongon*, to harm them, if they were too precipitately neglected. It was natural that people should take precautions, but what is more interesting is that the rear portion of the tent remained the most respected area, whether it was devoted to shamanist *ongons* or to Buddhist images.

The missionaries were the first Englishmen to study the Buryats closely and over a long period of time, but, like their accounts of their other experiences, their valuable observations have been overlooked by most later writers. The one exception seems to have been Alexander Michie, a Scot who set out from Shanghai in 1863, and drove and rode overland from Peking to St Petersburg. Michie made extensive use of the perceptive articles about the Buryats which William had published in the *Scottish Congregational Magazine* in 1841 and 1842, but his book, too, has long since gone out of circulation. Otherwise, William's articles, together with the missionaries' descriptions of shamanist ceremonies which they witnessed, and their reports on their visits to lamaseries and tents, seem to have gone quite unnoticed.

In his journal for 9 April 1827, for example, William described in detail a shamanist ceremony which reminded him of the biblical scape-goat rite. His account bears reprinting:

> This evening I learned that there were to be some Shaman rites performed at a tent about a mile from the house. After supper I went with my three young men to witness the ceremonies. They had not begun when we arrived. I was the more desirous to see this service, because, from what I had heard of it, I thought there was a remarkable resemblance in it to some of the ceremonies connected with the scape goat of the Mosaic economy. They call it the letting loose of the goat. Upon this occasion the animal provided was rather a kid than a goat. There were two Shamans, men, present, or as they are termed, *Boo*, and two female Shamans, or *Odagan*. A young man was sitting by the wall of the tent *dressing* the goat, that is, fastening little brass rings, corals, and other ornaments to its legs, neck, ears, etc. This occupied upwards of half an hour; two or three lighted lamps were placed on a table at the west side of the tent, before the sheep-skin images. Before

the table were placed the two Shaman sticks, called horses, being ornamented with the figure of a horses head on the top, and hung round with a number of iron rings and flat slips of the same metal, which make a tinkling noise when the stick is moved. A sword was stuck in the ground beside them. The use of these articles will be seen immediately. The younger of the two Shamans began the service by playing, for a few minutes, upon a Jew's harp, the instrument the Shamans use to invoke the objects of their worship, and, as they say, to bring their own minds into a fit state to hold intercourse with them. The harp was then handed across the tent to one of the Odagans, who began to play in the same strain. In the mean time the younger Shaman rose, laid aside his girdle, and hung a circular plate of brass round his neck. He then turned towards the table where the lamps were burning, and taking a taper in his hand, and, waving it with a slow continued motion over the table, began to mutter, in a low tone, a kind of prayer, or incantation. This was in the Mongolian language, but pronounced in so low a voice, and so indistinctly that I could not understand a single word. This lasted fifteen or twenty minutes, and then seizing the two sticks, one in each hand, holding also the sword in his left hand, with its point to the ground, he turned towards the fire in the middle of the tent, muttering all the while his invocations. A wooden cup was then given him, and a man stood by with a vessel containing some milk. The milk was poured, in small portions, into the cup and the Shaman threw the first part into the fire, then repeated portions out of the hole in the roof of the tent, towards the east, west, south and north. The Shaman then began to utter words in a louder tone, and to use more violent gesticulations. His whole frame became agitated, and after reeling about the tent for some time, he sat down in his place. The old Shaman, who was quite blind, and apparently very infirm, then rose, took the two sticks, (omitting the sword,) and began his prayers; at first his voice was low, and his motions gentle, but as he continued to strike the ground with his two rattling-sticks, he gradually became more active, began to make strange noises, hissing like a cat, and growling like an angry dog; his legs then began to tremble, his whole body shook violently, and at last he began to jump, with an agility and force which I did not think so feeble a man was capable of. This exercise lasted till he was quite exhausted, and he sunk down upon the floor.

  The other Shaman rose a second time, took his two sticks and sword. The people, who were crowded all round the tent, now drew back as far as possible, and the wooden posts, which partly support the roof of the tent, were removed, to allow more space for going round the fire. The man appeared now wrought up to a higher ecstasy; he walked, or rather staggered, round the fire, leaning on the two sticks, now and then jumping violently, and, to appearance, unconscious of the presence of any one.

The Buryats of Transbaikalia

In the midst of these feats, he threw off his boots, and began to rake out the burning cinders from the fire with his hands, and spread them by the side of the fire place. He took up a piece of live charcoal, and held it for some time in his hand, but, as I could perceive, in a way that could not burn him. Next he began to dance upon the glowing cinders with his naked feet, but neither did this seem very extraordinary, for the quickness of the motion soon scattered the ashes, so that he could not be burnt. The last part of the farce, for such I consider it to be, was his laying down the two sticks, and reeling about with the sword in hand, setting the point of it first against his side, then against his breast. He now staggered towards the door, and placing the hilt of the sword against the wall, with the point of it to his breast, leaned and pushed against it, as if he had been forcing it into his body; at last it seemed to go in, and he writhed and twisted his body, as if he had been really pierced through, and was making efforts to draw the weapon out; to assist him in this, he then went towards the young man, who had been all this while holding the goat, and the lad, taking hold of the handle of the sword, drew it with all his might; I observed, however, that the Shaman was holding it by the blade, and after various struggles and contortions, he let it slip through his fingers, and so it seemed to be extracted from his body with a jerk. All this was performed with his back towards the people present, and not one of them could see whether the sword entered his body or not, but I am persuaded the whole was a mere trick. And Gendung, my writer, did not scruple openly to say so before them all, and taking the sword, went through the whole ceremony of stabbing himself in the way of fun. This produced nothing but a smile from the spectators, and during the whole performances the people continued talking, laughing, and smoking their pipes with the greatest indifference. The old Shaman again rose, and went through his part, much in the same way as before, but not so violently; sometimes he suddenly stopped, and turning round his blind eyes, as if he wished to see something, mentioned a number of names, and inquired if such and such a one was well and happy. The other Shaman replied in a low voice, 'well.' Then were pronounced the names of the *dead friends*, and the old man pretended to see and converse with the spirits who had the charge of them in the invisible state. All these ceremonies were only preparatory to the letting loose of the goat, and now they began to talk of getting a horse provided for the 'fit man,' by whom the goat was to be sent away into the wilderness. Two other men were to go along with him, and the place to which the animal was to be taken was several versts distant, where there were no tents. On some occasions they told me the Shaman strikes the goat with a sword, but they never kill it, and after it is let loose they never inquire after it, nor is it ever more seen, as, no doubt, it soon becomes the prey of the wolves. I wished to wait till the whole was concluded, but I understood the Shamans were to repeat their tricks till day break, and not till then was the animal to be sent away. I therefore returned home with my companions, not a little struck with these singular ceremonies. I could not learn that these Shamans had any reference to the expiation of sin in this service, nor that their scape-goat was considered as bearing away their iniquities. Their view of it rather is, that this is an offering very acceptable to the *Ongoon*, or spirits they worship, renders them propitious, procures blessings upon their cattle, and all their undertakings; for all the Shaman services, as far as I can learn, have no higher design than the procuring of temporal good, or the averting of temporal evil; neither could these poor people give me any account of the origin, or source, whence they derived this ceremony. They trace their religion to no greater distance than the island Olchon, in the Baikal-lake, where, they believe, the objects of their worship have their most sacred and honoured residence.

There is another reason to regret the way the missionaries' ethnographic observations have been ignored. They had arrived in Transbaikalia at a most interesting stage in the spiritual development of the Buryats, and they were some of the very few informed eye-witnesses of the mass conversion to Buddhism which was then taking place among the adherents of shamanism. It is not that we do not have other records from which we can gain some impression of the methods used by Buddhist missionary lamas, and the impact which their campaigns had upon a population of another persuasion. The process has been described, as far as Mongolia proper is concerned, in chronicles and hagiographies, but of course in terms comprehensible primarily to Mongols, and from the point of view of the supporters of the victorious religion. The letters and journals of the three English missionaries give quite a different perspective on the situation, presenting it in a way easily intelligible to Western readers with a Christian background.

The conflict of religions was not a simple struggle for supremacy between the two 'heathen' faiths. It was complicated by the sporadic intervention of missionaries on the Orthodox church, while the English missionaries themselves provided a fourth, and more incongruous element, as they tried to interpose the tenets and ideals of English Congregationalism between shamanists and lamaists, and catch waverers from the former religion before they succumbed to the attractions of the latter. They were partisan, and made no bones about their prejudices. They did not pretend to be 'fair', but at the same time they were acute observers, and recorded what they saw and experienced as accurately as they could.

The missionaries were much better informed about the nature of the religions to which they were opposed, especially that of Buddhism, which had an infinitely more sophisticated theology than shamanism, than a casual

The Buryats of Transbaikalia

reading of their letters would suggest. At first sight they seem to have been interested only in the externals of lamaism, but they had actually gone quite deeply into its theoretical structure. Edward's library of Mongolian books, or part of it, is divided between the British Library and the Library of the BFBS, and can be examined, and the range of the missionaries' reading is hinted at here and there in their letters and journals. But when they presented the results of their studies to the public at home, they did so in anything but a neutral and academic manner. Their writings were so styled as to serve, deliberately, another purpose, that of shocking, and hence inspiring both themselves and their readers. That this was their intention can be deduced with some certainty from their correspondence.

The desire for self-mortification is apparent, for example, in a letter which Sarah wrote to her sister Ann in February 1820. Edward and William had gone to pay a visit to the Khamba at Goose Lake, and Sarah, who had not yet been inside a lamasery, decided to call on them. She had a dual intention. In her own words, 'I joined them for two days, in order to gratify my eyes and affect my heart. My desire was realized.' In other words, Sarah went to the lamasery partly out of curiosity, and partly determined to be shocked, so as to reinforce the disgust for lamaism which she already instinctively felt. And shocked she was.

This passage might be dismissed as a quirky device on the part of Sarah to enlist her sister's sympathy, if it were not that the attitude which she betrays in this letter seems to have been typical of the missionary group. One of the most revealing pieces of writing to be inspired by the experiences of the Buryat mission field is a long poem entitled *Idolatry* which William composed during the 1820s. It is not a good poem, either technically or in literary terms. William was handicapped by the verse form he chose, a nine-lined stanza containing eight decasyllables followed by a needless alexandrine. The rhyme scheme he chose intensified the feeling of uneasiness induced by the unbalanced stanza structure, for it divided the stanza into two interlocking quatrains, with the last line weakly echoing the shorter penultimate line.

William's poem was intended to have a didactic effect, and to act on the public conscience at a time when there was inadequate support for the LMS, in reinforcement of another, similar move he made a little earlier. In April 1824 he wrote to Alers Hankey;

> I am about to send to Scotland a few Mongolian Gods and other religious articles, which I have bought for the purpose. The friends to whom I send them are to employ these gods of the heathen in a new capacity. They are to be made collectors for the Missionary Society and so be made to serve in the cause which aims at their destruction.

One set of objects reached the Rev. Greville Ewing in Glasgow, and Ewing alluded to the gift in his preface to Swan's poem, which was published in 1827.

The Buryats of Transbaikalia

In the beginning of last year, Mr Swan sent me a picture of the Mongolian god, Shigemoni, surrounded by a group of inferior gods, painted by a Buriat lama. 'My intention,' he said, 'in sending home such things, is not merely to gratify curiosity, but, by the actual view of the objects of heathen worship, to excite in the minds of Christians greater abhorrence of idols, and tenderer and more operative compassion for the deluded worshippers.'

William developed this theme in a letter to Ewing which he sent with the manuscript of the poem:

The sheets herewith sent, may be considered as an accompaniment to the pictures of the gods formerly transmitted to you; and, as my intention in sending these, was not merely to gratify curiosity, but, by the actual exhibition of the objects of heathen worship, to excite in the minds of Christians a degree of abhorrence of the evils and absurdities of idolatry, and to rouse them to greater zeal in the cause of Christianity – so it is with the same view I presume to send you this production. . . . I have often thought, that, were it possible to bring the idolatrous practices – the low depravity – the gross ignorance – the unblushing sensuality of the heathen actually under the eye of Christians in general, a very different *degree* of impression would be the effect; and a very different measure of exertion from that which obtains at present, would become the standard of sincere and consistent attachment to the Christian cause. . . . I apprehend, too, that if Christians would take some pains to realize to themselves the scenes of heathen countries – characterized by all that is filthy, and blasphemous, and wretched – they might acquire a more adequate sense of their DUTY with regard to these their 'brethren.' I shall be glad if what I now send you shall have the effect to assist any one in acquiring a better knowledge of this part of Satan's usurpation – (I mean this country) – and impress a deeper conviction of the obligation, resting upon every Christian, to labour, according to his ability, to dispossess the enemy, and publish the news of freedom to his captives.

Here was a declaration of conviction and partisanship indeed, and William's poem lives up to the vehemence of its Preface. It occupies, or would occupy, if anyone remembered it, a unique position in English letters. Tirade though it is, it comes near to being a poetical treatise on shamanism and lamaism, and there is nothing to compare with it. To be fair, it casts its net wider, dealing with topics of missionary interest as diverse as Nestorian Christianity, the mission of St Francis Xavier, the foundation of the BFBS, the abolition of the slave trade, and the loss occasioned to Russia by the untimely death of the Emperor Alexander I. But it is the Buryat theme which concerns

The Buryats of Transbaikalia

us. It is possible that English readers of the poem may have found in it their first and perhaps only insight into the peculiarities of two religious themes which had hardly been touched upon in English up to the beginning of the nineteenth century. Between them, the poem, and the random notes attached to it, gave their readers a fairly comprehensive though totally one-sided and deliberately provocative picture of the externals, and some of the tenets, of Siberian shamanism, and the northern, Mongolian, form of Buddhism. But, let us repeat, its aim was not to instruct but to appal.

Idolatry is a phantasmagoria, thoroughly Gothick in its frightfulness, and it is difficult to believe that it was written by the same man who compiled the sober and informative articles in the *Scottish Congregational Magazine*. There are passages in it which can only be construed as a proleptic caricature of what William was to publish fifteen years later. Thus, in 1842, he published the following description of the appearance of Buryat women:

> Before marriage, the women wear their hair disposed in a number of plaits, hanging down behind, and at both sides of the head, strings of coral being suspended from the ends of some or all of these plaits, according to the wealth or taste of the wearer. After marriage, the hair is collected into two *ties*, one at each side of the head, and made to fall over the shoulder before. These ties are adorned with rows of coral beads. Silver ear-rings about two inches in diameter, form another item of their 'adorning.' The head is encircled with a fillet or tiara enriched with these favourite ornaments – red corals and other stones. They prefer the opaque to the transparent gems. White coral, malachite, lapis-lazuli, and such materials, are in great request among them.

In 1827 he saw the ladies in quite a different light:

> But lo! new cavalcades advancing, gain
> Yon swelling mound, tipt with the sun's first beam; –
> Sparkling they come abreast, and bit and rein,
> Saddle and crupper, dight with silver, gleam;
> Ten milk-white amblers prance, and proud they seem
> Of the bedizzen'd Buriat dames they bear.
> Eyeing the spectacle; ah! who would deem,
> That flaunting equipage, and ladyish air,
> Veil minds as barren as yon blasted sands are bare!
>
> By ornaments and looks that female group
> Aiming to fascinate the gazer's eye,
> Fancy may paint transform'd into a troop
> of trick'd out skeletons, who vainly try
> To hide their fleshless form, shrivell'd and dry; –
> The eyeless sockets show a brainless head; –
> They breathe – no – through their bones the breeze did sigh,

The Buryats of Transbaikalia

> Their clattering motion strikes the soul with dread:
> We see the mask of life, worn by the spectral dead!

Travelling one day in 1822 amongst the Khori, William chanced upon a tent where a shaman was performing an exorcism for a poor woman who was ill. His description of the ritual is a valuable record, and has fortunately been preserved in the pages of the *Quarterly Chronicle*:

> At length a groupe of tents, on the sheltered side of the hill, appeared in sight, and at a short distance beyond them two or three more. On approaching nearer, I perceived a number of people at the latter busily employed about something, and two great fires burning. I soon discovered that it was a company of Shamans engaged in their worship. I left my sledge at the tents on the hill, and walked down towards the poor idolaters. An old fierce-looking man was the chief actor in this scene of superstition. His dress was ornamented with a variety of long shreds of red cloth, and a large quantity of blue, green, and red feathers, formed into a sort of thong, hung down from his shoulders. He had in his hand a whip of the same materials, which he was incessantly smacking as he walked round and round a small circle, repeating all the while, in a loud voice, and with violent gesticulations, a prayer, or invocation. It was in the Mongolian language, but I could distinguish none of his words except *tengri* (heaven), which he frequently repeated. Beyond the circle which the old Shaman occupied, were two men, each holding a sheep, and a third man holding a goat. These animals were now to be offered in sacrifice. In a few minutes the old Shaman paused, and taking a pot, with something like butter in it, he forced a little into the mouth of the sheep and goat; another man did the same thing with some corn, and then threw the rest up into the air. The Shaman now made a sign, and the victims were immediately thrown upon their backs and killed. While this was going on, I entered into conversation with a man standing by, who informed me that a woman in the neighbouring tent was ill of a fever, and that this service was performed, and the sheep and goat sacrificed, for her restoration to health. Having left my fur shoob in the sledge, I found myself unable to remain any longer, from the excessive cold, and therefore telling them that I intended to spend the rest of the day at the adjoining tent, I walked back, expecting they would visit me when their business was over. They proceeded, after I left them to boil part of the flesh of the animals they had killed, but the skins were not taken off, and all the limbs were preserved entire. In this state the carcasses are suspended in the air by a long pole run through them, and firmly fixed in the ground. Being thus left, they soon become food for the ravenous birds, which in a very short time leave nothing but the bones. There are many more Shamans here, than

among the Selinginsk Buriats, and before almost every tent are the vestiges of such sacrifices, which have been offered either in the case of sickness, or to procure protection for their cattle and prosperity in their undertakings.

The same, or a similar, theme is treated in *Idolatry*, but here horror is piled upon horror, nature itself standing appalled at the grisly scene:

In yonder lowly hut, fast by the wood,
Where the white smoke, in curling volumes, slow
Ascends, lives a poor hunter and his brood
Of hardy children:– wherefore wail they so?
– Their mother to the grave is sinking low;
And now the wizard Shaman is at hand,
And neighbouring hunters gather to the show;
Amid the group the Shaman takes his stand,
And to prepare the feast, utters his loud command.

The goats are caught – the fire is lit – three knives
Unsheath'd and whetted, wait the expected sign,
To drink as many trembling victims' lives. –
'Tis done: and now upon a sapling pine
Suspended high the snow-white fleeces shine.
See next the wizard with his magic lash,
And iron cap, around which serpents twine;
His frantic arm inflicts the bloodless gash
Upon the demon air, and fierce his teeth do gnash.

To his Tengri again he howls a prayer,
Mingled with threatenings if they answer not;
The lynx and wolf are startled in their lair,
And the scar'd raven opes his croaking throat,
And wondering, perches near the noisy spot.
But now, his furious incantations o'er,
He sets him nearest the capacious pot,
Where boils the goat's flesh in its mantling gore,
And then the glutton feeds, and sweats at every pore!

William hoped that dramatic scenes like this would bring home to reluctant Christians in England the need to help the missionary cause more generously. As he put it:

– So be it! Yet, what if a Shaman crew
Should pitch their tent hard by your sacred wall,
And celebrate their rites full in your view? –
Could you, meanwhile, low at God's footstool fall,

> Beg HIM to save the captives from the thrall
> Of Satan, but yourselves make no essay
> To help them? – No – you'd weep – beseech, and call
> The heathen at your door; – but now you pray –
> 'From duty, Lord! – absolve; – Shamans are far away.'

Few of the external details of lamaist worship escaped William's notice, or his censure. He shows us the temple, in fact the great lamasery at Goose Lake ('the gorgeous pile on Gusine's ice-bound shore'), presided over by the Khamba Lama, and all prepared for the annual celebrations held in the White Month, or Tsagaan Sara, the first month of the lunar year. Buryats are riding in from all directions to take part. We watch them prostrate themselves before a 'haughty gelung' in his yellow robes, who sits twirling his coral rosary in his hand. The altars are piled high with offerings of food, and around them are the images which have been brought out of store to enjoy the annual feast. We pass the great prayer wheel in the porch, and come upon the rows of muttering lamas. Then we leave the temple, and go out into the open air, where we chance upon a *bunkhan*, a miniature temple pitched on a hillside, containing Buddha images and pictures, sacrificial vessels, and little figurines of clay and dough. Or we happen upon an *obo*, one of those pre-Buddhistic cairns, built of piled-up branches of trees, which dotted the Buryat countryside, and served as a shelter for the local spirits to reside in. Both *bunkhan* and *obo* were the venue for horse races and wrestling matches, marred alas, for William, by the drunken brawling which accompanied them:

> The horse-race now engages every eye –
> Then round the wrestlers forms the spacious ring;
> Meanwhile the noisy lamas ceaseless ply
> Th' intoxicating cup – some groan – some sing –
> Some quarrel – till the evening's sable wing
> Covers their shame – when sense and mind are gone.
> The youth, by their example profiting,
> Follow their steps; but wound and broken bone,
> That end the dark debauch, do not the sin atone.

Sarah witnessed this very scene, and wrote what is probably the first description in English of the *obo*-festivities. Its sight provoked in her some solemn, though predictable, reflections:

> On a hill, commanding an extensive view of the surrounding country, a sort of booth is formed of trees, called by the Buriats oboga, or obo, and in front a large circle of Lamas seated themselves upon their mats, leaving a space in front for the offerings to the gods. These consist of flesh, corn, etc. The head Lama, dressed in costly array, seated first in

the circle, began the service, giving signals by a little sceptre which he held in his hand, and by various motions of his fingers. These were observed by the others, who stood in the centre, scattering by a dextrous motion of the fingers, these different offerings; while the whole circle, consisting of about fifty other lamas, were reading prayers in the Thibetan language, – wholly unintelligible to the common people, and nearly so to the Lamas themselves. Around this group were seated all the spectators, the men taking the right, and the women the left side, – no one taking his seat till he has been in the circle to obtain a blessing from the chief Lama. Before the service closed, some water, esteemed holy, was handed round to the company, each one receiving a little in his hand, and drinking it. The last part of the ceremony was shooting with bows and arrows and a gun, into the air: and this was explained as expressive of the desire that all their enemies might be kept far from them. All now remounted their horses, descended the hill, and rode to the opposite side of the extensive plain below. There they again dismounted, seated themselves in ranks on the grass, and commenced their feasting, of which boiled mutton and araki form the principal materials. Horse-racing and wrestling closed the festival. We retired, to reflect on the hope which we entertain of being permitted to present them with higher sources of enjoyment, and to redouble our diligence for this end. While the worldly and irreligious would behold nothing in the practice, and even in the religion, of this people, to condemn, and would explain, that all was harmless; the Christian and the Missionary must lament the absence of God in all, and, as its necessary consequence, a debasing slavery, and every carnal lust.

Thus, the Christian missionaries condemned outright what the Buddhist missionaries had been content to annex and adapt.

In spite of its metrical and verbal infelicities and its bigotry, *Idolatry* is a remarkable achievement. Stripped of its fanaticism, it presents a lively and truthful picture of contemporary Buryat life, but, beyond that, it introduces us to the dynamic struggle for dominance which was taking place, in the 1820s, between the old shamanist faith and the new, vigorous, well-organized lamaism which was coming in from Mongolia and Tibet. The Russian authorities seem, on the whole, to have favoured the progress of lamaism, for reasons of political stability, though because of the presence of the Orthodox church in Siberia, with its Archbishop in Irkutsk, attitudes were sometimes ambiguous. On the one hand, Buryats were encouraged by the award of medals, and so on, to join the Orthodox church, while on the other hand lamas, and in particular the Khamba Lama, were also given medals in order to reinforce their loyalty to the Russian state in the person of the Emperor.

The English missionaries were very alert to what was taking place, and, appreciating the greater attractiveness of the gaudy Buddhist ceremonial compared with the shabby, often discredited mumbo-jumbo of the shamans, they viewed the new religion as the deadlier enemy. Both faiths were the work of Satan, but lamaism was doubly so:

> But though the Shaman neither book nor bead
> Employs, a letter'd though not better class –
> The Lamas – now oppose his mystic creed.
> *His* gods were sheep-skin; theirs cloth, wood, or brass,
> And as in figure, so in power surpass
> Their predecessors – and to them they bow,
> And sprinkle holy water, to amass
> A fund of merit, wherewith to endow
> Their souls! Say, Papist! who the mimic – they or thou?
>
> But I must hasten with the priceless boon,
> For Shigemoni's votaries prepare
> To attack the Ongoon mysteries, and soon
> They may obtain their purpose, for they spare
> Nor toil nor treasure – stratagem nor snare –
> To bow the necks of shamans to their yoke.
> And give them a more galling chain to wear,
> Than one which, though it awful terrors woke,
> Less varnish'd sin, and less hell's tyranny bespoke.

William ascribes the success of the lamas to their greater subtlety and duplicity, and to their greater skill in eliciting alms from the people, and in fact they seem to have been quite expert at swindling the credulous Buryats. J. C. Brown tells the following story, which he had heard from one of the missionaries:

> There have been visiting these parts lately, several lamas from Mongolia Proper, the country on the other side the boundary which separates this country from China. The people all considered them as a kind of living gods, and believed and told such things of them as would provoke a smile, even though involving something awful. They brought with them some shells, and they have made the people believe that one of these shells contains the virtue sufficient for their salvation, and that, if any one believe the sounds which pass through it from any lama's mouth, he will assuredly be saved. The poor people, anxious to get salvation on such easy terms, have given for one of these the sum of 3500 roubles, upwards of £160.

There is no denying that many lamas were mere mountebanks, but some had positive qualities, including a certain degree of medical skill, and William chose to ignore this redeeming feature. As with the Kalmucks, the Buryat shamans were nothing more than medicine-men, who claimed to be able to control the activities of the demons of disease. Many lamas, on the other hand, had studied Tibetan medicine. They knew how to feel the pulse and examine urine, and could prescribe herbal and other remedies, and some could perform acupuncture. Some of them kept detailed casebooks in which they recorded their experiences and observations. Even the missionaries could not ignore their ability as physicians. There was one dreadful occasion when Robert beat up a recalcitrant Buryat so badly that he needed medical attention, and sought it from the lamas, rather than from the missionaries, to the discredit of the latter. In the poem, though, any merits the lamas posessed as doctors could be, and were, conveniently ignored.

Shamanism is a specific term for a type of religion common among the peoples of northern Eurasia, including the Mongols, whose essential characteristic is a belief in good and bad spirits, which can be cajoled or controlled by a practitioner who possesses spirits himself, and can enter into an ecstatic trance in order to perform his functions. In a wider sense, the term 'shamanism' embraces the entire body of Mongolian folk religion, including beliefs and practices which do not necessarily require the participation of the shaman, and may be even more archaic than the institution of shamanism. Such practices were the worship of the fire as a domestic deity and guarantor of good fortune, the worship of the so-called White Old Man, or Tsagaan ebügen, the owner and protector of domestic animals, the worship of Manakhan Tengri, the owner of the beasts of the chase, and so on. However the term is applied, shamanism was in decline by the beginning of the nineteenth century, though it was by no means dead. Nor was there a clear conflict between Buddhism as a religion of the aristocracy and shamanism as a folk cult, though this was the way things were tending to go. For example, the progress of lamaism amongst the Khori Buryats was even frustrated for a while by the opposition of the mother of one of the taishas, who was a well-known shamaness.

The lamas did their utmost to discredit the shamans and to extirpate or at least neutralize the old religion. Following the pattern of events in Mongolia, they adopted as their own, and monopolized, certain shamanist rituals such as the ceremonies performed at the obos, which were too popular to eradicate. But there was a rougher way, too. Again following a familiar routine, the lama missionaries would make violent assaults on the shamans, breaking into their tents and destroying their costumes and their essential equipment such as their drums and drumsticks, and burning down their obos. Thus one reason for the rapid strides which lamaism made amongst the Buryats in the early nineteenth century was the vigour with which the lama missionaries promoted it. But, apart from that, it enjoyed an inherent advantage over Christianity, the other alternative to shamanism. The Buryats were the last of the Mongolian peoples to come under the influence of Buddhism, which was familiar to them as the prestigious faith of their cousins in Mongolia itself, whence radiated the fabulous charisma of the Jebtsundamba Khutuktu. To accept it brought them closer to that mysterious source of spiritual welfare, and, besides, it meant no change of 'nationality'. To the ordinary Buryat, conversion to the Orthodox church was the same as becoming a Russian, while the adoption of the English religion looked like an even more uncertain step into the unknown.

There is a report of Russians having come across a lama in the retinue of a Mongolian prince near the site of the future town of Selenginsk as early as 1652, but the systematic expansion of lamaism amongst the Buryats did not begin till rather later, around the turn of the century. The 'Six Tribes' were not originally lamaist, but the Mongols who were to form the 'Eight Fathers' mostly were, and they, and groups of migrant lamas, began to push into Russian territory, using the easy route of the Selenga valley. One of the most notable incursions was that of a band of 150 lamas who appeared in 1720. Fifty of them were Tibetans, fleeing from the turbulent Jungars, and the other hundred were Mongols, whom they had teamed up with on the way. The arrival of this band was reported to the Emperor, Peter the Great, and they were allowed to stay under Russian jurisdiction, on the grounds that their presence would be beneficial to the Buryats.

As early as 1701 a lama named Sangjai, who was an immigrant from Outer Mongolia, had set up a tent-temple on the banks of the river Khimni or Temnik, a tributary of the Selenga which joined it from the west a little south of Goose Lake. With his death, which occurred before 1740, this lamasery began to decline in importance, but it was re-established by another lama, one Jimba, a future Khamba, who had returned to Buryatia after studying in Urga. Jimba applied for, and received, imperial approval of his missionary activities. As a Buryat chronicle expresses it: 'At the time when our Khalkha Mongolian predecessors first came under the authority of the truly famous White Khan and Hero of Russia, acknowledging his great power, he greatly favoured us and, patronizing our religion, confirmed it as the second religion.'

At the same time, Jimba appears to have had an ecclesiastical rival, who also enjoyed imperial patronage, in the celebrated lama Dambadarjaa Caya-yin, who ultimately became the first Khamba. Caya-yin was born in 1711, and legend tells how at the age of fourteen he and two other Buryat lamas set out for Urga, intending to study there. Unfavourable omens, such as the fall of a thunderbolt at Urga, decided the Khutuktu there not to admit them, and they went on, one to the lamasery of the Setsen Khan of Khalkha, one to Amdo in Tibet, and Caya-yin to Lhasa itself. Here he studied under both the Panchen and Dalai Lamas, and then, in the 1740s, he returned to Buryatia, bringing with him religious books and images. He found that a tent-temple had been established among the Tsongol and Tabungut tribes by a lama named Pun-tsogs Noyan. Caya-yin defeated the latter in a theological disputation, and was immediately recognized and revered as a 'Lord of the Faith'.

In 1744 Caya-yin and the astrologer Batur-un, who had studied in Tibet also, performed some divination in order to select a site for a lamasery amongst the Tsongol, and they built a little temple which they later replaced by a much more elaborate lamasery, built in the Tibetan style. Then Jimba and some of his fellow-lamas from near Goose Lake asked the astrologer to carry out similar divination and select a site for a lamasery for them. He did so, and picked a site close to Goose Lake, in spite of warnings from Caya-yin that, by doing so, he was fostering a future rival to their own lamasery.

So much for legend. In 1764 the title of 'Bandido Khambo Lama' was devised, and conferred by the Empress upon Caya-yin. He died in 1777. For three years the Khamba's throne was occupied by another Tsongol lama, and then the appointment passed to Jimba, who held it until 1796. With this, the seat of the Khamba Lama was finally transferred from Tsongol to Goose Lake.

Thus, to begin with, the Goose Lake lamasery was by no means the most imposing foundation amongst the Buryats, and Pallas, surveying the state of lamaism in Transbaikalia in 1772, found it rather inferior to the Tsongol lamasery, which lay to the south-east of Selenginsk, on the right bank of the Chikoi river. But with the transfer of the office of Khamba to Goose Lake, the lamasery there grew rapidly in size and importance, and an excursion to inspect it was an almost obligatory part of the itinerary of every nineteenth century traveller, from Martos in 1823 and Erman in 1828, to Kennan in 1885. In the early part of the century, when Tibet and Mongolia were both more or less inaccessible to outsiders, Goose Lake was an exotic tourist attraction, affording a unique opportunity to inspect a lamasery and attend its services, and few of those who were privileged to see it failed to comment on its peculiarities, its Sino-Tibetan style of architecture, its noisy lama orchestra, its altars crowded with images and sacred vessels, its incense burners, and, most picturesque of all, the curious carriage on which the image of the Buddha Maitreya was paraded around the lamasery once a year, as it was also in lamaseries in Mongolia itself. When Kennan visited Goose Lake, the cart was apparently 'pulled', to judge by his sketch, by a model elephant. But when Martos and Erman were there, it was drawn by a brand-new, life-sized wooden horse, painted green, and flanked by six other horses of diminishing size. This team of seven was harnessed just as a Russian team would have been, and from the yoke of the central horse there hung a bell, reminiscent of the bell used by imperial Russian post couriers. Martos seems to have been under the impression that the horse was as important as Maitreya himself, rather than simply a draught animal for the carriage, for he tells us that the festival of the White Month, that is, the festival of the New Year, was celebrated in honour of the 'idol of Maitreya and of the Green Horse'.

The Russian Mongolist Pozdneev, writing up in 1887 his field researches carried out ten years earlier, traces the Maitreya festival back at least as far as AD 1409, when it was performed by the Tibetan Buddhist reformer Tsong-kha-pa. But he also recorded, with some reservations, the belief held by many lamas that the justification for holding the festival lay in a certain passage of the Buddhist scriptures, in the Vinaya section, thus giving it a far longer and more respectable ancestry. William, on the other hand, chose to link the circumambulations performed during the Maitreya festival with the cult of Juggernaut, and warned his Buryat hearers to beware of the latent dangers of what he understood as an innovation at Goose Lake, rather than a copy of what was done at all the wealthier lamaseries of Mongolia. He wrote in his Journal:

> April 22, Sabbath (1827). The Taisha called this morning and spent several hours with me. Read together several chapters of the Gospels of Mark and Luke, making observations as we read. His attention was then engaged by two of the Missionary Sketches lying on the table, viz. the Temple of Juggernaut, and the figure of the Indian goddess Doorga. I related to him some of the ceremonies performed in the worship of the former, pointing out, as represented in the Sketch, how the deluded victims placed themselves before the moving temple, that they might suffer death under its sacred, or, to speak more properly, its accursed wheels. I took the opportunity of making a remark, which seemed to touch him a little. 'India is the source whence your Lama superstition has proceeded. It has but recently reached these parts, and is but beginning to exercise its influence over the people, and many of them have as yet imbibed but little zeal in its ceremonies. But in the course of time it may increase, take a deeper hold of the minds of the people, and then its true character will be more manifest. The Buriats may become as infatuated as the Hindoos, and offer their lives in sacrifice to the idols of their vain worship. It is but two years since the Chamba Lama had a car made somewhat resembling that of Juggernaut, and the figures of seven horses, painted green, and harnessed to the car, complete the work of folly. The whole machine, horses and all, the Lamas drag round the Chamba's temple, once or twice a year, and for the present the people only gaze and wonder at this "new thing;" but perhaps the next generation will be more given to this idolatry, and think it a work of merit to throw themselves under the wheels of *Maidar's* car! Now you should think in time, whither this superstition may lead you and your children. By your encouraging it, or opposing and renouncing it, you may either be the means of setting future generations free from the delusion, or may entail the bondage of sin and death upon them to an extent you can never calculate.'

10

The Missionaries Separate

At first, the two missionary families had intended to live together when they reached Irkutsk. They hoped to find a house large enough for them to have a couple of rooms each, with another for common use as a dining room. Edward had been quite sure that they could all live together in harmony, but the few months' experience of sharing accommodation and housekeeping in the capital proved to them all that he was too sanguine, and almost as soon as they reached Irkutsk the two families separated. For the first few days they lodged together in rooms which the Governor had found for them, and where they were boarded for the modest sum of two and half roubles, or just over two shillings, each, per day. Then the Rahmns moved into Hedenström's house, which the Governor arranged for them to occupy, rent-free, at least until Betty had had her baby and recovered her health. Edward and Sarah soon found a house for themselves, some distance, as it happened, from where the Rahmns were living. Like most of the houses in Irkutsk, it was built of wood, and was only one storey high, but it had enough rooms for them to feel comfortable in, good cellars, and several outhouses. Here they stayed for the next sixteen months, before moving to Selenginsk, and here their first child, Thomas Edward, was born, on 6 August 1818, 'after a lingering season of sorrow'.

The move to Selenginsk took place at the beginning of July 1819. Edward heeded advice he was given, and took everything they owned with them, furniture included, for the loss in selling it in Irkutsk and buying new at their destination would have greatly exceeded the cost of packing and transport. The plan was to go by land to Lake Baikal, and then cross the lake by ship, and Edward thought that this would take no longer than a week. But, yielding once more to local advice, he finally decided to accompany the freight by road around the southern tip of the lake, and the tedious journey, which nowadays takes less than twenty-four hours by rail, occupied eleven or twelve days. The whole move, with the expenses of settling into their new, but still temporary, home, cost the Missionary Society an extra 1,500 roubles, or about £75, half of Edward's notional annual salary at the time.

The Missionaries Separate

Edward found a town house which he managed to rent for 25 roubles a month. Its owner had died some time before, and for nearly a year the local authorities had been thinking of taking it over for use as a post-house, but had still reached no decision. Tired of waiting, the executors offered it to Edward for 5,000 roubles, or about £250, and he would have snapped it up at once, without waiting for the Society's approval, but for his scruples about the government's prior claim. The house was nearly new, and apart from its living accommodation it had two kitchens, two ice-houses, and a number of outbuildings. Edward reckoned that it would cost at least twice as much to build a similar house, but he felt it prudent to reject the offer. This was in early September 1819. Anticipating the arrival of his future companions, he now began to look around for anywhere where he could put them up, and he was offered one house, a small building which he thought he could get for not much more than 1,000 roubles, or £50.

While house-hunting, Edward had an amusing interview with the Khamba at Goose Lake, the first of many fencing matches between the missionaries and the suspicious head of the church which they were intending to subvert. Edward had already met him once, during the course of his exploratory visit to Transbaikalia with Cornelius, and in July 1819 he called on him again, and gave him some tracts, which he asked him to distribute to the other lamas. Asked what he thought of the tracts, the Khamba said they were very good, – impressed, as other Buryats were as well, by the fact that they had been translated by Badma, himself a Buryat. But he then went on to interrogate Edward about his intentions in coming to Buryatia:

> He wished to know how long I intended to live there; I told him, probably my whole life. He asked what we wished to do? I told him we wished to circulate the gospel among his people – that I thought their religion was a dangerous one – that their gods could afford no help – that there was only one God who was almighty – and the gospel was the only safe religion upon which any man could rest. I told him I wished to live where he was if I could get a house. He said there was no good house. I said a bad one will do – There are no peaches [Russian *pech'*, or stove] in them: We will build a peach – There are no bricks – We will bring bricks from Selinginsk, if you will either give, let or sell us a house. He then said there was not a house at all to spare. It was evident he did not wish to have us as neighbours.

By early November, when Peter Gordon dropped in on his way from Okhotsk, the situation as regards housing had completely changed. Edward had found a suitable site for the mission station, and had begun to build. How he came to pick on this particular plot we do not know, though in his Memoir of the life of Sarah he hints that he and Cornelius had spotted it when they visited Selenginsk, and had more or less decided upon it then. It occupied a pleasant position on the left bank of the Selenga, opposite the gap between two islands, and under a high cliff, to which local legend has, in the meantime, given the name *Anglichanka*, or 'The Englishwoman'. This name recalls the supposed suicide of one of the ladies of the mission, who is popularly said to have ended her life by leaping from it into the river. Of the five women who took part in the mission, Betty Rahmn, Sarah and Charlotte Stallybrass, Martha Yuille and Hannah Swan, only Sarah and Martha ever lived at Selenginsk. Sarah moved away to Khodon with her husband five years before her death, leaving Martha, who died of typhus at the mission house in 1827, as the only possible heroine of this unlikely tale.

Once he had failed to find suitable accommodation for himself and his companions in the town, Edward acted quickly. Between the time of his letter to Alers Hankey of 8/20 September, in which he talked of buying the £50 house, and his next letter of 18/30 November, he had found the site and obtained an advance of 4,000 roubles from the new Governor General, Mikhail Speranskii – a loan repayable in St Petersburg through Asmus Simonsen – and the first stage of the building was far enough advanced for him and Sarah to contemplate moving in before the end of November. At this time, the house was only one storey high, and Edward planned to put on a second floor for the new arrivals. But the experience of the savage gales which swept the Selenga valley in spring-time, and which surpassed anything which he had thought possible, convinced him that the locals were right not to build higher than one storey, and it was decided that the best plan would be to let the Yuilles build a second house for themselves.

S. S. Hill, who visited Selenginsk in 1847, was enchanted with the siting of the mission house:

> The spot which these two families had chosen, or which had been appointed for their dwelling, is one of the most romantic in this part of Siberia. The river as we approached the site upon which the two houses stand, in turning to the left, seemed to terminate in a basin. The houses are situated upon the opposite bank of the river to that upon which the town of Selenginsk is seated; and they stand upon the edge of a narrow inclined plain, sinking from the abrupt base of steep and rugged hills, and immediately in front of a bold range of other hills, which rise upon the opposite side of the stream, and present more vegetation than the greater part of the hilly portion of the banks of the Selenga.

Most other nineteenth century visitors were equally charmed by the nostalgic appearance of the mission station. Erman wrote in 1829 of the 'remarkably picturesque and pleasing appearance' of the houses, while nearly sixty years later, in 1884, the Finnish Baron Henrik Wrede, then sub-agent of the BFBS at Irkutsk, was 'astonished at a truly European cosy little farmhouse between two sandstone heights'.

Only the supercilious Cochrane found something to carp at. Edward had deliberately sited the station outside the town, and across the river, so

The Missionaries Separate

Gordon tells us, in order to make it easier for the local Buryats to call on them, and also to minimize social contact with the Russians, which might be misinterpreted as illicit attempts to exert influence over them. Cochrane could not help admiring the appearance of the station, which he found to consist of 'two neat and homely dwellings'. But, mistaking Edward's farsighted prudence in settling outside the Russian community for self-interest, he found much to blame in the choice of site. 'The situation itself', he wrote, 'is in an inappropriate, although a romantic and secluded spot, and as it stands upon the opposite bank of the river to that of the city, the communication is difficult, dangerous, and expensive, but it is now too late to change it.' To make matters worse, he accused the missionaries of knowing that they had settled in what he termed the 'very worst field', but of being too self-indulgent to give it up and find somewhere better suited to their mission, though perhaps less agreeable. It is true that Selenginsk was not an ideal site for the mission headquarters, but the deficiencies of the town itself were graver than those of the country site of the mission. So far from being what Robert called the 'Place of Lamas', it was an entirely Russian town – not even the city, as Cochrane miscalled it – with only four or five destitute Buryat families living there as hangers-on of the Russians. Cochrane was prejudiced, and his strictures were a wholly unjustified slur on the professional honour of devoted men and women who had already made a considerable sacrifice of comfort in exiling themselves to Siberia. Moreover, though Cochrane himself would not live to see it, Edward and William were quite prepared to give up their sheltered life near Selenginsk, and find new homes amongst the Khori Buryats, when the best interests of the mission demanded that they move.

But Cochrane was out of humour with the idea of the mission to the Buryats altogether, and though he claimed to respect the missionaries as individuals, he showed no compunction in harming their reputations at home as a group. His gratuitous sneers at them, after enjoying their hospitality, gave great offence, and Edward was moved to refute his criticisms posthumously in his Memoir of Sarah. 'The author is gone', he wrote, 'to give in his account before a higher than any human tribunal: but his book survives; and for its sake I observe, that there is scarcely a sentence, respecting the Mission, but what abounds with either error or misinterpretation.' An indignant Richard Knill put Cochrane in his place even more firmly, though less publicly, when he wrote to John Arundel, the Home Secretary of the Missionary Society, to opine that 'perhaps it would be just as easy to convert a Mongolian as to convert Capt. C.'.

Today, there is almost nothing left to mark where the mission once lay. Originally, Martha Yuille's monument and the gravestones of her three children had been surrounded by a brick wall, and in the 1860s her son Samuel Yuille visited Selenginsk, travelling from China, and erected another wall around the little cemetery to protect it from the flooding waters of the

The Missionaries Separate

Selenga. A Russian book published in Irkutsk in 1829 remarks that at that time the inscriptions on all four monuments were still to be seen, but nowadays it seems that it is only the stout, white-painted brick obelisk which Robert erected to the memory of his wife which has continued to defy the years. This monument resembles many, including those to the Decembrists N. A. Bestuzhev and K. P. Torson who, from 1839, happened to be near neighbours of Robert's, which have been put up in Transbaikalia since those days. It consists of a tall truncated pyramid resting on two cubes. In the upper, and smaller, of these cubes, Robert set a metal plate with a memorial inscription in Latin. This inscription was published in a Russian magazine article by G. S. Rybakov in 1905, and was read again, with only a few minor differences, and copied, by a correspondent of the author's in 1977. Martha's memorial, forgotten by her fellow-countrymen for over 150 years, should be rescued from oblivion, and Robert's inscription is given here in the later transcription. It runs:

> Memoriae
> Marthae Cowie
> Fidelis Uxor
> Roberti Yuille
> et Fidelis Socia
> Londonensis Missionare Societis
> Nata in Scotia in urbe Glasguae
> Abit in Sibiriam
> ad urbem Selenginska
> in Anno Domino MDCCC XXVII
> Memoria justi est Benedicta
> Beati mortui qui in Domine moriuntur*

The cemetery itself became a place of mystery and legend. A local Buryat recalled, for example, how Samuel Yuille opened up the metal plate with the inscription, which was, he said, hung on hinges, when he visited the site, and behind the plate there could be seen the remains of Martha in a sitting position. Martha rested unquietly, and her ghost could sometimes be seen at night, wandering around her monument.

When William Swan and the Yuilles arrived at Selenginsk in February 1820, they would have found a small one-storey log house in the middle of a building site. We know something of its plan from one of William's letters. While he was in St Petersburg, he had lodged with the Patersons, and had become a favourite of their whole circle, but he had forged a particularly close relationship with Jean Paterson, which bears signs of having been a repressed infatuation. Not that there was anything overtly improper in it,

---

* Rybakov uses fewer capital initials; he prints lines 8 and 9 together as one line, and writes: societ.; Clascuae; Abiit; Selenginsca; domini; domino.

but its nature can be guessed at from the way in which William appears to have transferred his expressions of affection from Jean, whom he called his sister, to her baby daughter, whom he playfully referred to as his wife, and to whom he would send the kisses which he could not, and most certainly would not, have bestowed on her mother. Paterson was aware of this sublimated intimacy, and of the restrained flirtatiousness which passed between William and Jean, but he did not disapprove of it, or hide his knowledge, and it must have been a quite innocent relationship. So, in November 1818, he had written to Alers Hankey: 'We are quite delighted with Mr Swan here. He is an inmate with us and Mrs Paterson is constantly teasing him about staying in Petersburg. I dare not in conscience support her as I fear spoiling an excellent Missionary.' And when Jean fell ill, as a result of her assiduous prison-visiting, and died in 1820, Paterson hardly dared to write and break the news to William. 'The very thought of writing to him quite incapacitates me for putting pen to paper. They were much attached to each other, and I almost feel as much for him as for myself. He has a most feeling heart and I often fear that the mournful intelligence would be too much for him.' William was indeed deeply distressed, and gave vent to his feelings in a revealing sonnet:

> There is a tomb to which my fancy strays
> It rudely snatched from my embrace a form
> Once lovely and belov'd which now decays
> As sunbeams fade before the thickening storm.
> There is a heaven to which my hopes aspire
> There – mid the glorious spirits of the blest
> Is a bright spirit – cloth'd in white attire
> Wiped are its tears – and endless is its rest.
>
> There is an empty tomb my faith beholds
> Where once an uncorrupting body lay.
> That body death no more a prisoner holds
> It mingled not with earths polluted clay.
> Soon, like the *tomb of Christ*, earth's tombs shall empty be
> Then I, my sister, God and Christ and heaven shall see.

But he got over Jean's death, and came to contemplate it objectively enough to be able to compose a book-length Memoir of her.

What is important about this friendship for us is that, before leaving St Petersburg, William had arranged that he and Jean should write to each other. Paterson kept the few letters which his wife received, and today they form part of the Paterson Papers belonging to the BFBS. In this correspondence, William allowed himself a respectful informality quite different from the impersonally correct tone of his letters to his superiors. Once or twice he seems to have verged in them on a declaration of love:

The Missionaries Separate

I have more than once experienced that absence has both strengthened and refined my affection for christian friends, and never more than since I left you – and as we can now no longer see one anothers face in the flesh, and sit and walk and converse together, let us look more to Jesus – be diligent in his work – abide in him to the end and we shall walk with him in white! Courage! my sister – The Lord shall strengthen your heart – and I trust he will strengthen mine also – Perhaps he may make you the instrument if you write to me as a faithful monitor, and an affectionate christian friend.

Jean's early death deprived William of a friend, but it also deprived later readers of what promised to be a lively personal chronicle of life in Siberia. William wrote to Jean in February 1820, just two days after his arrival at Selenginsk, and included in his letter a roughly sketched ground plan of the still unfinished mission house. It formed a rectangle, with a kitchen tacked on to one end of the west front. The house was divided across the middle by a passage-way, on one side of which was a large common-room, and Edward's study. On the other side of the passage were three rooms, one for each family, and a small lobby. The east front faced directly on to the Selenga, offering a fine view of the town of Selenginsk, a little over a mile away, while William's own room, at the south-west corner of the house, looked along the range of hills which formed the background to the mission site. By 1823, when Martos called on the missionaries, the building operations had come to an end, and the engraving in his book of what he called the 'Colony of the Englishmen opposite Selenginsk' shows a range of buildings with quite an imposing façade. The two houses, one rather larger than the other, with their pitched roofs and dormer windows, their outhouses and their garden fence, are set cosily along the low bank of the Selenga, sheltered at the rear by bare-looking hills, and overshadowed by what may be the Anglichanka, and looking out across the tip of one of the islands which divided the river at this point.

Edward knew all along that the Emperor was willing to make a grant of land to the mission whenever it was needed, so that he could build free of doubt as to his ultimate right to the site. In the capital, the Society's business affairs were, from the end of 1820 onwards, in the hands of its new agent, the Rev. Richard Knill. Knill was very aware of the importance of patronage in an autocracy. 'To have an interest in the prayers and countenance and support of His Imperial Majesty and His Minister The Prince Galitzin and the good General Papof is not a trifle for a Missionary, nor will it be thought of small importance by the Directors of a Missionary Society when they consider how completely the Missionaries and their exertions (humanly speaking) are under the influence of the Powers that be' was the way he put it to George Burder, and through his 'kind and steady friend' Popov, the Secretary of RBS, he kept the Emperor and Golitsyn informed about the work of the Society and of other charitable organizations with which he was connected. In July 1821 he dropped a hint that the Society could do with some financial help towards its work in Russia, writing to Popov as follows:

> Stallybrass and Swan and Yuille have been much occupied in preparing a house to screen them and their families from the piercing cold of winter and although they have made it very plain, yet the materials and building have cost a good deal of money, which falls exceedingly heavy on the funds of the Society. As this is all done in hope to promote the eternal felicity of the subjects of this Empire, do you not think that His Imperial Majesty would graciously condescend to assist them in defraying these heavy expenses if He knew the circumstances. I think that the benevolent heart of the Emperor would feel a pleasure in ordering something for them.

In February 1822, Popov asked Knill to specify in more detail what he had meant by this begging letter, and Knill sent him his accounts, which showed that the mission settlement at Selenginsk had cost 7,000 roubles to erect. In the following April he was able to report to Alers Hankey that Alexander had made several donations to good causes in which he, Knill, was interested, one of which was of 7,000 roubles, payable in two annual instalments, which was intended to cover these building costs. A deed of gift was drawn up in Russian and English, and signed by Prince Golitsyn, specifying the amount of the gift, and also confirming the conditions under which the grant of land was made to the missionaries. The English text of the deed, which was in the form of a letter to Knill, ran as follows:

> According to the request of the Members of the London Missionary Society, the Rev. Messrs Stalybrass [sic], Swan and Yuille, the ground they have chosen for their station near Selenginsk, and where they have already built their dwelling house, in all 72 desiatines, has been graciously insured by His Imperial Majesty in the possession of these Missionaries upon the same principles, as land is accorded to the Members of the Scottish Missionary Society in the Government of Caucase.
> These principles consists [sic] in the following articles:
> 1. The land, accorded to them, must under no pretence pass from the Missionaries in other hands, not by selling, nor by mortgaging it, as they have no right to dispose of it for objects stranger to their views.
> 2. After the term of thirty years, since this land has been put in their possession, the Missionaries shall pay to the Government 15 Copeks yearly for every dessiatine of it, proper to be cultivated, and fulfil the services required from all possessors of grounds by the police.
> But they will be free from every other payment or charges, from military and civil services, as also from the obligation to give lodgings in their houses to the soldiers.

The Missionaries Separate

The Governor-General of Siberia has received the order of His Imperial Majesty, to make necessary dispositions, that the ground above mentioned may be delivered in lawful form into the possession of Missionaries of the London Missionary Society and to those, who after them will arrive there with full powers of that Society and the approbation of the Minister of ecclesiastical affairs and public instruction.

This Statement I pray you, Reverend Sir, to communicate to your friends, Messrs Stalybrass, Swan and Yuille, for their proper knowledge of it.

Besides this, I have not failed to lay before the Emperor, my August Sovereign, Your both letters of 17 July 1821 and of 21 February 1822 where the desire was expressed, that the whole or the part of the sum of 7000 Rubles expended for the buildings, the Missionaries have been in the necessity to erect on the same ground, now granted to them, may be defrayed, in order to give by it some assistance to the funds of the Society. His Majesty has been pleased therefore to comply also with this desire, in taking the whole of the said expense for buildings on His own account, one half of which is presently paid, and the other will be delivered in the next year.

In consequence of it, Three thousands and five hundred Rubles follow herewith, which sum you will forward to these your friends at Selenginsk, making them part of this favour of my Imperial Master.

May our Lord and Saviour give His blessing to all what is done on earth for the glory of His holy Name and for the salvation of mankind! May soon all the nations know Him, as the redeemer of their souls, and His kingdom come to realize the expectations of all who love Him!

    I remain with true esteem
      Revd Sir
        Your obedient servant
        Prince Alexander Galitzin.
No. 124 St. Petersburg April 19 1822.

A few years later, in 1825, the mission site was properly surveyed by Titular Councillor Stephen Bulatov, the District Landmeasurer, as the missionaries termed him, of Selenginsk, and a scale plan in colour was drawn, showing the position of the settlement relative to the Selenga and the high road from Irkutsk to Kyakhta, between the two of which it lay. The appended description of the site, witnessed by William and several local residents, both Russian and Buryat, shows that it comprised altogether over forty-five desyatins, from which had to be subtracted about three desyatins which were taken up by half the width of the road, deemed to be attached to the property. Taking one desyatin as equalling 2.7 acres, this means that the missionaries had been given a total of something over 121 acres of land. Over half this area was classified as pasture land; some 16 acres were stony, and described as useless; and a few acres were liable to flooding. Of the rest, there were over five acres of meadow land, a similar amount of shrubbery, and a fair amount of hilly ground. Altogether, it was a munificent gift to make to a group of foreign missionaries, though the real value of the grant was the tangible evidence it afforded of the Emperor's personal approval of the missionaries' presence in the field. At a more practical level, it allowed them generous space for the gardens they laid out, and for pasture and hay-fields for their horses, cows and sheep.

The missionaries begrudged the amount of time and energy they had to devote to supervising the building operations, but they tried to turn it to good account by talking to the labourers, partly in order to improve their own oral fluency, partly in order to put over some elementary notions of Christianity. Most of the work of site-supervision devolved, after his arrival, upon Robert, who, with his factory experience, was probably the most practical of the three men. Robert managed his small work-force with rather a heavy hand, and his strictness foreshadows the insensitivity, not to say brutality, with which he came, later, to treat those over whom he had authority. He considered himself entitled, and indeed duty-bound, not only supervise their work, but also to check and correct every aspect of their behaviour, however natural this was to the Buryat mind, if it conflicted with his own rigid interpretation of Christian morality. It is worth quoting at length from a letter he wrote in February 1823, in which he describes how he exercised this self-assumed authority:

I have to lament, now, and perhaps may yet lament for several years to come, that I should have been called to spend so much of my precious time on entering a heathen land as a housebuilder etc; yet in many respects these labours, I trust were not in vain, nor unprofitable; for while engaged in this, and the temporal things connected with it, the best of opportunities was afforded for becoming acquainted with the peculiarities of the Buriatee Character, which I closely observed, and also of detecting, and reproving many of the vices to which these people are prone. I always reproved on the principle that God sees and hates all evil – When I detected any of the workmen in crimes or when they were brought to my knowledge by information I usually endeavoured to bring them to a confession of their guilt, promising them that no more notice should be taken of it; provided they satisfied the offended party, and came under a promise not to transgress in future; and at the same time, endeavoured to impress on their mind, that they not only injured their fellow men, and hurt their own character, but lived as a continuous offence in the sight of God. This generally had a good effect, and afterwards I had no reason to call them in question. But on the other hand, when obstinacy, high mindedness, and lying was exhibited to cover their guilt, when I knew that they, or some one known to them must have been guilty, I then reproved them before all the workmen, gave them what money was due, and sent them away from my employ. Several of those so discharged I afterward employed, as a token of lenity, lest it should prevent our future access to them, for their better instructions. The crimes that I found most common among them were lying, stealing, drunkenness and sloth. I had also one case of *Fornication Prevented* under consideration, which proved ultimately somewhat curious, and caused a great deal of speculation, not only among the workmen but also to a distance of 40 versts in two different directions, where the young people lived. I kept the case more than three months in the Process and did not settle it, until the young man, to whom the girl was betrothed in marriage was made acquainted with the whole circumstance. My reason for protracting and making this affair so very public was, because it is said that this sin is very general among them, and is considered by the Buriats, rather an act of Gallantry than a transgression of the holy law of God. I found however, that the more sober, and decent, among them, highly condemned the ruinous practice, and acknowledged that the Lamas were the greater transgressors.

Robert was inexorable in his pursuit of righteousness, and seems to have been unsubtle in his dealings with the Buryats. He was, of course, a strict Sabbatarian, and insisted that the Buryats, for whom Sunday had no special significance, should observe the day as conscientiously as he did. He tells us how he once enforced Sunday observance on an unconverted Buryat lad. After searching for a year or so for a young Buryat who could read and write his own language, and who would be suitable to take on as a copyist, Robert finally got on the track of a candidate. This was Rintsin, whom we have met already in Chapter 8, and whom we shall meet again. At the time, Rintsin was about eighteen years old. He was one of a number of brothers, all of whom could read Mongol, something quite unusual at the time. He lived with his parents, about twenty-five versts, or fifteen miles, from the mission station, but at the time of the incident recorded by Robert, he was lodging at Selenginsk with someone who was teaching him Russian. Rintsin had talent and ambition, and would have been quite a catch for the mission. He had visited Robert once or twice already to borrow Russian books, and when he came on this particular occasion, Robert had made him a present of the Gospels in Mongolian, and had lent him the Gospels in Russian, on condition that he brought the book back in a week's time. Rintsin brought the book back a day early, and unfortunately this happened to be a Sunday. He told Robert that he had to go to see his parents the next day, and had come on the Sabbath so as not to overstep the period of the loan. He also said that he would like to come and work for Robert if there was any way he could be useful. Robert refused to have anything to do with either piece of business, telling Rintsin that he neither borrowed nor lent on the Sabbath, and would not make any bargains either, as God would be angry with him if he did, and Rintsin was sent away. He called again early on the Monday morning, before starting on the fifteen mile journey home, and Robert engaged him as a copyist. Rintsin turned out to be the mission's star pupil and the translator of the Psalms, though in the end he was lured away by the prospect of an official career.

The houses at Selenginsk were only the first of several premises to be acquired by the missionaries, either at the Society's expense or their own. William, who had come to know the Ona district well, decided to spend the winter of 1822–23 there by himself. On arriving there in late November he had first to find somewhere to stay. There was a village, or bazaar, as it was called, of wooden houses and booths near the kontora, where there was a fair every winter. Buryats came in from as far away as Barguzin on the shores of Lake Baikal, and Nerchinsk in the east, as well as from the surrounding Khori, bringing in furs of all sorts for sale to the Russian merchants who, in their turn, sold tea and tobacco, silks and cottons from China, and other Russian trade goods. There was such a coming and going at Ona that William's time was fully occupied on the spot, and he did not need to itinerate. At first he was offered a house right in the bazaar, but he preferred to take one a little way away which the taisha Jigjit himself offered to let him have. During the year 1823, he decided to buy a house of his own at Ona. The taisha offered him one, but it was inconveniently near the local lamasery, and was also used on occasion by the Shireetei, or 'enthroned lama', there. William was glad to accept the offer of another house, belonging to the taisha's mother, which she no longer used. It was not too near the temple, and he hoped the people would be less under the thumb of the lamas. The total price, with repairs and furniture, was 500 roubles. For some years, William used this house as a winter outstation, but when he and his wife Hannah settled permanently at Ona in 1837, and opened a little school there, the house proved too small, and he erected more spacious premises at his own expense.

Edward built a little log house, about 21 feet square, at a place called Barchigir, two or three miles from the mission house, in 1824, for the sum of 100 roubles, or about £5. He renamed the place Stepney, after his and Sarah's home church, and used it as a meeting place and chapel for the local Buryats. Five pounds was not a vast sum, even in those days, but still, it was significant, and Edward hoped to recoup it from free-will offerings from the congregation at Stepney in London. Robert, too, intended at one time to buy a building somewhere on the Temnik river, to be used for the same purpose, but it is not certain whether he did so or not. In 1832, he was planning a new school-house at Selenginsk, where he hoped to accommodate and teach both boys and girls, and one of his letters, as we have seen, gives a good idea of the costs of labour and material in Siberia at the time. The wood for the school came from two houses belonging to the local authorities, which he bought at a sale for 116½ roubles, not much more than £5. He employed five men at 50 kopecks a day each to demolish the old houses, and paid them a total of 35 roubles. To bring the wood a distance of 1¾ versts, a mile or so, across the frozen Selenga on sledges, cost almost as much as the wood itself. There were 772 sledgeloads, each costing 12½ kopecks, making a total of 96½ roubles. Robert's new school house was to measure 61 by 26 feet, and to build it would take only half the amount of wood he had bought. He was going to use the rest as firewood.

The controversy over Robert's abuse of the printing press, which led to the printing operations being taken out of his hands and transferred to Edward's station at Khodon in 1835, occasioned further unexpected expense, as a building had to be put up, at short notice, to house both the press and the printer, John Abercrombie, and his family. Robert, piqued at the loss of the press, which he always said was 'forced from him', sent it off to Khodon unannounced, and William, who was in charge of the station in Edward's temporary absence, had to make emergency arrangements. Fortunately, he had already had a quantity of wood cut for his own use, and he deferred building his new house and school-room, and used the wood instead for the printery and a house for the Abercrombies. The total extra cost to the Society was 1,500 roubles.

In 1828 the missionaries decided, at Edward's instigation, to reorganize the mission, and to occupy two additional stations some way from Selenginsk. They hoped that friends in England would help with cost of the move, but it still turned out, for reasons beyond their control, to be an expensive decision. William, of course, could, and did, take up permanent residence in the little house at the Ona, which up till then he had occupied for only a few months at a time, but whichever of the other two families left Selenginsk was going to need new accommodation, which would have to be paid for. As it happened, it was Robert who stayed where he was, while Edward, with his much larger family, moved to a house on the river Khodon. Not long after he moved into it, the house was destroyed by fire.

Edward's new station was only a few hours' ride from William's and the proximity of the two stations to each other seems to belie the most cogent of the reasons for the division of the mission which were put to, and accepted by, the Directors. This argument was that, now that the sedentary work of learning the language and translating the Old Testament was more or less behind them, it was time to go out amongst the nomads and evangelize them more systematically, giving them 'line upon line and precept upon precept'. The missionaries had found that the occasional journeys they had made, and the odd months spent at the house at Ona, were less effective than they had hoped, for the Buryats forgot what little they had imbibed during the long absences which separated these visits. It was hoped that residence amongst them would prove more effective and that, the more stations there were, the greater would be the number of heathen who could be reached. Selenginsk,

The Missionaries Separate

meanwhile, would remain a useful station, especially when the time came to print their translation of the Old Testament. Yet here were the two most effective missionaries of the trio setting up house, at considerable expense, almost on each other's doorstep, amongst a people who, as they told the Directors only a couple of years later, were not really nomadic at all. In October 1830, Edward informed Alers Hankey that 'the idea that the Boriats about the Ona and Khodon, *particularly*, are not stationary, is, I believe, not correct. They, like those about Selenginsk, have generally their summer, and their winter places; and some of them their spring and autumn ones: but these are generally within the compass of 4 or 5 versts, and often less.' The emphasis had changed since he told the same correspondent, only two years earlier, that 'for the purpose of finding pastures they remove from place to place, some times four or five times in a year: and what adds to the evil of it, in a Missionary point of view, each strives to keep as clear as possible of neighbours, so that many of them are not to be found together; consequently, the time and labour in preaching the gospel to them is greatly increased.'

As they presented it, their plan proved convincing to the Directors. They wrote to them as follows:

> It has therefore been deemed desirable by us to separate, and to establish ourselves more permanently in different stations; by which means it is hoped, that, although some of the advantages of cooperation may be lost, yet in the aggregate our means of usefulness will be increased.
> The state of the people presents to us a great mass of labour, all of which we are unable to accomplish; and our wisdom, we conceive, consists in choosing that, upon which we may reasonably entertain the greatest hopes of obtaining the Divine blessing. Educating, and imbuing with divine truth the minds of the young and especially of such young men from whom we may entertain the hope of future usefulness – are universally esteemed of great importance. Preaching and publicly declaring the gospel of salvation to all whom we can collect is esteemed by us another point most important. But we are unable to collect at any one station a sufficient number to occupy us all; and we entertain the hope that at each different station almost the same might be accomplished as is now doing at Selenginsk.

In a separate letter on the same subject, Edward mentioned the possible objections to the plan, only to dismiss them. He admitted that the missionaries would probably be less comfortable for a while, that extra expense might be incurred, that it was risky to disperse such a small group of colleagues and so deprive each of them of the immediate advice and help of the others. But it was a time for self-sacrifice, and, he declared: 'Although we ought to receive with gratitude all those temporal blessings and comforts which we enjoy, and not needlessly to deprive ourselves of them; yet it is

The Missionaries Separate

not always the time of greatest usefulness with us when we are in circumstances of the greatest ease and outward prosperity.'

On 5 January 1829, the Directors wrote to tell the missionaries that they approved of the division of the mission. In 1830, in retrospect, they confessed themselves puzzled as to how the missionaries, each in his individual station, could attend to such incompatible duties as school-teaching and itineration, but Edward assured them that it was all a matter of priorities, and his explanations seem to have satisfied them that the decision to occupy separate stations had, after all, been a wise one.

But the arguments they had accepted, while true, were not the whole truth. The move from Selenginsk was not such a sacrifice as it was made out to be. Edward and William would certainly be giving up a life of relative material comfort for a more pioneering existence on the Khori steppes, but at the same time they would be escaping from a situation which was progressively destroying their peace of mind, but of whose gravity the Directors had been kept in ignorance. The true reason for making what was represented to be a triple division of the mission, but was, in actual fact, a division into two parts only, was not that of professional advantage. The mission was torn apart by mutual distrust and dislike, and had been so almost from the time of its foundation, and Edward, supported by William, had forced the division on a reluctant Robert in the desperate hope of thereby saving it from complete disintegration. The separation did not take place amicably, but in an atmosphere of animosity and resentment. The Directors may have suspected something of the bickering and one-upmanship which was prevalent at Selenginsk, for Robert had complained about it in one or two of his letters, but they might never have needed to take official cognizance of the feud within the mission if it had not threatened, in 1834, to overflow into the public domain. To anticipate developments in our story, what happened then was that Robert, who, by staying at Selenginsk, had inherited control of the printing press, which had lain there for the last ten years, began to print Genesis. He took it into his head to make arbitrary alterations in the copy after it had been officially passed by the censor. This was not only discourteous to Edward, the translator, who had waited in vain for ten years for Robert to comment on his version, but it could easily have been turned into a public scandal. The mission had its enemies at Verkhneudinsk and Irkutsk, and Robert's irresponsible behaviour threatened to play into their hands, for it could be interpreted as wilful defiance of authority. Robert made matters worse by refusing to promise that he would not treat Exodus in the same high-handed manner as he had treated Genesis, and so the Directors had to be involved, and this meant letting them into the sordid details of what had gone before.

It fell to Edward to let the cat out of the bag, for Genesis was his responsibility, and on 1/13 October 1834 he wrote as follows to William Ellis, the Secretary of the Society:

The Missionaries Separate

There is another question to which I must beg to draw the Directors' attention, – one which is closely connected with our future printing operations. It will be remembered that our printing press was received at Selenginsk in 1824, before the division of the mission. In 1828 two of the Brethren saw it to be highly desirable for the *peace*, as well as *extension* of the mission that such a division should take place; I proposed it to the third, offering either to remain at Selenginsk, or to remove to another station. The latter was accepted; and while Mr Swan and myself removed to the Ona and Khodon respectively Mr Yuille was left at Selenginsk. We were led to the adoption of this measure in the hope that the blessing which we began to despair of receiving in our *united* capacity (– for there was, I am afraid, no true union and confidence –) might be bestowed upon us *separately*. And we humbly hope that our expectations on this head have been in a degree realized. – *This* reason for our separation has hitherto been kept from the Directors, as we were unwilling that their minds should be grieved and perplexed by any thing of the kind; and as we hoped to be going on in our different spheres, without any collison; which, so far as the little confidence which is placed in us by our Brother as to his movements enables us to judge, we believe has been the case hitherto. I trust I would gladly have borne in silence fourteen years more, the many unpleasant things which in the course of the past period of that length I have been called upon to endure, were merely private feeling and comfort concerned. But now silence would betray a criminal indifference.

Robert always maintained that he was acting in the best interests of the mission in 'correcting' Edward's translation at the last moment, and probably he was naive enough to believe this. But it is also possible that he was simply exploiting an opportunity to revenge himself on Edward for past snubs, real or imagined. The feud within the mission had originated between the Stallybrass and the Yuille families, though William, who was the same sort of man as Edward and always took his part, was inevitably drawn into the conflict too, and actually had to bear the brunt of the bitter and protracted dispute over Genesis as a surrogate for his friend, who was on furlough at the time.

Robert suffered from an inferiority complex, and was unforgiving by nature. He was always on the watch for any slight to his dignity or his professional standing, and he never forgot a single one. When he arrived at Selenginsk, Edward had apparently asked him to contribute his medicine box to their common stock. Robert, who was proud of his medical skill, took this to mean that Edward planned to monopolize the medical side of the mission, and was affronted. Then, when Edward asked his colleagues to put their books on the shelves near his study, Robert interpreted that too as a denigration. And after Martha's death, Sarah had tried to interfere in

The Missionaries Separate

the way the Yuilles' old nurse dressed Samuel. Each complaint was as trivial as the other, and they were dredged up a decade or more after they should have been forgotten.

Everyone knew that Robert was a prickly character. Paterson, Edward and William, and Richard Knill had all taken his measure, and Knill saw to it that the Directors knew as well. Robert seldom wrote to the Directors, but when he did, his letters were often weighed down with trivia or ranting. 'Weighed down' is the right expression. One letter, sent home in 1823 through Knill, would have cost fifteen shillings just to forward from St Petersburg to London by mail. 'Heavy postage for light matter,' said Knill, and got Paterson to carry it for him. Another heavy but vacuous letter turned up in 1826, and Knill copied out the few relevant bits, and sent the turgid original by ship to save money. He passed this incident off good-humouredly, writing:

> I have a very heavy letter of Mr Yuilles of 8 pages folio: it is addressed to Dr Paterson, Mr Venning, R. Knill and lastly to be forwarded to you. 7 of the pages are extraneous matter but I will send it by Shipping in the summer, and hope it will not be too late to be embodied in the Report as I think Mr Yuille is rather tenacious of his rights and a little capricious when all things do not please. Men, yea good men have such little things attached to them.

But Robert, who would turn out not to be a 'good man' in Knill's sense, was in earnest about his rights. He suspected Knill of suppressing his letters, and David Langton, the Society's Assistant Secretary, of ignoring their contents. In 1823 he told Langton:

> I have occasionally and not infrequently forwarded letters with extracts from my Journal, to our Dear friends in St. Petersburg, but they have either said nothing about them to the Directors, or perhaps you have considered my communications more suitable for the Dormitory than for Public use; but which of the two I do not stand to enquire. I shall, however, in future communicate with Mr Burder, and occasionally with one or other of the Directors, and at the same time not forget my Dear Friends, who are the invaluable Pillars of the cause of our Redeemer in the Capital of this Empire.

Things did not improve, and in 1830 Robert was complaining to Alers Hankey that Knill had actually destroyed a letter he had addressed to London.

Knill was thoroughly justified in delaying Robert's letters, and sending them on by the cheapest method, for they were often quite irrelevant to the work of the mission, and, at worst, could be of a startling banality. His poetry was even more painfully contrived than his prose. In January 1826 he wrote to inform Alers Hankey of the birth of his son Samuel, and to

The Missionaries Separate

explain that he had given him the second name of Bogue, in memory of Dr David Bogue, his old tutor at Gosport. He said that he had done this 'as a testimony of my Veneration for that invaluable Missionary, who, although not permitted to enter a foreign field of labour was like an Aaron and a Hur; Holding up the Cause of Missions until the very going down of his Sun:

And in his twilight oft had heard
From Servants of the Mighty Lord,
That Battles by these means were gain'd
And nations from their Idols wean'd.

Thus was he brought to Pisgah's top
View'd the land he fain would travel,
His home and friends would given up
and Blank! and Blank! would intermiddle
But proving faithful, in the end
One of the Blanks! became his friend.

Nonsense like this apart, there is a more informative side to Robert's unprofessional garrulity, for he tells us many little details about Selenginsk and its surroundings which are of passing interest. He examined a lama doctor's bag, and found out what was in it; he noticed rock inscriptions near Selenginsk; and he kept records of the weather there. But the Directors can hardly have been expected to pay postage on his casual jottings and his literary imbecilities gladly.

Unconsciously, Robert betrayed himself in other ways. In 1829 he sent home a couple of Tibetan–Mongolian dictionaries of which he had had copies made, with a request that the Directors should present them to the Royal Asiatic Society on his behalf. This was in any case a piece of self-advertisement. Robert claimed that the four dictionaries in his possession represented 'all the Tubetian learning, which is to be found in this part of the country', which was far from the true case, and no doubt he intended to ingratiate himself with the RAS by putting it in possession of this novel learning. Unfortunately, anticipating compliance with his request, Robert had written a dedicatory inscription on the flyleaf of each book, and these effusions were apparently so illiterate that the Society was ashamed to pass the books on, and waited until William came home on leave, and could substitute more worthy texts. Robert knew nothing about this till some years later, when William, irritated beyond measure by his persistent nagging, told him what had happened:

Since you still seem so desirous to be informed what I referred to when I said that both in St. Petersburg and London I had done what I could to 'remove bad impressions your own letters had produced,' I shall specify two instances – one at each place. . . . When I arrived in

The Missionaries Separate

London in 1831, I found that some books you had sent to the Asiatic Society a year or two before were still lying at the Mission House. On enquiring why they were not delivered I was told that the *title pages* and direction or address in your hand writing were so egregiously incorrect both in point of grammar and orthography, that they were ashamed to send them, adding that your letters sent from time to time were written in such a style that they could never allow any of them to appear in the publications of the Society. In short that your own writings had led them to form a very low opinion of your scholarship and general accuracy. I procured a sight of the books, and, with the concurrence of the official persons at the Mission Ho. who had them in charge, I wrote new title pages, and got the books conveyed to the Asiatic Society, and in relation to your letters etc I said all I could in your favour. Now I tell you all this – not to mortify you – but because you will not be satisfied without knowing it. Indeed it was from a wish not to mortify you that I did not tell you those things and others of the same description, on my return to Siberia. Another reason why I was very unwilling to bring in these things or any other extraneous matter into this correspondence was that it only multiplied points of discord and discussion and diverted the attention from the main and primary question.

William did not tell Robert either that the person by whom he had the books 'conveyed' to the RAS was, ironically, Cornelius Rahmn.

In 1833, Robert took the Directors to task for allowing Alers Hankey to give up the post of Treasurer which he had held since 1816:

I was very Sorry when I knew of it, especially as it appears that Mr Hankey himself was by no means tired of the office. It is not my sphere to make reflections on Such occurrences; nor is it my duty, nor am I able to tell the Sum of the Sin, which must be laid to the charge of those who *push* out the honoured Servants of the Lord, while faithfully and Successfully engaged in the work of the Redeemer: yet you will allow me to be sorry for Mr Hankey.

Robert cannot have been a favourite at the Mission House.

He had given early warning, too, that he was unhappy with the state of affairs at Selenginsk, and suffering from what nowadays would be called a persecution mania. In 1828 he complained to the Directors about the unfairness of his situation after the death of his wife:

Let the Directors be assured also that the work of Itinerancy cannot be dispensed with in the Situation of this Mission. Let them be assured also that I have paid as much attention to that part of the work as my leasure and situation would admit, and upon calculation, would not be found to be much less extensive than that of my Brethren, although I was not Privileged as they were; viz one at home while the other was on his journies. . . . While this must not be considered as throwing the very least reflection on my devouted Brethren, it cannot but point out to the Directors the difference of Privilege enjoyed by their Missionaries at this Station.

Unmistakable signs that Robert was in danger of losing his sense of proportion, if not his mental balance, are visible in a letter he wrote to William Orme on 18 January 1829. The letter starts with a petulant rebuke to the Directors for not writing to him often enough, and then flares up into a diatribe against the Stallybrasses:

You will be surprised, when I term your letter a very great rarity! But it truly is so, – for it is only the Second letter from a Director of our Society that I have seen in these wild regions! and I have been now here Eight years. And a week after your letter came to hand, I was favoured with the sight of another great rarity viz a Chronicle in which there is an extract of a letter from me to Dr Waugh, which is only the 2nd or 3d of the kind that I have seen in Siberia.

Orme was not so much surprised as offended. There is a pencilled note on the letter saying: 'His colleagues are as much entitled as Mr Yuille to write thus, but have they done so?' His rebuke to the Directors must have been a bad psychological preparation for what was to follow in the letter.

According to Robert, Martha had been a paragon of Christian virtues, but her efforts to help the mission had been thwarted by Sarah. She had planned a little school for the local girls, where she was going to teach them wool-processing and needle-work. Sarah had a rival plan to teach the girls to plait straw. The subject was talked over, and everyone appeared to be agreed that Martha's plan should be adopted, and that she should have the running of the school. So Robert went off to recruit pupils, and having done so, he set a Buryat carpenter to work to make spinning-wheels. Next day, he departed on a tour amongst the Buryats. 'The determination that we had come to respecting the Girls school was not the cause of my taking this journey, but for the purpose of visiting the people with the word of life.' *Les absents ont toujours tort*, and when Robert returned, he found that the school was being held in Sarah's house, and what the girls were being taught was straw-plaiting. No explanation was offered, and the Yuilles kept silent about the apparent affront, till Sarah asked Martha to help her out with the school, but proposed that *her* class should be held in the wash-house. Robert objected to this, but instead of offering an apology, Sarah 'spoke shortly, and in a degree unpleasantly and left the room'. According to his own account, Robert swallowed his resentment, and even did his best to advertise Sarah's school by using her products. And here his letter, trivial enough when we recall that it was an official communication between a missionary and the Directors of the Missionary Society, descends into unbelievable farce:

The Missionaries Separate

> I also bought Plait Straw for Mrs S which Mrs Y made into a Hat for me, with her own hands, and which I wore till it was in tatters; and then bought another ready made, which two Hats, I wore, frequently at the expence of a pained head, for they were not wind Proof, on all my Visits, and Journies, both to the Towns of Selenginsk, Kaichta and Udinsk, and to more distant places among the Boriates for the purpose of recommending this School. . . . I may add here, that perhaps these purchases of mine constitute about a 5th part of all the Free Sales, which has been made of the work of this School from its first commencement.

This little contretemps may have rather more than just anecdotal significance. Before going out to Siberia, Sarah had spent some time at Joseph Lancaster's school in Borough Road, Southwark, studying his educational methods. It is very probable that she learned about straw-plaiting there, for it was dealt with, as an occupation for girls, in the pages of Lancaster's book *Improvements in Education*. She would then have been in a position to pass on knowledge of the craft without descending from the superior level of a lady instructing the working class. Martha Yuille, on the other hand, though we know nothing of her background, may have been brought up to her husband's craft of weaving, and have belonged, in Sarah's eyes at least, to the artisan class. The petty rivalry over what was taught in the school may have had some subtle, wounding social undertones to it.

Martha had been dead for more than a year, and all this had happened long ago. What prompted Robert to rake it all up and discredit himself in the eyes of the Directors by such petulant whining? He gives us his own answer:

> Two reasons have prompted me to lay this Statement of facts before you, viz. First to shew to the Directors the cause, which prevented Mrs Yuille from being more actively and Publicly engaged in the work of the Mission. And Secondly, Because I have been led to suppose from hints occasionally given, that Mrs S had, or was intending to Solicit an assistant to this school from England; by which it might be supposed that no assistance could be had at Selenginsk; or that Mrs Y was either unwilling or unable to take any part in the Instructions of the Girls. Than which Suppositions nothing could be more contrary to the known ability, Humility, Complacency and anxious Solicitude of Mrs Yuille for the promotion of all good; for she was ready at a word, and stood engaged in an instant, without the least degree of Selfishness, on the behalf of the truth, and on the behalf of all the objects of the Mission. I Declare that I have no other intention of making this Statement to the Directors, than a Simple relation of the truth which, so far as it respects Mrs Yuille, they ought to be informed of. . . . I would be very sorry were the Directors in the least degree to alienate their affections and Support from Mrs Stallybrass: and be assured that I have not; and that I shall

The Missionaries Separate

continue to assist her, and my Brethren in all the work of the Mission.
– But should anything of the kind occur again among us, I cannot promise to be silent; for I am persuaded, that more evil results from forbearance on such occasions, than what could result from a speedy explaination of such a transaction.

Martha Yuille remains a shadowy figure. Everyone who spoke of her, including Sarah, did so kindly, and perhaps it was not with her, but only with her abrasive husband, that Edward and Sarah had their differences. But these were serious enough to threaten the survival of the mission, and so, in the spring of 1828, Edward and William set out to look over a house which had belonged to the late taisha Dembil, and which lay near the river Khodon, some 280 versts, or 190 miles, north-east of Selenginsk. The house had been valued at 2,500 roubles, but it had stood empty for five or six years, and the executors, who were anxious to realize something on it, were willing to let it go for 1,500 roubles. Edward calculated that this was equal to just over £61. He would have to draw on the Society for the money, but he hoped to recover some of the costs, at least, from gifts from friends at home. It was a slow process getting possession of the house, as the executors had to satisfy the authorities that there was no hope of getting more than the 1,500 roubles, and they had to obtain approval for the sale from the Senate in St Petersburg. No money had been handed over when Edward and his family moved in on 25 August 1828. Within a few months, disaster struck. On 10/22 December, while the family was assembled for prayer along with a few Buryats, one of the big brick stoves fell in and set the whole of the upper storey on fire. There was no pump to be had, and it was impossible to save the wooden structure, but, with the help of their neighbours, the Stallybrasses rescued most of their belongings.

They were not left entirely homeless. There was still the separate bath house, which Edward took over as a study, and there was another building, which had been used as a cattle pen, and which they adapted as a home for themselves and their servants. Edward also bought an old log house, and used the wood to erect a substitute kitchen. The work of the mission was interrupted for a while, but what was more serious was that the disaster provided their envious neighbours with a golden opportunity to harass them. The purchase of the house had still not been approved by the Senate, and the months dragged by without any news coming from the capital. The first pin-prick was an enquiry from the authorities at Verkhneudinsk as to whether Edward was willing to pay for the house which had been burned down, and if not, why not. He replied that although he did not consider he had been at all negligent, he was willing to pay for the house, as the fire had occurred during his occupancy, and probably would not have happened otherwise. The next step was to question Edward's right to reside at Khodon. What happened is best retold in his own words.

The Missionaries Separate

Some little difficulty has arisen about our removal hither. Before we made any proposals for buying this house, we signified our intention to the head of his district, informing him of our purpose (i.e. of me and my family) to take up our residence here. There was not the least objection made to it, nor any difficulty represented as being connected with it. The same head of the circuit gave orders to the executors of the late Taisha to make the necessary arrangements for selling us the house: and he advised me to remove hither without hesitation, as there was not the least probability of its not being decided in our favour. We removed in August last year, and waited till July this year before we received the decision; and then when the house was bought, and the money about to be paid, he told us it would be necessary to obtain the consent of the Governor before we could reside here. A representation was accordingly made from Verkhneudinsk, the district town, to the Governor at Irkutsk; and he wrote us that he could not decide it without authority from the higher powers. We wrote to the Governor, giving him a full account of the grounds on which, as well as the purposes for which we came here; – informing him that full liberty was given us by his Imperial Majesty to settle where we thought best in order to secure the attainment of our object; – that we did not think any new permission necessary, and that no such permission was deemed requisite when we thought it desirable to remove from Irkutsk to Selenginsk in 1819; – and that we thought it strange that no intimation was given of its necessity when we first made proposals for purchasing the house. – As he had kindly offered to make arrangements for obtaining the necessary authority we moreover requested him to do it, if he should *still* deem it requisite. This restriction is applicable to Mr Swan's removal to the Ona, as well as to that of us to his place. – When we received the Governor's letter the materials for building the new house were prepared, – the contract for building made, – the money in part paid, – and the time also which was fixed upon for commencing the building had arrived: so that in the opinion of my brethren as well as myself, it did not appear desirable to delay its commencement. The work is now commenced, and is to be carried on till the latter end of November – when it will cease till the 1st of March 1830.

We have not yet received an answer from the Governor, but hope that from the statement we made to him that he will not think any thing farther necessary. Should he, we hope it may be the means of letting us know more fully the mind of government respecting us; and I cannot think from the character of measures of his present Imperial Majesty that any thing worse can befal us. We should be more like exiles than Missionaries if we were to be confined to one spot without liberty to stir from it without obtaining permission from the civil powers *here*: for it has been intimated to us, that the gentlemen in Verkhneudinsk have felt

The Missionaries Separate

themselves aggrieved that we did not make our humble suit to them for permission to remove. We *consulted* them which was all we thought necessary.

Edward carried on building, and the intrigue against him subsided. But formal permission to move about and settle where they wished had still not been notified to the missionaries by the end of 1832 when William raised the matter with D. N. Bludov, the Minister of Ecclesiastical Affairs. We shall see in Chapter 17 how the central authorities in St Petersburg disposed of this minor matter.

11

Family Life in Siberia

The missionaries had no local income, and no prospect of making any money. As Edward explained to Alers Hankey:

> I am sorry to say that the prospects of supporting ourselves in any way are very distant; the pay of all kinds of officers is so small that they are obliged to do something else for a living, so that all means are employed to obtain money and none left by which an honest man may do anything in the way of getting a living.

Even school-teaching was to be a drain on the mission's resources, rather than a source of income, as it was impossible to recruit pupils without offering them board and lodging, and even then their parents sometimes expected to be paid for letting their children go to school. Hence all the money the missionaries needed for their own support, and for financing their works of charity, in particular their schools and their printing operations, had somehow to be sent in from outside. Their one regular source of income was, of course, the Missionary Society itself, which paid them each a half-yearly salary, and could be relied upon to cover extraordinary expenses, such as the cost of house-purchase and the occasional journey home. They had a few private benefactors as well. There was a group of patrons at St Petersburg, who sent them regular, though fluctuating, contributions towards the upkeep of their schools, and a church in London, Dr Morison's congregation at Brompton, supported their star convert, Shagdur, when he became a native preacher.

When the mission was first established, Paterson thought that £100 or £150 a year would be an adequate salary. Even after some experience of Siberia, where he found life comparatively expensive, Edward hoped to be able to manage on 3,000 roubles a year as a minimum, with a supplement of 250 to cover rent. Eventually, though, his level of salary, like that of Robert, settled down at twice that amount, or 6,000 roubles, and even so, what with incidental expenses such as doctors' fees, the cost of the move to Selenginsk, interest on a loan he had to take out, and so on, he was often overdrawn in the first few years. The exchange rate varied from time to time. In July 1816 the paper rouble was worth 11d; by March 1819 it had appreciated to 11½d; and in September of the same year Edward was calculating it at a shilling. In February 1821 it was worth only a little more than 10d. In 1828 it stood at 10¼d, and over the years this seems to have been its average strength against sterling. Thus the equivalent of the 6,000 roubles which Edward and Robert each drew in salary was accounted for in London as £250. This was not an over-generous income, for the missionaries had quite heavy responsibilities. Both Edward and Robert were married. Robert's family was small: three of his children died young, and only one, Samuel, survived to maturity. But Edward and Sarah had to support a steadily growing family. Between 1818 and 1826 Sarah gave birth to six children, of whom all but one survived, and in the late 1820s she was looking after two Buryat orphans as well. Edward had three more children, of whom two survived, by his second wife, Charlotte. William and Hannah Swan were childless, but they adopted a Buryat girl some time during the 1830s. Apart from their purely domestic responsibilites, all three missionaries had servants and copyists to pay, and they provided board and lodging for the children who joined their schools.

For some time after his arrival, William was less of a drain on the Society's resources than his colleagues. He was single, and had no house of his own, lodging with Edward and Sarah, whom he paid for his keep. He also had a small private income, much of it deriving from a patroness, a Mrs Puget of Totteridge, and for the first two and a half years he did not need to draw any salary at all. He then drew at the rate of 2,000 roubles, or about £90 a year, and by 1828 he was receiving 2,500 roubles, half of which went to Edward for board and lodging. By the mid-1830s, when he returned to Siberia as a married man after a period of furlough, he was drawing the same as his colleagues, 6,000 roubles a year.

Backed as they were by the Society, the missionaries were never out of credit, though laying their hands on cash was, to begin with, a complicated and uncertain process, as there were no proper banking facilities in eastern Siberia. When they left London, they carried letters of credit, which were honoured in St Petersburg by the Moravian house of Asmus Simonsen. The real difficulties arose after they reached their final destination. Edward and Cornelius left the capital with 3,000 roubles in cash, a credit of 1,000 roubles which they could draw at Tobolsk, and a further credit of 3,000 roubles payable at any of the offices of the Russian-American Company. By June 1818 most of this had been spent, and Paterson took it upon himself to send them the equivalent of £100 by mail. He did this without consulting the Society first, explaining that if he had waited for authorization, at least another four and a half months would have passed before the money could have reached Irkutsk, and the missionaries would have been without money for two months, 'which must not be'.

Family Life in Siberia

In view of such delays, a standing arrangement was essential, but it was some time before a reliable method of transferring money was found. To begin with, the missionaries relied on getting cash from local tradesmen as and when they could, repaying them with bills on Asmus Simonsen. But this *ad hoc* system had the disadvantage that cash was not always available just when it was wanted. The missionaries were obliged to draw at the convenience of the merchants, and this could mean drawing money well in advance of their needs, and so debiting the Society prematurely and irregularly. It seemed that the answer had been found when Speranskii asked Prince Golitsyn to arrange for the Russian-American Company to hold an annual credit of 5,000 roubles for the missionaries at its Irkutsk office. As Paterson said, this should be enough for their regular needs, and if they wanted more, he could always send it to them. Unfortunately, the negotiations were bungled. The Russian-American Company was a trading monopoly, not a banking house, and what Paterson thought was a running arrangement was interpreted by it as a one-time favour. The result was that the missionaries suddenly found themselves unable to draw money just as they were in the middle of their building operations. They had to stop the work and lay off the labourers, and borrow money locally at a high rate of interest for their day-to-day needs. In fact, they had been lucky to get any money at all from the Company, which did most of its business by barter, so that, in the remoter parts of Siberia at least, if not in Irkutsk itself, there was rarely cash enough on hand to honour casual bills.

Working through third parties was, in any case, not reliable. In December 1820 Henderson, in St Petersburg, drew 5,000 roubles for the mission, which he paid into the Russian-American Company there, but then he fell ill, and no letter of advice was sent to Selenginsk, so that the missionaries knew nothing of the transaction, and did not apply to the Company's office in Irkutsk for their money.

It was after the fiasco with the Russian-American Company that the missionaries adopted the method which perhaps they should have relied on from the beginning. Though it took longer than making local drawings, they drew directly on St Petersburg by mail, through Richard Knill, who got the money in bank notes from Asmus Simonsen, and sent it to them through the post. This procedure took about six weeks each way, and was not expensive. Thus, in 1825, postage and insurance on the sum of 6,000 roubles amounted to 85 roubles, while another transfer of 1,000 roubles cost 21. Asmus Simonsen, of course, recouped themselves from the Society through ordinary banking channnels. For a few years until 1820 their bills and letters of advice were written out, though anonymously, by none other than I. J. Schmidt.

The missionaries' accounts tell us something, but by no means everything, about the way they spent their money. Behind at least one apparently straightforward entry there lies a story of trickery which is indicative of the sort of treatment they had to put up with from local bigwigs, but which they did not usually describe so explicitly in their correspondence. But we should know nothing of the background to this particular transaction unless we could link up the accounts with an unusually outspoken private letter which William wrote to Paterson.

In March 1824, Edward wrote as follows to Alers Hankey in explanation of the odd sum of 6,695 roubles, for which he had just drawn, instead of 6,000 which was what he usually claimed every half-year on behalf of the Yuilles and himself: 'To be sent to the Bp. of Irkutsk for the carriage of books (i.e. Mong gospels) which he has paid on our behalf.'

The Mongolian gospels referred to were copies of the gospels as translated by Badma and Schmidt and printed in St Petersburg by the Russian Bible Society. The missionaries relied on regular supplies of these gospels to distribute among the Buryats, for, in order not to duplicate the work of translation, they themselves were concentrating on the Old Testament, leaving the New Testament entirely to the little team in the capital. On the face of it, this accounting entry can be interpreted as evidence of smooth cooperation between the two churches, with the Archbishop of Irkutsk making his official channels of communication available to the missionaries. That was far from the case. Archbishop Mikhail seems to have been rather two-faced in his dealings with the missionaries, and acting as an intermediary between them and the RBS in St Petersburg enabled him to control their operations and even sabotage them. He was quite capable of flattering them to their faces, writing to tell them how much he valued their work and how he prayed for its success, yet at the same time doing his best, behind their backs, to catch them out. The missionaries knew this only too well. In 1824, when the trumped-up crisis over the book by the German clergyman Gossner, which was aimed at Golitsyn, resulted in the Prince's removal from office and the sapping of the prestige of the RBS, the Metropolitan Seraphim had written to the bishops of the various dioceses, instructing them that 'for the easy and expeditious circulation of the Scriptures among the Heathen, that work be committed to the Priests of the Russian Church'. At Sarepta this instruction had resulted in the Moravians, either voluntarily or under pressure, handing in to the Archbishop in whose diocese they lay all the copies of Schmidt's Kalmuck Gospels which they possessed, and Edward was quite sure that 'should the Bp in our quarter receive authority to make a similar requisition, we have little hesitation as to the state of his mind toward us'. There was obviously no love lost between Irkutsk and Selenginsk.

Some two years before this, in May 1822, William was engaged in correspondence with Paterson about the Memoir of Jean Paterson which he had been persuaded to compile. The Memoir was now complete, and what was under discussion was the best way to get the manuscript from Selenginsk to the capital. Paterson had evidently recommended that William should send it through the Irkutsk Bible Society, and perhaps through the Archbishop himself, and William, in a mood of rare candour, had flatly declined to do so. We cannot be absolutely sure that it *is* the Bishop to whom he refers in his letter, as the operative word is scrawled in shorthand – probably Taylor's system, which was familiar to the missionaries – and is difficult to read, but it does look as if it might represent the letters 'Bp.' It would in any case not be surprising if William were to have accused the Archbishop of covertly trying to disrupt the activities of the mission which he overtly approved of, for he had suggested as much in an earlier letter to Paterson.

In December 1821, William had written:

> I am afraid something has befallen our two boxes with medicines and books sent from Petersburg last winter through the Bible Society to Irkutsk. We have repeatedly made enquiries, and have just learned from the Archbishop on application made to him, that he has heard of them 'being on the way' from Petersburg but that they have not reached Irkutsk. Our writing to Petersburg for a supply of gospels produces but little – and we are just as we were last winter *unsupplied*. It is a pity. 1000 copies it seems have been sent to the Irkutsk B. Society – but they may rot in their ware houses before the Buriats will buy them – expecially from Russians.

By the following May the boxes of medicines had arrived in Irkutsk, and had been opened in the Bible Society there, and, apparently, rifled by the Archbishop, and it was because of this that William refused to entrust his manuscript to the Irkutsk Bible Society.

> The Memoir I shall immediately send you by post direct from this place. Were I to send it by post in the way you direct I am afraid it would never reach you. The old drunken lying cheating —— is not to be trusted with anything – You have little idea my friend how things are carried on in that quarter – The detention of our boxes, the abstraction of articles from them which are still obstinately withheld did not surprise us after we heard of the letter concerning them which he addressed to the Committee in Petersburg for that letter was with the worst possible intentions both to you and to us.

The missionaries had approached the Archbishop, if indeed it was he who was the villain of the piece, through an English friend in Irkutsk, a Mr Bayton, who was told that the boxes had been opened under the impression that they were the property of the Bible Society. The medicines and some other things were released to Mr Bayton, but other things, including books, were kept, under the flimsy pretence of being set off against the cost of carriage. William was perplexed:

> What must we do? quietly submit and be laughed at, or insist upon the

delivery of our property? If there are any charges to be paid we are
ready to produce the money. When you enter upon the management
again you must reverse the foolish arrangement for our being supplied
with Mong. Scriptures etc through the Irkutsk Committee – such a plan
will subject us to endless vexation, besides increase greatly the suspicions
of the Buriats that we are only the tools of the Russians. We shall be
glad to get the copies already in the Irk. depository lest they should
lie there and rot, but that ought not to be the permanent channel through
which we are to be supplied.

But evidently the old arrangement was still in force in 1824.

It would be fascinating to know how English families, especially those with small children, organized their daily lives in Siberia in the early nineteenth century, but the missionaries never thought it worth while to give any of their correspondents a connected account of their worldly doings, or, if they did, such letters are no longer to be found. What with the work of the mission and family matters, Edward was always busy. Both he and Sarah were unwilling correspondents at the best of times, and begrudged every moment not spent upon mission work. 'To tell you the truth,' Edward wrote to Ann and Joseph Monds, 'I in general find letter-writing to be a sort of burden, and it is only when I am excited either by a sense of duty, or by a sense of the kindness of my friends that I can persuade myself to set about it.' Sarah was more fulsome, telling her 'dearest Ann':

If I did not know that my time was fully and perhaps more importantly
employed than in writing letters, the number of letters which I have
by me unanswered, would I believe wound my conscience. Ah, my Ann,
if time were generally estimated by us, by the number of Souls that
are every moment entering Eternity and that void of all hope beyond
the finite existence how willing should we be to make sacrifices not
only in our mental, but our bodily gratifications. I have never felt so
parsimonious of the time bestowed on dress, or company, or even lawful
mental gratifications, as I have done since I visited the great Temple of
the Idolatrous worshippers among whom we live.

When Joseph, who was evidently a keen geologist, suggested that Edward should write an account of the geology of the locality of Selenginsk, Edward replied that he had neither time, inclination nor ability for it, 'being almost buried in Biblical Studies, which I esteem the grand duty and pleasure of my life, at least till a version of the Old Testament in the Mongolian language be completed'. He did, though, find time to make a small collection of stones during the following twelve months, and promised to send it to Joseph as soon as he could find a cheap way to do so. Obviously there was no time for gossip, and most of what we know of the day-to-day life of the mission comes from little asides like this, in the missionaries' own correspondence or in other rare sources. So it is that we know that Peter Gordon approved of Sarah as a missionary's wife. 'I found a hearty welcome, and immediately got rid of my Ochotsk sensations, my Siberian misanthropy. Mrs Stallybrass soon convinced me that the ideas which I retained of my fair countrywomen were correct and true; my general admiration was not lowered by meeting with one eminently qualified for the delicate and arduous situation she fills to the admiration of all who know her.' But it was left to the Russian Martos to notice how Sarah tried, as far as possible, to follow an English pattern of life in her remote surroundings. When he called at the mission house in December 1823 it happened to be midday, and he found 'the mistress was seeing to lunch, absolutely in the national taste: she served tea with cream, biscuits and waffles'.

Even at Selenginsk, the mission families were to a considerable degree self-supporting. They kept their own domestic animals, sheep and cows as well as riding horses, and they baked their own bread, brewed their own beer and kvass, and manufactured their own candles. When they had to buy provisions, they preferred to buy them in bulk in Irkutsk and have them brought across Lake Baikal when it was frozen, for this was still cheaper than shopping retail in Selenginsk. They would lay in stocks of items like meat, flour and tea sufficient to last for several months, or even a year, at a time. Khodon was even more remote from civilization than Selenginsk, and James Steven Stallybrass, Sarah's youngest child, who deposited a number of his father's Mongolian manuscripts in the Library of the British Museum, recalls, in an accompanying memorandum, how they would make an expedition to Verkhneudinsk once a year in summer, for the purpose of buying a year's supply of tea, sugar, clothes, paper and so on.

Health care presented a major problem. There was no doctor in Selenginsk except the regimental surgeon, who interpreted the scope of his responsibilities very narrowly, refusing to treat anyone outside the town garrison. There were lama doctors, it is true, some of them possessing a certain limited amount of skill. These men would have been trained in the Tibetan classic of medicine, of which there were Mongolian versions as well, and which was known, from its four-fold division, as the 'Four Roots'. Edward himself possessed a copy. They would also have been conversant with herbals, and other manuals of drugs, which listed the names of medicines in Tibetan and Chinese, as well as Mongolian. Some knew how to administer acupuncture. The missionaries had little regard for the abilities of the lama doctors:

> They pretend to the knowledge of diseases by simply feeling the patient's pulse, and, like the Chinese physicians, have a set of rules describing the various states of the pulse, and the disease thereby indicated. The Lamas procure their medicines from China, almost all of them in a state of powders. Each medicine is kept in a small leathern bag, with a stick or bone tied to the mouth of it, on which is written the name of the

medicine in *Tangoot* characters, and the only utensil in their laboratory is a small copper spoon, with which they measure out the requisite dose.

Mongols and Buryats alike relied greatly on magic medicine, on the use of amulets, or of draughts containing only the ashes of paper on which a powerful spell had been written. The curious ceremony of constructing and then destroying a substitute figure of the sick person, practised in parts of Mongolia as late as the 1940s, was well described by William:

> It is a practice with the Shamans, and also with the Lamas, to offer to the Tengrie, or spirits of the heavens, or to the particular god they suppose to be concerned in the business, a sacrifice of a nature deserving to be mentioned. It is resorted to when a person is sick, as a most efficacious means of recovery. An effigy of straw, bearing a rude resemblance to the human form, is prepared, and clothed in the best garments of the sick person. After various preliminary ceremonies the officiating priests proceed to *slay* the victim, that is, to stab the effigy of straw with their knives, and then placing it upon a horse or ox, convey it to the distance of perhaps half-a-mile from the place, and then they burn it with fire. The dress is previously stripped off, and becomes a perquisite to the priest. This *Zolik*, as it is called, is made under the absurd notion, that by virtue of the prayers and incantations of the priests, the god who has brought the disease upon the sick person, and is trying to destroy him, will be deceived, and mistaking the effigy for the original will, upon it being stabbed and burnt, relinquish his hold upon the real sufferer!

One of William's acquaintances, the Shireetei, or head lama, of the Ona lamasery, was reputed to be a great doctor. One day, the taisha's little son, aged four, fell off a cart, and hit his head so hard that blood flowed out of his ears. The lama gave him some medicine, and then prepared some holy water as a lotion.

> This preparation consists in reading one or more of their holy books, and shaking the leaves immediately after being read over a pot, containing a mixture of milk and water. The Lama, at the same time that he shakes the virtue out of the leaves of his book, spits into the pot, thereby communicating to it, according to their ridiculous notions, a mysterious efficacy in removing diseases.

This particular lama, however, was probably not as much the prisoner of 'ridiculous notions' as William believed, but was rather pandering to popular superstition. Only a few days later, William got him to look at his own copyist, Rintsin from Selenginsk, who was suffering from an intermittent fever. William had managed to procure some quinine which was being sold off as part of the effects of the late taisha Dembil, and had administered this to Rintsin, but without effect. The back was probably inferior. So, 'thinking it would cheer him a little', William took Rintsin to the taisha's tent, to see if the lama could do anything for him. He confessed himself much impressed by the careful way in which the lama examined the boy, taking his pulse, and examining his eyes and tongue. Then he prescribed for him. The treatment consisted first of all in rubbing the body with some resinous substance. Then came a certain drug whose effect was to make the patient intoxicated for twenty-four hours. After this, a purgative had to be taken, and after two days the cycle of drugs was to be repeated. Rintsin followed the regimen, and no more is heard of his fever.

But there were other lamas who looked more to magic than to medicine, believing in the sympathetic power of their scriptures, and even transferring this efficacy to Christian tracts. A lama called on Edward one day complaining of sore eyes. Edward gave him some medicine and also a tract. Some time later the lama came back, his eyes much improved, to assure Edward how effective his *nom*, or sacred book, had proved. With dry irony, Edward adds: 'I wished him to go on reading, expressing my hope that if he continued to read, his eyes would in due time be completely opened.'

News of the wonderful skill possessed by the untrained missionaries, especially Edward, soon spread, and before the Stallybrasses had been at Selenginsk for a year, Buryats were coming in from as far away as 250 or 300 miles for treatment. Edward regretted having to give up so much time for what he considered to be a very secondary object of his mission:

> I am become very popular in these parts as a medical man, both amongst the Russians and the Bratsky, and more particularly the latter. Having been successful in a few simple instances, cases of every kind are brought to me. The only work which I have to consult is 'Buchan's Domestic Medicine' which I happily brought with me. . . . I am sometimes afraid of encouraging their applications, lest it should infringe upon the time which ought to be devoted to other purposes. It is, however, hard to deny a fellow-creature in distress any relief which may be afforded, in addition to which it is likely to gain the confidence of the Bratsky, and to prove an introduction to them for the impartition of better blessings.

These 'better blessings' consisted in preaching the gospel, obtaining conversions, and so saving souls from perdition. This alone, not healing the sick, was the justification for maintaining the mission, but in practice the missionaries found that their popularity as doctors had its compensations. It provided them with a captive audience for indoctrination and the distribution of tracts. Robert, characteristically, overdid it, and deliberately exploited the Buryats' dependence on the mission, making them hang about, or even attend church, before he would see them, even on weekdays.

Family Life in Siberia

> The Boriates now know that we do not attend to business on the Sabbath, and therefore we have few visitors at the two oclock worship, conducted by Mr Stallybrass. But as they must call occasionally for their own benefit, i.e. temporal benefit, they are therefore compelled to fall in with the general rule of the house viz. That no business is done, or visitor received till after worship in the morning; and all that intrude upon me for lodgings at night must be at both the evening and morning service.

As time went on, the demands upon Edward's services outran his elementary skill, and in 1823 he was writing home asking for a manual of surgery, or anything on the subject – back numbers of journals, or pamphlets about specimen cases – to be sent out, 'as we have frequently surgical cases which without proper works of reference I am at a loss to treat'.

Edward's professional reluctance to give up too much of his time to medical work was not shared by his more famous successor among the Mongols, James Gilmour, who saw in first aid the best way of approaching and influencing the people. By the time Gilmour went out to China in 1870, the concept of the medical missionary as such had evolved, and he found a flourishing LMS hospital in operation at Peking when he arrived there. But the institutionalization of medical work had brought with it a professional exclusiveness which the missionaries at Selenginsk, ill-prepared though they were, had at least been spared. They seem to have acquired some elementary knowledge of doctoring before they went out, and were able not only to treat the Buryats, but to carry out simple operations, like the reduction of a dislocated ankle or toe, on each other. Gilmour, fifty years later, was sent out with absolutely no medical training at all. He was prudent enough to pick up some hints in the mission hospital in Peking before risking days and weeks of isolation from civilization on the Mongolian steppes, and he then wrote back to the stay-at-homes at headquarters in London in forthright condemnation of what he considered their neglect of their responsibilities towards men going to occupy remote stations:

> At home it is all very well to stand before the fire in your room within sight of the brass plate on the doctor's door on the opposite side of the street and talk about the danger of a little knowledge; but when you are two weeks' journey from any assistance and see your fellow traveller sitting silent and swollen with violent toothache for days together, you fervently wish you had a pair of forceps and the *dangerous* amount of knowledge; and when in remote places you have the choice of burying your servant or stopping his diarrhoea, would you prefer to talk nonsense about professional skill rather than give him a dose of chlorodyne even though it should be at the risk of administering one drop more or less than a man who writes M.D. after his name would have done?. . . . I think it is little less than culpable homicide to deny

> a little hospital training to men, who may have to pass weeks and months of their lives in places where they themselves or those about them may sicken and die from curable diseases before the doctor could be summoned even supposing he could leave his post and come. Let it be understood that I speak now only of those intended for remote places, and the question I ask is this. 'Seeing they must [underlined four times] however unwillingly, have to do with sickness and accidents and seeing that, if they come unprepared to deal with such things, they must prepare themselves when they ought to be engaged in direct missionary work, would it not be much better to prepare themselves before leaving home even though they should know a few less Greek and Hebrew roots?'

This was strong stuff from a young missionary with only three years' experience in the field, and the situation it reflects suggest how much things had changed as mission practice developed from the happy-go-lucky amateurism of Selenginsk to the hierarchical formality of a big centre like Peking.

All the care of their own health and of that of their families too fell upon the missionaries. Of the two women at the Selenginsk station, Martha Yuille was strong and healthy, and it was a shock to everyone when she succumbed to typhus in 1827, after an illness of three weeks. Sarah, on the other hand, was often ill, and had to struggle along, watched anxiously by her husband, looking after her growing family, running the house, and teaching the Buryat girls, in defiance of one complaint or another. In 1819 it was a 'suppurating breast', which had troubled her ever since the birth of her first son the year before. Then it was dysentery. Then, in 1822, the birth of her little girl Sarah brought back the breast trouble again. In June 1828 Edward wrote to Ann and Joseph to say that 'my dear Sarah has never been so strong, as formerly, since the birth of James', and in fact James Steven was to be the last of their children. Sarah contracted a serious illness in 1831, from which she never recovered. Edward maintained that the root cause of her ill-health was a shock of some sort which she had experienced before she ever left home, but it is quite possible that repeated pregnancies in the harsh climate and not very hygienic surroundings of Transbaikalia may have taken their toll. She gradually declined, both physically and mentally, and died in February 1833.

Edward took the loss of his wife very hard. He wrote to Ann and Joseph:

> The mortal remains of dear Sarah are deposited within our own enclosure, in sight of my study window. Her tomb is built up in the form of an urn, and I am getting a cast iron plate, with an inscription in Latin for the top. When last I wrote you, although her spirit had escaped, yet *these* were still with me; and for some time they afforded me a melancholy consolation. But Oh the last glance of those undistorted, scarcely changed features, which will ever be deeply

inscribed upon my heart! Loth was I to let her go, but Mr Yuille kindly interposed, removed me, and closed her from my sight. He came post haste to me and performed the last sad office for her.

Gilmour saw the iron plate when he visited Khodon, and reproduced the Latin text of the inscription in his book.

When they went travelling, the missionaries preferred to stay overnight in the tents of the Buryats they were trying to influence, in spite of the squalor and discomfort, rather than lodge in the somewhat superior houses of the Russians. Russian eyebrows were raised at this eccentricity. As Edward wrote in 1819, soon after settling in at Selenginsk: 'Many of my Russian neighbours are surprised that I take so much trouble among the dirty Boriats. But I can truly say that I have enjoyed happiness here, which I never before knew.' The Russians never ceased to be astonished at the missionaries' unconventional behaviour. Three years later Edward recorded in his Journal:

> In the morning a Russian came from the village into the tents and expressed his great surprise at our sleeping in a Boriatt's tent when there were so many Russian houses near. We often met with similar instances of surprise, and if we had sought our own and not their good our conduct would have been surprising, but, glad to take the opportunities which long winter evenings afforded of imparting instruction to them, we willingly submitted to the inconveniences which our method subjected us to. The principal of these was the cold. As the Boriatt tents in general have no sort of floor, we were frequently unable to sleep, and obliged to arise in the middle of the night to kindle a fire.

The missionaries' Journals were meant for the Directors' eyes as well as their own, and stoicism in the cause of duty was in order. Privately, they admitted that the cold, and proximity to unwashed Buryat bodies, had their drawbacks. In January 1835 William wrote to Edward, who was on leave in St Petersburg, to keep him abreast of what was happening about the printing of Exodus, and giving him a little local news as well. At the beginning of January the temperature had dropped so low that his mercury thermometer was frozen, and on the 5th he had been able to record a morning temperature of −31° Reamur, the scale used in Russia, or about −40°C. This was hard enough to bear, though it happened regularly every winter, but having to sit in the same stuffy room with a class of Buryat boys who were none too clean was even more of a trial. William did not complain to his friend, but Hannah added a P.S. to the letter:

> I mean to make a request here which will make you smile and which I believe Mr Swan was too modest to do. You cannot sympathize with him as regards *smells* but I am sure you will *feel* for him when I tell you he is scarcely ever able to have the boys with him in his own room

without suffering severely from head ache and pain and the same reason which I suppose you can guess prevents him from being in the school room from which he returns quite sick. These things did not affect him in days gone by but now they do, and his frequent indispositions make me very anxious – he brought when we came here a little box of *Pastilles* which is now almost done – he has found them useful for fumigating his room – if such things are to be got in St. P. do send us a box in some packet that may be coming this way when convenient.

Of the thirteen mission children, only eight survived to adulthood. Little Susannah Stallybrass died in 1825, the year of her birth, in the same week as Elisabeth and Janet Yuille. Another little Yuille, Robert, who had been sickly from birth, died of a fever in 1823, and Edward's last child, Benjamin, died in extreme infancy in 1839. The tragic loss of three children within a few days was the result of an epidemic of what Robert called 'malignant sore throat', and may have been diphtheria. Strange to say, none of the children succumbed to smallpox, which was rife in Transbaikalia, and of which there was an epidemic almost every winter.

Smallpox seems not to have been an indigenous disease among either Mongols or Buryats. The Mongols probably acquired it through contact with the Chinese, and the first reliable reference to its occurrence among them is dated as late as the middle of the fifteenth century. The disease was familiar to the Chinese long before this, and the practice of inoculation against it is popularly supposed to have been introduced around the year AD 1000. According to Joseph Rehmann, the German doctor who accompanied Count Golovkin's abortive embassy to the Chinese court in 1805–6, it was the Russians who had introduced smallpox into Siberia, where it spread rapidly amongst the native peoples, including the Buryats. Immunization by means of variolation, the process of inoculating one person with matter drawn from another, was a familiar practice in Europe during the eighteenth century, and had probably been borrowed from the Chinese, who had originated it, by way of Turkey. Lady Mary Wortley Montagu witnessed what was at the time an exotic method of prophylaxis, and described it in a letter written from Adrianople in 1717. Only a few years later, Père d'Entrecolles, to whom we also owe a detailed account of the manufacture of porcelain, described different methods of immunization as practised by the Chinese. Almost at the same time, in 1730, the youthful second Khutuktu of Urga was immunized by the method which the Mongols termed 'sowing the flowers', meaning, most probably, the introduction of powdered crusts from a sick person into the nostrils of the patient. In England, on the other hand, matter would be introduced into an incision made in the arm, a procedure graphically described by William Hickey. By the beginning of the nineteenth century, true vaccination, that is, inoculation with cow pox, which Edward Jenner had demonstrated successfully in 1796, had reached eastern Siberia, and Rehmann extended the work amongst the Buryats by vaccinating them as and when he could. Supplies of vaccine were not always available, and this shortage affected the missionaries at Selenginsk, who were familiar with both techniques.

The Transbaikalian winter of 1823–24 was a hard one. There had been a severe drought in the summer of 1823. Sowing had been delayed, and little of the corn which was sown had germinated. Most of what did sprout failed to ripen and was cut for cattle feed. Animals had to be slaughtered for lack of hay, and this led in turn to depressed prices for meat. The dry summer was followed by a snowy winter, which was also bad for the cattle. In a cold spring with snow-cover the sun would melt the snow by day, and at night it would freeze hard, and the beasts, weakened after the long winter months, would be too feeble to scratch down to the withered grass beneath the ice. Cattle starvation, or *zud*, resulting from these conditions, was, and still is, a major source of disaster to the nomadic herders of Mongolia. To cap it all, 1824 saw a lethal outbreak of smallpox around Selenginsk. The first of the mission children to catch it was Elisabeth Yuille, and her illness provided the Khamba – who had rather unwillingly promised Robert to send him some lads, one of them his own nephew, for the new mission school at Selenginsk – with a good excuse for taking them away again. Edward's two eldest boys had been vaccinated, but he had been unable to get any vaccine for the two younger children, Sarah, aged three, and John, who was one. So he decided to immunize them by variolation from Elisabeth's pox. Robert gave him what he called a fine large pock, which he took home in his pocket, and applied to the arms of his small children. Robert was dubious about the wisdom of doing this, but it turned out satisfactorily. Sarah and John had smallpox but got over it, as did little Janet Yuille, who seems not to have undergone immunization.

For the children, Siberia was home, and they grew up like little Russians, dressed in Russian fashion, and speaking Russian as their first language, though they knew Mongolian perfectly as well, and could manage, though rather unwillingly, in English. To the end of their lives, the older Stallybrass children never entirely forgot their Buryat background. In 1850, nine years after the family came home, Edward's son James Steven noted down, with the help of his brothers and sisters, some of the songs which they had sung in their childhood. James died in 1888, and towards the end of his life his transcriptions came to the notice of the musicologist C. Stumpf, who edited them and published them in Germany in 1887, in what was then a pioneering analysis of Mongolian music. Stumpf writes as if he had met James, which is of course quite possible, saying of him:

> Mr Stallybrass, a highly cultivated man, is firmly convinced of the faithfulness of his notes, and stresses, with good reason, that, according to his experience, it is almost impossible to forget one's favourite

Family Life in Siberia

childhood melodies, especially when they have the closest relation to characteristic texts, and word and tune mutually recall each other.

Of Samuel Yuille we know almost nothing, except that he stayed on in Selenginsk with his father, and left with him in 1846, aged about twenty-two. Nor do we know what became of the Swans' adopted Buryat daughter, whom they had acquired because it was the only way they could get regular assistance for the school which they set up at Ona. Did she come back to Scotland in 1841, or did she stay behind in Transbaikalia?

The young Stallybrasses grew up somewhat aloof from their contemporaries, taking on the role of teachers and spiritual confidants of the young Buryats around them at an early age. Their entire upbringing and schooling, until Edward brought Thomas and William to England in 1834 to enter Silcoates school, was centred on their home. Sarah gave them their first lessons, and Edward took charge of them as they grew up, grounding them in the usual school subjects, including Latin and Greek. It was in their own home, too, that they went to church, and the church itself consisted solely of the mission families, for none of the Buryat converts was ever baptized, and so could not attain full membership.

Edward realized that artificial isolation from their contemporaries at home might cause his sons to grow up with too good an opinion of themselves. As he wrote:

> They have no stimulus from emulation. They have no superiors, no equals; none but those who are far inferior, to look to. The natural effect of this must be very evident, – a danger of self complacency. While they are looked upon by others as little oracles, it is hard to convince *them* that they are far behind what they should be. There are also many other things connected with the formation of their character which render it highly desirable that they should have intercourse with Christian Society.

It was, indeed, an inward-looking society to which the Stallybrass children belonged, and it was no wonder that they grew up with no ambition in mind but to become missionaries themselves.

This had been Sarah's constantly expressed wish. Writing to Ann and Joseph in 1834, Edward said:

> My two dear boys have come to the conclusion that they would prefer giving their lives to the Lord Jesus as Missionaries to any other employment upon earth. Oh, may they have grace to adhere to this resolution. Their desire is after enjoying some advantages in England, to return hither, where by their intimate knowledge of the language they would be fitted for immediate labour. Need I say that their wishes are in unison with mine? – with those of their dear, sainted Mother? Often has she said to them 'Remember, if you become anything but

Missionaries, I shall be disappointed.' She desired this, and laboured for it; and now her desires are realized, and her labours blessed.

Thomas and William were, respectively, sixteen and fourteen years old at the time. Their father brought them home in 1834, and sent them to Silcoates School, partly at the expense of the Society. Through no fault of their own they did not become missionaries, as Siberia remained closed to them, Chinese Mongolia was not yet open, and the LMS doubted whether they were constitutionally fitted for other fields. Their future lay in the ministry at home.

Some extracts from a letter which John Knox Stallybrass sent to Ann Monds in 1838, when he was about fifteen, illustrate how strict must have been the religious upbringing to which the Stallybrass children were subjected, and what a constricting effect it must have had on the development of their personalities. Even allowing that it was a party piece, it betrays John as a remarkable little prig. He writes:

> By the last letter from Aunt Prout, we heard of the death of Uncle James Stallybrass. May it be a warning for us to prepare for death. As we had no evidence of his end being that of the righteous, it was an afflictive stroke upon Papa, and all of us.

John went on:

> In your last letter you put a question to me if I had followed the example of my brothers and sister, in choosing the Lord for my God, and in making a covenant engagement to be the Lord's?. . . In the letter I wrote immediately after the receipt of your kind epistle, I could not reply in the affirmative and as I have not a copy of it I do not remember what I said then, but now I humbly hope I can tell you, that I have fled to the cross for Salvation. Since my last date the arrow of conviction has I humbly hope wounded my heart, and produced in me the fruits of repentance and faith. . . . We have just received some Evangelical Magazines from England, and are busy reading them. They are very interesting and profiting indeed. We were reading last night about the martyrdom of Rafaravavy, one of the converts of Madagascar. May we if called upon to endure suffering, or even *death* for Christ's sake, be faithful unto death, and afterward receive the crown of life.

These early impressions endured. When last we hear of John in his father's letters in 1842 he was expecting to go to a theological college, Coward or Homerton, and meanwhile he was preaching in Lincolnshire.

Rafaravavy was more fortunate than many of the converts in Madagascar, who were put to death in the most savage ways. After many adventures she managed to escape from the island, and from the persecutions unleashed there by Queen Ranavalona, and to get first to Mauritius and then to

England. John Knox's heroic dream of emulating her, though, was unlikely to be realized. The Buryats were the mildest of people, and the missionaries never felt the slightest threat to their safety amongst them. As Edward wrote, soon after settling in Selenginsk:

> They are a remarkably harmless, inoffensive sort of people; when upon my journeys amongst them, I lie down to sleep in their huts (upon a mat which they spread for me upon the ground) with the greatest composure and satisfaction. It is very frequently the case that before I can scarcely turn myself in their tents, I behold a sheep killed for me, meat of which is immediately cooked.

James Gilmour draws an exaggeratedly grim picture of what life must have been like for the missionaries – 'Banishment to Siberia! Exile in Siberia! Death in Siberia!' But life in Siberia – 'Dear Siberia', as the missionaries were known to call it – was not all hardship. It had its drawbacks, certainly. Transbaikalia had already become what it continued to be throughout the century, a dumping ground for convicts and other undesirables deported from European Russia and Poland. Criminals were constantly escaping from custody and roaming the countryside, and it was from them that what little danger there was could be anticipated. The mission house was rather vulnerable, isolated as it was from Selenginsk and all but a few Buryat neighbours.

Martha Yuille was alarmed one night, while her husband was away on a journey, by intruders who had got right inside the mission compound, though she never confessed to feeling any fear. Fortunately, the missionaries were men of sound common sense and, while trusting in divine protection, took practical steps to ensure that that protection could be rendered effective. As William wrote to George Burder in April 1822: 'Although we are *nightly* in danger of attacks from bands of desperate convicts who go about the country robbing and murdering we have hitherto been kept in safety. We are obliged to keep our fire arms etc in readiness, but our trust is in higher protection.' Burder professed himself sorry that the missionaries found it necessary to arm themselves. He trusted that 'the terror has been only of a very temporary duration and that the effect has in no respect been prejudicial to the feebler members of the Mission Families', and he prayed that 'the everlasting be your defence in all dangers'. He did not try to dissuade the missionaries from keeping guns in the mission house, but on the other hand, the trusting public at home was never allowed to know what precautions they had to take against their fellow men. The missionaries never mention in their letters any of the highly cultured exiles sent to Siberia after the suppression of the Decembrist uprising, though they were certainly aware of their presence in Transbaikalia. Thus, by a strange coincidence, the Decembrist D. I. Zavalishin ran across Charlotte, Edward's second wife, in the Khori steppes some time in the late 1830s, and the encounter reminded him of how, as a Russian naval officer, he had been entertained in the house of her father, whom he remembered as the Dutch consul, some twenty years before, at Elsinore. Robert, too, knew K. P. Torson and the brothers M. A. and N. A. Bestuzhev, who had settled only a short distance from him, on the left bank of the Selenga, opposite Selenginsk, in 1837 and 1839 respectively. But by the time their acquaintance began Robert was no longer in regular correspondence with the Directors of the LMS, and we know of it only because the Bestuzhevs mentioned it in one or two of their letters to their relatives.

Hardest to bear, for the adults, must have been the sense of separation from their families and friends at home, and of isolation amongst heathen Buryats and a few Russians. They did have the consolation of a fairly regular postal service, which seems to have been more reliable than Gilmour imagined when he wrote: 'No telegraph there, and postal services very meagre.' Letters could be sent in both directions through the Society's agent in St Petersburg, and the missionaries also kept in touch with colleagues elsewhere in Russia. We know, for example, that they corresponded with Cornelius in Sarepta, and with a Mr Mitchell in Astrakhan. When one or other of them went home on leave, letters sent by post could overtake the slower-moving passenger-sledges. The missionaries exchanged private letters with friends at home, as well as with their families, and also with relatives in the United States, from whom they managed to receive money on at least one occasion. Sometimes they even got parcels, containing gifts of books, samplers worked by Ann and Joseph's children, and so on. Isolation was by no means absolute, though Sarah hints darkly that not all of the letters they wrote actually reached England.

But England must have seemed very far away at times, with letters taking months in either direction, and with little prospect of home leave. Still, the missionaries had expected this when they accepted their call to the field, and it was part of the normal lot of their profession. Sarah certainly missed her father deeply, correctly anticipating when she left him that she would never see him again. Edward bore the loss of his own father with much greater stoicism, even indifference, perhaps because the older man had disappointed him by turning to Unitarianism in his later years. Edward also overcame any feelings of homesickness. Writing to William Ellis in 1834 about his projected visit home, he said:

> It is now more than seventeen years since I left my native land; and during that space I can safely say that my *back* has been turned towards it. I have many much loved friends, but have felt no hankering desire to see them. I have been willing to forego that pleasure till we see each other in a more perfect state. I know, too, that there is no need of Missionaries at home. So many are *compelled* to go home from sickness, and other causes, that the effect upon those who are able to *remain* ought

to be to bind them still closer to their stations. So I have thought and acted.

Of the three men, Robert never took furlough at all. William and Edward each paid one visit home during the period of their mission, but in neither case was it simply in order to take a holiday. In January 1829 William Orme, the Secretary of the LMS, invited William to come back, principally in order to advise the Directors about the state and prospects of the mission, and to give them information about the Buryats which it might have been imprudent to entrust to the Russian posts. No copy of Orme's letter survives, but it is clear from William's reply, dated 18 May 1829, that the Directors also thought he might wish to visit England for personal reasons – a delicate way of intimating to him that they appreciated that he might be thinking of marriage. It is quite possible that Orme may have been reacting to a suggestion put to him, half jokingly, by Paterson, only a few months earlier. Paterson had written to him in September 1828 with instructions about the format of the title page of William's Memoir of his wife Jean which was about to be printed. For some reason, now impenetrable, the author's name was not to be prefixed with the title *Revd*. He was to be identified simply as William Swan, Missionary at Selenginsk. Then Paterson had added; 'Poor fellow, I wish you could send out an amiable pious sensible young woman in some capacity or other who would make a good wife to him!!'

In fact, William was feeling the want of a wife, if only because, now that he was on his own at Ona, he saw how much more effective a married missionary could be than a bachelor. But in 1829 he still had doubts about the viability of the mission, and was not sure that it was advisable to bring out a bride to face the uncertain future. As he told Orme:

> I feel very sensibly the friendly concern you manifest for myself personally, in inquiring whether I have any desire to visit Great Britain for a season, expressing at the same time a wish for a general interview for the purpose of obtaining more particular information than we can communicate by letter concerning the scene of our labours. My mind in the matter is simply this, that were the state of things in Russia such that this mission could be considered as properly established I should be desirous, both for the more effectually carrying on of my work as a Missionary and for my own comfort, to seek a partner of my labours, joys and sorrows; but, things remaining in the uncertain state in which they have been for years past – neither openly for us nor openly against us, I am at a loss what to think.

By the end of the following year, William had made up his mind that there was more to be gained by visiting England than by not doing so, and early in 1831 he set out for home. His journey proved of crucial importance for the survival of the mission, for while he was in St Petersburg on the way home he conducted the negotiations with the authorities which led to the confirmation of the mission's status, and on the return journey he obtained permission to print the Old Testament in Mongolian. As far as his personal life was concerned, the journey was a happy one, for while in Scotland he married Miss Hannah Cullen, who was then in her early twenties, and took her back to Siberia with him.

William and Hannah arrived in St Petersburg during August 1832. In December, William wrote to William Ellis concerning matters which had delayed him, and to say that he hoped to be able to leave the capital some time in the next few weeks, so as to reach Transbaikalia before the winter snow-roads broke up. Then something unexpected happened, of such compelling importance that it detained him in St Petersburg for the best part of the coming year.

It was just at this time that the prospect of being able to print a Manchu translation of the New Testament, which had been completed a few years earlier by S. V. Lipovtsov, was occupying the thoughts of the Committee of the BFBS. At the beginning of January 1833 the Committee interviewed George Borrow, who had been recommended to them as an outstanding linguist, and by the end of July Borrow was on his way to Russia in their service, appointed to organize the printing of the Manchu Testament. Almost coincidentally, William discovered that it might be possible to lay his hands on a copy of most of the Bible, including the Old Testament, in Chinese and Manchu translation, which had been made in China at the end of the eighteenth century by a Jesuit priest named Louis Poirot. The Orientalist Baron Schilling von Canstadt had put him on the track of this manuscript in November 1832. It was owned by a 'gentleman formerly connected with the Russian Mission in Pekin', who turns out to be that Dr Voichekovskii who had been a student with the Tenth Mission which passed through Selenginsk on its outward journey in 1820, and who later in life occupied the chair of Chinese at the University of Kazan. This work would naturally have complemented Lipovtsov's New Testament, and Baron Schilling urged William to consult the BFBS. William wrote to that Society in November, describing the find. The owner refused to put a price on it, preferring to elicit an offer. The only advice William could offer the BFBS was that the work comprised over 10,000 pages, and that at a penny a page – the lowest rate for copying – the mere manual labour involved in its production would have been about £50. He supposed that the owner would not take less.

The Committee of the BFBS thereupon authorized William to offer £50 for the manuscript, giving him discretion to go as high as £100 if necessary. This rather meagre offer failed to match the expectations of Dr Voichekovskii, who valued the book at 50,000 roubles, or, so William calculated, upwards of £2,000. Naturally, no compromise could be reached, and William let the matter drop. But then he learned that there was a second copy of Poirot's version in the capital. This had been brought back by the Archiman-

Family Life in Siberia

drite Kamenskii, an old acquaintance from his Selenginsk days, and Kamenskii had presented his copy to the Holy Synod. William consulted Schilling about this new discovery, and the Baron offered to act as intermediary in negotiations to obtain the loan of the book so that a copy could be made. The question was, who should make the copy? There was really only one answer. William himself was the one man with a knowledge of Manchu who happened to be in St Petersburg at the time.

William was in a quandary. George Borrow's biographer, Miss Bigland, airily suggests that the discovery of the Manchu Old Testament drove all other thoughts out of his mind. She writes that 'understandably enough, the scholarly Mr. Swan forgot all about Siberia, sent an urgent message to the Bible Society in London, and sat down there and then to transcribe the Bible'. It did not happen quite like that. William was an employee of the LMS, not the BFBS, and could not decide, in a unilateral fit of amnesia, to abandon his mission for a whole year, even if he had wanted to. His dilemma had a personal dimension to it, too. All his heavy luggage had been packed up and sent off, and he and Hannah were within a few hours of leaving St Petersburg when the second manuscript turned up, and he could prolong his stay in the capital only at the cost of considerable inconvenience. He was also anxious to get back to Siberia and relieve Edward, who had been running the Khodon station by himself for two years. It was not an easy decision to take, but the deciding factor was no doubt the knowledge that, if the loan of the Manchu manuscript were declined now, there would probably never be a second chance to copy it. So William talked the matter over with Knill and with the leading members of the Congregational church in St Petersburg, and a corporate decision was taken that he should postpone his journey, and begin to copy the Old Testament, while awaiting the retrospective approval of the Directors. There was another factor which weighed with them. Everyone suspected that Schmidt would prove a dilatory censor of the Mongolian Old Testament, and the presence of one of the translators in the capital might stimulate him to get on with the task.

The Directors did give their approval in a resolution which they sent to Knill in April 1833, asking him to pass it on to William. A month later they wrote directly to William, repeating the text of the resolution, and adding the news that the BFBS had agreed to pay the cost of his unexpected stay in St Petersburg. The BFBS had received the news of the discovery of the second manuscript with a rather unholy joy. Joseph Jowett, the Editorial Superintendent, gloated in a letter to William in February 1833:

> It was no surprise to find, that the possessor of the first named Copy had attached a higher value to his property, than you had led us to suspect; but we *were* surprised, I may almost say amused, by the extravagance of the demand he now makes; nor can we greatly regret that his cupidity is likely to meet with a suitable disappointment.

Family Life in Siberia

Copying the Manchu Old Testament proved a far more demanding task than William had expected. He had hoped to finish it by the end of August 1833, by dint of working six days a week, and eight to twelve hours a day. But even with the help of George Borrow, whom he described as 'a gentleman who has made some progress in the study of Manchoo', and who arrived during the summer, the transcription was not finished and ready to be sent to London till almost the end of the year. Hannah and William finally got away from St Petersburg on 15/27 December 1833.

Edward left Siberia in October 1834. He had two reasons for taking leave. The first was that his sons were about to travel abroad for the first time in their lives, and he wanted to go with them, at least as far as St Petersburg. In that October, he was still uncertain whether his own affairs would take him further than the Russian capital, and this uncertainty was bound up with his second purpose. Sarah had been dead for over a year, and Edward was feeling the urge to remarry, both for his personal happiness and for the good of the mission. He had been planning this step for some time, and had taken William Ellis into his confidence in June 1834, when he wrote:

> But now you know, that 'the Lord has made a breach upon me,' – 'the hand of God has touched me.' The difference which this has produced in my circumstances is such that I cannot fully describe. This must necessarily produce a difference in some of my thoughts and feelings, and in my need too. I desire humbly to bow to his dispensation; and I desire also that the instruction and correction which He intended may be received and improved by me. But oh it has left such a solitariness of heart, such a desolation of spirits, as I often ill know how to bear; and such as, I feel fully convinced, I could not long bear without serious detriment to my health and usefulness. I regard it, therefore, as a duty which I owe to myself, in reference to my health and comfort; – to the Society, in reference to my usefulness; – and to my children, in reference to their future welfare, that I seek a reparation of the breach which has been made. Happy would I be had I the prospect of making such a reparation without leaving my station and incurring the expenses of a journey. But of that I have no prospect. I therefore desire to be left at liberty to act in respect of this as my circumstances may require, with this proviso, that it be with a view to the good of the Mission, – according as its circumstances may allow, – and with the entire concurrence of my Brethren.

Edward's colleagues approved of his intention to take leave and remarry, though Robert found something to carp at in his choice of bride. 'I never wish to middle with other peoples personal affairs,' he wrote to his two colleagues in September 1834, 'but I think as he was designed to go to Europe that he might keep from closing with —— till such [sic] he looks about him. Perhaps an English lady would prove at last more suitable.'

Family Life in Siberia

Edward left Khodon on 15/27 October 1834, just as the storm about the printing of Genesis was about to break over his head.

As Robert's letter shows, Edward was not going home to search for a bride, but to conclude an engagement already initiated. It is not certain when and how he persuaded Miss Charlotte Ellah, a member of the English family at Elsinore whom he and Sarah had called on in 1817, to become the second Mrs Stallybrass, but negotiations were already far enough advanced before he left Khodon for him to be pretty sure that she was going to accept him. On 4 October, the same day that he announced his impending departure to Ellis, he wrote to Ann and Joseph explaining and excusing the step he was about to take, and soliciting their approval. He also let them into the secret of his expected engagement, adding coyly:

> Shall I tell you more? That I have an object in view? But I could not speak this except in the ears of friendship – and that in a low whisper – for until my arrival in St. P. I can form no idea whether my intentions will be likely to be put into execution. Should we arrive thither in safety, I will write you more on this subject from that place. You will observe that I write this in perfect confidence – Memini!

The identity of Edward's bride became known in March 1835 when he wrote officially to Ebenezer Henderson, who was then chairman of the Eastern Committee of the Society, the committee which was responsible for the Siberian mission. Charlotte was in St Petersburg at the time, and stayed there until the beginning of May, when Edward saw her off for Elsinore in the company of his eldest son, Thomas, meaning to follow on with William as soon as he could. Amongst the family books now belonging to the Taylor Institution Library in Oxford are two which were once Charlotte's property. One is a copy of Schmidt's Mongolian Grammar, with her name, Charlotte Ellah, and the date, 27 March 1835, written in what appears to be Edward's hand on the flyleaf. In the bottom left-hand corner are the first words of the Lord's Prayer in Mongolian. The other is a copy of Schmidt's Dictionary, inscribed with Charlotte's name and the date in exactly the same way. But in this book, poor Charlotte's name has been overwritten with that of her stepson William Carey and is almost illegible. March 27 may have been a special day, but it can hardly have been her wedding day. For one thing, she is still called by her maiden name. For another, Edward, writing to Ellis on 18/30 May about his travel plans, still calls her Miss Ellah.

Most probably, Edward married Charlotte at Elsinore, where he left her while he went on to England with the boys. Charlotte, though English, had no connections with England, and preferred to wait with her family for Edward to pick her up on the return journey. He met her next in September 1835 at Lübeck, where she and her mother were staying with a sister, and by then he was referring to her as 'my dear Mrs S' in his letters. From Lübeck the three of them took a steamer to Copenhagen, and went on from

Family Life in Siberia

there to Elsinore. They spent the whole of October there, and then set out on Charlotte's last journey.

Edward says almost nothing about Charlotte in his letters. She was ill in St Petersburg, and ill on the journey to Siberia. In the four years of her marriage she gave birth to three sons, of whom two, Henry Martyn and Charles Ellah survived, and lived on into the twentieth century. She died at Khodon in the autumn of 1839, at the age of thirty-two, and was buried there alongside Sarah with her infant son Benjamin. Gilmour remembered seeing her grave, with an inscription in Russian on an iron plate set over it.

12

Missionary and Lama

The missionaries, like their sponsors, believed that, in organizing a Christian mission to Siberia, they were responding to a call for spiritual help from the Buryats. Nothing could have been further from the truth, and it was a painful revelation when they discovered that, while their presence excited some temporary curiosity, the Buryats were indifferent to the message they had brought. The LMS had been founded for a single purpose – 'to spread the knowledge of Christ among the Heathen and other unenlightened Nations' – and the missionaries were firmly convinced not only that they had the right and duty to pursue that aim, but also that, in God's good time, they were bound to achieve success. When success did come, it would be counted in Buryats converted and souls saved from perdition, not in the number of children educated in their schools or the number of invalids restored to health.

There was, too, though they tried to disguise it, considerable personal satisfaction to be found in the realization that they had been divinely chosen to undertake this noble task. Sarah, especially, had to try very hard to subdue her exalted emotions. When she felt doubt about the prospect before her, she found that 'the claim of perishing millions is a sufficient argument against all personal feelings'. What an honour it was, 'conferred upon mortals, to be employed for the promotion of His glory! And am *I* thus to be honoured? O may I never abuse the privilege, but may my future life witness for God.' For out there, in distant Siberia, were the 'deluded exiles of the plain', whom she was desperate to tell all that religion had done for her soul, and what it would do for theirs. Alas! the 'deluded exiles' were quite unmoved by Sarah's raptures and her solicitude for them.

With all their ostentatious humility, the missionaries were quite sure of themselves. The fundamental problem which faced them was not the identification of their purpose, but how best to accomplish it. They had all had a training of sorts. William had studied at the Theological Academy in Glasgow, Edward had attended Homerton College, and Cornelius had graduated from the University of Lund. Robert was the only one of the four who had anything approaching a specialized missionary training, at Dr Bogue's seminary at Gosport, where students had been admitted from 1801. But in none of these institutions, not even at Gosport, can there have been much systematic professional feed-back from the mission field. William's own *Letters on Missions*, first published in 1830, was itself an early handbook of missionary theory and practice based on first-hand knowledge of the field. So, far from being able to profit by the experience of others, it was the experience of the missionaries in Siberia themselves, digested and systematized by one of their own number, which provided one of the earliest comprehensive surveys of the profession of missionary. When they themselves entered the field, they had to feel their way.

William's book was not the first to deal with the subject of evangelical mission work, but, to judge from the introduction which William Orme contributed to it, it seems to have been the first to do so in a comprehensive way. Orme wrote:

> Before the writer of this Introduction had any idea of occupying the important office which he now fills in the London Missionary Society, he wrote the folowing remarks: 'Considering the period during which exertion had been made to propagate Christianity among the heathen, and the number of persons who are employed in the work, both at home and abroad, it is surprising that some work on what might be called the philosophy of missions, has not yet appeared.'

There were, admittedly, a couple of books by a certain James Douglas, one entitled *Hints on Missions*, the other dealing with the *Advancement of Society*, which Orme thought worthy of mention. But the former contained, as its title suggested, no more than a number of hints, while the latter covered many subjects besides missions. What Orme and others had felt the lack of was 'a condensed view of the knowledge and experience which have been acquired during the last thirty or forty years', a book which would answer a whole range of urgent questions about the nature and purpose of missionary work, and the ideal character, qualification, training and modes of operation of the individual missionary. William's book filled the gap, for it was 'the production not of a theorist, but of a practician; not of a spectator, but of an active operator in the fields which he describes; of one who has followed the path which he recommends to others, and calls for no sacrifice which he has not himself made'.

The implication is that Douglas was just such a theorist, and that his *Hints* were not a reliable guide to missionary practice. This was, in fact, William's view. Douglas was a rationalist, holding opinions which were not only contrary to practical experience, but also theologically unsound, and hence methodologically treacherous, in that they tended to inculcate reliance upon worldly wisdom rather than obedience to revealed truth. Douglas believed that the 'heathen' were as responsive to logic as he was himself, and that an appeal to reason would convince them of their religious as well as their secular errors. He maintained that 'a single glance through a microscope is sufficient to overturn their whole system'. William denied this. Douglas had failed to take into account that 'it is one thing to inform the judgment, and another to correct the obliquity of the will'. William took issue, too, with Douglas's view that 'servile ignorance is the *sole* support of the many superstitions of India'. That view would be tenable if ignorance meant ignorance of the revealed nature of God, and so on, but if Douglas was referring, as William thought he was, to ignorance of natural phenomena, he hoped he would not go on to maintain that 'philosophy may be substituted for the gospel, as the instrument of overturning the religion of the Bramins'.

William knew what he was talking about, for, some time before the appearance of his book, he had come near trying the experiment with the microscope on a Buryat, and the outcome had confirmed him in the correctness of his distinction between education and conviction, and in the futility of employing the observation of nature as a means of inculcating divine truth. One day in April 1827 he had had a long conversation with a Buryat named Ayushi, a local official, who had spent the night in his house at Ona. Ayushi was a Buddhist, and a convert from shamanism. He was a very intelligent man, who had read many Buddhist books, and was 'fully persuaded that they are all founded in truth, that they have all proceeded from God, and that in following them there can be no error'. William tried rational argument with him, and got nowhere:

> I endeavoured to convince him of the errors contained in his books on the subject of geography, the solar system, the doctrine of eclipses, etc. I found him, however, almost inaccessible to argument, and derived little aid from the exhibition and explanation of a pair of small globes, for as these were all contrary to the *noms*, they were, *of course*, unworthy of credit. I had not my microscope with me, and could not show him the animalculae in water, etc, but he said that he would not believe it although he saw them with his own eyes, for the appearance of animals in the water was a mere illusion produced by the glass. . . . A philosopher may think it a very easy matter to convince a heathen of his errors, but the actual experiment would, in many cases, lead him to question the correctness of his own views of the philosophy of the human mind. The scriptural account of the obliquity of the heart gives the only true and satisfactory explanation of the weakness of the human understanding, and its *incapacity* for the admission of unwelcome truth.

At least with respect to the Buryats, William was right and Douglas was wrong. Fifty years later, James Gilmour found that Buryat credulity had not altered a whit. They were quite capable of accepting, simultaneously, secular knowledge acquired from the Russians, and religious dogma which was incompatible with it:

Missionary and Lama

In an interview I had with a celebrated Lama of high position among the Buriats I was asked where my home was and by travelling in what direction I could reach it. This brought up the rotundity of the earth as opposed to the Buddhist *hearth stone* theory which is a fundamental doctrine of their sacred books. They manifested their knowledge and conviction of the truth of our theory and notwithstanding this they remained Buddhists and treated the matter as a joke. From this it is evident that mere knowledge cannot shake men's attachment to Buddhism. The fact is they are born into Buddhism, not reasoned into it, and are not be reasoned out of it. If they are to become Christians, it cannot be by the influence of the dead letter of knowledge, but by *coming into contact with the personal influence of living men*.

Some, but only a few, of the Buryats whose beliefs the missionaries were going to challenge, were as subtly sceptical as Ayushi. The population ranged in intellectual capacity and religious sophistication from masters of Buddhist theology who were able to expound their own system to the missionaries, down to bovine herdsmen and their passively ignorant womenfolk, who lived in fear of the spirit world, and were dependent on their idols of wood or felt. Some, the lamas, lived in sizeable communities, while others led a lonely existence on the open plains, nomadizing in small, isolated family groups which were hard to locate and keep track of. Most were completely illiterate, and even some of the lamas, who claimed to know Tibetan, could do no more than make out the words on the page, without understanding what they meant.

It was no easy task which awaited the inexperienced trio of missionaries at Selenginsk. Even Edward was not fluent in Buryat when he arrived, in spite of a year's language study in Irkutsk. What were they to do first, and how were they to set about it? In practice, their activities took three fairly distinct forms. One was a direct approach to the people, through the distribution of tracts and gospels, followed by conversations in which the contents of the books were explained. At a later stage, the missionaries held public services, accompanied by formal preaching. Secondly, they translated the Bible into Mongolian, printing the Old Testament on their own press. Thirdly, they opened schools both for boys and, a complete novelty in Buryatia, for girls too. Before they could do any of this effectively they had to master the language. On their early expeditions among the people they used interpreters, but what with constant travelling and the supervision of the builders at the mission station, they made rapid progress, and by the beginning of 1821 they could manage by themselves.

The missionaries themselves usually distinguished these three types of activity in their reports, and we shall consider them separately too, beginning in this chapter with itineration and preaching.

Except in the south, where Siberia touched China, the missionaries could see no definite limits to the pastures of the Buryats, which stretched out in all directions. In practice, though, they were to confine their activities almost entirely to the Selenginsk and Khori Buryats. The Selenginsk District formed a rough triangle, with the town of Verkhneudinsk near its apex. The Khori pastures lay further to the east. Some idea of the distances involved can be gathered from the facts that Selenginsk lay about 90 versts, more or less the same as 90 kilometres, from the Chinese frontier; Verkhneudinsk was 120 versts distant in the opposite direction; the mission houses at Khodon and Ona lay 200 versts to the east of Verkhneudinsk; and William's journeys to the Aga lamasery entailed a ride of yet another 400 versts or more. The Tungus around Nerchinsk lay even further away. The population was sparse. In 1828, Robert informed the Directors that the Selenginsk District contained about 96,000 Buryats, and that the Khori were perhaps three times as numerous. The Society itself, in its publications, used the figures of 10,000–12,000 and 30,000 respectively. Contemporary Russian figures are available, but are difficult to interpret. For comparison, it is known that, nowadays, there are something like 300,000 speakers of Buryat all told.

The true area of Buryatia, and the actual number of inhabitants, were, in any case, irrelevant, for the trio of missionaries had no hope of covering more than a small part of the country effectively. The population was so thin and scattered that they could make contact with only a fraction of it, and after 1828 they settled down to concentrate on two reasonably well-populated areas, the Selenga basin and the Ona plain. As Robert wrote:

> For my part, I do not think it a point of the first importance, where the missionary might fix his habitation among this people; for as we have experienced already, it is easy for them to remove thence to any convenient distance from his station, when they desire: and it is just as easy for them to come near his station, when they feel their wants. And I have no doubt, but when this people shall feel their need of the Gospel of Christ, that they will flock to the Missionary as the Doves fly to their windows.

But before this apotheosis – which was never to be realized – could be approached, a practical beginning had to be made with the scattered, shifting, and, as it turned out, psychologically resistant race. Edward made that beginning in two ways, with exploratory rides out amongst the ordinary Buryats, and with a formal visit, the first of many to different lamaseries, to the Khamba Lama, the superior of the Goose Lake lamasery, and the most influential cleric in the land.

The lamas formed a distinct class, and hence a recognizable target, but they were not a homogeneous group. Many lived at home, following a way of life which was hardly distinguishable from that of the ordinary herdsmen. The lamaseries themselves formed permanent communities – in fact the only permanent Buryat communities, for the towns and villages were still mainly Russian. Some lamaseries were of considerable size. Martos gives a figure of over 250 lamas attending service at Goose Lake. At festival times, crowds of Buryats would flock in from all around to be dazzled by the splendid ceremonies and deafened by the temple music, music which Erman compared to a roaring hurricane or the crash of a falling mountain. In the unstable, nomadic society of the Buryat plains, the lamaseries were the only fixed points where the missionaries could be sure of finding a big audience. The lamas also formed the one educated class, even though the missionaries complained that most of them were pitifully ignorant, though arrogantly self-satisfied at the same time. They enjoyed enormous prestige in the eyes of the common people, who actually worshipped them, and who relied on them as their intermediaries with the world beyond.

It might be expected, then, that the missionaries would have singled out the lamas as a special target for evangelization, arguing that if they could win over the priesthood, the conversion of the ignorant masses would follow automatically. But they do not seem to have thought along these lines. Their appeal was always to the individual conscience, and their aim was the salvation of individual souls, not the achievement of statistical, and hence meretricious, success. As Edward wrote to Alers Hankey in 1827:

> We are sometimes asked with a half sneer, what success we have had? This question is asked by our Christian neighbours, some of whom I believe sincerely pity us, as 'labouring in vain, and spending our strength for nought.' Their ideas of success are taken from the number who are immersed in the font without much regard to character: and they have often been told that this is not the kind of success which we desire; that we humbly wait for the bestowment of the Holy Spirit upon this people, when they shall become Christians, not in name only, but in deed and in truth.

That meant pounding away, year after year, with little to encourage them. But they were challenged rather than dismayed by the lack of response from the Buryats, recalling that in the South Seas it had taken twenty years for a gleam of hope to appear. They did use the lamaseries as centres for the distribution of their pamphlets, and they tried to interest the lamas, as well as the taishas, in the educational side of their work. But in the task of evangelization they made no distinction between lamas, shamans, nobles and commoners. To each they spoke directly, and it was the personal conscience, not the prestige of the office-holder, which was their target.

Within a week of his arrival at Selenginsk, and long before he could speak Buryat properly, Edward set out to explore the countryside and assess the prospects. On 15/27 July 1819 he wrote to Alers Hankey:

> I think there is abundant employment for the Missionaries of one station

about this spot, exclusive of the immense tribe of Chorinsk Boriats, 250 wersts and upwards to the north east of us. I have already begun my horseback expeditions among them, and the large quantity of ground which they occupy, and the great distance at which they live from each other, require much time to effect a little. The day before yesterday I rode upwards of 35 wersts from home, and found only one hoard of Boriates, consisting of about 10 tents, where any of the people were able to read. Here were three Lama's living, to each of whom I gave tracts, as well as to some others, who have children capable of reading them. They generally receive them gladly, and are very curious to know their contents. I waited about two hours in the tent, where the Lama's were sitting, to rest my horse, and the Lama's were all the time occupied in reading them. My own man, who is a Bratsky, and who speaks Russ fluently, goes with me and acts as interpreter, but I find it exceedingly difficult to convey the least instruction by means of him, and I must content myself with circulating these silent preachers, till I am able to speak more to them myself.

It was not until August 1823 that any of the missionaries began regular preaching at Selenginsk. Up till then, they used what time they could spare from language learning and supervising the builders to ride around the countryside giving out their tracts and, from early 1820, copies of the Gospels according to St Matthew and St John in Schmidt's translation. Both tracts and gospels were printed in St Petersburg with types developed by, and belonging to, the RBS. The RBS was responsible for producing the gospels, but the costs of the tract programme were borne by a little Tract Society, composed of enthusiastic volunteers, which had been formed in the capital during 1819. The Bible Society's Mongolian type was ready for use by mid-1818, and in May of that year some copies of the Lord's Prayer were printed off as a first test-piece. There was plenty of copy for the press. The two gospels and a tract composed in Mongolian by Schmidt were ready for printing, and Schmidt was at work on a second tract. The first one had been printed by the end of 1818, when Paterson wrote home that he was having several hundred copies bound up to send out to Siberia. A finished copy was sent to the Directors in February 1819 as a sample, and by May of that year, Edward, still in Irkutsk, had received the first hundred copies. These he prudently reserved until he could distribute them effectively from Selenginsk. Other tracts were to follow. In 1821, St Paul's speech at Athens was reprinted, and in July of the same year a triumphant Knill could report that he had received from Edward the latter's first original composition – a tract in Russian with a Mongolian version. Knill decided at once to print off 2,000 copies of the Mongolian text, but before doing so, and with an eye to public relations, he sent both versions to Popov, asking him to submit them to Golitsyn's inspection, and hinting, in his peculiarly unctuous style, that the Emperor might like to see them too. Knill wrote as follows:

> May it please your Excellency
> The last communications I had the honor to send you were respecting *foreign* nations, but now I have the inexpressible pleasure to forward you something from the *Russian Dominions* and prepared expressly for the happiness of His Imperial Majesty's subjects. The Manuscripts which accompany this were written by my Brother Mr Stallybrass at Selenginsk. The Mongolian is an exact translation of the Russ, from which you will plainly see with what simplicity and affection they are endeavouring to instruct the Buriats in the knowledge of our blessed Redeemer. I believe this is the first Tract that was ever written for the poor Buriats by an *European pen*, and I know your Excellency will rejoice to see it.
> It is my intention to print 2000 copies of the Mongolian and send to Mr Stallybrass for distribution, but I thought it my duty to show you the manuscript before it is sent to the Printer. It would be peculiarly kind if you would shew it to that good friend of Missionaries His Excellency the Prince Galitzin, as the Prince saw Mr Stallybrass and no doubt will be pleased to see what advancement he has made in the language of that very distant Region.
> O my dear Sir what a mercy it is that in the present day the Russian Eagle stretches his wings from the Baltic to Kiachta, by which means the glorious gospel of Christ is spreading and will continue to spread until the whole Empire be evangelized.
> His Imperial Majesty condescended to speak to Mr Stallybrass before he left Europe and if you think that it would gratify the Emperor to know what is doing in that remote part of his Realms, I hope you will let it be communicated unto him.

Early in 1820, Edward and his two colleagues began to carry their message into the lamaseries, and the friendly or, at worst, neutral way in which they were at first received encouraged them to undertake a regular programme of visits to all the lamaseries in their neighbourhood. To begin with, they paid brief calls, during which they handed out tracts and gospels, and when they felt they had saturated the market with literature, they extended the length of their stay in each lamasery, hoping to be able to reinforce the message through conversation. Robert's account of these modest little incursions makes them sound like flamboyant invasions of enemy territory. In 1823 he wrote:

> I had an opportunity of visiting Eight of the Buriate Temples belonging to the Selenginsk District, and one belonging to the Horinsky District. Three of these had not been visited before by any Missionary, and at

one of them I saw the greatest number of people I had seen anywhere, at one time, in Siberia. I continued to be surrounded by a changing crowd, from the multitude, for about three hours, asking them questions and giving books to as many as could read. In four out of the nine Temples that I visited, I had the pleasure of disturbing the Idolators in their worship, by putting the gospel of Salvation, if they would believe it, into their hands.

But it was not really so heroic as this. The lamas were quite used to seeing outsiders wandering round their temples during service. Nearly thirty years later, S. S. Hill attended a service at Goose Lake lamasery. He and his party were invited to walk up the main aisle of the temple, but, anxious not to disturb the service, he asked his interpreter to take them round the walls. The interpreter appreciated his concern, but assured him that it was superfluous, and in fact they did go straight up the centre of the temple without causing any disruption. Edward, too, remarked that 'as there is not much order or regularity observed in their assemblies, I was not thought an intruder for walking through their seats, which I did for the purpose of distributing a book to everyone who could read'. The missionaries used to ask permission before going into the lamaseries, and they did so in no arrogant or aggressive spirit, but, as Edward admitted, 'in weakness and fear, and much trembling'.

The lamas were, almost without exception, well-disposed towards the visitors, and at one lamasery they even took a hand in passing round the Christian books themselves. This complaisance was reassuring in one way, but in another it disappointed the missionaries, who felt that, as long as they could arouse no open opposition from those whom they already regarded as the enemy, they were failing in their subversive purpose:

> The lamas or Priests themselves not only come for the gospel but are sometimes seen sitting at our door reading it to a listening audience of their own people. They have not yet taken the alarm nor seem to be aware of the danger their lying vanities are exposed to from the introduction of the gospel. But we lay our account with opposition from them sooner or later. It will not be a good sign if there are not 'many adversaries,' and therefore when the offence of the cross begins to shew itself against us we shall neither be dismayed nor discouraged by its appearance.

That was how William felt only a few weeks after his arrival at Selenginsk in 1820, and before two years had passed, the missionaries had begun to experience the hostility they coveted. Towards the end of 1821, Edward paid another call on the Khamba, and succeeded in annoying him:

> I have sometimes before thought the Chamba shewed much uneasiness, but he spoke more plainly this time than ever. I had a long conversation

> with him upon the topics contained in the gospel, in which it was impossible to avoid touching upon some points which went near to him, and made him to suppose that I doubted the truth of their religion. He enquired with great warmth if their religion was a lie. I immediately told him that as we believe in only one God, so we believe that there is only one way of His appointment for the Salvation of the Soul, that as we believe the gospel to be that only way, so we must believe all other ways to be false. He immediately ordered the Boriatt man who was with me to take away the book which I had given him on the preceding evening, saying in great anger that he received by far too many of these books, that he had plenty of his own and did not need any others. – I went to him determining, in the strength of God, to tell him more plainly that I had ever before been able to do the truth as it is in Jesus, of *his own* need of an interest in the great salvation, – and his exposure to wrath and destruction without such an interest. At this he was offended and his offence was increased by the disrespectful terms in which their chief God Shegemóni is spoken of in the tract which I gave him. I was neither surprised nor alarmed at his dislike of these truths, but expect much of it before any good will be effected. Indeed it is a much better sign than the indifference which most of them manifest with respect to either side of the question, and one may apply to this the words of C. Wesley and say 'For more the treacherous calm I dread, than tempests bursting o'er my head.'

When the lamas finally woke up to what the missionaries were trying to do, their opposition did not take the form of active confrontation and debate, which the missionaries wanted, and would have known how to deal with, but of political intrigue and withdrawal into a baffling silence. By 1827, we read:

> A spirit of deep slumber has fallen upon the whole people. Most who attend our stated ministrations from Sabbath to Sabbath hear the most important truths of the Gospel and the exposure of the evils of their own faith with perfect apathy. . . . As for the Lamas, most of them now decline as much as possible all discussion, and indeed all but unavoidable intercourse with us. They are generally speaking unwilling to hear us when we would make known to them the way of salvation, and even avoid speaking in favour of their own tenets – well knowing that it is the wisest part to shun the discussion of all such matters. This is a 'dumb and deaf spirit.' They do not *speak* themselves and they refuse to *hear* us. Hence they seem inaccessible to any means we can use, and we are reminded in reference to them of the case of demoniacal possession recorded in the Gospel which the disciples could not cure. Some of these Lamas, either less cunning or more confident in the goodness of their cause, will still attempt to defend it, but they evidently shew that they

are neither willing to be convinced of their errors, nor to forsake them even could they be convinced. One of them, the chief Lama of a temple, lately closed a discussion with me to this effect: 'I am an old man; my system of faith I have held too long to change it now. It is therefore in vain for you to argue with me, for I will die as I have lived a disciple of Shigimoni.'

This was perhaps only to be expected, but in 1820 and 1821 the prospect looked much brighter, and there were several encouraging little incidents to report. In one lamasery, for example, Edward had been approached by a 'respectable shrewd Bratsky' who wanted to know why the missionaries were taking so much trouble to distribute their books, and who paid for it all. He warned Edward that if the idea was to turn them into Russians – a common expression for conversion to Christianity – they were wasting their time. The fact that the missionaries were not Russians proved to be much in their favour, and the Buryat promised to read the books that Edward gave him. But, as far as we know, this encounter, like so many others, could not be followed up.

The first visits to the lamaseries were made at the beginning of the lunar year of 1820, the Iron Dragon year. The whole of the first month of the Mongol calendar, the White Month, or Tsagaan Sara, as Buryats and Mongols still call it, was a period of festivities. The lamaseries were crowded with worshippers, for there were special services and ceremonies held on every day of the first half of the month, offering a continuous spectacle which would not recur for another year. In some Mongolian lamaseries, and amongst the Buryats too, these services culminated on the fifteenth day in the Maidari festival, when the statue of Maitreya was drawn around the temple by its wooden horses. During the White Month, the lamaseries acted as a magnet for the whole neighbourhood, and so the missionaries chose that period to make their first visits there. Their reception at Goose Lake in particular was so promising, that they planned to call on all the lamaseries within a hundred versts of Selenginsk in 1821, and stay in each for more than a few hours at a time. Edward and William took in Goose Lake itself, and other temples near the lake, the Tsongol lamasery – where they found over 200 lamas, and got rid of 150 books – and the lamaseries of the Ashibagat and Tabungut tribes to the east of Selenginsk. It was during their visit to Goose Lake that they were joined for a day or two by Sarah. She was the first English woman ever to visit a Buryat lamasery, and her account is now published for the first time:

> The present being the *White Month*, or first month in the calculation of the Mongolian Tartars, is devoted to services at the temples; though it is commenced with feasting and all sorts of animal gratification. You will recollect that our Gentlemen at the last year availing themselves of the opportunity, made a visit to one or two temples for the purpose

> of distributing the Gospel and tracts. The favorable reception they then met induced them to hope that more permanent good might be effected, by dividing their time during the whole month between the different temples within a circuit of a 100 versts. During their stay at the principal Temple, where the Chamba resides, I joined them for two days, in order to gratify my eyes, and affect my heart. My desire was realized. My Edward and his companion I found in a little apartment belonging to some of the Priests with the Prophets furniture, a Table and stool, and a *little* more than the Prophets fare. Here they were hourly visited by some of all description, partly from curiosity and partly to make enquiries respecting the books circulated among them. As the Chamba had expressed his wish to see me the reception I shortly met from him was a very gracious one. In a creditable little house not common to these people (as they live in Tents) I found this great Huge man sitting on the floor, surrounded by all the various objects and instruments of his worship, which to the eye were gaudy and glittering, but grovelling and debasing to the mind.

All the Khamba's visitors were fascinated by his enormous bulk. Peter Gordon was the first Westerner to be confronted by it, and comment on it.

> The Kumba or chief priest is the fattest man I ever saw; corporeal dimension is the qualification for the office. . . . He had not been able to visit the temple, which is about five versts from his house, for some months; and was anxious for snow, being able to go there only in a sledge, on account of his size.

Martos was just as impressed. When he called on the Khamba, he found him sitting on the floor, leaning against his divan, contentedly sniffing Russian snuff from a silver snuff-box. 'The Khamba', he wrote, 'is gigantic in both stature and bulk. In my whole life I have never seen such a colossal being.' When Erman was at Goose Lake in 1828, the Khamba was not even in a state to come and greet him. 'He was so prodigiously corpulent, that every motion must have been a labour to him. But in spite of this bodily grossness, the features of his dark brown face, and his calm self-possession, bespoke the cultivated man.' By the time S. S. Hill visited Goose Lake, the Khamba's successor had been installed. He shared his predecessor's characteristics. 'I never before saw so monstrous a specimen of humanity,' wrote Hill. 'The Khomba Lama, although, as I learned afterwards, only thirty-three years of age, was at once the tallest, the stoutest and the fattest, and at the same time the most deformed in feature, of all the men I have ever beheld.'

The gigantism may have been inherited. Erman was told that the young Khamba elect, who had welcomed him to the lamasery, was the Khamba's nephew, and he strongly suspected that the relationship was rather closer.

Missionary and Lama

Erman was the only visitor to Goose Lake to perceive, beneath the Khamba's gross exterior, the subtle prelate, though the missionaries came to appreciate his skill as an opponent. He mistrusted them, but he sent pupils to their schools. Even a nephew of his was a pupil at Selenginsk. He tantalized the missionaries with the prospect of his sending dozens of pupils, if only they would give up their hostility to Buddhism, knowing full well that their antagonism was the *raison d'être* of their mission. He professed good will towards them, and intrigued with the Russians against them behind their backs, never giving open cause for offence. Altogether, the Khamba was a worthy match.

To return to Sarah's account:

The Khamba's enquiries were not a few. The news of the little Town near where we live – The distance and extent of our native country. The mode of travelling etc etc. As Mr S had in a previous conversation when he had condescended to visit *them* enquired if he had read the Gospels and his Ideas on some of the most important subjects, it was not thought prudent at this time to introduce it, and it was proposed that I should see the Temples when he was pleased to give orders that all the priests should be summoned. In this short space of time I had an opportunity of witnessing that he was an object of *adoration* as well as respect by all subordinate to him. When any one entered the room, they prostrated themselves 5 times to the ground making the head touch the floor each time, and when they advanced to him for his blessing which he imparted by touching the head with his nom or religious book. Before he left he presented me with a prayer from this book which with his own hand he transcribed from the Tangut. When I am able to translate it you shall have a copy. All their prayers are written in this language though not one in a Hundred or the *Priests even* know the meaning of a word in the language. Thus they are 'Blind leaders of the Blind.' For they look for salvation from the reading of these books.

As we advanced to the Temples I was ready to exclaim Surely I am on Chinese ground, the exteriors assuming so much the appearance of the representations I had often seen of their Pagodas: nor were the interiors less remarkable; for then I thought I must be in a Chinese Museum: So little had the place the appearance of worship except that the long robes of the priests, their voices and the frequent prostrations might serve to inform the beholder that it was a place for worshiping the Gods. Alas not the one living and true *God*. In the outer court is placed a moveable Machine in the form of a Kettle Drum, which as each worshiper advances he turns with his hand and contributes to the motion of the prayers which it contains, and which by this means he is supposed to present to the Gods. On entering the inner Court, he prostrates himself to the picture of Zarlee Kahan [probably Erlik Khan] the chief Deity, a Hideous figure. In all aspects the object of terror. He next bows to the chair held sacred for the Dalai Lama and then receives the blessing of the Chief Lama present, by a touch of his book on the head. These Lamas including all ranks from the Chamba to the beater of the drum; and aged from the Hoary head to the little playful boy, are placed by gradation on benches a little raised from the ground, and as they sit on their legs crossed, have a very motionless appearance.

The clash of trumpets, cymbals and drums in the gathering twilight made Sarah feel for a moment that she was a prisoner of the Inquisition, but then she recognized the lamas for what they were – the mildest of men – and sat down alongside them, to muse that

the day was perhaps not distant when the gospels now in circulation among them would be substituted for their prayers; their instruments attuned to the praises of the most High; and the great Chair occupied as a Pulpit, by one of our devoted Missionary Brethren. With what pleasure did I reflect that my husband Edward was already in possession of such a knowledge of their dialect, as to be able to converse with them on the things relating to their everlasting salvation and my Soul panted for a similar attainment.

The letter to Ann from which these quotations are taken may have been passed on to the Directors, for in a letter written in September 1823 Edward had to curb their extravagant expectations. 'It was surely a lapsus pennae,' he wrote, 'when the worthy Editor of the Quarterly Chronicle expressed it as my hope that we should soon preach in the heathen temples of the Boriatts – I have no foundation for such a hope.'

Everywhere the lamas treated the missionaries with respect as individuals, but ignored their message. At the Tabungut lamasery, for example, during the White Month of 1821, they found the lamas

very much disinclined to hear anything against their worship, and some of them have even refused to accept of tracts, saying, by way of excuse, that they cannot read. They are curious and inquisitive about every thing, except the one thing needful. They treat us with great ceremony and respect, as if we were great personages, but we would a thousand times rather be considered by them as nothing, and our *message* as of infinite importance.

Studied politeness and cool indifference became the standard way in which their approaches were fended off by the lamas, and, as far as we know, not a single lama was ever converted. Did Edward ever stop to ponder how a wandering Buryat lama would have been received by the Rev. Mr Fletcher or the Rev. Mr Ford, if he had made his way into the church at Stepney and started handing out lamaist prayers?

Missionary and Lama

The missionaries found the lamas, generally speaking, ignorant and smug. An encounter Edward had in 1828 is typical of many others:

> The Lamas, as might be expected, are extremely ignorant, having never, as Dr Watts expresses it, seen beyond the smoke of their own chimney; but their confidence or impudence supplies the place of knowledge, in the minds of the deluded multitude. Their boasted knowledge of the Thibetan, their sacred language, is an empty puff; as it is confined to the *reading* of the language, which every lama is required to learn. I was yesterday visited by a Lama, and among other things asked him if he could read the Mongolian language: he replied in the negative but with a considerable degree of confidence professed to be able to translate the Thibetan. I immediately reached a book written in that language and desired him to translate a piece to me; when he hung down his head and confessed his ignorance of it.

Some lamas may have taken refuge in silence to hide their ignorance, but not every one can have been so stupid and conceited as they were made out to be. One proof of this lies in the immense amount of printing that was done in Buryat lamaseries during the nineteenth century. According to a list drawn up in 1911, there were thirty-one lamaseries which had their own printing shops, and from these, nearly 1,700 items had been issued over the years. Most of these were in Tibetan, but there were Mongolian books, too – canonical and extra-canonical scriptures, lives of famous lamas, and secular works such as grammars and dictionaries. The missionaries inspected the printing offices at Goose Lake and other lamaseries, and must have realized that the organization of book production on the scale they saw – 'immense numbers of prayers', as Edward put it – was not the work of indolent ignoramuses.

However inept some of its members might have been, the Buddhist church as an institution was flourishing and expanding. From the centre in the Selenginsk District, its influence was radiating vigorously throughout the countryside, from Irkutsk in the west to beyond Aga to the Tungus people in the east, and the sheer quantitative success that its missionaries were scoring must have given the lamas much of the self-confidence with which they condescended to the quaint strangers in their midst.

> There are heathen Missionaries as well as Christian Missionaries in this very field [wrote William in 1825], and were we servants of the Dalai Lama, and had you sent us hither to propagate his faith, we could send you accounts of success which would fill your heart with joy – we could tell of the burning of idols, of the erection of places of worship – of the increasing number and influence of the priests – of the zeal of the people for the new system and their liberality in supporting it. But alas, these are triumphs not of the gospel but of Dalai Lamaism. The teachers and

the taught are deceiving and being deceived. They present an affecting picture of the blind leading the blind.

The ordinary lama owed everything to the Buddhist church. Through it he enjoyed personal respect and prestige far beyond what he could have expected as a layman, and, as a member of a lamasery community, he was entitled to a share of the lamasery revenues. What possible reason could there be to apostasize, to give all this up, to cut himself off from his fellow Buryats and earn their scorn for going back on his vows and abandoning the clerical life, all for the sake of what must have looked like a fly-by-night novelty from afar. The men at Selenginsk came from who knew where. Their numbers were never reinforced, and they could offer no guarantee of continuity. They appeared to enjoy the support of secular authority to begin with, but as the political balance changed in the late 1820s and the 1830s, so that support looked more and more uncertain. They claimed to be the sole possessors of true religion, but what evidence was there that they did, beyond their own assertions? Looked at from the lamas' point of view, there was little to recommend the exotic mission at Selenginsk as a spiritual home, when almost all the rest of Buryatia was turning from shamanism to the lamaism which enjoyed the allegiance of all other Mongols.

Naturally, the three missionaries did not see things in the same light. They were the only ones in step, and they made no secret of their belief that lamaism was a fraud. In his Journal for March 1821, William described some of the conversations he had had with some lamas, and some of the ceremonies he had attended, and concluded:

> The view given in the foregoing pages of Lamaism, as practised here, certainly exhibits it as comparatively of a harmless character. It has no features of cruelty, and presents none of those shocking spectacles which are common among some idolators. And so far well. But the whole system is a delusion. The people believe a lie: they take pleasure in unrighteousness, and none more than the Lamas themselves. Their books teach them no morality, for they are in an unknown tongue. Their restraints from criminal indulgence are confined to the short time they spend at the temples, and when they return home it is to commit all uncleanness with greediness. Their services are unmeaning forms, and they hesitate not to confess them to be irksome and disagreeable, but think their performance of them, on this account, so much the more meritorious.

Whether this was a fair view of the state of lamaism amongst the Buryats is beside the point. From a practical point of view, for a little band of uninvited strangers to abuse the clergy of what was to all intents and purposes a national church, accusing them of ignorance, fraud and dissipation, was, to say the least, a questionable way of influencing either them or the credulous Buryats who doted on them as almost divine.

The growth in the number of lamaseries was one indication of the vigour of the Buddhist church. In 1822 the missionaries reported that there were four lamaseries amongst the Khori, while in 1825 the number had increased to six. In 1829 William wrote from Ona to say that 'in this country' there were now more than twenty lamaseries. By then, lamaism was making strides even among the Tungus, who had two temples of their own. One day in the early summer of 1829, Edward was preaching at the mission house at Khodon, when the service was interrupted by one of two Tungus visitors from the Onon river area, south-east of Chita. The man wanted to know whether the sermon meant that the gods in the lamaseries ought not to be worshipped. Edward told him it was both pointless and wrong to worship things made by human hands, but the Tungus was not satisfied, and interrupted again to say that he and his companion were on a begging tour, collecting money to build a temple. Should they continue or give up? After service, Edward took them aside. They were in a real quandary, thinking he had forbidden them to build their temple. He told them he had no authority to do so, but that what they were doing was contrary to the word of God. The men went off with copies of the Gospels and the Acts, and what became of them we do not know.

The missionaries suspected – and their suspicions were confirmed by local people – that it was the threat which they themselves posed which was partly responsible, around 1829, for the increased activity of the lamas and the wave of conversions which followed. The trouble was, as William recognized, that once a small band of missionaries had 'roused the latent spirit of heathenism to augmented energy', their own tiny numbers were insufficient to cope with the hostility they had stirred up. This was a familiar phenomenon, encountered at home as well as in the mission field, but it provoked sombre reflections, especially as the missionaries gradually came to realize that the Directors, disappointed by the lack of progress, and doubtful about the political situation in Russia, were not going to reinforce their numbers. Not only were they a mere handful of missionaries, openly opposed, as William put it, 'to thousands of lamas, and the tens of thousands of their abettors', but they also suffered under psychological disadvantages. The teaching of the lamas was one which found 'a ready entrance to the heart of depraved human nature', while the gospel had 'every avenue of the heart shut against it'. The missionaries saw themselves engaged in a war, where they seemed to be fighting at every disadvantage, sustained only by their confidence that God was on their side.

The Khamba did not exert direct authority over the more distant lamaseries, but his charismatic prestige made itself felt as far afield as Aga and beyond. In March 1822, William was at Aga, and he joined the chief lama, a gelong who was deputizing for the absent shireetei, and three lamas who had come from the west on a tour of inspection organized by the Khamba, at the temple service. At that time, Aga was still a small lamasery. Of its complement of some forty lamas, only twenty were at service, and about half of these seemed to be mere boys. William was moved to sad reflection by the paradox of the date, 1811, expressed according to the Christian calendar, displayed on the façade of this 'heathen temple', and trusted that better times would come.

The presence of the lamas from Goose Lake had a perceptibly inhibiting effect on the local lamas. The gelong had been quite forthcoming when William had talked to him earlier at the taisha's headquarters, but now he proved devious and non-committal. In the end, William gave up trying to make conversation, as he was getting nowhere. He moved to the tent of another lama, who seemed to be a

> courteous, open, unassuming man, and desired me, if I staid all day, to make this tent my resting-place. I have had much conversation with him, and with others, in the course of the day. The more zealous of them expressed great disapprobation of the Gospel, because of its exclusive character – condemning every other system, and refusing the very shadow of alliance with them. The Lama just referred to, either from politeness or stupidity, pretended that he saw no reason why their religion and ours might not be both true; and he evidently wished to let the matter pass, and suffer my statements to remain uncontradicted, rather than risk a discussion. I urged him, and all present, however, to hear and examine this doctrine of Christ, saying that we did not shrink from any investigation of our system, for it was THE TRUTH, and they would sooner or later find it to be so.

There lay the difficulty. The lamas were prepared to accommodate Christian doctorine and morality, as far as they could, within their own religion, just as they had adapted shamanist beliefs and ceremonies, and they could not understand the intransigent exclusivity of the missionaries. Over and over again, in the missionaries' letters and journals, we find evidence that this was the great stumbling block, the philosophical divide which prevented any understanding between the two sides. It was bound to be so. The Buddhist church was syncretist in practice if not in principle, while the conviction that they were the bearers of the unique truth was the justification for the missionaries' presence in Siberia. There could be no compromise between these two stances, and inevitably the weaker side, the one with no roots in local tradition and culture, and no political pull, was the loser.

The lamas' imperviousness to logical reasoning must have infuriated the tidy-minded missionaries, for, when the lamas did get involved in argument, the level of debate could be absurdly low, and the opinions they upheld were, to trained minds, too frivolous to warrant serious rebuttal. The policy which gradually evolved was to avoid wrangling about the merits of the two religions, and to concentrate on the absolute truth of Christianity. In 1821 William wrote:

> During our stay many came to us, received books, and conversed about the Gospel. We could not always avoid disputing with them about their ridiculous pictures or gods, but we found it always more calculated to impress their minds, as well as more agreeable to ourselves, by sound doctrine, both to exhort and convince the gainsayers; setting before them the great doctrines of the Gospel. Some seriously attended to what was spoken, some were indifferent, and some were angry. We met with some very acute, shrewd men among them, but our imperfect knowledge of the language laid us under great disadvantages; and we found it very difficult to do anything through our interpreter. It would be tedious to relate particular conversations. It may be stated in general, that we commonly introduced our grand subject by asking if they knew that the soul was immortal, and what would become of it after it left the body; if they were sinners – if they were afraid to die. To these last two questions they always replied in the affirmative; they trust for the pardon of sin to their making many prayers, but their fear of death still remains, and indeed is universal among them. We took advantage of this to point out the insufficiency of their system to give them peace of conscience, in the prospect of death and eternity. When we had exposed the futility of their arguments for a multitude of gods, etc. they would say, 'This is too much for our minds,' (meaning such subjects were beyond their reach.) In fact, they are in general very ignorant, even of the tenets of their own superstition, nor is it requisite, according to their ideas, that they should know them, their duty consisting merely in reading prayers in an unknown tongue, and performing other bodily exercises; so that they are saved completely *the trouble of thinking*; on this account their religion is more suited to the indolence of their minds, as well as the depravity of their nature, than one which addresses the understanding and the heart.

Sometimes, though, direct confrontation could not be avoided. The lamas adopted either or both of two positions which the missionaries were bound to reject. One was that, while Christianity was suitable for Europeans, lamaism was best for Buryats. Edward quoted an instance of this in a letter which he wrote home in 1828:

> I was lately reasoning with another Lama of some note, and among other *weighty* reasons for his adhering to the Lama's system he said: Shigimoni's language was Boriat, therefore it is proper for the Boriats to worship him; but as Jesus Christ spoke the Russian language it is right that they worship Him. You may easily suppose that to convince such a man was no easy task. I could only tell him that he was as ignorant

of Shigimoni whom he professed to worship as of Jesus Christ, of whom he evidently knew nothing. And yet such a man passes for an oracle with many.

The other heresy was that Christianity and Buddhism were aspects of the same religion. The missionaries never succeeded in convincing the lamas of the untenability of this position. In 1827 Edward reported as follows to Alers Hankey:

> There is one thing which bears no bad aspect, and that is that the Lamas become more hostile to us. They would be glad to have it acknowledged that the religion of us both are essentially the same; that Christ and Shigemoni (i.e. their belial) are the same under different names. I have combatted these declarations a good deal lately, and have found that they have been carefully inculcated on the minds of many. I have shewn that their origin, place of residence (for they profess to believe that Shegemoni came from heaven too), manner of life (for they acknowledge that Shegemoni had no less than 500 wives), doctrine, laws, methods of salvation etc. etc. are all different, so that it is not in the name merely in which a difference exists, but that in every respect they were *totally* different; this they are obliged to concede.

But having to concede a rational argument did not produce any deep convictions, and the lamas ignored the logical conclusions to which they had been driven, and went quietly away.

13

Preaching to the People

Talking and arguing with the lamas made little impression, and itineration and distribution of Christian literature among the people proved almost as unfruitful, though at first the missionaries entertained high hopes of success. In 1820, Edward wrote:

> We intend to continue our journeys among them as the last summer; this is advantageous and desirable, not merely as it gives us an opportunity of distributing books, but also for the opportunity of conversing with the people, and knowing more of them – I rejoice in our prospects. God has been pleased to give us an introduction to this interesting people, destitute of the Word of Life, the way of salvation; and shall this be in vain ? that He has put (as I trust He has) a desire in to our hearts to impart unto them that gospel which is to be preached 'to all nations for the obedience of faith' and shall our efforts, feeble and humble as they are, be in vain ? and especially shall His word be translated into their language, be distributed among them, read by them, and ultimately be without effect ? Oh no! it is *His* word, concerning which He has declared that 'as the rain cometh down and snow from heaven – ' so shall *His* word be etc. My sanguine hopes may be in some way or degree disappointed, but surely it becomes us to sow in faith and hope, and to labour diligently in the certain expectation of a glorious issue.

The missionaries drew their confidence, not from observable signs of progress, which were few and ambiguous, but from their faith in God. In 1820, though, the prospect was not entirely bleak. 'We are now distributing the gospels and tracts very widely,' wrote Edward that February, 'and surely these shall not return void.' People seemed glad to take their books, even if they did not always study them. But by the time he sent home the Journal of a tour which he and William had made amongst the Khori Buryats in January 1822, the main obstacles in their way were becoming identifiable. Foremost among them was the physical difficulty of making contact with

Preaching to the People

the Buryats, and then of calling on them a second or a third time to reinforce the message. 'Surely they need "line upon line and precept upon precept," but what are we among so many' is a cry which echoes through the missionaries' letters. They were always far too few to be able to keep in touch with the elusive nomads.

All too often, when they did catch the people at home, the whole lot of them, from the taishas downwards, would be drunk, especially in spring, when the mares' milk began to flow again, and was turned into the new season's kumis. And mostly, when they were sober, they could not be bothered to talk about religion. Religion was something for the lamas, not the laymen, and was best left to them.

What did the two men find, when they set off on a bitterly cold day in January 1822 to visit the Khori? Their first call was at the tent of a lama whom they knew already. They began to talk about the gospel, but the lama, as they discovered, 'was not a man of much enquiry, and could not be prevailed upon to give any attention, evidently thinking that the system was new to him and too much trouble for him to enquire about: that it might be very well for us, but that his own was better for him'. On the next day they stopped at a Buryat tent to boil up some of the meat they were carrying with them, and talked to the old man who owned it. The only thing that interested the old man, who was childless, was to know whether he would have any children in heaven, and whether he would be rich there. Here, and elsewhere, Edward felt 'a great depression of spirits at the idea of these poor people being willing to listen to what was spoken, but the impracticability of our paying them more attention than that of a *passing visit*'. From there they moved on to another tent, where they spent the night, and were upstaged by an arrogant lama who 'kept the people employed waiting upon him'.

Next day, the 17th, they handed out medicines, and did their best to address the people, before moving on to visit a local taisha, one Tseden. Their visit proved useless, for Tseden was entertaining the chief taisha Dembil, the one who tried so hard to get baptized, and the two of them were settling down happily to a hard drinking session. There was nothing to be done there, so they went on to another tent, belonging to a Buryat called Sokto. Edward unwittingly maligns Sokto in his Journal. The name 'Sokto' means 'Splendid', but Edward confused it with another, similar, word, meaning 'drunk', and commented: 'as his name, so was the man'. Not that the mistake matters. Hardly had the missionaries entered the tent than Sokto, who had been tippling with the two taishas, rolled up gloriously drunk, and making such a commotion that there was nothing to be done at that tent either. As Edward put it: 'Little opportunity offered for speaking upon our great subject, nor were there here any persons disposed to listen to us.'

Alcoholism was a curse to Mongols and Buryats alike, and proved one of the biggest frustrations the missionaries had to face. In 1830 Edward wrote to Alers Hankey on the subject in pained tones:

> Owing to the peculiar state of the Boriat nation, in travelling amongst them much time is consumed while very little is effected. During the summer season a great part of those who have come to years of maturity, (perhaps the greater part,) are buried in intoxication; their tent where we meet them is the common receptacle for children, cattle, and every thing else which belongs to them; and we have often found it impossible to introduce those subjects to which we wish to draw their attention, amidst the confusion which prevails: so that in returning home we have had the distressing persuasion that the time, labour and expense which have been involved in travelling have been to no purpose.

This was no new discovery. Eight years earlier, Edward had also written, apropos of the deplorable Sokto and his weakness for mares' milk: 'This is a sin very prevalent amongst them, but in their apprehensions it does not deserve the harsh appellation.'

This is a little hard on Mongol tradition. True, there had always been the temptation to drink too much, for mares' milk was a staple item of the Mongolian diet, and fermentation and distillation was the only means of preserving it in liquid form in hot weather. Those in authority had often tried to curb excess, usually without result. Some early maxims and anecdotes attributed to Genghis Khan show that, in folk memory at least, the great founder of the nation disapproved of heavy drinking. On the other hand, his immediate successor, Ogodai, died of alcoholism. The acts of milking the mares and processing the milk were institutionalized as a religious ritual, but we have no evidence that dignifying an everyday activity by transforming it into a cult practice promoted moderation, though it may have helped. In later, Buddhist, times, too, tracts were composed and printed, condemning indulgence in tobacco and drink, and threatening sinners with dreadful retribution in case of disobedience. At the popular level there were, and still are, satirical songs in which all the different types of drunkard are described and castigated – perhaps only tongue in cheek, though. Nothing changed. The hard climate, dependence on milk as a food, and no doubt sheer boredom, led to regular over-indulgence, as the missionaries lamented over and over again.

From Sokto's tent, Edward and William went on to that of a taisha called Badma. Badma was drunk and incapable, but one of his wives took pity on the travellers, and let them stay in a 'miserable room'. Next day they had a talk with the taisha, but he was preoccupied with preparations for a journey, the most important of which seemed to be getting drunk again, so the missionaries 'judged it desirable to depart, having no prospect of doing any more here'.

Their next call was at the tent of a shaman. Here,

as amongst the Chorinsky Boriatts in general, were the insignia of Shamanism, which consist of several ugly figures rudely cut in wood and rendered black by the smoke and other dirt with which all the tents abound, as well as some skins of lambs and other animals. They suppose that these are the guardians of their cattle, and that if they were destroyed their cattle would die. This, however, is renounced by the Boriatts in our vicinity, (called the 18 tribes) and all the Shamanic apparatus burnt. Many of them enquired of our Boriatt Servants, with much ignorance, if the Cattle were still safe since Shamanism was renounced, and with equal surprise heard that there was no difference. We enquired with apparent surprise, what those ugly things could mean, and being informed that they were gods, in whom they trusted for the safety of the cattle, we endeavoured to shew them the folly of trusting to things like these for the least good, reminding them that they had *souls* exposed to everlasting ruin which needed salvation, and pointing them to Him alone who is able to save.

This was only one of many encounters with the *ongon* or shamanist idols, in which many of the Khori still trusted, and from which it was difficult for the missionaries to wean them. In February of the same year, William called in at the tent of a Khori shaman:

Pointing to his two black idols, I asked what these things were? 'They are gods.' 'No. I think they are two black sheep-skins, and their heads are made of wood, with blue beads instead of eyes; do they see?' 'No.' 'Can they walk?' 'No.' 'Can they speak, or hear, or move?' 'No.' 'Then what can they do, and what is the use of them?' 'They save the cattle from the wolves, and keep diseases from my family. See! we are all in health.' 'How can that be? These idols know nothing of the wolves, and the wolves know nothing of them; and how can they preserve the health of your family, if they could not save themselves from being burnt, if you should throw them into the fire?' In this manner I reasoned with the poor man, and recommended to him the gospel of Christ as a more excellent way.

But probably it was to no effect. William saw the man again a month later, and nothing seemed to have changed.

From the shaman's tent, Edward and William went on to that of a lama, where they spent the night and left some books. On the 21st they called on a 'surly old Shaman', who would have nothing to do with them. They were forced to spend the night in a Buryat tent on the edge of a Russian village called Tarbagatai. Here, one of Edward's horses fell sick, and he went back to Selenginsk to get another, arranging to meet William at Verkhneudinsk. A few days later they resumed the trail, and called on an old man who seemed very suspicious of them. They tried to convince the old man and his wife that they should be concerned about the state of their souls, and were met with incredulity. Probably the old people were baffled by the concept of a single soul, for Buryat popular belief admitted a multiplicity of souls, or 'lives', some of which might even lead an independent existence outside the body. The two old people just laughed at the missionaries, and said that the state of their souls was nothing to do with them – that was what the lamas were for. Several other people joined in the conversation, and for the first time on that journey the two missionaries felt cheered at having aroused some slight curiosity. They had managed to thaw the suspicious atmosphere, too. When they turned up at the tent, the people had tried to overcharge them for a little corn they needed for their horses, but by the end of the evening they were pressing corn on them for nothing. Something had been achieved, if only the creation of a little good will.

Next day, they had first to satisfy the curiosity of an old man who had ridden in from twelve or thirteen versts away just to see what an Englishman looked like. They handed out a few books and then separated, planning to meet again at the Khori kontora. Edward had an interesting conversation with a *shulinga*, or minor official, who took him in for the night, and next day called on an old man who was living with a blind woman. He tried to persuade them that their idols were impotent, and upset the old man, who said that 'until a command should come from the Emperor, they would not be persuaded to burn them'. Edward disavowed any intention of making them burn their idols, and mildly advised them simply to believe in God.

The next night was spent at a post-house. Edward was woken up about midnight by a man who had been following him for miles, hoping to get him to attend to a sick relative. In the morning, Edward rode back to the tent, and found the patient 'afflicted with a severe bilious attack'. He gave him all his little stock of pills, though he feared, justifiably as it turned out, that they would not have much effect. The opportunity to do a little preaching was too good to be missed, but Edward found the man so preoccupied with his upset stomach that 'I could scarcely gain his attention to any other subject'. He handed out some tracts and left.

That night was spent at the house of a 'respectable Boriatt' where, once again, Edward failed to attract an audience, this time because everyone was gambling. They even took the cards to bed, and then got up for another round. 'It was not a little mortifying,' he wrote, 'to find that in addressing a number of five or six, they began to converse amongst themselves, till by degrees they were all engaged in different conversations, and we found ourselves speaking without any to listen to what we said.'

Some Buryats were suspicious:

> I called at the tent of a poor man who had a son that could read and to whom I wished to give a tract. But when the old man understood what tracts they were he would by no means consent, fearing we should

afterwards require him to be baptized. I was surprised at his conduct, but afterwards understood that these tracts had been distributed and upon a second visit the Boriates who received them were given to understand that the receipt of them laid them under obligations to be baptized. I assured this old man that we had no such end in view. But no arguments of mine were sufficient to induce him to take the book.

No doubt Nomtu, or someone like him, had been doing a little quiet extortion.

Next, Edward called on an old retired shulinga, to whom he spoke about eternity, something which interested him 'from his being an old man and having in all probability but little time to remain here'. But the old shulinga had no intention of changing his beliefs. He was going to leave the lamas some cattle when he died, and they would come and pray for him, and everything would be all right. 'I in vain tried to convince him to the contrary. This is a piece of Priestcraft, and, of course, the more the people are persuaded to give, the more *meritorious* is the donation, and the more happiness will they obtain hereafter'. This was not the only occasion on which the missionaries had to deplore the gullible generosity of the Buryats toward the lamas, and what seemed like a compensatory avariciousness as far as the Christian missionaries were concerned.

So, in 1837, Edward called to see a poor old Buryat, who had 'frequently heard and read the word of truth', having learned that he was ill:

> In my last visit, a few hours before his death, although perfectly sensible, his whole thoughts and attention were engrossed in the subject of his burial, – whether I would not give him some linen to wrap his body in, and some boards to make a coffin. The attention which he would give to what I said about his deathless part was most forced; and after listening for a few minutes, he would interrupt me with 'the linen' – and 'the boards'. His soul, he said, God would care for; the body was *his* only concern. It was a truly affecting scene; and two of our *pious* young men whom I took with me, were deeply impressed with what they saw and heard. So strong did the ruling passion among those Boriats – 'give, give' – appear (even in death) that after I had left him, only a few minutes before he for ever closed his eyes upon all earthly scenes, he desired his wife to come to me and say, that he had died *in our faith*, and hoped I would take the charge of his burial. A few days after this, I met with another old man upwards of 70 who told me he had heard that I had given linen to the man above mentioned, and as he was an old man, and soon expected to die, he hoped I would do the same for him. I scarcely need say that I embraced the opportunity of exhorting him to attend to the infinitely more important concerns of his soul; but alas! with no apparently good effect.

Preaching to the People

The people did not mind scrounging from the missionaries, but they could be generous patrons of the lamaseries. An extract from a letter written by William to George Burder in April 1822 describes the frustration felt by the little band at Selenginsk. From a tour in the Khori pastures he wrote:

> The religion of Dalai Lama has not gained so much ground among this tribe as among the Selenginsk Buriats. The Shamans are still numerous, and the rites of Shamanism observed by many even of those who profess to be votaries of the other system. The Lamas are few in number and their influence proportionately small. The Selenginsk Buriats amount to only about half the number of their brethren the Chorinsky tribe, but they have *ten* temples and not less than two thousand lamas while the latter have only four temples and scarcely two hundred lamas. Shamanism however is on the decline. Many have recently renounced it, and embraced Dalai Lamaism, and many more are at present halting between these two opinions. What a pity these poor heathen should be left thus to exchange one system of delusion for another, instead of being turned from darkness to light, and from the power of Satan to God.
>
> The Lamas exert their influence to overthrow shamanism, in other words to advance themselves and establish their own dogmas. Their zeal has carried some of them beyond the Baikal to the unlettered tribes around Irkutsk, among whom they are acting as Missionaries, building temples etc. and thus preparing to set up their unintelligible mummery in regions where it has hitherto been unknown. I am sure my dear Sir, you cannot read this statement with indifference. Is it not enough to provoke the Society – the churches to jealousy? Shall no soldiers of the cross be sent to take *that* field against these emissaries of Dalai Lama? – Some may think that *we* ought to wage the war there; but I could easily fill my sheet with arguments to shew why we should not desert our present post – On this side of the Lake we have enough – abundantly more than enough to employ our hearts and hands even were our numbers increased seven fold. The work among such a people is not to be effected by an occasional visit. They must have line upon line, precept upon precept. Missionaries must reside amongst them and shew them daily and from tent to tent, in season and out of season what neither shamanism nor Lamaism can – the way of salvation.
>
> I have another *provoking* circumstance to mention – the liberality of heathens in the support of their superstition. During my last journey, some Buriats in my presence were conversing about the flocks and herds of the Taisha Djigjit. They said he was not so very rich in sheep. I asked him how that happened since I had been told that his father Damba, to whom properly he succeeded, had upwards of ten thousand – 'Yes – his father at one time had ten thousand, but *seven thousand*

sheep, (beside other property) were disposed of for the building of the temple!' Shall greater sacrifices be made by individuals to uphold or propagate the mass of lies and nonsense of which Dalai Lamaism consists, than Christians who have it in their power are willing to make for the furtherance of the gospel of the Lord Jesus Christ? Will not such munificent heathen offerings as these rise up in the judgment against some who are withholding more than is meet? Perhaps this is out of place – the facts speak for themselves, but I am moved when I see such calls for more missionaries, and the Society, unable to meet them!

But that was how things were. The Society's resources, made up of voluntary donations from ordinary church-goers, were too small to pay for enough missionaries to counter the flood of lamas, even if the men could have been found and the Russian government persuaded to admit them. Besides, the outwardly drab religion which the missionaries purveyed had little pulling power with the Buryats to counteract the attractiveness of lamaism. The missionaries discovered that, some ten years before their own arrival in Siberia, one tribe had been willing to give 12,000 head of cattle to pay for thirty wagonloads of sacred books from Tibet. For their part, the missionaries usually found little difficulty in giving away their tracts and gospels. But it was galling to know that only too often the people wanted them merely because they had good uses of their own for the paper and leather they were made of.

When Edward reached the kontora, he found the taisha Dembil there, along with the equally disreputable Nomtu. The two were busy getting drunk together, and invited Edward to join them. They were surprised when he refused. The sight of Nomtu led Edward on to describe and condemn the type of Buryat who became an Orthodox Christian. The Buryats, he found, were just as mercenary in their dealings with the Russian church as they were with him and his colleagues, but the Russian priests exploited the situation shamelessly. As a result, without making any systematic attempt at proselytizing, they obtained hundreds of conversions over the years. A few Russian missionaries had been appointed in 1834, and the sinister implications of the coincidence that they had been sent to work near Selenginsk, Khodon and Ona did not escape the missionaries. But mostly the Orthodox church got its converts without making any special effort.

There were reasons for this success, none of them very creditable. Converts were given rewards of money or medals, or they were exempted from taxation for as much as three years. Sometimes, as happened in 1824, a Buryat taisha would be baptized, attracted by the prospect of a minor order of nobility, and would be able to take a number of his fellow tribesmen with him. These methods were similar to those which the lamas had employed themselves in Mongolia in making conversions from shamanism, and they worked, at least in the statistical sense. There was one other

Preaching to the People

powerful inducement to become a Christian: a Buryat who would otherwise be liable to punishment for some crime or other could escape prosecution by allowing himself to be baptized, and taking a Christian name.

There were even more trivial reasons for seeking, or pretending to seek, baptism into the Orthodox church. In one letter we read:

> It is by no means uncommon, when a husband and wife quarrel, for the latter, as soon as her husband has left the house, to flee to the nearest priest of the Greek church, and request to be immediately baptized. The priest will in all probability desire her to wait, for he knows that in a short time she will be followed by her husband. He returns to his home, and finding that his wife is absent, concludes at once that she has gone to the priest's, whither he also directs his steps, and enquiring for his wife learns that she is there. 'Is she baptized?' he enquires with earnestness. – 'No,' is the reply of the priest, 'Not yet.' 'Well then, I will give you a cow, or I will give you two sheep, if you will not baptize her.' 'Oh,' replies the priest, 'I am just preparing to baptize her, and I cannot refuse. But let me see. If you will give me four sheep I will not do it.' In this way frequently several hours will be spent, haggling within hearing of the poor woman about the sum to be paid to prevent her being baptized. But why the desire of baptism on her part, – it will be asked. Is she convinced of the truth of Christianity? No; but she has learned that according to the law of the empire, no authority can be exercised over a christian by a pagan; and if once baptized should her husband maltreat her, she may leave him whenever she pleases. And why is he so desirous of preventing her baptism? Does it arise from conjugal affection? No, no. It is a mere mercenary consideration by which he is actuated. If his wife leave him he must purchase another wife, and while the priest may be induced by the bribe of two, or of three sheep, to refuse baptism, another wife would cost him four sheep or perhaps six! And why does the priest hesitate to baptize? Does he suspect the motive of the woman? No, no. He knows it, he knows all, and delays only that he may make as advantageous a bargain for himself as he can.

No attempt was made to instruct the new converts in the doctrines of Christianity, and consequently they differed from their erstwhile co-religionists only in a few externals. Becoming a Christian meant no more than changing a few habits – living in a house instead of a tent, wearing the hair short instead of in a pigtail, eating fish on Wednesday or Friday, making the sign of the cross and so on. 'By reason of these things,' Edward sighed, 'the way of truth is evil spoken of, and the name of Christ is sometimes received from our lips with a sneer, or as a theme for diversion.' All too often, nominal conversion engendered arrogance. As William said: 'The Baptized Bratsky here are in the sight of all men who have eyes "the worse for washing" – proud, ignorant – without God as well as without gods – and what is most affecting thinking that all is well with them for eternity while we dare not tell them the contrary.'

Edward turned back at the kontora and went home, calling in on some of the Buryats he had visited on the outward journey. The tour had been uneventful, and probably unproductive too, and in that sense it was typical of all the other tours which the missionaries undertook.

From time to time the missionaries travelled to less familiar parts. Here, where they were not known, their reception was even cooler than among the Khori. In December 1826 William made a journey to the Kudarinsk Buryats who lived near the mouth of the Selenga. Ethnographically the visit was interesting, but otherwise it was unrewarding. Most of the people could speak Russian, but they were completely illiterate. They were farmers and fishermen rather than herdsmen, and were still exclusively shamanist. Neither lamas nor the Orthodox clergy had made any headway among them, and William made no impact either. The people were suspicious of him because he was offering something ostensibly for nothing. He admitted that time and patience would be needed to gain their confidence, but the missionaries were never able to pay much attention to this tiny outlying population of less than 1,800 males. Robert was equally disappointed by his visit to Ol'khon, the 'sacred' shaman island in Lake Baikal. He found the islanders even more backward and primitive than the Buryats in general. 'They have no letters,' he wrote, 'and therefore not one of them can read. Bū, or Būgēr, the god of Shamans is their God. [Robert seems to have confused the Mongol word for shaman, *böö*, with that of a god.] There are no Lamas among them yet. They are Barbarous Islanders.' So much for the inhabitants of Ol'khon, who told Robert plainly 'that they did not wish to be instructed in any thing', and sent him on his way.

The missionaries operated at various levels of argument. One method of proving the truth of Christianity with which they experimented, apparently to little effect, was that drawn from the evidence of Christ's miracles. The lack of success of this approach is hardly surprising, as the Buddhists were well supplied with miracles of their own. Of one such encounter Edward wrote, in 1821:

> He then asked us how we know that Christos was the true God? We answered, one class of arguments was drawn from the miracles which He performed, which could not be contradicted by his greatest enemies, and which could not possibly be performed by any mere man. We then read to him some of the miracles which our Lord performed, as recorded in the gospels of Matt and Jno. He seemed however more disposed to be angry that he was unable to answer than willing to be convinced by what was said to him.

The Directors may have doubted the efficacy of this argument when

Preaching to the People

addressed to a champion of a sophisticated religion, for this part of Edward's conversation with a high lama at Goose Lake was omitted when the relevant pages from his Journal were published.

Talking to ordinary Buryats whom they met on their journeys, the missionaries used even simpler arguments than this, and it was not till they got permanent classes of young men going, in the 1830s, that they could engage in anything like systematic exposition of the Bible. In 1822 Robert described how he had tried to reason with a tentful of Buryats, one of them a lama:

> I directed their attention to the object of my Mission, by inquiring who is their chief God? They said his name is Shigomony. I asked what sort of god he is? They answered there is no god greater than he, for he knows all things. I then directed my questions to a man, who had come on a visit, and with whom I was before a little acquainted. Then, my friend, if your god Shigomony knows all things, he must know that we are in this tent, and that we are talking about him. Yes – He must know that you were one of the ferry-men last summer on the Temnik? Yes. That the ice now on the river prevents you from crossing it with your boat? Yes . . . . Well then, my friend, Shigomony must know all the evil that you have done, and all the evil that is in your heart. He would not answer this question; but I told him it must be so, if he knows all things. Where is your Shigomony? In that chest, pointing to it. When do you take him out of it? During the white month, and when the Lamas come to pray for us. I told him I did not believe him else he is not such a god as he represented him to be. You could not put a man there; therefore he must be less than a man! You could not put that dog there; therefore he must be less than a dog! You could not even keep a living mouse there, for it would either eat its way out, or die; he must therefore be less than a mouse! My friend, you are quite mistaken about your god Shigomony; but I tell you what I think: Your Lamas deceive you, causing you to pay 18, 20 or 30 Roubles for that which is but a bad drawn likeness of a man, by saying, it is necessary to have it in your tent, to preserve you from evil, and to do you good, since it is evident it can do neither – you fear him and bow to him, when you might as well do it to the ashes from the fire – If you give him to me I shall burn him in the fire, and you shall find that we shall sleep as sound tonight, and rise as well in the morning without him, as with him. They seemed to wonder at my boldness, or presumption, but said nothing.

By late 1830, Edward and William seem to have come to terms with the futility of itineration as a major activity on their part. They decided that it would be more productive to stay at home and encourage the local Buryats to visit the mission stations. But they did not altogether neglect the outlying areas. As late as 1839 they were still making occasional journeys, but the main burden of itineration fell on the shoulders of their young convert Shagdur, who undertook long evangelistic tours when he was not teaching at one or other of the mission schools. For the last ten years of the life of the mission, the time of its European members was taken up by lengthy periods of home leave, by the care of their schools, and by the printing of the Old Testament.

It never proved possible to establish a proper Congregational church in Siberia, which would include the Buryat converts, since the missionaries were never able to baptize their converts. But they did manage to gather together small groups of interested Buryats, whom they persuaded, cajoled, and sometimes even tried to compel, to attend their regular church services. Their public preaching started at Selenginsk in August 1823, when Edward first admitted some Buryats to services held at the mission house. The services he held at his 'Stepney' chapel failed to invite many listeners, and by the end of the 1820s we hear no more of Stepney in his letters.

At first the services excited a little interest, no doubt because of their novelty, but once the freshness had worn off, it was the old story. The missionaries never refer to their church services in their letters without complaining of the apathy of the local people towards them. Only a year after he had started preaching, Edward had to report that 'there is a spirit of great slothfulness and carelessness manifested by this people. Some sitting almost within hearing will not be prevailed upon to come out of their tents to attend to what is going forward. There is scarcely any curiosity in them to know anything about religious things; they act as if they had no concern in them.' There was plenty of opportunity for the Buryats to attend church if they wanted to. In 1826, for example, before the missionaries separated, there were services at three different places every Sunday, at the mission house, at Stepney, and at another place where there were usually some Buryat tents. In 1828 Robert reported that he was preaching two sermons each week day, in Mongolian in the morning and in Russian in the evening, while for years Edward had been holding a daily service in Mongolian, a practice he kept up at Khodon. It was no use. Hardly any people came, sometimes none at all, and those who did come were mostly employees of the mission, who were afraid of losing their jobs if they failed to turn up. As William wrote in 1827, in a general review of the first nine years' work of the mission:

> There is scarcely one individual of our Buriat congregation who is not in some way dependent upon the Mission for assistance or support, and they are induced to attend our services rather from the fear of displeasing us, than from any interest they take in what they hear.

Robert, who worked hard to drum up a congregation, felt equally frustrated:

Preaching to the People

I myself at the hour of meeting went round all the Tents, every sabbath for more than two years, thus inviting them to attend. I even opened their tent doors, to know who was at home, that they might not excuse themselves. But it was hinted to me, that perhaps my trouble was unnecessary: and from that moment I desisted from that duty personally, but continued to send one or other of the students, or the Boriate servant. All the people at the tents generally absented themselves, except one, two, or three, when they were not working for the Mission! The women seldom attended: and except one Blind Woman none of them regularly; and this woman was in the habit of receiving perquisites from the Mission. For a considerable time I had a meeting every Sabbath evening, at which all the workmen and students attended, and also the people from the tents were invited; but none of the tent people attended regularly except the above mentioned blind woman.

It was all very discouraging, and in 1827 Edward wrote to say that he would not be surprised if the Directors compared the mission to the barren fig tree in the Bible. As a matter of fact, this was rather the view they took. By 1829, they realized that the Society was not getting value for money, and that the resources applied in Siberia might have been used more productively elsewhere. 'Had the Mission in Siberia been now commencing,' it was minuted by the Northern Committee, 'the Committee would not have recommended a mission to be undertaken in that quarter.' But the Society had committed itself to Siberia, and the Directors were unwilling to cut their losses, though they were, understandably enough, reluctant to send reinforcements.

Towards the end of the life of the mission, the congregations at Khodon and Ona seem to have grown in size, and in 1839 William could report as many as thirty or forty Buryats turning up for service at Ona. There were conversions, too, and a few drop-outs, but all the converts came from the ranks of the pupils in the mission schools and their families, not from the Buryats whom the missionaries had met on their travels. Quite early on, they had reached the conclusion that it was not much good preaching haphazardly to the odd ignorant adult. If they were to make any impression at all, it could only be on the unformed and receptive minds of lads whom they could be sure of having under their care for years on end. To this end they organized schools, first at Selenginsk, later at Khodon, and finally at Ona as well. In spite of some backsliding, a few Buryats became genuine Christians, and one of them, Shagdur, was still a believer when Gilmour visited Siberia over thirty years later. The Missionary Society hoped to bring Shagdur to Inner Mongolia as an evangelist, but nothing came of the idea.

14

The Mission Schools

One of the main branches of Protestant missionary work, from the beginning of the great period of expansion which began around 1800 onwards, was the education of young people of both sexes in elementary schools and more advanced institutions which the missionaries founded themselves. The pioneers were the Baptist missionaries Carey, Marshman and Ward. Carey set up his first little school in Bengal in 1794, and as early as January 1795 he was writing about his vision of establishing colleges in terms which seem to anticipate the foundation of the Serampore College in 1818. Other societies, too, began to occupy Bengal early in the nineteenth century and to found schools there. Missionaries of the LMS took part in this fundamental work in Bengal itself, elsewhere in India, and in other mission fields. Richard Knill, for example, the Society's future agent in St Petersburg, promoted education in Madras, where he arrived in 1816. Two years later he moved to Travancore, and when he left there his work was continued and developed with conspicuous success by his successor, Charles Mault. By 1822 there were reported to be twenty village schools in operation, as well as a seminary for training young Indian evangelists. Further east, schools were being established for the instruction of young Chinese, though here progress was slower. Robert Milne's school at Malacca, and Robert Morrison's Anglo-Chinese College at the same place, were both founded in 1818. A very progressive feature of missionary education was the foundation of girls' schools. Knill's seven Madras schools included one for girls; the Maults had a girls' boarding school; and in Penang, Mrs Samuel Dyer's school, which opened in late 1827, had twenty-two girl pupils by May 1828. These are only random examples of a phenomenon characteristic of nineteenth-century Protestant missionary work. In Siberia, too, schools were founded which, though on a smaller scale, followed a similar pattern of grading, and welcomed pupils of both sexes.

India and China were two areas where unpretentious beginnings led to a vigorous growth in missionary education. By contrast, the contemporary Protestant missionary educational effort among the non-Russian peoples of

The Mission Schools

Russia and Siberia, principally the Kalmucks and the Buryats, has gone more or less unobserved, and is completely forgotten today. These schools were run by missions which were themselves short-lived. Hence they failed to develop beyond a rudimentary stage, and were still entirely dependent upon the missions when the latter were withdrawn. Lacking local roots, they vanished without trace.

One of the pupils at Selenginsk made something of a name for himself as an antiquarian, and taught for a few years at the military school at Troitskosavsk, and one or two other budding intellectuals passed through the missionaries' hands. But their early Protestant training seems to have left little or no impression upon their personalities or upon the course of educational development in Siberia. Proof of this lies in the fact that, within a single generation, the local people had more or less forgotten about the mission and its ideals, while the few European travellers who went out of their way to enquire about it could pick up no more than scraps of folk memory from a dimly remembered past. Gilmour met the convert Shagdur and another former pupil of one of the mission schools who had become a lama. Henry Lansdell, passing through Selenginsk ten years after Gilmour, discovered that popular superstition had already transformed the missionaries into spooks, who came out of their graves at night to roam their old haunts. He did run across a Russian called Melnikoff who had gone to school there as a boy. Melnikoff had not opened a book for forty years, and had forgotten how to read. He had lost track of his Buryat school-fellows, but he thought that with one exception – probably Shagdur – who had joined the Orthodox church, not one of them had become a Christian. Lansdell also met the nephew of another former pupil, and heard of one more old Buryat, still alive, who had attended a mission school. All in all, it was a dismal record of devoted effort and early promise which had come to nothing.

The pattern of educational enterprise in Siberia followed that familiar from other mission fields. The missionaries set up small elementary schools, located in their own homes, and also founded an Academy or Seminary, as it was also called, for the advanced training of promising pupils. They had two main objectives. The first was to dispel the cloud of intellectual darkness which, in their estimation, shrouded the whole land. It was uphill work. The Buryats were found to be dull, ignorant and apathetic. As Robert put it, crudely but forcefully: 'It is like drawing a Cow out of the Mud to get this people to act.' They had to be made to think, and to be shown the value of independence of mind, before there was any point in putting new ideas in front of them. There would be a practical advantage also in teaching them to read. The three missionaries could not hope to cover anything but a small part of the population, and would have to rely to a great extent on their tracts and gospels to spread the message. Unless the people could read,

The Mission Schools

these 'silent missionaries' would be useless. The second objective was to train selected young men as teachers and evangelists.

In 1827 William defined what he considered to be the purpose of mission education, in the course of a general report to the Directors:

> Means should be taken to excite in them a spirit of enquiry. The people should be taught to *think*, and to consider this as their undoubted privilege. When they learn that freedom of thought and action in religious matters is their inalienable right, their eyes will then begin to open upon the deceitful maxims of their own priesthood. They will then be led to examine the foundations of their belief, and the true nature of their religious observances; and no supposed holiness of persons or things should exempt them from being subjected to examination. Every Christian Mission established in such a country has the direct tendency thus to excite and keep up enquiry, and much may be done in sapping the foundations of an erroneous system before any outward change is apparent. . . . We had not been long here before we saw the peculiar importance of adopting some plans for the promotion of General Education among the people in connection with the preaching of the Gospel and the translation of the Scriptures; and every succeeding year has deepened the conviction that the *young* demanded our especial attention. And when we speak of the education of the young it must be understood, that this includes not merely instruction in the arts of reading, writing, etc., but the inculcation of Christian principles, both by the use of Christian Schoolbooks, and the direct instruction communicated by the teacher; so that it is, strictly speaking, a *Christian education*. Some friends of the cause not perhaps properly adverting to this, think and speak slightingly of Schools, as but an inferior object of attention to a Missionary. But even were nothing more done than teaching the youth of a heathen nation to read, by means of native teachers, surely this, when the Scriptures are ready for circulation among them is no small matter. Ignorance is emphatically the mother of their devotion, and, in many cases, ignorance of their own as well as of other religions. And you are aware that the Lamas of these parts, as if they were sensible of this, while they themselves must learn to read in order to utter the words of their voluminous *noms*, prudently keep the meaning of them concealed under the veil of an unknown tongue.

William's letter underwent considerable editing before it was read in Committee in July 1827. In particular, the Directors shied away from the possible implications, at home, of his advocacy of uninhibited freedom of thought amongst the heathen, and deleted much of what he had written to that effect. But his opinions on the importance of education went uncensored, and so presumably enjoyed the approval of the Directors. These opinions also reflected Edward's philosophy of education. Robert, though,

The Mission Schools

seems to have held conflicting views, and to have favoured education for its own sake. In particular, he wanted to introduce Tibetan, the sacred language of lamaism, into the curriculum, while his colleagues were resolutely opposed to such a step. They took the anti-intellectual view that mastery of Tibetan could serve no purpose but that of making it easier for the people to study the very 'heathen' scriptures which they proposed to eliminate. As William wrote:

> I am no foe to literature, but instead of assisting the Buriats whether lamas or laity to read the voluminous lies and nonsense of their books – and there is nothing else in the language for them to read – I would rather assist in sweeping the whole mass of their Tibetan noms out of the country.

Robert was interested in Tibetan for its own sake. He also wanted to show up the lamas, by demonstrating that he and his pupils were better Tibetan scholars than they were. He also considered that his work in the Tibetan language, principally the compilation or copying of dictionaries, would be of great use to the Buryats, though he did not explain in what way it would be useful. The pro and anti Tibetan views could be argued. After all, in Bengal it was thought prudent not to divorce Western education from traditional native culture, and the study of Sanskrit was encouraged. But the Siberian situation was different, in that Tibetan was itself a foreign language, only recently introduced, and serving solely as the vehicle of a rival missionary religion. William was right. To teach Tibetan would do nothing for the mission and nothing to advance native Buryat culture either. It could serve only to make lamaism more readily accessible, and his advocacy of freedom of thought did not stretch that far. For him and Edward, education was a *praeparatio evangelica*, whereas to Robert it had a value in itself, wherever it led. In this difference of approach lay some of the seeds of discord which were to grow and split the mission.

It is impossible to be sure what educational models the missionaries had in mind when planning their schools. Their letters and reports tell us little or nothing about their theoretical standpoint, and the textbooks they compiled and sent copies of to the Directors, which might have provided a clue, seem to have disappeared. We do have a prospectus of the Academy, and one report on its work, but both these documents were drawn up by Robert, and suffer from his characteristic prolixity and superficiality.

As far as the elementary schools are concerned, the model was probably Joseph Lancaster's school in Southwark. Lancaster's brand of monitorial teaching was fashionable in Nonconformist circles, and we know that the Directors favoured it, and that Sarah had undergone a little training at the school. But the Siberian programme of elementary education was too restricted in scope, too short-lived, and too vaguely described in the mission correspondence for us to be able to form any clear idea as to its possible

The Mission Schools

affiliations. The same goes for the Academy. It is tempting to see it as an imitation of the more famous institution at Serampore. We know that Edward was a great admirer of Carey, and named his second son William Carey after the famous Baptist missionary. But that is the sole possible link between the two institutions, and it is an extremely fragile one. For one thing, the Serampore College is not mentioned in the mission correspondence. For another, it was not Edward, but Robert, who was the moving spirit behind the Academy, and there is nothing to suggest that he had any special regard for Carey or his college. Most probably, if the Selenginsk Academy represents anything more than a local response to a situation similar to that faced by missionaries in other fields, it may owe its inspiration to the Dissenting academies at home, perhaps even to the Gosport Seminary, Robert's old college. But this is pure surmise. We know nothing for sure about the theoretical origins of the Selenginsk institution.

Curiously contradictory judgments have been expressed about the nature and extent of missionary education in Siberia. At one extreme the missionaries have been blamed for doing nothing at all in this direction, and merely alienating the Buryats by making insensitive assaults upon their beliefs. At the other, they have been praised for acting as something like an early equivalent of development experts. The truth can be ascertained from their own papers, and bears little relation to either of these eccentric opinions.

S.S. Hill, who began his Siberian adventure in mid-1847, did not, of course, meet the missionaries personally. He called at the former mission house, then occupied by an exiled naval commander of Dutch origin, and learned about them from one of the ladies of the family who could speak French. Hill's knowledge of mission work in general, and of the Siberian mission in particular, looks rather superficial. He made artificial distinctions which were not supported by fact, and he completely misunderstood what had happened at Selenginsk and the other stations. He wrote as follows:

> It appears to me, however, in relation to Central Asia, that there is a more certain means than the labours of missionaries, for the introduction of the religion of civilized man even into the heart of the country; and this means is, the promulgation of a knowledge of the most useful arts of civilized life, together with the elements of natural science. These very words indeed thus employed may seem like empty sounds. But let us suppose, that even the missionaries above spoken of as soon as they had completed the grammars and dictionaries of the Mongolian tongue, had begun to teach their scholars the means of acquiring knowledge – that is, writing, reading and the use of figures – and that they had followed this up by the elements of such knowledge as tends most to benefit the condition, or excite the curiosity of men. . . . What obstacle, for instance, can it be supposed would be put in the way of the agriculturalist who would double the crops of the land?

The Mission Schools

> What opposition can we anticipate would be offered to the introduction of gardening, as one of the fine, as well as useful, arts? And above all, in what corner under heaven has the art of medicine found any opposition to its introduction, save when it has been in the hands of men who have degraded their profession by suffering avarice to predominate over every other passion they possess? Men who should carry these immediately apparent boons with them and among whom would appear none of these disputes and denials of each other which are found among missionaries of opposite sects, could not fail to gain a degree of respect and obtain an ascendancy that would throw education completely into their hands, and thus pave the way for the promulgation of the religion which the missionaries whose feelings are ever too strongly engaged in the prime object of their mission to act with coolness and deliberation, may never accomplish. . . . It was because I entertained these opinions, that I did not hesitate to express to the *Khomba Lama* an unfavourable opinion of the English mission.

The Khamba must have smiled, if he recalled how the missionaries struggled to get their schools going during the time of his predecessor, who played cat and mouse with them and did so much to thwart their work. Hill was naive in his analysis of the general situation, but apart from that, he was simply misinformed. In the twenty years that separated his visit from the dispersal of the mission in 1828, memories in Selenginsk had perhaps had time to grow dim, though it is surprising that no one seems to have remembered Robert, who had left Selenginsk only a year or two earlier, and the Academy he had run.

On the other hand, some present-day scholars, relying apparently on Russian sources, present the missionaries as being more interested in secular than spiritual progress, and as having devoted themselves wholeheartedly to precisely what Hill chided them for neglecting. Marc Raeff, the biographer of Speranskii, suggests that the reforming Governor General had welcomed them in Buryatia and patronized them because he found them ready to assume the leadership in the intellectual, cultural and social development of the natives, and to encourage them to realize their potential in these secular respects, rather than persuade them to seek baptism. He sees the missionaries as having acted as advisers and teachers of agriculture and medicine. Raeff's sources may support this interpretation of the work of the missionaries, but their own writings do not. Admittedly, they did not press very hard for permission to baptize their converts, but this was only because they had applied to the Emperor for such permission in 1835 and had been refused, and they were acute enough not to draw attention to themselves by courting a second refusal. In the end, their inability to form a church of their own, with baptized converts, proved an almost fatal discouragement, and some time before they were expelled they were seriously thinking of abandoning

The Mission Schools

Siberia for this very reason. Nor is there any reason to believe that they taught agriculture, or even understood it. The nearest they got to improving Siberian farming was to arrange for the Governor of Irkutsk to be supplied with an English plough, which, incidentally, he never paid for. N.A. Bestuzhev, philosophizing in a letter written in 1841 about how change and innovation can only be effective if the time is ripe, tells the following amusing anecdote about Robert, which hardly suggests that he was an accomplished farmer:

> There lives by us an English missionary. He knows that in England, after sowing and harrowing the corn, they roll the soil solid with a roller. By means of this, the corn grows more thickly and evenly. He did the same here last year, and we all envied his enterprise and vowed to introduce the same thing ourselves in the future. But what happened? Strong winds prevail here in spring. These dry up the soil and it is only the clods which remain after the harrowing and retain moisture which provide protection for the shoots. In his field, the clods crushed and pulverised by the roller were turned to sand by the first strong wind, and carried away with the seeds into the neighbouring fields, and our Englishman was left with an empty hole rather than a level field.

Nor were they notably skilled in medicine. Their services were in demand simply because they knew more than their ignorant neighbours, and were willing to help. It is possible that Robert may have made a name for himself as a jack-of-all-trades, especially after he left the service of the LMS, but this is a period of his life about which we know practically nothing, and during which he was not entitled to call himself a missionary. On the whole, it is hard to see what can have given rise to an evaluation of the missionaries' activities which is in direct conflict with their own estimation of their position.

This position is defined in a letter which William addressed to Prince Golitsyn in May 1831, justifying himself and his colleagues in the face of what he felt were unfair accusations which had been brought against them. William stressed the spiritual nature of the mission:

> The sole object of our Mission being the spread of the gospel among heathen tribes – the glory of God, in the Salvation of men – and being sincerely desirous of promoting the welfare both spiritual and temporal of the country, we trust we shall receive the countenance and favour of His Imperial Majesty the Emperor, so long as we devote ourselves to the work of enlightening the heathen people among whom we have for so many years been permitted to labour. We engage in no commercial or other secular pursuits; have no connection with any political affairs, and are wholly supported by the Missionary Society in London, whose Christian character and objects are known all over the world.

The Mission Schools

He went on to speak of being 'engaged for the spiritual good of a people sunk in heathenism' and submitted that 'all we ask is to be allowed peaceably to perform our sacred duties'. The tenor of his remarks in this official communication, made at what was a critical time for the mission, is unmistakable.

Education is not mentioned in the Directors' Instructions to Edward. Perhaps it was taken for granted that the teaching of the young formed part of a missionary's duties, and certainly the opening of schools both in Siberia and amongst the Kalmucks was fully approved of in London.

It was in late 1821 that Cornelius Rahmn, recently transferred to Sarepta, opened a rudimentary school there for Kalmuck boys, which he planned to run on Lancasterian lines. This school slightly antedates those of the missionaries in Siberia, and though there was no connection between the two enterprises, the problems he encountered – laziness, superficiality, unpunctuality, parental indifference and opposition from the lamas – are so reminiscent of those complained of in correspondence from Siberia, that it is worth looking briefly at this abortive, and now quite forgotten, attempt to give Mongolian children a Christian education.

Cornelius was not a pioneer at Sarepta. The Moravians before him had tried to instruct Kalmuck boys, but without success. As far back as 1801, a young Kalmuck boy had persuaded the Moravian schoolmaster, Brother Wendling, to teach him German, and for a short while a few other young Kalmucks were excited by the same whim. But the novelty soon wore off, and the boys stopped coming to school.

Cornelius reached Sarepta in the late summer of 1819, and in January 1821 he got his first Kalmuck pupil. This was a lad of fifteen named Dschimba, who was apprenticed to a Moravian joiner. Dschimba decided that he wanted to learn German and, with his master's approval, Cornelius agreed to teach him every afternoon. The boy came to school fairly regularly for a while, though his attendance was interrupted by illness. Then, in October 1821, Cornelius seized the opportunity he had been waiting for to extend his activities. He writes as follows in his Journal for Tuesday 2 October:

> I have often wished to be able to take up Calmuc children and give them regular instruction in a day school. This plan has repeatedly been tried by the Moravians, but without success and permanency, owing partly to the fickleness of mind, which is a peculiar trace in the Calmucs' character, partly to the want of controul over the children, especially as long as the parents do not countenance the matter. Today when I went out, four Calmuc boys came to me begging. I told them to come to my lodgings. 'Now, I said, children! I will teach you to read and write, if you are willing to learn, but you must come daily to my house. If you do well I shall give you somewhat to eat.' As they agreed to my proposal

time was fixed to begin the school, and their and their parents name was written down. When these four boys were gone away two other boys came and wished to have their names written down also.

Next day, the school opened at nine in the morning, with two more pupils, making eight in all. Cornelius was quite pleased with the first day's progress, and gave them each a bun at the end of the lesson. On Thursday, three boys were absent, but three others turned up in their place. 'If I am able to keep two or three continually in school, till they can read fluently, I would consider myself very happy and successful', wrote Cornelius, but that was asking too much. On Friday there were nine pupils, but these included only three of Wednesday's intake, and on Saturday none turned up at all, as they were all working in the water-melon fields. None came on Monday either, and when Cornelius interrogated one of them, he just got a cheeky answer. On Tuesday he met four of his pupils, but they told him they were too busy to come to school.

This was only a week after Cornelius had opened the school for the first time, and not until 13 December does he mention it again in his Journal. His letters show that for a while he gave up hope of making a go of it. On 19 October he wrote to George Burder to say that he had recently had the idea of opening a school, but that, although it had promised well at first, the pupils had all given up and deserted him. But in December Dschimba turned up again, and once more it was arranged that he should come back every day for two hours. On 1 January, four more of the pupils came back. Cornelius taught them for a couple of hours, and was surprised at how much they had remembered. By 20 January he had six boys. The school was going on 'with great cheerfulness' and he was confident enough to adopt the Lancasterian pattern, intending that these six boys should become monitors in due course. The enthusiasm lasted until 5 February, and then attendance began to fall off again, till on the 10th there were no pupils at all, and only three on the 11th.

This is the last entry about the school in that part of Cornelius's Journal which has survived, but from his letters we know that he managed to keep it alive for another six months. Although he had 'to struggle with the craftiness of the heathen priests, those miserable and unhappy workers of iniquity', there were times when it seemed to be almost flourishing. The Lancasterian system was being applied, and Cornelius wrote in July that he was busy composing standard lessons for the use of his pupils. Unpunctuality remained a problem, and so was the lack of discipline and self-discipline:

> I am at a loss what to do in order to accustom the children to more
> punctuality. I can exercise no moral or social control over them. This
> is almost the case with the parents themselves, which, even if they were
> decidedly on my side, are yet unable to exercise any authority over
> their children. A Calmuc child is its own master completely, and no pen

can draw, no tongue can utter all the perverseness, malignity, uncleanness and desperate wickedness which a Missionary here must witness.

In the same letter, Cornelius reports that in May he had had as many as fifteen children at the school, seven of whom attended more or less regularly. Teaching occupied five hours a day. His next report, also sent in July, was still cheerful, in spite of the obstruction he was having to face from the lamas. But by December the school was dead. In autumn all his pupils had gone off to work in the tobacco fields, and after harvest time he was unable to persuade them to come back. That was the end of missionary schooling at Sarepta, and Cornelius himself left the scene only six or seven months later.

Cornelius saw what was wanted. If only a few young Kalmucks could be taught to read and write, and educated according to Christian principles, they could be infiltrated into the illiterate mass of the people, where they might 'imperceptibly operate on their minds by removing now existing prejudices and paving a fair way for the reception of the Gospel of Christ'. To achieve this, it would be necessary to set up what he called Ambulatory Schools in each of the aimaks, or subdivisions of the hordes, so as to keep up with the nomadic population. This would require the approval of the Russian government, followed up by definite orders to the local chiefs. After that, it would be necessary to recruit 'a sufficient number of exceedingly well qualified, pious, zealous and persevering schoolmasters'. Cornelius thought such men would only need a year to become fluent enough in Kalmuck to do the job. But all this was mere visionary dreaming. Even if the Russian government were to take an interest in Kalmuck education, the LMS never had any intention of hazarding resources on this scale – or indeed any scale at all – in so uncertain a field as Sarepta, where they would never have had a missionary at all but for Betty Rahmn's neurasthenia.

When Edward and Cornelius arrived in Irkutsk, they would have found a few schools in existence in eastern Siberia, though there was nothing even remotely resembling an educational system. The first school to be founded in the whole region had been a monastery school set up by order of Peter the Great at Irkutsk in 1725, and intended for the children of the clergy. Mongolian was taught there until 1737. There were no institutions of secular education in eastern Siberia until 1754, when the Irkutsk Navigation School was opened. In 1780 the Irkutsk Religious Seminary opened its doors, and in 1781 a town school was set up. This was a fair-sized institution for its time: in 1782 it had three teachers and 133 pupils. Popular education was advanced to some degree after new regulations were promulgated in 1786. Three years later, two 'popular' schools, a major and a minor one, were opened in Irkutsk. The former, as its name implies, was the more advanced, and for a few years it offered an ambitious programme of teaching which included Mongolian, Chinese, Manchu and Japanese. In 1794 these subjects were discontinued, though in 1799 the teaching of French and German was begun. In Transbaikalia very little had been done by the end of the century. A garrison school had been opened at Selenginsk, and for a year or two there had been a navigation and mining school at Nerchinsk.

Thus, by 1800, very little had been done for Russian children, especially outside the few large towns, and nothing at all for the Buryats. Government may have approved of the establishment of schools, but even after the promulgation of further regulations, in 1804, which provided for the replacement of the two types of popular school by a triple system of parish and district schools and gymnasia, inertia on the part of the local administration under its absentee Governor General Pestel helped ensure that progress was slow. Schools depended for finance mainly on private generosity, and lack of money meant that some elementary schools which did manage to open their doors during the first two decades of the century, were forced to close them again in a few years. Just before the end of the eighteenth century, a popular school was opened in Verkhneudinsk, the first in Transbaikalia. In 1806 it was turned into a district school. A district school was opened in Irkutsk in 1806, at the same time as a gymnasium, and in 1811 the Troitskosavsk district school was established. These were all modest enterprises, and catered mainly for Russian children.

It was during the same years that public provision was first made for Buryat education. Balagansk boasted the first Buryat minor popular school, which was opened in 1804, and lasted till 1811. In 1805 a school was opened at the Khori kontora, though it had no regular teacher until 1815. Until that time, instruction was given by any clerks who could spare the time for it. Other Buryat schools were opened successively at other kontoras, but not all managed to survive, because of lack of money and flagging interest. The numbers of pupils remained low. So, for example, in 1850 there were three Buryat parish schools in the Verkhneudinsk district, with a total of forty-five pupils between them.

It was one thing to open schools for the Buryats, and another to get the children to attend. In 1828 Edward reported to Alers Hankey that, while each kontora had a school attached to it, and a teacher provided by Government, the schools were almost empty. What shocked him most, and what he thought would shock 'many persons who are able to appreciate the advantages of education', was that children had to be paid to attend, the sums varying from sixty to a hundred roubles a year. There was a good economic reason for this, even if it was not the sole reason. Ordinary Buryats had to pay an annual tribute, which in past days had been collectable in kind, but which had become commuted to a money payment. The tax may not have been very high, but many families were poor, and if a boy could not earn his share of the family income he represented a real burden on his parents. The missionaries were to run up against the same obstacle themselves as soon as they tried to set up schools, and from time to time they were driven to consider the same solution, but the Society never allowed them to use its money for the purpose of making cash grants to needy students.

There were many disincentives to learning, as the missionaries soon discovered. The people were passively ignorant, and saw no point in sending their children to school when they could be helping with the animals. The lamas, obscurantist by definition, battened on the popular ignorance which served their interests. Some brighter sparks had seen that a mission education opened the way to a good career in government service, and out of sheer selfishness did their best to discourage others from going to school and so qualifying themselves to compete for the few openings available. Finally, the nomadic way of life meant that it was impossible for most children to attend school regularly, unless their parents took the imaginative step of letting them become boarders at the mission schools. The schools themselves became more and more suspect as the missionaries began to make converts. The people were inhibited by the fear that their children would 'become English'. As Edward wrote in 1838: 'Since the separation of the few converts from the mass has taken place, hatred of our innovations in some, and fear of their superiors in others, is superadded to their former extreme apathy on the subject of education.'

Early on, in 1825, Edward hinted at another, more complex, disincentive. Fearing censorship, he expressed himself obliquely, but what he had in mind was the political situation in Siberia. He observed that some recent changes in administrative procedures, those arising from Speranskii's reforms, might encourage more Buryats to learn Russian, and continued:

> It will not appear surprising to you that there should be so much difficulty in stirring up an ignorant people to avail themselves of the opportunity of procuring education for themselves and their children. They cannot appreciate its advantages and so are not disposed to make any sacrifices to obtain them – while those of them who are better informed have not benevolence or public spirit enough to exert themselves for the good of others. But in addition to this, their political situation operates strongly against such things by taking away the chief motives for bettering their condition in an intellectual point of view. I cannot on this head go into explanation but you can easily conceive the difference between a free and independent people, and a people in a state of vassalage. It restrains them from freedom of thinking as well as freedom of acting.

Edward was perhaps being a little unfair in accusing all educated society of indifference to the needs of others. There were both Russians and Buryats who were prepared to put themselves out to provide what schooling they could for the children. One example is that of Igumnov, who taught Russians and Buryats each other's language in his private school at Verkhneudinsk.

The Mission Schools

The names of some of those private individuals who financed the early Buryat schools, too, have been recorded. But on the whole he was right. These were exceptions to the general state of apathy and indolence. His other point is an intriguing one. He does not make it clear whether, in blaming the political set-up in Siberia for stifling initiative, he is thinking of the population as a whole, Russians and Buryats alike, or whether he sees the Buryats as suffering under some special disability as a sort of colonial people. In this connection it is worth recalling the favourable impression which the Kazan Tatars had made on William during his journey to Selenginsk. Amongst their positive qualities he noticed that they were 'exemplary in the education of their children, and distinguished by their taste for reading'. Nearly a century later, Douglas Carruthers drew attention to the great disparity in well-being which existed between the shabby Mongols of west Mongolia and the prosperous Kirei-Kirghiz, their immediate neighbours. The former were Buddhist by religion, the latter Muslim. Edward's analysis, while thought-provoking, is too narrow to be satisfying.

The first hint that the missionaries were actually teaching young Buryats comes in an indirect way in a letter written by Robert towards the end of 1822. In it he complains that Richard Knill had not sent him a Russian arithmetic book and some arithmetical tables, as he had promised to do. 'My young Buriate is longing very much for them', he wrote. The young Buryat was Rintsin, the same lad whom Robert refused to do business with on Sunday. Rintsin had been with him since some time in 1821, and in September 1823 he was joined by his brother Sebek. By then, Edward too had a lad of about fifteen years of age studying with him. Sarah had her little school, attended by six or more children who came in every day to study elementary Mongolian. These were extremely modest beginnings, and the missionaries were looking for ways to formalize and extend their activities.

As far as we can tell, the question of the practicability and desirability of educating young Buryats first arose in an official way in correspondence between the missionaries and the Directors during the year 1823. On 3 February, Robert remarked in a letter that 'this people must be instructed before they can have knowledge; they must understand before they can believe'. He continued with an account of the work of young Rintsin, to whom he was at that time teaching Mongolian, Russian, English and Arithmetic. In what is evidently a reply to this and other letters, though the file copy, like many others, is faded and partly illegible, George Burder took up the topic encouragingly, though with caution. On 7 July he wrote:

> We have already hinted at the indisposition to read prevalent among the Buriats. This and the indolence of their general character, of which it may be regarded as an evidence, naturally leads us to inquire whether it be practicable to adopt any plans for the instruction of their children

The Mission Schools

in the elements of Christian knowledge. We presume, that hitherto you have found the superstition and the prejudices of the people what has appeared to you as an insurmountable barrier against all such attempts. We however, cannot help thinking, that whatever obstacles may exist, the subject is one that may deserve your very attentive consideration. We learn that among the Hindoos the inducement presented to the poor by the advantage of gratuitous elementary learning, in many instances, overcomes the aversion generated by their religious prejudices. We are aware that the strength of this inducement must depend on the value which the parents attach to learning and that this again will be regulated by the circumstances of the country as well as the degree of its civilization. Perhaps, however, it might be possible to succeed in making favourable impressions as to the object on a few minds, and that the advantages which, in a very few instances, might be reaped by the children first instructed, might produce a wish in the Parents of others to send their children to the School. The attractions that the *New System* of instruction represents to children appears to us of considerable importance and could the influence of the Priests and the prejudices of the parents be only in a comparatively few instances overcome, it is probable, that a foundation might be laid for a School in which, *gradually*, Christian Instruction might, perhaps, be introduced, and sound moral instruction *immediately*. The confidence which the people at Selenginsk must now have in the general integrity and uprightness of your character would we presume, in some degree facilitate success. At all events it would be desirable for us to receive the results of your reflections and observations on this important subject and we are persuaded that in the meantime you will keep your attention alive to the object.

This letter reached Selenginsk at the latest by the beginning of October 1823, when Edward referred to it in a letter to Alers Hankey, and it was answered in some detail in a joint letter from all three missionaries written in November. After outlining the difficulties which faced their mission, they took up Burder's suggestion of making a cautious start with schools in which there would, at first, be no overt attempt to proselytize:

It has occurred to us that some of the popular objections might be obviated by the establishment of schools in various parts of the country, to be wholly under the superintendence of native teachers, and for this purpose to get the Taishas and other principal men to form themselves into a kind of society, and by voluntary subscriptions support the expense of the schools. In this case the instruction would be merely of a moral kind, for we could not at present propose the introduction of our books, without exciting suspicions, and so defeating the plan. But before we can bring the matter to bear it will be previously necessary to

The Mission Schools

lay the plan before the individuals whom it is of consequence to interest in the business, which we have not yet been able to do.

Early in 1824 Edward and William called on the Khamba and on Yumdeleg, the recently appointed taisha, to try to interest them in setting up schools in each of the eighteen tribes of the Selenginsk Buryats. They hoped to raise enough money locally by subscription to pay for the scheme, but they offered to supply the school books and other equipment themselves. The Khamba nibbled at the bait, even tentatively offering to send them three young men from his own entourage as pupils. But evidently the two missionaries were not sanguine about the prospects, for Edward added, in his letter of March 1824 describing the démarche:

> In case nothing is done by the summer, I think I shall be inclined to hire a person qualified for teaching, which may be done without a great expense, and open a school as an example to them. I have already the offer of a house free for the purpose by the lama who gave us the use of it last summer for a temporary residence. Perhaps my brethren will do the same, in another quarter.

A year or so later, in January 1825, Edward went to Ona and made a similar proposal to the chief taisha of the Khori Buryats. He reported as follows on that episode:

> You have learned from former letters that we have been on the best terms with the chief Taisha of the Chorin Buriats ever since our first acquaintance with him upwards of three years ago. . . . I have again brought before him the subject of the establishment of district schools, concerning which we formerly wrote you. He and all others seem to approve and admit that to afford the people generally the means of education is a good thing; but I think there is little encouragement to hope that the plan will be heartily taken up by them. Many of their principal men were assembled at the Comptoir, when I arrived here, and I went thither for the purpose of ascertaining what countenance they were likely to give to the proposed schools. I found them however so occupied with a multitude of their own affairs, and so disinclined to take up any new subject, that I could do nothing more than converse separately with a few of them; but this gave me an opportunity of making known more fully the plan and present state of our Seminary at Selenginsk for the instruction of Buriat youth, and we entertain hopes that, if we are permitted to continue in the field of labour, a greater number of young men will yet be brought under our instructions.

The taisha was Jigjit, who was himself inclined to favour the missionaries, and rather enjoyed learning a little English, but who had inherited a difficult position following the fiasco of Dembil's flirtation with the Orthodox church,

The Mission Schools

and was not self-confident enough to promote the spread of Christianity. There is nothing in the mission correspondence to suggest that the missionaries ever got beyond the exploratory stage in their plan to set up schools in collaboration with Buryat notables, in either of the areas where they made the attempt. Those schools which they did set up were located at their own stations. They were managed solely by the missionaries, and were financed entirely from their own resources.

Long before they gave up hope of working through the local authorities, the missionaries had taken the first steps towards giving shape to their tentative educational enterprise. On 4 December 1823 they wrote to the Directors to give them 'a few particulars concerning the Liberal Education of the Buriate youth' at Selenginsk. The letter seems to be lost, but its contents were fortunately summmarized in a lengthy 'Memorial' concerning the foundation of what became known as the Selenginsk Academy. This Memorial, which was sent to the Directors under cover of a letter dated 12 August 1824, shows that the missionaries had evaluated the local circumstances, and had decided to set up the Academy, well before the end of 1823.

The Memorial and its covering letter are signed by all three men, but they are written in Robert's hand, while a P.S. appended to the Memorial is initialled by him alone. Subsequent correspondence about the Academy, including the one and only Report on its work, is also in his hand and name. This is not accidental. There are clear indications that he was, or very soon became, solely responsible for running the Academy. Thus in a report to the Treasurer dated 24 January 1826, William pointedly declined to say anything about the Academy, saying only: 'For particulars on this head I shall refer you to the communications of Mr Yuille.' Three years later, in the course of the long letter in which he rehearsed the misdeeds of Edward and Sarah over the management of the girls' school at Selenginsk, Robert recalled that he 'had taken the whole charge of the Academy'. It is quite probable, then, that the concept was his from the beginning, and that his colleagues, already doubtful about his ability to do anything properly, had decided to keep aloof from the Academy, while allowing their names to be attached to his proposal as a matter of form.

The covering letter of 12 August outlines the developing situation. Renewed approaches to the local Buryats had at last aroused some interest in the topic of education, and the missionaries felt confident of attracting enough candidates to make the project viable. They had no doubts as to the purpose of the Academy. As Robert wrote, they felt it their duty 'to endeavour to call in some fresh aid to assist in the Particular Branch of Labour, which, without controversy, is one of the most important in which Missionaries can be engaged, namely, that of Training up a certain number of Heathen youth, with a view to their usefulness, as Teachers and Preachers of Salvation to their fellow men'.

The Mission Schools

'Calling in fresh aid' meant tapping fresh sources of income. The school would be expensive to set up and run, and, not wishing to burden the Society further, the missionaries had already, in April 1824, sent the first copy of their Memorial to John Venning in St Petersburg. John was an expatriate merchant and philanthropist, the brother of Walter Venning the prison reformer, who had been Edward's companion on the voyage to Cronstadt, and who had, like Jean Paterson, died not long afterwards as a result of illness contracted during his charitable activities. The Vennings were great benefactors of good causes, and it was another member of the family, James, who remained in Russia after his father John retired to Norfolk in 1830, who proved a helpful friend to George Borrow when he arrived at St Petersburg in 1833.

One hopes that Robert had been less condescendingly patronizing when he wrote to Venning than he was in the covering letter:

> The Memorial is drawn up exclusively to John Venning Esq, St Petersburgh, with a view to secure an interest in this work with our Friends in that City – The Importance of which we are well aware of – and although we are aware that Mr Venning Supports Three Native Preachers in India!! And otherwise Aids the London Missionary Society; and also that the Christian Charity of this worthy Gentleman is by no means confined to our Society alone; yet we could not deny ourselves the Privilige[sic] of requesting him to take the Patronage of our Humble Institution upon him, which we believe shall grow in importance, as Prophecy ripens to Maturity – Besides, if that Worthy Gentleman should consider it an Honour conferred on him by us, we assure you that he merits it at our hand; for the marked attention and kindness which he and his Dear Relations, some of them are in the Rest beyond the grave, manifested to every member of this Mission during our respective residence in St. Petersburgh, and for the many tokens of continued Friendship which we have since received; but of this the Directors are already acquainted, and some of whom know Mr Venning better than from our information from these remarks, we humbly trust, that the Directors, with whom we stand more immediately connected, and our other Friends whom we wish to be interested with the Seminary in connection with this Mission, will see the Propriety of this *first Public step* we have taken, as it regards this Institution.

John Venning had responded with an immediate gift of 500 roubles and a promise of more when it was needed, but Robert now wanted the Memorial circulated more widely at home. He proposed various recipients in Glasgow, Dundee and what he was pleased to call Hampshare, including Ralph Wardlaw and Greville Ewing, his old tutor David Bogue, and Dr Dodds of Haslar Hospital.

The Memorial is a long, rambling document, characteristically uncouth

The Mission Schools

in style and idiosyncratic in spelling. It opens with an exposition of the difficulties encountered in evangelizing the Buryats with the limited resources available, and acknowledges that the Missionary Society could hardly be expected to supply enough missionaries to overcome these difficulties in the near future. Accordingly, after much consideration and prayer, the missionaries had decided that 'a Seminary at this Station should immediately be attempted, for the Liberal Education of the Buriate youth, with a view to qualify them, under the Blessing of our Three One God, to take a part with us in the concerns of this Mission'.

The proposed curriculum was an ambitious one, and was to be of a Christian character from the outset. The boys were to be taught languages – Mongolian, Russian, Latin, Greek, Hebrew and English – or as many of these as each individual could manage, together with whatever of the 'useful arts and sciences' the missionaries considered appropriate. Religious instruction was a *sine qua non*: 'We did not think it necessary to make any clause as it respects the one thing needful, namely divinity, as we suppose that no objections will be made to it, and as we are determined that this Branch shall make a daily exercise.' So much, then, for Burder's advocacy of a gradualist approach. It was typical of Robert's bad judgment that he thought there could be no objection to giving religious instruction. Predictably enough, it was just this which aroused the suspicions, not only of the people, but of the influential Khamba, and frightened off many potential pupils over the years.

The students were to agree to study for a period of three years – none too long, it would seem, in the light of the formidable curriculum. They were to have one week in seven as a holiday, and their families were to be allowed to visit them at any time. Tuition would be free, and those pupils who could not support themselves would be boarded and lodged for nothing.

These conditions had been advertised for about two years, with little response, and the missionaries were on the point of asking the Directors to let them pay cash grants to the poorer families, when a few students began to arrive. At the time of writing there were, apart from Rintsin and Sebek, six regular students and one candidate. Robert names them, and discusses each individual lad. They ranged in age from eleven to twenty-two. Three were lamas, one of them the Khamba's own nephew. Rintsin was, of course, the most advanced. He already knew Russian quite well, and had copied various rare books for the mission, including a Manchu–Russian dictionary belonging to William. He was busy, too, translating the Book of Psalms from modern Russian into Mongolian. Most of the other pupils could at least read and write Mongolian, though one or two were not even capable of that when they joined the Academy. Their lack of an elementary foundation makes Robert's course of study look quite chimerical, but in fact several of them were to make very respectable progress.

Most of the works copied for the mission were, incidentally, printed

The Mission Schools

books, not manuscripts. There was a good reason for this laborious task. The Manchu dynasty, 1644-1912, was a period of intense activity in the printing of lamaist works in Mongolian. Some lamaseries had their own printing shops, but the centre of this printing activity lay in Peking, with certain Chinese shops. There was no retail book trade through which a would-be purchaser could easily place an order in Peking, and it was cheaper and more reliable to pay a scribe to copy out the desired text by hand. There are several such copies in European libraries today where it is quite certain that the originals were printed books, for the scribes have faithfully included the colophons, which frequently contain the names of the patron who paid for the printing, the scribe who wrote the text which was cut on the blocks, and the Chinese shop which acted as publisher, and the dates between which the blocks were cut. So we know, for example, that Edward's copy of the Geser Khan epic was transcribed from the 1716 Peking printing. It was no sinecure being a mission copyist. The missionaries made a serious attempt to learn all they could about lamaism and Mongolian literature, and had copies made of everything they could lay their hands on which they felt would be useful, even of some books like fortune-tellers' manuals which they condemned as nonsense. Edward's Mongolian library alone, the surviving parts of which are today divided between the British Library and the Library of the BFBS, consisted of several thousand bound sheets. His books included some bilingual Tibetan–Mongolian dictionaries, whose transcription demanded the mastery of two quite different languages, and the neat arrangement of two scripts which went in different directions. There were, finally, the missionaries' own productions to be copied out as well, principally the entire Old Testament, in two or three copies of several successive revisions.

Just before Robert left St Petersburg, Paterson had reminded him, and William too, of the vastness of their field of labour, and had cautioned them to 'beware of having contracted ideas, and thereby shorten the hand of God towards you'. No doubt what he had in mind was his dream of evangelizing China and Siberia, but it was dangerous advice to give to Robert, who needed no encouragement to act extravagantly. Already he could see his infant Academy gleaming like a beacon of enlightenment over all east Asia. 'There is every possibility', he wrote, 'that from this Mission Station the Light of Divine Truth may shine to meet our brethren in Western Tartary; and our Brethren on the farther shore of China; and to the Eastern and Northern Sea, places where Missionaries and Truth have not yet been known to travel.' But meanwhile the need was to disarm potential scepticism at home, 'as we do not wish to be understood as going beyond the limits of our Mission'.

Still, Robert intended that one day his Academy should be open to boys from all over Siberia, and so he gave it the grandiose title of 'The Selenginsk Missionary Seminary, Instituted for the instruction of a Select Number of the youth of the Heathen Tribes of Siberia'. The principal argument which he put forward to justify this extravagant conception of the Academy's function was the fact that the Emperor himself had given the missionaries his explicit permission to learn the various languages of Siberia, to translate the Scriptures into those languages, and to teach in them. This was, then, an argument from what was thought to be permissible, rather than what was practicable, though Robert did try to whet the Directors' appetites by telling them that he had enquiries from 'a Mohammedan Tartar from near Tobolsk' and a young Jew. His argument was also founded upon rather shaky premises. Robert was relying on the wording of some letters, signed and sealed by Prince Golitsyn, which the missionaries had been issued with to present to the authorities through whose jurisdiction they passed on their outward journey, in case they needed assistance. Some of these letters had not been used, and remained in their hands. But they were, after all, only letters of recommendation, given for a specific, temporary purpose. Besides that, the political situation had changed since the letters were issued, and Robert probably did not realize how fragile his evidence might prove if put to the test. Still, the Directors accepted the validity of his argument, at least to the extent of using its wording in introducing the topic of the Selenginsk Academy in their 31st Report, issued in 1825. They also announced Venning's gift, and published Robert's request for donations of school books.

Otherwise, though, they moved with caution. The Memorial was considered by the Society's Northern Committee at a meeting in July 1825, and the Board accepted its recommendation that 'under present circumstances, the *Memorial* on the subject of the Seminary lately instituted at Selenginsk, for the Education of Boriat Youths be exclusively confined to the Society's Office'. They did, however, authorize a single extra grant of £50 towards the expenses of the institution.

No reason is given in the Board's Minutes for the decision to keep the Memorial confidential. One possible explanation may be that the Directors foresaw accounting complications if they had to look after a large number of small subscriptions. Certainly, only a few years later, they were positively discouraging small earmarked gifts in favour of donations to their general funds. They may also have been unwilling to expose Robert's Memorial to public scrutiny on account of its illiterate drafting, which is exactly what happened to his dictionaries a few years later. Thirdly, they may have been deterred by advice from St Petersburg from seeking too much publicity in Russia itself. Writing to George Burder on 26 August 1824, Robert remarked: 'We received a letter from our friends in St Petersburg by last post, dated 25 June O.S. saying that our Memorial had arrived safely, but that nothing could be done for us at present, because that some very material changes had taken place in the management of the Bible Society in that City.' The 'friends' are not named, but they must have included Knill, who had written an agitated letter to London earlier that month, advising Alers

The Mission Schools

Hankey of the crisis affecting the RBS, but reassuring him that Princess Meshcherskaya had personally petitioned the Emperor to see that the Society's missionaries came to no harm. The Directors must have taken this seriously. But if this is the true explanation for their refusal to circulate the Memorial, it is a puzzling one. They were going to announce the foundation of the Academy in their 31st Report, and one wonders what damage could have been done in Russia by circulating the Memorial which the printed Report would not already have caused.

Robert was not too impressed by the news from the capital, and put forward sixteen points which he thought adequate counter-arguments. These dealt with such matters as the favours the missionaries had already received, their reputation for benevolence, the training they had given some Buryat workmen (presumably those who had built their houses), the Russian government's policy of encouraging foreign settlement, and so on. No doubt the arguments were factually accurate, but they were irrelevant to the political crisis which had blown up at the capital, and was worrying Knill and others there. Robert knew that something had happened, but he probably did not appreciate all the implications of the furore which had been whipped up over the alleged indiscretions of the German cleric Gossner, Gossner's expulsion from Russia, the fall from office in Government and the RBS of Prince Golitsyn, and the dismissal of Popov as Secretary of the Society. By the time his letter can have reached St Petersburg on its way to London, Popov was actually under arrest and facing trial for his alleged association with Gossner, and it is unlikely that the LMS representative in the capital would have done anything in mid-1824 to draw attention to the extension of the activities of its missionaries.

Since Edward and William ignored the Academy in their letters, we can only look to Robert's for enlightenment about its work and the history of its existence. His letters are unfortunately less informative than we could wish. Long periods of silence were punctuated by bursts of loquacity, and it is difficult to extract what is significant from the verbose and irrelevant detail with which he packed his letters. Within ten years of the foundation of the Academy, too, Robert had become estranged from the Directors, and after the end of 1833 he ceased to write regularly or to report to them at all. Apart from the initial Memorial we have only one Report, in spite of Robert's promise to submit annual reports. To be fair to him, he does seem to have prepared reports for 1824 and 1825, which he then felt it unwise to entrust to the Russian posts. Pressure from St Petersburg and an open hint in the Society's 32nd Report, issued in May 1826, that news from Selenginsk was overdue, spurred him to risk sending a triennial report at the end of that year – the only account we now possess of the Academy's activities.

The Report occupies twenty-eight pages, and, like the Memorial, it is a meandering composition, almost incoherent in passages. It dwells heavily on trivia, and its bucolic style cannot have reassured the Directors about the

The Mission Schools

educational standards of the Academy. On the other hand, it does suggest that some substantial progress had been achieved, and this impression is confirmed by three examination papers, worked by some of the pupils, which Robert also forwarded. His boys came, as he said, 'from the inhabitants of the wilds of Siberia, whose real character is but little elevated above the beasts of the field'. But he confessed himself fairly satisfied with their progress, which was 'as good as possibly could have been expected, considering that all of them came to me from the Sheep fold, and from the midst of ignorance'.

The first section of the Report, on 'the increase and decrease of students', must have tried the Directors' patience. Robert devoted valuable space and postage to such nonsense as describing, in what he no doubt thought graphic detail, how he had taken his telescope to look out for the arrival of a student he was expecting; how, 'elevating my telescope a little, I discovered four persons on foot making for the woods towards a foot path, which leads across the mountains on the east side of the town', and so on. But they would also have learned how the Khamba had at first been quite willing to send Robert some pupils, but had been put off by the latter's refusal to consider dropping religious instruction – something the Directors, to judge from Burder's letter, might have allowed as a first step in gaining the confidence of the Buryats. Robert was uncompromising:

> I with my family visited the Humba again in the month of August last, when he told me very plainly, that it was because of our Religious instruction that he had taken the young men from me; but said that he would send me our complement of students, i.e. 30, if we promise to teach nothing about the gods, or if we would teach that *Shigomoni* was as great a god, as our God. This led to a long and warm conversation, during which I was three different times called to Silence, which orders I obeyed immediately: But he wishing to extricate himself out of his difficulties again and again renewed the discourse.

So it was all the Khamba's fault, and as a result Robert did not get his thirty pupils. By 1826 the Academy had actually attracted fourteen students in all, aged from eleven to twenty-six. Of these, eight had given up without finishing the course. Several Russians had asked to be admitted, but Robert had thought it best not to accept them unless and until the Emperor declared himself more positively in favour of the Academy.

The second section of the Report deals with teaching methods. It shows once more that Robert was running the Academy on his own, though in the course of time it had become possible to delegate the supervision of the beginners first to Rintsin, and then to another lad called Delek.

The most interesting section of the Report is the third, in which Robert outlines the progress made by his students. The ambitious programme outlined in the Memorial had been realized. The boys were expected to learn Mongolian, Russian, Latin, Greek and English grammar; arithmetic, geometry, trigonometry, mensuration, algebra, geography, history, composition, translation and logic. They varied in their accomplishments. Rintsin, the top pupil, had 'finished' the grammar of Mongolian, Russian, Latin and Greek, and had done some English and mathematics. The slowest student, one Tsidep, had learned the grammar of Mongolian, and had done a little Russian and arithmetic.

This was by no means bluff. Robert reports what his pupils had actually done in their examinations, whose difficulty was graded to suit each individual. Rintsin had had to read passages of Scripture in Mongolian and translate them into Russian, and vice versa; to read other portions in Greek and English; to write out a passage in all the languages read; to do examples in arithmetic, mensuration and algebra; and to make a public speech on the advantages of education and the knowledge of salvation by Christ. The three extant examination papers prove that the boys who worked them could at least write a decent hand in two, three or four languages, and do simple sums – multiplication, division and reduction – in arithmetic, and some elementary algebra.

In the last section, Robert describes what the students had done to advance the work of the mission. They had transcribed several Mongolian books, including some dictionaries, and had also helped him translate the Book of Psalms and most of the New Testament. They had also taken part in translating a text-book of geometry and one of trigonometry into Mongolian for use in the Academy, while Robert himself was busy with a version of the Assembly Shorter Catechism and a grammar of Greek in Mongolian.

There are a few scattered references to Robert's educational work in his subsequent letters. In 1828 he started a Tibetan class. In 1832 he had nine pupils, and was building a new school house, where he hoped to accommodate girls as well as boys. By 1833 the number of pupils had fallen to four. Rintsin left the mission service in 1827 to better himself, and was succeeded as teacher by Delek, of whose abilities Robert had no great opinion: 'This young man is exceedingly Stable. He has been with me for nearly five years under titles of Bichigechi and Bakshi, after he had honourably finished his term of three years Education. His talents however do not come up to line of mediocrity at least as Europian [sic] would judge.' (Robert liked to mystify. The two Mongolian words he uses, without explanation, mean only 'scribe' and 'teacher'.) We learn, finally, that in the early 1830s Robert was approached by several lamas who thought they wanted to study. But they had no idea of discipline and wanted to come and go at will, and he declined to admit them.

We can follow the story of the Selenginsk Academy in the mission papers only as far as the end of 1833, but probably Robert kept it going for some years after his estrangement from his colleagues and the Society. What became of it in the end we do not know.

The Mission Schools

Edward and William opened schools of their own which had rather a different thrust from that of the Academy. They were in reality what the Academy was only in theory – forcing grounds for young converts. Edward had had a few pupils at Selenginsk and so had Sarah, but it was only after the dispersal of the mission in 1828 that his plans began slowly to mature, and even so, they were held up by the fire at the new mission house. It was well on into 1829 before he got a school going at Khodon. William did not open a school of his own at Ona before he left Siberia on home leave in January 1830, and on his return in 1834 he lived for three years at Khodon, where, for part of the time, he looked after the station in the absence of Edward. It was not till 1837 that he once again occupied the Ona station full-time and opened a school there.

Like the pretentiously named Academy, the schools at Khodon and Ona were quite modest domestic enterprises, with some or all of the pupils living on the premises. We know, for example, that in 1832 Edward had thirteen pupils living at his expense, while in the following year the average was ten. In 1834 there were four or five little girls coming in every day as well, to learn to read and write and sing hymns, no doubt using a copy of Edward's own Mongolian hymn book, which still survives. The total of boys and girls at Ona in 1839 was twenty-five, the highest number ever attained, and there were also from time to time some adult pupils. At Khodon, Sarah had helped with the teaching up to the time of her death in 1833, and she was followed by her daughter, another Sarah, who taught the girls and some grown-up women. The two elder Stallybrass boys, Thomas and William, also gave some help, and some of the more advanced pupils were employed as teachers. Shagdur, the evangelist, taught at both Khodon and Ona, and other named teachers include Badma and Wangdang. Unlike the Academy, we have no list of the names of the pupils at Khodon and Ona, though we know that amongst them were the sons of the former taisha Dembil, and his successor Jigjit who held office till 1835. Dembil's son, Rinchindorji, became a Christian in 1842: he was baptized into the Orthodox church under the name of Nikolai, with the Emperor standing as his godfather. The other boy, Tarba, seems to have been rather unremarkable. William wrote of him: 'He is not a youth of great parts, otherwise he would have stood a fair chance of succeeding his late father into his high office, but he is mild and teachable, and very desirous to improve.' Tarba acquired something of a reputation for learning, and in 1852 he did actually become chief taisha. But certain misdemeanours, apparently connected with the control of money, led to complaints being lodged against him with the Governor of Transbaikalia, and in 1857 he was removed from office. Rinchindorji turned against the missionaries in the late 1830s, and Tarba proved a nonentity, so that, as far as we can tell, the schools at Ona exerted little influence for the good on the few members of the upper class who attended them.

All three institutions aimed at making conversions and turning out a select band of young evangelists. The Bible was used in all of them as a text-book for lessons in reading and writing, and as an inspiration for essays which the pupils had to write. Robert, for example, set a subject for a scriptural composition every Saturday. The compositions would be read aloud and criticized on Saturday evening, and the young authors had to hand in corrected versions on the following Monday. Edward interrogated his pupils every Sunday evening on what they had heard during the day, while Shagdur and another senior pupil used to take notes of his sermons and produce compositions based on them. Examples of these essays, which Edward sent home in his own English translation, show that the young men had a good grasp of Christian teaching, and could express themselves fluently and at some length in writing.

There was, however, a considerable difference of emphasis in the reports and letters relating to the education given in the two groups of schools, the Academy at Selenginsk on one hand, and the schools at Khodon and Ona on the other. This difference undoubtedly reflects a difference in practice. Robert tended to stress what most interested him, that is, the purely academic progress made by his pupils, while Edward and William more or less ignored this aspect of the work of their schools, concentrating upon the long-term goal – the spiritual development of their protégés. In the conversion of a few of them, which took place in the mid-1830s, they found the climax to which they had aspired, and the justification for the existence of their schools. Each group of schools had its star pupils, and in what was said about them by the missionaries we can discern how the ethos at Selenginsk must have differed from that at Khodon and Ona.

The Academy turned out one scholar of note, Rintsin, who was to play a leading role in the intellectual development of his people and in the emergence of the language and culture of the Mongols as a subject worthy of academic investigation. Rintsin Nima Wangchikov joined Robert at Selenginsk in 1821, and stayed with him for six years as student, copyist, translator and teacher. It was his own father who had persuaded Robert to take him on in the full-time service of the mission. A formal agreement was drawn up with the Cossack officer who was his superior, and who agreed to exempt him from all taxes, in anticipation of the services he would one day be capable of rendering his own people as headmaster of the Academy. Up to that time, Rintsin had been studying only Mongolian, Russian and arithmetic, but Robert now devised an individual curriculum for him, which included Latin, Greek, Hebrew, mathematics, geography and Scripture as well. Rintsin made excellent progress, but unfortunately for the mission his growing reputation as a scholar went to his head. At least, that was how Robert saw, and condemned, his developing ambitions: 'He got great praise, to which he fell a victim; for by the advice of his relations and others who praised him he began to think of rank, of honours of a worldly kind.'

Rintsin's former Cossack officer eased him out of the mission in 1827, and took him on as his own interpreter and clerk. A little later, Rintsin was sent to Irkutsk to help Kowalewski and Popov, the former of whom became the most celebrated Mongolian scholar of the century, to learn Mongolian. From Irkutsk he was summoned in 1830 to the capital, where he was received in audience by the Emperor, and decorated by him. On his return to Siberia he became, in 1833, a teacher in the newly established Russo-Mongolian Military School at Troitskosavsk, where Dorji Banzarov, the celebrated Buryat Mongolist, was a pupil. Apart from his share in teaching Kowalewski, Rintsin is remembered as being one of the first scholars to attempt to decipher the so-called 'Stone of Genghis Khan'. It was probably he, too, who helped the Archimandrite Bichurin improve his knowledge of Mongolian, when the learned monk was in Kyakhta in the early 1830s, assisting him in particular in translating his Mongolian–Chinese dictionary into Russian and rearranging it. Rintsin was not exactly ruined, and indeed, he enjoyed a remarkable career. But from the missionaries' point of view his secular success was something of a disappointment, though they made the best of it. As Robert wrote:

> I should have wished that this young man had remained with me, for
> the benefite [sic] of others: but since it is ordered otherwise, and
> perhaps for good ends, or rather I am persuaded for good ends!
> Therefore I shall continue to teach and Preach the Truths of the Blessed
> Gospel of Christ, to whom the Most High shall Direct me, in Faith and
> Hope, leaving the Event with God, who has the Residue of the Spirit!

In curious contrast to this note of humble resignation to the ways of Providence, we find Robert simultaneously hoping that something of Rintsin's worldly success would rub off on him:

> I hope His Emperial [sic] Majesty will not forget me, when he bestows
> His Favours on my Student. – I am Persuaded that his Majesty is full of
> Favours to every deserving person, whom he gets notice of in his Empire;
> therefore I am sure, when he hears of my Public, and Private Labours,
> I shall not be forgotten: for all my labours are for the good of His
> Empire; and for the Glory of the Kingdom of Christ Jesus, without
> any personal motive, or Interest, or Deceit whatever!

Rintsin's defection was not the only disappointment, but there were also missionary triumphs to report. In 1829 Robert could inform Knill that one of his pupils had conducted divine service in the mission house, and preached what was surely the first Nonconformist sermon ever given by a Buryat.

But it was at the schools of Khodon and Ona, where a more concentrated spiritual atmosphere prevailed, that true converts were produced, by methods which combined the continuous lavishing of affection, and unrelenting psychological pressure. The missionaries hoped to produce some good scholars who would become effective teachers, but what they wanted above all for their pupils was that 'in the midst of a people given up to idolatry and iniquity, they may have the grace to turn from idols, to flee youthful lusts, choose and follow the way of life, and adorn the doctrine of God their Saviour in all things'. There was an all-pervading emphasis on the reality of sin, and the need for self-examination, repentance and forgiveness, as William's description of a normal Saturday evening's teaching at Ona illustrates:

> On the Saturday evenings we continue to hold a meeting intended as a preparation for the Sabbath. It is regularly attended by ten or twelve, and we think it is generally found to be a profitable season for all. The review of the past, confession of sin, the need of the spirit's influences, self examination, the great ends of the institution of the Sabbath, the necessity of earnest prayer for the presence and blessing of God – the duty of seeking and maintaining a spiritual frame of mind, prayer for each other, intercession for the unconverted around, the value of gospel privileges, the sin and danger of abusing, neglecting or despising them, are some of the subjects to which the attention is more or less directed on these occasions.

To speak of the missionaries having exerted extreme psychological pressure on their pupils is, unfortunately, no exaggeration. Their aim was to provoke a crisis of self-confidence, partly by means of sheer terror, and so produce an irreversible change in the personalities of the boys. The sort of crisis which was welcomed when it came is described in an exultant letter from Edward, dated 8 May 1834, in which he rejoiced that 'the time is at length come – the time which we have been looking for till our eyes had well nigh begun to fail – in which God is making it appear that the hard and frozen hearts of Boriates are not impervious to the entrance of His Blessed Spirit'. It had all begun with his own children, who had undergone conversion, and whose example had started to affect their young Buryat companions, to whom, as life-long companions and native speakers of the language, they were no doubt rather closer than their father was. Two or three lads confessed that they were becoming convinced of the truth of Christianity, among them one named Badma, who was then about sixteen years old. Edward describes what happened:

> This lad has been under instruction for about three years. He has on several occasions discovered a mind susceptible of impression.
> Sometimes convictions have appeared to be produced; but they have been like 'the morning cloud and early dew,' and have passed away without producing any permanent or saving change. But on the occasion referred to when Mr Swan was preaching his mind was so much affected by some things which were said that towards the close of the service he could not refrain from weeping and sobbing aloud. This was something

The Mission Schools

quite new. He had no precedent for it; so that it could not be regarded as any thing like imitation. But we were induced to believe that he was alarmed on account of his sins. He was taken aside after the service and asked what it was that affected him. He said his sins were so great that he was fearful of the consequences; adding Lord save me!

What can have provoked this hysterical outburst on the part of the sixteen-year-old Badma? The missionaries knew very well how impressionable boys of that age – an 'interesting age' as they termed it – could be. By chance, too, we possess the text of a short article which William contributed to a missionary magazine, which illustrates how far they were prepared to go in playing upon the susceptibilities of their unsuspecting pupils. That these thoroughly upright men could behave in what might be thought so unscrupulous a manner with the personalities of boys whom they knew were psychologically vulnerable, is an indication of the thinness of the frontier which separates conviction from bigotry.

William's article, which is called 'Extracts from a Missionary's Journal', begins:

Two or three more of the boys appear to be in an enquiring state of mind. One was with W—— last night, weeping on account of his sins. On Sabbath I spoke of sinners while going on in their vain wicked course as *fuel* about to be bound in bundles and thrown into hell fire to feed its flames that shall never be quenched. This seems to have been fixed with power by the Spirit of God on some of their hearts. In several instances a lively and affecting view of the wrath to come has been remarkably blessed in my preaching both here and elsewhere. It was something said about the poor tormented sinner enduring the torments of the pit of woe, having no gospel any longer to listen to, no sound of mercy, no goodness of a Saviour any longer to receive or reject, that first impressed T——'s mind.

Later on, the article mentions a conversation with another 'converted heathen', referred to as S——, who had burned his idols, and had been roundly abused by a 'priest' for doing so.

The writer of the article definitely approves of the use of terror in the evangelization of boys and young men, of threatening them with everlasting damnation in hell fire, forsaken by an unforgiving God, if they reject Christianity. The article may be only a literary fiction, but it probably reflects actual experience. W—— is probably William himself; T—— is probably Tekshi, a Buryat convert who wrote an emotional letter to a correspondent in St Petersburg, describing how he had nearly become 'a partaker in everlasting death' but had fortunately been 'turned from this fearful road'. S—— is probably Shagdur, who made a special trip from Khodon to his

The Mission Schools

home on purpose to burn his idols, encouraged to do so by the Stallybrass children.

Acceptance of Christianity exposed the young men to physical danger as well as emotional disturbance. One of them, Bardo, came to a sorry end. Poor Bardo was warned by Edward 'of what he must expect from his unbelieving countrymen if he became a follower of Jesus', and indeed, he had his share of insults and ostracism. Worse still, he worried that that he would be separated for all eternity from his mother, who died soon after his conversion, still a Buddhist. Bardo was destined to be the first, and only, Nonconformist 'martyr' among the Buryats. J.C. Brown quotes from a letter he received in St Petersburg:

> One of our youths made the remark, some time ago, that he thought it would be no bad thing for the cause of Christ, if their enemies should beat and trouble them, 'for this,' said he, 'will make the more noise, and many may hear of it in this way, and be led to enquire what these things mean.' Happy youth – little did he know for what God was then preparing his soul!

What actually happened to the 'happy youth' was that a lama hit him on the head with a club, and injured him so severely that after several weeks of feverish illness he died. Tekshi took part in the funeral service, and all found it a most improving occasion 'to hear one converted Buriat, who firmly trusts in his saviour, joining thus in the funeral service while we committed to the dust the body of another young Buriat, who had died in the faith'.

The schools at Khodon and Ona were closed in 1840 when the mission was suppressed. We have no evidence on which to judge whether they made a lasting impact on Buryat cultural development. Had the mission been able to continue, it is possible that the schools might have lived down the suspicion in which they were widely held, and have developed from their rudimentary state to the point where they could become a self-perpetuating institution, and exert a permanent influence on educational ideas and practice in eastern Siberia. But this did not happen, and we cannot tell if any of the ideas introduced by the missionaries, particularly the quite revolutionary concept of education for girls, took root.

15

Translating the Bible

Protestant Christianity is the religion of the Bible, and wherever Protestant missionaries have penetrated, they have made it their business to translate the Scriptures into the local language, and put them into the hands of the people at large. The Siberian mission was no exception to this general rule. As we have seen, Edward was instructed to translate the Bible, giving priority to the New Testament, as soon as he had mastered the Mongolian language. He and William, with a little help and a great deal of obstruction on the part of Robert, translated the whole of the Old Testament during the first ten years or so of their mission, and printed it on their own printing press. They began to translate the New Testament as well, and were seeking permission to print it, when the order came for the dismantling of the mission. This part of their task was completed after their return to England, and the New Testament was printed in this country for the Bible Society, from type ingeniously, if awkwardly, adapted from a Manchu fount.

If the missionaries in Siberia are remembered at all today – and it is perhaps only a small circle of enthusiasts for things Mongolian who do remember them – it is for their translation of the Bible. This was no easy task. The Bible Society itself was less than twenty years old when they set to work, and there was little general experience in translating the Bible into Oriental languages to go on. In preparation they had first of all to learn Russian and some Manchu, the contemporary keys to a mastery of Mongolian, the target language. They then had to analyse the Mongolian language and reduce it to order. They had to distinguish between the written language, with its archaic grammatical system and spelling, and the spoken Buryat, which differed considerably from it, and to compile their own grammars and dictionaries. To do this with understanding, they had to plough their way through hundreds of pages of uncongenial Mongolian literature, Buddhist sutras, cosmologies, legends, medical treatises, handbooks of divination and so on. Edward's manuscript copies of some of the books he studied in order to perfect his knowledge of the language and his appreciation of the theology of Buddhism are painstakingly annotated. The contents of some are summarized and systematized. The end-papers of a few are filled, in his minute, tidy handwriting, with his definitions of difficult or doubtful words, in Latin, English and Russian. With the exception of the Book of Psalms, which was translated first of all by Rintsin, the missionaries did not take the easy way of translating from Russian or English, but worked from the original languages. They had some printed commentaries, but there was no one they could consult over difficult problems. When all was done, the Old Testament, being printed under Russian law, had to pass the scrutiny of the censor, and came under the eye of no less critical and exact a scholar than I.J. Schmidt. Schmidt took his duties seriously, as inspection of some surviving versions shows. He checked the manuscripts both for the literal accuracy of the translation and for its conformity with other Protestant versions of the Bible. His annotations, made partly in pencil, partly in red ink, range from queries and suggestions to peremptory alterations which the missionaries had to accept. Altogether, the Bible in Mongolian is a monument to the scholarship, the tenacity and the fortitude of the only Englishmen of their day who had mastered the Mongolian language, and it is right that it should not be forgotten.

The Moravians at Sarepta were the first Protestants to translate any parts of the Bible into a Mongolian language, around the turn of the eighteenth century, and it was after hearing of their pioneering, though unsystematic, venture that the BFBS voted them a sum of money in 1808 with which to buy a fount of Kalmuck type. But the Moravian versions, which seem in any case to have been harmonies of parts of the Gospels, and paraphrases of other portions of the Bible, rather than literal translations, were never printed, and were of little or no significance in the history of biblical translation.

Apart from what the Moravians had done before 1808, the Bible was being translated into Kalmuck and Mongolian almost simultaneously at three different places in Russia in the early part of the nineteenth century. Encouraged by the interest shown by the BFBS, the Moravians commissioned Schmidt to translate the Gospel of St Matthew into Kalmuck. He began the work in 1809, and in October a correspondent of the BFBS in St Petersburg told the Society that the translation was finished and ready for printing. It did not appear, though, until 1815. It has been suggested that the delay was caused by the destruction of the manuscript, along with the rest of Schmidt's Mongolian library, in the great fire of Moscow in September 1812. This seems unlikely to be true. For one thing, in a letter to the Rev. C.F.A. Steinkopff of the BFBS, written on 29 May 1814, Schmidt tells how 'a pretty collection of Mongolian manuscripts and copies of my own, which I possessed, together with my whole fortune have become a prey to the flames and the plundering in Moscow'. Steinkopff would have had a particular interest in the fate of St Matthew if it had been lost, but Schmidt makes no mention of it. For another thing, it was, almost without a doubt,

Translating the Bible

John Paterson who had told the BFBS that the Kalmuck St Matthew was ready for printing, and it was only a month earlier that he had dashed from Moscow to St Petersburg in company with Schmidt. If the translation had been abandoned in the occupied city, he would certainly have known, and would not have sent the Bible Society a misleading report. It is much more reasonable to suppose that Schmidt brought the translation to St Petersburg with him, and that the only reason for the delay in printing it was the fact that, until mid-1814, there was no Kalmuck type in existence from which it could have been printed.

Schmidt did little or nothing in the way of biblical translation for two years or more between the publication of the Kalmuck St Matthew and the arrival of the two Buryat zaisangs in St Petersburg at the end of 1817. The only progress made was the reprinting of St Matthew in late 1817 in a new format. The first edition had been in quarto size, bound like a European book, but the second was oblong in shape, printed on separate leaves, so imitating the appearance of a traditional Buddhist book. This format, which was doubtless intended to flatter the religious susceptibilities of its eventual readers, became standard for all later St Petersburg printings, up to the termination of Schmidt's programme in 1827.

With the arrival of the two zaisangs, there began a period of intensive translation work which lasted for several years, up to and beyond the death of Badma in November 1822. Schmidt, too, was able to devote himself more whole-heartedly to the task when he was relieved of his commercial duties by the Moravians in 1819, and appointed full-time translator of the Scriptures into Kalmuck for the RBS. To begin with, Schmidt translated the three remaining Gospels and the Acts of the Apostles into Kalmuck, while the Buryats – principally, of course, Badma – turned these into Mongolian. All the books so translated were printed by 1821, and subsequently the remaining books of the New Testament were translated into both languages, while the Gospels and Acts were revised. Badma was unable to finish the translation of the New Testament into Mongolian before his untimely death, but we do not know how much he left unfinished for his interpreter, who also worked under Schmidt's direction, to complete. The complete New Testaments were printed in the years leading up to 1827, set up in a new, smaller type. As things turned out, the entire enterprise was frustrated by the refusal of the Holy Synod to allow the Testaments to be published, as part of the religious reaction following the suppression of the RBS in 1826.

As Badma gained in experience and improved his knowledge of Russian, he broke away from literal dependence on Schmidt's Kalmuck versions, and began to translate direct from the Russian or Slavonic New Testaments. But, to begin with, his task was one of transcription and adaptation, rather than true translation. This is certainly true for the Mongolian St Matthew, St John and Acts, as we learn from Schmidt's own account and the colophon to Acts. St Matthew did not take long to turn into Mongolian, not more than two or three months. By the beginning of March 1818 the work was done, and Schmidt reported in glowing terms on the achievement of the two Buryats in the Moravian journal *Periodical Accounts*. He gave the entire credit to Nomtu and Badma. Their translation was, in his opinion,

> the best that can be procured. No European could have executed it so well, nor will any one be able to do it, for a long time to come. These persons are not only most profound scholars in their own vernacular and learned dialects, in so much that they could explain the meaning of many words and phrases to me, in a way, which I have sought for in vain among the Calmucks, but they are well versed in the language of Tibet, and can read the Tibetan characters with as much ease as the Mongolian.

The Buryats were keen to get on with the translation of St John next, 'the first chapters having excited within them the greatest possible interest'. However, by that time Schmidt had translated no more than seven chapters of that gospel into Kalmuck.

Schmidt's effusive approval was premature, especially in the case of Nomtu, who had to be sent back to Siberia in the following year because of his incompetence and instability. His enthusiasm for Badma, which had probably been aroused by the excitement which the conversion of the two Buryats had provoked, subsided too, and he openly took for himself the entire credit for the translation of the New Testament. There is more than one proof of this rather unseemly appetite for glory. In spite of what Schmidt wrote in *Periodical Accounts*, when the Mongolian St Matthew came to be printed in 1819, it carried his name on the title page as that of the translator, to the exclusion of those of the two Buryats. Badma's name is mentioned in only one edition of one book of the Mongolian New Testament. The first printing of Acts, dated 1820, incorporates a long colophon, which summarizes the main tenets of the Christian faith, and describes the genesis of the translation. This colophon is almost identical in wording to that in the corresponding Kalmuck version, from which it has obviously been adapted, and where the latter names Schmidt as translator, the former names Badma. But when Badma's translation was incorporated in the complete New Testament of 1827, the individual colophon was dropped, naturally enough, while the entire Testament was ascribed to Schmidt as translator, without any mention of the large part played by the deceased zaisang. Whoever may have been taken in by this misappropriation of another man's work, the missionaries in Siberia were not. They knew that what was generally called Schmidt's New Testament was largely the work of Badma and his interpreter, and they told the Secretary of the Missionary Society as much in 1828.

Independently of the St Petersburg programme, Cornelius Rahmn translated some parts of the Bible into Kalmuck at Sarepta. His progress was not remarkable and it was cut short by his decision to abandon his station in

June 1823. By mid-1822 he had finished the First Epistle of St John, and had started on the Book of Psalms. We do not know how far he got, nor do we know what happened to his versions, which were apparently never printed. His diaries and private letters were deliberately destroyed by fire early in the present century in Sweden, and the Bible translations may have shared their fate. On the other hand, four volumes of linguistic materials, including his own Kalmuck grammar and two dictionaries, have survived the years, and are now in the possession of the Library of the University of Uppsala. There is a slim chance that the translations may yet turn up.

Cornelius's efforts may seem to have duplicated what Schmidt's group was doing. But there was a good reason why he, and the missionaries in Siberia, felt justified in going on with their independent translation programmes. They were unhappy with Schmidt's versions, and disapproved of his principles and methods, and their dismay was shared by Paterson, who communicated it to the Directors, while warning them not to make too much of it publicly. Paterson's reservations were forcefully expressed in a joint letter from himself and Ebenezer Henderson to Alers Hankey, written from Tiflis in October 1821, not long after they had called in at Sarepta to see Cornelius. Referring to the recently printed Kalmuck Gospels and Acts, they wrote:

> We were truly sorry to learn that this translation is so imperfect that it is scarcely fit to be put into the hands of the people. This is a source of great grief to Mr Rahmn as well as to us. We are with him fully convinced that a new translation must be made and that by your own missionaries, which is another and very important reason why you should send him a suitable companion as soon as possible. The Brethren's missionaries are good men but not men of learning. The same observations apply to the Mongolian; but Stallybrass and Swan will remedy the defect. This is for your own private eye. Let none but a confidential Burder know a word of this or you will injure us as also your own cause and Missionaries.

No doubt it was with this encouragement that Cornelius now set to work on the New Testament. It is significant, too, that even as early as this, it was to Edward and William alone, not to Robert whom he disliked and distrusted, that Paterson was looking for a satisfactory translation of the Bible into Mongolian.

The missionaries in Siberia were very critical of the way the St Petersburg translators had handled the text of the Scriptures. It was not the adequacy of Schmidt's scholarship which worried them so much as his free and easy way with the word of God. In May 1820 Edward wrote to Alers Hankey, to tell him that he was planning to compose a catechism in Mongolian, and added:

This will be chiefly taken from the tracts translated by the Buriats from Mr Schmit's [sic] Calmuck: but as I conceive they are in many parts defective, I intend to supply these defective parts as may appear desirable. For example, the first tract begins with an account of the creation, and is taken from the first Chapter of Genesis; it relates to the work of six days, but takes not the slightest notice of God's sanctifying and setting apart the seventh. The fraternity of Mr S it is well known, pay very little regard to the sabbath day; but surely in translating the word of God, although in detached parts, and not professedly as the translation of the *scriptures*, yet it becomes us to give the *whole sense* to any particular passage which we may wish to convey to the Heathen. This is not a solitary instance.

In spite of their dissatisfaction with the St Petersburg translations, the missionaries do not seem at first to have contemplated setting up a full-scale programme of their own, separate from, and ostensibly in competition with, Schmidt's group. Their position was somewhat delicate. They were dependent on the RBS for supplies of tracts and copies of the Gospels and Acts, which that Society alone was in a position to supply them with, and they realized that it was good policy to keep in with the RBS, which was under the direct patronage of the Emperor, and of which Schmidt was an influential office-holder. Nor did they look on translation as necessarily the most important occupation of a missionary. Preaching the gospel took first place. As William wrote in January 1822:

We shall only add that while we consider the translation of the Scriptures should occupy an important place among the various labours of a Missionary, we view it as *second* to the direct preaching of the gospel, and as we have happily the prospect of abundant room for this *first* work, we should gladly have left the other to be performed by those who are now engaged in it if it had been done as it requires to be done, and we thus furnished with the word of life to be distributed among those who are dying around us for want of it.

Implicit in these words, though, is a determination somehow to improve the quality of the St Petersburg translations, and in fact in April 1821 William had put a concrete proposal before the Directors. Could they not be sent a press for their own use? Explaining the frustration they felt, he wrote:

You will perceive from these statements that our stock of gospels was exhausted before these journeys were commenced so that we could not avail ourselves of these excellent opportunities of distributing them. It is *long since* we wrote to St Petersburg for a supply, but the multifarious engagements of our friends there render them unable to attend so promptly to such requests as the case demands. We are likewise extremely concerned to find various defects and unfortunate mistakes in the version of the gospels, and our distance from the press puts it out of our power to lend any assistance in correcting or improving the other parts now going forward. These things together with our widening prospects of usefulness in this field have made us think seriously of the advantages, we may say, necessity, of having a press established here. And we now beg to call the particular attention of the Society to the subject. I think the following plain statements will recommend themselves to you and to all the directors as so many arguments for immediate compliance with our request.

William supported his proposition by arguing that, if they had their own press, he and his colleagues could print correct versions of the Scriptures, not those done in the 'mutilated manner' which was sufficient to satisfy Schmidt. Secondly, it would be possible to print the tracts which they themselves were composing. Thirdly, and this was the nub of the matter, if there was a press at Selenginsk, Badma might feel inclined to leave St Petersburg, come back to his own country, and continue the good work there. Paterson was in favour of such a move, if we are to believe William. Fourthly, William believed, though on what authority is not disclosed, that the RBS would bear all the expenses of the printing operations planned for Selenginsk, operations which might be expanded to include printing in Manchu and other languages of northern Asia. The fifth point was a purely practical one: the mission house was already capacious enough to accommodate a printer, his family, and the printing shop, with only the minimum of conversion.

Thus the missionaries had two complaints. They were starved of supplies of the Scriptures, and when they did get them the translations proved inadequate. But to take both the translation and the printing out of Schmidt's hands and transfer them to Selenginsk would have injured the pride of the pioneer translator, and Pinkerton, whose advice the Directors sought, was surely right if, as William claimed he did, he argued that Badma was more useful to the cause in St Petersburg than he would be in Siberia, and that for the missionaries to set up a press at Selenginsk to print the Scriptures would be tantamount to 'erecting a battery against the Russian Bible Society'. Pinkerton was not against the missionaries' having a press: what concerned him was merely the use to which it would be put. In fact, he advised the Directors about the sort of press which might be appropriate to the needs of the mission, and it was he who was authorized, along with Knill, to buy such a press, together with type and other equipment, and have it all sent out to Selenginsk. So, in spite of William's suspicions, it was, ironically, Pinkerton, the rival of his confidant Paterson, to whom the missionaries owed their press.

The Directors did, however, insist that for the time being the press was to be used only for printing tracts, and not for printing the Scriptures. Yet, curiously enough, they announced just the opposite in their 28th Report, issued in May 1822. In this it was stated that:

> the purpose to which the Press will be in the first place applied, is the printing of the Gospels and tracts in Mongolian. As the brethren are prosecuting the study of this language chiefly with a view to a Version of the whole Scriptures therein, it is also intended that the different portions of such Version, as they are successively completed, should be printed at Selenginsk, under the inspection of the brethren. The St Petersburg Bible Society have engaged to defray the whole expense attending the printing of the Scriptures in the Mongolian, or any other of the languages of Northern Asia. Part of the present mission premises at Selinginsk will afford the accommodation necessary for a Printing Office.

This announcement is so wildly at variance with the Directors' policy as explained to the missionaries, that one can only suppose that it was carelessly put together from the wrong source, perhaps even from William's letter, which its wording recalls.

This was not the only inaccurate report. Two or three times in their letters home the missionaries felt concerned enough to complain that careless mistakes had been made. Edward was disturbed to read in the report for 1823 that he was engaged in preparing a translation of Genesis, and in that for 1825 that he was about half way through. 'I trust our anxiety is to approve ourselves faithful to God rather than to obtain the applause of men,' he wrote, 'but I fear an attentive reader of the reports would suppose, either that the reports are made up without great preciseness, or that we think lightly of the importance of translation.'

The press was in the missionaries' hands by the middle of 1824, but then it lay idle, pending the appointment of a printer, for ten years. It was not till the late summer of 1833 that William, then in St Petersburg, was authorized to take on a printer. Printing began in 1834 and continued until the end of 1840. There were reasons for what might seem dilatoriness on the part of the Directors, in allowing the capital cost of a printing shop to be tied up unproductively for so long. In all their activities, they were handicapped by the slowness of communication. A letter could take anything from two and a half to six months to reach London from Siberia. It then had to be considered by the appropriate Committee: in earlier years the Northern Committee, and later on the Eastern Committee. Committee recommendations were submitted to the Board very promptly, often on the same day that they were made, but the Board's decisions also took months to reach Siberia. Secondly, the Directors, none of whom had experience of life in Russia, had to reconcile submissions and advice received from very differently placed members of the Society. Requests from Siberia naturally reflected local interests, but the missionaries' correspondence was regularly read, and often commented on, by the Society's agent in the capital, whose views were coloured by events of national importance during a critical time in Russian history. Thirdly, the years 1824 to 1826 saw a change in the individuals in St Petersburg through whom the Society conducted its business. Golitsyn and Popov fell from office in 1824, and in 1826 Paterson, discouraged by the collapse of the RBS and the reassertion of Orthodoxy, left Russia. Knill, who comes through as a much more cautious man than Paterson, was left to represent the Missionary Society with Russian authority, bereft of the comforting buffer of the RBS.

In a letter dated 4 January 1822, the missionaries reluctantly accepted the restrictions placed by the Directors upon their use of the press. At the same time they justified themselves in the face of what they thought was unfounded criticism of their motives. They denied that they had ever intended to act in a manner contrary to the interests of the RBS, explaining that their plan 'of having the printing of the Mongolian Scriptures carried out here contains in it nothing inconsistent with the most perfect harmony and co-operation with the measures of the R. Bib. Society'. They rehearsed all the old arguments: the RBS would pay for the work; their translations would not compete with what was being done at St Petersburg, for Schmidt's group was proceeding so slowly that duplication was not feared for a long time to come; Badma could be employed more effectively at Selenginsk than in the capital, unless, of course, he took the disastrous step of joining the Orthodox church. All this may have been true, but it was not the essential truth. In this very letter, the missionaries stressed that 'it is not to a few incidental errors we object, but to the *principles* and style of the whole translation', something which could not be rectified as long as Schmidt was in charge of the programme. And in November of the following year they were again expressing the radical hope that 'the translation of the Mongolian Scriptures carrying on at St Petersburg may soon be superseded by those which we are attempting'.

The question of engaging a printer for Selenginsk was raised again from time to time. To a letter sent home in 1823, the Directors replied questioning whether the missionaries had enough work in hand to justify the expense of such an appointment: 'We have considered that you receive from time to time supplies of the Gospels and Tracts from St Petersburg, and that these, together with what after a while you may be able yourselves to print, will probably be sufficient for your immediate purpose.'

In June 1825 the missionaries tried to attract a Mr Mitchell, who up to then had been working as a printer for the Scottish missionaries at Astrakhan, to come to Selenginsk after the closure of his own station. They sent him an invitation on their own responsibililty on 18/30 June, and wrote to Paterson on the same day, advising the Directors of their démarche on 6 July. The explanation of their action given to the latter took little account of the critical political situation in St Petersburg:

> We were gratified to observe in the Report of the Society for 1824 that our request had been complied with, and instructions issued to our friends at Petersburg, to engage and send from that place to Selenginsk a suitable person as a printer. We accounted for this not being put into execution from the turn of affairs with regard to the Rn. Bible Society. But we consider that the relaxation of the efforts of that Society in printing and distributing the Scriptures, instead of deterring us from going on with our translations and printing them as we wished and intended, is an additional reason for our exerting ourselves more than ever; for if the Rn. Bible Society declines such work, there is no prospect at present of the Mongolian Scriptures being translated and printed at all unless we accomplish it. . . . Taking all this into view, after separate reflection and mutual conference and prayer, it appeared to us very desirable in present circumstances to endeavour to secure Mr Mitchell's services . . . . The only possible objection we can think can be started against this measure is on the score of expense.

Paterson wrote to the Directors on the subject from St Petersburg on 15/27 August 1825. He did not disapprove of what the missionaries had done, and he thought that if the Directors did decide to send a printer to Selenginsk, Mitchell would be an excellent choice, even though he was too old to learn a new language. But he then went on to advise the Directors about the general situation in a way which ensured that they would reject the approach. He reminded them that the missionaries were legally obliged to submit anything which they proposed to print to the censor, and warned them that, with Prince Golitsyn out of power, there would be no chance of by-passing this regulation, as had sometimes been the case in the past. The men now in office had no faith in the missionaries

> and would willingly find fault even where there was none. Since the Bible Society was formed all versions of the Scriptures printed in Russia or imported from other places were submitted for approbation to the Committee and no more was required. As things are at present this could not be obtained for any version made by foreigners and I should certainly not advise our friends to submit their version to us, as it would certainly be condemned right or wrong. Perhaps the version may be printed without our knowing any thing about it provided it be done quickly, and before it comes to be circulated such changes may have taken place as to secure its being approved of. Another thing to be noticed is that if printed it must be at the expense of your Missionaries. For reasons hinted at above the Bible Society here will do nothing. You may obtain assistance from the Bible Society in London but then not a vestige of this must appear in their Reports or it will ruin us. In short as long as matters stand as they do now the whole must be done in a clandestine manner.

Translating the Bible

In October 1825 the Directors resolved to reject the request to employ Mitchell at Selenginsk. They minuted three reasons for their decision: that he did not know Mongolian, and was probably too old to learn the language; that the strict censorship would frustrate the project; and that great expense would be incurred for little gain. A year later they once more declined to send out a printer, pending the receipt of further information, but they encouraged the missionaries 'to proceed to the extent of their power in advancing the translating and the printing of the Mongolian Scriptures'.

The Directors came very near to appointing a printer in 1828 when, in response to a fresh approach, they accepted the necessity of sending out another missionary, and considered reappointing Cornelius Rahmn. They also accepted that the time was ripe to begin printing the Selenginsk translations of the Bible locally. Anticipating that the Russian authorities might balk at admitting an ordinary tradesman from abroad, they decided that Cornelius should learn the trade before going out, and should act as both missionary and printer. In October of that year Knill was instructed to approach the Russian authorities for clarification of their attitude. The missionaries were informed of these resolutions, but by the same post they also received a letter from Knill informing them that the 'friends in Petersburg' were advising against sending out any new missionary, and especially Cornelius. The Directors, briefed by their Northern Committee, accepted the same advice, and, once again, the appointment of a printer was postponed. It is not clear what had prompted the discouraging advice from the Russian capital. Knill may have been overcautious, as William on this occasion judged him to be, but as he was close to the centre of events, the Directors no doubt felt obliged to accept his advice rather than that received from provincial Siberia.

A year later, Knill counselled further delay. In 1829 the missionaries ran into trouble locally, at the same time as Knill was thinking about engaging a printer in Russia, instead of bringing one from England. By May 1830 the difficulties had been smoothed out, but Knill was anxious not to act too hastily. 'Of course,' he wrote, 'I have not made any further proposals respecting the Printer, while the Brethren were in this unsettled and uncomfortable state: but I suppose *now* as things appear settled, we may proceed, but I should like to hear further from the Directors on this subject.' Nothing more seems to have been done, however, until William himself arrived in St Petersburg in the spring of 1831, and initiated negotiations about the future of the mission. Before he left Siberia, the missionaries had been given permission by Baron Schilling von Canstadt, who was carrying out a mission on behalf of the Asiatic Department of the Ministry of Foreign Affairs, to operate their press without further delay, as long as they printed nothing but text-books like grammars, dictionaries, manuals of arithmetic, and so on. They would still need the express permission of the Holy Synod before they could print their translations. William did not think this restricted use of the press would justify the expense of sending out a printer, and he directed his efforts to gaining the required approval.

Between March and June 1831, William had a number of interviews in the capital with influential serving and former officials. Most of those whom he lobbied were sympathetic, but they had little encouragement to offer. There was an atmosphere of timidity abroad, for which 'the spirit of the times', as Popov put it, was to blame. Golitsyn put William in the picture, explaining the ascendancy of the Holy Synod. Towards the end of his life, Alexander had been swayed by those who feared the dangers which might arise from unorthodox bodies like the RBS. Golitsyn, seeing which way the wind was blowing, 'had seen it expedient to devolve the care of the instruction of the people and providing them with the Scriptures, upon the body constituted for the purpose – the Holy Synod'. The Emperor Nicholas was unlikely to change his late brother's religious policies. The RBS had been irrevocably abolished, and though there was no objection to the circulation of books which it had published, this, and all the rest of the business, had reverted to the Synod.

William's most disconcerting interview must have been the one he had with Baron Attercos, an official in the office of Prince Meshcherskii, who was the Ober-Prokuror of the Synod. Attercos was pious but pusillanimous, afraid to touch anything which might prove not to be entirely in accord with the views of the 'dominant party' in the church. 'Upon learning my wishes as to the printing of the Mongolian version of the Scriptures,' wrote William, 'he was evidently afraid to have any hand in it. He declined even to introduce me to the prince thinking that my application in that quarter would not merely be ineffectual, but might bring him under suspicion as favouring objects not approved of under the present system.'

Even William's old friend Mikhail Speranskii was sceptical about his plans, and advised him that the most he could hope for would be to have the Old Testament printed under the eyes of a censor at St Petersburg. The missionaries should not expect to be able to print it themselves in Siberia. He sent William off to see Schmidt, who was even more gloomy. Schmidt told him that the first step was to make an application to the Synod, which would then appoint a committee to examine the project. After that, an expert might be appointed to examine the version itself, and report on it. If the report was favourable, permission to print might be granted. 'But the present spirit of that body is such that they refuse at once, and without examination all proposals for new versions.' The Synod was pursuing a Russian nationalist policy of encouraging the exclusive use of the Slavonic version of the Bible, intending that the heathen should acquire Slavonic and Russian along with Christianity.

At this point, William seems to have taken advice offered him by Popov to let the question of printing drop for a while, and concentrate on the more basic request for a restatement of the privileges which the Emperor Alexander had granted. This point was gained. Through D.N. Bludov, Minister of Ecclesiastical Affairs for Foreign Religions, Nicholas formally re-authorized the missionaries to continue their work in Siberia on precisely the same basis as before. It was on his return journey from England that William achieved his second aim. In September 1832 he resumed his negotiations with Bludov, who by then held the additional post of Minister of the Interior. Bludov felt obliged to consult Prince Lieven, the Minister of National Instruction. Lieven refused to take cognizance of the matter, but just as William was contemplating the last, desperate step of making a direct appeal to the Holy Synod, where, 'from all that we can learn of the Counsels which sway it at present, delay and difficulty and opposition would in all probability have harassed me', it occurred to Bludov that matters might be arranged if Schmidt would agree to act as censor, while continuing to reside in the capital. Schmidt did agree, and on 30 December 1832 Bludov was able to write officially to William, giving the missionaries permission to print their Old Testament.

In the late summer of 1833 the LMS negotiated a financial agreement with the BFBS by which the latter Society undertook to pay £500 towards the costs of translating the Old Testament into Mongolian which had already been incurred, and to pay all the expenses of printing and binding an edition of 1,000 copies. William and his friends in St Petersburg had located an experienced and willing printer, who happened to be free to move, in John Abercrombie, a young man of just over thirty years of age. In spite of his Scottish-sounding name, John was a native of the Caucasus, a 'Circassian Scotsman', as he called himself. He was one of several young tribesmen who had come by their Scottish names in an extraordinary way. The Scottish settlers at Karass had, in 1806, been granted a charter by the Russian Government which allowed them, amongst other things, to ransom slaves from the surrounding tribes, and to keep them in their service up to the age of twenty-three. A young lad whose name was recorded as Teeona, a member of the Cabardian people, was one of several slaves, male and female, thus ransomed. He was supported by the generosity of the celebrated Edinburgh doctor John Abercrombie, from whom he took his name. John trained as a printer at Karass, where he also learned to speak fluent Scots as well as Russian and one or two local languages. While at Karass he had been useful to Paterson and Henderson on their biblical travels through the Caucasus, and he was known and trusted, as a result, in missionary circles at St Petersburg. In 1827 he had left Karass to work for the Basel missionaries at Shusha. By a fortunate coincidence, the Basel missionaries were forced to stop printing in 1833, and John, at a loose end, was glad enough to accept the post at Selenginsk. He and William met by arrangement in Kazan, and travelled on together in early 1834. William was carrying with him the censored copy of Genesis, and by June John had rigged up the press and was ready to start work. With this, there began the final phase of the activities of the mission, during which the entire Old Testament was printed, and much of it distributed.

Mention of the 'censored copy' takes us back to 1822. How had the completed manuscript of Genesis come into existence and reached the stage where Schmidt could pass it for printing? In late 1818 Edward was studying Mongolian at Irkutsk, and finding it hard going, for lack of reading matter. Amongst the texts which were to hand, there were, though, eleven, and later on, eighteen chapters of Genesis. These had been put into Mongolian by his teacher Novoselov, from a Manchu translation made in China by a Jesuit, perhaps by that very Father Poirot whose Manchu Old Testament William was to transcribe, with the help of George Borrow, many years later. Predictably, the missionaries did not think much of the accuracy of this version, but at least it served as an introduction to the art of biblical translation. As William wrote in 1822:

> As you may easily suppose, there were so many departures from the original that the revision of it proved actually a re-translation. I for my part engaged in this task chiefly with a view to improvement in the language, and with this view we carefully sifted every phrase and expression – we on this account proceeded very slowly through the work – but with regard to so important a task it is a good maxim *festina lente*.

This early preoccupation with Genesis was, then, a matter of practice, not the beginning of the work of translation. At some time, perhaps during 1822, Edward began to translate the New Testament, no doubt with his Instructions in mind. Two things complicated the course of events. First of all, in June 1822, the missionaries were reliably informed by Pinkerton that Badma was not going to leave St Petersburg, but was going to stay on there until the whole New Testament, and perhaps Psalms as well, had been translated. In the same letter, Pinkerton advised them to turn their attention to the Old Testament, and to prepare to translate Genesis, and his advice was followed. That very month, Edward began carrying on the translation of Genesis from chapter 19, where Novoselov had broken off. William was helping him. Writing home in November 1822, he remarked: 'During the weeks of harvest, Mr S and I sat down to the translation of Genesis.'

The second disturbing event was the death of Badma in November 1822. For some time the missionaries were left wondering what would happen to the St Petersburg programme, but by April 1823 the pattern was once more clear. Badma's interpreter, who is not named in the mission correspondence, was commissioned to continue the translation of the New Testament. Edward was in a quandary. He had already translated the Epistles of John, and had begun that of James, and was planning to go on with those of Peter and Jude. But he knew that the order of books in the Russian New Testament differed from that current in England. The epistles he was working on preceded, rather than followed, those of Paul, and there was thus a risk that his work might duplicate what the translators in the capital were doing, and they had a press in action, while he did not. For fear of wasting his time, Edward decided to drop the New Testament for a while, and devote all his time to Genesis. The Directors would not have minded his making an alternative version of the Epistles, and encouraged him not to be distracted by the news from the capital. Looking forward to the time when a more definitive translation could be undertaken, they opined that it would be advantageous to have two versions for comparison, citing the case of the almost contemporaneous Chinese versions by Morrison and Milne on the one hand, and Marshman on the other. But Edward and William would not be deflected, and went on systematically with the Old Testament.

The bulk of the work of translation was finished by the time the missionaries took up their separate stations in 1828, with the exception of Isaiah, which had to be done as a rush job at the end of the 1830s. However, the missionaries were never satisfied that they had reached perfection, and went on revising and correcting their work right up to the moment of censorship. Genesis, for example, had been translated by November 1823, but a year later Edward was revising it with the help of a lama. Ten years later he was still at work on it, honing and polishing the translation, hardly daring to let it out of his hands. When William went to St Petersburg in 1831 he took a copy of Genesis with him, but this was not the version which was censored. Only in July 1833 could Edward bring himself to send his manuscript off to St Petersburg in the definitive form which would be checked by Schmidt and thereafter become unalterable.

At some time it was agreed that Edward and William should divide almost the whole of the Old Testament between themselves, leaving Robert with only a relatively small part of it, that is, the Books of Psalms and Isaiah. Robert also took on the New Testament. One wonders why he accepted this arrangement, knowing, as he must have done, that Edward had already abandoned the New Testament because it was being translated at the capital. Explaining the situation to Alers Hankey in 1826, Robert did not hint at anything but a free choice. He wrote, in ignorance of, or ignoring, information that had been available for three years:

> I was induced to turn my attention to the New Testament for the following reasons, namely, 1st, we have heard nothing concerning the translation of the New Testament since the Death of Badma. 2nd, We are perfectly ignorant as to the State of Progress in which he left it.

But then he added, enigmatically:

> But although I have thus turned my attention to the New Testament it is my hope that I may yet be favoured to assist my Beloved Brethren

with part of the Old; at least with the Book of Isaiah, of which I have purposed a beginning, by the will of God.

Reading between the lines, we may surmise that Robert's 'beloved brethren' had already summed him up, and had come to the conclusion that it would be foolish to leave in the hands of someone they thought totally incompetent anything which, if botched or delayed, could delay the completion of their task. Little damage could result from the arrangement which was made. By 1826, Rintsin had finished translating the Book of Psalms, and Edward and William had revised it, while the New Testament had been in the press in St Petersburg for several years. The only hostage they gave to fortune was Isaiah, and perhaps they reckoned it was worth risking delay with that one book so as to avoid provoking Robert too much. As a matter of fact, they held his linguistic abilities in utter contempt, though it was not until the rift in the mission became public knowledge that they felt obliged to say anything officially about his regrettable deficiencies.

Edward alerted the Directors to Robert's ignorance in the same letter, written in October 1834, in which he warned them of the coming storm over the printing of Genesis. He denied both Robert's right to meddle with his work, especially after it had been passed by the censor, and his competence to do so:

> In every body's opinion but his own, I am persuaded Mr Y would appear, *primâ facie*, a *most improper* person to undertake any thing of the sort. If his letters to the Directors are in any way similar to those which he writes to us, I need only refer you to them, in order to give you a tolerable idea of his critical acumen.

In 1837, Edward and William expressed themselves more explicitly. In that year it was still possible that Robert might go home for consultations, and in particular to explain his part in the controversy over the printing of Genesis. Edward and William wrote to warn the Directors not to be taken in by his plausible advocacy of his own cause:

> In the event of Mr Yuille going to England, and setting up a defence of his proceedings in the disputed matter of his correcting Mr Stallybrass's Mongolian version of Genesis, he may contend for his *right* to alter it, and on this part of the subject we have nothing to add to what is already before the Directors. But we have presumed not merely to deny his right, but to question his *ability* to be the final judge and corrector of a version of the word of God. He may think himself safe from any danger of having his deficiencies as a Mongolian scholar detected in England. He may think it easy to vaunt of his attainments in this language before the Directors, but we beg leave to suggest that they

may try his skill in *any language* he professes to know – *English* – Latin – Greek – Hebrew – Russ – and the result of such examination may lead them to something near the truth of his Mongolian scholarship.

This contemptuous view of Robert's attainments was apparently shared even by his star pupil Rintsin. At some time the question of the revision of Robert's translations of certain books of the New Testament had been under discussion, and he had proposed to revise some of them himself. Edward recalls how, on that occasion, Rintsin, with a sneer, had said: 'He – revise! he cannot!'

So Robert was more or less eliminated from the translation programme. What, after all, did he translate? Of the two books of the Old Testament which he took on, Psalms, much revised, was eventually printed at Khodon, but that book was mostly the work of Rintsin. What about Isaiah? According to a schedule in the mission archives, he had translated it by 1828, and in 1834 he claimed that the book had been finished 'long ago', though he never produced a copy for inspection and correction. Edward and William, anxious to submit the book to the ageing Schmidt for censorship, and anticipating continued delay, finally made their own version, using a rough draft prepared by Edward's eldest son, Thomas. It was this version which they printed in 1840, just before the mission was suppressed. But in 1839 Robert included passages from Isaiah in the Mongolian primer which he printed on his own press, along with the Lord's Prayer, the Ten Commandments, some catechetical questions, and extracts from other books of Scripture, including Psalms and Proverbs. So most probably he had translated Isaiah after all.

Robert reported that the translation of the New Testament had been completed by 1826, and he may have been right. The question is, who made it? At one time he took all the credit for himself; at another he admitted that his pupils had 'assisted' him. The Directors took his claim seriously, and published the news in their 33rd Report, dated May 1827. Robert says, too, that he brought his manuscript copy back with him from Siberia in 1846 and, if we can believe him, he was prepared to lay it before the Directors in London in 1847, as evidence of the priority of his version over that commissioned by the BFBS from Edward and William, which had been published, to his chagrin, the year before. By that time, though, Robert seems to have been wandering in his mind, brooding over what he felt to be his quite unjustified fate, and living in a world of fantasy. Forgetting all that had happened, he was seriously trying to persuade the Directors to re-appoint him to Selenginsk, or, failing that, to Tibet, or perhaps to Peking, where no missionary had yet penetrated. From any of these places he thought he might get to Kalgan which, of all places, was now the goal of his ambitions, for in his deluded mind, it had become 'the Centre of Mongolia'. 'I have had good wishes,' he told the Directors, 'and the gift of a Book sent to me from the Hotoctoo – Chief Lama of Khalgan, to whom I had previously sent Portions of the Holy Scriptures; and who read a portion of what I sent to him every day, until all were finished – Every morning on his Knees, and with all the Lamas of his Household with him.' Robert probably meant Urga rather than Kalgan, but the improbability of this fantastic scene cannot have impressed the Directors with his reliability.

Robert was not asked to produce his manuscript in 1847, but it must have existed, because his two colleagues had seen it, or considerable parts of it, and had even revised some of the translations. The only thing was, whose work had it really been? On that point there can be little doubt. As early as 1826 the Directors had been informed that it was Rintsin who was the translator of Psalms and the New Testament, and that he was working, not from the Greek, but from the Russian and Slavonic versions. Nevertheless, when the BFBS began to enquire about the availability of this version in 1837, it had evidently come to be accepted that Robert had been responsible for it, for William felt obliged to tell William Ellis that 'if the real history of what is called "Mr Yuille's translation of the epistles" were laid before you, it could be seen whether he or some others had more to do with the production of it'. By then, of course, Robert was out of the running, and even if the LMS had been convinced of the reality of his work, they would not have been rash enough to embroil themselves with him yet again.

Edward and William may have started to translate Genesis together, but their work assumed the character of a co-operative venture rather than a joint one. Edward took as his share the Pentateuch, the books of Solomon, Daniel, and the Minor Prophets, together with those parts of Ezra which were in Chaldee. He also assumed responsibility for the final revision of Rintsin's translation of the Book of Psalms. William took what remained, less Isaiah. The censored copies of Edward's manuscripts have survived, the Pentateuch in the British Library, and the remainder in the Library of the Bible Society, and they confirm that this division of labour was really followed.

In 1833, when the Bible Society was considering whether to take over financial responsibility for the production of the Old Testament, the two missionaries were asked to submit statements of the principles they had followed in performing their task. Their method of working was as follows. Each would first translate a book or books using the Hebrew Bible and whatever aids to textual criticism and exegesis were at hand. The rough translation was then gone over in detail with a learned Buryat, generally a lama, though only to ensure linguistic accuracy. A fair copy would then be taken, and would be revised itself during the process of transcription. This revision would then be sent to the other two translators, who would have copies made which they could examine and comment on at leisure. Later revisions were also carried out. Critics and commentators were consulted with reserve, and variant readings were accepted, but the translators preferred to err, if at all, on the side of conservatism. The style adopted was one halfway between that used for letter writing, and the more difficult style of the Buddhist scriptures.

16

Printing the Old Testament

The printing of Genesis began in 1834, probably in June, and the last sheet was ready in proof towards the end of October. The censor's imprimatur, for which Russian types were needed, and the title page, were set up and printed by 25 December. A few copies were completed and bound up by the end of the year, but it was some weeks before as many as 135 bound copies could be sent from Selenginsk to Khodon. The edition totalled 500 copies in quarto size, bound up like European books. Presentation copies were sent to both the LMS and the BFBS, but none can be traced in the libraries of those Societies today. The first edition of Genesis is, in fact, a bibliographical rarity, for reasons which will become apparent.

Every page, or at least every leaf, had to be signed by the censor, though not with his full name. Schmidt split up his name and titles into syllables, writing one syllable on each page, and at the end of the book he appended the imprimatur, which Edward translated as follows for the Rev. G. Browne of the Bible Society:

> Commissioned by the Ministers of the Interior, and National Education,
> I have examined this version of Genesis in Mongolian and have found
> it consonant with the various Protestant versions: as such I recommend
> it for publication.

The imprimatur was signed in full: Academician, Collegiate Councillor and Cavalier Yakov Schmidt. Some time later, Schmidt was promoted in rank, and the imprimatur to Isaiah describes him as Councillor of State.

The remoteness of Selenginsk gave rise to practical problems, though these were overcome. Paper had to be brought from a great distance, from St Petersburg or, on one occasion, from the old Scottish mission at Astrakhan. Schmidt, too, was inclined to be dilatory, and was too preoccupied with other things to be an expeditious censor. The missionaries had anticipated that he might prove positively obstructive. They believed that he held their criticisms to be partly responsible for the suppression of his Kalmuck and Mongolian New Testaments of 1827, and feared that 'if his love to the cause do not triumph over his love to retaliate, he may easily find occasion to retard or even yet prevent the printing of our version'. Their fears proved groundless. Certainly, Schmidt needed jogging now and again, but fortunately both Edward and William spent several months in St Petersburg at different times during the 1830s, and were able to speed things up. Thus William managed to retrieve the censored copy of Genesis, and bring it back to Selenginsk in early 1834, while Edward was able to send off Exodus while he was in the capital in early 1835. When he was there the following year, Schmidt even delegated much of the actual work of censorship to him. Edward told William Ellis; 'I am now censor', but this was a slight exaggeration. It is Schmidt's name which appears on all the manuscripts, and Edward's function was limited to making any alterations which were required to ensure that his translation corresponded with the accepted Protestant versions.

Shortage of paper, and delay in receiving censored copy from the capital, were minor irritants. What plunged the printing enterprise into unnecessary and potentially disastrous trouble was Robert's wilful mismanagement of the press. The press had originally been consigned to Selenginsk, and when the missionaries parted company in 1828, it was Robert who stayed there, and so automatically succeeded to its control. By the time John Abercrombie arrived to take up his post in 1834, the estrangement between Robert and his colleagues was complete. The unsuspecting Circassian printer was dropped straight into a complex and explosive situation, an innocent third party in a feud of fourteen or fifteen years' standing. He had been engaged by William, his first task was to print Edward's translation of Genesis, and his immediate boss was Robert. There could not have been a plainer recipe for disaster.

The first thing Robert did was to upset John. Within six months, what with bullying and abusing him, and treacherously undermining his authority with the untrained Buryat assistants, a couple of his own students, he had driven the cheerful, pipe-smoking printer to what would nowadays be called a nervous breakdown. There is a letter in the mission files, written to William at the end of 1834, badly spelt and almost incoherent, in which John pours out all the resentment of his wounded spirit, contrasting the bright hopes with which he had accepted his appointment with the black despair to which Robert's coarse and brutal behaviour had reduced him, and begging somehow to be rescued from the dreadful trap into which he had unwittingly fallen. Robert fancied himself as a printer, and tried to make John do things his way, and when John refused, Robert called him a rogue, a dog and a beast. What was worse, he said it in Russian, so that the Buryat boys could understand him, and he laid hands on John and threatened to throw him out of the house. It was a sad melodrama, and poor John was distraught at what was happening to him, far from home and among strangers. He wrote to William:

Sir, if you please to hear these things, and who can stay here in such a
manner; for we did not come here to be treated so in this way, and
did not leave our Fathers dear country, our dear friends and nears, and
even ofered our lives, and our little one, near to death; by the soward by
hunger, by the cold, and being not in safe for Robers, traviling through
the disert watching by night, starving for cold, and hunger, and did
not know, at what moment we would loose our lives, and all what we
had, all thises things we indured, and comd here in order to help to
the poor *Buriats*, and now we are to be so abused in such a manner, and
to be called by these bad Russian words by Mr Youle, as if I was one
of His Sarvents, or if He had brought us here, or if we had come by
His good will; and if it was so? Still He ought not to give such
nams. . . . Sir therefore I would beg you most humbly, to let me hear
as soon as possable then we would leave the house, for as I corresponded
with you, before we left Our Country and comd here together, so I
thought to let you know of all these things, beging you again if it is
possable, to let me hear as soon as possable.

Robert, too, wrote to Khodon complaining about John, and telling his colleagues what he was going to do. He had decided, as if he had the authority to do so, to dismiss John immediately and send him back to Karass, and ask the Directors to send out another printer. The absurdity of his position was lost upon him, but not upon William. 'It is painful', he wrote to Edward, then safe at Irkutsk or beyond, 'to have to do with people that are infallible.'

We have already looked at the beginnings of the quarrel which isolated Robert from his companions and from the Society. It began as an expression of personal incompatibility, but the source of the trouble lay far deeper. In the eyes of Edward and William, Robert's profession was marred by a fatal flaw. He did not possess the character of a missionary, and many happenings over the years tended only to reinforce this assessment of him. There can be little doubt that William was tacitly using Robert as a model when he wrote in one of his *Letters on Missions* about the ease with which a missionary who had mistaken his vocation could degenerate, when he was too far away to be supervised:

If we follow an individual of an improper character, such as we are here
supposing, into a distant scene of labour, remote from the view of all
whose presence might be a spur to good, and a check to evil, it is easy
to conceive the almost certain consequence; at liberty to think his own
thoughts, and speak his own words, and do his own deeds, and that for
a long season; while there are no means by which his friends, or
constituents may ascertain the true state of matters, and so his real
character may remain long undiscovered and unsuspected. His
unconscientious waste of time – his engagements in pursuits foreign to

his proper work – his deviation from sobriety, and dignity and
consistency of conduct – his dereliction of principle, and utter breach
of his most solemn engagements, are never known and never heard of,
because he will not criminate himself, and he is at a safe distance from
the observation of his brethren. With all this, there may be such a
measure of attention paid to the language of the country, and to the
duty of holding occasional intercourse with the natives, as will furnish
matter for an occasional letter, for the satisfaction of those at home,
whom it may be his interest to please. He may find it no difficult matter
to keep on good terms with his constituents, and delude them with the
vain idea that he is labouring faithfully to disseminate the gospel among
his heathen charge, while he is leaving them without the smallest
concern, and, as yet, without remorse, to their wicked delusions.

And he went on, apparently aiming more directly at Robert:

The case is in some respects, but not essentially altered, where there are
several labourers together, and one such character among them. There
must be here more circumspection, more care to preserve appearance.
But as it is generally found conducive to the performance of the work,
and most suited to the variety of taste and qualification in a body of
missionaries to make a division of labour, each in his own department
is rendered more independent and left more at liberty. And in the
supposed case of an unfaithful member of a missionary establishment,
there is more room for the practice of hypocrisy, and less liability to
suspicion; while delicacy, and the spirit of forbearance, and hope of
amendment and charitable allowance for peculiarity of natural
disposition, may make his brethren very tender of exposing one whose
improprieties cannot escape their notice. The truth is, a Judas may
remain undetected for years among his brethren and fellow labourers.

So there it all was – deviation from sobriety, hypocrisy, a Judas – hard
words indeed, expressed as an impersonal hypothesis, as early as 1830. The
Directors must have wondered how William, be he never so perceptive a
psychologist, could have analysed the downward course of a false missionary
so tellingly, unless he had had a case history to study. They may of course
have recognized the sad truth, and kept it to themselves as long as they
could. They took no open notice of it until the crisis over Genesis forced
them to.

The point at issue over the printing of Genesis was a simple one. Robert
had made arbitrary alterations to Edward's translation while he was printing
it. These alterations went beyond the tacit correction of copyists' slips, and
touched the substance of the text. He refused to see that this was discourteous to his colleague, especially as he could have suggested emendations at
any time during the past eight or ten years, but had not done so. He was

also blind to the fact that, by altering the text which had been passed by the censor, he was acting illegally, and also endangering the reputation of all three missionaries for trustworthiness. The normal requirement was that three copies of everything printed with the censor's approval had to be submitted for checking before the edition could be published. The missionaries had been exempted from this provision as a special concession, and Edward and William were conscious of the particular delicacy of their position. Robert obstinately declined to admit that he had done anything reprehensible. Rather the opposite – he claimed to have acted with good intentions, and in the best interests of the mission by ensuring that the translation was as accurate as possible, and he would not promise not to do the same with Exodus when he got the chance. He was all injured innocence.

Edward asked the Directors to consider transferring the printing of the Old Testament to Khodon, and Robert agreed that this would be the best course for all concerned, now that his kind attentions had been spurned:

> I shall by no means oppose you in this resolution; for independent of John, or anything connected with him it is absolutely necessary that the printing should be carried on under your own eyes, since I cannot be allowed to discover any errors which have escaped the eye of the translator and the pen of the copyist – Since my brethren would rather that errors were put into print than that I should correct them or point out any means to have them corrected.

Locally, this controversy was the start of an interminable correspondence between Robert and the unfortunate William, who was left to bear the brunt of the dispute, since Edward, Robert's real antagonist, was absent on leave for the next two years. On William's side the tone is patient and logical, though he does not hide the irritation he felt at having to waste time on such a tedious and unseemly wrangle. On Robert's side the correspondence is verbose, diffuse, and frequently absurd, betraying his increasingly fragile hold on reality. For a while he can be lucid and almost convincing, once one succeeds in decoding his stilted English style, but then some irrational stimulus takes possession of his thoughts, and he plunges into an incoherent farrago of irrelevant triviality and abuse. As the correspondence progresses, it becomes increasingly obvious that Robert must have been mentally disturbed in some way, as his colleagues thought he was.

In the wider sphere, the outcome of the dispute was Robert's downfall as a missionary. The Directors could no longer ignore his eccentricities, which threatened the security of the mission. First of all they ordered him to send the press and the printer to Khodon, which he did in April 1835, pointedly omitting to warn William and give him time to make preparations. Then they asked him to come home for consultations. He simply ignored these instructions. In the end, the Directors had no alternative but to terminate his appointment, and they dismissed him with effect from 7 September 1838.

It would be a waste of time to try to analyse the contents of the exchange of letters between Robert and his colleagues, mostly with William, unless the purpose were to make a psychological study of the former's deteriorating personality. One can only offer a sample or two, to illustrate the surrealist quality of what William had to cope with, the nonsense he felt obliged to consider and to answer in a civil and rational manner, despite the bafflement he felt at its absurdity. The tone is set by one of the very first letters. Edward had obviously objected to something Robert had done, and the latter retorted:

> I wonder that you did not think on what Moses might be thinking of
> you when you wrote your Deprecations against me! – I suppose you
> would like to know what I thought when I read your letter, and how
> my thoughts were exercised when thinking on your Deprecations!
> Well, I will write you one of them. – I looked up to the Skies and
> thought Surely Moses, instead of Deprecations, would Bless us both
> for endeavouring to put his Book into Such good order for the Boriates!
> – I earnestly invite your Remarks, Criticisms, and advice. I hope you will
> let no Error pass without noting it particularly. But your Deprecations
> I think Surely might be thrown into the Khodon.

Then there was John to be torn to pieces, with his supposed professional incompetence and his personal idiosyncrasies. He was even to be held responsible for Robert's poor state of health:

> He is very inconsiderate. He is jealous and doubtful of every body –
> That his hay may not be stolen, he has it placed near to hand. It took
> *fire* on Thursday night last at 9 o'clock, by what accident I cannot tell,
> but the people and his own servants suppose that it was by fire from
> his Tobacco pipe; for he visits his hay frequently, it is said, for fear of
> thieves. . . . It cost me, 12 Boriates, he and his wife, and 3 Russians
> about 2½ hours hard work to extinguish it. I caught cold at this fire,
> and have not been well since.

Nothing was too petty for Robert to take offence at, or too distant to be remembered. Just as Colonel Maslov's snub had provoked his outburst about his dignity as a former student at the University of Glasgow, so anything said by Edward or William could be twisted into a jibe, and in Robert's distorted fancies these imagined jibes gave birth to resentment which turned in on itself and grew to grotesque and comic proportions, before bursting forth in an unstoppable torrent of reproach. One day he asked after William's health, and offered his help. Quite innocently, William replied: 'I have been somewhat better since I last wrote, and although still not well I use little medicine, and have only to thank you for your kind offer of advice and assistance.' Back came the answer:

> Did you really think that I expected any more than thanks? And what was it that you thought I would expect? And what reasons can you give for supposing that I expected any thing *at all* for my advice? Be pleased to explain yourself, that I may have an opportunity to defend myself against all kinds of accusations! I can say in all truth that my advice was given to you, in all affection and sympathy for your state as a sick man, and according to the representation of your letter, without have any view *even* to receive thanks! and this is my state of mind in all the help in all kinds of help which I render to my fellow men! – so if you have thought otherwise, be pleased to correct yourself of the mistake.
>
> And if your state of mind toward me is such, which leads you to despise my advice, I shall only say for myself that very many have been benefited by it: and that it is not only in this region of the world that I have benefited, or began to benefit my fellow men, as it respects advice and medicine; for about three years, and more before I left Glasgow I was in the habit of both giving advice and medicine occasionally among my friends, and after I left Glasgow I lived for about three years near to Haslar Hospital, where I became well acquainted with Dr Dodds, who at that time was at the Head of that Hospital. That Gentleman counted me as a distant Relation, but at any rate I counted him as a *friend*; for at all my leisure hours, his house was open to me, and his advice and instructions were ever at hand, and I had the Privilege of visiting the sick of that Hospital, and I believe that it is one of the Largest in England. This Gentleman also employed me at times, to give my joint advice when things were doubtful: and one of these cases, in which I was employed, was at the instance of our Directors, who had appointed him to examine their student Mr Nicolson before he went to India. I was made a party in that examination, and the result, with my name, I believe in the document, was sent to our Board. I was unwilling that a Missionary should be kept back; but I say on the occasion, that I thought India was not for him – Mr Nicolson died shortly after he went out to India. . . .
>
> I considered this statement as having been called for, and I have made [it] to shew that my attention was called to medicine before I was in my present calling. . . .

There was more of the like. In December 1834 Robert complained to William about the state of his eyesight. That was William's fault:

> I hope that this may be the last letter that I shall be called on to write on this, or any similar grievous subject. I never had occasion to write

with eye glasses to month of Oct. last. But I got badly for nearly two weeks at that time, and since which my eyes have become dim. The cause of the disease was from the Khodan; Therefore if you have any spare spectacles be pleased to send me a pair.

It was not the last letter by any means. The correspondence between Selenginsk and Khodon rumbled on throughout 1834 and 1835 up to the end of 1836. In November of that year Robert was demanding that his colleagues should subscribe to a set of 'Articles of Peace' which he had drawn up. By this peace treaty, Robert would have been authorized to print Psalms, Isaiah and the New Testament on his new press which he had acquired, and which would be recognized as a mission press by the Directors. All three men would agree to forget everything unpleasant which had happened. The Directors would cancel the letter in which they had requested Robert to come home, and a joint request would be sent to the Directors to send out another missionary to join him in Selenginsk. Obviously the time had passed when there could be rational discussion with Robert, and in December William broke off the correspondence, refusing to answer any more of Robert's letters unless he adopted 'a very different strain'.

Mixed up with the argument over the printing of Genesis was another dispute. Robert did not object to the printing of the Old Testament going to Khodon, along with the printer, as long as he could have a press of his own at Selenginsk, either the original one or a substitute. When he saw that there was no hope of keeping the mission press at his station – that his colleagues had succeeded, in his words, in forcing it from him – he had the impudence to urge Edward, then on his way home on leave, to buy another press, perhaps in Kazan, acquire a new set of type in St Petersburg, and send the whole lot out to him across the length of Siberia. He realized that the Directors might not feel disposed to underwrite this transaction, so he proposed that the members of the mission should contribute towards the cost in equal shares out of their own resources. This arrangement would include Mrs Swan, who, he hoped, would shoulder a quarter of the expense, leaving him with only a quarter to carry himself. Robert had to be reminded that if this plan were adopted, the Directors would still be financing the press, since it was they who provided the missionaries with all their funds. The plan, of course, fell through, because the others would have nothing to do with it, but by April 1835 Robert had found another solution. He had a new press made for the Selenginsk station, partly to his own design.

What was he going to print? In December 1833 he sent his last full report to the Directors, and in it he included the news that he had two alphabetically arranged dictionaries ready for printing, a Mongolian one, and a Mongol-Tibetan one. Though he did not mention it in this letter, there was a third one on the stocks as well, a Russo-Mongolian dictionary, and he was also wanting to print Psalms and Isaiah and about twenty little booklets of his on various subjects. Local Buryats, he told the Directors, had spoken well of both his dictionaries, and he thought there would be a good sale for them, perhaps even enough to cover the printing costs and make a profit for the Society. To help on the good work, he had had iron matrices made for a fount of Tibetan type, and had already cast some type. He had sent one set to the learned physicist and Orientalist Baron Schilling, and he enclosed some samples with his report for the Directors' inspection.

The Directors considered his proposal, and in October 1834 they requested him to consult his colleagues, and submit a unanimous recommendation as to whether or not the dictionaries should be printed, what the cost would be, and what the chances were of breaking even. October 1834 was not a good time to promote objective discussion between Selenginsk and Khodon, and in any case, Edward and William, who knew the history of Robert's dictionaries, had already made up their minds about them. They considered his Mongolian dictionary to be little more than a copy of Edward's. To have made such a copy was perfectly legitimate as far as the practical needs of the mission were concerned, but for Robert to print it under his name was quite another matter. In any case, there was no need for such a work any more, after the publication of Schmidt's Dictionary. The verdict on the Tibetan dictionary was even less favourable. It could do the mission no good to publish something whose effect could only be to enable the Buryats to study their 'heathen scriptures' more thoroughly. And in any case, Robert was an incompetent lexicographer who did not know Tibetan properly. Robert was not convinced. He maintained that he was properly qualified, and he refused to see that there could be any difference between a scholarly work and a missionary one, and he put his colleagues' negative assessment down to ignorance, jealousy and prejudice.

The loss of the mission press was only a temporary setback to Robert's ambitions. In April 1835 he told William, in response to an enquiry, that he was going to print all his books, including the New Testament and 'other books of a missionary nature' which we can tell from other letters included his dictionaries, on his own new press. What, if anything, did he print? Mention of the Book of Psalms slightly worried his colleagues, for Robert had had something to do with the translation of that book, and might be thought to have a moral claim to it. In December 1836 Edward explained the whole history of the translation of Psalms to William Ellis, showing that it had been Rintsin who had translated the book from the Russian, and that he had revised it from the Hebrew, helped by William. 'I regard it', he said, 'as having cost me more labour than most of my translations – i.e. the part which I revised: – and I am persuaded that the labour of making an entirely new version would have been far less.' Nevertheless, he did not want to assume the responsibility of printing Psalms without express authority from the Directors, for 'Mr Y charges me with having forcibly wrested the press from him, and we are unwilling that he should have the colour of such a charge respecting the book of Psalms. We have therefore deferred the printing of it till we hear from you. This is truly an humbling and melancholy subject, and the aspect which it has upon the mission is far from cheering.'

In April 1838 the Directors instructed Edward and William not to let the manuscript of Psalms, or any other censored copy, get into Robert's hands. 'It is almost needless to assure you,' wrote Ellis, 'that we never intended the press Mr Yuille has set up at Selenginsk to be employed in printing any of the Sacred Scriptures under Mr Yuille's separate and independent control, and if Mr Yuille really entertained such an impression he must have strangely misconceived the nature of his relation with the Society.'

So Psalms was safe, and so was Isaiah, and nothing more is heard of the printing of Robert's New Testament or his dictionaries in the mission correspondence. However, he did put his press into operation. The most substantial work to come from it was a primer of the Mongolian language which contained, in its 124 pages, tables showing the letters of the Mongolian alphabet and their combinations, some passages for reading, and elementary arithmetical tables. This book was passed by the censor, not I.J. Schmidt, but one P. Korsakov, in 1837, and was printed in 1839. Two copies of it are known to exist in England, one in private possession, the other in the Bodleian Library, Oxford. The second item to come from the Selenginsk press was a single sheet, also dated 1839, but without a censor's imprimatur, printed on both sides and containing twenty-eight four-line devotional poems or prayers. A copy of this sheet is also in the possession of the Bodleian Library.

Like so much else in Robert's ambiguous life-story, the question of what, and how much, he printed at Selenginsk is confused, and cannot be answered with certainty. There is, however, no doubt that the primer was the first thing he printed, and that it was printed, as we might expect, from moveable types. The Bodleian copy was previously owned by the Rev. Dr S.C. Malan, the eminent nineteenth-century Orientalist and vicar of Broadwindsor in Dorset, and formed one item of the gift of books which he made to the Indian Institute in Oxford in 1884–85. Another item in the gift was a folio volume containing manuscript copies of some Mongolian and Tibetan texts. Both books display the bookplate of the Malan gift.

The manuscript volume is dedicated to Malan in what is almost certainly Robert's handwriting. The only disturbing element is the legend 'Dr Yuille' added beneath the dedication. As far as we know, Robert never held, or even claimed to hold, a doctor's degree. This legend, however, is in a different hand from that of the dedication. A letter which is indisputably in Robert's hand has been affixed to the recto side of the first leaf of the primer, and though it does not bear the name of any addressee, it must surely have been sent to Malan. At the foot of the letter is the legend 'Robert Yuille Missy in Siberia', in what appears to be the same hand as the 'Dr Yuille' of the manuscript volume. This letter describes the genesis of the primer as follows:

> Sir, This Book I have called the *Mashy Saiin Belek*; It contains various Peices of Instruction; I composed it of hand; i.e. without made arrangements for it before hand; I made the Press on which it was printed, and on which I made a New Invention, for which the Russian Government offered me a Patent; I made Matrises also and Cast and prepared two Fonts of Types from them, one in Mongolian and the other in Tibetian languages; my Mongolian Students and Workmen whom I had taught from the A.B.C. of their own Language were the only helps I had in this work. I had not any knowlede [sic] of type making or Printing until I went to Eastern Siberia; but I picked my knowlede of printing there while I had to be Interpreter to a man who had some knowledge of printing in his Youth, but knew not anything of Mongolian, and my students and workmen were all of them Mongolians; and they all became Expert young men both in printing and in their Classical learning; some of them obtained from me a little knowledge of Latin, Greek, Hebrew and English, and I had some of them very tolerable Russian, Mongolian, Manjurian and Tibetian Scholars.
>
> This being my first Essay at Type making and Printing, I hope that you will be pleased to Criticise Sparingly.
>
> My Types were made of too Soft Metal, and with use soon became defaced; and I had not time to cast them over again!

Facing this letter, and affixed to the inside of the front cover of the book, is what can pass as a preface, printed in Mongol, and with Robert's name, also in Mongolian type, appended to it. The text is somewhat barbarous, but it can be translated as follows:

> Notice to all readers of this book. The press on which this book was printed, and the types and everything used in the printing, I caused to be wrought and perfected by my Buryat pupils and Buryat friends, for the sake of instructing them in the art of printing. Thus this book has not been elegantly wrought. But this is an innovation for the Buryat nation, and new to them, and never before this time has so difficult a work been seen in this country, wherefore, dear readers, pray do not blame me or my Buryat friends too harshly.

The primer has no title in any European language. Robert called it *Excellent Gift*, in Mongolian, in his letter to Malan, but this is only part of its full title, which may be translated: *The Book known as the Excellent Gift, displaying beneficially and clearly to Persons desirous of learning, the Letters of the Mongolian Language, their Combinations, and other elementary Matters*. At the foot of the title page is a pious motto in Tibetan and Mongolian to the effect that 'Merit consists in instructing others in good understanding'. The only wording in a European language is the legend in Russian: 'Composed by Robert Yuille'. The book is dated in a colophon on page 123 *bis*, not on the title page.

Detail of this order should be adequate to identify copies of the primer. The books which Robert printed at Selenginsk have always been bibliographical rarities, but they have not entirely escaped notice in specialist literature. Yet, of the four separate descriptions I have seen, none corresponds to the copies I have examined.

The first Western European scholar, to my knowledge, to draw attention to Robert's printing activities was B. Jülg, in an article on the current state of Mongolian researches published in the *Journal of the Royal Asiatic Society* in 1882. One of the books he enumerated was 'Robert Yuille, *Short Mongolian Grammar* (in the Mongolian language)', which he described as follows: 'Xylography from the English mission press before Selenginsk beyond the Baikal, 1838. This book will always remain unique.' Jülg's description is credible in some respects, questionable in others. If what he had before him was the 1839 book – and Robert himself says that this was his first attempt at printing – then the date 1838 can only be a mistake. On the other hand, the curious attribution of the book to 'the English mission press before Selenginsk beyond the Baikal' corresponds, at least in part, to the wording of the Mongol colophon to the 1839 edition, which reads: 'Printed in 1839 at the mission press before the town of Selenga.' This claim, incidentally, need cause no surprise. Robert always contested the validity of his expulsion from the Society, and it would have been quite consistent with his stubborn, irrational nature to have gone on regarding his press as the legitimate mission press. But why did Jülg call the book a xylography? Again, one can only suppose that he made a mistake. Robert would hardly have gone to the trouble of having wooden blocks made and developing a separate printing process when he possessed his own printing press, and types designed by himself, of which he was extremely proud.

The next to draw attention to Robert's work was a German Mongolist and priest of the Orthodox church, W.A. Unkrig. In 1914 Unkrig initiated a correspondence with the BFBS on the subject of translations of the Bible into Mongolian. He was studying at the time at the Spiritual Academy at Kazan. In one of his letters he told the Rev. Dr Kilgour of the Bible Society:

> You may be interested to know that yesterday, while rummaging with the Archimandrite Gurii in our library, I found, quite by accident, a little primer or chrestomathy of the Buryat language, printed with Mongolian type (1837), which was composed by the missionary Robert Yuille, and which, as appears from information in Mongolian and Russian on the inside of the cover, is the first printed Buriat book. A bibliographical rarity indeed!

The dating to 1837 can easily be accounted for, if it needs to be explained away, since that is the year of the imprimatur granted by the censor. But the copy seen by Unkrig evidently had a statement in both Russian and Mongol, where the Bodleian has only one in Mongol. This can hardly be a mistake, due to a lapse of memory, since Unkrig wrote to the Bible Society the day after he had seen the book. The notation in Russian must have figured in the Kazan copy, but was it printed or handwritten? Unkrig does not say.

The third and most baffling reference is that by Neville Whymant, who, in 1926, listed, in his *Mongolian Grammar*, under the heading *In Latin*, 'Juille, R. *Syllabarium Mongolicum* Selenginsk 1837'.

Finally, in 1948, the Polish Orientalist W. Kotwicz published a description of a book printed by Robert which recalls the gist of the preface to the Bodleian copy. After mentioning Robert's fount of Tibetan type, he goes on to say:

> In fact, the Mongol type came to be cast later, and when in 1837 Yuille printed a grammar of the Mongolian language with it, he was by then in possession of a small printing press, prepared entirely by the hands of the Buryats. In the preface to the reader he could declare, with real pride, that 'the press on which I printed, the cutting and preparation of the matrices of the type, the casting and cleaning of the type, the printing and binding, in a word, everything which is connected with this book (except the layout and the paper) was prepared and carried out by my Buryat students in my house, situated in the vicinity of the town of Selenginsk, with the aim of enlightening the local people and making them apt for good works, and also for the public good and the reputation of this area. . . . It may be the first book from the beginning of time which was printed by this method among the people of Siberia.'

Whymant's aberrant identification is inexplicable. In spite of the obvious discrepancies, there are enough points of similarity among the other three descriptions, and between them and the 1839 edition, to suggest that they all refer to that book. How the discrepancies may have arisen is another matter and probably of no real importance, serving only as a reminder that there is more than one loose end left in the enigmatic story of Robert Yuille and his failed mission.

The autumn of 1834 and the next three or four years were an unhappy time for everyone in the mission. By this time, it was becoming too late to reason with Robert. He was beyond rational argument, and after the end of 1836 his two colleagues had as little to do with him as possible. Replying in the spring of 1836 to a series of enquiries about Robert's character and actions from William Ellis, Edward wrote:

> Do you ask, 'has he been remonstrated with?' I answer, we have long since discontinued it. We have so often been convinced, by painful

experience, that his overweaning conceit of his own wisdom and abilities is such as to leave us without the hope of convincing him, and that all such attempts lead to useless quibbling and disputings. It has often occurred to me whether, thinking as I did, I ought or ought not to make the Society acquainted with my views. But I feared lest I should judge rashly or harshly. I hoped – for I have always thought him sincere, that, although much appeared to me which I thought defective, there might be that which God approved, and which he might be pleased to make useful. . . . But now I must say it appears a hopeless case, and that, especially for the last three or four years, he appears so pertinaciously and incorrigibly wilful as to afford very little hope of a change.

Even before receiving this letter, the Directors had decided to recall Robert for consultations, and they did so on 5 December 1835. He ignored the invitation, as he ignored similar instructions sent in April 1837 and March 1838. In the five years following his report of December 1833 he wrote home only three times. His first two letters were mainly about money matters, though in February 1835 he had the grace to tell the Directors that the reason why he had not reported on the previous year's work was that he had been suffering from eye-trouble, which prevented him from writing letters. Curiously enough, the state of his eyes had not interrupted the flow of ever more offensive letters from Selenginsk to Khodon. A letter of 1835 included a petulant complaint about what he considered his colleagues' folly in applying for permission to baptize their converts. Then there was silence for three years, until Robert suddenly presented a draft for 18,000 roubles on account of salary he had not drawn for, accompanied by details of a draft he had submitted in 1834. In trying to debit the Society with his salary at this time he was deliberately ignoring, or challenging, a notification sent to him by the Directors in April 1837 that they had suspended his credit with Asmus Simonsen.

Robert had been sending hurt and hurtful letters to Khodon until William broke off the correspondence, but only with this letter, written at the beginning of December 1838 to the Treasurer of the Missionary Society, did he attempt to justify his conduct to any one of the Directors. It was not an impressive performance, for it consisted of nothing but a string of dogmatic assertions of his own rectitude and the malignity of his two colleagues. Ignoring everything that had happened, he continued to protest that he was 'a humble, upright and faithful missionary by the rich Grace of God', who had fallen victim to a vicious conspiracy:

> I request no favour. I only wish for impartial Justice; because I am a faithful, humble, zealous, prudent and able missionary of the Society. . . . I am forced to defend myself against a stream of what I am led to suppose are Selfish Politics, which has been flowing against me, at times, and ever ready to overflow me, for 18 years. I strongly

suspected Dr Henderson to be no friend to me; and that his Politics with
Mr Swan, or vice versa, while in England, was the reason Mr Swan
ultimately effected nothing, neither favour nor help for my branch of
the Mission: Although at his first arrival in England, it was otherwise
determined by the Board. But for what reason the Board of Directors has
not fulfilled their resolution of assistance to this Branch of the Siberian
Mission, I have not even received information. And it is probable that
these Selfish Politics have been in Exercise for a long time among them:
yea, perhaps from the very commencement of our mission. I think it
my duty to state these suppositions, in order to prevent the Directors
from going farther, than necessary in my case, until I know their
reasons for it.

And Robert went on to question the judgment and actions of the Directors
themselves:

I expected also that the Directors would have been so kind as to lay
before me the complaints, or accusations alleged against me, from
whatever quarter they had come, before they should begin to Judge and
condemn me: But they have not, in the most distant way, given me any
reason for their rising up against me, in order that I might answer for
myself: thereby appearing to endeavour to cut me off also, from the
Privileges of the Law of the Gospel, and also from the Law of Nations.
They have also Since the very time, this unpleasing crisis first
commenced, Entirely cut me off from all friendly correspondence, with
themselves, by their resolutions against [me]; and by one of their letters
it will appear that they wished others to be of the same mind as
themselves. I beg that these things may be considered! for These very
things, Dear Sir, frequently cut me to the very heart, and both prevented
me from writing to the Directors, and from sending some letters forward,
which have been written.

This was nothing but prevarication, and Robert's tacit refusal to come home
could have only one result.

When they asked Robert to come home in April 1837, and cut off his
credit with Asmus Simonsen, the Directors empowered Edward and William
to take over from him all the Society's movable property at Selenginsk, and
to secure the mission premises. They also authorized them to draw any
money he might need for the journey, and to issue it to him as requisite.
This was, as might have been anticipated, an unworkable arrangement.
Robert tried to drum up sympathy from the local Russians, by letting it
appear that his colleagues were planning to evict him from his station so
that they could take it over themselves. It would have been damaging to the
interests of the mission to insist on ejecting him, and Edward and William

asked the Directors to relieve them of all responsibility for dealing with Robert, and to put his affairs in the hands of J.C. Brown at St Petersburg.

In February 1839 the Directors' patience finally ran out, and they wrote to tell Robert that he was now regarded as 'not having sustained the character of a missionary' for flouting their peremptory instruction of 5 March 1838 to come home, and that they were disowning him as from 7 September 1838, the latest day he should have left Selenginsk. Brown was instructed to settle his arrears of salary up to that date, and sent 16,000 roubles to Khodon for that purpose. Edward and William were once again authorized to take possession of the Society's property, and in May 1839 they went to Selenginsk to carry out their instructions, but were rebuffed. They therefore withheld the money, which was by then in their hands, a course of action which the Directors approved: indeed, the Directors were even considering deducting part of it as rent for the now illegally occupied mission station. To cover all eventualities, the Society informed the Russian government, in the person of Count Stroganov, the Minister of the Interior, that Robert was no longer in their employ. This was a wise step, as well as a formally correct one, for in 1840 Robert wrote to Brown, demanding his back pay, and mischievously sent his letter care of the Minister of the Interior.

By now, Robert was trifling with the Russian government as well as with the Society. In October 1839, after they had been notified of his dismissal, the local authorities asked him to notify them of his expected date of departure from Siberia. Robert once again prevaricated. Months passed, and then he told them that he was still awaiting a formal decision from London. Edward was outraged by his duplicity, writing, in April 1840: 'It is a most deplorable and humiliating statement to make, yet I make it not unadvisedly, that there is scarcely any species of equivocation, prevarication, or falsehood of which Mr Yuille has not proved himself capable.' Altogether it was a sorry tale, in which Robert showed himself repeatedly to be his own worst enemy, for the Directors took action against him only after a series of intolerable provocations.

In the autumn of 1840 it became urgently necessary to make a financial settlement with Robert, as Edward and William, under notice to quit, still held his 16,000 roubles. What they did was to hand over 12,000, keeping back the remainder as security against the mission premises. At the time this seemed a satisfactory solution, and the Directors gave it their approval.

But the trouble did not go away; it merely subsided for five years. In October 1845 Robert suddenly wrote to the Directors demanding 4,115 roubles which he claimed was still due to him in respect of arrears of pay. By the time he wrote this letter, it had become, in his mind, the retention of this money by Edward and William which alone had forced him to stay on in Siberia, against his will:

I have been obliged unwillingly to remain at this place to the present day; and the Directors know that it was for the want of these Monies; and no reason was given to me only I should leave my Station, that prevented me from doing so when they first requested me, and it is easy for any person of common judgment to conceive that my state here under such circumstances was what I truly did not in any way deserve at any person's hand. . . . My own conscience approves of my faithfulness and diligence in all the work of this Mission.

This was sheer impudence. Robert knew, but refused to acknowledge, that he had not been an accredited member of the mission, which had ceased to exist in 1840, since 1838. Besides, his colleagues had been authorized to pay his passage home in 1838, but he had not taken advantage of the offer.

The reason for this sudden demand on the Society was that the Russian government had grown tired of Robert's presence in Siberia, and were expelling him. They had promised him an order for horses and money for his travelling expenses, but of course they were, in his eyes, still at fault. They had not specified the number of horses, nor had they allowed him enough money to cover the carriage of all his effects. So there he was, marooned in Siberia, applying to the Governor of Irkutsk for permission to extend his stay, and to the Directors for his back pay. And what was he to do with the house? Abandon it, and let it revert to Government? Sell it for almost nothing? Or should the Directors not keep it on against the time when they and the Russians would let him resume his mission? Robert was as detached from reality as ever, still believing himself to be, as he signed himself, 'a faithful Missionary of our Society'.

Robert finally left Selenginsk in February 1846, and reached St Petersburg in April, having left behind everything belonging to the Society and most of his own possessions. Incredible as it may seem, he was still expecting to go back one day. He wrote to the Minister of the Interior on the subject, but unfortunately for him, though perhaps not surprisingly, his letter 'did not effect any thing to favour my strong desires on behalf of the continuance of my Mission at Selenginsk'. He also managed to persuade the British Embassy, whose officials may not have been *au fait* with the full facts, to send in a petition on his behalf to the Emperor, but before a reply could be received, he was obliged to leave Russia. His money was running out, and he could not face another winter in St Petersburg. On 14 October 1846 he and Samuel landed at Hull.

With Robert's return to this country there began the last phase of his long duel with the Society – a duel protracted by intervals of silence, during which his failing eyesight prevented him from composing his rambling epistles to the Directors. After all the years of exclusion from the Society, he was still trying to establish that he continued to be a missionary. His claim for arrears of pay now included the five years and one month between the time when the mission was closed and the time he left Selenginsk. After all, had he not been acting as a faithful missionary all that time, and so earning his salary though, for some incomprehensible reason, kept incommunicado by the Directors?

In April 1848 the Directors made a final compromise offer. They would pay him the salary he was owed up to the date of his dismissal, together with £150 for travelling expenses, and they would assume responsibility for a loan he had taken out with the Russian authorities at Selenginsk, and which he had left Russia without repaying. Take it or leave it, they said, and Robert seems to have left it. When last we hear of him, in a letter dated 3 May 1848, he is still contesting the Society's offer. They had, he complained, allowed him nothing for his last seven years' service, and his travelling expenses did not even cover 'the simple interest on my salaries due to me even before the year 1838', a novel and incomprehensible factor in his calculations. Robert passes from our view with a last complaint that he had been treated impolitely when he called at the Mission House. His story closes with a typical non-sequitur: 'During the time I was waiting, I read a good deal, and learned something.' If only he had learned earlier.

To return to the Old Testament. Once the press had been moved to Khodon in April 1835, the printing went on smoothly, as and when copy came in, and John gave satisfactory service, though he proved to have a 'peculiar temper', and needed careful handling. Edward and William were authorized to suppress the first edition of Genesis if they thought fit, but it soon went out of print in any case, and they decided to issue a new printing of the entire Pentateuch instead. Genesis was restored to what it should have been in the first place, and a few typographical improvements were introduced into the other four books. Psalms was printed in two sizes, the only book to receive such treatment. A non-standard, octavo, edition was printed, without revision, at the expense of the Bible Society of New York. In late 1840 the operations were held up for lack of paper. There was plenty of paper, belonging to the BFBS, at Selenginsk, but Robert sat on it, alleging that, as his salary had not been paid, he could not afford the cost of sending it to Khodon. It was only the timely arrival of a delayed consignment from St Petersburg which enabled the missionaries to complete the Old Testament before they left. Ezekiel was the last book to be printed, and it actually went through the press in November, long after the order to close the mission had been received. Edward and William salved their consciences by submitting an appeal to be allowed to finish the printing, and meanwhile carried on, confident that they would have done so before an answer could be received from the capital.

During the course of printing, individual books, or small groups of books, appeared with their separate imprimaturs. There was no systematic pagination. When complete Testaments were bound up in 1840, these imprimaturs were dropped, and were replaced by a single one, dated to that year. Fortunately, the Mongolian colophons were not deleted at the same time, and they allow us to reconstruct the chronology of the printing. As might be expected, it was the second printing of the Pentateuch which was incorporated in the complete Old Testament. Genesis and Exodus, first printed in 1834 and 1835 respectively, are from the 1837 impressions, while Leviticus and Numbers, first printed in 1835, and Deuteronomy, first printed in 1836, are from the 1839 impressions. The other books of the Old Testament were printed between 1836 and 1840. The Mongolian colophons regularly give Khodon as the place of printing. This has been ingeniously, but erroneously, explained by Darlow and Moule, in their monumental catalogue of translations of the Bible, as meaning 'the City', and hence referring to Selenginsk. The confusion is made possible because the name Khodon, in Mongolian script, looks remarkably like the word *khota*, which means 'city'. But Selenginsk was not a city (though Robert misled the Directors into thinking it was, until Edward put them right), and the colophons faithfully locate the printing where it was carried out after so much bitter controversy.

When Edward and William left Siberia, they left behind not only the press and all its equipment, including most of their last consignment of paper, but most, if not all, the printed Testaments. These, both complete volumes and individual parts, were packed in eight cases; the press in two more; and the types in four boxes. There were eighteen bales of printing paper, each holding a hundred reams, and one keg of printer's ink. This all belonged to the Bible Society. At first, that Society tried to sell the Testaments to the Holy Synod, but the offer was ignored. It was then decided to bring them home. Mr Archibald Mirrielees, a St Petersburg merchant who was correspondent of the Bible Society, arranged this through Mr Bocharov, the post-master at Verkhneudinsk. The Testaments travelled slowly across Siberia. They left Verkhneudinsk on 12 January 1843, were due in Kazan by July, and finally turned up at the capital, with the packages all smashed, and the books rain-soaked and muddy, in early 1844. Mirrielees had them cleaned and repacked, and the last we hear of them in the correspondence of the BFBS is that they were due to leave St Petersburg for England on 25 May 1844.

After much uncertainty, the press and types were sold on the spot in early 1843. It was an unhappy coincidence that at the same time Edward was advising the Bible Society that, contrary to what he had said some time earlier, it might prove economical to get them sent home for use in printing the New Testament which he and William were then preparing.

With the printing of the Old Testament well under way, the Bible Society began, in 1835, to take an interest in distributing the New Testament in Mongolian as well. To begin with, they set their sights on the version printed in St Petersburg before 1827 under Schmidt's name, but which the Holy Synod had kept out of circulation.

This translation had a curious history. The printing was completed by 1827, but the edition was successfully kept out of the public eye. Nearly a

Printing the Old Testament

century later, the BFBS itself still did not have a copy of it in its uniquely comprehensive library of Bibles. The reason was that it had been one of the last products of the discredited Russian Bible Society, and the Holy Synod had begun to have doubts about its validity. To test this, they decided to submit it to impartial criticism, before allowing it to be issued, and for this they turned to the English missionaries.

Paterson had anticipated that something like this might happen, and in February 1827 he had warned the missionaries to be on their guard:

> Mr Schmidt has received the charge of correcting the Mong. N.T. When ready they are to be sent to some body to pass judgment on them before circulated. Should they come your way you had better excuse yourselves as well as you can from giving any opinion. Keep quiet and make no enemies. You will get no thanks from any party whatever opinion you might give.

At first sight it may seem strange that the Holy Synod should seek an evaluation of the translation after all the expense of printing it had been incurred, but there is a simple explanation. The printing had been begun far back, in 1822, when the RBS had been in favour, and it was only after the bulk of the work had been done that the Synod was in a position to interfere.

In November 1827 Archbishop Mikhail of Irkutsk sent the missionaries a copy of the New Testament, with a request for advice as to its quality. He intimated that the decision whether or not to publish would probably hinge on this advice. The missionaries temporized, awaiting divine guidance, but in principle they felt obliged to accede to the request. Edward told Alers Hankey:

> We shall take time for consideration on the subject, but it does not appear to me, at present, how we can be silent, exactly consistently with duty. If the version be a good one we ought surely to do all we can to promote its circulation: and if otherwise it is our duty at least to give a faithful report and to point out wherein the errors consist and to leave it with those whom it concerns to make the application. But I trust we shall be directed as to the path we ought to take.

By May 1828 they had had time to examine the translation and found it better than they had feared. 'There are many things in it which, according to our ideas of Biblical translation would require correction', William told William Orme, 'but there is nothing like any systematical or radical error in the work, so far as we have observed, and it is in many places in a more improved state than the first Edition of the gospels and Acts which we have been circulating among the Buriats.' He went on to suggest that it might be worth while for the Society to get hold of twenty or thirty copies and send them to India, for possible infiltration into Tibet, where he thought the

Mongolian language was understood. But no copies were ever released for this or any other purpose.

We do not know whether the missionaries communicated their assessment of the New Testament to the Archbishop, but presumably they did do so, for the Holy Synod decided to have the translation revised. The work was entrusted to Bobrovnikov, the Mongolian teacher at Irkutsk, and in 1829 the Archbishop again approached the missionaries, soliciting their help with the revision. Wisely, they declined the invitation:

> Knowing the character and acquirements of the man, knowing also that by this measure we should be in a degree responsible for the work, without the power of controlling it, as our suggestions would be either received or rejected as he thought proper, we respectfully declined, alleging our own engagements for several years in that department, and our having the whole Bible in a state of considerable forwardness.

With equal tact and suavity the Archbishop accepted their refusal, and congratulated them on what they were doing. He even looked forward, so he said, to seeing the whole Bible printed on their press. The missionaries had evaded what might have been planned as a trap, and the Directors wrote approvingly of their skill and prudence:

> We consider your respectfully declining the proposal of the Archbishop of Irkutsk as dictated by prudent caution and the reasons which you assigned for doing so appear to have been satisfactory to him. It is both gratifying and encouraging to find him congratulating you on having accomplished the work of translating the whole Bible, and expressing a desire to see it printed at the mission Press.

What the Archbishop's real sentiments were is a matter for conjecture. More to the point, as far as we are concerned, is the fact that this letter shows the Directors still undeceived as to the true state of affairs in the mission and confidently anticipating the printing of the whole Bible in Mongolian, comprising the Old Testament as translated by Edward and William, and the New Testament as translated by Robert.

Even after the revision had been undertaken, the New Testament still remained sequestrated. Nor did a request for its release, made probably in 1832, by Bludov, produce any effect.

In August 1835 Edward had a meeting with the Committee of the Bible Society in London on the subject of the various Mongolian versions of the Scriptures, and embodied the substance of the discussions in a letter to the Rev. Joseph Jowett, the Editorial Superintendent, which he drew up on the spot, at the Earl Street headquarters of the Bible Society. He reminded the Committee that the Holy Synod still had the whole edition of the New Testament in its hands, and told them that the Metropolitan of Moscow had promised to help him secure it for distribution among the Buryats. Would

Printing the Old Testament

the Committee agree to his buying up the edition, if it could not be got for nothing? The Committee did so agree, and Edward, back in St Petersburg a year later, tried to negotiate the purchase through a Mr von Poll, a friend of Paterson's and one-time Secretary to D.N. Bludov. Von Poll had succeeded in extracting other translations from the clutches of the Synod, and Edward thought the BFBS stood a good chance with the Mongolian New Testament if they made a formal approach to him themselves. They did so, but in January 1837 von Poll had to admit defeat. The Synod would not release the Testaments.

Frustrated in this direction, Jowett looked into the back history of the Mongolian New Testament, and discovered that the Reports of the LMS, in particular the Report for 1827, indicated that Robert had been working on the New Testament during the 1820s, and that the translation had been completed during the course of 1826. Here was an easy solution to the problem. In February 1837 he wrote to William at Selenginsk, where he mistakenly thought he was living, to suggest a composite version of the New Testament. Could not the missionaries combine Schmidt's Gospels and Acts, of which they had copies, with Robert's Epistles and Revelation, and so make up a complete Testament at once? And would it not be a good idea to apply for permission to print it straight away?

William was embarrassed by this suggestion, as he and Edward were determined to have no more truck with Robert. On 1 May he replied to Jowett, saying that he thought it very desirable to follow up the Old Testament with a version of the New. But as he and Edward, with whom he had discussed Jowett's letter, did not have a translation ready to submit for censorship, it would be premature to apply for permission to print. Besides, it might be tactless to raise the subject so soon after their offer to buy the existing New Testament had been rejected. Meanwhile, there was no reason why he and Edward should not get on with the preparatory work. And he added, disingenuously, in view of all that had happened:

> We happen not to have a copy of the Report of our Society for 1827, and are not aware of the statements there published with regard to the translation of the Epistles. But you may be able by communication with Mr Ellis our respected Secretary to receive any explanation or make any arrangements that may be deemed needful.

Meanwhile, on 27 April, William had written to William Ellis, informing him of the delicate turn of events, and dumping the whole matter in his lap:

> I have thought it needful to apprize you of this correspondence, as Mr Jowett's proposal seems to place us in a very awkward and delicate position with respect to Mr Yuille: for as Mr Jowett has applied to myself along with Mr Stallybrass to prepare a version of the N.T. thus virtually excluding Mr Y from any share in the matter, I presume he

may know something of what is thought of his (Mr Y's) competency as a translator. But as Mr Y may now have *his* N.T. in what he may consider a *correct* state, and as he will not, I am persuaded, either allow his brethren in the Mission to touch it, or to have the charge of printing it, even were it approved and censored, it remains for the Society to decide in the case as they may see proper. Were Mr Y considered competent to furnish the version required, it would be a superfluous as well as an invidious task for Mr S or myself to undertake it. But as the case actually stands, what do you advise us to do?

After the painful correspondence that passed between us and Mr Y for 1834-6, I shrink from any further collision with him, and must beg leave respectfully to leave it with you to make any arrangements that may be thought needful about the share Mr S or myself are to have in the Mongolian N.T.

The initiative was now with the Directors. They conferred with Henderson and Jowett, and by November 1837 they were in a position to authorize Edward and William to carry on with their translation of the New Testament, provided that this did not get in the way of their more immediate work. Both men set to work, and William, at least, had finished the rough draft of his share of the translation by 1840. The project was far enough advanced by February of that year for the missionaries to put in a request that the censor be authorized to examine their New Testament as well as the Old, and they were able to accompany their application with a sample copy of St Matthew. The BFBS agreed to finance an edition of 3,000 copies. But, before anything more could be done, the missionaries were ordered to close their mission.

After their return to England, Edward and William discussed the future of the Mongolian New Testament with the Bible Society in the summer of 1841. There seemed to be no prospect of distributing it in the near future, and it was decided to let the matter rest. In October 1842 the two men raised the subject again, feeling age stealing upon them, and fearing that their knowledge of the language was fading away. The Bible Society was by then entertaining hopes that the recently concluded Treaty of Nanking, which ended the First Opium War, might improve their chances of introducing their books into China. Discussions were held with the LMS, and in February 1843 it was agreed that the latter Society should re-employ Edward and William to finish the translation for the BFBS, and that the latter should refund the costs when the translation had been approved. Printing presented a problem, as the mission's types had just been sold in Siberia, and it was decided to adapt the Bible Society's Manchu types. Printing began in early 1845 and was completed in 1846, the resulting text being readable, if rather disturbing in appearance.

The Old Testament was never reissued in full, but the New Testament was reprinted several times. In 1880 it achieved the dignity of appearing in a proper Mongolian type, the same as that used for Schmidt's 1827 version, and his other books, when the BFBS had it reprinted on the press of the Imperial Academy of Sciences at St Petersburg. A few individual books of both the Old and the New Testaments were revised and published early this century, while the 1880 impression of the latter continued to be reproduced by photographic reproduction up to as late as 1939. Today the New Testament has been replaced by a new translation made, after the Second World War, by the Rev. Joel Eriksson and others, and the Stallybrass and Swan version retains only a historical significance. But this does not diminish the achievement of the translators as pioneer scholars who, if they had so chosen, could have secured for themselves an academic reputation equal to that of any of the great Mongolists of the nineteenth century.

17

The External Relations of the Mission

The mission to the Buryats lasted for almost twenty-two years, but in the end it failed in both its main aims. Quite early on, during the 1820s, the missionaries were forced to accept that Russia's interest in good relations with its southern neighbour, China, would preclude the extension of their activities across the frontier into Outer Mongolia. Eastern Siberia thus turned out to be a cul-de-sac, rather than a jumping-off place for the conversion of the Chinese for which it had been intended. In the long term, too, though a few Buryats were converted, the missionaries were unable to baptize them and form them into a church, for reasons of internal Russian politics. Towards the end of the 1830s, discouragement and disillusion began to cloud the missionaries' lives, and though they struggled hard against feelings of defeatism, they themselves came to view withdrawal as the only way out of the impasse. But the effective cause of the termination of the mission in 1840 was not its failure to achieve results, which might have led to a loss of confidence on the part of the Directors, but the victory, at the seat of power in St Petersburg, of that section of the Russian ecclesiastical hierarchy, represented by the successive Archbishops of Irkutsk and elements within the Holy Synod, which had always opposed its continuance.

As an English Evangelical mission working in a Russian Orthodox environment, the mission in Siberia was a political and ecclesiastical anomaly, and so in a chronically precarious position. Moreover, its very constitution was paradoxical. The true aim of any mission must be to make converts to Christianity, and then to confirm them in their new faith by administering the rite of baptism and admitting them into a church. Only within the institutional framework of a church can new converts find the stability and reassurance which they need to strengthen them against hostility from without and doubts from within, and prevent them from lapsing.

The LMS, however, had not obtained permission for its missionaries to baptize their eventual converts when it negotiated the establishment of the mission with the Russian government. This omission was probably not a mere oversight on the part of the Directors. They had taken Sarepta and its charter as a model for their thinking when they first considered planting a colony in Russia. The Sarepta privileges did not include freedom to baptize the heathen, and, until the issue was tested in 1822, there was no reason to anticipate difficulties on that score. The Directors can be forgiven for thinking, several years before the Moravians were brought up so sharply, that what was apparently adequate for Sarepta would be good enough for them. Besides, their advisers on Russian affairs, Paterson and Pinkerton, had misled them. They had advocated a gradualist, not to say opportunist, approach to the establishment of a Siberian mission. They seem to have trusted that something would turn up when the time came. In their eyes, a door was ajar in Russia, and the main thing was to get a foot in it at once, in the hope that, once an entrance had been effected, on whatever initial terms, all the rest would follow. That was how they had advised the Directors in their memorandum of 7 November 1814:

> All that you will require from the Russian government at first will be, liberty for the missionaries to go to Irkutsk to endeavour to learn the languages of the heathen tribes, to promote the translation of the Scriptures into their languages and to instruct them in the principles of the Christian religion. . . . You will need no other privileges until such time as your missionaries may see it proper to form a settlement, when, judging according to the present spirit of the Russian Government, you can rest confident of obtaining any privilege for your missionaries which you can reasonably demand.

With hindsight, this can be seen to have been far too sanguine an appraisal of the situation. There was no reason why the favourable stance of the Russian government should be maintained, dependent as it was on nothing more than the personal will of the Autocrat, as modified by cliquish pressures. Alexander's extreme religious tendencies, his fad for such fancies as Quakerism and Evangelicalism, offended the Orthodox establishment. They were an aberration, doomed to reversal sooner or later. Besides, there was, in the background, the impediment of Russian legislation, formulated in the previous century. When the question of baptizing the Kalmucks arose, recourse was had to a law of 1724, which apparently reserved the conversion of the heathen to the Holy Synod, and to a law of 1746 which expressly stated that converted heathens or Muslims could only be baptized into the Orthodox church. Failure to secure agreement on matters of detail at the outset exposed the missionaries to harassment in later years over such relatively minor matters as their freedom to move house and acquire fresh property, let alone their right to baptize the Buryats. But whether the mission would have been accepted at all if the Directors had insisted on settling every detail in advance is of course another matter.

If the missionaries were to be able to fulfil their true purpose and baptize their converts, they would either have to seek exceptional privileges, or else act illicitly. Both courses of action were contemplated at different times, and the former was actually adopted. In 1834 Edward petitioned to be allowed to baptize some Buryat lads, but his request was refused. The rejection of their petition underlined the false position which the missionaries had occupied all along. Like it or not, they were condemned to do nothing more than preparatory work from which others, that is, the Orthodox church, would profit, and their realization that this was so finally induced a mood of near desperation. Watching their converts lapse for want of the spiritual support which church membership would afford, they considered administering the rite of baptism illicitly. They asked the Directors time and time again for guidance as to whether they should take this step. The Directors, perhaps understandably, stalled until it was too late. By the time they did send an answer, ambiguous though it was, the order for the closure of the mission had been issued and received.

What sustained the missionaries' self-confidence for more than twenty years, in the face of what must have been a growing conviction that they were heading down a blind alley? The general answer must be that, as true missionaries, they expected and welcomed confrontation, and trusted in divine help to see them through. They did not believe in the possibility of failure. This conviction is voiced over and over again in their letters. Success itself they rejected as a criterion by which the viability of a mission should be assessed. William devoted a whole chapter of his *Letters on Missions* to the development of that proposition, showing that, as ultimate success was assured through God's promises, intermediate signs of success should not be considered as an encouragement to continue, nor should their absence count as an excuse for giving up.

This was all very well as a general theoretical justification for persisting in a mission in the face of disappointment, and as an expression of the nature of personal dedication and obedience to the Divine Will in the face of setbacks. But it ignored practical considerations. The LMS never had enough men or enough money to occupy every field, and unproductive missions were bound to come under scrutiny as wasteful luxuries. In 1831 William had to defend the Siberian mission against arguments put forward by a Mr X for closing it down. The anonymous opponent asked what was the justification for continuing to lavish men and money on a field which had shown itself to be barren, while so many other promising fields were lying fallow for want of resources. He attributed Siberian sterility to the malign influence of the Orthodox church upon the minds of the local people, Christian and heathen alike:

> The way in which the Greek religion operates as hindering the heathen Buriats from receiving the gospel through the instrumentality of the Missionaries, is, that it awakens the suspicions of these poor idolaters, that their Rulers would not permit them to embrace our form of

The External Relations of the Mission

Christianity; and it excites the jealousy of so-called Christians lest the heathen should embrace it. This prompts many of the adherents of the established church there to thwart our endeavours and weaken our hands – for they would prefer that the Buriats should remain heathens to their becoming Christians of a profession different from their own.

This was a shrewd analysis of the situation, and one which the missionaries might easily have made for themselves. It was as an argument for terminating the mission that William refuted it. The example of the Kalmucks convinced him that it was possible to make converts under precisely the conditions mentioned. Secondly, the fear of the consequences of conversion might deter some Buryats, but it would prove no more serious an impediment than the prospect of losing caste did among the Hindus. Thirdly, in spite of all the real and imaginary difficulties, the missionaries did manage to talk to the Buryats every day, to expose the 'follies and lies' of their own religion to them, and to distribute copies of the Scriptures. Fourthly, the presence of the missionaries enabled the Buryats to appreciate what real Christianity was, in contrast to the 'corrupted form' of it presented by the Orthodox church, which would otherwise be their only source of evidence. Fifthly, the mission provided what he called a 'disturbing force', which could be inserted in the 'machinery of their superstition' so as to clog its movements, diminish its power, and in time, perhaps, effect its complete destruction. Preaching an alternative religion would excite a mood of scepticism among the Buryats, and, once this was done, all that was needed was the 'descent of the divine influence'. Lastly, no one could be really sure what the true situation was, how much latent success had already been achieved. There might well be embryo converts, as he called them, hidden among the people and only waiting for the right moment to emerge. It would be a tragedy if this consummation of so many years' work were to be frustrated by last minute timidity on the part of the Society.

For many years the mission in Siberia enjoyed an exceptionally charmed existence, for which it is hard to account, but which in a way justified William's persistence. The fiasco over the baptism of the Kalmuck converts at Sarepta in 1822 and 1823 did not affect it at all, nor, in spite of gloomy prognostications, did the crisis of 1824. In November of that year Edward wrote to Alers Hankey lamenting that the general turn of events looked like resulting in the exclusion of all but the clergy of the Orthodox church from any work connected with the Bible, and in December the missionaries, in a joint letter, anticipated that the outcome of the changes which had taken place in the management of the RBS, that is, the elimination of Golitsyn and Popov, would be that Bible distribution work would either be severely restricted or totally forbidden. 'There is every reason to conclude,' they wrote, 'that Foreign Missionaries will not be allowed much longer to have any share in it. . . . Affairs at present wear a gloomy aspect, but our faith we trust is not shaken.'

Their confidence was justified. As early as February 1825 Edward could write, from Ona, to say that their work had not been interrupted in any way, and that they could even travel about from place to place as before. They may have owed this immunity to the personal intervention of Princess Meshcherskaya with the Emperor some time in mid-1824, but it seems more likely that they were simply profiting from a general disinclination on the part of Government to interfere unnecessarily with any foreign missions. Though the atmosphere in the capital was unfavourable to Evangelicalism for several years after 1824, the mission pursued its way unhindered except by petty harassments, and by 1831 William judged it not only expedient, but also safe, to negotiate a restatement and an extension of its privileges.

Other Protestant missions did not share the same good fortune in those years. The Scottish mission, founded at Karass early in the century, and the Basel mission, which began its work at Astrakhan in 1822 and soon afterwards extended it to Shusha, were both compelled to curtail or cease their operations in 1835. Both enjoyed the exceptional privilege of being allowed to baptize their converts, subject, it seems, to certain rather stringent limitations. In 1822 a case did arise at Karass. The Scots thought it incumbent upon them to put in a request for specific permission to baptize the individual concerned, and this was granted by Prince Golitsyn. Knill rather disapproved of them for drawing attention to what he considered a grey area by making the application. 'Paul never made any', he wrote. 'When I was at Madras we made *one* application, and it was denied – with an intimation to go on and say nothing. I am fully of the opinion that this is the way. When we ask for this and that and the other thing we as it were bind down persons who will not be bound.' But no doubt the Scots were acting as they thought their charter obliged them to. The Basel missionaries, too, did not enjoy unfettered discretion. They were required to inform the religious authorities before administering the rite of baptism, and the latter had to submit the request through the competent ministry for final decision by the Emperor.

Their comparatively privileged position did not confer any special immunity upon these two missions. In 1835 both were brought to book, though for different reasons, in a single decree issued by the Ministry of the Interior. The Scots were criticized for not having made effective use of their privileges, having succeeded in converting no more than nine persons in the course of thirty-two years. This miserable record proved to the satisfaction of the Russian authorities that they did not need a privilege which was so under-exercised, and accordingly it was withdrawn. The Basel missionaries, on the other hand, had been too zealous, in the wrong direction. There were some 500 Armenian Christian families near their station at Shusha, with five churches and twelve priests, and one aim of the missionaries had been to breathe new life into what they saw as a stagnant Christian community, or, as they put it themselves, to lead the Orient by means of the Occident to the Kingdom of God and the acknowledgment of his salvation.

The Basel missionaries began their work by opening a school at Shusha in January 1825 which they intended should become a model for other schools. By 1829 they had also opened a small teacher training college, and had begun to print in both Arabic and Armenian. Unwisely, as it turned out, they concentrated on the Armenian side of their operations. Their list of publications show that by 1832 they had printed eight books in Armenian, including a grammar, excerpts from the Bible, and some tracts, as against a single pamphlet of fourteen pages in Arabic. Fourteen more tracts, translated from English and German originals, were issued in 1833. They had not made a single convert from Islam, and their activities were beginning to upset the Armenian clergy. The Russian government objected to what they saw as interference with a Russian church, and ordered the Swiss to halt their missionary work, and to cease teaching Armenian boys in their schools. By contrast, the missionaries in Siberia, who by 1835 had made, at most, only four converts, and who had been the subject of complaints from two Archbishops of Irkutsk, not only escaped censure, but had their conditions of residence confirmed once more in that year. The Governor General of Siberia, S.B. Bronevskii, was instructed that they might remain and carry on working, as long as any converts they made were baptized into the Orthodox church.

William's arguments for continuing the mission are supplemented in another paper, dated 1832, in the same group as the one in which he refuted his anonymous opponent. In it, he analysed the religious situation in Buryatia for the benefit of the Directors. He was fully conversant with the laws which reserved the right to baptize converts to the dominant church, and he admitted that this legislation caused political and religious difficulties additional to those normally encountered in a mission field. But he still thought it worth while keeping the mission in existence, though he anticipated that sooner or later a collision with the Russian authorities was likely to occur, and that this might lead to the suppression of the mission.

Partly because of the very progress the missionaries were making, he said, the Russian ecclesiastical authorities were beginning to launch their own missions. The Mongolian language was being taught at the seminary at Irkutsk to priests who would be sent to Transbaikalia. As a matter of fact, a couple of years later, in 1834, three Russian missionary priests were sent, one each to Selenginsk, Khodon and Ona respectively, of all places, obviously to shadow the English missionaries. Part of the Russian liturgy had already been translated into Mongolian. The new Archbishop of Irkutsk, Irene, who had succeeded Mikhail in 1830, was a vigorous promoter of missionary work among the Buryats, and, William concluded:

The External Relations of the Mission

> It is not impossible, therefore, that in the course of time, there may be a clashing of interests and operations between our Mission and the Russians. . . . If the question be put what success we may expect on the supposition that the Siberian Mission is to be continued? I answer – I cannot tell – I cannot be responsible for the consequences of our attempts – It may be proper to say however that it is not impossible that our labours may, in the course of time, be restricted or suppressed. The Russian authorities may ere long find out what indeed some of them are already aware of, that our labours have no tendency to predispose the Buryats, upon their being convinced of the truth of Christianity, to embrace the Russian form of it.

Even after their petition to baptize their converts had been rejected in 1835, William remained optimistic about the future of the mission, and argued for its continuance. 'Some', he wrote, 'may regard this as a signal directing them to recall their Missionaries, and others may be disposed to wait for the breaking of the clouds. I believe another appeal to the highest authority will yet be made, but supposing even that to be unsuccessful, it becomes us to consider well what course ought to be followed.' He restated the arguments he had used before, and in addition he was able to point to the significance of the new phase the mission had entered upon with the beginning of the printing of the Old Testament. Either the mission should be closed down at once, or the decision should be taken to continue it as long as possible. The worst course would be to hang on until the printing was completed, and then withdraw the missionaries, leaving the printed Testaments in the hands of the Orthodox clergy, who would, without a doubt, do nothing constructive with them. The time had come to rethink the purpose of the mission, but William himself was in no doubt that they ought to carry on their work as vigorously as possible, reinforcing the message where they had already preached it, and carrying it to some of the thousands of Buryats who had never yet set eyes on them.

Perhaps the main factor in the charmed life of the mission was the fact that, at the beginning, it had enjoyed the explicit protection of the Emperor Alexander, and that the effect of this patronage outlasted Alexander's life. Certainly, the missionaries relied on this manifestation of imperial favour to see them through difficult times. Thus in 1824, when reaction against all that the RBS stood for was in full swing at the capital, they wrote as follows to George Burder:

> Our views and intentions in coming to this country were explicitly stated to the Russian government and fully recognized by them – and therefore without assigning a sufficient cause we cannot be dispossessed of this field of labour, and the mere exercise of the rights and privileges granted to us to teach and preach to the people the gospel and disseminate among them the word of God, cannot be considered a

reason for removing us. Yet we have too good ground to conclude that there is every disposition in certain quarters to effect our removal, because we are labouring to bring the Buriats to the knowledge of Christ. As this cannot however be ostensibly held up as the ground of any proceedings against us, other means must be resorted to. What these may be we are not careful to enquire, humbly trusting that we shall be upheld in our integrity.

This is a clear hint of a pattern of intrigue and covert plotting against the mission, and the mission correspondence does in fact disclose to us something of how the conspiracies anticipated in 1824 developed during the following years.

Fortunately, for many years the missionaries enjoyed the active friendship of a small number of powerful men, and the disinterested regard of others. Until almost the end of Alexander's reign, that is, until the opportunist alliance of the fanatical Archimandrite Fotii and the unscrupulous Arakcheev brought about a reaction in Russian politics which led, amongst other things, to the eclipse of Prince Golitsyn, the position of the mission, favoured as it was by men like Golitsyn himself, Popov and Speranskii, must have seemed impregnable. Until 1817, Golitsyn was Ober-prokuror of the Holy Synod, the Emperor's personal representative in the governing body of the Orthodox church. In that year he moved to a yet more influential position, as Minister of Ecclesiastical Affairs and Public Instruction. Even after his fall from office he remained worth cultivating, and he was among the first of the public figures whom William consulted in 1831, when he was negotiating the confirmation of the mission's privileges.

Popov was a more ambiguous figure, and though William consulted him too, he seems to have been something of a broken reed. Knill admired him as 'one of the most holy and devoted men in the world', not surprisingly, for Knill, a tearful, sentimental zealot himself, adored any exaggerated expression of godly sensibility. That was why Cornelius Rahmn appealed so deeply to him. Cornelius wore his 'bleeding heart and weeping eyes' on his sleeve, and Knill loved him as 'an eminent pattern of piety and zeal – full of love and compassion to perishing souls – and full of good will to all men'. He loved his letters, too, for the 'exalted piety' which they breathed, and for the unction which they exuded, an unction 'worth going to China for, if China would afford it.'

Popov stood equally high in his esteem, but there was something queer about Popov which perhaps Knill and his circle never guessed at, or which they chose to overlook. He was a ghastly fanatic, a leading member of the curious group of mystics led by the zealot Ekaterina Filippovna Tatarinova. Tatarinova's group attracted official displeasure as early as 1822, while Popov was still in office in the RBS, and she was expelled from the castle where she directed it. Nothing daunted, she bought alternative accommodation, and revived her group. It seems to have been harmless enough in itself, though it provoked scandalous gossip, and for some years Government tolerated its existence. Popov not only belonged to it himself, but tried to force his daughters to do the same, and when his middle daughter showed some reluctance, he subjected her to regular weekly beatings, and kept her a close prisoner. In 1835 the police were obliged to intervene. The circle was broken up, and the leading members were confined to various monasteries. Popov himself was sent to a monastery in the government of Kazan, where he died in 1842.

As long as he remained Governor General of Siberia, Mikhail Speranskii patronized the missionaries. He showed his favour publicly, by calling on them, and he lent them money when they needed it. Speranskii's sympathies may have been aroused partly by his personal connection with England. He had enjoyed a happy, though sadly brief, marriage with Miss Elizabeth Stephens, a relative of Joseph Planta, one-time librarian of the British Museum. But he was also a statesman, a man who took the long view, and his patronage of the mission was founded upon more than personal inclination. Entrusted as he was with the reform of the administration of Siberia, he could appreciate that the Buryats could only benefit from the disinterested civilizing work being done at Selenginsk, and so he did his best to further the aims of the mission.

Another such statesmanlike patron was Baron Paul Schilling von Canstadt. Schilling was of Baltic German extraction, and was a man of the widest interests – army officer, administrator, physicist and collector of Orientalia. Born at Reval in 1786 he gained diplomatic experience abroad as a very young man in the Russian embassy at Munich, before taking part in the campaigns of 1812–14 in the Russian army. After the conclusion of peace, he found employment in the Russian civil administration, and it was during the course of a scientific expedition in eastern Siberia in the years 1830–2, mounted by the Asiatic Department of the Ministry of Foreign Affairs, that he made the acquaintance of the missionaries, and came to appreciate what they were doing. He was able to restore public confidence in them on the spot, when it had been rather shaken by local intrigues, and he promoted the work of both the LMS and the BFBS at the capital after his return. In William's words: 'He has uniformly shown the greatest attention and friendliness to the Missionaries, and the Mission owes much to his influence with the people in restoring their confidence in the Missionaries, which had been shaken by the secret acts of some designing men – abetted by the priests and seconded by certain members of the government.' It was Schilling who helped William gain access to the Manchu Old Testament which belonged to the Holy Synod, when the owner of the copy which had first attracted his attention demanded such an outrageous price, and it was through his benevolent interest that George Borrow was able to make such rapid progress in getting permission to print the Manchu New Testament, buy the paper, and get the copies bound up. Schilling richly deserved the gift of a couple of books which the Directors of the LMS sent him in 1832 in recognition of his good offices.

At least until the mid-1830s, the highest authorities in eastern Siberia itself were more or less well disposed towards the work of the mission. Speranskii's immediate successor as Governor General, Alexander Stepanovich Lavinskii, who held office until 1833, had some reservations about them at first, wondering if they were not spying on Russian trade through Kyakhta, under cover of their evangelistic work. But he soon became convinced of their sincerity, and recognized that he was the victim of rumours put about by the merchants of Kyakhta themselves. Hansteen, who came to know Lavinskii well, gives us a sympathetic portrait of him. In 1829 he was a man of around fifty, capable, broadminded, and renowned for his integrity. He had not enjoyed a particularly academic education, but common sense, strict attention to routine, and the possession of a conscientious executive secretary, enabled him to perform his duties in a creditable manner. He sang well, appreciated the fine arts, and spoke French like a native. The one thing Hansteen regretted was that Lavinskii was an epicure, who kept an excellent table, which he liked to share with his friends. Not only did Hansteen find that he had to eat and drink more than was good for him, but as Lavinskii dined at midday, his invitations invariably clashed with the Norwegian scientist's observations.

The long-serving Governor of Irkutsk, Ivan Bogdanovich Tseidler, who held office from 1821 to 1835, seems also, to judge from the sparse references to him in the missionaries' correspondence, to have been no enemy of theirs. It was only later Governors and Governors General who began to look askance at their presence in Transbaikalia.

Right from the start, though, the missionaries had enemies on the spot, ever ready to plot against them, but unable to achieve much as long as they had powerful friends. The general pattern of events was, as far as we can tell, one of local intrigue, in which the ecclesiastical authorities connived with minor officials, those below the level of Governor, while it was at St Petersburg that the accusations brought against the mission could be refuted, either by the missionaries themselves, or through their well-wishers.

It goes without saying that the Khamba, however bland he seemed on the surface, was an enemy. But he was scared to do anything off his own bat, in case he stepped out of line with the Russian authorities. Given a lead, though, he was ready enough to act as their catspaw. There were enemies, too, in the administration, and amongst the ordinary Russians. The only one we can identify is the District Captain at Verkhneudinsk. We do not know his name, but he may have been that Shaposhnikov whom the Governor General Rupert incited in 1838 to report unfavourably on the activities of the missionaries, but who disconcertingly gave them a clean bill of health. No others can be identified by office or by name, but it seems that the post-master at Verkhneudinsk, Bocharov, was not amongst their number.

Rumours of all sorts circulated about the nefarious undercover activities the missionaries were supposed to be engaged in. They were even suspected of stooping to espionage. C.H. Cottrell reported that it was believed at one time that the British government, cherishing designs on Tibet, had sent them to Selenginsk to learn Tibetan, in preparation for serving as political agents in Tibet. They would somehow win over the Dalai Lama, and then all the Kalmucks, Mongols, and other Buddhists of Inner Asia, to the detriment of Russia's continental interests.

Whatever the anxieties of the local officials and traders may have been, they did not spring from concern with the doctrines which the missionaries preached, even though, in the end, these proved to be the Achilles heel which invited attack. If the missionaries can be believed, and surely they can, their motives were baser. Once a Buryat had become a Christian, of whatever persuasion, it was much more difficult to exploit him like the wild animal he was deemed to be as a heathen. So all conversions were unwelcome, because they narrowed the scope for profiteering. This may look like an obsessive denigration of the local Russian mentality, but it was what Edward assured the Directors of in 1830, basing himself, so it seems, on inside information given him by Hedenström many years before:

> I dare say Mr Rahmn will remember the impression produced upon his mind the first time he and I visited the Ispravnik in Verkhneudinsk in 1818, viz that these people have no wish to see the Boriats converted. By this craft, i.e. by imposing on them, they have their wealth. So long as the Boriats are wild beasts, these hunters have a right, or think they have, to take them as they can. But if they were brought within the pale of the church they would sustain a different relation towards them – they would be more like cattle – private property. They are not much in fear from the zeal of their own clergy.

There was an additional reason why the local Russians were suspicious of the missionaries. They were known to correspond directly with the capital, and might tell tales. Edward went on:

> Their extortions must be in some degree known to us, and though we have never in a single instance in any way interfered – much as our feelings would sometimes have disposed us – yet they cannot be without apprehension that we make reports of their actions. Thus we are the innocent occasions of trouble and unpleasantness to them. We are also sometimes preventives to the accomplishment of their wishes.

Those concerned would have had reason to be apprehensive if the missionaries had not behaved with such scrupulous correctness, for officials at the capital did try on occasion to force their confidence. When William was there in 1831, one of those he called on was a certain Mr Rodofincken, a counsellor of state, who asked him directly whether he could tell him anything about maladministration in Siberia. Wisely, William refused to be drawn, and answered only 'in general that His Excellency might be aware that in the nature of things abuses would creep in, and many affairs required the vigilant inspection of the higher members of government'. He took the opportunity of mentioning Schilling by name, saying that 'such men of independent character, and above the temptation to connive at evils committed by inferior officers, were those who should be employed to investigate and correct abuses'.

The invitation to criticize Schmidt's New Testament and then to assist in its revision may or may not have been a trap, but the first real opportunity to harass the missionaries came in 1829, after the house which Edward was buying at Khodon had been burned down. We have seen earlier how Edward committed himself to paying the agreed price, even though the house no longer existed, and how, once he had done so, the local authorities at Verkhneudinsk began to dispute the missionaries' legal right to live anywhere but at Selenginsk. Characteristically for Siberian trickery, it was the same individual, the District Captain, who, having first encouraged Edward in his plan to move to Khodon, was now trying to immobilize him and so cheat the mission out of the cost of the house. Edward saw through his chicanery, and reported it home in May 1830:

> That movement, contrary to our expectations, seems to have given umbrage to some of the people in authority in Verchneudinsk, the head town in this circuit. In order that this might *not* be the case, we took no step in purchasing the house of the late Taisha, until we had consulted with the Captain of this district. He could say nothing against it; but rather forwarded our views; nevertheless, that very person, in an underhand way has, we have every reason to believe, been the cause of all the trouble we have experienced. The house was put up for sale by auction, and decided in our favor by the authorities in Irkutsk more than a year after we had bid for it. In the mean time the house had been destroyed by fire, notwithstanding which the money was paid for it. But no sooner had this been done, than we were questioned as to our right to remove thither; and obstacles were thrown in the way of building another house, although I had been told that no obstacle existed and was advised to purchase materials, by the very person who now questioned us.

The matter was then passed to the Governor of Irkutsk, Tseidler, who asked the missionaries to explain their move, telling them that he had no authority to sanction it, but that he would submit the case to higher authority if they wished. They made a spirited defence, answering that such a move was superfluous, since they already had permission from the highest authority

The External Relations of the Mission

of all, the late Emperor Alexander, to reside, not just at Selenginsk, but anywhere amongst the Buryats. Tseidler submitted the case to Lavinskii for decision, and meanwhile allowed the missionaries to go on building their new house. In December 1829 Lavinskii gave his approval to their move to Khodon, though with the provision that they were not to acquire any landed property in future without the express approval of the local authorities.

This was still not the end of the matter. William took it up again with Bludov at the end of 1832, explaining how necessary it was for the missionaries to be able to follow the Buryats about, not only because of their normal migrations, but for another reason too. By the end of the 1820s an increasing number of exiles were reaching Siberia every year, and complicating the pattern of nomadic life. They were located in villages, or concentrated at various sites to be employed in public works, and the Buryats were anxious to put as great a distance as possible between themselves and the unwelcome newcomers. William asked, therefore, for express instructions to be given to the authorities in Siberia to allow the missionaries to settle where they saw fit, and to build, rent or buy houses at new stations as it might prove expedient. Bludov replied that he would have to consult the Governor General before giving a reply. Lavinskii raised no objection, and in February 1833 permission to occupy stations other than Selenginsk was finally granted, at ministerial level.

The next unsettling thing to happen was that William was warned by a certain Buryat official that he had been put under pressure, presumably by the same District Captain, to sign a complaint, in which the missionaries were accused of disseminating doctrines which were different, not only from the Buryat faith, but from the Russian as well, and asking that they be expelled. He had resisted the pressure, but this sinister development prompted the missionaries to write to Speranskii in St Petersburg, asking him to use his pull with the highest authorities to elicit some clear hint from them of their attitude towards the mission, so that they could get on with their work in peace. Speranskii made a personal approach to Lavinskii, who promised to do all he could to protect the missionaries, and this cloud, too, passed over.

This took place in St Petersburg in May 1830. Meanwhile, and apparently in connection with these events, things in Siberia were verging on melodrama. On 1 February of that year, Edward received an anonymous letter. The sender informed him that 'a certain personage in Irkutsk who wishes you well' had sent a warning that the missionaries could expect to be deported at any moment: a courier might be on the way to them already. In true conspiratorial style, Edward was instructed to return the note to the bearer, or to tear it up before his very eyes. At first he could not decide what was going on, whether the letter really did come from a friend, or whether it was a provocation. But in the end, it turned out that there was no well-wisher in Irkutsk at all. The letter had been originated by the sender, a friend in Verkhneudinsk, who was passing on a warning of his own, under an assumed identity. When he met the friend, Edward discovered the background to the hasty warning.

It was just about this time that the gendarmerie Colonel Maslov, Robert's bête-noire, was making his tour of inspection in Siberia, in obedience to direct orders received from the Emperor. Maslov seems to have inspired terror wherever he went. Hansteen, who was not subject to his authority, came across him in Irkutsk and elsewhere, and described him as having been sent by the Emperor to inspect 'the records of all lower and higher officials, right up to the Governor General, in the capacity of an Inquisitor or General-Fiscal over all Siberia. – a man at whose name the knees of all officials trembled'.

Maslov had passed through Buryatia some time in 1829, and had summoned Edward and William to a meeting at a post-station near Ona. William did not get the message in time, but Edward turned up, and the interview passed off satisfactorily. Maslov spoke approvingly of what the missionaries were doing, especially of their schools, and went so far as to hint that he thought the authorities would probably help them to recruit more pupils. With this little pat on the back he pursued his way eastwards, promising to call again on his return journey. When he did, the atmosphere had changed.

William met Maslov at the Khodon post-station early in 1830, and noticed a distinct chill in his attitude. Robert, too, felt the Colonel's displeasure. Warned to expect a call, he sat up till late at night with lamps burning, but the Colonel passed by his house – at a distance of forty-two feet, to be exact – without deigning to call on him, evidently expecting Robert to run after him. What had happened was that the Khamba had denounced them, accusing them of trying to subvert the Orthodox church, and in particular of teaching the Buryats that Russian icon-veneration was no better than their own idolatry. The Khamba's complaint stuck, apparently, because it had been accompanied by a suitably large bribe.

Edward did not believe that the Khamba would have had the temerity to take this step if he had not been put up to it by Russians in authority. No doubt the District Captain was up to his tricks again. There were other strange rumours flying about, too. In the same month of February, Robert was visited by two monks of the Orthodox church, one of whom had come all the way from Irkutsk. First of all, they spoke encouragingly to him. They had seen the Archbishop quite recently, and knew the difficulties the missionaries were experiencing, but they assured Robert that there was nothing to worry about. When they called a second time, it was obvious that they were after something. They questioned him closely about his beliefs – whether he and his colleagues had a creed, and if so, whether it was the same as the Roman Catholic one; whether they believed that the Holy Spirit proceeded from the Father or the Son; what fast and feast days they observed, and so on. On this occasion they had some clergy from Selenginsk, and a 'hermit monk from a place about 200 versts S.E. from this place' with them, and Robert learned that they had been nosing around amongst the people of Selenginsk as well. He conjectured that they were trying to discover some connection between the mission and the Roman Catholic church, and said he was not at all surprised that an evil rumour to that effect should circulate, for 'faithfulness has always created enemies, but the good people of Selenginsk know us, and it is at them that inquiry should be made for our character!'

Once the accusation had been made against the missionaries, and its progress assured by greasing the Colonel's palm, it took its natural course. It reached the Synod, and the Synod wrote back to the Archbishop, instructing him to look into the matter, and reprimanding him for not keeping better control over his diocese. But this time, too, the trouble petered out. In February 1830, Edward happened to be in Selenginsk at the same time as Tseidler was there. The Governor proved affable, even offering to try to persuade the Khori Buryats to send some of their children to the mission schools – a promise he apparently kept – and offering also to act as intermediary if the missionaries decided to apply for permission to put their printing-press into operation. In November, Edward could report that all was quiet again in Siberia, thanks, he thought, to Speranskii. But the calm was not to last for long.

In May 1831, William was in St Petersburg, negotiating the renewal of the mission's privileges with Bludov. This step should not have been necessary, as he and his colleagues enjoyed the categorical approval of the late Emperor Alexander, to which no term had been set. But times had changed. A new ruler was on the throne, and in Siberia the missionaries sensed that some of those in authority took the view that the changes in the capital had somehow impaired the status of the mission. It was time to reassert themselves.

William's strategy in these negotiations was to present the mission as a civilizing influence, hindered in its benevolent work by no more than misunderstanding on the part of the lamas, and perhaps of a handful of Russians, but, on the whole, co-operating harmoniously with everyone of importance in Siberia. Then, without making any direct accusations, without pointing a finger at any individual, he went on to imply that the mission was somehow under attack, and needed a restatement of imperial favour. If his presentation of his case did not altogether correspond with reality, it was, nevertheless, difficult to refute.

The Buryats, he said, were chiefly to blame, though it was not altogether their fault. By nature they were timid and jealous, and hence terrified of doing anything which might offend their superiors, and, above all, the Russian administration. Knowing this,

The External Relations of the Mission

some of their own Lamas, and perhaps Russians also of those parts, have taken advantage of their fears of giving offence, and represented that their attending to our instructions or receiving the Holy Scriptures from our hands was displeasing to the government, and might bring them into trouble. In consequence of this, the young people who were receiving Christian instruction, and useful education under our care were called away by their parents, and others were afraid to come. Meanwhile the Lamas were making converts from Shamanism and rivetting the chains of idolatry faster upon the minds of their poor countrymen.

William was careful not to identify these Russians, at the same time excluding from suspicion all those in high positions:

We have lived these twelve years in the most perfect confidence and good understanding with their Excellencies the Governors and other inferior officers of the government of every description and have received from many of them marks of peculiar respect and confidence. The late Archbishop of Irkutsk frequently wrote to us in the most friendly manner, and the present Archbishop was pleased to express his good opinion and good wishes when I had the honour to see his Grace in Irkutsk in January last.

And yet it is possible that some individuals occupying offices of trust, either from not properly understanding or enquiring into the real object of our Mission – the evangelization of the heathen people, or suspecting that this our professed object was but the cover of some other design gave ear to suspicions and prejudices, and might speak so as to cause such prejudices to spread among an ignorant people credulous of evil reports. Had we not been living at a place so remote from the seat of government, we might easily have brought proof that we were fully sanctioned and authorized by his Imp. Majesty in 1817 and 1818 and afterwards confirmed by his granting us a portion of land to belong to the Mission, with peculiar privileges and exemption from taxes and all public burdens, as may be seen from the printed Reports sent along with this letter. It was supposed and said that subsequent changes of public affairs had affected our rights, and that we were now without protection and sanction. I therefore thought it my duty on arriving in St Petersburg to bring this matter forward in the full confidence that His Imp. Majesty upon ordering proper investigation of facts to be made, and finding our Mission to be such as has now been represented would be graciously pleased to express his favor towards us, and our object, in the enlightening and christianizing of an important class of his Majesty's heathen subjects.

All we ask is to be allowed peaceably to perform our Sacred duties, and to be recognized and approved as our Character and objects shall seem to deserve in the eyes of an enlightened Christian Government.

William obviously hoped to provoke a full investigation of the mission's activities at the highest level, as a result of which its privileges would be openly confirmed, and the slate wiped clean. That done, it should prove awkward for its enemies to bring up the old slanders yet once more.

Before recommending that the Emperor should approve the continuation of the mission, Bludov made enquiries from the Ministry of the Interior as to whether there was anything discreditable to the missionaries on their files. Being informed that there was nothing, he applied for, and obtained, the Emperor's approval, and informed William of it in the following letter:

> Dear Sir,
>
> His Imperial Majesty upon my most humble report has, in condescension to your petition, willed that the Mission of the London Missionary Society in Selenginsk, continue its labours for the conversion of the Buriats to the Christian faith; and, besides this, His Majesty is pleased to permit the arrival of new Missionaries from England for this purpose, with this understanding however that they exceed not the bounds of operation and right granted them by the Emperor Alexander 1st of blessed Memory.
>
> Communicating to you this His Majesty's will I have the honour to be with perfect respect, Dear Sir, Your most humble Servant,
>
> D. Bludof.
> No 1137
> 30th May 1831.

This should have proved a lasting settlement, but it did not.

Two years later, when William was once again in St Petersburg, Bludov found himself in the embarrassing position of having to allow the old attacks upon the integrity of the mission to be reopened. The Ober-prokuror of the Synod had got hold of what purported to be a statement made some years earlier by the late Archbishop Mikhail, which was damningly critical of the missionaries. Bludov was obliged to send them a formal reprimand:

> The chief procurator of the Holy Synod, in fulfilment of a commission given to him, has communicated to me that the deceased archbishop of Irkutsk Michael, when making a representation to the Holy Synod respecting the augmentation of the number of Greco-Russian priests, appointed to propagate the word of God among the Buriats, found that the English Missionaries residing at Selenginsk, introduce among the Buriats the opinion that the Russian picture-veneration is the same as the worship of idols.
>
> Directing your attention to this, I reckon it at the same time necessary to state, for the purpose of your informing your companions in Selenginsk,

that unless they refrain from all discourses that may spread false meanings, not conformable with obligations placed on them by the very generous toleration of our government, they will expose themselves to be answerable according to the full severity of the laws.

This was a serious charge, contrived by the mission's most consistent opponent, the then Archbishop of Irkutsk. If it could be proved that the missionaries had defamed the dominant church, it would have been an easy matter to discredit them and engineer their expulsion. William prepared a most competent defence, and presented it to Bludov in the form of a long and closely reasoned justification of all their activities. He began by querying the good faith of the accusation. If it was true that the late Archbishop Mikhail had complained about them, why had it taken so long for the complaint to come to light? Why had nothing been heard of it while he was still alive, and could speak of it personally? Why had his successor Irene received him, William, in such a friendly manner when he called on him in Irkutsk? What about all the approving letters they had received from Mikhail during his lifetime? Bludov must surely remember, too, how in 1831 William had informed him that

> certain persons, hostile to our efforts to enlighten the heathen Buriats, had endeavoured to persuade some of the leading people among them to prefer a false accusation against us; but they did not succeed. I had the honour, upon my arrival from Siberia two years ago, to confer with your Excellency, and also to present a written statement of our proceedings; and I then adverted to these facts. But when your Excellency, in consequence of my Memorial, made enquiry at the different offices and departments connected with Siberia, to ascertain whether any complaints had been lodged against us, there was found none.

Indirectly, William implied that the whole thing was an impudent fraud.

Nevertheless, he agreed, it was natural that such charges should be brought against them, however ill-founded they were, and it was necessary to refute them. Adopting a more conciliatory tone, he suggested that the ignorance of the Buryats was at the bottom of it all. Such unsophisticated people could easily confuse the two types of religious practice in their own minds, and then transfer this confusion to the missionaries. The lamas, being jealous of the missionaries and anxious to see the back of them, would eagerly exploit any opportunity of discrediting them with influential members of the Orthodox church. The latter would surely have brought them to book long ago if the charges had any substance, but nothing of the sort had happened.

In any case, William continued, turning to the content of the complaint, it would not have been in the missionaries' interest to libel the Orthodox church so grossly. They would have been inviting retaliation, and they were not so stupid as deliberately to put their mission at risk. Secondly, to have taught what they were charged with having taught would have exposed them as ignoramuses, for who in their right mind could suppose that they did not know the difference between a Christian icon and a lamaist tangka? Could it be supposed that they would confuse 'the doctrines and practices of a church which acknowledges the One living and True God, Father, Son and Holy Ghost' with the idolatrous worship of heathens? Thirdly, there would have been no advantage in undermining the Orthodox church. Interconfessional sniping was not the right way to promote the cause of Christ: 'We believe that no policy can be worse than that of endeavouring to prejudice the minds of idolators against any of the forms or confessions of the Christian faith.' It was in everyone's interest to maintain Christian solidarity, and stress what united the churches, rather than what divided them. How could anyone imagine that the missionaries did not understand this, and did not act accordingly? Finally, said William, the timing of the accusations against them denied them credibility. What they were charged with must either be their common practice or have happened on a single occasion. The former alternative could not be true, for they had been working in Siberia for fourteen years, cheek by jowl with priests of the Orthodox church, who had not detected any systematic teaching of heresy. On the other hand, if a single instance was being complained of, this too was incredible, for it would suggest that they were inconsistent in their teaching, telling one thing to one person and another thing to another. Could Bludov really imagine them to have behaved so frivolously?

These ingenious but not altogether convincing pleadings prevailed with Bludov. Probably he wanted to be convinced. Personally, he was not ill-disposed towards the work of either the LMS or the BFBS, as George Borrow, in his turn, was to discover, and he may have wanted to spare himself unnecessary trouble. At any rate, by October 1833 William could report to London that he had received a semi-official assurance that his explanations had been accepted as having completely refuted the accusations which had emanated from Siberia, that his letter had been filed in government records (though the Russian historian Vagin could not find it there in 1871), and could be produced if similar charges were laid again in the future. The trouble blew over. For form's sake, Lavinskii sent Edward and Robert each a friendly admonition to be careful. He was conciliatory in tone, saying only that 'although in his visits to these parts he has met with nothing to confirm the truth of such a report, yet he feels it consistent with the duties of his office to *request* that we should cautiously guard against such interference etc etc.'. Robert, predictably, reacted explosively in the self-justification he sent to Thomas Wilson, then Treasurer of the LMS, in December. 'The Laws of Christianity are not Licentiousness: – But are Moral and Spiritual: – and they ae given to us by the Everlasting God, who made all things, and who has put a Just, and Due restraint on all the works of his hands,' he declared, inscrutably. But he denied categorically ever having taught anything discreditable to the Orthodox church, as did Edward too, though with more moderation:

> This, I am persuaded, has ever been our object of desire, both with myself and my Brethren. It is impossible almost to conceive that, in religious conversations with the heathen, our opinions on these points should not have been elicited; but we have made it a *rule* to evade such questions; although it has been more difficult to satisfy such enquirers, as well as to steer clear of Acts xx, 27. You may form some idea of our difficulties on these points.

Edward's letter implies that there may have been a grain of truth in the allegations, and that the missionaries may have spoken to the detriment of the dominant church, if only involuntarily. That possibililty becomes a probability in the light of what we know of their true attitude towards the practice of icon-veneration, which, of course, they whole-heartedly rejected. In the advice which he gave to the Directors in 1832, William put quite a different complexion upon both the views he held and the tactics he employed in dealing with this tricky topic. The policy of the missionaries was to let it be seen that they, at least, would have no truck with images of any sort, and to leave the Buryats to draw their own conclusions:

> The use of pictures of the Saints in the Russian Churches, and indeed in every Russian house, strikes the mind of the Buriat as so identical with his own idolatrous adoration paid to the gods of his own mythology, that the only difference in his view, is the difference of the names of the respective objects of worship. Accordingly, one of the first objects in discussion with an enquiring Buriat is to set his mind right upon this point, and to convince him that *we* are not idolators – that we worship one God – and use no representations whatever in our addresses to Him whom unseen we adore and love and serve. The avowal of our belief, and the exhibition of our practice therefore, are a tacit condemnation of the Russian modes of worship; and in proportion as a pagan Buriat thinks favourably of our profession, in the same proportion must he think unfavourably of the Christianity he had been accustomed to witness.

The next potential confrontation arose in 1834, and was resolved, at least for the time being, in the following year. By 1834, two of the schoolboys at Khodon had become converted to Christianity, and were anxious to be baptized. The missionaries were in a dilemma. At one stage, William toyed with the idea of going ahead regardless of the consequences, but after much prayer and deliberation, he and Edward came to the conclusion, in which they were supported by the leading members of the English church at St

The External Relations of the Mission

Petersburg, that they ought to follow the proper procedure and send in a petition for permission to administer the rite. Edward must have sent in the text of such a petition to J.C. Brown for presentation, though it is not preserved in the mission papers, for on 6 August 1834 Brown reported to London that 'the petition referred to in Mr Stallybrasses inspiriting communication' had been received, and had been submitted to the Ministry of the Interior. This direct approach had its dangers, for it was always risky to importune authority, but Brown and his colleagues thought it a risk worth taking. Some time in 1835, probably in May, the petition was rejected. It was not till 14 July that Edward, then in the capital, was formally notified of the outcome by Bludov, but he knew it earlier, and had sent the news to William at Khodon in May or June. The cloud had a silver lining, in that the missionaries were assured once more that they might go on with their work, but it was evident that there was a considerable body of opinion within the church, and especially within the Synod where it mattered, which favoured the immediate suppression of the mission.

18

The End of the Mission

Lavinskii gave up his Governor Generalship in 1833, and Tseidler ceased to be Governor of Irkutsk in 1835. Little or nothing is known of the view which Lavinskii's two immediate successors, N.S. Sulima and S.B. Bronevskii, took of the mission, but in any case, neither of them held office for long. In 1837, the Governor Generalship changed hands once more. Vil'yelm Yakovlevich Rupert, who was appointed to the office in July, was an officer of German extraction, good-hearted, plodding, and reportedly none too decisive. His feats of maladministration brought a Senatorial investigation about his ears, and led to his enforced resignation in 1847. The Governorship of Irkutsk fell into the hands of one Pyatnitskii, a shallow-minded bureaucrat, whose notorious ignorance allegedly included his interest in a supposed tunnel under the Seine in London.

Rupert and Pyatnitskii seem to have formed an alliance with, or succumbed to the influence of, the earnest new Archbishop of Irkutsk, Nil, who occupied the see from 1838 to 1853, at least as far as the fate of the mission was concerned. It was this combination of forces which finally brought the mission down. Had the missionaries still enjoyed the protection of St Petersburg which had helped them during the twenties and thirties, it is possible that they might have weathered the hostility of Nil as well as that of his predecessors. But Speranskii had died in 1837 and Schilling following him in 1839, and there was no one left at the capital who had influence, personal, local knowledge of the work of the mission, and the intellect to appreciate its value, just at the moment when incompetent administrators, to whom it was of no significance, and an ambitious cleric to whom it was anathema, came to power in Siberia.

Rupert, who at the beginning of his term of office knew nothing of Transbaikalian affairs at first hand, relied heavily on Pyatnitskii for advice, and the Governor played down the work of the mission, letting Rupert believe that not a single Buryat had been converted, that the only pupils in the schools were a few poor boys (whereas in fact they included members of the taishas' families), and that even they had stopped attending. Rupert

The End of the Mission

was all for getting rid of this useless mission, but Bludov warned him that this could be done only for just cause, for example if local conditions demanded it, so as to prevent the Buryats gaining a false impression of the dominant church.

Rupert, lacking a plausible pretext, set about looking for one. In September 1838 he sent Shaposhnikov at Verkhneudinsk a curiously worded order to keep the missionaries under observation. He told the District Captain that, living as they were in such an out-of-the-way place, with no history of past success and no prospect of future success to sustain them, and subject to privations of all sorts, they must have some ulterior motive to explain their persistence. Shaposhnikov was to keep a sharp lookout. He was to ascertain whether they were not perhaps carrying on a correspondence with the British government, or with relatives living in England, and, if so, what its subject matter was. Were they giving the Buryats a false idea of the faith of the dominant church? In general, was there anything in their activities which might be construed as detrimental to the interests of the Russian government or of Transbaikalia?

Shaposhnikov's reply must have disappointed the Governor General. He could only report that the missionaries were minding their own business – preaching Christianity – though they were, admittedly, finding success elusive. They themselves attributed this lack of results to the influence of the lamas, who were trying to dissuade the Buryats from learning to read and write, and to the lack of a press on which they could print their translations of the Bible. However, they had recently set a press going, and were now anticipating greater success. They corresponded only with the Missionary Society, to whom they submitted their reports, and with some private individuals in England. Shaposhnikov disclaimed all knowledge of the purport of their correspondence. The post-master at Verkhneudinsk had refused to reveal what their letters contained – which suggests that the District Captain had tried asking him to open them and been rebuffed. Nor, said Shaposhnikov, would there be much point in it if he had agreed, for he, the District Captain, could not read English. No doubt, too, if they had anything political to report, they would not entrust it to their letters, but would have passed it on personally during the course of their visits to England. Some people thought that the missionaries were keeping an eye on the Kyakhta trade, while others thought that they were spying on the activities of Government. But Shaposhnikov himself had observed nothing suspicious in any of their activities.

This exchange of letters took place between September and November 1838, at the same time as an unsettling event which occurred at Khodon and Ona. In October William wrote to Thomas Wilson that some local people, including 'men of influence and authority', had sent in a written complaint about the missionaries to higher authority, alleging that they were teaching customs which the Buryats could not lawfully observe. No doubt

The End of the Mission

it was the old canard about icon-veneration again. On account of this complaint, an official had called on the Buryats who lived near the two mission stations, and had summoned the people to attend at his office and answer an accusation that they had 'embraced some unknown and unauthorized religion'. Edward and William had accompanied the Buryats from their respective stations, so as to give them moral support. The Buryats confessed their faith in Christ, their renunciation of idolatry, and their determination to obey God's word. The examining official had touched upon the subject of baptism, and suggested to the people that they might be willing to receive it from the hands of an Orthodox priest. But apparently he had no brief to pursue this topic, and it was not pressed.

This episode sowed doubt and dismay among the converts, especially as one of its principal instigators had been the son of the former chief taisha Dembil, who had been a pupil of Edward's for ten years, but had turned against the missionaries once they were no longer of any use to him. The Buryats were apprehensive about what might be in store for them, and the missionaries feared that an unavoidable crisis in the affairs of the mission was looming up. It may have been this realization that things were taking a decisive turn for the worse which emboldened them to consider taking a desperate step – the unauthorized administration of the rite of baptism.

Success in making converts had brought its problems. Lacking the discipline and sense of belonging which membership of a church would have given them, some of the Buryats evidently felt themselves lost in a no-man's-land between the lamaist church which they had deserted, and which had no more use for them, and the Christian church which could not offer them full communion, and they began to lapse. The missionaries felt conscience-stricken. In August 1840 they wrote, in a joint letter:

> The question – 'What is our duty in relation to the baptism of Buriat converts?' remains in all its original importance; and painful facts have tended much to increase our fear that we have not been acting the part we ought. Within the last two years several of those who professed to believe in Christ, and of whom we had reason to hope well have given up their christian profession, and returned to their former idolatrous and sinful customs. The question irresistibly forces itself upon us – 'if these individuals had been baptized, and thus visibly recognized as disciples of Christ, might not that, by the Divine blessing, have been a happy preservative against apostacy?' – and have we not reason to fear for those who continue to the present day to walk as disciples, that they too, living in the neglect of an acknowledged duty, may be left to fall from their stedfastness?

At the beginning of 1839, Edward and William had evidently reached the point where they were willing, if the Directors approved, to risk everything by baptizing their converts without seeking permission. We do not know exactly what course of action they had in mind, because the letter in which they must have sought the Directors' advice, written in March 1839, is no longer traceable in the LMS archives. Moreover, there is an unusually long gap in the correspondence from Siberia at this time, lasting from January 1839 to April 1840, and we do not know whether the missionaries repeated or amplified their original request. We can only surmise that the Directors were unwilling to commit themselves, and put off making a decision for the best part of eighteen months, until, as it turned out, there was no point in making any decision at all. Neither the Board Minutes nor the file of Outgoing Letters for this period hints at any formal discussion of the letter of March 1839. We know of its existence, and of the tricky moral and political issues it raised, only indirectly. Four times between April and November 1840, Edward and William wrote to London complaining that they had been left without guidance. Month after month the Directors went on temporizing, and it was not till 9 December 1840, by which time they knew their advice had been overtaken by events, that, rather shamefacedly one hopes, they wrote to tell the missionaries what advice they had been thinking of giving them. Even then, the advice was ambiguous, and Edward was fully justified in complaining in a private letter to Ann Monds, written in May 1841, that 'our Directors whose advice we earnestly sought, could afford us no assistance in deciding upon the path of duty, but left it to us to decide . . . . Thus we were left as much to ourselves as if we had not asked their opinion.'

The Directors had written as follows:

> It may be of some satisfaction to you to know the views which the Directors entertained on the subject of the Baptism of the Buriat converts, although they are quite aware that the affair is now superseded by the measures of the Government. The Resolution adopted was as follows:
> 'The Directors of the London Missionary Society cannot advise the Missionaries to baptize the Buriats, because they have been prohibited by the authorities to which they appealed, and because such a measure would prevent the completion of the translation and publication of the Holy Scriptures, an object of *paramount* importance. But the Directors will not dissuade, much less prohibit the Missionaries from baptizing any whom they may deem proper subjects for that ordinance, but leave them at perfect liberty to act in all such cases on their own conviction of Christian duty, the Directors being prepared to indemnify their Missionary Brethren against any and all consequences it may involve.'

If Edward and William felt let down, it is no wonder. It had taken the Directors over a year and a half to formulate even these elastic guidelines, and the two men must have been well on their way home, probably as far west as St Petersburg, before they received them. But the Directors were

The End of the Mission

not entirely to blame for the dilemma in which all concerned now found themselves. The missionaries had closed their options by applying for permission to baptize in 1834. The refusal of their application had formalized a situation which it might have been better to leave fluid. At least, that was the opinion of John Paterson, whom the Directors had evidently consulted in connection with the letter of March 1839. Paterson agreed that, once they had been forbidden to baptize, and had opted to stay in Siberia on that condition, it would be dishonourable to break their agreement. Nevertheless, he regretted that they had ever asked for permission, claiming, for the very first time, that Alexander had actually given them verbal permission to baptize their converts, when they were received in audience by him. What they should have done was to go ahead and form a church as soon as they had converts. They might have got away with it for a time, and, with luck, they might have got away with it for good. 'The laws of Russia,' he said, 'are not like the laws of the Medes and Persians. They do alter and alter often.' The trouble was that Alexander used to act according to his perception of what was right, while Nicholas preferred the constitutional path, referring everything to the competent authority. The question of baptism would naturally be referred to the Synod, whose rejection was a foregone conclusion. It was a pity that the missionaries had acted as they did, but it was too late now to retrieve the situation. Representations might be made, but they should not go back on the agreement:

> The Government has in all things, the prohibition excepted, treated them kindly, and they ought to shew their sense of this. Both our Brethren are wise and prudent men and the final decision ought to be left entirely to them after you have candidly stated your opinion and given your advice. And you ought to assure them in the very strongest terms, that you will not only hold them blameless, whatever determination they come to; but that you will afford them your most cordial support. They know much which they cannot safely communicate to you, and there may be circumstances which demand their acting promptly without your advice and even contrary to it. Indemnified they must be against any and all consequences which this important question may involve.

The wording of this letter, dated 6 November, is so reminiscent of the Directors' subsequent Resolution, as to suggest that the latter was merely a paraphrase of Paterson's advice. One can only wonder why they took so long to elicit it.

Apparent neglect on the part of the Directors at an anxious time may have been partly responsible for the growing tone of despondency which marks the few letters which Edward and William wrote during 1840. But they were losing heart for other reasons too, and when the blow fell in the autumn of 1840 it was, in a way, not unwelcome. The two men were willing to toil away in Siberia as long as there was a chance that younger men would be

The End of the Mission

sent out to take over from them, but if the Directors were thinking of abandoning Siberia, they thought it might be just as well to give up at once, and start work in more promising surroundings while they were still vigorous and adaptable enough to do so. As William put it:

> After being borne up for twenty years under discouragements not a few, I think, for my own part, I would be content to spend the uncertain remainder of my days in Siberia, were it only *to keep the door open* for successors, who might enter into our labours, and reap what we have sown. But the case is altered if the Mission is to be suffered to expire, when the present labourers die, and it becomes a serious question, whether the days and strength that yet may be given me ought not to be devoted to the work of the Lord in some sphere, where my labour is not foredoomed, like the blossom of the wicked, 'to go up as dust'.

Edward, too, looking back in May 1841 over the final days of the mission, confessed that he had been on the point of giving up just as the Russian authorities forced them to leave the country. He wrote to Ann as follows:

> For the present we were occupied in a most important work, printing the Sacred Scriptures in a language in which they (as a whole) had never appeared. . . . It was our intention to remain as we were till that work should be completed, which had we been permitted to go on uninterruptedly, might have been in about two years. Our increasing conviction was that at the close of that period, we must relinquish that field, and seek some other sphere in which we could without restraint act as ministers or missionaries of Jesus.

It was a sad decline from the bright hopes of the morning of their lives, when they had ridden out confidently over the broad Buryat plains, their prospects of success limited only by the dispositions of Providence. Now they were old and chastened, and they looked for some spiritual satisfaction before it was too late. In a way, though, their expulsion was providential. It enabled them to put the entire blame for the inevitable ruin of their mission on the Russians. Edward told Ann:

> Although we had become increasingly convinced that our ground was untenable, yet we shrank from the responsibility of breaking up the mission. Now, however, the Holy Synod, by forbidding and preventing us from preaching the Gospel 'That they may be saved' have taken that responsibility upon themselves, and *they* must bear its tremendous weight.

This was no doubt a comforting thought, but Nil and the Holy Synod, having gained their point, probably bore the responsibility for their actions lightly enough.

Edward attributed the decision on the part of Government to close the mission down to the fact that William and he had drawn attention to themselves in the spring of 1840 by applying for permission to print the New Testament in Mongolian. His letter to Ann of May 1841 is scathing about the part played by the Synod:

> You require a relation of the suppression of our Mission. About March last year, having the prospect of completing the printing of the Mongolian Old Testament we applied for permission – we are not in America – to print the N.T. This was transferred to the *Most Holy Synod* for its decision. It might as well have been referred to the Sanctissima inquisitio. We have reason for supposing, that this application was the means of stirring up the latent hostility of that *most holy* body.

He and William waited for months for a reply to their petition, and at the end of September 1840 they were summoned to an interview with a government official. Half hoping that permission had been granted, half apprehensive that it had been refused, they obeyed the summons, and were brusquely served with the order to dismantle their mission, in the form of a communication from the Ministry of the Interior, signed by the Emperor. What had happened was that Nil had formulated a comprehensive list of complaints against them, and sent it to the Synod. The thing that most angered Edward, and aroused his contempt for Nil, was that, only a year earlier, the Archbishop had visited the Khodon station and inspected the printing shop. He had expressed his approval of what he termed their 'godlike' desire of publishing the Scriptures, and positively encouraged them to persist in their work. And now he had been revealed as the instigator of the move against them.

The official who had brought the order had no authority to do anything but serve it, and was reluctant even to let the missionaries make a copy of it. They insisted, and in the end he grudgingly allowed Edward to jot down some extracts, but only in English. Edward's hasty notes are preserved in a letter he wrote to Thomas Wilson in October 1840:

> It is a letter of instructions from the Minister of the Interior to the Genl Govr of Eastern Siberia, in which the Minr states:
> 'The Ober-procurator of the most holy Synod communicated to me that the Archbishop of Irkutsk, in consequence of evident signs of opposition to the dominant faith observed by him on the part of the Boriats who dwell in the vicinity of the Baikal, near those places where the English missionaries reside, who were permitted by his Imp. Majesty, in 1817 to engage in the work of converting the heathen to Christianity in Siberia, – expressed in his report to the most Holy Synod his fear that their teaching produces the effect of extending lying subtleties concerning the faith. He adds, moreover, that the Boriats who have received instruction in the schools of these Missionaries remain in their

The End of the Mission

former heathenism; while in places remote from the Missionaries, they of their own accord request baptism to which they are called by grace. The Procurator shewed also that in 1833 etc (A repetition of what was then brought against us, and which was answered apparently in a satisfactory manner by Mr Swan who was at the time in St Petersburg.) When they afterward requested permission to baptize Boriats, – by virtue of existing laws, they were forbidden and threatened with the utmost rigour of the law in case of their refusing to comply with the commands then given etc.' (See letter of Mr Bludoff addressed to Mr Stallybrass, June 1835.) Having all these circumstances in view, in consequence of the above mentioned reasons, that the English Missionaries not only do not act to the advantage of the Orthodox faith, but even secretly propagate the errors of infidelity, the Holy Synod regard it as indispensably necessary to forbid the Missionaries any longer to act as, or to call themselves by the name of Missionaries. This resolution Count Potasoff laid before His Imperial Majesty, who was pleased to confirm it, and to order that measures might be taken to put it into execution.

So, after two decades of sniping, the Orthodox church had won, and Nil now had a clear run for his own missionaries. There was something of a lull under his two immediate successors, the Archbishops Afanasii (1853–56) and Evsevii (1857–60), but the task of converting the Buryats was then taken up vigorously by the Archbishop Parfenii (1860–73). He founded two missions, one on either side of Lake Baikal, but their history does not concern us.

The missionaries were required to give their written consent to comply with the terms of the order to the official who had brought it. They flatly refused to refrain from calling themselves missionaries, on the reasonable ground that the Russians could not take away a title they had not conferred. They also managed to spin out their term of residence until the printing of the Old Testament could be completed. But nothing further could be done. The order was absolute, and they had no opportunity to defend themselves against what they bitterly resented as a cruel slur on their characters. Edward poured out his contempt for the actions of the Holy Synod in his letter to Ann:

> You will not, perhaps, be prepared to admit at once that we really did propagate 'lying subtleties' and 'the errors of infidelity,' although asserted by such a venerable body of most *holy men*. You may even so far forget yourself, as to aver, that they ought to be made to *prove* the slander, but remember *who* they are, and do not presume to judge them by the same laws, to which we every day mortals are expected to yield obedience. They are too elevated to descend to such a vulgar Process, and when they are able to effect their purpose, by mere assertion, it is often, by far, more convenient to have nothing to do with such a

The End of the Mission

stubborn thing as proof! And so, my dear Sister, they wrap it up, 'and perhaps it may not be unveiled till the day shall declare it.'

He wrote in similar vein to Wilson, who, he thought, might well find it strange that they had been condemned without being given the chance to defend themselves. But that was how things were done in Russia. Even imperial Rome had not descended to such depths of injustice, and he quoted Acts 25: 16, to prove his contention.

All that remained was to salvage as much as possible of the Society's property, and return to England. The premises at Khodon were sold to the chief taisha of the Khori Buryats for 2,500 roubles, and the Society's buildings at Ona fetched 1,500 roubles upon their sale to the family of the late taisha Jigjit. The press and types were ultimately sold, too, as we have seen, and the copies of the Old Testament reached England in due course. The Abercrombies were sent back to Karass. Edward and William paid John's travelling expenses and advanced him his wages up to the estimated time of his arrival there. They also suggested to the Directors that it might be appropriate to give him a gratuity. He had worked faithfully for the mission for nearly seven years, and now, through no fault of his own, he was suddenly thrown out of work. He had a wife and five young children to support, and nothing to look forward to in Karass. He might be able to earn a little by casual bookbinding, but there was little prospect of regular printing work, and he would probably have to go back to tilling the land like an ordinary colonist. Would the Directors please consider the matter, and let them know their decision while they were in St Petersburg on their way home, as it would be easier to pay the money before they left Russia. Even at this last gasp in the mission's life, the Directors proved sadly dilatory. There was no answer awaiting Edward and William when they reached the capital in April 1841, and towards the end of the month they wrote again. There is a touch of impatience in the way they regret that their letter has not been answered, and their intimation to the Directors that, if they have not been authorized to send John the money, which he urgently needed, before their departure, they would advance him 500 roubles on their own responsibility. Probably that was the way things turned out, for it was not till August that the Directors finally got around to sanctioning John's leaving present of £40.

Having suppressed the mission, the Russian authorities acted correctly towards the missionaries. The Directors requested Count Stroganov, the Minister of the Interior, in a letter authenticated with the seal of the Lord Mayor of London, to afford Edward and William every protection on their way home, and Stroganov issued the necessary orders. Before leaving Russia, the missionaries made one final effort to re-establish their good name, which they felt had been impugned by the tone of the order for their expulsion. While still in St Petersburg they presented the Emperor Nicholas with a

The End of the Mission

copy of their Old Testament, together with a long letter in which they reviewed the history of their mission. They rehearsed the terms in which both Nicholas and Alexander had sanctioned it; they refuted the alleged reasons for its suppression; and they defended themselves against the aspersions cast upon their characters. With nothing left to lose, they wrote in rather stronger terms than the Emperor was perhaps accustomed to hear from petitioners. They utterly rejected the charges which had been made, and which he had approved:

> These grounds of objection to our Mission, a sense of what we owe to our own character and to the character of the Christian Community to which we belong, constrains us to declare to be unfounded in fact, and unsupported by proof – having no pretext but the opinions or fears of Individuals, or the suggestions of persons, hostile to *all* efforts to convert the heathen Buriats to the Christian faith.

And they maintained to the last that they had never taught any objectionable doctrines. They accepted that the Emperor could cancel any privileges which he himself had granted, but they appealed to his sense of honour and love of justice not to allow their characters to remain stained by intolerable slurs and stigmas. They rejected any suggestion that they had ever engaged in political activities, or had interfered in anything unconnected with their missionary work, and they expressed the hope that they might be allowed to return home with their characters as Christian teachers unsullied, 'conscious as we are that we have done nothing to forfeit the confidence of your Imperial Majesty's Government, or the approbation of our own constituents'.

Such a step was necessary, not merely to relieve their own feelings which, as can be seen from their other letters, were deeply wounded, but also to set the record straight. At the time, it produced no effect at all, something for which the two men were, doubtless, quite prepared.

With the mission at an end, one of its members, John Abercrombie, drops more or less out of sight. He lived on at the Scottish colony till the 1870s at least, but nothing more might have been heard of him, had not a Scottish traveller, one Mackenzie Wallace, found him there, 'a venerable old man, with fine regular features of the Circassian type, coal-black sparkling eyes, and a long grey beard that would have done honour to a patriarch'. John still spoke genuine broad Scots.

Robert Yuille recedes from view during the 1850s. Whether or not he ever patched up his quarrel with the LMS we do not know, but probably he did not, as his obsessively self-righteous nature would surely have prevented him from admitting himself to be at fault in the slightest detail. How he supported himself during his last thirteen years is as much a mystery

The End of the Mission

as how he earned his living for seven years or more in Siberia. Robert died in Glasgow in 1861.

Neither Edward nor William ever served as a missionary again, the former because no suitable post could be found for him, the latter by his own wish. In July 1841 William resigned from the Society's service, assuring the Directors that he 'was never more attached to the Missionary cause, and never felt more deeply interested in the prosperity of the Missionary Society than at the present moment'. He had private means, and these were sufficient for him to make a generous final reckoning with the Society. He renounced his claim to more than 2,000 roubles which were owing to him, and donated a further £100 to its funds. Many years of active work remained to him. In 1844 we find him teaching at the Glasgow Theological Academy, his old college, and in 1845 he became Secretary of the Scottish Congregational Union. He held this post for ten years, and during the same period he edited the *Scottish Congregational Magazine*, writing much of the material for it himself. He was the Edinburgh correspondent of the BFBS, acted as consultant for the LMS, and took a great interest in organizations such as the YMCA, the Book and Tract Society for Scotland, and the Medical Missionary Society. As we have seen, he worked once more for the LMS and the BFBS in a contractual capacity, co-operating with Edward in translating the New Testament into Mongolian. He remained interested in missionary work among the Mongols, and less than a year before his death he was in correspondence with members of the LMS about the prospects of resuming it from the Chinese side. But he did not live to see James Gilmour go out. He died on 1 January 1866, survived by his wife Hannah, who lived on in Edinburgh until 1890.

Edward enjoyed a rather less settled life during the first few years after his return from Siberia. While the Swans took care of his motherless children for a while, earning their life-long gratitude, Edward plunged into deputation work, exhausting himself in travelling the country, speaking at missionary meetings, and preaching missionary sermons. The frantic life did not appeal to him, and he was anxious to give it up. He would have liked to go out as a missionary once more, perhaps to the Cape, where he thought that, with his knowledge of German, he could soon pick up enough Dutch to be useful, or to the West Indies, where there would be no language problem. But it was not to be. After the long years in Siberia, it was thought that a hot climate would not suit him, and the Directors never sent him abroad again. Instead, as he wrote plaintively to Ann in January 1842, it was a long round of hectic travelling and speaking, through Norfolk and Essex, Lancashire, Yorkshire, Lincolnshire and Northamptonshire. 'This work I have regarded and performed rather as a duty than a pleasure,' he told her. 'I do not wish to continue long in this employ.' But the travelling continued for a while. In October 1842 he was writing from Glastonbury and in December from Stroud, and in January 1843 he was back in Stepney again.

The End of the Mission

On 14 April 1844 Edward was writing from Bishops Stortford, and this, though the contents of the letter do not betray it, was a sign that he was about to settle down again. All his life he was dependent upon marriage to complete his happiness, and in 1844 he married a Miss Sarah Bass, daughter of the Rev. James Bass of Halstead in Essex. Miss Bass had run a girls' school at Bishops Stortford for a while, and after her marriage she and Edward had an Academy for young ladies at Dalston, where Sarah died in 1855. Edward's life was once again centred on East London, familiar from days long past at Homerton, and with the Robinsons at Stepney. In 1861 he took a fourth wife, marrying Mary Ann Oughton at Hackney. Mary Ann predeceased him too, dying in 1874. By then, Edward was eighty years old, and some of his children, too, were coming to the end of their lives. His dear daughter, Sarah Robinson Stallybrass, who had married Adolf Sonnenschein in 1850, was the first to go. She died at Hackney in 1871, at the early age of forty-nine, seven years before her son, William Swan Sonnenschein, established his celebrated publishing firm. John Knox died in 1879, and Thomas Edward in 1883. Two sons of Edward's first marriage survived him. James Steven died in 1888, while William Carey, twice married, lived on to the age of eighty-one, dying at Birkenhead in 1901. Edward himself died in 1884, at the age of ninety, at Shooters Hill. His last service to the missionary cause had been to make a second copy of the Manchu Old Testament for the Bible Society, in the years from 1849 to 1851. A scheme had been mooted by the Chinese Foundation at Kassel in Germany to have the Testament printed by the missionary Karl Gutzlaff, and it was thought prudent to have a duplicate copy of it made before parting with the original. Alas for Edward's efforts – the Testament was never printed.

So ended a unique episode in mission history, and a strange passage in Anglo-Mongolian relations. What good the mission did to the Buryats it is hard to say. Few of them were converted, and none was baptized by the missionaries. By contrast, the Orthodox church was to win thousands of new adherents in the latter part of the nineteenth century. The most important catch in the 1840s was the Khori taisha, Dembil's son, once a pupil at Khodon. Great things were hoped from his baptism, in which the Tsar himself stood godfather, but he apparently proved a disappointment. By 1851 there were over 9,000 baptized Buryats, but how many of them were Christians it is hard to tell. Conversions continued to swell in number. By 1891 there were 35,000 baptized Buryats, and at the turn of the century there were 85,000. Seventeen years later came the Soviet revolution, and the whole work was undone.

The missionaries may have made a slight contribution towards the awakening of Buryat national self-consciousness through the training they gave in their schools, but such things are impossible to evaluate from the sources available to us. More concretely, the mission was the precursor of the mission to the Mongols of China, opened by James Gilmour in 1870. Gilmour was

The End of the Mission

inspired and encouraged by the personalities and the work of his predecessors, and their translation of the Bible saved him much spadework. But Gilmour's mission itself was a gallant failure. He made one or two converts, and treated countless sick people. But after his time, the LMS gradually abandoned the Mongolian mission field, which was taken over by missionaries from elsewhere. There is some anecdotal evidence of the part played by the mission, or rather by the missionaries as individuals, in influencing other people's lives. William was gratified on one occasion to learn that a reading of his *Letters* had inspired the American medical missionary Peter Parker to adopt the profession. On the other hand, the copy of his book in the library of the LMS had never been read until 1980, when some of its pages were cut open for the first time.

Edward had his little triumphs too. One day, while staying at an inn in Market Deeping, he got into conversation with an old gentleman. It turned out that the latter's son had been a passenger on the same ship on which Edward had taken passage from Russia in 1841, and it was through listening to Edward that he had been converted, and had joined the Baptist church. Another young minister told Edward that he had been critically affected by reading the *Memoir* of Sarah. But these isolated incidents, however gratifying in themselves, were not a justification for the effort and expense of twenty years of missionary work in Siberia, and, with regret, we have to conclude that the mission had proved futile in both its main objects – the conversion of the Buryats and the opening up of China to Christianity.

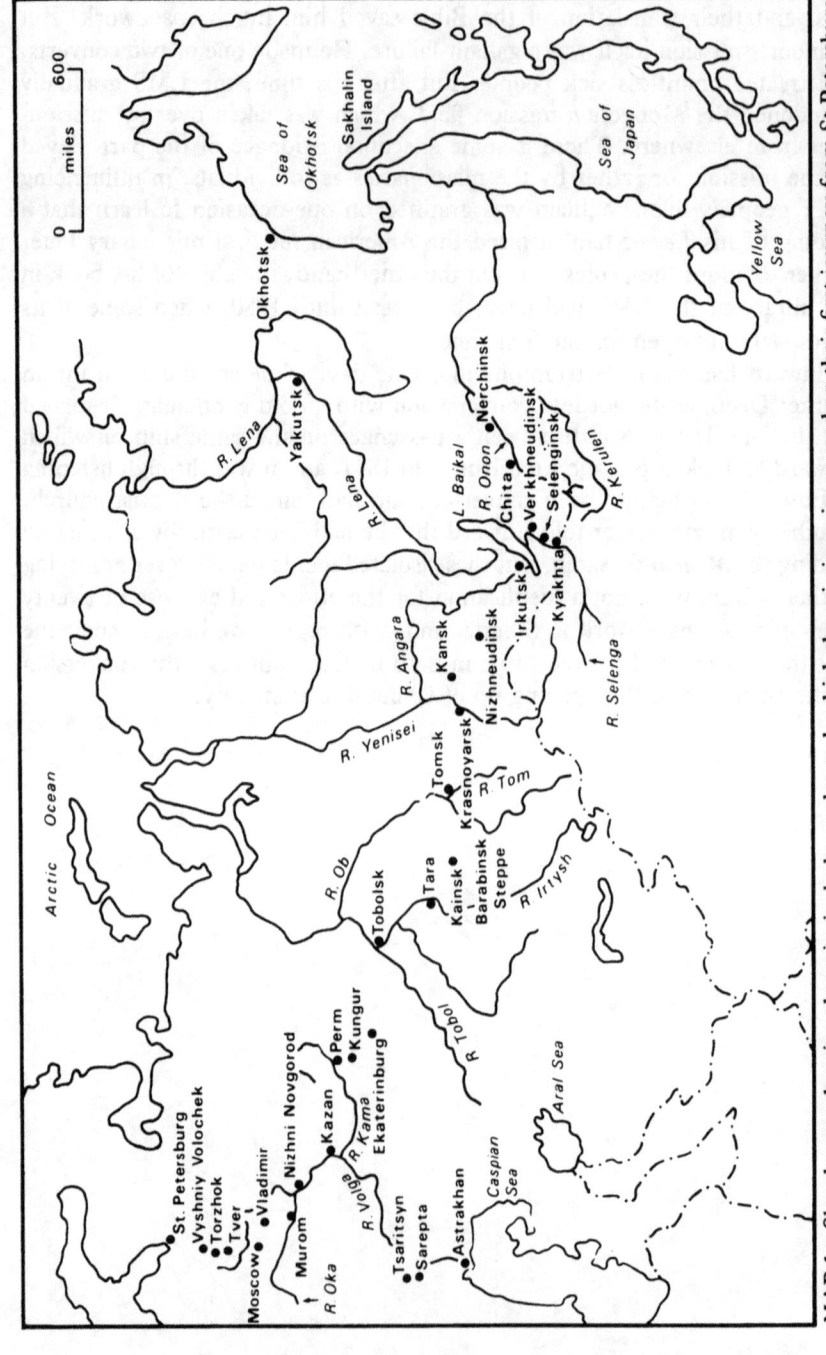

MAP 1 Sketch map showing the principal places through which the missionaries passed on their first journey from St Petersburg to Irkutsk

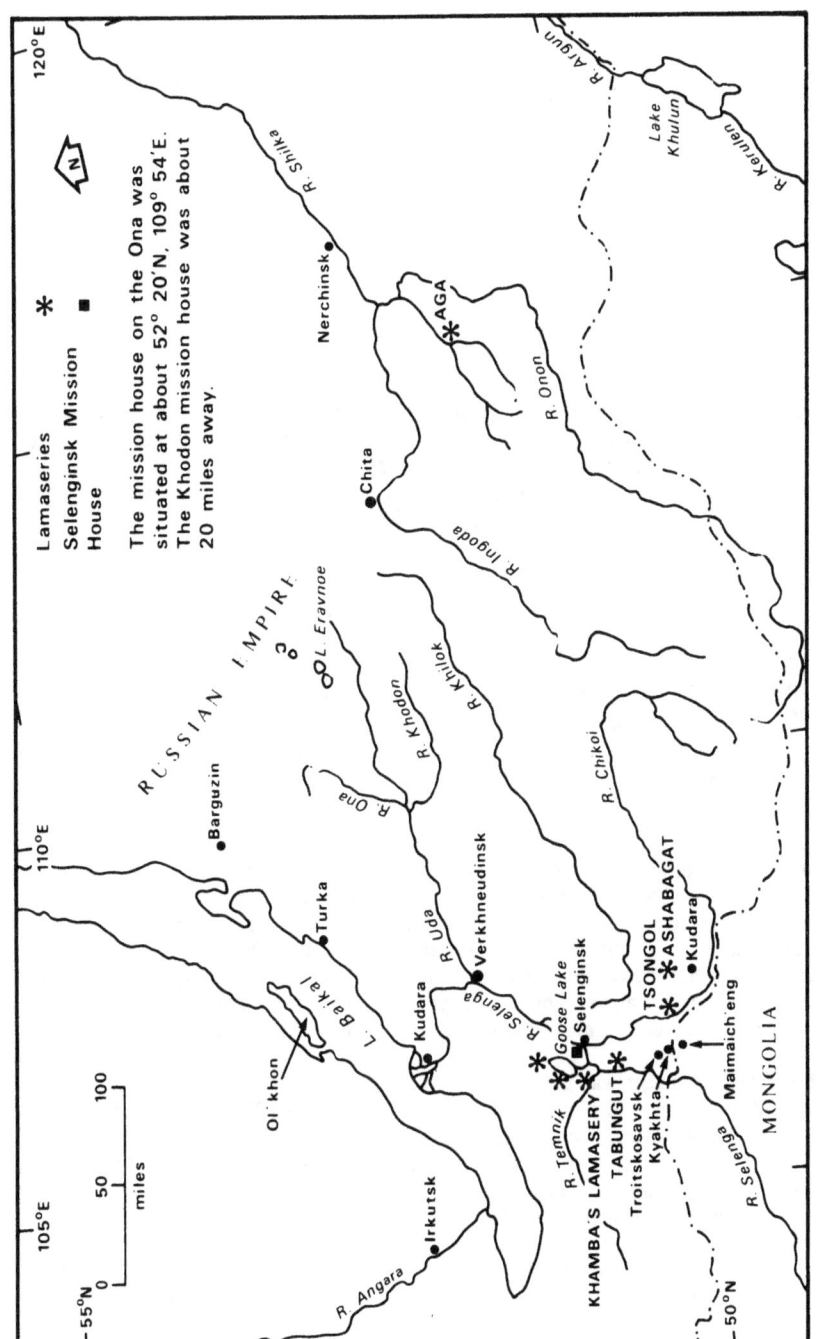

MAP 2   Sketch map showing the area of the missionaries' activities

APPENDIX

The Printing of the Bible in Mongolian

The only book of the Bible to be printed officially and in full at Selenginsk was Genesis, which was completed by the end of 1834, in an edition of 500 copies. Three copies of this rare first edition are known so far to exist, one each in the Bodleian Library, the British Library, and the Royal Library, Stockholm. The last-named copy was that owned originally by Cornelius Rahmn.

The books of the Old Testament were printed at Khodon as follows:

1835   Exodus
1836   Leviticus, Numbers, Deuteronomy, Joshua, Judges, Ruth, Proverbs, Ecclesiastes, Song of Solomon
1837   Genesis, Exodus (second editions), 1 and 2 Samuel
1838   1 and 2 Kings, 1 Chronicles, Psalms (quarto and octavo editions)
1839   Leviticus, Numbers, Deuteronomy (second editions), 2 Chronicles, Ezra, Nehemiah, Esther, Job, Daniel, Hosea, Joel, Amos, Obadiah, Jonah, Micah
1840   Isaiah, Jeremiah, Lamentations, Ezekiel, Nahum, Habbakuk, Zephaniah, Haggai, Zechariah, Malachi.

Dates are ascertainable from the Mongolian colophons, which also site the printing at Khodon, as well as from the mission correspondence. A typical colophon runs, in translation: 'Printed in 1835 at the missionaries' press at Khodon.'

In 1840 the missionaries made up a number of complete Old Testaments from the original parts. One copy, described by Darlow and Moule, is said to have the original part titles and imprimaturs. The only copies examined by the author have a general title, in Mongolian only, and a single imprimatur, dated 1840, replacing the original ones.

The New Testament was printed in London in 1846 by William Watts, using an adapted Manchu type. A new edition was undertaken in 1877. The first few sheets were corrected by Edward Stallybrass himself, but the edition was supervised thereafter by A. Schiefner, and, after his death in 1879, by A.M. Pozdneev. This edition was printed from a fount of type specially cast from matrices in the printing-office of the Academy of Sciences in St Petersburg, and hence uniform with that used for Schmidt's New Testament of 1827. Photographic reprints of parts of this edition were subsequently issued, and the whole New Testament was reissued as late as 1939 in Shanghai.

Bibliography

WESTERN SOURCES

Anon., 'Death of the Rev. E. Stallybrass, formerly of Siberia', *Chronicle of the London Missionary Society*, 1884, p. 313.
Anon., 'The late Rev. William Swan', *Scottish Congregational Magazine*, New Series, vol. 16, 1866, pp. 102–8.
Anon. (Mrs Swan), *Reminiscences of the Mission in Siberia*, Edinburgh, n.d.
Babinger, F., 'Isaak Jakob Schmidt, 1774–1847. Ein Beitrag zur Geschichte der Tibetforschung', *Festschrift für Friedrich Hirth*, Berlin, 1920, pp. 7–21.
Barnard, H.C., *A History of English Education from 1760*, 2nd edn, London, University of London Press, 1961.
Barthold, V.V., *La Découverte de l'Asie. Histoire de l'orientalisme en Europe et en Russie*, Paris, Payot, 1947.
Bawden, C.R., 'Two Mongol texts concerning obo-worship', *Oriens Extremus*, vol. 5, no. 1, 1958, pp. 23–41.
Bawden, C.R., *The Jebtsundamba Khutuktus of Urga. Text, Translation and Notes*, Asiatische Forschungen, Bd 9, Wiesbaden, Otto Harrassowitz, 1961.
Bawden, C.R., 'On the evils of strong drink: a Mongol tract from the early 20th century', *Tractata Altaica*, ed. W. Heissig et al., Wiesbaden, Otto Harrassowitz, 1976, pp. 59–79.
Bawden, C.R., 'Nomtu, Badma and the English Missionaries in Siberia', *Journal of the Anglo-Mongolian Society*, vol. 5, no. 1, 1979, pp. 1–24.
Bawden, C.R., 'The English Missionaries in Siberia and their translation of the Bible into Mongolian', *Mongolian Studies*, vol. 6, 1980, pp. 5–39.
Bawden, C.R., 'W.A. Unkrig's correspondence with the British and Foreign Bible Society', *Zentralasiatische Studien*, vol. 14, no. 1, 1980, pp. 65–108.
Bawden, C.R., 'English mission schools among the Buryats, 1822–1840', *Zentralasiatische Studien*, vol. 16, 1982, pp. 211–52.
Bell, John, *Travels from St Petersburg in Russia to diverse parts of Asia*, Glasgow, 1763.
Bell, John, *A Journey from St Petersburg to Peking 1719–22*, edited with an introduction by J.L. Stevenson, Edinburgh, Edinburgh University Press, 1965.
Bergmann, B., *Nomadische Streifereien unter den Kalmüken in den Jahren 1802 und 1803*, Riga, 1804–5. Reprinted Oosterhout, Anthropological Publications, 1969.
Bigland, E., *In the Steps of George Borrow*, London, Rich & Cowan, 1951.

Bibliography

Broomhall, M., *The Bible in China*, London, The British and Foreign Bible Society, 1934.
Brown, J.C., *First-Fruits of a Mission to Siberia by the Revs. Messrs. Yuille, Stallybrass, and Swan, Agents of the London Missionary Society*, Cape Town, 1847.
Brown, W., *The History of the Christian Missions of the Sixteenth, Seventeenth, Eighteenth, and Nineteenth Centuries*, London, Thomas Baker, 1864.
Browne, G., *The History of the British and Foreign Bible Society*, London, 1859.
Bryson, Mrs (Mary Isabella), *James Gilmour and the Mongol Mission*, London, The National Sunday School Union, n.d. (1928).
Bullen, G., *Catalogue of the Library of the British and Foreign Bible Society*, London, 1857.
Carruthers, D., *Unknown Mongolia*, London, Hutchinson, 1913.
Ch'en, Ch. H., 'The decline of the Manchu language in China during the Ch'ing period (1644–1911)', *Altaica Collecta*, ed. W. Heissig, Wiesbaden, Otto Harrassowitz, 1976, pp. 137–54.
Cochrane, J.D., *Narrative of a Pedestrian Journey through Russia and Siberian Tartary from the Frontiers of China to the Frozen Sea and Kamtchatka; performed during the Years 1820, 1821, 1822 and 1823 by Capt. John Dundas Cochrane, R.N.*, London, John Murray, 1824.
Collie, M., *George Borrow, Eccentric*, Cambridge, Cambridge University Press, 1982.
Collins, P.M., *Siberian Journey. Down the Amur to the Pacific, 1856–1857. A new edition of A Voyage down the Amoor by Perry McDonough Collins*, edited with an introduction by Charles Vevier, Madison, University of Wisconsin Press, 1962.
Cottrell, C.H., *Recollections of Siberia in the Years 1840 and 1841*, London, 1842.
Craig, S. Stuart, *The Archives of the Council for World Mission*, London, School of Oriental and African Studies, 1973 and 1980.
Darlow, T.H. (ed.), *Letters of George Borrow to the British and Foreign Bible Society*, London, Hodder & Stoughton, 1911.
Darlow, T.H., and Moule, H.F., *Historical Catalogue of the Printed Editions of Holy Scripture in the Library of the British and Foreign Bible Society*, London, The Bible House, 1903 and 1911.
Erman, A., *Travels in Siberia*, London, 1848.
Evander, S., *Londonsvenskarnas Kyrka genom 250 år, with a Summary in English*, Lund, Berlingska Boktryckeriet, 1960.
Evangelical Magazine and Missionary Chronicle, vol. 22, 1814, to vol. 52, 1844.
Falivene, M.R., and Jesson, A.F. (eds), *Historical Catalogue of the Manuscripts of Bible House Library*, London, The British and Foreign Bible Society, 1982.
Gerish, W.B., 'Obituary of John Morse Mullinger 1802–80', *East Herts Archaeological Society, Transactions*, vol. 5, 1912–14, p. 292.
Gilmour, J., *Among the Mongols*, London, Religious Tract Society, 1883. Reprinted, with an introduction by Denis Sinor, New York, Praeger Publishers, 1970.
Gilmour, J., *More about the Mongols*, London, Religious Tract Society, 1893.
Glazik, P. Dr Josef, 'Die russisch-orthodoxe Heidenmission seit Peter dem Grossen', *Missionswissenschaftliche Abhandlungen und Texte*, vol. 19, Münster, Westfalen, Aschendorffsche Verlagsbuchhandlung, 1953.
Glitsch, A., *Geschichte der Brüdergemeine Sarepta im östlichen Russland während ihres hundertjährigen Bestehens*, Nisky, Berlin, Verlag von L. Glitsch, 1865.
Gordon, Peter, *Narrative of the Imprisonment and Escape of Peter Gordon, Second Mate in the Barque Joseph, of Limerick, Capt. Connolly*, London, 1816.

Bibliography

Gordon, Peter, *Fragment of the Journal of a Tour through Persia in 1820*, London, 1833.
Gordon, Peter, *A Petition to the House of Commons*, London, ?1836.
Gordon, Peter, *Petition of P.G. relative to his Imprisonment*, London, 1841.
Gowing, L.F., *Five Thousand Miles in a Sledge. A mid-winter Journey across Siberia*, London, Chatto & Windus, 1889.
Hafa, H., 'Die Brüdergemeine Sarepta', *Schriften des Osteuropa-Institutes in Breslau*, Neue Reihe 7, Breslau, 1936.
Hansteen, C., *Reise-Erinnerungen aus Sibirien*, Leipzig, 1874.
Hawes, C.H., *In the uttermost East*, London and New York, 1903.
Heissig, W., 'A Mongolian source to the lamaist suppression of shamanism in the 17th century', *Anthropos*, vol. 48, 1953, pp. 1–29, 493–536.
Heissig, W., 'Neyici Toyin. Das Leben eines lamaistischen Mönches (1557–1653)', *Sinologica*, vol. 3, no. 4, 1953, pp. 1–44; vol. 4, no. 1, 1954, pp. 21–38.
Heissig, W., 'W. A. Unkrig', *Central Asiatic Journal*, vol. 3, no. 1, pp. 21–2.
Heissig, W. (ed.), *Mongoleireise zur spaeten Goethezeit. Berichte und Bilder des J. Rehmann und A. Thesleff von der russischen Gesandtschaftsreise 1805/06. Verzeichnis der orientalischen Handschriften in Deutschland*, Supplementband 13, Wiesbaden, Franz Steiner Verlag, 1971.
Heissig, W., *The Religions of Mongolia*, London, Routledge & Kegan Paul, 1980.
Henderson, E., *Biblical Researches and Travels in Russia; including a Tour in the Crimea, and the Passage of the Caucasus: with Observations on the State of the Rabbinical and Karaite Jews, and the Mohammedan and pagan Tribes, inhabiting the Southern Provinces of the Russian Empire*, London, 1826.
Henderson, Thulia S., *Memoir of the Rev. E. Henderson, DD PhD, including his Labours in Denmark, Iceland, Russia etc etc*, London, 1859.
Henderson, Thulia S., *Memorials of John Venning, Esq. (Formerly of St Petersburgh, and late of Norwich), with numerous Notices from his Manuscripts relative to the Imperial Family of Russia*, London, 1862.
Hill, S.S., *Travels in Siberia*, London, 1854.
Hommaire de Hell, X., *Travels in the Steppes of the Caspian Sea, the Crimea, the Caucasus, etc*, London, 1847.
Horne, C. Silvester, *The Story of the L.M.S.*, London, London Missionary Society, 1904.
Jansson, E. Alfred, *Cornelius Rahmn, 1800-talets förste svenske Missionär*, Stockholm, Evangeliska Fosterlands-Stiftelsens Bokförlag, 1951.
Jenkins, H., *The Life of George Borrow*, London, John Murray, 1912 and 1924.
Jones, M.G., *The Charity School Movement. A Study of eighteenth century Puritanism in Action*, Cambridge, Cambridge University Press, 1938.
Jones, M.V., 'The sad and curious story of Karass, 1802–35', *Oxford Slavonic Papers*, New Series, vol. 8, 1975, pp. 53–81.
Jülg, B., 'On the present state of Mongolian researches', *Journal of the Royal Asiatic Society*, New Series, vol. 14, 1882, pp. 42–65.
Kennan, G., *Siberia and the Exile System*, New York, 1891.
Kennan, G., *Tent Life in Siberia. A new Account of an old Undertaking. Adventures among the Koraks and other Tribes in Kamchatka and Northern Asia*, New York and London, G.P. Putnam's Sons, The Knickerbocker Press, 1910. Reprinted, New York, Arno Press and the New York Times, 1970.
Kingston, A., *A History of Royston, Hertfordshire, with biographical notes of Royston Worthies, Portraits, Plans and Illustrations*, London and Royston, 1906. Reprinted, Royston, Warren Bros & Cooke, 1975.

Bibliography

Kirchner, W. (tr. and ed.), *A Siberian Journey. The Journal of Hans Jakob Fries, 1774–1776*, London, Frank Cass, 1974.

Knox, T.W., *Overland through Asia. Pictures of Siberian, Chinese, and Tartar Life*, Hartford, Conn., American Publishing Company, 1870. Reprinted, New York, Arno Press and the New York Times, 1970.

Kohls, W.A., 'German settlement on the lower Volga. A case study. The Moravian community at Sarepta 1763–1892', *Transactions of the Moravian Historical Society*, vol. 22, no. 2, 1969, pp. 47–99.

Kotwicz, W., *Józef Kowalewski Orientalista (1801-1878)*, Wrocław, 1948.

Laird, M.A., 'The contribution of the Serampore missionaries to education in Bengal, 1793–1837', *Bulletin of the School of Oriental and African Studies*, vol. 31, no. 1, 1968, pp. 92–112.

Laird, M.A., *Missionaries and Education in Bengal 1793–1837*, Oxford, Clarendon Press, 1972.

Lange, K., 'Maidari-Fest im Ivolginsker Kloster', *Jahrbuch des Museums für Völkerkunde zu Leipzig*, vol. 27, pp. 90–8.

Lansdell, H., *Through Siberia*, London, 1882.

Laufer, B., 'Skizze der mongolischen Literatur', *Keleti Szemle*, vol. 8, 1907, pp. 165–261. Reprinted in H. Walravens (ed.), *Kleinere Schriften von Berthold Laufer*, Wiesbaden, Franz Steiner Verlag, 1976, Teil 1, Bd 2, pp. 1120–1216.

Levin, M.G., and Potapov, L.P., *The Peoples of Siberia*, Chicago and London, University of Chicago Press, 1964.

Lovett, R., *James Gilmour of Mongolia. His Diaries, Letters and Reports*, London, Religious Tract Society, 1892.

Lovett, R., *James Gilmour and his Boys*, London, Religious Tract Society, 1894.

Lovett, R., *The History of the London Missionary Society 1795–1895*, London, Henry Frowde, 1899.

Marthinson, A.W., 'The revision of the Mongolian New Testament', *The Bible Translator*, vol. 5, 1954, pp. 74–8.

Massey Stewart, John, 'Early travellers, explorers and naturalists in Siberia', *Asian Affairs*, vol. 15 (Old Series vol. 71), Part 1, February 1984, pp. 55–64.

Mazour, A.G., *The first Russian Revolution 1825. The Decembrist Movement. Its Origins, Development and Significance*, Stanford, California, Stanford University Press, 1937.

Meignan, V., *De Paris à Pékin par Terre. Sibérie-Mongolie*, Paris, 1876.

Mende, Erling von, 'Einige Bemerkungen zu den Druckausgaben des mandjurischen Neuen Testaments', *Oriens Extremus*, vol. 19, 1972, pp. 215–22.

Michie, A., *The Siberian overland Route from Peking to Petersburg, through the Deserts and Steppes of Mongolia, Tartary, etc.*, London, 1864.

Missionary Magazine, vol. 1, June 1836 to December 1837; vol. 2, 1838; vol. 3, 1839.

Missionary Sketches, no. 23, October 1823; no. 39, October 1827; no. 72, January 1836.

Mumby, F.A., and Stallybrass, F.H.S., *From Swan Sonnenschein to George Allen and Unwin*, London, George Allen & Unwin, 1955.

Nairne, W.P., *Gilmour of the Mongols*, London, Pickering & Inglis, n.d. (1932).

Neill, Stephen, *A History of Christian Missions*, The Pelican History of the Church, vol. 6, Harmondsworth, Penguin Books, 1964, and London, Hodder & Stoughton, 1965.

Owen, J., *The History of the Origin and First ten Years of the British and Foreign Bible Society*, London, 1816–20.

Bibliography

Pallas, P.S., *Reise durch verschiedene Provinzen des russischen Reiches*, St Petersburg, 1771–6. Reprinted, Graz, Akademische Druck- u. Verlagsanstalt, 1967.

Pallas, P.S., *Sammlungen historischer Nachrichten über die mongolischen Völkerschaften*, St Petersburg, vol. 1, 1776; vol. 2, 1801.

Pallas, P.S., *Travels through the Southern Provinces of the Russian Empire in the years 1793 and 1794*, London, 1802.

Palmer, A., *Alexander I, Tsar of War and Peace*, London, Weidenfeld & Nicolson, 1974.

Paterson, J., *The Book for Every Land. Reminiscences of Labour and Adventure in the Work of Bible Circulation in the North of Europe and in Russia. By the late John Paterson D.D. Edited with a prefatory memoir by William Alexander D.D. F.S.A.S.*, London, 1857.

Periodical Accounts relating to the Missions of the Church of the United Brethren established among the Heathen. London, published by the Brethren's Society for the Furtherance of the Gospel, No. 10 Nevil's Court, Fetter Lane. vol. 1, 1790, to vol. 7, 1819.

Pinkerton, R., *Extracts of Letters from the Rev. Robert Pinkerton on his late Tour in Russia, Poland and Germany, to promote the Object of the British and Foreign Bible Society*, London, 1817.

Pinkerton, R., *Russia: or miscellaneous Observations on the past and present State of that Country and its Inhabitants*, London, 1833.

Poppe, N., *Mongolische Epen IX. Übersetzung der Sammlung C. Ž. Žamcarano, Proizvedenija narodnoj Slovesnosti mongol'skikh plemen*, t.I, Asiatische Forschungen, Bd 65, Wiesbaden, Otto Harrassowitz, 1980.

Pozdneyev, A.M., *Religion and Ritual in Society: Lamaist Buddhism in the late 19th-century Mongolia*. Edited by John R. Krueger. Translated from the Russian by Alo Raun and Linda Raun, Bloomington, Indiana, The Mongolia Society, 1978.

Quarterly Chronicle of Transactions of the London Missionary Society, London, vol. 1, 1821; vol. 2, 1825; vol. 3, 1829; vol. 4, 1833.

Rachewiltz, Igor de, 'Some remarks on the stele of Yisüngge', *Tractata Altaica*, ed. W. Heissig et al., Wiesbaden, Otto Harrassowitz, 1976, pp. 487–508.

Raeff, M., *Siberia and the Reforms of 1822*, Seattle, University of Washington Press, 1956.

Raeff, M., *Michael Speransky Statesman of Imperial Russia 1772–1839*, The Hague, Martinus Nijhoff, 1957.

Ramstedt, G.J., *Seven Journeys Eastward 1898–1912*. Translated from the Swedish and edited by John R. Krueger, Bloomington, Indiana, The Mongolia Society, 1978.

Reports of the British and Foreign Bible Society. Third Report, 1807 to 73rd Report, 1877.

Reports of the Directors to the Twenty Fourth General Meeting of the Missionary Society, May 14, 1818, and subsequent reports up to the 47th, 13 May, 1841.

Rinchen, *Four Mongolian Historical Records*, Indo-Asian Literature, vol. 2, New Delhi, International Academy of Indian Culture, 1959.

Robinson, C.H., *History of Christian Missions*, Edinburgh, T. and T. Clark, 1915.

Rosén, Staffan, 'Ur den Mongoliska Bibelns Historia', *Svensk Missionstidskrift*, Årgang 70, 1982, no. 2, pp. 23–49.

Rupen, R.A., *Mongols of the Twentieth Century*, Uralic and Altaic Series, vol. 37, Bloomington, Indiana University; The Hague, Mouton and Co., 1964.

Salmon, D. (ed.), *The Practical Parts of Lancaster's Improvements and Bell's Experiment*, Cambridge, Cambridge University Press, 1932.

Sandschejew, G., 'Weltanschauung und Schamanismus der Alaren-Burjaten', *Anthropos*, vol. 23, 1928, pp. 576–613, 933–86.

Schlatter, W., *Geschichte der Basler Mission, 1815–1915*, Basel, 1916.

Schmidt, I.J. (ed.), *Geschichte der Ost-Mongolen und Ihres Fürstenhauses, verfasst von Ssanang Ssetsen Chungtaidschi der Ordus; aus dem Mongolischen übersetzt, und mit dem Originaltexte, nebst Anmerkungen, Erläuterungen und Citaten aus anderen unedirten Originalwerken*, St Petersburg, Leipzig, 1829. Reprinted, The Hague, Europe Printing, 1961.

Serruys, H., 'Smallpox in Mongolia during the Ming and Ch'ing dynasties', *Zentralasiatische Studien*, vol. 14, no. 1, 1980, pp. 41–63.

Shorter, G.K., *George Borrow and his Circle*, London, New York, Toronto, 1913.

Sibree, J., *A Register of Missionaries, Deputations etc. from 1796 to 1923*. Fourth Edition, London, London Missionary Society, 1923.

Stallybrass, E., *Memoir of Mrs. Stallybrass, Wife of the Rev. Edward Stallybrass, Missionary to Siberia*, London, 1836.

Stallybrass, J.S., Memorandum on the Mongolian M.S.S. offered to the British Museum by J.S. Stallybrass, manuscript, The British Library, OR 2266.

Stumpf, C., 'Mongolische Gesänge', *Vierteljahrschrift für Musikwissenschaft*, 3 Jahrgang, zweites Heft, April 1887, pp. 297–304.

Swan, W., *Memoir of the late Mrs. Paterson, wife of the Rev. Dr. Paterson, St. Petersburg: containing Extracts from her Diary and Correspondence*, Edinburgh, Glasgow, Dublin, London, 1824. Third edition.

Swan, W., *Idolatry; a Poem in four Parts by the Rev. William Swan, Missionary at Selinginsk, and Author of Memoirs of Mrs. Paterson*, Glasgow, 1827.

Swan, W., *Letters on Missions*, London, 1843. Second edition.

Van Hecken, J., 'La littérature mongole chrétienne', *Neue Zeitschrift für Missionswissenschaft*, vol. 3, 1947, pp. 118–27.

Van Hecken, J., *Les missions chez les Mongols aux temps modernes*, Peiping, Imprimerie de Lazaristes, Petang, 1949.

W.S. (William Swan), 'The Buriats', *Scottish Congregational Magazine, New Series*, vol. 1, 1841, pp. 397–400; vol. 2, pp. 39–44, 103–7.

Watrous, S.D. (ed.), *John Ledyard's Journey through Russia and Siberia 1787–1788. The Journal and selected Letters*, Madison, Milwaukee, London, University of Wisconsin Press, 1966.

Whitehouse, J.O., *Register of Missionaries, Deputations etc. 1796-1896*. Third edition, Centenary, London, 1896.

Widmer, E., *The Russian Ecclesiastical Mission in Peking during the eighteenth Century*. Harvard East Asia Monographs 69, Cambridge, Massachusetts, and London, 1976.

Williams, D.S.M., 'The "Mongolian Mission" of the London Missionary Society: an episode in the history of religion in the Russian empire', *Slavonic and East European Review*, vol. 56, no. 3, July 1978, pp. 329–45.

Williamson, A., *Journeys in North China, Manchuria, and Eastern Mongolia*, London, 1870.

Wrede, H., *I Sibirien för 30 År sedan*, Stockholm, 1918. Finnish edition; *Siperiassa 30 vuotta sitten*, Porvoo, 1923.

Zacek, Judith C., 'The Russian Bible Society, 1812–1826', unpublished thesis, Columbia University, 1964.

Žamcarano, C.Ž. *The Mongol Chronicles of the seventeenth Century*, translated by Rudolf Loewenthal, Göttinger Asiatische Forschungen, Bd 3, Wiesbaden, Otto Harrassowitz, 1955.

Zwick, H.A., *Calmuc Tartary; or a Journey from Sarepta to several Calmuc Hordes of the Astracan Government; from May 26 to August 21, 1823. Undertaken on behalf of the Russian Bible Society, by Henry Augustus Zwick and John Golfried Schill, and described by the former*, London, 1831.

RUSSIAN SOURCES

Андрей Ефимович Мартынов 1768-1826. Акварель, Рисунок, Гравюра, Литография. Каталог, Ленинград, Государственный Русский Музей, 1977.

Алексеев, М. П., 'Русско-Английские литературные связи XVIII век — первая половина XIX века', Литературное Наследство, том девяносто первый, Москва, Издательство "Наука", 1982.

Асалханов, И. А., 'О Бурятских родах в XIX веке', Этнографический Сборник, вып. I, Улан-Удэ, 1960, стр. 68-83.

Вагин. В. И., 'Английские миссионеры в Сибири', Известия Сибирскаго Отдела Императорскаго Русскаго Географическаго Общества, I, 4 и 5, 1871, стр. 69-77.

Востриков, А. И. и Поппе, Н. Н., Летопись Баргузинских Бурят. Тексты и исследования, Труды Института Востоковедения VIII, Москва-Ленинград, 1935.

Декабристы М. и Н. Бестужевы. Письма из Сибири, вып I, Селенгинский Период 1839-1841, Иркутск, 1929.

Денисов, П. В., Никита Яковлевич Бичурин, Чебоксары, 1977.

Жмакин, В., 'Английская миссия за Байкалом 1817-1840', Христианское Чтение, 9-10, 1881, стр. 458-60. (not seen)

Завалишин, Д. И., Записки Декабриста, München, 1904.

Залкинд, Е. М., Общественный Строй Бурят XVIII и первой Половине XIX века, Москва, 1970.

Залкинд, Е. М., (ред.), Очерки Истории Културы Бурятии, том I, Улан-Удэ, 1972.

Костарев, С. П., Исторические Памятники Бурятии, Улан-Удэ, 1959.

Кудрявцев, Ф. А., История Бурят-Монгольского Народа, Москва-Ленинград, 1940.

Мартос, А., Письма о Восточной Сибири Алексея Мартоса, Москва, 1827.

Поппе, Н. Н., Летописи Хоринских Бурят, вып. I. Хроники Тугултур Тобоева и Вандана Юмсунова. Текст издал Н. Н. Поппе, Труды Института Востоковедения IX, Москва-Ленинград, 1935.

Поппе, Н. Н.. Летописи Селенгинских Бурят, вып. I. Хроника Убаши Дамби Джалцан Ломбо Церенова 1868 г. Текст издал Н. Н. Поппе, Труды Института Востоковедения XII. Москва-Ленинград, 1936.

Поппе, Н. Н., Летописи Хоринских Бурят. Хроники Тугулдур Тобоева и Вандана Юмсунова. Перевод Н. Н. Поппе, Труды Института Востоковедения XXXIII. Москва-Ленинград, 1940.

Пучковский, Л. С., 'Монгольская феодальная историография XIII–XVII вв.', Учение Записки Института Востоковедения, том I, Москва-Ленинград, 1953, стр. 131–66.

Пучковский, Л. С., 'Собрание Монгольских рукописей и ксилографов Института Востоковедения Академии Наук СССР', Ученые Записки Института Востоковедения, том IX, Москва-Ленинград, 1954, стр. 90–127.

Пучковскйй, Л. С., 'Александр Васильевич Игумнов', Очерки по Истории Русского Востоковедения, сборник 3, Москва, 1960, стр. 166–95.

Румянцев, Г. Н., 'Селенгинские Буряты (Происхождение и родо-племенной состав)', Материалы по Истории и Филологии Центральной Азии, вып. 2, Улан-Удэ, 1965, стр. 87–117.

Рыбаков, Г. С., 'Английские миссионеры в Забайкальской Области', Исторический Вестник 99, 1905, стр. 224–35.

Санжеев, Г. Д., (ред), Доржи Банзаров. Собрание Сочинений, Москва, 1955.

Устюгов, Н. В., Златкин, И. Я., Кушева, Е. Н., (ред.), Очерки Истории Кальмыцкой АССР. Дооктябрьский Период, Москва, 1967.

Хаптаев, П. Т., (ред.), История Бурят-Монгольской АССР, том I, Улан-Удэ, 1954.

Харчевников, А., 'Обзор исторических памятников Селенгинска', Сборник "Изучайте свой Край", Чита, 1924. (not seen)

Шамов, Г. Ф., 'Научная деятельность О. М. Ковалевского в Казанском университете', Очерки по Истории Русского Востоковедения, сборник 2, Москва, 1956, стр. 118–80.

Шастина, Н. П., 'Значение трудов Н. Я. Бичурина для Русского Монголоведения', Очерки по Истории Русского Востоковедения, сборник 2, Москва, 1956, стр. 181–97.

Шастина, Н. П., 'Из переписки О. М. Ковалевского с Бурятскими друзьями', Материалы по Истории и Филологии Центральной Азии, вып. 2, Улан-Удэ, 1965, стр. 210–21.

Шафрановская, Т. К., 'Монголист XVIII века Иоган Иериг', Страны и Народы Востока, вып. 4, Москва, 1965.

Index

Abercrombie, John, 7–8, 181, 291, 299–300, 302, 315, 351, 352
Abercrombie, Dr John, 291
Åbo, 77, 82
Abudai Khan, 39, 41
Academy of Sciences, Imperial, 24, 31, 123, 321
'Account of the manner . . .', 111–12, 114
Acts of the Apostles: in Kalmuck, 281, 282; in Mongolian, 233, 281, 282, 319
Advancement of Society, 218
Afanasii, Archbishop, 350
Aga lamasery, 148, 221, 231, 233–4
aimak, 259
Åland islands, 82
Alers Hankey, Miss, 75
Alers Hankey, William, 75, 78, 93, 96, 101, 114, 117, 122, 135, 136, 147, 157, 171, 174, 176, 182, 185, 187, 222, 236, 239, 260, 263, 269, 283, 293, 317, 325
Alexander I, Emperor, 4, 13, 14, 24, 25, 52, 53, 54, 57, 61, 76, 99, 100, 107, 108–9, 125, 147, 158, 175, 176–7, 191, 224, 269, 270, 290, 323, 326, 328, 329, 334, 336, 337, 338, 347, 352
Alexander, William, 49, 102
Altai range, 35
Altan Khan, 39, 40, 41, 110
Altan Tobchi, 133
Amdo, 166
America, United States of, 210, 349
Among the Mongols, 1, 3, 12, 204
Amsterdam, 33

Angara, river, 117, 131, 139
Angerstein, John Julius, 75
Angerstein, Juliana, 75; *see also* Sablukov, Juliana
Anglichanka, 17, 175
Antiburghers, 89
applications to become missionaries, 63–4, 85–7, 89–92
Arakcheev, 329
araki (distilled kumis), 163, 239
Argun, river, 32, 149
Arianism, 100
Armenians, 326–7
Arminians, 33
Arundel, John, 172
Ashibagat lamasery, 227
Asiatic Department of the Ministry of Foreign Affairs, 289, 330
Asmus Simonsen & Co., 23, 104, 171, 194, 195, 311, 312
Assembly Shorter Catechism, 272
Astrakhan, 13, 16, 18, 19, 23, 36, 77, 99, 210, 287, 298, 326
Attercos, Baron, 290
Avalokiteshvara, 39
Ayuka Khan, 135
Ayushi, 219, 220

Badma (convert), 276–7
Badma (taisha), 239
Badma (teacher), 273
Badma Morchiunayin, 109, 111–16, 147, 170, 196, 281–2, 285, 287, 292, 293
Baikal, Lake, 5, 28, 55, 110, 112, 117,

Index

119, 131, 133, 138, 149, 150, 151, 246
Baltic Sea, 66, 224
Bambar, 19
Bandido Khambo Lama, 167
baptism, 108, 112, 114–15, 120, 147–9, 244–5, 255, 323, 325, 326, 327, 328, 341–2, 345–7, 350, 354; and conflict with Russian law, 14, 19, 26, 115, 248, 255, 322, 324, 327, 347
Barabinsk steppe, 129
Barchigir, 180; *see also* Stepney (Siberia)
Bardo, 278
Barguzin, 151, 180
Basel mission, 7, 13, 291, 326, 327
Bass, Rev. James, 354
Bass, Sarah, 354
Batur-un, 167
Bayton, Mr, 197
Bell, John, of Antermony, 11, 123, 127, 142
Benares, 43
Bengal, 250, 253
Berg, Count, 138
Bergmann, Benjamin, 21, 24
Bestuzhev, M. A., 210
Bestuzhev, N. A., 173, 210, 256
Bible: in Chinese and Manchu, 212; in Finnish, 51, 52; in Kalmuck, 46; in Manchu, 31, 58, 60; in Mongolian, 3, 11, 31, 58, 107; *see also* Gospels; New Testament; Old Testament; Scriptures and tracts; and individual books
Bible House, St Petersburg, 75, 104
Bible in Spain, The, 60
Bible Societies, 13, 54, 77
Biblical Researches and Travels in Russia, 77
Bichurin, Iakinf, 32, 137, 275
Bigland, Eileen, 30, 31, 213
Bishops Stortford, 354
Black Faith, 36
Blackwood, Andrew, 51
Blackwood, Betty, 51; *see also* Rahmn, Betty
Blomdahl, Rev. J. U., 81, 82
Bludov, D. N., 192, 291, 318, 319, 334, 336, 338–40, 350
Bobrovnikov, Aleksei, 137
Bobrovnikov, Alexander, 76, 121, 133, 137, 318
Bocharov, post-master, 316, 332

Bodleian Library, 307, 310
Bogue, Rev. David, 7, 62, 92, 93, 94, 95, 186, 218, 266
boo, böö, 153, 246
Book for Every Land, The, 49, 52, 110
Booker, John, 97
Bookless Faith, 36
Boriats, Boriates, Boriatts, *see* Buryats
Borrow, George, 30, 31, 55, 84–5, 212–14, 266, 292, 330, 340
Bratsky, *see* Buryats
British and Foreign Bible Society (BFBS), 8, 22–3, 30, 46, 47, 48, 57–8, 60, 78, 80, 158, 171, 212–14, 279, 280, 281, 288, 291, 296, 309, 316, 318–19, 320, 321, 330, 340, 353, 354; Library of, 8, 157, 268, 296, 298; Reports of, 58, 114, 288
British Library, 157, 268, 296
British Museum, Library of, 8, 10, 199, 330
Bronevskii, S. B., 327, 343
Brothers (ship), 54
Brown, Rev. John Crombie, 9, 11, 110, 164, 278, 313, 342
Brown, Mr, 23, 77, 99, 132
Browne, Rev. G., 298
Brunton, Henry, 23, 47
Bü, Büger, 246
Buchan's Domestic Medicine, 201
Buddhism, *see* lamaism
Bulatov, Stephen, 177
bunkhan, 162
Burates, Buräts, *see* Buryats
burchan, see idols, images, Buddhist
Burder, Rev. George, 56, 63, 81, 99, 117, 175, 185, 209, 243, 258, 262, 263, 269, 283, 328
Burghers, 90
Buriats, Buriatts, *see* Buryats
Burjats, *see* Buryats
Burns, Rev. Dr, 96
Buryates, *see* Buryats
Buryatia, 59, 91, 107, 150, 151, 166, 327
Buryats: language of, 58, 105, 109, 138; as a Mongolian people, 47–8; and donations to the RBS, 54, 56–7, 110, 112; and conversion to Christianity, 107, 111, 134, 165–6, 207, 222, 227, 249, 261, 276–8, 332, 345, 352; their culture, 138–9, 152–3; and baptism, 148, 163, 244–6; distribution of,

368

Index

149–152; and conversion to
  Buddhism, 156, 219, 233; as printing
  assistants, 299, 308, 310
Buryats, the two, see zaisangs

Cabardians, 291
Calmuc, Calmuck, see Kalmuck
Cambuslang, 50
Campbell, Miss, 101
Canton, 16
Capetown, 9
Carey, William, 1, 12, 50, 250, 254
Carruthers, Douglas, 262
Caspian Sea, 16
Catherine II (the Great), Empress, 13, 17, 18, 27, 167
Catharinenbrunnen, 18
Cathcart, Lord, 97
Caucasus, 19, 20, 23, 27, 291
Caya-yin, Dambadarjaa, 166–7
censor(ship), 288, 289, 290, 320
Chamba, see Khamba
Ch'ien-lung emperor, 35, 111
Chikoi, river, 167
children, missionaries', 194, 205, 206–8
China, 14–16, 28, 35, 39, 107, 143, 151, 199, 212, 268
Chinese (people), 15, 43, 205, 322
Ch'ing dynasty, 151; see also Manchu dynasty
Chita, 233
Chopin, F., 138
Chorin, Chorinian, Chorinsk, Chorinsky, see Khori
Christianity, 38, 42, 45, 46, 116, 122, 134, 147, 158, 165, 178, 227, 234–6, 245, 325
Christians, 122, 158, 161, 222, 245, 325
church, missionaries' inability to form in Siberia, 207, 248, 255, 345, 347
Church of England, 99
Church of Scotland, 89, 99
Cisbaikalia, 139, 150
Clavering, 63
Cochrane, Captain John Dundas, 88, 142, 171, 172
colonies, foreign, in Russia, 18; privileges of, 17, 24, 25–6, 29, 323
Committee of Examination, 7, 24, 61, 62, 65, 66, 67, 74, 92, 93
Congregationalism, 156
Constantine, Prince, 128

Cook, Captain James, 123
Copenhagen, 50, 215
copyists, 179, 180, 194, 267–8, 272, 301
correspondence, of mission, 9, 14, 96, 106, 147, 148, 156–7, 185, 198, 210, 286, 344, 346
Cossacks, Buryat, 133, 150, 152, 274
Cottrell, C. H., 332
Council for World Mission, Library of, 10
Coward College, 208
Cowie, Martha, 6, 94, 95, 96, 145; see also Yuille, Martha
Crimea, 77
Cronstadt, 66, 74, 75, 97–8, 104
Cullen, Hannah, 212; see also Swan, Hannah

Dalai Lama, 5, 37, 38, 39, 40, 41, 43, 45, 139, 166, 230, 231, 332
Damba, 243
Dambadarjaa Caya-yin, see Caya-yin
Darlow and Moule, 8, 316
Davidson, Mr, 24, 29
Decembrists, 76, 173, 209
Delek, 271, 272
Dembil Galsanov, 112, 114, 120, 147–9, 151, 201, 238, 244, 264, 273, 345, 354
d'Entrecolles, Père, 205
Dictionaries, 30, 31, 32, 33, 59, 87, 88, 89, 115, 135, 136, 137, 186, 215, 254, 267, 268, 269, 305, 306
disease, demons of, 38, 164
Dissenters, 99, 100
District Captain, 331–5, 344
divination, 37, 38
Djigjit, see Jigjit
Dodds, Dr, 266, 304
Don, river, 35
Doorga, 168
Dorji Banzarov, 133, 134, 275
Douglas, James, 218–19
drunkenness, 44, 76, 120, 238–9
Dschimba, 257–8
Due, Lieutenant, 125
Duff (ship), 17
Dundalk, 89
Duntocher, 49
Dyer, Mrs Samuel, 250
dzaisang, see zaisang

East India Company, 12, 50
Eastern Committee of LMS, 215, 286
Edinburgh, 10, 77, 84, 353;
  Congregational churches at, 50;
  University of, 84
education: as a missionary activity,
  250–1; for girls, 250, 278; objectives
  of, 251–2; Swan's views on, 252;
  Yuille's ideas on, 253; and
  Lancasterian system, 253; at Sarepta,
  257–8; government provision for,
  259–60; disincentives to, 261; begins
  at Selenginsk, 262; and conversions,
  275–8
Eight Fathers, 151, 166
Eighteen Tribes, 240, 264
Ekaterinburg, 129
Ekhrit-Bulgat Buryats, 138
Elders' Conference of the Unity, 112
Ellah, Charlotte, 74, 215; see also
  Stallybrass, Charlotte
Ellah, T., 74, 210
Ellis, William, 183, 210, 212, 214, 215,
  296, 299, 306, 310, 319
Elsinore, 50, 74, 215, 216
Erdene Juu, 41
Erdeni-yin Tobchi (Schmidt's chronicle),
  32, 39, 110, 136
Eriksson, Rev. Joel, 321
Erlik Khan, 229
Erman, Adolph, 131, 141, 167, 171,
  222, 228–9
Erskine, Ebenezer, 90
Evangelical Magazine, 9, 67, 114, 119,
  208
Evangelical movement, revival, 1, 49
Evangelicalism, 323, 326
Evsevii, Archbishop, 350
Ewing, Rev. Greville, 50, 77, 85, 86,
  90, 92, 157, 158, 266
exiles, 71, 209, 334
Exodus, Book of, 183, 204, 302
expenses, mission, 120, 169, 170, 171,
  176, 180, 181, 190, 193
'Extracts from a Missionary's Journal',
  277
*Extracts of Letters from the Rev. Robert
  Pinkerton*, 49
Ezekiel, Book of, 315

Fife, 83
Fifteen Fathers, 150

fire-worship, 37, 165
First-Fruits of a Mission to Siberia, 9–10,
  11, 110
Fleming, Mr, 92
Fletcher, Rev. Mr, 230
Ford, Rev. George, 65, 230
Fotii, Archimandrite, 329
'Four Roots', 199
*Fragment of the Journal of a Tour through
  Persia*, 56
Fries, Jakob, 124
frontier, Russo-Chinese, 59, 134, 142,
  148, 150, 151, 152, 164, 221, 322

Galdan, 152
Galitzin, *see* Golitsyn
Galsang Gomboev, 133
Galsang Mardaev, 54, 112, 147
Gelugpa lamaism, 36, 39
gelung (gellong, gelong), 44, 46, 162, 233,
  234
Gendung, 155
Genesis, Book of: translated by
  Stallybrass, 7, 183, 286, 292, 293;
  printed at Selenginsk, 7, 298; dispute
  over printing, 7, 183–44, 215, 294,
  301–3; censored copy, 7, 291, 292,
  293, 294, 299, 302; translated by
  Novoselov, 135, 292; rarity of first
  edition, 298; suppression of first
  edition authorized, 315; corrected,
  315
Genghis Khan, 32, 36, 38, 39, 41, 239;
  Stone of, 32, 275
George Town, 12
ger, 35, 152
*Geschichte der Ost-Mongolen und Ihres
  Fürstenhauses*, 111
Geser Khan epic, 32, 268
Gesundbrunnen, 18, 145
Gilmour, James, 1–12, 101, 125, 202–3,
  204, 209, 216, 219, 249, 251, 353,
  354–5
Glasgow, 49, 83, 85, 89, 91, 93, 96, 353;
  Theological Academy at, 85, 217,
  353; University of, 49, 83, 91, 92, 303
Glen, Mr, 99
Glitsch, Alexander, 21
Gmelin, J. G., 123
goat, as sacrificial animal, 160, 161
Gobi Desert, 151
'Golden Summary', 133

370

Index

Golitsyn, Prince A. N., 13, 14, 52, 53, 54, 57, 76, 98, 100, 107, 113, 116, 148, 175, 176, 195, 196, 224, 256, 269, 270, 287, 288, 290, 325, 326, 329
Golitsyn, Princess, 13, 47, 53
Golovkin, Count, 134, 205
Gombodorji, 42
Goose Lake lamasery, 112, 140, 157, 162, 167, 168, 221, 222, 227, 234, 247
Gordon, Captain Peter, 15, 54–7, 73, 121, 122, 132, 143, 170, 172, 199, 228
Gospels: in Kalmuck, 196, 281; in Mongolian, 119–20, 179, 196–8, 233, 281, 286, 319; in Russian, 179
Gosport, Seminary at, 7, 62, 80, 92, 93, 95, 218, 254
Gossner, 196, 270
Gothenburg, 50, 51, 78–82
Gowing, Lionel, 124, 126
Grammars, 30, 88, 89, 215, 254
Grant, Mrs, 101
Greek church, *see* Orthodox church
Greenland, mission to, 51, 82
Gregor, Rev. C. F., 23, 24
Greig, Admiral, 79
Greig, Jean, 79, 104; *see also* Paterson, Jean
Gurii, Archimandrite, 309
Gutzlaff, Karl, 354

Hablitz, Privy Councillor, 52
Haldane, James, 77
Haldane, Robert, 49, 50, 77
Hall, John, 51
Hamel, Christian, 43, 44, 45
Hansteen, Professor C., 125, 131, 331, 335
Haslar Hospital, 266, 304
Hasse, J. H., 19
Hedenström, Mattias, 135, 140, 169, 332
Henderson, Ebenezer, 20, 49, 50–1, 65, 75, 76–80, 104, 105, 114, 195, 215, 283, 291, 320
Herrnhut, 18, 22, 44
Hickey, William, 205
Hill, Rowland, 77
Hill, S. S., 171, 225, 228, 254–5
Hindus, 43, 168, 325

Hints on Missions, 218
Hollinder, Katarina, 50; *see also* Paterson, Katarina
home leave, 193, 210, 211
Homerton College, 63, 64, 65, 208, 217, 354
Hommaire de Hell, Xavier, 21, 36
Horne, C. S., 16
horse tax, 126
horses, order for, 125, 126; *see also* passports
horses, wooden, 167, 168, 227
house-building, 170, 176, 178, 180, 190–2, 223
Hübner, Brother, 22
Humba, *see* Khamba

icon veneration, 335, 338–41, 345
idolatry, 158, 276, 335, 340
Idolatry, 157–64
idols, images: Buddhist, 139, 140, 153, 157–8, 162, 276, 277–8, 338; shaman, 153, 231, 240; *see also* ongon
Igumnov, A. V., 76, 133, 134, 135, 261
Ilinskaya, 125
Improvements in Education, 189
independency, independents, 49, 67, 82, 89, 90, 100
India: Edinburgh mission to, 50, 77; schools in, 250
Indian Institute, 307
Ionian Islands, 93
Irene, Archbishop, 327, 339
Irkut river, 131
Irkutsk: mission to, 4–5, 13, 14, 47, 48, 51, 58, 60–1, 78, 80, 81, 103–4, 138, 144–5; (Civil) Governor of, 105, 108, 130, 131, 169, 191, 256, 314; (Arch)bishop of, 108, 163, 196–8, 322, 327, 335, 336, 337, 339; Government of, 110, 130; life at, 131–4, 169; Spiritual (Religious) Seminary at, 137, 259, 327; Bible Society at, 197–8; schools at, 259–60
Irtysh Line, 27
Isaiah, Book of, 91, 293–5, 305, 307
Ishi gelung, 44, 45
itineration, 187, 220, 237, 247; *see also* journeys
Ivanova, Maria, 76
Izmailov, L. V., 123

Index

Jaehrig, Johannes, 21, 44
Jäschke, H. A., 32–3
Jebtsundamba Khutuktu, 40, 41, 42, 166, 205
Jenkins, Herbert, 30, 31
Jenner, Edward, 205
Jesuits, 85, 107, 212, 292
Jew's harp, 154
Jigjit Dambadugarov, 149, 151, 180, 243, 264, 273, 351
Jimba, 166–7
John, First Epistle of: in Kalmuck, 283
John, Gospel of: in Kalmuck, 282; in Mongolian, 223, 281–2
John Williams (ship), 2
journals, 9, 106, 108, 120, 156, 185, 204, 237, 247, 257, 258
journeys, 181, 204, 209, 220, 223, 237–44, 246; *see also* itineration
Jowett, Rev. Joseph, 30, 213, 318, 319, 320
Juggernaut, 168
Jülg, B., 309
Jungaria, 35, 152
Jungars, 35, 142, 152, 166

kabitkie, see kibitka
Kaichta, *see* Kyakhta
Kalgan, 295–6
Kalmuck alphabet, 36, 54, 58
Kalmuck language, 36, 43, 44, 58, 109
Kalmucks, 16–17, 18, 19, 21, 24, 26, 27, 34–7, 44–6, 47, 112, 257–9; Moravian mission to, 23, 26, 37, 42–6, 53
Kalv, 4
Kamenskii, Archimandrite, 136, 137, 213
Kan, river, 149
K'ang-hsi emperor, 35, 42
Kansk, 130
Karass, Scottish colony at, 7, 13, 23, 25, 29, 47, 291, 326, 351, 352
Karakorum, 39, 41
Kazan, 27, 127, 128, 137, 262, 291, 305, 316; Government of, 330; Spiritual Academy at, 309–10; University of, 32, 133, 137, 212
Kennan, George, 124, 131, 167
Khalkha, 39, 41, 42, 143, 166
Khamba, 112, 140, 141, 157, 162, 166, 168, 170, 206, 221, 225–6, 228, 229,
230, 233–4, 255, 264, 267, 271, 331, 335
Kharganatskii tribe, 111
Khimni, river, 166; *see also* Temnik
Khoatsaiskii tribe, 111
Khodon, river and mission station, 5, 171, 181, 182, 184, 190, 199, 204, 213, 215, 216, 221, 327, 334, 335, 349, 351; Old Testament printed at, 7–8, 315, 316; house at, burned, 181, 190, 333; trouble over reoccupation of, 190–2, 333–4; congregation at, 249; school at, 249, 273, 274, 275, 278; girls taught at, 273
Khomba, *see* Khamba
Khori Buryats, 54, 111, 112, 115, 121, 143–4, 147–9, 150–1, 165, 172, 180, 221, 223, 233, 237, 238, 246, 264
Khoridai, 151
Khorinsk, 151
Khoshut, 36
Khubilai Khan, 39, 40, 41
khürüm, 44–5
Khutuktu Setsen Khungtaiji, 39, 40, 110
Kiachta, *see* Kyakhta
kibitka: (tent), 35; (vehicle) 124, 140
Kilgour, Rev. Dr Robert, 309
King's Head Society, 63, 65
Kirei-Kirghis, 262
Kirkcaldy, 84
Kneesworth Street, church in, 62
Knill, Rev. Richard, 22, 93, 100, 175, 176, 185, 195, 213, 223, 224, 250, 269, 270, 275, 285, 287, 289, 326, 329
Knox, Thomas, 125
Kochubei, Count, 52, 53
Kokonor, 35
kontora, 150, 151, 180, 241, 244, 260, 264
Korsakov, P., 307
Kotwicz, W., 310
koumiss, *see* kumis
Kowalewski, J. E., 32, 76, 133, 134, 135, 136, 137–8, 275
Krasnoarmeiisk, 18
Krasnoyarsk, 130, 149
Krüdener, Julie von, 13
Kudarinsk, 134
Kudarinsk Buryats, Kudarintsy, 151, 152, 246
Kumba, *see* Khamba
kumis, 140, 238

Index

Kungur, 129
Kyakhta, 15–16, 21, 28, 55, 101, 109, 117, 133, 134, 135, 142, 143, 189, 275, 331; Treaty of, 28, 142, 150

lamaism, 11, 14, 36–42, 43, 45–6, 48, 59, 106–7, 113, 139–40, 151, 153, 156–7, 158–9, 163–5, 166, 167, 231, 232–6, 243, 268
lamas, 14, 37, 38, 44, 45, 54, 57, 107, 140, 141, 150, 152, 156, 162–3, 164–5, 199–201, 220, 221–3, 225–7, 230, 231–6, 243–4, 261, 337, 344
lamaseries, 35, 88, 140, 152, 166, 221–2, 231, 233, 243–4, 268; visits to, 14, 157, 221, 224, 227–8
Lancaster, Joseph, 189, 253
Lancasterian system, 253, 257, 258, 263
Langton, David, 118, 185
language learning, 17, 43–4, 66, 100, 104, 105, 106, 134, 135, 146, 181, 220, 223, 269
Lansdell, Henry, 124, 251
Latrobe, Rev. C. I., 23
Lavinskii, A. S., 331, 334, 340, 343
leave, *see* home leave
Ledyard, John, 123–4
Leighton, Dr, 130
Leith, 98
Letters on Missions, 17, 42, 74, 87, 218, 300–1, 324, 355
Lhasa, 43, 166
Lieven, Prince, 104, 291
Life of George Borrow, 30
Ligdan Khan, 40
Linn, The, 77
Lipovtsov, S. V., 30, 212
'List of Queries', 85
Living Buddha, *see* Jebtsundamba Khutuktu
Livingstone, David, 1, 87
Lockhart, William, 10
London Missionary Society (LMS), 1, 16, 217; Board of, 7, 62, 65, 66, 79, 80, 92, 93, 94, 95, 96, 269, 286, 304, 346; Directors of, 7, 15, 16–17, 25, 28–9, 57–61, 62, 65, 66, 72, 78, 83, 85, 86, 94, 95, 96, 97, 98, 103, 104, 106, 127, 128, 143, 144, 145, 148, 183, 185, 187, 188, 189, 211, 213, 230, 233, 249, 252, 253, 262, 265, 271, 283, 284, 285, 286, 287, 288, 289, 293, 294, 295, 296, 302, 305, 306, 307, 312, 313, 314, 315, 318, 320, 322, 323, 324, 331, 341, 345–8, 351; Library of, 10, 23, 298, 355; Reports of, 8, 9, 185, 269, 270, 286, 288, 295, 319
Lord's Prayer, 223
Lot, the, 18
Love, Rev. John, 16
Lovett, Richard, 1–2, 10
Lübeck, 215
Lund, University of, 51, 81, 217
Lutheran church, 22

Mack, Captain, 97
Madagascar, 208
Madras, 55, 93, 250, 326
Madura, 55
magic, 37, 200, 201
Maidar, *see* Maitreya
Maidari (Maitreya) festival, 167–8, 227
Maimaicheng, 133, 142, 143
Maitreya, 167, 168, 227
Malacca, 62, 92, 93, 94, 143, 250
Malan, Rev. Dr S. C., 307, 308
Maltsch, J. F., 43, 44
Manakhan Tengri, 165
Manchu alphabet, 58, 59
Manchu dynasty, 35, 268; *see also* Ch'ing dynasty
Manchu language, 15, 58, 59, 60, 150
Manchus, 35, 56, 142, 151, 152
Mandjur, Manjur, *see* Manchu
mares' milk, 35, 238, 239
Marieberg, 81
marriage: LMS and, 58, 60, 66, 67, 74, 79, 94, 95, 96, 103, 145
Marshman, Joshua, 250, 293
Martos, A., 167, 175, 199, 222, 228
Mashy Saiin Belek, 308
Maslov, Colonel, 91, 303, 335–6
Matthew, Gospel of: in Kalmuck, 46, 53, 58, 109, 110, 111, 112, 113, 280–1; in Mongolian, 109, 112, 113, 146, 223, 281
Mault, Charles, 250
Mead, Mr, 62
medical work, missionaries', 44–5, 107, 184, 199, 256
medicine, Tibetan, 164–5, 199–201
Meignan, Victor, 101–2
Melnikoff, 251

Index

Memoir of the late Mrs Paterson, 174, 196–7, 211
Memoir of Mrs Stallybrass, 67, 75, 170, 172, 355
'Memorandum on the Mongolian MSS', 199
Merchants, Guilds of, 26, 56
merchants, Russian, 107, 130, 140, 180, 195
Meshcherskaya, Princess Sofiya, 13, 47, 53, 76, 270, 326
Meshcherskii, Prince, 290
Methodism, 99
Michael, *see* Nomtu
Michie, Alexander, 153
Mickiewicz, Adam, 137
Mikhail, Archbishop, 196–7, 317–18, 327, 338, 339
Milne, Robert, 250, 293
Ming dynasty, 151
Minister of ecclesiastical affairs and public instruction, 177
Minister (Ministry) of the Interior, 129, 314, 326, 338, 342, 349
Mirrielees, Archibald, 316
mission(aries), the English, 2–16, 47, 48, 53, 57–61, 62, 71–80, 88, 94–6, 104–10, 116, 134, 138, 143–6, 147–8, 156, 169, 172, 180–90, 191–2, 193–6, 201–3, 204, 209, 210, 217–18, 246–9, 255–6, 279, 283–90, 317, 322–6, 327–42, 344–52, 354–5
mission colonies, 17–18, 23–9
Mission House, 187, 315
Missionary Chronicle, 97, 188
Missionary Magazine, 9
Missionary Sketches, 9, 168
missionary work, 17, 43, 86–7, 105–8, 138, 217–20, 246, 254–6
Mitchell, Mr, 210, 287–9
Monds, Ann, 56, 67, 68, 69, 76, 80, 100, 102, 127, 128, 132, 157, 198, 203, 207, 208, 215, 230, 346, 349, 350, 353
Monds, Joseph, 68, 100, 101, 132, 198, 203, 207, 215
money supply, 194–6
Mongolia, 2, 9, 39, 40, 41, 150, 152, 163, 164, 165, 167, 206
Mongolia, Inner, 35, 39, 151, 249
Mongolia, Outer, 35, 39, 40, 143, 151, 152, 322
Mongolian alphabet, 36, 112

Mongolian language, 15, 32, 36, 38, 58, 105, 115, 116, 133, 150, 154, 160, 206, 207, 231, 279
Mongolian literature, 32, 138, 268, 279
Mongolian music, 206
Mongolian peoples, 35, 47–8, 58, 109, 165
Mongolian studies, 11, 87–8, 111, 133, 134, 321
Mongols, 2, 15, 31, 47, 48, 59, 110, 111, 143, 150, 156, 166, 200, 205, 227, 262; mission to, 1–2, 12, 354
Mongols, eastern, 35, 36, 38, 40, 111
Mongols, West, 35
Montagu, Lady Mary Wortley, 205
Moravians, 13, 18–23, 25, 42–6, 50, 53–4, 82, 106, 143, 196, 257, 280, 323; *see also* United Brethren; U.F.
Moreham, 127
Morison, Dr, 193
Morrison, Robert, 1, 15, 250, 293
Mortimer, Mr, 99
Moscow: fire of, 19, 34, 280; Bible Society at, 47, 52; Metropolitan of, 318
Murom, 127–8; Bible Society at, 128
Muslims, 26, 27, 47, 262, 323

Namkhaijamtso, 43
Nanking, Treaty of, 320
Napoleon I, 13, 52
Neitz, Conrad, 43, 44, 46
Nemptchinof, Madame, 101
Nerchinsk, 134, 150, 180, 221
Nestorian Christianity, 158
Neuwied, school at, 33
New Testament, *see* Testament, New
New York, Bible Society of, 315
Nicholas I, Emperor, 3, 13, 91, 92, 191, 255, 273, 275, 290, 291, 335, 338, 347, 349, 351–2
Nicolson, Mr, 304
Nikolai, *see* Rinchindorji
Nikolai, Baron, 51
Nil, Archbishop, 134, 343, 348, 349, 350
Nizhni Novgorod, 102, 125, 128
nom, 201, 219, 252, 253
Nomadische Streifereien unter den Kalmüken, 24
nomads, nomadism, 35, 150, 152, 182, 206, 220, 221, 238, 259, 261

Index

Nomtu Uutayin, 109, 111–21, 147, 242, 244, 282
Northern Committee of LMS, 80, 145, 249, 269, 286, 289
Novgorod, 77
Novo-Selenginsk, 143
Novoselov, Vasilii, 76, 110, 133, 136, 292
Novosil'tsev, N. N., 24, 25, 28, 29

obo, oboga, 37, 162–3, 165
Ocean of Stories, 32
Ochotsk, *see* Okhotsk
odagan, 153, 154
Ogodai Khan, 239
Oirat language, 58
Oirats, 35, 39, 152
Olchon, *see* Ol'khon
Old Testament, *see* Testament, Old
Okhotsk, 15, 54, 55, 122, 170, 199; Bible Society at, 13
Ol'khon, island of, 151, 156, 246
Ona, river and mission station, 3, 5, 151, 180, 181, 182, 184, 191, 211, 221, 233, 327, 335, 351; congregation at, 249; school at, 249, 273, 274, 275, 276, 278; girls taught at, 273
Onagen Dome, 5
ongon, ongoon, 36, 153, 156, 164, 240; *see also* idols
Onon, river, 233
Opium War, First, 15, 320
ordination, 65, 85, 92
Ordos, 110
Orenburg, Scottish missionaries at, 13
Orme, Rev. William, 72, 188, 211, 218, 317
Orthodox church, 5, 12–13, 14, 20, 26, 45, 55, 100, 104, 106, 108, 112, 115, 116, 117, 120, 121, 143, 148, 149, 163, 166, 196, 244–5, 251, 322, 323, 324, 325, 328, 335, 339–40, 354
Orthodox missionaries, 156, 244, 327, 338, 350
Oscar (ship), 74
Otaheite, 129
Otrada, 20
Oughton, Mary Ann, 354

Pagspa Lama, 39, 40, 41
Pallas, P. S., 20, 21, 23, 123, 167

Panchen Lama, 41, 166
Pangloss, Dr, 60
Papof, Papoff, *see* Popov, V. M.
Parfenii, Archbishop, 350
Parker, Peter, 355
passports, 25, 96–8; *see also* horses, order for
Paterson, Jean, 85, 118, 119, 174–5; *see also* Greig, Jean
Paterson, Rev. John: and the beginnings of the mission, 6–7, 14, 16, 29, 57–61, 65, 66; his memoirs, 7, 49, 58, 73, 79, 80, 109, 114; distrust of Yuille, 7, 96, 185, 283; and the RBS, 13, 14, 49, 53–4; and Bible work, 20; visits Sarepta, 20; and Moravian translations, 22, 283; and Schmidt, 33–4, 53–4, 281; and Pinkerton, 48–9, 52–3; early life, 49–50; and Henderson, 50, 77, 78–82; fails to reach India, 50; in Scandinavia, 50–1; goes to Russia, 51–2; and Rahmn, 51, 103, 144–5; visits Moscow, 52–3, 281; and Kalmuck type, 54; and Mongolian language, 58–9; recruits Rahmn, 78–82, 85; and married missionaries, 94, 96; and the British in St Petersburg, 99; and the journey to Irkutsk, 101, 102, 126, 130; character of, 102; marriage to Jean Greig, 104; and Stallybrass's Instructions, 104–5; and the zaisangs, 109–10, 114–15, 118; and the move to Selenginsk, 138, 144; and Jean's death, 174; and money supply, 195; and the *Memoir of Mrs Paterson*, 196–7, 211; leaves Russia, 287; and Mitchell, 288; and Abercrombie, 291; and Schmidt's New Testament, 317; and baptism, 323, 347
Paterson, Katarina, 52, 53, 66; *see also* Hollinder, Katarina
Paterson Papers, 174
Patterson, Alexander, 23, 47
Pauly, J. F., 34
Pearse, Rev. James, 63
Peking, 15, 59, 101, 110, 123, 134, 295; printing at, 59, 111, 136, 268; LMS hospital at, 202–3
Penang, girls' school at, 250
Pentateuch, 31, 296, 315
Periodical Accounts relating to the

Index

Missions of the United Brethren, 23, 111, 282
Perm, 128, 129
Persia, 19, 23, 55
Pestel, I. B., 48, 56, 61, 125, 148, 260
Peter the Great, Emperor, 123, 166, 259
Pinkerton, Rev. Robert: and the beginnings of the mission, 29, 48, 57–61, 110, 323; and Schmidt, 33; at Karass and Moscow, 47; and Paterson, 48–9, 52–3; and the Buryat donations, 54; and Stallybrass's Instructions, 104–5; and Badma, 116; and the mission press, 285; and translation of Old Testament, 292
Pitt, Pastor, 13
Pitt, William, 24
Planta, Joseph, 330
podorozhnaya, 126; *see also* horses, order for; passports
Poirot, Louis, 212, 292
police, 135, 140, 150, 176, 330
Poll, Mr von, 319
Polo, Marco, 40
Popov, A. V., 76, 133, 137, 275
Popov, Vasilii Mikhailovich, 52, 53, 98, 99, 100, 107, 147, 175, 176, 223, 270, 287, 290, 325, 329–30
Potasoff, Count, 350
Pozdneev, A. M., 167
prayer wheel, 140, 162, 229
preaching, 106, 107, 201, 220
'Precious Summary', *see Erdeni-yin Tobchi*
Presbyterian church, 49
Prins Oskar School, 82
printer, 95, 286–9, 291, 300
printing-press: of mission, 6, 7, 95, 181, 183, 284–7, 299, 302, 315, 316, 318, 344, 351; Yuille's, *see* Yuille, Robert
prison visiting, 47, 174
'Products of Home Industry' exhibition, 32
Prout, Aunt, 208
Psalms, Book of: in Kalmuck, 283; in Mongolian, translated by Rintsin and Yuille, 180, 267, 272, 280, 293–4, 296; Yuille and printing of, 305–7; octavo edition of, 315
Pugachev, 19
Puget, Mrs, 194
Pun-tsogs Noyan, 166
Pyatnitskii, 343

Pye Smith, Dr, 64, 66, 79

Quakerism, 323
Quarterly Chronicle of Transactions of the London Missionary Society, 9, 88, 108, 120, 127, 139, 160, 230

Raeff, Marc, 255
Rafaravavy, 208
Rahmn, Betty, 66–7, 73–4, 76, 96, 101–2, 103, 127–8, 144–5, 169, 259
Rahmn, Rev. Cornelius: opens the mission, 4, 10, 110; at Sarepta, 22, 145, 257–9; early life of, 51, 81–2; and Henderson, 51; friction with the Stallybrasses, 73–4, 169; accepted by the LMS, 78–82; at St Petersburg, 82, 100; described, 101; Paterson and, 102–3, 144–5; Memoir of, 108; received by Alexander I, 108–9; studies Mongolian, 134; journey to Kyakhta, 135–6, 139–43; leaves Irkutsk, 144, 146; in Russia and London, 145; life at Irkutsk, 169; translations, 282–3; his books, 283; proposed return to Selenginsk, 289
Rahmn, G. S., 81
Rahmn, Hannah, 81, 82, 108
Ranavalona, Queen, 208
Rehmann, Dr Joseph, 205–6
Reminiscences of the Mission in Siberia, 10
Reval, 330
Riga, 24, 135
Rinchindorji, 273
Rintsin (copyist), 200–1
Rintsin Nima Wangchikov, 32, 91, 133, 179–80, 262, 267, 271, 272, 274–5, 280, 295, 296, 306
Robinson, Sarah, 65, 66, 67–74; *see also* Stallybrass, Sarah
Robinson, Thomas, 65, 68–9, 71, 210
Robinson, Thomas (junior), 76, 127
Rodofincken, Mr, 333
Roman Catholic church, 38, 100, 336
Roman Catholicism, 335
Rostock, University of, 31
rouble, 126, 194
Royal Asiatic Society, 8, 88, 186–7
Royston, 62
Rupert, V. Y., 331, 343–4

Russia: or Miscellaneous Observations, 49
Russian American Company, 126, 131, 194–5
Russian authorities, 14, 23, 26, 29, 45, 72, 143, 148, 163, 190, 269, 287, 289, 315, 326, 327, 331, 333, 335, 337, 348
Russian Bible Society (RBS), 13, 33, 47, 48, 52, 53, 54, 56, 58, 77, 106, 109, 111, 112, 114, 147, 175, 196, 197, 223, 269–70, 281, 284, 286, 287, 288, 317, 325, 328, 329
Russian church, *see* Orthodox church
Russian Ecclesiastical Mission in Peking, 15, 110, 134, 136, 137, 212
Russian government, 10, 26, 45, 259, 270, 323, 326, 327, 328, 330, 333, 344, 348
Russian language: spoken by Jesus Christ, 235
Rybakov, G. S., 173

Sablukov, Juliana, 75, 76, 99; *see also* Angerstein, Juliana
Sablukov, General N. A., 75, 76, 99
Sagang Setsen, 110
St Petersburg: Congregational church at, 9, 23, 77, 99–100, 213, 342; LMS agent at, 9, 22, 100, 210, 287; Moravian chapel at, 22, 23, 99; British community at, 99; pastor at, 100
saisang, *see* zaisang
salaries, missionaries', 193–4
Sam, 75
Sangjai, 166
Sanskrit language, 253
Saratov, 18, 19, 34, 45
Sarepta, Moravian colony at, 13, 18–24, 35, 42, 44, 196; Rahmn at, 4, 103, 210, 282; privileges of, 25, 27, 29, 323; Schmidt at, 34; Rahmn's school at, 257–9; translation work at, 280
Sarepta House, Moscow, 34, 52
Sarepta House, St Petersburg, 23, 53
Sarpa, river, 18, 20, 44
Satlonkoff, *see* Sablukov
scape-goat, 153–6
Schilling von Canstadt, Baron Paul, 76, 212, 289, 306, 330–1, 333, 343
Schmidt, Isaac Jacob: as a Mongolist, 11, 31–2, 88; as censor, 11, 30, 31, 213, 280, 291, 298–9; as Treasurer of RBS, 13, 33; and the beginnings of the mission, 29; life and work, 33–4; loss of library, 34, 280; and the 'Precious Summary', 32,39, 110–11, 136; and Gospel of Matthew in Kalmuck, 46, 53, 110, 112–13, 280–1; and Treskin, 48; and Paterson, 53–4; and the Buryat donations, 54, 56; and the zaisangs, 111–16; and the New Testament in Mongolian, 281–2, 284, 285, 287, 316–17; and the renewal of the mission, 290
Schmidt, Jan, 33
Schönbrunn, 20
schools, 5, 45, 72, 95, 134, 188–9, 193, 220, 249, 250–78, 336, 343
Scott and Gordon, 80
Scottish Congregational Magazine, 153, 159, 353
Scottish Congregational Union, 353
Scottish missionaries, 13, 29, 47, 99, 106, 176, 287, 298, 326
Scriptures and tracts, distribution of, 138, 143, 196, 220, 222, 224, 225, 228, 244, 284, 318, 325
Sebek, 262, 267
Secession church, 89, 90
Selenga (Selinga), river, 142–3, 171, 173, 175
Selenginsk (Selinginsk): as the site of the mission, 3, 141–4; Peter Gordon at, 55; girls' school at, 72, 188–90, 262; society at, 76; grant of land and money, 108, 143, 175–8; servants at, 132; mission moves to, 169, 191; missionaries at, 169–84; mission station at, 170–2, 209; preaching at, 223; S. S. Hill at, 254
Selenginsk, Academy (Seminary) at, 32, 91, 206, 229, 251, 254, 255, 265, 273, 274; Report, 253, 265, 270–2; Memorial, 265–7, 269, 270; curriculum, 267, 271–2, 274
Selenginsk Buryats, 112, 143, 150–1, 221
Senate, Russian, 190, 343
Serampore, 12, 33, 43, 50; College at, 250, 254
Seraphim, Metropolitan, 196
services, religious, 201–2, 220, 248–9
Setsen Khan, 166

377

Index

Seven Fathers, 151
Shagdur, 6, 10, 193, 248, 249, 251, 273, 277–8
Shakyamuni (Shigemoni, Jagjamooni, Shigimoni, Shigomony, Shigomoni), 120, 139, 158, 227, 235–6, 247, 271
shamanism, shamanists, 5, 11, 12, 36–8, 41, 57, 133, 138, 150, 153, 156, 158–9, 165, 240
shamanist séances (ceremonies, rituals), 11, 88, 153–6, 160–1
shamanist spirits, 37, 156, 162, 165
shamans, 36–8, 153–6, 160–2, 164, 165, 239–40; dress and equipment, 154, 160, 165, 240
Shaposhnikov, 331, 344
sheep, as sacrificial animal, 160
Shilka, river, 150
Shira Uighur, 39
Shireetei lama: at Ona, 180, 200; at Aga, 233
shorthand, 14, 197
shulinga, 241, 242
Shusha, 7, 13, 291, 326, 327
Siberia: Governor General of, 108, 176; General Post Director of, 129; Governor General of eastern, 131, 349
Silcoates School, 207, 208
Simonsen, Asmus, 19, 34, 47
sisang, *see* zaisang
Six Tribes, 151, 166
sledge-roads, *see* snow-roads
smallpox, 205–6
Smith, Rev. John, 12
Smolensk, 52
snow-roads, 12, 66, 81, 95, 101, 102, 212
Socinianism, 100
Sokto, 238–9
Sonnenschein, W. S., 354
Soublikoff, *see* Sablukov
soul, 36, 37, 241
South Sea Islands, South Seas, 17, 87, 129, 222
Speranskii, Mikhail, 57, 61, 76, 121, 122, 126, 131, 134, 148–9, 150, 171, 195, 255, 290, 329, 330, 331, 334, 336, 343
Stallybrass, Benjamin, 205, 216
Stallybrass, Charles Ellah, 216
Stallybrass, Charlotte, 5, 73, 171, 194, 209–10, 216; *see also* Ellah, Charlotte
Stallybrass, Rev. Edward: at

Selenginsk, 3, 6, 55, 76, 143, 170, 273; at Khodon, 5, 7, 213, 233; translates Genesis, 7, 286, 292, 296; leaves Siberia, 8, 316; and Mongolian studies, 11; translates Pentateuch, 31, 296; acts as censor, 31, 299; at Irkutsk, 51; Instructions to, 103–6, 257, 279; early life, 62–3; joins LMS, 63–5; marriage to Sarah Robinson, 65–7, 74; friction with the Rahmns, 73–4, 169; at St Petersburg, 75–6, 99–100; hopes for a married colleague, 96; requests help from Alexander I, 107; received by Alexander, 108–9; and the zaisangs, 110, 115; and Nomtu, 117, 120; journey to Irkutsk, 124–30; and death of Sarah, 132, 203–4; studies Mongolian, 134–6, 146; journey to Kyakhta, 135–6, 139–43; visits the Khamba, 140, 157, 170, 225; and the Taisha's affair, 146, 147–8; his Mongolian MSS, 157, 199, 268, 279–80; at Irkutsk, 169; moves to Selenginsk, 169; at Barchigir, 180; moves to Khodon, 181–4; and printing of Genesis, 183–4, 294, 298, 301–2, 305, 315; house burned, 190; difficulties with authorities, 190–2, 333; and money affairs, 193–5; and letter-writing, 198; as a doctor, 201–2; and his sons, 207; and home leave, 210, 214–16, 302; marriage to Charlotte Ellah, 214–15; and itineration, 222–3, 237–47; composes a tract, 223; visits lamaseries, 224–5, 227, 230, 231; and lamas, 231, 235, 236; and Tungus visitors, 233; and distribution of tracts and Scriptures, 224–5, 226, 237; preaching, 248–9; admires Carey, 254; and payments to pupils, 260; and plans for Buryat schools, 264; school at Khodon, 273–4; his hymn book, 273; and the conversion of Badma, 276–7; translation of the Bible, 279, 284–5, 293, 296–7; translation of Exodus, 299; and the New Testament, 318–19, 320, 353; and baptism, 324, 342, 345–6; and Colonel Maslov, 334–5; and the closure of the mission, 348–51; and deputation work, 353; marriages to Sarah Bass

378

and Mary Ann Oughton, 354; death at Shooters Hill, 354
Stallybrass, Henry Martyn, 216
Stallybrass, Uncle James, 208
Stallybrass, James Steven, 199, 203, 206–7, 354
Stallybrass, John Knox, 206, 208, 354
Stallybrass, Sarah: grave at Khodon, 5, 203–4, 216; character, 67–74, 217; pregnancy, 66–7, 102; difficulties with Martha Yuille, 72; death, 74, 203; isolation in Siberia, 96, 145; and the Rahmns, 101–2; and servants at Irkutsk, 132; illness, 146, 203; visits Goose Lake, 157, 227–30; and *obo*-festivities, 162–3; and girls' school at Selenginsk, 188–90, 262, 273; and her children, 194, 207; and letter-writing, 198; and Martos, 199
Stallybrass, Sarah (junior), 203, 206, 273, 354
Stallybrass, Susannah, 205
Stallybrass, Thomas Edward, 139, 169, 206, 207, 208, 214, 215, 273, 295, 354
Stallybrass, William, 62, 210
Stallybrass, William Carey, 206, 207, 208, 214, 273, 354
Starrkärr, 81
Steinheil, Count, 51
Steinkopff, Rev. C. F. A., 48, 280
Stephens, Elizabeth, 330
Stepney (London), 65, 180, 230, 353–4
Stepney (Siberia), 180, 248
Steven, Robert, 78, 80
Stewart, D., 97
Stockholm, 50, 51, 78, 80, 81, 82
Stroganov, Count, 313, 351
Stumpf, C., 206
substitute figure, 200
Sukov, General, 128
Sulima, N. S., 343
Sumeru, Mount, 37
Sunday observance, 75, 127, 128, 129, 130, 179, 201–2, 262
Surat, 50
Swan, Hannah, 5, 10–12, 171, 180, 194, 204, 353; *see also* Cullen, Hannah
Swan, Rev. William: at Selenginsk, 3, 7, 175, 225; leaves Siberia, 8, 316; and J. C. Brown's book, 10; and the duties of a missionary, 11, 87, 300–1; and missionary methods, 17, 218–19, 235; and Schmidt, 30–1; and Moravian missionaries, 42; and the Manchu Bible, 60, 84, 212–14, 292; and George Borrow, 60, 84, 214; early life, 83–5; conversion, 84; joins LMS, 85–8; ordained at Greenwich, 85; and Mongolian studies, 87–8; views on married missionaries, 94–6; preaches at St Petersburg, 99; and Badma's letter, 115–16; journey to Irkutsk, 117–19; and Nomtu, 117–21; obtains books from Peking, 136–7; describes shaman rituals, 153, 160, 200; and *Idolatry*, 157–64; and Maidari festival, 168; and Jean Paterson, 173–5; at Ona, 180–1, 191; and Yuille's dictionaries, 186–7; adopts a Buryat girl, 194, 207; and the *Memoir of Mrs Paterson*, 196; and the Archbishop of Irkutsk, 196–8; negotiations in St Petersburg, 211–12, 289–91, 326, 329, 334, 336–40; home leave, 211–14; marriage to Hannah Cullen, 212; returns to Siberia, 214; visits to lamaseries, 227; at Aga, 233–4; itineration, 237–40; and religious situation in Buryatia, 243–4, 327–8; visits Kudarinsk Buryats, 246; views on education, 252; and objectives of the mission, 256; and Kazan Tatars, 262; and school at Ona, 273–4; conversion of pupils, 276–7; and translation of Bible, 279, 284–5, 293, 296–7; and Abercrombie, 299–300; and dispute with Yuille, 302–5, 306, 311–13; and the New Testament, 317–20, 349, 353; argues against closure of mission, 324–5, 327; and icon-worship, 339–41, 344–5; and baptism, 345–6; and the end of the mission, 348–9; last years and death, 353
Swedish church in London, 4
Synod, Holy, 213, 289, 290, 291, 316, 317–19, 322, 323, 329, 330, 336, 338, 342, 347, 349, 350

Tabungut lamasery, 227, 230
Tabungut tribe, 166
taischi, see *taisha*
taisha, 54, 57, 112, 120, 139, 147, 150,

168, 191, 234, 244, 263–5, 273, 351, 354
Taisha's affair, 146–7
Tanggŭ meyen, 135
Tangoot, Tangut, *see* Tibetan
Tara, 129
Tarba, 273
Tarbagatai, 240
Tartars, *see* Tatars
Tartary, 16
Tatarinova, Ekaterina, 329
Tatars, 26, 27, 47, 262, 269
Tauride Palace, 114
Taylor Institution Library, 115, 215
teaching, 14, 17, 107
Teb Tenggeri, 38
Teeona, 291
Tekshi, 277, 278
Telford, Thomas, 51
Temnik, river, 166, 180, 247
'Tenfold Virtuous White Chronicle of the Faith', 40
tengri(e), 160, 161, 200
tents, 35, 140, 152–3, 239
Testament, New: in Chinese, 15, 59, 143; in Kalmuck, 33, 58, 281, 298; in Manchu, 30, 60, 212, 330; in Mongolian (translated by the missionaries), 3, 105, 349, (translated by Schmidt and Badma), 5, 31, 33, 59, 112, 115, 137, 196, 281, 282, 292, 294, 298, 316–19, 321, 333, (translated by Stallybrass and Swan), 279, 292–3, 295, 316, 320, 321, 353, (translated by Yuille and Rintsin), 91, 272, 293–4, 295, 296, 307, 318, 319
Testament, Old: in Manchu, 60, 84, 85, 212–14, 292, 330, 354; in Mongolian, 14, 181, 182, 196, 198, 213, 268, 279, 293–4, 296–7, 315–16, 318, 320, 321, 328, 349, 351, 352, printing of, 3, 7–8, 14, 182, 183–4, 212, 220, 248, 279, 280, 291, 292, 302, 315–16, 318–19, 320, 328
Thibet(an), *see* Tibet(an)
Tibet, 35, 36, 38, 39, 59, 163, 166, 167, 244, 295, 317, 332
Tibetan language, 38, 163, 200, 229, 231, 253
Tibetan learning, 186
Tibetans, 31, 166
T'ien-shan range, 35
Tiflis, 50, 77, 283

Tobolsk, 101, 129, 131, 145, 194, 269; Archbishop of, 129; Bible Society at, 129; Governor of, 26, 129
Tochmut, 43
Tomsk, 28, 121, 129; Government of, 27, 28, 130; Governor of, 130
Torguts, 135
Torpa, 81
Torson, K. P., 173, 210
Towne, Thomas, 62, 63
Tract Society, 223
tracts, 47, 170, 201, 223–4, 285, 286 (*see also* Scriptures and tracts); Buddhist, 239
Transbaikalia: Governor of, 273; population of, 150, 209
Travancore, 250
travel, Siberian, 66–7, 95, 101–2, 108, 117, 119, 123–30
Treskin, N. I., 34, 48, 56–7, 59, 61, 112, 113, 121, 122, 134, 143
tribes, Buryat, 150–1
tribute, 260
Troitskosavsk, Military School at, 251, 275
Tsagaan ebügen, 165
Tsagaan Sara, 162, 227; *see also* White Month
Tsaritsyn, 17, 18, 19
Tseden, 238
Tseidler, I. B., 331, 333–4, 336, 343
Tsidep, 272
Tsong-kha-pa, 168
Tsongol lamasery, 167, 227
Tsongol tribe, 166
Tubetian, *see* Tibetan
Tulishen, 135
Tümen, Major, 36
Tümen Jasagtu Khan, 41
Tümet, 39, 41
Tungus, 150, 221, 231, 233
Tura, river, 28
Tushetu Khan, 42
Two Principles, 40, 41
type, founts of: Kalmuck, 23, 46, 53–4, 280; Manchu, 279, 320; Mongolian, 109, 223, 281, 305, 316, 321, 351; Yuille's Mongolian, 308, 310; Yuille's Tibetan, 306, 308, 310
tysha, *see* taisha

Uda, river, 151

Index

Udinsk, 6, 117, 189; *see also* Verkhneudinsk
U.F. (Unitas Fratrum), 22; *see also* Moravians; United Brethren
Unitarianism, 92, 210
United Brethren, 17, 18, 33, 112; *see also* Moravians; U.F.
Unkrig, W. A., 309–10
Unofficial Committee (of Alexander I), 24, 52
Uppsala, University of, 283
Uren, Charles, 124, 126
Urga, 40, 42, 134, 166
Ushakova, river, 131

Vagin, V. I., 340
Van Dam, Anna, 33
Vassilich, Lieutenant, 76
Venning, James, 266
Venning, John, 185, 266, 269
Venning, Walter, 75, 97, 98, 266
Verkhneudinsk, 11, 55, 117, 134, 135, 142, 151, 190, 191, 199, 221, 261, 316, 332, 335; *see also* Udinsk
Vilno, University of, 137
Vladimir, 127
Voichekovskii, Dr, 137, 212
Volga, river, 16, 18, 19, 24–8, 35, 36, 128
Volgograd, 18
Voroshilov, 76

Walford, Rev. William, 64
Wallace, Mackenzie, 352
Wangdang, 273
Ward, William, 250
Wardlaw, Rev. Ralph, 50, 85, 86, 89, 90, 92, 93, 96, 266
Warsaw, 137
Watts, Dr, 231
Waugh, Rev. Dr Alexander, 24–9, 188
Weber, C. M. von, 131
Wendling, Brother, 45, 257
Wesley, Charles, 226
Western Union Telegraph Company, 124
White Khan, 166
White Month, 141, 162, 167, 227, 230, 247
White Old Man, 165
Whymant, Neville, 310

Wier, Dr, 20, 44, 45
Wigand, Johann, 34, 47, 48
Wigand, Maria Helene, 34, 47
Williams, John, 1, 87
Wilson, Thomas, 340, 344, 349, 351
Wrede, Baron Henrik, 171

Xavier, St Francis, 158

Yakuts, 58
Yakutsk, 123
Yellow Faith, 36, 39
Yellow River, 110
Yenisei, river, 28
Yisüngge, 32
Yüan dynasty, 38
Yuille, Elisabeth, 205, 206
Yuille, Janet, 205, 206
Yuille, Martha: grave and monument at Selenginsk, 5, 12, 172–3; difficulties with Sarah Stallybrass, 72; and girls' school at Selenginsk, 188–90; illness and death, 203; and intruders, 209; *see also* Cowie, Martha
Yuille, Mrs (senior), 89
Yuille, Rev. Robert: Gilmour and, 6–11; and the printing of Genesis, 7–8, 183–4, 301–5; his printing press, 8, 91, 305, 306–7; dismissal, 8, 303, 315; death, 9, 353; difficulties with the Stallybrasses, 72–3, 184–5, 188–90; character, 83, 86; his textbooks, 88, 253; his dictionaries, 88, 186–7; early life, 89; conversion, 89; application to LMS, 89–92; and Colonel Maslov, 91, 335; his appointment, 92–5; at Gosport, 92; appointment to Siberia cancelled, 94; marriage to Martha Cowie, 94–6, 145; at Cronstadt, 97–8; criticizes Directors, 98, 187–8, 311–12; and Nomtu, 117–18; and Kowalewski, 137; treatment of Buryats, 165, 178–80; at Selenginsk, 171, 173, 181, 183–4, 313–14; and Rintsin, 179–80, 262, 274–5; disagrees with his colleagues, 183–4, 300–5, 310–11; his correspondence, 185–6; salary, 194; and the Decembrists, 210, 256; disapproves of Charlotte Ellah, 214; visits to lamaseries, 224–5; visits

Ol'khon, 246; as an evangelist, 247; preaching, 248; and the teaching of Tibetan, 253, 272; and the Selenginsk Academy, 265–72, 274; ignores the Directors, 270, 302; his translations of the Psalms, 293–5; his translation of Isaiah, 293–4; his translation of the New Testament, 293–6, 319–20; alleged ignorance, 294–5, 306; his primer of Mongolian, 295, 307–10; mental state, 295–6, 302; and Abercrombie, 299–300, 303; correspondence with Swan, 302–4, 311; recalled, 302, 311, 312, 313, 314; his 'Articles of Peace', 305; proposes purchase of a second press, 305; his printing activities, 305–10; credit suspended, 312; financial affairs, 313–15; returns to Scotland, 314; keeps back paper, 315; last years and death, 352–3

Yuille, Robert (junior), 205

Yuille, Samuel Bogue, 8, 11, 93, 172, 173, 185, 207, 314

Yumdeleg, 264

zaisangs, 43, 111, 112, 150; the two, 5, 45, 109–16, 138, 143, 281–2

Zakamennyi Buryats, 151

Žamcarano, C. Ž., 138

Zarlee Khan, *see* Erlik Khan

Zavalishin, D. I., 209–10

Zaya Pandita, 36, 43

Zelotes, 84

zolik, 200

zud, 206

For Product Safety Concerns and Information please contact our EU
representative GPSR@taylorandfrancis.com
Taylor & Francis Verlag GmbH, Kaufingerstraße 24, 80331 München, Germany